"With good attention to first-century background, thorough engagement with contemporary discussion, and careful judgments on the text, David Starling has provided a sound guide to 1 Corinthians from an evangelical, Reformed perspective—a gift which will benefit many, both pastors and laity."

—**Mark A. Seifrid,** *emeritus professor of exegetical theology, Concordia Seminary*

"With all the exegetical controversies surrounding 1 Corinthians, it is unrealistic to expect a new commentary to agree with all of one's own perspectives, yet David Starling's volume comes close. Even when we disagree, he is always clear, fair-minded, aware of all the major options for interpretation and cogent in his conclusions. Abreast of all the most important recent literature, this commentary nevertheless wears its learning lightly, with particularly helpful 'Bridge' sections that focus one's attention on everything needed for contemporary application without actually doing the applicational work itself."

—**Craig L. Blomberg,** *distinguished professor emeritus of New Testament, Denver Seminary*

"David Starling's commentary deftly handles the many perplexing and controversial subjects one finds in Paul's first letter to the Corinthians. It engages deeply with primary scholarship while at the same time proves to be a very readable work that both students and ministers alike can appreciate. An added bonus is his section on biblical and theological themes that addresses in a clear and convincing way relevant topics in this letter such as Christ's resurrection, the Spirit, wisdom, grace, salvation, eschatology, baptism, and much more."

—**B. J. Oropeza,** *professor of biblical and religious studies, Azusa Pacific University and Seminary*

"David Starling has written an informative and edifying commentary on 1 Corinthians that is a great guide for teachers and preachers seeking to navigate their way through one of Paul's most complex and contested letters."

—**Michael F. Bird,** *deputy principal, Ridley College, Melbourne, Australia*

"This series is based on biblical theology. Starling has given us an up to date and detailed commentary based on considerable scholarship and an impressive command of both the Greco-Roman and Jewish background to 1 Corinthians. It meets the needs of both biblical scholars and church groups."

—**Alanna Nobbs,** *emeritus professor, Macquarie University, Sydney, Australia*

"This commentary is a rare combination of learned interaction with primary source material, sensible exegetical judgments and also the joy that the engagement with Scripture elicits. Preachers and teachers will benefit enormously from Starling's methodical and deep engagement with the text, as well as from the very helpful introduction on the historical background and theology of the letter. A trustworthy guide to an often difficult epistle!"

—**Simon Gathercole,** *professor of New Testament and early Christianity, University of Cambridge, United Kingdom*

"On the surface, 1 Corinthians appears to be Paul's random responses to a diverse range of problems in a troubled church. However, in this engaging commentary David Starling exposes the deep logic of the letter as Paul's attempt to reframe the Corinthians' understanding of all things in light of the gospel of the death and resurrection of Christ. This commentary, along with rigorous exegesis, provides a rich resource for understanding the grand biblical narrative and its relevance to everyday life."

—**Brian Rosner,** *principal, Ridley College, Melbourne, Australia*

"Even as some of the Corinthians had brought elite cultural assumptions to bear on their understanding of the story of Israel and Israel's Messiah, modern readers may do so too. Starling's commentary offers a corrective that should be any student of the letter's first stop. With lucid and engaging prose, and with command of recent scholarly discussions, David Starling's expertise in both 1 Corinthians and the New Testament's use of the Old brings alive the ancient text, even while tackling perennial concerns of biblical theology."

—**A. Andrew Das,** *Niebuhr Distinguished Chair and Professor of Religious Studies, Elmhurst University*

"David Starling's new commentary on 1 Corinthians is a rich resource for scholars, students, and pastors alike. Grounded in thorough knowledge of the Greco-Roman world, Starling demonstrates how Paul's responses to the Corinthians' problems and questions challenged the prevailing beliefs and customs of the inhabitants of Roman Corinth. First Corinthians emerges from Starling's illuminating exposition as a deeply theological letter that interprets the salvation-history of God's dealings with Israel and reveals the dramatic, life-changing consequences of God's intervention in the darkness of the present age through the crucifixion and resurrection of Jesus Christ."

—**Larry L. Welborn,** *professor of New Testament and early Christianity, Fordham University, New York*

1 CORINTHIANS

1 CORINTHIANS

Evangelical Biblical Theology Commentary

General Editors

T. Desmond Alexander, Thomas R. Schreiner, Andreas J. Köstenberger

Assistant Editors

James M. Hamilton, Kenneth A. Mathews, Terry L. Wilder

David I. Starling

1 Corinthians
Evangelical Biblical Theology Commentary

Lexham Academic, an imprint of Lexham Press
1313 Commercial St., Bellingham, WA 98225
LexhamPress.com

Print ISBN 9781683598183
Digital ISBN 9781683598190
Library of Congress Control Number 2024952171

General Editors: T. Desmond Alexander, Thomas R. Schreiner, Andreas J. Köstenberger
Assistant Editors: James M. Hamilton, Kenneth A. Mathews, Terry L. Wilder
Lexham Editorial: Derek Brown, John Barach
Cover Design: Joshua Hunt
Typesetting: Mandi Newell

25 26 27 28 29 30 31 / IN / 12 11 10 9 8 7 6 5 4 3 2 1

To my wife Nicole,
whose daily presence and encouragement immeasurably enrich
our shared journey of life and ministry.

CONTENTS

GENERAL EDITORS' PREFACE

In recent years biblical theology has seen a remarkable resurgence. Whereas, in 1970, Brevard Childs wrote *Biblical Theology in Crisis*, the quest for the Bible's own theology has witnessed increasing vitality since Childs prematurely decried the demise of the movement. Nowhere has this been truer than in evangelical circles. It could be argued that evangelicals, with their commitment to biblical inerrancy and inspiration, are perfectly positioned to explore the Bible's unified message. At the same time, as D. A. Carson has aptly noted, perhaps the greatest challenge faced by biblical theologians is how to handle the Bible's manifest diversity and how to navigate the tension between its unity and diversity in a way that does justice to both.[1]

What is biblical theology? And how is biblical theology different from related disciplines such as systematic theology? These two exceedingly important questions must be answered by anyone who would make a significant contribution to the discipline. Regarding the first question, the most basic answer might assert that biblical theology, in essence, is *the theology of the Bible*, that is, the theology expressed by the respective writers of the various biblical books *on their own terms* and *in their own historical contexts*. Biblical theology is the attempt to understand and embrace *the interpretive perspective of the biblical authors*. What is more, biblical theology is the theology of the *entire* Bible, an exercise in *whole-Bible theology*. For this reason biblical theology is not just a modern academic discipline; its roots are found already in the use of earlier Old Testament portions

[1] D. A. Carson, "New Testament Theology," in *DLNT* 810.

in later Old Testament writings and in the use of the Old Testament in the New.

Biblical theology thus involves a close study of *the use of the Old Testament in the Old Testament* (that is, the use of, say, Deuteronomy by Jeremiah, or of the Pentateuch by Isaiah). Biblical theology also entails the investigation of *the use of the Old Testament in the New*, both in terms of individual passages and in terms of larger Christological or soteriological themes. Biblical theology may proceed *book by book*, trace *central themes* in Scripture, or seek to place the contributions of individual biblical writers within the framework of the Bible's larger overarching *metanarrative*, that is, the Bible's developing story from Genesis through Revelation at whose core is *salvation* or *redemptive history*, the account of God's dealings with humanity and his people Israel and the church from creation to new creation.

In this quest for the Bible's own theology, we will be helped by the inquiries of those who have gone before us in the *history of the church*. While we can profitably study the efforts of interpreters over the entire sweep of the history of biblical interpretation since patristic times, we can also benefit from the labors of scholars since J. P. Gabler, whose programmatic inaugural address at the University of Altdorf, Germany, in 1787 marks the inception of the discipline in modern times. Gabler's address bore the title "On the Correct Distinction between Dogmatic and Biblical Theology and the Right Definition of Their Goals."[2] While few (if any) within evangelicalism would fully identify with Gabler's program, the proper distinction between dogmatic and biblical theology (that is, between biblical and systematic theology) continues to be an important issue to be adjudicated by practitioners of both disciplines, and especially biblical theology. We have already defined biblical theology as whole-Bible theology, describing the theology of the various biblical books *on their own terms* and *in their own historical contexts*. Systematic theology, by contrast, is more topically oriented and focused on contemporary contextualization. While there are different ways in which the relationship between biblical and systematic theology can be construed, maintaining a proper distinction between the two disciplines arguably continues to be vital if both are to achieve their objectives.

---

[2] The original Latin title was *Oratio de iusto discrimine theologiae biblicae et dogmaticae regundisque recte utriusque finibus.*

The present set of volumes constitutes an ambitious project, seeking to explore the theology of the Bible in considerable depth, spanning both Testaments. Authors come from a variety of backgrounds and perspectives, though all affirm the inerrancy and inspiration of Scripture. United in their high view of Scripture and in their belief in the underlying unity of Scripture, which is ultimately grounded in the unity of God himself, each author explores the contribution of a given book or group of books to the theology of Scripture as a whole. While conceived as stand-alone volumes, each volume thus also makes a contribution to the larger whole. All volumes provide a discussion of introductory matters, including the historical setting and the literary structure of a given book of Scripture. Also included is an exegetical treatment of all the relevant passages in succinct commentary-style format. The biblical theology approach of the series will also inform and play a role in the commentary proper. The commentator permits a discussion between the commentary proper and the biblical theology it reflects by a series of cross-references.

The major contribution of each volume, however, is a thorough discussion of the most important themes of the biblical book in relation to the canon as a whole. This format allows each contributor to ground biblical theology, as is proper, in an appropriate appraisal of the relevant historical and literary features of a particular book in Scripture, while at the same time focusing on its major theological contribution to the entire Christian canon in the context of the larger salvation-historical metanarrative of Scripture. Within this overall format, there will be room for each individual contributor to explore the major themes of his or her particular corpus in the way he or she sees most appropriate for the material under consideration. For some books of the Bible, it may be best to have these theological themes set out in advance of the exegetical commentary. For other books it may be better to explain the theological themes after the commentary. Consequently, each contributor has the freedom to order these sections as best suits the biblical material under consideration so that the discussion of biblical-theological themes may precede or follow the exegetical commentary.

This format, in itself, would already be a valuable contribution to biblical theology. But other series try to accomplish a survey of the Bible's theology as well. What distinguishes the present series is its orientation toward Christian proclamation. This is the Evangelical Biblical Theology Commentary series! As a result, the ultimate purpose of this set of volumes is not exclusively, or even primarily, academic. Rather, we seek to relate biblical theology to our own lives and to the life of the church. Our desire is to equip those in Christian ministry who are called by God to preach and teach the precious truths of Scripture to their congregations, both in North America and in a global context.

The base translation for the Evangelical Biblical Theology Commentary series is the Christian Standard Bible (CSB). The CSB places equal value on faithfulness to the original languages and readability for a modern audience. The contributors, however, have the liberty to differ with the CSB as they comment on the biblical text. Note that, in the CSB, Old Testament passages that are quoted in the New Testament are set in boldface type.

We hope and pray that the forty volumes of this series, once completed, will bear witness to the unity in diversity of the canon of Scripture as they probe the individual contributions of each of its sixty-six books. The authors and editors are united in their desire that in so doing the series will magnify the name of Christ and bring glory to the Triune God who revealed himself in Scripture so that everyone who calls on the name of the Lord will be saved—to the glory of God the Father and his Son, the Lord Jesus Christ, under the illumination of the Holy Spirit, and for the good of his church. To God alone be the glory: *soli Deo gloria.*

ACKNOWLEDGMENTS

This book was written with the help and encouragement of many, and I am glad of the opportunity to express my thanks to them.

I am grateful to the editors of the series for the invitation to contribute this volume and to Lexham Press for taking up the baton from the original publishers. Working on this project has been a great delight, and the team at Lexham have been wonderful collaborators in it.

Over the years I have had the privilege of sharing the teaching of classes on 1 Corinthians with friends and colleagues including Brian Powell, Tim MacBride, Elim Hiu, and Cass Kwakye. I am thankful to all of them for the conversations we have enjoyed and the insights they have shared. Other friends with whom I have had the opportunity to discuss issues that arose within the course of working through the letter include Con Campbell, Lynn Cohick, Chris Forbes, Andy Naselli, Brian Rosner, Larry Welborn, Cynthia Westfall, and Bruce Winter, as well as numerous others with whom I have enjoyed interacting via email and in face-to-face conversations at academic conferences and in various other contexts.

The team in which I serve at Morling College continues to be a great source of encouragement and stimulus, and I am grateful to the college (and to the Australian College of Theology, with which it is affiliated) for the provision of study leave periods and conference attendance grants that assisted enormously in making the writing of this commentary possible.

Closer to home, I am as always filled with deep and joyful gratitude to Nicole, my wife, for her love and support in every stage of our shared journey of life and ministry. I could not have completed this project without her, and it is a privilege to have the opportunity to dedicate this book to her as a token of my thanks.

LIST OF ABBREVIATIONS

JOURNALS, SERIES, REFERENCE WORKS, AND TECHNICAL TERMS

BBR	*Bulletin for Biblical Research*
BDAG	Danker, Frederick W., Walter Bauer, William F. Arndt, and F. Wilbur Gingrich. *Greek-English Lexicon of the New Testament and Other Early Christian Literature.* 3rd ed. Chicago: University of Chicago Press, 2000 (Danker-Bauer-Arndt-Gingrich)
BECNT	Baker Exegetical Commentary on the New Testament
BETL	Bibliotheca Ephemeridum Theologicarum Lovaniensium
BHGNT	Baylor Handbook on the Greek New Testament
BibZeit	Biblische Zeitschrift
BNTC	Black's New Testament Commentaries
BTB	*Biblical Theology Bulletin*
BZ	*Biblische Zeitschrift*
BZNW	Beihefte zur Zeitschrift für die neutestamentliche Wissenschaft
CBET	Contributions to Biblical Exegesis and Theology
CBQ	*Catholic Biblical Quarterly*
COQG	Christian Origins and the Question of God
CSB	Christian Standard Bible
DLNT	*Dictionary of the Later New Testament and Its Developments.*
EKK	Evangelisch-katholischer Kommentar zum Neuen Testament

ESV	English Standard Version
EVV	English Versions
ExAud	*Ex Auditu*
HNT	Handbuch zum Neuen Testament
HTA	Historisch-Theologische Auslegung
HTR	*Harvard Theological Review*
ICC	International Critical Commentary
JAAR	*Journal of the American Academy of Religion*
JBL	*Journal of Biblical Literature*
JGRChJ	*Journal of Greco-Roman Christianity and Judaism*
JETS	*Journal of the Evangelical Theological Society*
JRASup	*Journal of Roman Archaeology Supplements*
JRS	*Journal of Roman Studies*
JSNT	*Journal for the Study of the New Testament*
JSNTSup	Journal for the Study of the New Testament Supplement Series
JTI	*Journal of Theological Interpretation*
JTS	*Journal of Theological Studies*
LCL	Loeb Classical Library
LEB	Lexham English Bible
LNTS	Library of New Testament Studies
LSJ	Liddell, Henry George, Robert Scott, Henry Stuart Jones. *A Greek-English Lexicon.* 9th ed. with revised supplement. Oxford: Clarendon, 1996
LXX	Septuagint
MT	Masoretic Text
NCBC	New Century Bible Commentary
NCCS	New Covenant Commentary Series
Neot	*Neotestamentica*
NETS	A New English Translation of the Septuagint
NIGTC	New International Greek Testament Commentary
NICNT	New International Commentary on the Greek New Testament
NIV	New International Version
NovT	*Novum Testamentum*
NovTSup	Supplements to Novum Testamentum
NRSV	New Revised Standard Version
NTC	New Testament Commentary
NTS	New Testament Studies
NTTSD	New Testament Tools, Studies, and Documents
PJBR	*Pacific Journal of Baptist Research*

PKNT	Papyrologische Kommentare zum Neuen Testament
PNTC	Pillar New Testament Commentary
ResQ	*Restoration Quarterly*
RNT	Reading the New Testament
RTR	*Reformed Theological Review*
SNTSMS	Society for New Testament Studies Monograph Series
STR	Southeastern Theological Review
s.v.	sub verbo, under the word
TNIV	Today's New International Version
TNTC	Tyndale New Testament Commentaries
TynBul	*Tyndale Bulletin*
UBS[5]	Aland, B., K. Aland, I. D. Karavidopoulos, C. M. Martini, B. M. Metzger, H. Strutwolf, and American Bible Society. *The Greek New Testament.* 5th ed. United Bible Societies, 2014
WBC	Word Biblical Commentary
WUNT	Wissenschaftliche Untersuchungen zum Neuen Testament
ZECNT	Zondervan Exegetical Commentary on the New Testament

APOCRYPHA AND SEPTUAGINT

1–4 Macc	1–4 Maccabees
2 Kgdms	2 Kingdoms (MT, EVV 2 Samuel)
Bar	Baruch
Sir	Sirach
Sus	Susanna

DEAD SEA SCROLLS AND RELATED TEXTS

1QSa	Rule of the Congregation (Appendix to 1QS)
1QM	War Scroll

OTHER SECOND TEMPLE JEWISH WRITINGS

1–2 En.	1–2 Enoch
4 Ezra	4 Ezra

Jos. Asen.	Joseph and Aseneth
Josephus, *Ant.*	*Jewish Antiquities*
J.W.	*Jewish War*
LAB	Liber antiquitatum biblicarum (Pseudo-Philo)
Philo, *Alleg. Interp.*	*Allegorical Interpretation*
Cherubim	*On the Cherubim*
Creation	*On the Creation of the World*
Dreams	*On Dreams*
Embassy	*On the Embassy to Gaius*
Migration	*On the Migration of Abraham*
Spec. Laws	*On the Special Laws*
Virtues	*On the Virtues*
Worse	*That the Worse Attacks the Better*
Sib. Or.	Sibylline Oracles
T. Benj.	Testament of Benjamin
T. Iss.	Testament of Issachar
T. Job	Testament of Job
T. Jos.	Testament of Joseph
T. Jud.	Testament of Judah
T. Levi	Testament of Levi
T. Reu.	Testament of Reuben
T. Sol.	Testament of Solomon

TARGUMIC TEXTS

Tg. Onq.	Targum Onkelos

MISHNAH, TALMUD, AND OTHER RABBINIC WRITINGS

B. Meṣ.	Baba Meṣiʿa
Gen. Rab.	Genesis Rabbah
Ketub.	Ketubbot
m.	Mishnah
Mek.	Mekilta
Num. Rab.	Numbers Rabbah
Pesaḥ.	Pesaḥim
Qidd.	Qiddushin
Šabb.	Shabbat
t.	Tosefta

CLASSICAL AND ANCIENT CHRISTIAN WRITINGS

1 Clem.	1 Clement
Alciphron, *Ep.*	*Epistles*
Aphthonius, *Prog.*	*Progymnasmata*
Apuleius, *Metam.*	*Metamorphoses* (*The Golden Ass*)
Aristophanes, *Thesm.*	*Thesmophoriazusae*
Aristotle, *Hist. an.*	*History of Animals*
Athenaeus, *Deipn.*	*Deipnosophistae*
Augustine, *Civ.*	*The City of God*
Chrysostom, *Hom. 1 Cor.*	*Homiliae in epistulam i ad Corinthios*
Cicero, *Agr.*	*De Lege agraria*
Off.	*De officiis*
Rep.	*De republica*
Tusc.	*Tusculanae disputationes*
Demosthenes, *Fals. leg.*	*False Embassy*
Dio Chrysostom, *Or.*	*Orations*
Diodorus Siculus, *Bib. hist.*	*Bibliotheca historica*
Diogenes Laertius, *Lives*	*Lives of Eminent Philosophers*
Dionysius of Halicarnassus, *Ant. rom.*	*Antiquitates romanae*
Epictetus, *Diatr.*	*Diatribai*
Herm. Vis.	Shepherd of Hermas, Vision(s)
Herodian, *Hist.*	*History of the Empire from the Death of Marcus*
Herodotus, *Hist.*	*Histories*
Hippocrates, *Epid.*	*Epidemics*
Horace, *Ep.*	*Epistles*
Ignatius, *Rom.*	*To the Romans*
Livy, *Ab urbe cond.*	*Ab urbe condita*
Lucian, *Merc. cond.*	*Salaried Posts in Great Houses*
Marcus Aurelius, *Med.*	*Meditationes*
Pausanias, *Descr.*	*Description of Greece*
Plato, *Resp.*	*Republic*
Pliny the Elder, *Nat.*	*Natural History*

Plutarch, *Mor.*	*Moralia*
Per.	*Pericles*
Quaest. rom.	*Quaestiones romanae et graecae*
Tim.	*Timoleon*
Polybius, *Hist.*	*Historiae*
Seneca, *Ep.*	*Epistulae morales*
Strabo, *Geogr.*	*Geography*
Suetonius, *Claud.*	*Divus Claudius*
Tacitus, *Ann.*	*Annales*
Theodoret, *Interp. Ep. 1 ad Cor.*	*Interpretatio epistulae primae ad Corinthios*
Xenophon, *Mem.*	*Memorabilia*
Xenophon of Ephesus, *Eph.*	*Ephesiaca*

PAPYRI AND INSCRIPTIONS

IG	Packard Humanities Institute Database of Greek Inscriptions
P. Oxy.	Oxyrhynchus papyri
P. Oslo.	Papyrus Osloensis
P. Tebt.	Tebtunis papyri

INTRODUCTION

I. Paul and the Beginnings of Corinthian Christianity

In late AD 50 or early 51 Paul arrived for the first time in Corinth. According to the narrative that Luke provides in Acts 18 (which is consistent with the information we can glean from Paul's first letter to the Thessalonians), he arrived on his own, having left Silas and Timothy behind in Thessalonica in hopes that they would rejoin him when they were able.[1] He found a welcome in the home of Aquila and Priscilla, fellow Jews who had been expelled from Rome under the edict of Claudius, and joined in working with them in their shared trade as σκηνοποιοί (CSB: "tentmakers").[2] During this initial phase of his ministry in Corinth, his missionary activity included not only the conversations that would doubtless have accompanied his activities as he practiced his trade but also the weekly opportunities for evangelism and debate among Jews and interested gentiles, as he "reasoned in the synagogue every Sabbath and tried to persuade both Jews and Greeks" (18:4).

[1] For a summary account of Paul's first visit to Corinth, see N. T. Wright, *Paul: A Biography* (San Francisco: HarperOne, 2018), 209–30.

[2] The traditional translation of this word, retained in most English versions, is "tentmakers." Cf. BDAG, s.v. "σκηνοποιός," and Michael Wolter, *Paul: An Outline of His Theology* (Waco: Baylor University Press, 2015), 10–11, for arguments in favor of "maker of stage properties," rather than the traditional "tentmaker" or "leatherworker," as the most likely meaning that Luke would have intended the word σκηνοποιός to carry. For further discussion of that possibility and its implications for our interpretation of Paul's letters, see L. L. Welborn, *Paul, the Fool of Christ: A Study of 1 Corinthians 1-4 in the Comic-Philosophic Tradition*, JSNTSup (London: T&T Clark, 2005), 11–12.

The arrival of Silas and Timothy from Thessalonica triggered a second phase in his Corinthian ministry, in which he "devoted himself" (presumably full-time, and in a wider range of contexts) "to preaching the word and testified to the Jews that Jesus is the Messiah" (18:5). This intensification and expansion of his missionary activities evoked a hostile reaction from the leadership of the local Jewish community, to which Paul responded by shaking out his clothes in a dramatic sign of judgment and declaring that "from now on I will go to the Gentiles" (18:6). Even then, however, he did not go far, shifting the base of his activities just one door up the street to the house of Titius Justus, a worshiper of God who lived next door to the synagogue (18:7). He was joined there, according to Luke, by "Crispus, the leader of the synagogue," and all the members of his household (18:8), and his activities of teaching and evangelism continued unhindered for another eighteen months (18:9–11).

At some point during this period, according to Luke's narrative, "the Jews made a united attack against Paul and brought him to the tribunal," alleging that Paul was persuading people to worship in ways that were contrary to the law (18:12–13). It is not entirely clear whether the "law" Paul was accused of undermining was the Jewish law or the Roman law, or perhaps a combination of the two. The fact that the accusation was brought before Gallio the proconsul suggests that in his accusers' minds the transgression was in some way relevant to the jurisdiction of the Roman authorities—either because of the politically subversive overtones of Paul's message about the crucified Messiah Jesus (cf. 17:7) or because Paul's departures from what they considered to be authentic Jewish tradition disqualified him and his followers from enjoying the toleration that Rome typically extended to Jewish religion.[3] Gallio, however, displayed no interest in entertaining the accusation, declaring that the matters in dispute were merely "questions about words, names, and your own law," over which he refused to adjudicate (18:14–16). The mob then turned on Sosthenes the synagogue leader and beat him, with Gallio showing no interest in intervening.[4]

---

[3] Cf. the discussion in Craig S. Keener, *Acts: An Exegetical Commentary*, 4 vols. (Grand Rapids: Baker, 2012–2015), 3:2768.

[4] It is possible that this Sosthenes was the same person as the co-sender named in 1 Cor 1:1, and that he had already declared himself a convert to Paul's message or in sympathy with it; if that is the case, then the "all" who turned on him may have been a Jewish mob who were present to support the charges against Paul. The more likely explanation is that

The events that Luke narrates, along with Paul's own reflections (e.g., in 1 Cor 1:18–2:5) on his first visit to Corinth, help to explain the distinctive shape and ethos of the church that developed out of Paul's missionary activity in the city, the unique character of his relationship with its members, and some of the particular features of his correspondence with them that are of special relevance to a commentary focused on the biblical-theological themes of the text. Although the majority of Paul's converts appear to have been gentiles (and are described as such by Paul in 1 Cor 12:2), the group that Paul gathered included from its earliest days a core of Jewish believers and gentile God-fearers, who could assist gentile converts in accessing and understanding the Jewish Scriptures that Paul quotes and alludes to with frequency and freedom in his letters. The peremptoriness with which Gallio dismissed the charges brought by Paul's accusers and his clear lack of interest in protecting their leader from the violence of the mob vividly illustrate the thinly veiled contempt with which many among the Greco-Roman elite regarded Jews and their traditions. And the implicit legitimacy that Gallio's ruling conferred on the group that Paul had gathered together gave them a place within the social order of the city that enabled them to maintain social and commercial contacts and aspire to a degree of advancement that might elsewhere have been unthinkable.[5]

The combined effect of these three circumstances goes a long way toward explaining the extent of Paul's engagement with Old Testament passages and themes in 1 Corinthians, the pervasiveness of biblical-theological ideas within the letter, and the range of issues Paul addresses as he brings this biblical theology to bear on the lives of the readers. The Corinthian believers (and especially the more wealthy and privileged among them) were blessed—as Paul acknowledges in 1:5—with an unusual degree of knowledge, including access to and familiarity with the Scriptures of the Old Testament, and probably also a grasp on at least the rudiments of the

---

the members of the mob who turned on Sosthenes were of gentile background, and that Sosthenes's conversion (if indeed he was the same person as the Sosthenes of 1 Cor 1:1) took place only subsequently.

[5] Cf. the discussions in John M. G. Barclay, "Thessalonica and Corinth: Social Contrasts in Pauline Christianity," *JSNT* 47 (1992): 56–72, and Bruce W. Winter, "Gallio's Ruling on the Legal Status of Early Christianity," *TynBul* 50 (1999): 213–24.

popular pagan philosophies of the day.[6] They were also (especially, once again, the more privileged among them) connected to an unusual degree with the social and educational elites of the city that they inhabited and aspired to a place among them—or, at least, to a way of maintaining their approval and patronage. It is true, as Paul reminds them in 1:26, that "not many" of them were "wise from a human perspective, not many powerful, not many of noble birth." But it is also true that he feels the need to remind them of that fact, and goes on at a subsequent point in the letter to paint a searingly sarcastic portrait of how "wise," "strong," and "distinguished" they are, in their own opinion at least (4:10). This was not a congregation of docile or compliant listeners, content to believe what they were told to believe and do what they were told to do.

It is no surprise, therefore, that Paul's letter to them includes so much by way of theological argumentation, as Paul engages with their questions and ideas, rebuking them at the points where they have, in his view, departed from basic Christian understanding and practice in a quest for social acceptance and advancement, while still taking seriously their questions and their desire for a coherent account of the world and the way one ought to live within it. And it is no surprise, too, that in doing so he is able to make such frequent reference to the Scriptures of the Old Testament and the overarching shape of the story that they tell, interpreted in light of its surprising climax in the resurrection of the crucified Jesus and its anticipated consummation in the age to come. There are few places within the literature of the New Testament that are as thick with Old Testament quotations and allusions as 1 Corinthians,[7] or as explicitly theological in the mode of engagement with them.[8]

---

[6] Cf. Timothy A. Brookins, "The Wise Corinthians: Their Stoic Education and Outlook," *JTS* 62 (2011): 51–76.

[7] Among Paul's letters, the density of Old Testament quotations in 1 Corinthians (17 direct quotations from Scripture across the 16 chapters of the letter) is exceeded only by Romans (60 quotations in 16 chapters) and Galatians (10 quotations in 6 chapters).

[8] For a discussion of what "theology" meant within the first-century context and its relevance to the mode of Paul's engagement with Old Testament Scripture in 1 Corinthians, see David I. Starling, "'Nothing Beyond What Is Written'? First Corinthians and the Hermeneutics of Early Christian *Theologia*," *JTI* 8 (2014): 45–62.

II. The Corinthian Context

The broad range of issues to which Paul applies the biblical theology of 1 Corinthians is likely, therefore, to have been a consequence, at least in part, of the Corinthians' desire for acceptance and esteem within the pagan social context that they inhabited. Many of those issues would have arisen in any first-century Greco-Roman city of a comparable size, but the distinctive cultural ethos and economic conditions that prevailed in Corinth were also influential in determining the particular matters that were most pressing for Paul to address.

Although the ancient Greek city of Corinth had enjoyed a long and storied past, the Corinth of Paul's day was a relatively young city, established by Julius Caesar in 44 BC after the original city of Corinth had been destroyed in 146 BC and the site left largely (though not entirely)[9] unoccupied for a century (cf. Strabo, *Geogr.* 8.6.23). The colonists sent by Rome to refound the city belonged for the most part (as Strabo tells us, based on his own visit to the city in 29 BC) to the "freedmen class," and the establishment of a new city gave them a rare opportunity to increase their social standing and acquire wealth through commercial activity.[10]

The commercial opportunities that were available in Corinth were enhanced by the city's strategic location on the narrow neck of land that linked the northern portion of Achaia with the Peloponnesian peninsula, as Strabo explains:

> Corinth is called "wealthy" because of its commerce, since it is situated on the Isthmus and is master of two harbors, of which the one leads straight to Asia, and the other to Italy; and it makes easy the exchange of merchandise from both countries that are so far distant from each other. (*Geogr.* 8.6.20)

Corinth's reputation as a wealthy city was matched by its reputation for the venality of its citizens; it is no accident that the second-century writer

---

[9] Cicero (*Agr.* 2.87; *Tusc.* 3.22.53) recounted visits that he had made to Corinth in his youth and interactions with people that he referred to as *Corinthii*; cf. Marcin N. Pawlak, "Corinth after 44BC: Ethnical and Cultural Changes," *Electrum* 20 (2013): 148–49.

[10] Worth noting, however, are the cautions against overstating the degree of social mobility in Roman Corinth that are voiced in Benjamin W. Millis, "The Local Magistrates and Elite of Roman Corinth," in *Corinth in Contrast: Studies in Inequality*, ed. Steven J. Friesen, Sarah A. James, and Daniel N. Schowalter, NovTSup (Leiden: Brill, 2014), 38–53.

Apuleius chose Corinth as the venue for a tale about greed and corruption (*Metam.* 10.18–35). The city was famous, too, for the contempt that its wealthier residents displayed for the miserable condition of the poor. The Athenian writer Alciphron has one of his fictitious letter writers, a "parasite" whose brief observations of the city had exposed him to some of the seamier aspects of its culture, comment bitterly on "the sordidness of the rich there and the misery of the poor" (*Ep.* 3.60). Although the social order in all Greco-Roman cities was highly stratified and the distribution of wealth extremely unequal, the particular circumstances of Corinth, with its relative shortage of land and surplus of labor, exacerbated those tendencies, and the city's reputation for both the luxury and excess of its landowning elite and the misery of its numerous slaves and wage laborers is borne out by the surviving archaeological evidence. In between those two extremes, the economic conditions that prevailed in the city also created space for a smallish subelite group, whose businesses provided goods and services to the wealthiest and highest-status residents of the city and whose success and prosperity depended on their patronage and custom.[11]

Two particular (and closely interrelated) subcategories of the trade and commerce that enriched the city were the trafficking of men and women as slaves and the readily available services of the prostitutes that constituted a key element of the city's reputation. Strabo's frequently quoted reference to "more than a thousand temple slaves, courtesans," whom the men and women of the city had dedicated to the service of Aphrodite at her temple, was, of course, made in relation to the old Greek city, not the Roman Corinth of his own time. The number of "more than a thousand" that he quotes, too, may well have been significantly inflated by the passage of time and the hyperbole with which such stories about the old city were passed down. Nevertheless, the sentences that follow suggest a shrewd awareness of the economic realities of life in a port city and go on to refer to a proverb that had continuing currency in Strabo's own time: "And therefore it was also on account of these women that the city was crowded with people and grew rich; for instance, the ship captains freely squandered their money, and hence the proverb, 'Not for

[11] Cf. especially the analysis in L. L. Welborn, "Inequality in Roman Corinth: Evidence from Diverse Sources Evaluated According to a Neo-Ricardian Model," in *Roman Corinth*, vol. 2 of *The First Urban Churches*, ed. James R. Harrison and L. L. Welborn (Atlanta: Scholars Press, 2016), 47–84.

every man is the voyage to Corinth.'" (*Geogr.* 8.6.20).[12] It is clear from the context in which the second-century orator Favorinus praises Corinth as "a city favoured by Aphrodite beyond all that are or ever have been" (Pseudo Dio Chrysostom, *Or.* 37.34) that he is referring not only to the symbolic role of the goddess as the city's patron deity but also to the culture of the city over which she presided and the ready availability of sexual services for those who had money to procure them. Kyle Harper sums up:

> In recent decades the reputation of Roman Corinth has enjoyed the sort of undeserved rehabilitation that comes only when generations of gross exaggeration allow overcorrection to pass as healthy revision. It is true that Corinth had first earned its notoriety in centuries long past. But the laxity of the Corinthians in venereal affairs was not just hoary legend. ... The eroticized atmosphere of Corinth was the predictable attribute of a wealthy, imperial crossroads; even against the indulgent background of late pagan sensuality, Corinth stood out as louche.[13]

The reputation of Corinth for excess, display, and crass competitiveness extended beyond the brothel and the marketplace to the cultural and intellectual life of the city. When the first-century orator Dio Chrysostom retells the famous story of the visit made to Corinth centuries earlier by Diogenes of Sinope, the Cynic philosopher, he has the philosopher explain that his journey there was made not because of the city's wisdom but because of its folly:

> For he observed that large numbers gathered at Corinth on account of the harbours and the *hetaerae*,[14] and because the city

[12] The same proverb is quoted by Horace (*Ep.* 1.17.36). Cf. the similar comments made by Cicero on the reputation of maritime cities, such as (old) Corinth, for "corruption and degeneration of morals," due to the influence of foreign customs and the ready availability of opportunities for extravagance and luxury (*Rep.* 2.7–9).

[13] Kyle Harper, *From Shame to Sin: The Christian Transformation of Sexual Morality in Late Antiquity* (Cambridge: Harvard University Press, 2013), 87.

[14] The word ἑταῖραι as it was used in the Hellenistic and Roman periods refers sometimes to courtesans or mistresses and sometimes (euphemistically) to the prostitutes who worked in the city's brothels. On the blurry line (both in language and in reality) between these categories, see Laura McClure, *Courtesans at Table: Gender and Greek Literary Culture in Athenaeus* (New York: Routledge, 2003), 9–17; Harper, *From Shame to Sin*, 47–50; Dominic Montserrat, *Sex and Society in Græco-Roman Egypt* (London: Kegan Paul, 1996), 107–8.

> was situated as it were at the cross-roads of Greece. Accordingly, just as the good physician should go and offer his services where the sick are most numerous, so, said he, the man of wisdom should take up his abode where fools are thickest in order to convict them of their folly and reprove them. (*Or.* 8.4–5)

The description of the city that he goes on to provide for his readers is ostensibly placed in the time of Diogenes but is almost certainly colored by his own experience of Corinth in the first century. It paints a vivid picture of a public square in which the sophists who were adulated by the crowds touted their wares within a public square in which they competed for attention with a motley assortment of "writers ... poets ... jugglers ... fortune tellers ... lawyers ... and peddlers":

> That was the time, too, when one could hear crowds of wretched sophists around Poseidon's temple shouting and reviling one another, and their disciples, as they were called, fighting with one another, many writers reading aloud their stupid works, many poets reciting their poems while others applauded them, many jugglers showing their tricks, many fortune tellers interpreting fortunes, lawyers innumerable perverting judgement, and peddlers not a few peddling whatever they happened to have. (*Or.* 8.9)[15]

As was the case in any typical Greco-Roman city of the first century, the urban landscape of Corinth included numerous temples dedicated to the worship of the various gods whose rites were observed by the city's inhabitants. A description of the city written by the second-century geographer Pausanias mentions shrines for the worship of deities including Poseidon (the patron god of the city), Aphrodite (Corinth's traditional protector, whose shrine watched over the city from the pinnacle of the Acrocorinth), Palaemon, the Cyclopes, Bellerophontes, Artemis, Isis, Dionysus, Fortune, Apollo, Hermes, Athena, Zeus, Asclepius, Serapis, Demeter and Kore ("the maid," i.e., Persephone), Hera Burnaea, and the deified Octavia (sister of Augustus).[16]

---

[15] Cf. the discussion in C. P. Jones, *The Roman World of Dio Chrysostom* (Cambridge: Harvard University Press, 1978), 47–49.

[16] Pausanias, *Descr.* 2.1–5. Cf. the discussion of the surviving archaeological evidence from Roman era Corinth in Nancy Bookidis, "The Sanctuaries of Corinth," *Corinth* 20 (2003): 256–58, and Nancy Bookidis, "Religion in Corinth: 146 B.C.E. to 100 C.E.," in *Urban Religion*

The Temple of Octavia, an imposing structure at the west end of the forum,[17] was the principal site in Corinth for the observance of the Roman imperial cult, in which honors were offered to deified emperors and their families, the genius of the emperor of the day, and the deity of personified Rome.[18] The imperial cult was of particular importance in Corinth because of the city's status as a Roman colony and the capital of the province of Achaia, and it gained still greater prominence in AD 54 when the city became the host of an annual province-wide imperial cult celebration.[19] Corinth's ties with Rome were a matter of pride for Corinthians and, at times, a focus of envy and criticism from other Achaians.[20] When Paul wrote to the believers in the city about the "many 'gods' and many 'lords'" (8:5) who were venerated and served by their pagan neighbors, his words would likely have evoked images of both the wide array of shrines within the city and the special place of the shrines and symbols that asserted the claims of Rome at its emperors.

Unmentioned by Pausanias but important to Paul was the synagogue in which Jews of the city gathered to pray, hear from the Scriptures, share community meals, and conduct community business. The partial remains of a stone lintel survive, bearing the inscription, "Synagogue of the Hebrews,"[21] and although the date of the building it came from is uncertain, Philo's *On the Embassy to Gaius* (written approximately a decade before Paul's first visit to Corinth) makes reference to a substantial "colony" of Jews living in Corinth in his time (*Embassy*, 282). It was in close connection with that synagogue and the circle of Jews and God-fearing

---

in Roman Corinth: Interdisciplinary Approaches, ed. Daniel N. Schowalter and Steven J. Friesen (Cambridge: Harvard University Press, 2005), 151–64.

[17] Assuming that the building Pausanias describes as the Temple of Octavia is to be identified with the building that archaeologists have labelled as Temple E. For an argument in favor of that identification, see C. K. Williams II, "A Re-evaluation of Temple E and the West End of the Forum of Corinth," in *The Greek Renaissance in the Roman Empire*, ed. Susan Walker and Averil Cameron (London: University of London Press, 1989), 156–62.

[18] Cf. Bruce W. Winter, *Divine Honours for the Caesars: The First Christians' Responses* (Grand Rapids: Eerdmans, 2015), 184–92; Panayotis Coutsoumpos, *Paul, Corinth, and the Roman Empire* (Eugene: Wipf & Stock, 2015), 52–56.

[19] Winter, *Divine Honours*, 196–225.

[20] Cf. the accusations leveled against Corinth on behalf of the citizens of Argos in the letter that is summarized and discussed in Antony Spawforth, "The Achaean Federal Cult Part 1: Pseudo-Julian, Letters 198," *TynBul* 46 (1995): 152–68, and Bruce W. Winter, *After Paul Left Corinth: The Influence of Secular Ethics and Social Change* (Grand Rapids: Eerdmans, 2001), 19–20.

[21] Cf. J. Murphy-O'Connor, *St. Paul's Corinth: Text and Archaeology*, 3rd ed. (Collegeville: Liturgical, 2002), 78–80.

gentiles who were attached to it that Paul's ministry in Corinth began and spread rapidly outward along lines of friendship, trade connections, and household membership.[22]

III. The Corinthian Church

The church that grew out of the ministry of Paul and his coworkers in Corinth brought together a mixture of Jews (7:18) and gentiles, at least some of whom had before their conversion been active participants in the cultic veneration of the traditional gods (8:7; 12:2). Although the instructions Paul gives in chapters 8–10 suggest a context in which this variety of different religious backgrounds created difficulties for some of the more recent converts from paganism, and the passing comments in 7:18–19 suggest at least the possibility that some Jewish and gentile congregation members may have felt anxiety regarding matters of circumcision and uncircumcision, there is no evidence within the letter of the sort of entrenched ethnoreligious divisions and estrangements Paul addresses in Romans 14–15. As far as we can tell from the contents of Paul's letters, gentile and Jewish believers in Corinth acknowledged one another as fellow members of a single ἐκκλησία and met together in mixed Jewish-gentile gatherings for their community meals.

The same sort of visible unity was not, however, consistently evident between the wealthier members of the Corinthian church and their poorer brothers and sisters, as Paul is compelled to point out in 11:17–34. Judging by the evidence of Paul's letters and the narrative in Acts 18, the members of the Corinthian church appear to have been drawn from a wide range of different socioeconomic circumstances. A handful belonged to the elite of the city and/or the relatively wealthy subelite, who enjoyed their patronage and profited by supplying them with goods and services. This group would have included such people as Erastus, who is named by Paul in Romans 16:23 as the "city treasurer" (οἰκονόμος τῆς πόλεως),[23]

---

[22] Cf. the imaginative reconstruction of the social matrix within which the growth of the Christian community in Corinth took place during the period of Paul's original residency in the city, in L. L. Welborn, *An End to Enmity: Paul and the "Wrongdoer" of Second Corinthians*, BZNW (Berlin: De Gruyter, 2011), 392–400.

[23] This Erastus may or may not have been the same person as the Erastus who is referred to in the pavement inscription adjoining the courtyard at the northeast entrance of the theater. Although the pavement adjacent to the inscription was probably laid in the second

and Gaius, described in the same verse as "host to me and to the whole church." Other possible members of this category include Stephanas, whose household constituted "the firstfruits of Achaia" (1 Cor 16:15), Crispus, who is named in 1:14 as a householder and in Acts 18:8 as a "leader of the synagogue" (ἀρχισυνάγωγος),[24] and the Chloe whose "people" (slaves? household members? house-church members?) are referred to in 1:11—if indeed she was a member of the Corinthian church at all.[25] At the other extreme were those whom Paul describes in 11:22 as "those who have nothing" (τοὺς μὴ ἔχοντας)—or perhaps "those not having homes" (τοὺς μὴ ἔχοντας [οἰκίας])[26]—language suggesting either the insecurity of those who did not have homes of their own or a secure place within the household of another, or the even more precarious situation of those who had no possessions at all to speak of and lived on the edge of subsistence.[27] Between these two extremes there were, no doubt, a significant number of others who lacked the wealth and privileges of the former group but possessed somewhat more by way of social and economic capital than the latter. The members of this middling group (including shopkeepers, skilled workers, and the minority of slaves whose situation was advantageous enough for them to have a realistic prospect of purchasing their freedom or otherwise advancing their status) would likely have felt a

century AD, the inscription itself is not quite flush with the other paving stones and is laid at a slightly different orientation, and may be a reused stone from an earlier pavement in that same location or nearby. On the likely second-century date of the paved courtyard, see Charles K. Williams, "Corinth, 2011: Investigation of the West Hall of the Theater," *Hesperia* 82 (2013): 493–94. On Latin pavement inscriptions as a first-century (mainly Augustan or Tiberian) form, see the discussion and list of examples in Steven J. Friesen, "The Wrong Erastus: Ideology, Archaeology, and Exegesis," in *Corinth in Context: Comparative Studies on Religion and Society*, ed. Steven J. Friesen, Daniel N. Schowalter, and James C. Walters (Leiden: Brill, 2010), 242–45. For arguments for and against identifying the Erastus of Rom 16:23 with the Erastus of the inscription, see John K. Goodrich, "Erastus of Corinth (Romans 16.23): Responding to Recent Proposals on his Rank, Status, and Faith," NTS 57 (2011): 583–93, and Friesen, "The Wrong Erastus," 231–56.

[24] The title of ἀρχισυνάγωγος was an honorific one and was generally conferred on a person who had been a source of substantial benefaction for the synagogue community. Cf. Tessa Rajak and David Noy, "*Archisynagogoi*: Office, Title and Social Status in the Greco-Jewish Synagogue," *JRS* 83 (1993): 84–89; Murphy-O'Connor, *St. Paul's Corinth*, 80.

[25] As argued below in the comments on 1:11, I suspect "Chloe's people" were probably Ephesian visitors to Corinth, not Corinthian visitors to Ephesus.

[26] Note the contrast with the group described in the first half of the verse as having "homes in which to eat and drink."

[27] See especially the discussion in Welborn, "Inequality in Roman Corinth," 66–67.

strong pull to maintain and strengthen their connections with those who were above them on the social ladder and a corresponding temptation to minimize the shame that would have come from associating too closely with those who were below them.

It is difficult to be certain regarding the size of the Corinthian church at the time of the writing of 1 Corinthians. One important clue can be found in Paul's reference to Gaius in Romans 16:23, where (writing from Corinth) he describes him as "host to me and to the whole church" (ὁ ξένος μου καὶ ὅλης τῆς ἐκκλησίας).[28] The language of this description suggests both that the church was small enough that all of its members could congregate together in the venue that he provided and that it was large enough to require a verbal distinction between occasions such as these in which the "whole church" assembled and the smaller gatherings in which believers met together week by week.[29] Depending on the size of the venue that Gaius made available, the number of smaller subgroups within the congregation, and the proportion of the smaller groups' members and adherents who attended the gatherings of the "whole church," the total number of those who belonged to the Corinthian church could have been as few as thirty or forty or as many as one or two hundred.[30]

---

[28] An alternative interpretation is suggested by John Kloppenborg, who argues that the description of Gaius as ξένος of Paul and the church was more likely referring to him as the "guest" than as the "host." John S. Kloppenborg, *Christ's Associations: Connecting and Belonging in the Ancient City* (New Haven: Yale University Press, 2019), 85–86. Kloppenborg's proposal is linguistically possible, but it is difficult to picture Gaius as the "guest" of Paul (who was himself a visitor—albeit a long-term visitor—in the city), or to explain why Paul would go out of his way to say that it is the "whole church" that is playing host to Gaius.

[29] Cf. Robert J. Banks, *Paul's Idea of Community: Spirit and Culture in Early House Churches*, 3rd ed. (Grand Rapids: Baker, 2020), 25–34.

[30] Cf. Murphy-O'Connor, *St. Paul's Corinth*, 178–84 (forty or fifty, with the upper limit set by the assumption that the venue was the atrium of a typically sized urban domus); Craig Steven De Vos, *Church and Community Conflicts: The Relationships of the Thessalonian, Corinthian, and Philippian Churches with Their Wider Civic Communities*, SBLDS (Atlanta: Scholars Press, 1999), 203–5 (more than one hundred if the venue was a public space rented by Gaius on behalf of the congregation); Kloppenborg, *Christ's Associations*, 97–130 (fifteen to thirty members, in keeping with the normal size of Greco-Roman cultic associations); Chrys C. Caragounis, "A House Church in Corinth? An Inquiry into the Structure of Early Corinthian Christianity," in *Saint Paul and Corinth: 1950 Years Since the Writing of the Epistles to the Corinthians*, ed. Constantine J. Belezos (Athens: Psichogios, 2009), 1:413 ("hundreds of members," on the assumption that the "whole church" could have met in a public venue as large as a rented civic basilica); Welborn, *An End to Enmity*, 324, 48–55 (approximately one hundred, meeting across various spaces within the domus of Gaius and assuming a large house such as the House of the Opus Sectile Panel, the remains of which were excavated in 1928–1929).

If we assume that the smaller gatherings within which believers assembled week by week typically took place within a household context, then the potential hosts of such groups could have included householders such as Stephanas, Crispus, Gaius, Erastus, Chloe (if she was a member of the church or open to having its members meet in her house), and Aquila and Priscilla (who could have hosted a moderately sized gathering in the workspace attached to their dwelling, as they appeared to have done during their later periods of residency in Ephesus and in Rome; cf. 16:19; Rom 16:3–5). It is possible, too, that other subgroups of the congregation may have met in non-domestic settings, including any of the wide variety of indoor and outdoor spaces surveyed by Edward Adams as possible venues for early Christian gatherings.[31]

The wording of Paul's endorsement of Stephanas and his household in 16:15–18 suggests that Stephanas was not only (in all likelihood) the host of a regular household gathering but also, along with various others including Fortunatus and Achaicus (probably slaves or freedmen within his household), one of a number of congregation members whose service extended beyond these smaller gatherings to the activities and ministry networks of the entire ἐκκλησία. The references elsewhere in the letter to the Corinthians' "countless instructors in Christ" (4:15) and to the plenitude and diversity of the gifts with which the church had been blessed (1:4–7; 12:1–31) convey the impression that ministry and leadership within the Corinthian church took a wide variety of forms. These varied forms of ministry and leadership appear to have been exercised within a complex matrix of household and patronage relationships, generating crisscrossing lines of influence and responsibility and (to Paul's consternation) partisan divisions and hierarchies of status that were sharply antithetical to the value system implied by the gospel Paul had handed on to the church.

IV. Paul's Letter: Occasion, Aims, and Coherence

It was tensions such as these (including both the internal divisions and debates within the congregation and the various instances of discordance Paul perceived between the Corinthians' attitudes and practices and the

[31] Edward Adams, *The Earliest Christian Meeting Places: Almost Exclusively Houses?*, LNTS (London: T&T Clark, 2013), 137–97.

gospel that he had preached to them) that appear to have created the occasion for the writing of 1 Corinthians.

The travel plans Paul describes in the final chapter of the letter indicate that it was written from Ephesus, at a time of year that was not long before the festival of Pentecost (16:8), suggesting a date in the spring of AD 54 or 55, during the two-year period of ministry in that city that Luke describes in Acts 19. During the interval of time between the end of Paul's first eighteen-month period of residence in Corinth and the writing of 1 Corinthians, Paul had evidently maintained close contact with the church, with the assistance of various members of both churches who had made trips to and fro between the two cities,[32] and had already written them the earlier letter that he refers to in 5:9.

Between the sending of that earlier letter and the decision to write 1 Corinthians, Paul appears to have received several fresh communications from Corinth, in both oral and written forms. Included among the oral communications that he had received were the report of leadership-related divisions that he refers to in 1:11 (conveyed to him by "Chloe's people"), a report of an ongoing sexual relationship between a congregation member and his father's wife (5:1), and a report of status-based divisions within the congregation when they gather to celebrate the Lord's Supper (11:18). Further to these matters, about which Paul explicitly says that he had "hear[d]" (11:18) or received a report (1:11; 5:1), it is also likely that he had received oral reports about some of the other matters that he responds to within the letter, including predatory lawsuits initiated by members of the congregation against their fellow believers (6:1–11) and a culture of sexual permissiveness that extended well beyond the particularly egregious instance referred to in 5:1 (6:12–20 and 7:2).

In addition to the oral communications regarding the Corinthian church that Paul had received, a letter had been sent to him by the church (or perhaps by a subset of its members). Paul first makes explicit mention of this letter in 7:1 ("Now in response to the matters you wrote about ..."), and the following chapters contain a series of topics introduced by the same phrase, "now about" (περὶ δέ), probably referring back to issues that the Corinthian letter had raised (see 7:25; 8:1, [4]; 12:1; 16:1,

[32] According to the assumptions relied upon by the Stanford Geospatial Network Model of the Roman World (https://orbis.stanford.edu/), a sea trip from Corinth to Ephesus at a favorable time of year, such as the spring, took just three or four days, with the return trip taking only slightly longer.

12). Although these are the only places within Paul's letter that make explicit reference to the letter from the Corinthians (assuming that this was the intended function of the περὶ δέ formula) it is possible that other assertions and questions contained within the Corinthian letter are also alluded to by Paul at other points (e.g., in the clarification that he offers in 5:9–11 regarding the intent of the instructions in his earlier letter; in his response in 11:2 to an apparent claim made by the Corinthians that they "remember [him] in everything and hold fast to the traditions"; in the "other matters" that he refers to in 11:34, promising further instructions when he next visits; or in the reference in 15:12 to the fact that "some of you say, 'there is no resurrection of the dead'").

Given the kinds of issues to which Paul responds in the sections of his letter that commence with the περὶ δέ formula and the tone of his responses, it appears that the Corinthian letter was not a polite and deferential request for information but a rather pointed series of assertions and questions put to Paul by a privileged subgroup of the congregation who were conscious of their superior knowledge and spiritual prowess.[33] If that was the case (and if the letter carriers who brought the letter to Paul were expected by its senders to function as their representatives and to advocate for the viewpoints that the letter put forward),[34] then it is unlikely that this delegation from Corinth was the same as the group from the household of Stephanas that Paul endorses so warmly in 16:15–18.[35] A scenario that more plausibly accounts for the tone of both Paul's commendation of Stephanas's household members and his responses to the Corinthian letter would be one in which Stephanas, Fortunatus, and Achaicus were already with Paul when the letter from Corinth arrived (perhaps having wintered with him in Ephesus), and "the brothers" (16:12) Paul sent back to Corinth with his letter included both this trio and the group who had brought the Corinthians' letter to him.

---

[33] Cf. Gordon D. Fee, *The First Epistle to the Corinthians*, 2nd ed., NICNT (Grand Rapids: Eerdmans, 2014), 295–96.

[34] Cf. the comments on the expected function of letter carriers in Peter M. Head, "'Witnesses Between You and Us': The Role of the Letter-Carriers in 1 Clement," in *Studies on the Text of the New Testament and Early Christianity in Honor of Michael W. Holmes*, ed. D. M. Gurtner, J. Hernández, and P. Foster, NTTSD (Leiden: Brill, 2015), 492–93, and the longer discussion in E. Randolph Richards, *Paul and First-Century Letter Writing: Secretaries, Composition, and Collection* (Downers Grove: InterVarsity Press, 2004), 188–209.

[35] Contra Fee, *First Epistle to the Corinthians*, 7.

If the immediate occasion for the sending of 1 Corinthians was the need to reply to the letter he had received from the Corinthians, it is striking that he leaves it so long before he finally makes mention of their letter in 7:1. The decision to deal first with the reports that he has received of divisions, immorality, and predatory lawsuits is a strong implicit reminder of his pastoral authority over the Corinthians; he is happy to respond to the theories and questions that the Corinthian letter writers have put to him, but there are other things (presumably not mentioned in their letter!) that he insists on addressing first.

Interpreters of 1 Corinthians differ widely on the question of whether there is a single thread of coherence that ties together Paul's responses to the diverse range of issues that have been reported to him or raised within the Corinthians' letter and (if so) what that thread of coherence is. According to one influential school of thought, the thesis statement for the entire letter is to be found in the appeal for unity Paul makes in 1:10,[36] with all of the various topics that follow functioning as arguments in support of that appeal. It is certainly true that issues of division, disunity, and disorder are a recurring concern within the letter, not only in chapters 1–4 but also in subsequent passages such as 11:17–34 and chapters 12–14. As other commentators have pointed out, however, it would be unreasonable to expect that a letter as long as 1 Corinthians, addressing a situation as complex as the one Paul is faced with in Corinth, should have the kind of tight unity of theme and neatness of structure that one might look for in a textbook piece of deliberative rhetoric.[37] The attempt to read the entire letter through the lens of 1:10 as the propositio requires

---

[36] E.g., Margaret Mary Mitchell, *Paul and the Rhetoric of Reconciliation: An Exegetical Investigation of the Language and Composition of 1 Corinthians* (Louisville: Westminster John Knox, 1993), 197–200; Ben Witherington, *Conflict and Community in Corinth: A Socio-Rhetorical Commentary on 1 and 2 Corinthians* (Grand Rapids: Eerdmans, 1995), 69, 94. Cf. the criticisms of this approach in Anthony C. Thiselton, *The First Epistle to the Corinthians: A Commentary on the Greek Text*, NIGTC (Grand Rapids: Eerdmans, 2000), 33–34; Roy E. Ciampa and Brian S. Rosner, *The First Letter to the Corinthians*, PNTC (Grand Rapids: Eerdmans, 2010), 19–21; and the more nuanced position articulated in B. J. Oropeza, *1 Corinthians*, NCCS (Eugene: Cascade, 2017), 9–10, 16, emphasizing the close interrelationship between reinforcement of insider solidarity and resistance to assimilation with outsiders.

[37] Cf. the comments in Raymond F. Collins, "Reflections on 1 Corinthians as a Hellenistic Letter," in *The Corinthian Correspondence*, ed. Reimund Bieringer, BETL (Leuven: Peeters, 1996), 39–61.

us to force quite a number of its sections out of shape to make them fit.[38] The call for an urgent exercise of church discipline that Paul issues in chapter 5, for example, certainly includes a depiction of the church as a single "batch of dough" (5:6), but the function of that image is not to speak about the divisive consequences that the man's actions might give rise to but to highlight the contagiousness of unrepentant sin when it is tolerated within the community.[39] The section that follows, in which Paul responds to reports regarding the lawsuits that members of the congregation have initiated, is focused at least as much on the injustice that the lawsuits have perpetrated as on the disunity between "brother" and "brother" that they have created. The response in chapters 8–10 to the Corinthians' questions about food sacrificed to idols is framed not as an adjudication or mediation between two warring factions but as a warning to the "knowledgeable" members of the congregation about the dangers of arrogance and complacency (both to themselves and to their weaker brothers and sisters). And even in chapter 12, where the unity and solidarity of the congregation are undeniably evoked by the image of the church as the body of Christ, Paul's use of the metaphor transcends and at several points sharply subverts its conventional function as a reinforcement of the harmonious ordering of a hierarchical political community and becomes, instead, a vigorous appeal for the special honor that ought to be given to the body's weakest and most vulnerable members. All things considered, the range of issues Paul addresses and the various ways in which he frames his responses suggest that his concern is at least as much for the ethical distinctiveness of the Corinthian community and the maintenance of its boundaries with the surrounding culture as it is for the preservation of the community's internal unity and concord.[40]

---

[38] For an extended discussion and evaluation of Mitchell's reading of 1:10 and its implications for the interpretation of the letter, see David I. Starling, "'In the Same Mind and the Same Purpose': 1 Corinthians, Unity, and the Graeco-Roman Political Tradition," in *Paul in His Jewish and Graeco-Roman Contexts*, ed. Constantine R. Campbell and James R. Harrison (Sydney: SCD Press, 2025), from which several of the sentences in this paragraph and the following two are adapted.

[39] Contra Mitchell, *Paul and the Rhetoric of Reconciliation*, 112.

[40] Cf. the comments in Ciampa and Rosner, *The First Letter to the Corinthians*, 21–25, and Frank Thielman, *Theology of the New Testament: A Canonical and Synthetic Approach* (Grand Rapids: Zondervan, 2005), 291–99, and the analysis in Eckhard J. Schnabel, *Der erste Brief des Paulus an die Korinther*, HTA (Wuppertal: Brockhaus, 2006), 33–34.

But acknowledging the inadequacy of approaches that attempt to read everything through the lens of the call to unity in 1:10 does not require us to give up altogether on the idea that there might be some form of underlying coherence that ties the letter together or a pastoral/rhetorical logic that informs the sequence and arrangement of its parts. As we have already argued above, there is an implied pastoral/rhetorical strategy at work in the structuring decision Paul makes to address (most of) the reports that he has received before he turns to the questions and theories that have been conveyed to him within the Corinthians' letter. A further indication of how the various issues addressed within the letter cohere within Paul's mind can be seen in the recurring rhetorical question, "Don't you know that ... ?" (οὐκ οἴδατε ὅτι ... ;), which Paul asks ten times across the various sections of the letter (cf. 3:16; 5:6; 6:2, 3, 9, 15, 16, 19; 9:13, 24), frequently followed by a reminder of basic entailments of the gospel and the Corinthians' experience of the outpoured Spirit (3:16–17; 6:2, 3, 9, 15, 19) or of other elementary facts, drawn from Scripture or from common knowledge, that a congregation as "knowledgeable" as the Corinthians ought to have been well aware of (5:6; 6:16; 9:13, 24). In addition to these are the various other rhetorical questions Paul puts to the Corinthians, frequently expressing his incredulity at their apparent forgetfulness of the gospel and its immediate implications or of the events surrounding their own conversion (e.g., 1:13, 20; 4:7), and the points at which he offers the Corinthians extended and explicit reminders of core gospel tradition (e.g., 11:23–26; 15:1–11). As a remedy for this apparent forgetfulness, manifested in a wide variety of attitudes and practices that are antithetical to the values implied by the gospel, Paul begins and ends the central core of the letter body with passages that remind his readers of the message he preached to them during the time of his original ministry in Corinth.[41] The former of these two reminders, in 1:18–2:5, focuses on the message of the cross as the judgment of God on all human arrogance and the heart of the wisdom Paul urges the Corinthians to live by; the latter, in chapter 15, focuses on the apostolic testimony to the resurrection as the foundation for the assurance Paul gives to the Corinthians that all who live by that humble, countercultural wisdom will one day be vindicated and glorified with Christ as participants in his victory over the rulers of

[41] Properly speaking, the letter body of 1 Corinthians commences at 1:10 and extends to 16:12, but its theological core is contained in 1:18–15:58.

the present age.[42] Everything between is framed by these two reminders and applies the wisdom that is revealed in the message of the cross and vindicated in the resurrection to the multiplicity of issues that have been raised by the Corinthians in their letter or made known to Paul in the reports that he has received.[43]

The various points at which the Corinthians have departed from this wisdom or voiced their skepticism regarding aspects of it are probably best explained not as the product of an explicitly theological teaching, such as a developed and fully articulated "over-realized eschatology,"[44] or as a consequence of overtly theological disputes between the factions named in 1:12.[45] A more plausible explanation, given the way in which Paul frames his responses, is that the Corinthians (or, in the case of most issues Paul addresses within the letter, a privileged and relatively well-educated subgroup among them) have uncritically permitted their attitudes and practices to be shaped by assumptions that are basic to their culture but antithetical to the gospel.[46] For some of the Corinthians at least, the shaping influence of these tacit cultural assumptions was heightened by their desire for social acceptance and advancement (cf. 3:18–20; 4:8–13; 15:33–34), crystallized in a collection of maxims and principles drawn from Greco-Roman philosophical sources,[47] and reinforced by the way in which they experienced the manifestations of the Spirit and practiced the Spirit's gifts. It would be a mistake, however, to conclude from this that the Corinthians' problems were "non-theological" in nature or that the corrective Paul applies is merely to assert his own authority and issue a series of rebukes and instructions on matters of conduct and character. If "theology" is to be understood not in the sense that it later came to carry in Christian usage (referring to a systematic,

---

[42] See especially Matthew R. Malcolm, *Paul and the Rhetoric of Reversal in 1 Corinthians: The Impact of Paul's Gospel on His Macro-Rhetoric*, SNTSMS (Cambridge: Cambridge University Press, 2013), 231–66.

[43] Cf. David I. Starling, "'As to Sensible People': Human Reason and Divine Revelation in 1 Corinthians 8–10," in *Revelation and Reason in Christian Theology*, ed. David I. Starling and Christopher C. Green (Bellingham: Lexham, 2018), 113–26.

[44] Contra Anthony C. Thiselton, "Realised Eschatology at Corinth," NTS 24 (1978).

[45] See the discussion on that verse below.

[46] Cf. David E. Garland, "First Corinthians," in *Theological Interpretation of the New Testament: A Book-by-Book Survey*, ed. Kevin J. Vanhoozer (Grand Rapids: Baker, 2008), 97–98.

[47] See especially Timothy A. Brookins, *Corinthian Wisdom, Stoic Philosophy, and the Ancient Economy*, SNTSMS (New York: Cambridge University Press, 2014).

scholastic, and exclusively Christian discourse) but in something more akin to the broader, looser sense that word implied in the first-century context, then both the Corinthians' departures from the wisdom of the gospel and the corrective Paul applies were pervasively theological in nature.[48] In order for the Corinthians to live the way in which the gospel calls them to live, they must reframe their understanding of all things in light of the gospel announcement of Christ's death and resurrection (cf. 15:1–11), proclaimed as the fulfillment of Scripture and the inbreaking of the ends of the ages (cf. 10:1–13) and as the anticipation of a day when all things will be placed beneath Christ's feet and handed over to the Father, so that God may be all in all (cf. 15:20–28).[49]

Paul's letter is, therefore, a rich resource for us to draw upon if we wish to understand the grand biblical narrative that shaped the various reminders, rebukes, and encouragements that he brought to bear upon the lives of the congregations that he ministered to. It also offers us an illuminating glimpse into the way in which he brought that grand narrative into critical conversation with the assumptions and beliefs of the prevailing culture about God and the gods, the nature and purpose of reality, and the wisdom that ought to shape the practices of everyday life. It is, in other words, a richly theological letter, which cries out for the kind of interpretation that is attentive to biblical-theological themes and their application to the way in which we think and live within our own cultural context. In the pages that follow, that will be our task.

V. Biblical and Theological Themes

Almost the entirety of 1 Corinthians is made up of Paul's responses to the various issues that have been raised in the reports that have reached Paul and the letter that has been sent to him. This is not a treatise or oration on a single, theological theme but a letter in which Paul works his way through a series of issues, responding to them one by one.[50] Nevertheless, it would be a mistake to read this letter as if it were merely a series of ad hoc reactions to various Corinthian problems and questions. Paul's

---

[48] Cf. Starling, "Nothing Beyond What Is Written?," 45–62.

[49] See especially Richard B. Hays, "The Conversion of the Imagination: Scripture and Eschatology in 1 Corinthians," *NTS* 45 (1999): 391–412.

[50] Cf. the comments in Garland, "1 Corinthians," 98; Collins, "Reflections on 1 Corinthians," 39–61.

responses to the issues he addresses are not formulated at random; they are, rather, deeply grounded in a theological framework that he wants to teach and reinforce throughout the letter. They also repeatedly connect and collide in a variety of complicated ways with key elements of the pagan *theologia* that was presupposed and practiced as the mainstream belief system of the city's Greco-Roman inhabitants and continued to exercise a powerful influence on the thinking of at least some of the Corinthians.[51] First Corinthians is not a theological *treatise*, but it is, in multiple important and interconnected senses, a deeply *theological* letter.

It is also a letter that is pervasively informed by a *biblical*-theological perspective. The apostle Paul was, as scholars including J. Christiaan Beker and J. Ross Wagner have rightly recognized, a "hermeneutical theologian,"[52] whose theological reflections on the topics that he addresses were shaped at every point by the Scriptures of the Old Testament and by the various configurations of the story of Israel and the nations that they narrate and project, interpreted in light of the surprising climax to that story that Paul perceived in the gospel of the crucified Christ.[53] If we are to understand the way in which Paul responds to the issues in the Corinthian church that have been brought to his attention and discern the significance of his responses for our own understanding and practice today, we will need to pay attention not only to the immediate circumstances of the Corinthian congregation (insofar as we are able to discern them) but also to the much larger story of Scripture and its fulfillment in Christ, that functions as both the frame within which Paul encourages the Corinthians to interpret their circumstances and the bridge between their circumstances and our own.

---

[51] On the connections and conflicts between 1 Corinthians and the Greco-Roman *theologia* of the time, see Starling, "Nothing Beyond What Is Written?," 45–62.

[52] J. Christiaan Beker, "Recasting Pauline Theology: The Coherence-Contingency Scheme as Interpretive Model," in *Thessalonians, Philippians, Galatians, Philemon*, ed. Jouette M. Bassler, vol. 1 of *Pauline Theology* (Minneapolis: Fortress, 1991), 15; J. Ross Wagner, *Heralds of the Good News: Isaiah and Paul "in Concert" in the Letter to the Romans*, NovTSup (Leiden: Brill, 2002), 1.

[53] On the narrative dimensions of Paul's theology, see especially Ben Witherington, *Paul's Narrative Thought-World: The Tapestry of Tragedy and Triumph* (Louisville: Westminster, 1994), 2; Francis Watson, "Scripture in Pauline Theology: How Far Down Does It Go?," *JTI* 2 (2008): 192; Bruce W. Longenecker, ed., *Narrative Dynamics in Paul: A Critical Assessment* (Louisville: Westminster, 2002); Ian W. Scott, *Implicit Epistemology in the Letters of Paul: Story, Experience and the Spirit*, WUNT (Tübingen: Mohr Siebeck, 2006), 159–276.

The story that underpins Paul's arguments within the letter is explicitly salvation-historical in its shape and content.[54] Paul's assertion that the gospel announcements of Christ's death for our sins and resurrection on the third day are "in accordance with the [Old Testament] scriptures" (15:3–4 NRSV) is consistent with the salvation-historical hermeneutical framework that is implied and assumed throughout the whole of 1 Corinthians.[55] Within this framework, convictions about the oneness and self-consistency of God invite us to understand the church's present and future in narrative continuity and typological correspondence with the story of God's actions in the past.[56] Thus, the gentile believers in Corinth are invited to view the Israelites of the Exodus generation as "our ancestors" (10:1) and to understand the things that happened to them as "examples" (τύποι) ... "for our instruction" (10:6, 11), illustrating and reinforcing convictions of permanent validity about enduringly relevant attributes of God (in this instance, God's jealous love and faithfulness).

The stability and unity of this grand narrative are critical for the hermeneutical bridge that Paul builds across the ditch between historical assertions about unique, particular events and theological truth-claims of universal validity and relevance. The events to which Paul and his fellow apostles bear witness line up within a single story, with a single, divine protagonist about whom statements can be made that have enduring truth and applicability; on the basis of the narrative logic of that story,[57] Paul is confident that he can commend such statements to the Corinthians as "sensible" people (10:15), asking them to "judge for [them]selves" the implications for their conduct.[58]

Nevertheless, a reader of Paul's letters cannot help noticing that this narrative, as Paul configures it for his readers, is not a *smoothly* linear one in which the covenant-faithfulness of God is met with the answering faithfulness of his people and the glorious triumph of their cause. Readers familiar with the original context of his Old Testament quotation in 1

---

[54] The material in the following paragraphs is adapted from David I. Starling, "Not a Wisdom of This Age: Theology and the Future of the Post-Christendom Church," in *Theology and the Future*, ed. Trevor H. Cairney and David I. Starling (London: T&T Clark, 2014), 93–96.

[55] See especially Witherington, *Paul's Narrative Thought-World*, and Richard B. Hays, *Echoes of Scripture in the Letters of Paul* (New Haven: Yale University Press, 1989), 84–121.

[56] See especially Hays, "Conversion of the Imagination," 391–412.

[57] Cf. Ian W. Scott, *Paul's Way of Knowing: Story, Experience, and the Spirit* (Grand Rapids: Baker, 2009), 277–88.

[58] Cf. Starling, "As to Sensible People," 113–26.

Corinthians 10:7, for example, will be reminded of the shocking gash that the account of Israel's apostasy in Exodus 32 tears in the fabric of that book. More than that: Paul's picture of the church as the community "on whom the ends of the ages have come" (10:11) is a reminder of the sharp disjunctions between the old age and the new that are characteristic of the mode in which he renders the story of Israel and the church, in the light of God's saving intervention in Christ. In this sense, the narrative of God, Israel, Christ, and the world that Paul evokes in his letters can be described not only as a "salvation-historical" narrative but also, more specifically, as an "apocalyptic" narrative—apocalyptic being the particular form that salvation history takes when the blackness of the present is understood to be so thick that God's purposes can neither be perceived nor fulfilled without a new and direct divine intervention in both revelation and salvation.[59] A Christian theology that is true to its apocalyptic roots will resist the temptation to offer a neat, static providential system that explains and justifies the world as it is and assumes that the explanation it offers will be universally accepted by all reasonable people. Instead, it will take serious account of the hiddenness of God's hand in the world that we see and the desperately unsatisfactory condition of the world that is presided over by "the rulers of this age" (2:6), and it will insist on asserting propositions that appear laughably foolish from within the plausibility structures erected by the elites of this present age.

The narrative within which the New Testament describes the work of God in Christ is not only a *salvation-historical* and *apocalyptic* narrative. It is also, as an integral element of the outworking of both those characteristics, an explicitly *cosmic* narrative: "for us there is one God, the Father. All things are from him, and we exist for him. And there is one Lord, Jesus Christ. All things are through him, and we exist through him" (1 Cor. 8:6). The grand finale of the story is one in which, through the victory of Christ

---

[59] "Apocalyptic" refers properly to a particular corpus of early Jewish writings: "a genre of revelatory literature with a narrative framework, in which a revelation is mediated by an otherworldly being to a human recipient ... envisag[ing] eschatological salvation and involv[ing] a supernatural world ... intended to interpret present earthly circumstances in light of the supernatural world and of the future, and to influence both the understanding and the behavior of the audience by means of divine authority." Adela Yarbro Collins, "Introduction: Early Christian Apocalypticism, Genre and Setting," *Semeia* 36 (1986): 7. More broadly, and by extension, the adjective "apocalyptic" can also be used with reference to the literary and theological aspects of many other texts from early Judaism and early Christianity that share an affinity of outlook with these apocalyptic writings.

over every hostile power, God will be "all in all" (15:28). The scope and scale of this narrative embolden Paul, as he writes to the Corinthians, to make repeated, sweeping assertions about "all things"—almost forty times within the sixteen chapters of the letter. Not all of these references to "all things" are cosmic in scope: at times, Paul is speaking about the "all things" that one encounters in daily life, or the "all things" that are done in the Christian gathering, or the "all things" that he is willing to become in the service of a mission to "all people." But it is still striking to note the confidence with which Paul constructs these utterances of general or universal applicability. Because of the cosmic scope of the story Paul tells, he unhesitatingly assumes that it will in some way inform our understanding of every corner of the universe and every aspect of life.

§1 God

Foundational for the theological framework Paul teaches in 1 Corinthians is the creational monotheism that was taught in the Old Testament Scriptures and remained fundamental to the religious and ethical distinctiveness of first-century Jews and Christians.[60] The weightiest and most sustained reflection on this theme within the letter (and, indeed, within any of Paul's writings) is contained within chapters 8–10, where Paul addresses the questions that the Corinthians have put to him about participation in temple meals and the eating of food that has been offered to idols.

Paul begins his response to the Corinthian letter writers' question in 8:1–4, by speaking about the "knowledge" that they have appealed to in justifying their attendance at temple meals:

> 1 Now about food sacrificed to idols: We know that "we all have knowledge." Knowledge puffs up, but love builds up. 2 If anyone thinks he knows anything, he does not yet know it as he ought to know it. 3 But if anyone loves God, he is known by him.
> 4 About eating food sacrificed to idols, then, we know that "an idol is nothing in the world," and that "there is no God but one."

[60] For an account of the various dimensions of Paul's "creational monotheism" and its relationship to his confession of Jesus as Lord, see especially N. T. Wright, *Paul and the Faithfulness of God*, COQG (London: SPCK, 2013), 619–773.

Despite the sharp rebukes in verses 2–3 to the arrogance expressed in the way that the Corinthians have asserted and made use of their knowledge, Paul's response in the following verses makes it clear that the core content of the creational monotheism expressed in the slogans of verse 4 is still entirely compatible with (and required by) the Christian confession of Jesus as Lord:

> 5 For even if there are so-called gods, whether in heaven or on earth—as there are many "gods" and many "lords"—6 yet for us there is one God, the Father. All things are from him, and we exist for him. And there is one Lord, Jesus Christ. All things are through him, and we exist through him. (8:5–6)

Paul's language in verse 6 ("one God ... one Lord") has a solemn creedal character that echoes the form and substance of the Shema (Deut 6:4). But the Deuteronomic formula is not reproduced unchanged. First, and most importantly, Paul expands the assertion of the Shema about "the Lord our God" into two parallel clauses about "one God, the Father," and "one Lord, Jesus Christ," making it clear that the traditional confession of fidelity to one God, YHWH, must now be refracted through the prism of faith in Jesus, who participates in the very identity of the God of Israel as the one Lord of all.[61] And second, within those clauses, he incorporates two carefully constructed elaborations ("All things are from him, and we exist for him ... All things are through him, and we exist through him") that echo the terminology and grammar of Hellenistic Judaism and Stoic natural theology.[62] The effect of this is to bring the Deuteronomic call for covenant loyalty into conversation with the popular beliefs and philosophical theology of Paul's day, making explicit its cosmological implications.[63]

The discussion that follows, in verses 7–13, shifts the focus from the common knowledge possessed as axiomatic by all believers (as encapsulated in the slogans of vv. 4–6) to the more theologically sophisticated inferences that some, though not all, of the Corinthians have succeeded

---

[61] See especially Richard Bauckham, *God Crucified: Monotheism and Christology in the New Testament* (Grand Rapids: Eerdmans, 1999), 36–40; Wright, *Paul and the Faithfulness of God*, 661–70.

[62] E.g., Philo, *Cherubim* 125–26; *Spec. Laws* 1.208; Marcus Aurelius, *Med.* 4.23; Pseudo-Aristotle, *De Mundo* 6; Seneca, *Ep.* 65.

[63] Cf. the discussion in Starling, "Nothing Beyond What Is Written?," 55–56.

in drawing from them (v. 8). Even here, Paul still implicitly identifies his own theological opinions with those of the "knowledgeable" Corinthians, affirming the validity of their assertions, if not their adequacy, and focusing his criticisms on the carelessness with which they have made use of their knowledge.

When Paul returns to the subject in 10:19, asking, "What am I saying then? That food sacrificed to idols is anything, or that an idol is anything?" the implied answer of verse 20 is still a clear no; but it comes this time with a fresh qualification: "No, but I do say that what they sacrifice, they sacrifice to demons and not to God. I do not want you to be participants with demons!" The truth claim at the heart of the Corinthian slogans is still upheld, but Paul now makes it clear that there is somewhat more to be said about the meaning of participation in a pagan temple meal or the ontological status of a pagan god than the glib Corinthian slogans might imply. An idol is, indeed, a nothing; but it is a nothing through which powerful demonic deceptions can be at work. The effect of these deceptions can be enslaving and ultimately destructive, not only for the "weak" but also for the "strong," who think that they are immune from danger (cf. 10:12–13, 22).

The vigilance that Paul urges on the Corinthians in 10:1–22 does not, however, do away with the strong monotheistic affirmations with which the discussion commenced in chapter 8 or reduce the sovereign and transcendent God to the status of merely one spiritual power among many, wrestling against hostile forces for the control of the universe. The advice with which Paul concludes in the final verses of the chapter (10:23–11:1) makes it clear that the God whom the Corinthians worship is to be honored as the creator of all things, the giver of all good gifts, and the only judge whose verdict is of any eternal consequence.

The sum total, when all the parts of Paul's argument in chapters 8–10 are put together, is a multifaceted and deeply practical doctrine. Belief in one God, for Paul, includes within it a joyful embrace of the goodness of the creation, a firm and fierce commitment to the exclusive claims of Christ, and a doxological orientation toward the glorification of God in all things. It finds expression in his confidence that "the earth is the Lord's and all that is in it" (10:26, quoting Ps 24:1), in his determination to ensure that the social and religious behavior of the Corinthians communicate a consistent message of unqualified allegiance to Jesus as Lord, and in his insistence that the Corinthians, in every facet and aspect of life, are to "do everything for the glory of God" (10:31).

The same basic assumptions of the unity of God, the undivided allegiance that believers are to give to the Lord Jesus, and the orientation of the Christian life toward the glory of God as creator and redeemer inform the instructions, reminders, and admonitions that he offers to the Corinthians across the entirety of the letter. Boasting, Paul insists, must be only in the Lord (1:31), and it is to God alone that believers should look as the ultimate source of judgment and approbation (4:5); faith must rest not on human wisdom but on God's power (2:5); the bodies of believers have been made and redeemed by God, so they are to use their bodies for his glory (6:13); the daily life of believers, whatever their situation, is to be lived "with God" (7:24); the interrelationship between men and women should be understood in accordance with a creational and providential order in which "woman came from man ... man comes through woman, and all things come from God" (11:12); the exercise of prophecy within the gathered community is to function in a way that exhibits the presence of God among his people, promotes his worship (14:25), and is consistent with his character of peace (14:33); the Christian life is to be lived in thankfulness to the God who gives victory to his people in Christ (15:57) and in confident anticipation of the day when God—that God—will be "all in all" (15:28).

Because the one God, who has made himself known through Christ, is the creator of all things and the one for whom all things exist, Paul is able to frame his responses to the various and particular details of the Corinthians' situation within a larger picture that embraces "all things" (e.g., 2:10, 15; 3:21–22; 6:12; 10:23, 25; 11:12; 13:7; 14:40; 15:24–28; 16:14), "all people" (e.g., 1:29; 7:17; 9:19–23; 10:33; 11:3–5; 15:22, 51), and "every place" (1:2; cf. 4:17; 14:33), and orders them all in relation to the glory of God in Christ.

§2 Christ

The monotheism of 1 Corinthians is, as we have already seen, tightly integrated with the christological claims that Paul advances as the core content and necessary entailments of his gospel. Belief in "one God," from whom and through whom are all things, goes hand in hand with allegiance to "one Lord, Jesus Christ," through whom are all things and through whom believers exist (8:6).

§2.1 Christ the Lord

This pattern, in which the exclusive devotion of believers to Jesus is included within the worship of the one God, can be seen in a variety of ways across the rest of the letter, the most striking of which is the use Paul makes of the title "Lord" (κύριος) with reference to Jesus. What is important about the function of this title in 1 Corinthians is not merely the *fact* that Paul uses it (the word κύριος, after all, can be used in a variety of senses, e.g., as a form of respectful address or a way of referring to the bearer of some form of authority) but the *manner* in which he does so, using the word to refer to Jesus in contexts closely corresponding to those in which the LXX uses it to refer to YHWH. The pattern is established at the very beginning of the letter, where Paul reminds the Corinthians in his opening greeting that they possess their identity as the church of God in common with "all those in every place who call on the name of Jesus Christ our Lord—both their Lord and ours" (1:2)—an unmistakable echo of the numerous Old Testament passages in which the people of God are identified as those who "call on the name of the Lord" in worship and invocation (e.g., Gen 4:26; 1 Kgs 18:24; 2 Kgs 5:11; Joel 2:32 [LXX Joel 3:5]; Zeph 3:9). It recurs across the following chapters, in contexts such as the call in chapter 5 for the urgent exercise of church discipline, where the OT expression, "the day of the Lord," is appropriated to refer to "the day of the Lord [Jesus]" (5:5; cf. Isa 13:6; Joel 2:1; Amos 5:18; Mal 4:5), and the reminder in the previous chapter of the exclusive prerogative of judgment that the Lord (in context, the Lord Jesus) will exercise at his coming (4:4–5; cf. Pss 96:13 [LXX 95:13]; 98:9 [LXX 97:9]).[64] The prayer, "Our Lord, come!" (Μαράνα θά), that Paul includes in 16:22, within the final greetings at the end of the letter, is a further expression of this fusion between the invocation of Jesus as Lord and the expectation of his return as the fulfillment of the Old Testament promise of the coming of YHWH.

References to Jesus as "Lord" within 1 Corinthians typically occur in connection with one or more of three closely interrelated themes,

[64] A similar phenomenon, though without the use of the title κύριος, can be seen in the way that Paul retells the story of the Israelites' wilderness wanderings in 10:1–13, identifying Christ with the "rock" from which Israel drank (10:4; cf. Deut 32:4, 15, 18, 30–31, 37) and drawing a close functional parallel between the Israelites' testing of God and his warning to the Corinthians against "test[ing] Christ" (10:9; cf. Exod 17:2–3, 7; Pss 78:18; 106:14). Cf. Thomas R. Schreiner, *First Corinthians: An Introduction and Commentary*, TNTC (Downers Grove: InterVarsity Press, 2018), 22.

highlighting the exclusive claims of Christ over the acts of cultic devotion that believers are to participate in (e.g., 8:5–6; 10:20–22; 12:3), the authority of Christ over believers' ethical conduct and ministry labors (e.g., 3:5; 4:4; 6:13; 7:35; 9:1; 15:58), and the centrality of Christ in believers' eschatological expectations (e.g., 1:7–8; 5:5; 15:57; 16:22).[65] In addition to these (and closely related to them) are the places in which the expression "in the Lord" is used to refer to the sphere of belonging within which believers are bound to one another and to Christ (e.g., 4:17; 7:39; 9:2; 11:11).[66]

Paul's inclusion of devotion to Jesus as the central focus of the worship and obedience that are owed to God does not imply the obliteration of all distinctions between Jesus and the Father. The blessing in 1:3 that concludes the opening greetings of the letter ("Grace to you and peace from God our Father and the Lord Jesus Christ") does not imply a mere juxtaposition between Christ and the Father, setting them up as separate deities from whom distinct and disconnected blessings might be sought, but it does suggest a distinction between them that is basic to the grammar of Christian prayer and devotion. Here, and throughout the rest of the letter, the picture that Paul's language implies, consistent with the creedal affirmation in 8:6, is one in which the blessings which he prays that his readers will experience originate (like all things) in "one God, the Father," and are extended to believers through their union with the "one Lord, Jesus Christ." The ordered relationship between God the Father and the Lord Jesus that is implied by Paul's formulation in 8:6 is also reflected at various other points in the letter, including 3:22–23 ("everything is yours, and you belong to Christ, and Christ belongs to God"), 11:3 ("But I want you to know that Christ is the head of every man, and the man is the head of the woman, and God is the head of Christ"), and 15:28 ("When everything is subject to Christ, then the Son himself will also be subject to the one who subjected everything to him, so that God may be all in all"). The cosmic, all-inclusive scope of verses such as these and their explicit placement against the horizons of the creation (8:5–6) and the eschatological consummation of all things (8:5–6; 15:28) suggest that they should be taken not only as a reference to a temporary state of affairs that existed during the time of Christ's earthly ministry

[65] Cf. Paul Gardner, *First Corinthians*, ZECNT (Grand Rapids: Zondervan, 2018), 759–61.

[66] Cf. Constantine R. Campbell, *Paul and Union with Christ: An Exegetical and Theological Study* (Grand Rapids: Zondervan, 2012), 171–75.

but also as offering a glimpse into Paul's understanding of the eternal, inner-Trinitarian relationship between the Son and the Father.[67]

§2.2 Christ Crucified

Crucial to the theological meaning and social significance of the high Christology Paul affirms in statements such as these is the fact that the Christ of whom they are predicated is the one whom Paul identifies elsewhere in the letter (explicitly and emphatically) as "Christ crucified" (1:23; cf. 2:2). The incongruity of this combination of ideas is not lost on Paul, but he insists on holding them together in paradoxical juxtapositions. It is not merely that the sufferings of Jesus were reversed by his subsequent exaltation; the one whom the rulers of this age crucified was (already) "the Lord of glory" (2:8). Paul's claim is not merely that God's wisdom is greater than human wisdom, or that the strength of God is greater than human strength; it is that "God's *foolishness* is wiser than human wisdom, and God's *weakness* is stronger than human strength" (1:25).

As Raymond Pickett correctly points out, the primary function of assertions such as these within the pastoral rhetoric of 1 Corinthians is to hammer home Paul's point about the shameful discordance between the arrogance and self-indulgence of the Corinthian elite and the content of the gospel that they claim to believe:

> Paul's aim in 1 and 2 Corinthians was to ensure that behavior within the community was governed by the "word of the cross" (cf. 1 Cor. 1.18–25). In order to secure the kind of conduct commensurate with the values mediated by the preaching of Christ crucified he called the community's attention to the social significance of this soteriological symbol.[68]

---

[67] This point should not be overpressed. Paul's reference to Christ as "the Son" in 15:28 does suggest that he has in mind not only the earthly, messianic mission of Jesus but also the continuing fidelity and submission of the exalted Son to the Father. But the final consummation that he goes on to depict in the remainder of the verse is one in which it is not merely "the Father" but "God" (ὁ θεός) who is "all in all." The Son is indeed subject to the Father, but his rule over all things is not swallowed up within the rule of the Father but perfected within in the universal rule of (the Triune) God. See the more detailed comments within the discussion of this verse in the commentary above, and the nuanced and careful discussion in Wesley Hill, *Paul and the Trinity: Persons, Relations, and the Pauline Letters* (Grand Rapids: Eerdmans, 2015), 120–34.

[68] Raymond Pickett, *The Cross in Corinth: The Social Significance of the Death of Jesus*, JSNTSup (Sheffield: Sheffield Academic, 1997), 33–34.

The emphasis Paul places on the social significance of the cross does not take away from the soteriological dimension of his message. Paul is able to assume that the Corinthians will already be familiar with the meaning of the brief, unelaborated formulations that he reminds them of across the letter: Christ is "our Passover lamb," who has been "sacrificed" (5:7); the bread that Christ broke on the night when he was betrayed was interpreted by him as "my body, which is for you" (11:24), and the cup that he took after the supper was "the new covenant in my blood" (11:25); the message that Paul received and handed on to the Corinthians included within it the assertion that Christ died "for our sins according to the Scriptures" (15:3). These things are foundational for Paul, included among the things that are of first importance and integral to the message on which the Corinthians have taken their stand and by which they are being saved (15:1–3). The reason he spends so little time explaining or defending them is not that they are of secondary importance for him. It is simply that the sacrificial, soteriological content of the message of the cross is not the aspect of the message that the Corinthians have overlooked or taken issue with. Paul's purpose in reminding them of the message that they are already so familiar with is to point out, again and again, the various ways in which their conduct is out of line with it. It was Christ who was crucified for them, not Paul, yet they insist on elevating Paul (and Cephas, and Apollos, and who knows how many other teachers and leaders) as if it was he that they belonged to and were saved by (1:12–13); God's choice was to make known his salvation in the foolish proclamation of a crucified Messiah, yet the Corinthian elite have persuaded themselves that they are able to belong to him and still be "wise in this age" (1:18–31; 3:18–23); the weaker believer is a "brother or sister for whom Christ died" (8:11), yet the more knowledgeable members of the Corinthian church insist on making full use of their own freedom without regard for the impact of their actions on other members of the fellowship; the meal that the community shares in together is meant to proclaim the Lord's death, yet the way in which the wealthier Corinthians conduct the meal makes it clear that they "despise the church of God and humiliate those who have nothing" (11:22, 26). To live by the word of the cross, Paul insists, is not merely to luxuriate in the forgiveness that Christ's death has procured but to imitate the crucified one, embracing the apparent foolishness of a life of servanthood and sacrifice, in solidarity with those whom the rulers of this age exploit and despise.

§2.3 *Christ's Resurrection*

While it is the word of the cross that is the central theme of the countercultural wisdom that Paul explicates and applies across the first fourteen chapters of the letter, it is the message of the resurrection that he brings into focus in chapter 15, at the letter's climax.[69] The function of this focus on the resurrection at the climax of the letter is not, however, to qualify or counterbalance the cruci-centric message of the letter's earlier chapters. The resurrection, according to Paul, will be the great and final vindication of those who have lived by the wisdom of the cross, endangering themselves hourly and facing death every day (15:30–31), pouring out their lives in sacrifices and labors that would ultimately turn out, were it not for the resurrection, to have been foolish, pitiable, and futile (15:13–19, 32, 58).[70] A similar, mutually reinforcing relationship between the word of the cross and the promise of the resurrection can be seen in Paul's brief, earlier reference to the resurrection of Christ in 6:14. In that instance, Paul's reminder that "God raised up the Lord and will also raise us up by his power" is given in support of the previous verse's claim that "the body is not for sexual immorality but for the Lord, and the Lord for the body," and is followed several verses later by a parallel reminder to the readers that they have been "bought at a price" through the death of Jesus (v. 20a), before the chapter arrives at its conclusion in verse 20b: "So glorify God with your body."

The world-transforming significance of Christ's resurrection is, at least in part, a consequence of his representative role as Messiah and second Adam (or, if we are to follow Paul's language more precisely, as "second man" and "last Adam"). Paul's claim in 15:20 that Christ has been raised as "the firstfruits of those who have fallen asleep" is supported in the immediately following verses by the parallels and contrasts that he draws between the death that came through Adam and the life that comes through Christ to all who belong to him (15:21–23). The verses that follow go even farther, making it clear that in Paul's understanding the consequences of Christ's resurrection include not only the resurrection

[69] For a classic exposition of the climactic role that ch. 15 plays within the letter, see Karl Barth, *The Resurrection of the Dead* (London: Hodder & Stoughton, 1933). For a more recent study, see Malcolm, *Paul and the Rhetoric of Reversal.*

[70] Cf. especially Michael J. Gorman, *Cruciformity: Paul's Narrative Spirituality of the Cross*, 2nd ed. (Grand Rapids: Eerdmans, 2021), 304–48.

of individual believers but the reordering and restoration of the entire creation:

> 23 But each in his own order: Christ, the firstfruits; afterward, at his coming, those who belong to Christ. 24 Then comes the end, when he hands over the kingdom to God the Father, when he abolishes all rule and all authority and power. 25 For he must reign until he puts all his enemies under his feet. 26 The last enemy to be abolished is death. 27 For **God has put everything under his feet.**

The language Paul uses in verse 25 ("For he must reign until he puts all his enemies under his feet") splices together strands that he has taken from both Psalm 110:1 ("Sit at my right hand until I make your enemies your footstool") and Psalm 8:6 ("you put everything under his feet"), with the latter verse quoted explicitly in verse 27. This conflation has important implications for how Paul wishes us to understand both psalms and the nature of their fulfillment in Christ. On the one hand, it reframes our reading of Psalm 110, representing the messianic rule of the figure addressed in that psalm as embracing not merely the conquest of the nations but the transformation of the entire creation (in keeping with the scope of the vision of human dominion that is depicted in Psalm 8). On the other hand, it highlights the eschatological nature of the vision that is celebrated in Psalm 8, linking its fulfillment to the messianic figure whose conquests are spoken of in Psalm 110. The implications of this linkage are far-reaching, as Oliver O'Donovan correctly emphasizes:

> The resurrection carries with it the promise that "all shall be made alive" (1 Cor. 15:22). ... And so this central proclamation directs us back also to the message of the incarnation, by which we learn how, through a unique presence of God to his creation, the whole created order is taken up into the fate of this particular representative man at this particular moment of history, on whose one fate turns the redemption of all. And it directs us forward to the end of history when that particular and representative fate is universalized in the resurrection of mankind from the dead. "Each in his own order: Christ the first fruits, then at his coming those who belong to Christ" (15:23). The sign that God has stood by his created order implies that this

order, with mankind in its proper place within it, is to be totally restored at the last.[71]

§3 The Spirit

Paul's summons to the Corinthians to devote themselves exclusively to Jesus as Lord, shaping their lives by the wisdom made known in the word of the cross and setting their hope on the resurrection life of the age to come, establishes the framework in which he speaks about the spirit of God in 1 Corinthians.

The first explicit reference to the Spirit within the letter is in 2:4, in the context of a contrast Paul draws between "persuasive words of wisdom" and the "demonstration of the Spirit's power" (i.e., the way in which the message of the cross was used by God to bring about transformative conviction in the hearts of the hearers). The discussion that follows, in 2:6–16, gives further evidence of the close connection in Paul's mind between the wisdom of the cross and the person and work of the Spirit. Since the wisdom of God that is revealed in the message of Christ crucified is a "hidden" wisdom (2:7), rejected as foolishness by the rulers of this age, it is only by the work of the Spirit that it can be understood and accepted by those who receive it (2:10–16). What the Spirit reveals is not merely a package of information that God has provided; the Spirit "searches ... even the depths of God" (2:10) and "knows the thoughts of God" (v. 11), so that what is made known to believers is nothing less than "the mind of Christ" (v. 16).

Paul's description of the person and work of the Spirit within this chapter gives a revealing insight into how he understands both the unity of God and the distinctions between the three divine persons. The Spirit's work, on the one hand, is described in language that suggests not merely energy or instrumentality but personal agency: the Spirit searches (v. 10), knows (v. 11), teaches (v. 13), and explains (v. 13). While the last two of these actions are descriptions of the work of God ab extra, the first two appear to offer a glimpse into Paul's understanding of the inner-Trinitarian dynamics that stand behind that revealing work.[72] But (on the other hand) any tempta-

---

[71] Oliver O'Donovan, *Resurrection and Moral Order: An Outline for Evangelical Ethics*, 2nd ed. (Leicester: Inter-Varsity Press, 1994), 15.

[72] Cf. the comments on 2:10 in Volker Rabens, "The Development of Pauline Pneumatology: A Response to F. W. Horn," *BZ* 43 (1999): 177.

tion we might feel to construct a notion of the Spirit's personhood that dissolves the unity of God into an exclusively social Trinitarianism is pulled up short by the implied analogy in verses 10–11 between the way in which the Spirit "searches" and "knows" the mind of God and the way in which the thoughts of a human person are known by that person's own spirit. The Spirit, according to Paul, is not merely the Spirit who knows God and is sent by God, but the Spirit "of God" (v. 11).

The lengthiest and most substantial discussion of the Spirit's work within 1 Corinthians can be found in chapters 12–14. The jumping-off point for the discussion in 12:1 ("Now concerning spiritual gifts: brothers and sisters ...") appears to be a reference to a question that the Corinthians have asked or a comment that they have made within their letter. As discussed in the comments on that verse within the commentary, the most likely sense in which Paul is using the phrase περὶ ... τῶν πνευματικῶν here is probably not the narrow and semitechnical sense implied by the CSB translation ("concerning spiritual gifts") but a slightly broader sense ("concerning matters of the Spirit") that embraces both spiritual gifts and spiritual people. In response to the views and practices of an elitist group within the Corinthian congregation who consider themselves to be "spiritual" in a sense that their fellow believers are not (cf. 3:1; 14:37), Paul argues vigorously for an inclusive, Christocentric notion of spirituality that embraces all who belong to Christ (12:12–13), leaves room for the wide diversity of the gifts with which the Spirit blesses the body of Christ (vv. 4–11, 27–30), and gives special honor to the body's weakest and least presentable members (vv. 14–26). The essential criterion underlying all of these aspects is allegiance to Jesus as Lord, made known in verbal confession (12:3) and lived out in practices of mutual honor and humble service within the community of believers (12:5).

Paul's understanding of the Spirit's work is thus a deeply communitarian vision; it is not only the individual believer (6:19) but the believing community as a whole that can be spoken of as a "temple" in which the Spirit dwells (3:16–17). The gifts of the Spirit, too, are to be understood and practiced as having been given not merely to the individual believer for his or her own private benefit but to the whole community for the common good (12:7). It is for this reason that Paul's accent in chapter 14 falls so heavily on the priority of prophecy, as a gift that "builds up the church" (14:4) by strengthening, encouraging, and consoling the hearers.

§4 Wisdom

Prominent among the blessings bestowed by the Spirit on the Corinthian church are the gifts of "speech" (λόγος) and "knowledge" (γνῶσις) that Paul makes mention of in the thanksgiving report at the start of the letter (1:4–7). There is no reason to doubt that Paul's thanksgiving report is intended as a sincere and serious statement of his gratitude to God (albeit one that is strikingly limited in its scope, including no mention, for example, of the works of faith and labors of love for which he typically offers thanks to God in his letters to other churches). It soon becomes clear, however, that the framework within which these gifts have been exercised by a number of the Corinthians (including those most conscious of their eloquence and understanding) amounts, in Paul's view, to a form of "wisdom" that is fundamentally irreconcilable with the true wisdom made known by God in the word of the cross.

The critique of this false and distorting wisdom that Paul offers across the following chapters suggests that its source was probably not an endemically Christian teaching but the continuing influence on the Corinthian church of mainstream Greco-Roman values and beliefs, and that it included attitudes and assumptions relating to both the rhetorical form in which ideas were communicated and the content of the ideas that were taught (and/or tacitly assumed) as the framework for shaping a well-lived life.[73]

Paul's critique of the pagan wisdom that the Corinthians were being influenced by is a major theme in chapters 1–4, as he responds to the reports he has received about the divisive way in which the Corinthians were adulating and assessing their leaders. In place of that sort of wisdom, Paul offers a confronting reminder that it is Christ (in context, the *crucified* Christ) who has become for us "wisdom from God" (1:30), and commends a sharply countercultural set of dispositions and understandings that he sums up in 3:16 as "the mind of Christ."[74]

At the heart of this alternative wisdom that Paul advocates to the Corinthians is the insight into God's plans and purposes that is revealed in the message of the cross:

---

[73] See especially Timothy A. Brookins, "Rhetoric and Philosophy in the First Century: Their Relation with Respect to 1 Corinthians 1–4," *Neot* 44 (2010): 233–52, and Brookins, "The Wise Corinthians," 51–76.

[74] See especially Harm-Jan Inkelaar, *Conflict over Wisdom: The Theme of 1 Corinthians 1–4 Rooted in Scripture*, CBET (Leuven: Peeters, 2011).

> 20 Where is the one who is wise? Where is the teacher of the law? Where is the debater of this age? Hasn't God made the world's wisdom foolish? 21 For since, in God's wisdom, the world did not know God through wisdom, God was pleased to save those who believe through the foolishness of what is preached. 22 For the Jews ask for signs and the Greeks seek wisdom, 23 but we preach Christ crucified, a stumbling block to the Jews and foolishness to the Gentiles. 24 Yet to those who are called, both Jews and Greeks, Christ is the power of God and the wisdom of God, 25 because God's foolishness is wiser than human wisdom, and God's weakness is stronger than human strength. (1:20–25)

As Paul points out in these verses, the divine "foolishness" made known in the word of the cross collides not only with the rhetorical and philosophical conventions of the Greco-Roman tradition (v. 22: "Greeks seek wisdom") but also with the kind of triumphalistic political expectations that flourished in some versions of Second Temple Jewish messianism (v. 22: "the Jews ask for signs"). It would be a mistake, however, to draw the conclusion that the wisdom Paul has in mind involves the kind of apocalyptic disruption that demolishes any possible basis for rational conversation with those outside the faith, or eliminates all sense of salvation-historical continuity with the Old Testament Scriptures and the history of Israel.[75] Even the "fool" whom Paul rhetorically addresses in 15:36 is still engaged in conversation and encouraged to give consideration to a string of rhetorical questions based on analogies of various kinds between the claims of the gospel and the observable realities of everyday life (15:36–44).[76] If that is the case with the common knowledge made available to all through general revelation, it is even more the case with the special revelation of God made known to Israel in the Scriptures. The continuing truth and power of Scripture is assumed by Paul throughout the letter as a reliable basis for Christian knowledge and understanding. In the verse immediately prior to the passage quoted above, for example, Paul has just made use of a quotation from Isaiah 29:14 ("I will destroy the wisdom of the wise, and I will set aside the intelligence of the intelligent")

---

[75] For an example of an assertion of this sort, see Alexandra R. Brown, *The Cross and Human Transformation: Paul's Apocalyptic Word in 1 Corinthians* (Minneapolis: Fortress, 1995), 92–93.

[76] On the role played by appeals to "logical coherence" and "rational thought" within the argument of ch. 15 and the "basicality" of the truth-claim regarding the resurrection within the belief-system that Paul is commending, see Thiselton, *First Corinthians*, 1217–18.

to highlight the continuity between the challenge posed to conventional human wisdom by the word of the cross and the similar challenge posed by the message of the Old Testament prophets. Paul continues to appeal to the Old Testament Scripture in a similar manner across the remaining chapters of the letter,[77] with the intention of shaping both the thinking and the behavior of the Corinthians. The Scriptures, according to Paul, were "written for our instruction" (10:11),[78] and it is this normative function of Scripture that Paul appears to have in mind when he appeals in 4:6 to the saying, "Nothing beyond what is written."[79]

According to Paul's diagnosis of the Corinthians' situation, the attachment to the false wisdom that has distorted their thinking and practice goes hand in hand with their aspiration to be well-regarded by their social superiors and potentially even included within their ranks; they are not only "wise" in their own estimation but also "rich," "strong," and "distinguished" (4:8, 10). Paul goes out of his way, therefore, to point out to the Corinthians that the "rulers of this age," whose approval the Corinthians are seeking, are the same people who presided over the crucifixion of Jesus (2:8), and that the apostles who brought the gospel to Corinth were (and continue to be) "fools," "weak," and "dishonored" in the eyes of the world (4:10). If the Corinthians are to become truly wise, they will need to imitate them, becoming fools in the estimation of the current age in order to find the wisdom of the age to come (3:18–19; 4:16–17).

The nature of true wisdom and its contrast with the ideas that the Corinthian elite have absorbed from their pagan context continues to be a theme throughout the remainder of the letter, where Paul applies it not only to the way in which the Corinthians regard their leaders but also to the way in which they shape their own lives.[80] In 6:4–5, for example, Paul excoriates the behavior of the Corinthian believers who have initiated lawsuits against their brothers and sisters, accusing them of acting in a

---

[77] For a discussion of the function of Scripture in informing the ethical teaching of chs. 5–7, see Brian S. Rosner, *Paul, Scripture and Ethics: A Study of 1 Corinthians 5–7* (Leiden: Brill, 1994), 61–94.

[78] For a discussion of the way in which Paul reappropriates law as wisdom, within and beyond 1 Corinthians, see Rosner, *Paul and the Law: Keeping the Commandments of God*, NSBT (Downers Grove: InterVarsity Press, 2013), ch. 6.

[79] Cf. Inkelaar, *Conflict over Wisdom*, 62–63; Starling, "Nothing Beyond What Is Written?," 54–55.

[80] For a discussion of how this theme is developed in chs. 8–10, see Starling, "As to Sensible People," 113–26.

manner that implied there was, in their view, "not one wise person among you who is able to arbitrate between fellow believers." In 8:1–13 he urges those within the church who boast in the "knowledge" that elevates them above their fellow believers to repent of their arrogance and learn to use whatever knowledge they may have in the humble services of others. In 13:1–2, similarly, he describes the person who has "all knowledge" but does not have love as "nothing." And in 15:35–36 he confronts as a "fool" the person whose reductive thinking has no room for the possibility of a bodily resurrection made possible by the power of God. Those among the Corinthians who have come under the influence of a mentality such as this are to "come to [their] senses" and turn away from a mindset that is "ignorant of God" (15:34).

§5 Grace

Like all of Paul's letters, 1 Corinthians begins and ends with grace, in the form of the blessings that Paul includes within his opening and closing greetings (1:3; 16:23). The intervening chapters containing nothing that is directly equivalent to the arguments Paul offers in Romans or Galatians to defend his gospel against the idea that the justification of believers can be obtained through the works of the law, but it would be a mistake to draw the conclusion that the idea of grace plays a role that is peripheral or merely ornamental within this letter. Even when the grace of God is not under attack from the proponents of a gospel of justification by the works of the law, it remains central to Paul's understanding of the message that he preaches, and therefore to the shape of the Christian life and the conduct of his own ministry.[81] The Corinthian church may not have been under threat from a teaching that explicitly denied the sufficiency of God's grace for the salvation of believers, but the gracious character of God's salvation is still a key theme of Paul's letter to them; Paul's letter to them is not so much a defense of the gospel of grace as a "reproclamation" of the message with an accent on this theme, aimed at reshaping the values and behaviors of the Corinthians so that they cohere with this central gospel component.[82]

---

[81] Thus, for example, in 2 Cor 1:12, Paul sums up the "boast" that he makes about his ministry as the claim that he and his fellow missionaries have conducted themselves "not by human wisdom but by God's grace."

[82] Thiselton, *First Corinthians*, 34.

Nowhere in 1 Corinthians can this be seen more clearly than in chapters 1–4 (including the response Paul offers in 1:10–4:21 to the reports that he has received of divisions within the Corinthian community). The prominent role that reminders of God's grace will play within this section is anticipated in the thanksgiving report of 1:4–7, at the very beginning of the letter. Paul commences his account of the prayers of thanksgiving that he offers to God by speaking of "the grace of God given to you in Christ Jesus" (1:4), unpacking that reference by reminding his readers of the way in which they have been "enriched in [Christ] in every way, in all speech and all knowledge," with the consequence that they "do not lack any spiritual gift" (1:5, 7). Already, without any explicit word of rebuke or correction, Paul has made it clear to the Corinthians that each and every gift (χάρισμα) they enjoy, including the gifts of knowledge and eloquence that they possess in such abundance, is a manifestation of the "grace" (χάρις) of God and a reason for gratitude to him. The implications of this reality are spelled out across the following chapters, as Paul confronts the self-congratulatory arrogance of the Corinthians and the adulation with which they regard the particular leaders and teachers with whom they associate themselves. The differing ministries of Paul and Apollos (and all other leaders within God's church) are given to them "according to God's grace" (3:10), each of them serving in "the role the Lord has given" (3:5). The faith of the Corinthians may well have come about "through" their labors (3:5), but its ultimate source is not in them but in God (3:6–7; cf. 1:30).

The corrective of grace that Paul offers within these chapters applies not only to the way in which the Corinthians regard their leaders; it also applies to the way in which they regard themselves and the various social privileges and spiritual endowments that they enjoy. "Who makes you so superior?" Paul asks his readers in 4:7. "What do you have that you didn't receive? If, in fact, you did receive it, why do you boast as if you hadn't received it?" Here, as elsewhere in Paul's letters, grace operates to the exclusion of human boasting (see 1:29, 31), and the boasting that is ruled out by grace includes not only the kind of boasting in ethnic identity and moral performance that he condemns in Romans and Galatians (see Rom 3:27; 4:2; 11:18; Gal 6:13–14) but also the kind of boasting in social prestige and spiritual giftedness that he critiques in his letters to the Corinthians.[83]

[83] Cf. the similar comments in Thielman, *Theology of the New Testament*, 282–83.

The grace at the heart of Paul's gospel is an incongruous gift, given without regard to the standing or the merits of its recipients.[84] But it should not be reduced (as it sometimes is in preaching and popular piety) to mere indulgence or forgiveness, as if it left its recipients unaltered by the gift they have received. As we have already seen in the thanksgiving report of 1:4–7, Paul's understanding of grace includes within it not only the forgiveness of sins but also the outpouring of the Spirit and the various gifts and enablings with which the Corinthians have been blessed. It also includes the transformative power that God exerts by his Spirit within the life of believers and the energy with which he enables them to labor in his service. Thus, when Paul speaks about his own encounter with the risen Christ, he lays heavy emphasis on the efficaciousness of the grace he has received, placing that aspect of God's grace side by side with its unmeritedness and seeing both within his own story:

> 9 For I am the least of the apostles, not worthy to be called an apostle, because I persecuted the church of God. 10 But by the grace of God I am what I am, and his grace toward me was not in vain. On the contrary, I worked harder than any of them, yet not I, but the grace of God that was with me. 11 Whether, then, it is I or they, so we proclaim and so you have believed. (1 Cor 15:9–11)

A similarly transformative effect can be expected in the lives of all believers. It is no accident that chapter 15 ends with an exhortation that encourages the readers to be "always excelling in the Lord's work" and reassures them that "[their] labor in the Lord is not in vain" (15:58). Nor is it an accident that in the opening verses of the following chapter Paul's mind turns immediately to the topic of the collection for the saints, as a "gift" (χάρις) that the Corinthians will be able to give out of the abundance with which they have been blessed (16:1–4); the grace that God pours out in Christ transforms its recipients, not least in the way that it produces in them a joyful, active generosity that imitates God's own kindness and participates in its extension to others.[85]

---

[84] Cf. especially John M. G. Barclay, *Paul and the Power of Grace* (Grand Rapids: Eerdmans, 2020), ch. 10.

[85] Cf. the much lengthier and more developed unfolding of how Paul sees the relationship between the grace of God and the collection for the saints in 2 Cor 8–9, and the discussion of those chapters in David I. Starling, "'The Harvest of Your Righteousness': Scripture, Bread

§6 Salvation

As mentioned above in relation to the theme of grace, the situation Paul was addressing in 1 Corinthians does not appear to have included a group advocating for a theology of justification through the works of the law or the necessity of gentile circumcision. The salvation of uncircumcised gentile believers, by faith in Christ and apart from the works of the law, is something that Paul can safely take as a given within this letter, arguing *from* the fact of his readers' salvation in Christ rather than needing to argue *for* it, as he is compelled to do in some other contexts. But this does not mean that 1 Corinthians is a soteriology-free zone. Repeatedly, across each of the major sections of the letter, Paul reminds his readers of various aspects of the story of their salvation, applying it to the different issues that he is addressing and urging his readers to live in accordance with it.

In 1:10–4:21, as Paul addresses the factionalism and boasting of the Corinthian church, his accent falls on the crucicentric nature of the gospel message through which God has made his salvation known and the sovereign election that he exercises in determining those by whom his salvation will be experienced. His exposition of these themes within this section of the letter has a deliberately and overtly corrective emphasis, pushing back against the divisive and elitist attitudes of the Corinthians. As a cure for the arrogance underlying the Corinthian factionalism, Paul emphasizes the sovereignty of God in the work of salvation, exercised in both his choice to bring about the salvation of believers through "the foolishness of what is preached" (1:21) and his choice (bound up in that decision) about the kinds of people whom he purposes to save:

> 27 God has chosen what is foolish in the world to shame the wise, and God has chosen what is weak in the world to shame the strong. 28 God has chosen what is insignificant and despised in the world—what is viewed as nothing—to bring to nothing what is viewed as something, 29 so that no one may boast in his presence. (1 Cor 1:27–29)

Election for salvation is not (according to the picture Paul paints in these verses) a random choice; still less is it one that is based on the foreseen merits of those who are chosen. Nor does Paul's depiction of the

---

and Benefaction in 2 Corinthians 8–9," in *Scripture, Texts, and Tracings in 2 Corinthians and Philippians*, ed. A. Andrew Das and B. J. Oropeza (Minneapolis: Fortress Academic, 2022), 139–51; David I. Starling, "Meditations on a Slippery Citation: Paul's Use of Psalm 112:9 in 2 Corinthians 9:9," *JTI* 6 (2012): 248–49.

basis for God's choice rely on an elaborate metaphysical theory regarding the presence or absence of a free will on the part of those who are chosen, or of the compatibility or incompatibility of such a will with God's predestining purposes. His point is simply, and subversively, the assertion that God's choice for salvation is an exercise of his wisdom and good pleasure, and that God chooses not according to who people *are*, but (for the most part, in general) according to what they are *not*: wise, strong, significant, or esteemed. The implications for the Corinthians are clear: if they are in Christ, included among God's chosen ones, then it is "from him" (v. 30) and not because of anything in them that might serve as a ground for boasting (v. 31).

In chapters 5–6, as Paul turns his attention to the reports that he has received of immorality and lawsuits among the Corinthians, the accent of his reminders to the readers regarding the story of their salvation falls on the sanctifying and transformative dimensions of the event. If Christ is "our Passover lamb," who has been "sacrificed" for our salvation (5:7), then the implication for us is that we should "observe the feast, not with old leaven or with the leaven of malice and evil, but with the unleavened bread of sincerity and truth" (5:8). The warning in 6:9–10 regarding those who will not inherit the kingdom of God is followed in the next verse by a reminder that "some of you used to be like this. But you were washed, you were sanctified, you were justified in the name of the Lord Jesus Christ and by the Spirit of our God" (6:11). Here, as in 1:30, the experience of being justified in the name of the Lord Jesus goes hand in hand with the experience of being "washed" and "sanctified" by the Spirit.[86] Similarly, in 6:20, the reminder to the readers that they have been "bought with a price" through the death of Jesus is followed immediately by a call to "glorify God with your body." The same reminder recurs in 7:23, in the central section of the following chapter, where it functions in support of the call that Paul issues in the previous verse to live as "Christ's slave."

The next major section of the letter, in chapters 8–10, responds to the questions that the Corinthians have asked regarding food that has been offered to idols. Within this section of the letter, reminders of the saving work of God play a key role in each stage of Paul's argument. In

[86] On the depiction of conversion in 6:9–11 as a multi-faceted transformation of identity, see Stephen J. Chester, *Conversion at Corinth: Perspectives on Conversion in Paul's Theology and the Corinthian Church* (London: T&T Clark, 2003), 125–48.

chapter 8, as Paul rebukes the arrogance of those who use their knowledge and freedom without regard for the effect of their actions on weaker fellow believers, he sharpens the edge of his critique by reminding the readers that the fellow believer so affected is "[a] brother or sister for whom Christ died" (8:11). In chapter 9, as Paul directs his readers to the example of the way in which he has used his own rights and freedoms, he frames his ministry as a participation in and extension of the saving work of Christ, the Servant: like Christ, he has made himself "a slave to everyone" (9:19), becoming "weak in order to win the weak"—indeed, becoming "all things to all people"—with the aim that "I may by every possible means save some" (9:22; cf. 10:24, 33). And in chapter 10, when his focus shifts from the call to act in a way that promotes the salvation of others to a warning that the Corinthians' own salvation is at stake, he makes it clear that final salvation requires perseverance in faith, urging his readers to beware of the risk of apostasy and pointing them to the faithfulness of God as the one who can bring them safely through times of trial and strengthen them to endure to the end (10:1–22; cf. 1:8–9).[87]

The instructions Paul gives in chapter 11 on issues to do with the gathering of believers and his response in chapters 12–14 to the Corinthians' questions regarding matters of the Spirit and spirituality are also informed by his understanding of the church as a community shaped by the story of salvation that they have been given to proclaim. The divisions at the Lord's Supper between the haves and the have-nots within the Corinthian congregation are made even more scandalous than they would otherwise be, because the meal is meant to be an enacted proclamation of the death of Christ (11:23–26). Likewise, in chapters 12–14, the strength of Paul's concerns about the chaotic competitiveness of the way in which the Corinthians are exercising the gifts of the Spirit when they gather is amplified by the role that the gathering ought to have in the extension of God's saving work: when things are happening as they should and the Spirit is at work through the exercise of intelligible and edifying prophecy, Paul's hope is that the unbeliever or outsider who is present will find themselves "convicted by all" and "called to account,"

[87] On the relationship between warnings such as 10:1–12 and assurances such as 10:13 and 1:8–9, and the implications for how we are to understand Paul's theology of perseverance and apostasy, see Andrew Wilson, *The Warning-Assurance Relationship in 1 Corinthians*, WUNT (Tübingen: Mohr Siebeck, 2017).

so that they "fall facedown and worship God, proclaiming, 'God is really among you'" (14:24–25; cf. Isa 45:14; Zech 8:23).[88]

Reminders of the story of salvation play a key role, too, in the response to issues regarding the resurrection that Paul offers in chapter 15, the last major section of the letter. Here, Paul begins the chapter by reminding the readers about the core content of "the gospel I preached to you, which you received, on which you have taken your stand and by which you are being saved" (15:1–2). He then goes on, across the remaining paragraphs of the chapter, to highlight the centrality of bodily resurrection (both the resurrection of Christ and the future resurrection of believers) within the salvation story that the Corinthians have believed. If Christ has not been raised, then "our proclamation is in vain, and so is your faith" (15:14). But if Christ has been raised, then salvation for those who are in him means both forgiveness of sins (15:17) and participation in his victory (15:50–58).[89]

§7 Eschatology

It is not until the climax of the letter, in chapter 15, that Paul provides a sustained and focused discussion on matters of eschatology. Nevertheless, the entirety of the letter, anticipating this climax, is permeated by the perspective of an inaugurated eschatology that encourages the Corinthians to perceive themselves as a community on whom "the culmination of the ages has come" (10:11) and to wait patiently for the full consummation that will come at Christ's return (1:7–8; 4:5).[90] This perspective serves as a corrective against the Corinthian tendency to focus on the pursuit of prosperity and honor in the present (4:8–10) and the spiritual gifts and empowerments they already possess (13:8–12).

Some interpreters of 1 Corinthians have mirror-read the eschatological correctives that Paul brings to bear within the letter as indications that the Corinthians had come under the influence of an explicit and fully developed "over-realized eschatology," along the lines of the doctrine

---

[88] For a discussion of these verses and the understanding of conversion that they imply, see Chester, *Conversion at Corinth*, 114–25.

[89] For a discussion of the larger biblical-theological and dogmatic question of the relationship between the cross of Christ and the kingdom of God, see Jeremy R. Treat, *The Crucified King: Atonement and Kingdom in Biblical and Systematic Theology* (Grand Rapids: Zondervan, 2014).

[90] See especially Hays, "Conversion of the Imagination," 391–412.

Paul refers to in 2 Timothy 2:18.[91] The simpler and more likely explanation, however (consistent with the way in which Paul frames his reminders and rebukes), is that the Corinthians had let go of the eschatological emphasis of the gospel that was originally preached to them (or had never fully absorbed and embraced it), under the influence of a cultural context that encouraged a focus on power, prestige, and prosperity in the present.[92]

The first indication of the eschatological perspective that Paul wishes to bring to bear on the Corinthians' situation can be seen as early as the thanksgiving report in 1:4–9. Here, having expressed in verses 4–7a his gratitude for the gifts with which the Corinthians have been blessed, Paul goes on verses 7b–9 to describe their present situation as one in which they "eagerly wait for the revelation of our Lord Jesus Christ" (1:7b), reassuring them that "he will also strengthen you to the end, so that you will be blameless in the day of our Lord Jesus Christ" (1:8).

The chapters that follow contain repeated reminders of this eschatological perspective, bringing it to bear on a wide range of different issues that Paul is addressing. In 1:10–4:21, responding to the boasts that the various groups within the Corinthian church are making in their respective leaders and teachers, Paul offers a series of reminders that the only assessment of his ministry and the ministry of his fellow teachers that ultimately matters is the assessment that will be made by Christ on the last day (e.g., 3:8, 13–15, 17; 4:3–5). Side by side with those reminders, and closely related to them, is the sharp and sarcastic rebuke that he delivers in 4:8–13 to those among the Corinthians who are "already full" and "already rich," and have already "begun to reign" (4:8)—language that suggests they consider themselves entitled in the present to comforts and privileges that Paul and his fellow apostles await in the age to come. The repentance that he calls them to is also eschatological in nature, taking the form of a renunciation of one form of wisdom—the wisdom that is "wise in this age" (3:18; cf. 2:6)—and the embrace of an alternative wisdom that is grounded in the promise of what "God has prepared ... for those who love him" (2:9).

The prospect of the coming day of the Lord, already invoked in 1:10–4:21 as a corrective to the premature and worldly assessments that the

---

[91] E.g., Fee, *First Epistle to the Corinthians*, 187–88; Thiselton, "Realised Eschatology at Corinth," 510–26.

[92] E.g., Garland, *1 Corinthians*, BECNT (Grand Rapids: Baker, 2003), 138–39; Ciampa and Rosner, *The First Letter to the Corinthians*, 179–80; Hays, "Conversion of the Imagination," 396.

Corinthians are making of their leaders, reappears in chapters 5–6 as a stimulus to the necessary and proper judgments that the Corinthians must make in matters of church discipline and in the resolution of intra-communal disputes. The urgency of such disciplinary judgments, according to Paul, derives in part from the desire that the persons subject to them might be "saved in the day of the Lord" (5:5). The coming judgment of God is also highlighted by Paul within the following paragraphs as both a reason why the believers should *not* be passing judgment on outsiders (5:13) and as a reason why the church—even its lowliest and least privileged members—should be capable of carrying its responsibility of fostering justice and resolving conflicts that arise within the community (6:2–3). In addition to these repeated references to the coming judgment, chapters 5–6 also contain a brief but important reminder of the future bodily resurrection of believers, which Paul points to as proof that "the body is not for sexual immorality but for the Lord, and the Lord for the body" (6:13–14).

The consistently eschatological nature of Paul's perspective can also be seen in chapter 7, when he turns to address the questions regarding marriage and celibacy that have been raised in the Corinthians' letter. While Paul cannot endorse the philosophy of celibacy-for-the-sake-of-spirituality that appears to have been advocated in the Corinthians' letter, he does give strong encouragement to those who are not yet married to consider remaining in their current situation, not only because of the immediate circumstances of the "present distress" (7:26) but also because of the eschatological nature of all Christian existence in the last days:

> 29 The time is limited, so from now on those who have wives should be as though they had none, 30 those who weep as though they did not weep, those who rejoice as though they did not rejoice, those who buy as though they didn't own anything, 31 and those who use the world as though they did not make full use of it. For this world in its current form is passing away. (1 Cor 7:29b–31)

The particular focus of Paul's advice within this paragraph is the situation of believers who are not yet married, but the list of examples that he offers fans out broadly from matters of marriage and celibacy, making it clear that the mindset he is advocating is one that applies to all believers, in every facet of life. Believers are still to participate in the activities and structures of the present age, but they are to do so in a way that takes account of the fact that "this world in its current form is passing away" (7:31) and does not seek in this life the security and permanence that belong in the age to come.

In chapters 8–10 Paul turns to the matter of food that has been sacrificed to idols and the question of whether, if at all, believers should eat in a pagan temple or at the table of a pagan god. Here, too, his instructions and warnings have an explicitly eschatological character. Believers are to read the scriptural story of Israel as having been "written for our instruction, on whom the ends of the ages, have come" (10:11). To do so involves understanding their own time as having been prefigured in the wilderness wanderings of the Israelites, who had been "baptized" in the Red Sea (see §8.1) but had not yet entered into the land of promise:

> The Corinthians are not only to see how Scripture points to its fulfilment in their own community but also to see that God's final judgment stands over their present experience. The prospect of future apocalyptic judgment, symbolized by the destruction that came upon the idolatrous Israelites in the wilderness, hovers over the entire passage. If the "strong" persist in provoking God's jealousy, they will suffer loss and destruction (cf. 3.10–17; 4.1–5; 5.1–5; 6.9 10; 11.27–32). Because Paul and his readers stand at the turn of the ages, they must envision their present experience both as the fulfilment of the scriptural figures and, at the same time, as a hint of the eschatological consummation that is still to come.[93]

As Hays correctly points out, the prospect of future judgment that hovers over Paul's rebukes and warnings in chapters 8–10 does not disappear at the end of this section of the letter. In chapter 11, as Paul instructs the Corinthians on matters relating to their gatherings, his response in the second half of the chapter to the status-based divisions that are perpetuated in their community meals includes a reminder that the recurring remembrance of the Lord's death in the community meal of the church takes place "until he comes" (11:26), followed by a sobering reference to the anticipatory judgments that have already fallen on some members of the congregation, which he interprets as an experience of being "disciplined, so that we may not be condemned with the world" (11:27–32).

93 Hays, "Conversion of the Imagination," 401.

Similarly, in chapters 12–14, the eschatological frame within which Paul's comments on spirituality are set includes not only the humbling anticipation of a day when the "partial" will be superseded by the "perfect" (13:8–13) but also the sobering warning in 14:37–38 that a person who ignores Paul's instructions "will be ignored" (by implication, by God, both invisibly in the present and visibly on the last day).

The climax of Paul's eschatological corrective to the Corinthians' thinking and practice is in chapter 15, where it becomes evident that some among the Corinthians have drifted so far away from the gospel that was preached to them as to say that "there is no resurrection of the dead" (15:12).[94] The primary focus of the chapter's eschatology is on the future bodily resurrection of believers as climax of Christ's victory over every enemy, including even death itself (cf. 15:20–28, 50–58). But around that center Paul draws a circle with a wide circumference, embracing the renewal and reordering of the entire cosmos, so that "God may be all in all" (15:28). The time between Christ's resurrection and the final consummation, too, is described in a way that suggests something more than merely a vacant interval in which the church waits passively for Christ's return: the multiple "enemies" Paul makes reference to in verses 25–27 and the description of Christ's resent reign as one that will continue "until" (ἄχρι, v. 25) they have all been placed beneath his feet suggests a story in which the reign of Christ is progressively extended through the proclamation of the gospel and the labors of believers, in anticipation of its final consummation in the age to come.

§8 The Church

1 Corinthians is not only a letter that is *addressed to* the church; it is also, from start to finish, a letter that is *about* what it means to be the church—or, more precisely, to be "the church of God at Corinth, ... sanctified in Christ Jesus, called as saints, with all those in every place who call on the name of Jesus Christ our Lord" (1:2).[95]

The description of the church that Paul offers in the opening greeting places heavy emphasis on its status as a community that has been "sanctified in Christ Jesus" and "called as saints." This emphasis continues

---

[94] For a discussion of the ways in which Paul's eschatological perspective in ch. 15 contrasts with mainstream Greco-Roman beliefs, see Starling, "Nothing Beyond What Is Written?," 58–61; Witherington, *Conflict and Community*, 295–98.

[95] Cf. especially Hays, "Ecclesiology and Ethics in 1 Corinthians," *ExAud* 10 (1994): 36–40.

through the rest of the letter, and is especially evident in those sections where Paul chastises the readers for their failure to uphold the distinctions of allegiance and behavior that demarcate them from their pagan neighbors (e.g., chs. 5–6, 8–10, 15).

The proper placement of the boundary lines that delineate the edges of the believing community is, therefore, a recurring concern across the letter. If (as Paul insists) the visible church's boundaries are to serve the mission of God and promote his glory in the world, then it is important not only that they exist, and that they can be seen, but also that they are drawn in the right places. Boundaries drawn too narrowly (e.g., the elitist Corinthian boundaries drawn around the "spiritual" people with their special gifts and the wealthy people with their special meals) dishonor Christ by dividing his body, humiliating and excluding people who ought to have been welcomed and cherished (11:23–34; 12:12–31). Boundaries drawn too loosely dishonor Christ by implying that there is no difference between those who know him and those who do not, and that his saving rule over the church is an empty ceremonial rule that can be disregarded with impunity (5:1–13; 6:9–20; cf. 2 Cor 6:14–7:1). Boundaries that are drawn in the right place do not in themselves create or guarantee the church's holiness, but they do present a reminder to the church and a representation to the world of the ways of the God who dwells in the church as his temple (cf. 3:16–17), and the shape of the repentant and believing response to the gospel to which the church is called.[96]

Hand in hand with this emphasis on the holiness of the church, the opening verses of the letter place stress on what later generations of Christians would come to speak of as its "catholicity," i.e., that the church in Corinth possesses its identity in solidarity with "all those in every place who call on the name of Jesus Christ our Lord—both their Lord and ours" (1:2). This reminder at the outset of the letter is followed by a series of more pointed references to the same reality across the following chapters, in which Paul poses repeated challenges to the Corinthians' sense of their own uniqueness and calls them back to the core beliefs and practices that are adhered to by all believers everywhere (e.g., 4:17; 7:17; 11:16; 14:33, 36).

In addition to this solidarity that the Corinthian believers have with those who assemble in other places, Paul also encourages them to

[96] The content of this paragraph is adapted from Starling, "Good Fences, Good Neighbours? Holiness, Boundaries and Mission," *PJBR* 8 (2013): 24–25.

understand their identity as the church in salvation-historical continuity with the people of God in generations past. The death and resurrection of Christ and the outpouring of his Spirit constitute, in Paul's understanding, an inbreaking of "the ends of the ages" (10:11) that creates a clear and important distinction between the Israelite "them" of the time before Christ and the new covenant "us" to which Paul and the Corinthians belong (10:13). Nevertheless, the Corinthian believers (including the uncircumcised gentiles who made up the majority of the church) are still encouraged to think of the people of Israel as "our ancestors" (10:1) and to regard them as having been "baptized" into Moses when they passed through the sea, having eaten "spiritual food" in the wilderness, and having drunk from the "spiritual rock" that Paul speaks of as "Christ" (10:1–4).[97]

A third key element of the letter's ecclesiology emerges in 1:10, with the call to unity of mind and purpose that Paul issues in response to the reports that he has received of rivalry and divisions within the congregation. Read within the larger context of chapters 1–4, Paul's call for the Corinthians to "agree in what you say," united in "the same understanding" and "the same conviction," implies something more than merely an affirmation of the traditional Greco-Roman preference for harmony over conflict and division.[98] The "understanding" that he wishes the Corinthians to have in common is the mindset that he goes on in the following chapter to describe as "the mind of Christ" (2:16), and the message on which they are to agree in their speech is the message that has been given to them, "not in words taught by human wisdom, but in those taught by the Spirit" (2:13).[99] The focus of their unity is, therefore, the message of the gospel, which is to be clearly and cogently proclaimed in their speech (cf. 14:1–25), consistently demonstrated in their actions (cf. 4:17; 11:17–26), and pervasively influential within their inward thoughts and desires (cf. 2:10–16; 8:1–13; 15:1–2). It is to be lived out in practices that embrace the plurality and diversity of the members within Christ's body and the gifts they have been given (12:4–30; 3:21–23), give special

[97] Cf. Hays, "Conversion of the Imagination," 391–412.

[98] For an elaboration and defense of this assertion, see Starling, "In the Same Mind."

[99] For a discussion of the meaning of Paul's claim in 2:16 and its implications for our interpretation of the letter, see David I. Starling, "'But We Have the Mind of Christ': 1 Corinthians, Wisdom, and the Interpretation of Israel's Scriptures," in Campbell and Harrison, *Paul in His Jewish and Graeco-Roman Contexts*.

honor to those of its members who are weakest and most vulnerable (11:17–34; 12:15–26), and act toward all in the patience and humility of love (13:1–13).

§8.1 Baptism

Paul's understanding of the church and the gospel by which it is constituted finds symbolic expression in the ritual of Christian baptism, to which he makes repeated reference within the letter.

The first cluster of baptism references within 1 Corinthians occurs in 1:13–17, commencing with the string of rhetorical questions that he puts to the readers in 1:13: "Is Christ divided? Was Paul crucified for you? Or were you baptized in Paul's name?" The point that is emphatically asserted by all three questions has to do with the christological basis of the Corinthians' unity. They are *Christ's* body, and to tear apart the church into rival functions is to dismember the body of Christ; it was *Christ* who was crucified for them, not Paul (or Cephas or Apollos); and it was into *Christ's* name that they were baptized, not Paul's (or Cephas's, or Apollos's). At this point in the letter, therefore, the accent of Paul's reference to baptism falls on its significance as a badge of allegiance to Christ and a basis for the unity of all who have experienced that baptism within the one community of his people—with implications for both the internal unity of the Corinthian church and for the catholicity of its relationships with other communities of believers in the same Lord Jesus (cf. 1:2 and the comments in §8, above).

In the verses that follow, Paul answers his own rhetorical question with a list of the (very few) people whom he did baptize during his time in Corinth (1:14–16). The fact that he speaks here in terms of not only the baptism of individuals (Crispus and Gaius) but also the baptism of a whole household (that of Stephanas) is sometimes appealed to as evidence for a first-century practice of infant baptism, on the assumption that Stephanas's conversion would have led to the baptism of his whole household, including any infants that may have been within it.[100] To draw this conclusion would go beyond the evidence, however, and beg a number of important questions regarding the meaning and function of the

[100] E.g., Jeremias, *Infant Baptism in the First Four Centuries* (Philadelphia: Westminster, 1960), 19–24, 40–41.

ritual. It is certainly worth highlighting the way in which Paul (along with others within earliest Christianity) saw the gospel as a message addressed not only to individual men and women but also to whole households as collective social units (cf. Luke 10:5–7; Acts 16:31), and called for not only the repentance of individual believers but the renewal and transformation of the entire household. A telling example of this can be seen in the final chapter of this same letter, where the members of the household of Stephanas, whose baptism was recalled in 1:16, are described by Paul as "the firstfruits of Achaia," who "devoted themselves to serving the saints" (16:15). Undoubtedly, the capacity of the various individual household members (including Fortunatus and Achaicus, who were likely slaves or freedmen depending on Stephanas as a patron) to give time and energy to the service of the church would have been greatly enhanced by the fact that the entire household, including Stephanas the householder, had given its allegiance to Christ. But the authority of a first-century householder was not so absolute or the bonds of solidarity within the household so strong as to override any need in Paul's mind for the individual household members to confess Christ with their own mouths and from their own hearts. On occasion (as the evidence of 1 Corinthians and the rest of the New Testament makes clear) a householder might be baptized into Christ without all the members of the household following suit, or a number of the individuals within a household might come to faith in Christ even though the householder himself was not a believer.[101] Even within a marriage, a pagan husband might find himself living with a Christian wife, or a Christian wife with a pagan husband (cf. 1 Cor 7:12–16).

The advice Paul gives to believers in a situation such as this suggests that he viewed the situation of a non-believer married to a believing spouse as a special and privileged one, with "the unbelieving husband ... made holy by the wife," and "the unbelieving wife ... made holy by the husband"; something similar can be said of the children of believing parents, whom he describes as "holy," rather than "unclean," due to the faith of their parents (7:14). But the fact that an unbelieving spouse is "made holy" in this sense, and should therefore not be abandoned and disowned by their Christian husband or wife, does not imply that they are automatically

[101] Note the differences of language between Rom 16:3–5, Rom 16:10b and Rom 16:11b, and the comments on these verses in Robert Jewett, *Romans: A Commentary*, Hermeneia (Minneapolis: Fortress, 2007), 954–60, 966–68.

saved by virtue of their marriage (cf. 7:16); the same logic would presumably have been applied by Paul to the situation of children within the household who had not yet professed Christ as Lord, though they may well have attended and participated in gatherings of the church in a way that an unbelieving spouse would not have. It would be going beyond the evidence, therefore, to conclude that children in a situation such as this would have been baptized as infants, as an imitation or fulfillment of the old covenant practice of circumcision. The question of whether the children of believers should be baptized as infants cannot ultimately be given a conclusive answer based solely on our attempts to reconstruct what we think the practice of the first-century church would have been; it requires us, in addition, to reflect on the various layers of *meaning* that the New Testament writers attribute to the practice.[102] These include (within 1 Corinthians) a dramatization of the saving events proclaimed in the gospel (cf. 10:1–2, where the gospel events are depicted as having been prefigured in the saving events of the exodus), a declaration of allegiance to Christ as Lord (e.g., 1:13),[103] and a symbolic display of the forgiveness of sins (6:11) and incorporation into the body of Christ (e.g., 12:13) that are experienced by believers in Jesus.[104]

§8.2 The Lord's Supper

A second symbolic practice that Paul implicitly places alongside baptism in 10:1–4—and that also speaks of the story of the salvation that is proclaimed in the gospel (e.g., 10:3–4; 11:26), the unity of believers with one another (e.g., 10:17), the exclusivity of allegiance that believers owe to Christ (e.g., 10:21)—is the meal that Paul refers to in this letter as "the Lord's supper" (κυριακὸν δεῖπνον; 11:20).

---

[102] For a brief but insightful discussion of some of the larger hermeneutical issues that arise when passages such as this are appealed to as the "evidence" basis for competing claims within debates about infant baptism, see Anthony C. Thiselton, *The Hermeneutics of Doctrine* (Grand Rapids: Eerdmans, 2007), 511–14.

[103] On the likely meaning of the εἰς Χρίστον formula (cf. Rom 6:3; Gal 3:27) that Paul appears to be alluding to in 1:13 and 10:2, see Thiselton, *The Hermeneutics of Doctrine*, 538–39, citing Rudolf Schnackenburg, *Baptism in the Thought of St. Paul: A Study in Pauline Theology*, trans. G. R. Beasley-Murray (New York: Herder and Herder, 1964), 22–29.

[104] Water baptism is not directly referred to in either 6:11 or 12:13, but it is reasonable to assume the likelihood that Paul would have expected his hearers to find an allusion in both these passages to the conversion-initiation events that baptism symbolizes. Cf. the discussions of these passages in Thiselton, *First Corinthians*, 453–55, 997–1001, and in this commentary.

As is the case with baptism (10:2), Paul describes the eating and drinking of the Lord's supper as practices that were typologically prefigured by events within the history of the Exodus generation of the Israelites—in the case of the Lord's supper, by the "spiritual food" (10:3; cf. Exod 16:31) and "spiritual drink" (10:4; cf. Exod 17:6; Num 20:7–13) that were provided for the children of Israel to eat and drink during the years of their wilderness wanderings. Paul's reminder of this prefigurement leads to a warning to the Corinthians to "flee from idolatry" (10:14), based on the fact that "the cup of blessing that we bless" is "a sharing in the blood of Christ" (10:16), and "the bread that we break" is "a sharing in the body of Christ" (10:16). The reality Paul has in mind as being depicted in this act of symbolic participation is not merely the communion of an individual soul with the Lord Jesus; the meal, in his view, is an irreducibly ecclesial event, signifying both the union that each believer has with Christ and the solidarity that all believers have with one another, since "all of us share the one bread" (10:17).

The subject of the Lord's Supper returns in the following chapter (11:17–34). Here, the focus of Paul's warnings shifts from the symbolic boundaries of exclusive allegiance that the Lord's supper inscribes around the church to the content of the salvation story that ought to shape the church's community life and be displayed in its gatherings. A community meal celebrated in a manner that leaves in place the divisions of status between haves and have-nots within the church is, in Paul's view, a catastrophic failure to recognize and honor the body of Christ (11:29) and "proclaim the Lord's death" in a worthy manner (11:26–27). The kind of self-examination Paul calls for in 11:28–31, therefore, is probably not a process of individual introspection, in which believers separately and independently take a moral inventory of their own personal conduct across the previous week; it is, rather, a searching critical assessment of the attitudes and assumptions that believers bring to the meal itself, that should lead to the kind of radically revised and repentant manner of celebrating the supper that Paul goes on to command in 11:33–34a.

At the heart of the story that the Lord's supper dramatizes and proclaims is the death of Jesus and its significance as an event that took place "for you" (ὑπὲρ ὑμῶν), inaugurating a "new covenant in my blood" (11:24–25)—language Paul says he received "from the Lord" and—on an earlier occasion—passed on to the Corinthians (11:23). This focus on the death of Jesus and its salvific significance is consistent with the way in which Paul later formulates his summary of the "most important" things at the heart of the gospel he originally preached to the Corinthians (15:1–5)—a summary that he also says that he "received" and "passed on" (15:3)—and underlines the closeness with which Paul understood the relationship between the practice of the Lord's supper and the proclamation of the message of the gospel.

§9 Leadership and Ministry

Given that the divisions to which Paul is responding in 1:10–4:21 are caused, at least in part, by the attitudes of some within the church toward its various leaders and teachers, it is no surprise that this section of the letter contains one of the longest sustained discussions within Paul's letters on the theme of leadership and ministry. Within it, Paul offers a corrective not only to the arrogance that fuels the Corinthians' boasting in their leaders but also to the false estimation of Christian leadership that informs it. Leaders within the church, Paul reminds the Corinthians in 3:1–4:5, should be regarded not as competitors in a quest for status and recognition but as servants collaborating in a common project.[105] Any abilities they possess should be viewed as gifts from God (1:4–7), as should the leaders themselves (3:21–23) and the work they are granted the opportunity to perform (3:10). Evaluation of leaders and their ministry is the prerogative of God himself, and his verdict will be announced on the last day (3:10–4:5); when situations arise, as they will, in which believers need to make evaluations of their own regarding the conduct and teaching of others, including their leaders (e.g., 5:12; 6:5; 14:29), such assessments should be made in humility and with care, informed by the criteria of God's eschatological judgment rather than the distorted value systems of the present age (3:1–5, 18–20).

Paul's teaching on ministry within 1 Corinthians is not focused exclusively on the question of how believers should regard the ministry of

---

[105] See especially James R. Harrison, *Paul and the Ancient Celebrity Circuit: The Cross and Moral Transformation*, WUNT (Tübingen: Mohr Siebeck, 2019), 331–45; Andrew D. Clarke, *Secular and Christian Leadership in Corinth: A Socio-historical and Exegetical Study of 1 Corinthians 1-6* (Eugene: Wipf & Stock, 2006), 109–27; James Thompson, *Pastoral Ministry according to Paul: A Biblical Vision* (Grand Rapids: Baker, 2006), 124–29; John L. Hiigel, *Leadership in 1 Corinthians: A Case Study in Paul's Ecclesiology*, SBEC (Lewiston: Mellen, 2003).

those who teach and lead; it also addresses at some length the question of how the readers should understand their own ministry and the ministry of their fellow believers within the church. Paul's discussion of this issue is foreshadowed in the thanksgiving report of 1:4–9, where he sets the gifts of speech and knowledge that the Corinthians themselves possess within the same frame of grace that he later places around the ministries of their teachers and leaders. It is not until chapters 12–14, however, that he turns to discuss the topic at length and in detail. Here, as the opening verses of the section make clear, he is writing not to offer a comprehensive treatise on gifts and ministry but to respond to a particular attitude toward the topic that has been voiced within the Corinthians' letter. The attitude taken by the Corinthians appears to have been one in which particular gifts, most notably the gift of speaking in tongues, are elevated as the mark of a "spiritual" elite within the congregation and the gifts of others, if they are acknowledged at all, regarded as of little value. The basic contours of Paul's response are sketched out in 12:4–6, where his carefully constructed threefold formula reframes the activities that the Corinthians are accustomed to viewing as status-conferring manifestations of the Spirit, recasting them as acts of service performed for the Lord Jesus and labors performed through the enabling power of God. The paragraphs that follow stress the diversity of forms that such service and working can take and the fact that all are given "for the common good" (πρὸς τὸ συμφέρον; v. 7).

While Paul emphatically affirms the wide diversity of the gifts that Spirit bestows and the forms that the service of believers can take, he does not regard all gifts as equal in the contribution that they make to the building up of the community. The chapter thus concludes with an encouragement to the Corinthians to "desire the greater gifts" (12:31), which is reiterated and unpacked in 14:1 as the introduction to an extended discussion of the advantages of prophecy over tongues-speaking as a means for the church's upbuilding (14:2–25). Sandwiched between the initial encouragement in 12:31 and its reiteration in 14:1 is the encomium to love that Paul inserts as the centerpiece of his discussion regarding the exercise of gifts and ministry within the church. Above all else, believers are to "pursue love" (14:1), which will inform their assessments of which ministries and gifts to prioritize, transform the dispositions with which the gifts are exercised (13:4–6), and energize believers to persevere in the service of others when the work of ministry involves struggles, toils, and trials (13:7), anticipating the perfections and joys of the age to come (13:8–13).

The eschatological note that is sounded in the final stanzas of chapter 13 anticipates the perspective on ministry that Paul offers in the climactic discussion regarding the resurrection of believers that follows in chapter 15. What is at stake in the discussion is more than just a theoretical difference between two different viewpoints on life in the age to come; across the chapter it becomes increasingly clear that Paul is contending not only for a set of ideas but also for a pattern of life and ministry that coheres with them. As early in the chapter as verse 10, he hints at this emphasis in the passing reference that he makes to the labors that he performed through the empowerment of the grace of God that was with him. A similar note recurs in verses 30–32, where he contrasts the risks and struggles that he and his fellow missionaries daily embrace, emboldened by the hope of the resurrection, with the life of comfortable self-indulgence that is the logical outworking of a belief that "tomorrow we die" (v. 32). The chapter concludes with a call to believers to persevere in the "work" and "labor" of ministry, motivated by the resurrection-based assurance that their toil is not in vain. In place of the model of ministry that is celebrated and exemplified by the Corinthian elite—a model that focuses on virtuosic displays of knowledge and spirituality performed by the most privileged and prominent members of the community—Paul champions a model that focuses on the expenditure of toil and effort for the good of others, empowered by the grace of God and motivated by the hope of the resurrection. The exhortations and commendations of the final chapter reinforce that message by shining a light on the work of Stephanas, Fortunatus, and Achaicus, who have "devoted themselves to serving the saints" (16:15), and urging the Corinthians to "submit to such people, and to everyone who works and labors with them" (16:16). The closing words of the letter, in 16:19–24, direct our minds toward the matrix of relationships within which all ministry takes place, the grace that enables and empowers it, and the love for the Lord Jesus and his people that belongs at its heart.

VI. Outline

EXPOSITION

I. Letter Opening (1:1–9)

The first two paragraphs of 1 Corinthians contain the typical elements of a Pauline letter opening: a greeting that identifies and describes the sender and recipients, wishing the latter "grace ... and peace, from God our Father and the Lord Jesus Christ," and a thanksgiving report, in which Paul shares with the readers a brief account of the matters for which he gives thanks to God as he prays for them. Both of these elements of the letter opening adapt and expand on the traditional formulae that commenced a Greco-Roman letter, infusing them with distinctively Christian content and anticipating some of the major themes and concerns of the letter.

A. Greeting (1:1–3)

> 1 Paul, called as an apostle of Christ Jesus by God's will, and Sosthenes our brother:
>
> 2 To the church of God at Corinth, to those sanctified in Christ Jesus, called as saints, with all those in every place who call on the name of Jesus Christ our Lord—both their Lord and ours.
>
> 3 Grace to you and peace from God our Father and the Lord Jesus Christ.

Context/Structure/Form

The greeting (vv. 1–3) follows the same pattern as Paul's other epistle greetings. The typical Greek letter commenced with a simple, one-sentence greeting: "A to B, greetings." Paul expands on that form in all his letters, changing "greetings" (χαίρειν) to "grace ... and peace" (χάρις ...

καὶ εἰρήνη), and adding content to the descriptions of the author and addressees. These additions are often in response to relevant aspects of the situation that the letter addresses and anticipate the letter's themes and emphases. Here, the main expansion is in verse 2, which emphasizes the identity and calling of the addressees as the church of God, foreshadowing the ecclesiological themes of the letter and the recurring challenges throughout the letter to the various ways in which the believers in Corinth are failing to live out the holiness to which they have been called.

Comments

1:1. Although Paul's self-description in the opening line of the greeting is not as assertive as his self-descriptions in some of the other letters (e.g., Gal 1:1; Rom 1:1) it still contains a clear and explicit reference to his apostleship and its source in the calling and will of God, which he sees no need to include in some other letters (cf. Phil 1:1; 1 Thess 1:1; 2 Thess 1:1; Phlm 1:1). Fee is perhaps going beyond the evidence in the extent to which he reads this as a reaction against a "decidedly anti-Pauline sentiment" that has infected "nearly the whole" of the Corinthian church,[1] but the letter body does contain a number of indications of Paul's awareness that there are some at least among the Corinthians for whom his authority and apostleship are not something that can be comfortably taken for granted (cf. 9:1–2; 14:37–38; 15:8–11).

The particular claim Paul makes by describing himself in this manner is both assertive and self-effacing. As an apostle, Paul speaks as an authorized representative of the Lord Jesus, testifying to the events of his death and resurrection (1:17; 9:1–2; 15:1–11), giving directions in his name (14:37), and exercising a fatherly authority within the communities that he has established (4:14–21; 5:3–5). His commissioning as an apostle originates in the will of God, involving purposes for which he was set apart from birth (Gal 1:15; cf. Jer 1:5), made known to him when he was called into God's service through his encounter with the risen Christ (Gal 1:15–16; 1 Cor 9:1; 15:8). But the authority bestowed on him by his commissioning is not an authority to speak and act in his own name, for his own advancement. He is a representative of Christ, not himself, and his solidarity with Christ and with the other apostles demands a pattern of ministry that is humble and collaborative (3:5–7) and a willingness to

[1] Fee, *First Epistle to the Corinthians*, 8–9, 24–25.

work hard, endure suffering and social dishonor, and relinquish rights and privileges for the good of others (4:8–13; 9:5–18; 15:10, 30–31).

As in most of his early letters (though not in Romans, Ephesians or the Pastorals) Paul includes a co-sender in the greeting—an unusual feature compared with other letters from the period.[2] "Sosthenes our brother" is possibly the same Sosthenes mentioned as the "leader of the synagogue" in Acts 18:17. If that is the case (assuming Sosthenes's subsequent conversion and his presence with Paul in Ephesus), then his inclusion here may function not only as an expression of Paul's characteristic preference for collaboration (cf. 2 Cor 1:1; Phil 1:1; Col 1:1; 1 Thess 1:1; 2 Thess 1:1; Phlm 1:1) but also as a way of linking his ministry to that of another known and trusted figure.

1:2. In verse 2 Paul turns to the recipients, whom he describes as "God's church at Corinth." His use of the singular "church" (not "the churches" as he addresses the Galatians) suggests that he viewed the various house-churches of the city as part of one larger church that met from time to time (cf. 5:4; Rom 16:23). ἐκκλησία ("church") is the word that was commonly used for a political assembly (cf. Acts 19:39, 41) and was used in Greek translations of the Old Testament to refer to the assembled nation of Israel (e.g., Deut 4:10). It is these backgrounds, along with the usage of the word within Paul's letters and other early Christian writings, that should be our primary points of reference in determining its meaning, rather than the etymology suggested by the form of the word (ἐκ + καλέω), from which some have argued that it includes a reference to the "called-out-ness" of the church.[3]

Paul's further description of the recipients as "those sanctified in Christ Jesus, called as saints" stresses by repetition that the church of God is called to be a holy community (see §8). "Sanctified" (ἡγιασμένοις; perfect passive participle) depicts their sanctification as a present reality resulting from the past event of their conversion and baptism into Christ (see §8.1), with implications for their conduct and vocation as the

---

[2] Cf. E. Randolph Richards, *The Secretary in the Letters of Paul*, WUNT (Tübingen: Mohr Siebeck, 1991), 47.

[3] Cf. Charles Hodge's comments on the church as "called out from the world" in Charles Hodge, *First Epistle to the Corinthians*, 5th ed. (Edinburgh: Banner of Truth, 1958 [1858]), 3, and the critical observations in Thiselton, *First Corinthians*, 75. The church's "called-out-ness" is, however, implied by Paul's description of it in the following phrase as "those who are sanctified in Christ Jesus and called as saints."

holy and set-apart people of God. These implications are immediately reinforced in the following phrase (κλητοῖς ἁγίοις; "called as saints"), in which the word "called" probably implies an authoritative summons or appointment, in line with its use in the previous verse ("called as an apostle"). This reminder to the readers of their distinctive identity and vocation anticipates a theme that is to be a major emphasis in the letter, challenging the various ways in which the Corinthian believers have accommodated themselves to the mindset and behaviors of their pagan neighbors (cf. 3:1–4, 16, 18–19; 4:8–10; 5:1; 6:1–23; 7:29–31; 10:1–22; 12:2; 15:33–34).[4]

The shared identity of the believers in Corinth as the holy people of God is a status that they possess in solidarity with "all those in every place who call on the name of Jesus Christ our Lord—both their Lord and ours." In reminding them of this at the outset, Paul anticipates a series of challenges that he will make in subsequent chapters to the Corinthians' arrogant sense of specialness (e.g., 4:17; 7:17; 11:16; 14:33, 36).

His description of Christians as "those ... who call on the name of Jesus Christ our Lord" is consistent with the central place he gives to the confession of Jesus's lordship as the heart of Christian faith (cf. 1 Cor 12:3; Rom 10:9) and the act of "call[ing] on" in him in prayer as the most basic and definitive expression of that allegiance. The language that he uses to describe that relationship of dependent allegiance is an echo of LXX Joel 3:5 (EVV Joel 2:32: "everyone who calls on the name of the Lord will be saved"). Paul's appropriation of that verse, here and elsewhere, implies a very high estimation of the identity and authority of Jesus, sufficient to warrant taking a text about YHWH, the covenant God of Israel, and applying it to the Lord Jesus (see §2).

An additional Old Testament text that is also (somewhat more faintly) echoed in this verse is Malachi 1:11: "'My name will be great among the nations, from the rising of the sun to its setting. Incense and pure offerings will be presented in my name in every place because my name will be great among the nations,' says the Lord of Armies." The precise phrase "in every place" (ἐν παντὶ τόπῳ) that constitutes the echo is only a brief one and it would be difficult to mount a convincing argument that Paul is intending an allusion that would have been discernible by the original

[4] See especially Paul R. Trebilco, *Self-Designations and Group Identity in the New Testament* (Cambridge: Cambridge University Press, 2012), 128–37.

hearers of the letter and necessary for the basic meaning of the verse to be grasped. Nevertheless, the prominent place of the phrase within the opening greeting and its recurring use in Paul's letters (cf. 2 Cor 2:14; 1 Thess 1:8; 1 Tim 2:8)—frequently in connection with references to prayer (1 Cor 1:2; 1 Tim 2:8) and incense imagery (2 Cor 2:14) that correspond to the ideas of the source-text in Malachi—combine to support the likelihood that the language and concepts of Malachi's prophecy are present at the back of Paul's own mind and have exerted an influence on the way in which he frames his vision for the churches that he plants in fulfillment of his missionary calling.[5]

1:3. The blessing with which the paragraph concludes is a characteristically Pauline expansion and Christianization of the customary Greek letter greeting, converting "greetings!" (χαίρειν) to "grace ... and peace" (χάρις ... καὶ εἰρήνη), and adding, "from God our Father and the Lord Jesus Christ." The "grace" for which the blessing prays can refer (here in 1 Corinthians and elsewhere in Paul's letters) both to the divine disposition of favor and kindness from which all of God's blessings proceed and to the outpoured gifts that flow from that generous disposition (cf. 1:4) (see §5). The "peace" that is joined to it refers principally to the harmony and well-being that God's salvation creates, both "vertically," between God and his people, and "horizontally," within the human relationships of the reconciled community (cf. 7:15; 14:33).

Both the grace and the peace that Paul wishes for his readers are spoken of as proceeding "from God our Father and the Lord Jesus Christ." Here as elsewhere in Paul's letter greetings, this form of words does not imply that "God our Father" and "the Lord Jesus Christ" are to be thought of as two separate sources of blessing; rather, as Paul spells out later in the letter, the picture he wishes to convey is one in which the agency of God and that of Christ are exercised in an inseparable unity, such that the gifts and graces that originate, like all things, in the will of "God, the Father," are extended to believers through their participation in the person and work of the "one Lord, Jesus Christ" (8:6). Nor is the relationship between Christ and the Father represented as a merely instrumental one; in speaking of "the Lord Jesus Christ" (1:3; cf. 1:2: "Jesus Christ our Lord"), Paul is

[5] Cf. the discussion in Ciampa and Rosner, *The First Letter to the Corinthians*, 33–35, and the criteria for evaluating proposals regarding the presence of Scriptural echoes in Paul's letters in Hays, *Echoes of Scripture*, 29–32.

implying that the risen Jesus participates in the very identity of YHWH himself as "Lord" (κύριος), in line with the high Christology implied by his appropriation of the language of LXX Joel 3:5 (EVV Joel 2:32) in the immediately preceding verse (see §§1, 2).

Bridge

The greeting Paul extends to his readers in the opening verses of the letter establishes vitally important connections between Paul and the Corinthians and, in turn, between the Corinthians and us. For us as twenty-first century readers of Paul's letters, the greetings with which they commence are an important reminder that the texts we are reading originated as artifacts of communication created for readers in a time and place remote from our own, and were (in the case of the Corinthian letters, at least) part of an ongoing correspondence between the author and a community of readers with whom he was closely and personally acquainted. But the expansions Paul includes within his descriptions of himself as the sender and the communities to which he is writing stress aspects of their identity and situation that connect us to, rather than alienating us from, the original parties to this correspondence.

Paul, for his part, is writing not merely as the founder of the Corinthian church (cf. 4:14–15) but as "an apostle of Christ Jesus" (1:1), with a commissioning that embraces all the nations (Rom 1:5)—and, by implication, all future generations, our own included, that exist within the time opened up by the inauguration of the ends of the ages in Christ (1 Cor 10:11). And the Corinthians, despite their well-developed sense of uniqueness, are joined to Paul not only by their shared history and experiences but also, and even more basically, by an identity that they possess in common with "all those in every place who call on the name of Jesus Christ our Lord" (1:2).

We would be wise, therefore, to read the chapters that follow with the double awareness that the greeting establishes for us at the outset, giving proper attention both to the particularities of the Corinthians' situation and their unique relationship with Paul and to the extended relevance, applicability, and authority that the letter possesses for believers in all times and places, including our own.

B. Thanksgiving Report (1:4–9)

> [4] I always thank my God for you because of the grace of God given to you in Christ Jesus, [5] that you were enriched in him in every way, in all speech and all knowledge. [6] In this way, the testimony about Christ was confirmed among you, [7] so that you do not lack any spiritual gift as you eagerly wait for the revelation of our Lord Jesus Christ. [8] He will also strengthen you to the end, so that you will be blameless in the day of our Lord Jesus Christ. [9] God is faithful; you were called by him into fellowship with his Son, Jesus Christ our Lord.

Context/Structure/Form

The thanksgiving report (vv. 4–9), like the greeting, is a recurring feature of Paul's letters, in keeping with the common (though by no means universal) practice of ancient letter-writers to follow the opening greeting with a prayer and/or a statement of thanksgiving to the gods for the health and well-being of the recipient.[6] Paul's letters occasionally omit any thanksgiving report altogether (cf. Gal 1) or replace or precede it with a benediction (cf. 2 Cor 1:3–7; Eph 1:3–14), but in the majority of cases he retains it as the item that follows immediately after the letter greeting. Where Paul does retain a thanksgiving report, he typically adapts and expands the traditional thanksgiving formulae to reflect the shared relationship with God that he and the readers have in Christ and prepare the way for the issues he will address in the body of the letter.

Here, in the thanksgiving report that he shares with the Corinthians, the emphasis falls primarily on the gifts with which God has blessed the Corinthians (see §5) and the confidence Paul has that God will show his faithfulness by strengthening and keeping them as they wait for the day of the Lord Jesus (see §7). This twofold emphasis on God's grace and the future day of Christ paves the way for the challenges that Paul will mount in the subsequent chapters against the arrogance and complacency that he sees evidenced in the conduct of the Corinthians and the letter that they have sent to him. At this point in the letter, however, there are no direct or obvious indications that this is the direction he will go on to take, and the rhetorical effect of the thanksgiving report is broadly consistent with that of the *exordium* in a typical Greco-Roman speech, reminding the

[6] Cf. the examples discussed in Peter Arzt-Grabner, "Paul's Letter Thanksgiving," in *Paul and the Ancient Letter Form*, ed. Stanley E. Porter and Sean A. Adams, Pauline Studies (Leiden: Brill, 2010), 132–49.

audience of the bonds that connect them with the speaker and reinforcing the goodwill they feel toward him.[7]

Comments

1:4. The prominent place Paul gives to thanksgiving reports in his letters models thankfulness as a basic Christian attitude, responding to the graciousness of God. His thanksgivings also frequently serve a didactic and paraenetic purpose, anticipating the teaching and exhortations of the letter.[8] Here, Paul begins by thanking God for the "grace" given to the Corinthians (probably intended as an overarching reference to everything they have received from God, including their salvation but also—as Paul goes on to spell out explicitly in vv. 5–7—the gifts with which they have been enriched in Christ).

The constancy with which Paul asserts that he is "always" able to give thanks to God for the Corinthians is in keeping with the similar statements that he makes in other letters (cf. Eph 1:16; Phil 1:3–4; Col 1:3; 1 Thess 1:2; 2 Thess 1:3; 2 Tim 1:3; Phlm 4). This recurring motif in Paul's thanksgiving reports is partly an expression of the closeness of his relationship with the recipients and the frequentness of his prayers for them (cf. the assurances of consistent and continuing petitionary prayer in Rom 1:9–10; Col 1:9; 1 Thess 1:2; 2 Thess 1:11; 2 Tim 1:3) and partly an outworking of the fact that his prayers of thanksgiving focus on blessings and benefits that are reliably grounded in the gracious work of God in Christ and by his Spirit, not contingent on the vicissitudes of fortune or the fickle will of the gods.[9]

1:5–7a. Paul goes on in verses 5–7a to express his thankfulness for "everything" with which the Corinthians have been enriched by God, with a particular focus on the gifts of "speech" (λόγος) and "knowledge" (γνώσις) that they enjoy. In view of what Paul goes on to write about

---

[7] Cf. Witherington, *Conflict and Community*, 39–48.

[8] Cf. Peter T. O'Brien, *Introductory Thanksgivings in the Letters of Paul* (Leiden: Brill, 1977).

[9] Cf. Peter Arzt-Grabner's observation regarding the thanksgiving reports in typical Greco-Roman letters of the period: "whereas these opening phrases are expressed in a formulaic way and may be used in almost *every* private letter, regardless of the individual situation of the sender, the expressions of thanksgiving have to be described differently: They *cannot* be used in *every* letter, for if a sender expresses his thanks, this has to be seen in connection with his or her present situation. If he or she has received good news, this may cause him or her to thank the gods for the recipient's welfare." Arzt-Grabner, "Paul's Letter Thanksgiving," 149 (emphasis original).

knowledge (esp. chs. 8–10) and gifts of speech (esp. chs. 12–14), it is difficult to avoid the conclusion that he has deliberately omitted any mention of more important qualities such as love (which are the primary focus of the thanksgiving reports in almost all of his other letters).[10] Paul does nothing at this point, however, to draw attention to that omission, and Fee is still likely to be correct in his claim that the thanksgiving is genuine and not ironic.[11] Paul still thanks God for the very gifts that the Corinthians abuse; in so doing he also reminds them that their fundamental attitude to their own gifts should be one of thankfulness, not pride (cf. 4:7).

Verse 6 ("In this way, the testimony about Christ was confirmed among you") connects the experience of the gifts with which the Corinthians have been enriched to the message of the gospel,[12] which God (the implied subject of the passive verb) has "confirmed" in Corinth by gathering together a congregation of believers and blessing them with the gift of his Spirit. Paul's description of the gospel as a "testimony" (μαρτύριον) that was "confirmed" (ἐβεβαιώθη) implies a metaphor drawn from the domain of commercial law,[13] similar to his references elsewhere to God as having "sealed" believers with the Spirit (σφραγισάμενος; 2 Cor 1:22; cf. Eph 1:14; 4:30) and given the Spirit to them as a "down payment" (ἀρραβών; 2 Cor 1:22; 5:5; Eph 1:14) of the future realities promised in the gospel.

In affirming, as a consequence of this,[14] that the Corinthians "do not lack any spiritual gift" (v. 7a), Paul is perhaps choosing his words carefully, painfully conscious of other ways in which they *are* lacking. Nevertheless (as was the case in v. 5) Paul does nothing here to draw attention to that, and the negative expression in verse 7 ("you do not

---

[10] Cf. J. Murphy-O'Connor, *Paul the Letter-Writer: His World, His Options, His Skills* (Collegeville: Liturgical, 1995), 62–63.

[11] Fee, *First Epistle to the Corinthians*, 33–34.

[12] The conjunction καθώς (CSB: "in this way") is probably best read as conveying a causal sense; cf. BDAG, s.v. "καθώς," 3; Timothy A. Brookins and B. W. Longenecker, *1 Corinthians 1–9: A Handbook on the Greek Text*, BHGNT (Waco: Baylor University Press, 2016), 9. On that reading, the flow of thought is something like this: God enriched you in every way, in all speech and all knowledge (v. 5); this was a result of the action that he took to confirm the gospel promises by granting you the Spirit (v. 6), in consequence of which you do not lack any spiritual gift (v. 7a).

[13] Cf. Fee, *First Epistle to the Corinthians*, 38–39.

[14] The conjunction ὥστε (CSB: "so that") signals a result clause

lack any spiritual gift") is essentially equivalent to the positive expression in the earlier verse ("you were in enriched in everything—in all speech and all knowledge").[15]

1:7b–9. Having expressed his thanks for the Corinthians' present enrichment and gifts, Paul reminds them of what they seem less conscious of—that they have not yet arrived, and still await the day of the Lord Jesus and depend on God to strengthen them as they wait. Paul's reference in verse 7b to the (future) "revelation" (ἀποκάλυψις) of the Lord Jesus is a reminder of the apocalyptic framework that is basic to his worldview (if not the Corinthians'). Although Christ "appeared" (ὤφθη) to numerous witnesses in the aftermath of his resurrection from the dead (15:5–8), vindicating his claims and anticipating his final triumph over every enemy (15:23–28), the reality of his universal rule is still, in the present age, hidden from those who have not embraced the paradoxical wisdom made known in the message of the cross (2:6–9; 4:8–13). Those, like Paul, who have believed that message "eagerly wait" (cf. Rom 8:19, 23, 25; Gal 5:5; Phil 3:20) for the day when what is presently hidden will be made manifest for all to see, and all things will be put under the feet of Christ. Paul's inclusion of the Corinthian believers among those who adopt this stance stands in some tension with the indications later in the letter that this does not in fact appear to be the case for some of them (cf. 4:8; 15:12); here, it is probably best taken as a reminder of what is (or at least ought to be) a "fundamental orientation for all believers" (cf. 1 Thess 1:10) and an anticipation of the rebukes and admonitions in the following chapters.[16]

In speaking of the event that will usher in that promised future as "the day of our Lord Jesus Christ," Paul appropriates the "day of the Lord" language of the Old Testament prophets (e.g., Isa 13:6–9; Amos 5:18–20; Joel 2:31; Mal 4:5) rewording it in light of the same christological convictions that informed his earlier description of believers as those who "call on the name of Jesus Christ our Lord" (v. 2; cf. Joel 2:32). The christological fulfillment of this prophetic expectation does not eliminate the element of divine judgment that the phrase carried in its original Old Testament contexts (cf. 3:13; 4:5; Rom 2:5, 16; 2 Cor 5:10).

---

[15] Cf. Gardner, *1 Corinthians*, 62.

[16] Ciampa and Rosner, *The First Letter to the Corinthians*, 66.

With that fearful prospect in mind, Paul assures the Corinthians that God "will also strengthen [them] to the end";[17] the same God by whom the gospel promises were "confirmed" (ἐβεβαιώθη) among the Corinthians through the outpouring of his Spirit will also "strengthen" (βεβαιώσει) them to the end, so that their initial faith does not turn out to have been in vain. The anticipated consequence of that strengthening work of God is that the Corinthians will be "blameless" (ἀνεγκλήτους) on the day of Christ. Paul's use of this word and its near-synonyms, here and elsewhere (cf. ἀνέγκλητος in Col 1:22; 1 Tim 3:10; Titus 1:6–7; ἄμωμος in Eph 1:4; 5:27; Phil 2:15; Col 1:22; ἄμεμπτος in Phil 2:15; 1 Thess 3:13) does not imply perfect sinlessness (either by personal achievement or by imputation of the righteousness of Christ) but does imply the absence of the kind of habitual, unrepentant sin that would give rise to a verdict of condemnation at the final judgment (cf. 6:8–10; 10:1–13).[18]

The ultimate ground of Paul's confidence is the faithfulness of God (v. 9; cf. 10:13; 1 Thess 5:24), whose strengthening work will provide the Corinthians with the help that they need to resist temptation and persevere in Christ. It was his work that initiated the Corinthians' Christian experience ("You were called by him into fellowship with his Son") and he, by implication, will honor the commitment that this fellowship (κοινωνία) involves.[19]

Bridge

Because of Paul's tendency to focus his thanksgiving reports not on the fluctuating fortunes of his letters' recipients but on those things about their situation that are grounded in the unchanging purposes of God, it is not difficult for us as fellow believers with the Corinthians to use

---

17 The word "he" at the start of v. 8 translates the relative pronoun ὅς, the antecedent of which is probably not "our Lord Jesus Christ" (v. 7) but God, as the one to whom Paul's thanksgivings are directed in v. 4 and the implied subject of the passive verbs in vv. 5–6.

18 Cf. Schreiner, *1 Corinthians*, 56. Fee's distinction between ἀνέγκλητος as a "last judgment" word and ἄμεμπτος and ἄμωμος as "words that carry more of the more of the moral or religious sense" (Fee, *First Epistle to the Corinthians*, 42) is not well supported by the pattern of the three words' usage in Paul's letters.

19 The syntax of the CSB translation unhelpfully converts the relative clause structure of the original (πιστὸς ὁ θεός, δι' οὗ ἐκλήθητε εἰς κοινωνίαν ... ; "God, by whom you were called into fellowship ... , is faithful") into two apparently separate, free-standing assertions, or perhaps implies by the semicolon between them that the faithfulness of God is *manifested in* the Corinthians' calling, rather than demonstrated in his *ongoing fidelity to* the commitment that their initial calling entailed.

them as a source of guidance and encouragement for our own prayers of thanksgiving for ourselves and others. We too have been abundantly blessed by the grace of God, equipped with gifts for ministry that have been supplied by his Spirit, and given the promise of Christ's return as the focus of our hope and a spur for our holiness.

Nevertheless, in taking Paul's thanksgiving report and making it our own, it is still worth reflecting on those elements of it (including both the things it includes and the things it leaves out) that are colored by his awareness of the particular circumstances of the Corinthian church. If the Corinthians experienced an array of gifts and manifestations of the Spirit somewhat wider than the range of gifts that we experience this may stimulate us to pray for him to supply us with some of the gifts that we do not currently possess (cf. the encouragements in 12:21). There is, however, no reason for any such prayers to be tinged with unease or dissatisfaction on our part; it is, after all, God who "has placed each one of the parts in one body just as he wanted" (12:18) and the thanksgiving report at the start of the letter is a reminder that our basic stance in relation to the gifts we have received, whatever they are, should be one of gratitude to him. If we, like the Corinthians, possess more of the Spirit's gifts than we do of the graces such as faith, hope, and love that should accompany them, then the omissions in Paul's thanksgiving report may supply a focus for the prayers to which our thanksgiving will be joined. And if, by God's kindness, we can see in ourselves (and in the people we are praying for) evidences of the qualities that were not so abundant among the Corinthians, that should be a matter for heartfelt thanks to God.

II. Response to Reports of Division over Leaders (1:10–4:21)

Chapter 1 verse 10 commences the first major section of the letter body, running from 1:10 to 4:21, in which Paul responds to reports about the divisions over leadership that have arisen within the Corinthian church. It is probably overstating the importance of the call to unity in 1:10 to treat it (as some commentators do) as an announcement of the main theme that will dominate the whole letter.[20] It does, however, introduce a

[20] E.g., Mitchell, *Paul and the Rhetoric of Reconciliation*, 197–200; Oropeza, *1 Corinthians*, 16; Witherington, *Conflict and Community*, 69, 94. Cf. the criticisms of this approach in Thiselton, *First Corinthians*, 33–34; Ciampa and Rosner, *The First Letter to the Corinthians*, 19–21.

concern that will remain in view (either as foreground or as background) throughout the remainder of chapters 1–4 and will recur from time to time in subsequent chapters (e.g., 11:17–34; 12:4–26) (see §8).

Paul's initial response to the reports of division (1:10–17) is followed in 1:18–2:16 by what may appear at first to be an extended digression or a new section addressing a separate issue, in which he seeks to reframe the readers' understanding of wisdom in light of the message about the cross that Paul preached when he was with them in Corinth. The close connection between this theme and the presenting problem of the Corinthian divisions becomes apparent, however, in 3:1–4, where Paul revisits the initial reports of Corinthian factionalism that he had cited in 1:11–12 and ties them back to the immature and fleshly approach to wisdom that he has been critiquing in the previous chapters. A second, closely related reframing exercise then follows in 3:5–4:5, focusing this time on the way in which leaders and leadership should be viewed in light of the coming judgment. Finally, in 4:6–21, Paul brings this section of the letter to a conclusion with a climactic challenge to the "boasting" of the Corinthians and an appeal to them to imitate the pattern of humble service displayed to them in the ministry of Paul and his fellow apostles (and Timothy, whom he has sent to them to remind them of these things).

A. Initial Response to Reports of Division (1:10–17)

> [10] Now I urge you, brothers and sisters, in the name of our Lord Jesus
> Christ, that all of you agree in what you say, that there be no divisions
> among you, and that you be united with the same understanding and
> the same conviction. [11] For it has been reported to me about you, my
> brothers and sisters, by members of Chloe's people, that there is rivalry
> among you. [12] What I am saying is this: One of you says, "I belong to
> Paul," or "I belong to Apollos," or "I belong to Cephas," or "I belong to
> Christ." [13] Is Christ divided? Was Paul crucified for you? Or were you
> baptized in Paul's name? [14] I thank God, that I baptized none of you
> except Crispus and Gaius, [15] so that no one can say you were baptized
> in my name. [16] I did, in fact, baptize the household of Stephanas; beyond
> that, I don't recall if I baptized anyone else. [17] For Christ did not send
> me to baptize, but to preach the gospel—not with eloquent wisdom, so
> that the cross of Christ will not be emptied of its effect.

Context/Structure/Form

Within 1:10–17, Paul makes his initial appeal (v. 10), briefly outlines the reports that have concerned him (vv. 11–12), then begins in vv. 13–17 to offer his response, using the story of his own association with the Corinthians to set the scene for the following paragraphs, in which he will go on to reframe their understanding of leaders and wisdom in light of the centrality of Christ and the message of the cross.

Comments

1:10. The opening words of Paul's appeal neatly illustrate the way in which he understands and makes use of his apostolic authority: "I urge you" (Παρακαλῶ) is an example of Paul's preference for appeal and persuasion over direct command;[21] "brothers and sisters," Paul's characteristic way of addressing his fellow Christians, frames his arguments and appeals within a family-shaped relationship of mutual belonging and affection; "in the name of our Lord Jesus Christ" is a reminder that Paul speaks not merely on his own authority but as a representative of Christ.

The nature of the unity to which Paul calls the Corinthians is not merely mutual affection or an institutional affiliation but a unity of message and purpose: "that all of you agree in what you say" (ἵνα τὸ αὐτὸ λέγητε πάντες). Commentators since J. B. Lightfoot have recognized in this phrase the echo of a classical Greek idiom for political communities that are free from factions, united in a common policy and aim.[22] While Paul clearly sees enormous room for diversity of gifts and ministries (ch. 12) and some room for differences of conscience and opinion on disputable matters (chs. 8–10), he is not a thoroughgoing theological pluralist. It matters to him that the Corinthians agree with one another on the fundamentals of the message that they have been given to speak and are "united with the same understanding and the same conviction" (κατηρτισμένοι ἐν τῷ αὐτῷ νοΐ καὶ ἐν τῇ αὐτῇ γνώμῃ). The latter phrase,

[21] Thiselton is probably correct in his assessment that the primary function of Paul's Παρακαλῶ language, here and elsewhere in his letters, is not to signal the commencement of a piece of persuasive rhetoric but to make a request based on the preexisting relationship that he has with the addressees, including his role as a representative of the Lord Jesus. Cf. Thiselton, *First Corinthians*, 111–14, citing the survey of usage of παρακαλῶ in the papyri in C. J. Bjerkelund, *Parakalô: Form, Funktion und Sinn der Parakalô Sätze in den Paulinischen Briefen* (Oslo: Universitetsforlaget, 1967); see also the examples and discussion in Peter Arzt-Grabner, *1 Korinther*, PKNT (Göttingen: Vandenhoeck & Ruprecht, 2006), 58–59. Nevertheless, that Paul's requests and appeals are frequently (as is the case here) followed by supporting argumentation and other rhetorical devices suggests that the persuasive sense the word can sometimes carry is not entirely absent from Paul's mind as he uses it.

[22] Cf. J. B. Lightfoot, *Notes on the Epistles of St. Paul*, 5th ed. (London: Macmillan, 1895), 151; Mitchell, *Paul and the Rhetoric of Reconciliation*, 68–80.

like the earlier appeal for the Corinthians to "agree in what [they] say," is soaked in the idioms of Greek political discourse and calls for the Corinthians to be (re)united with one another as relationships within the community apart are healed and repaired (κατηρτισμένοι; cf. 2 Cor 13:11; Matt 4:21). Paul's desire for the members of the Corinthian church to be united in "the same understanding" and "the same conviction" is not merely an expression of the traditional Greco-Roman preference for concord (ὁμόνοια) over conflict; he has in mind a very definite idea, as he will make clear in the following paragraphs, regarding the content of the understanding in which he wishes them to agree and the message that he wishes them to speak (1:18–2:16; cf. Phil 1:27–2:11), and it is in *that* message and mindset, rather than merely in a commitment to harmony and good order, that he wishes to see them united.[23]

Nevertheless, from the way in which Paul responds to the problem in 1:18–4:21, it seems unlikely that the "divisions" (σχίσματα) within the Corinthian church were (as F. C. Baur famously argued) fully developed theological parties based on differences of doctrine.[24] More likely, they seem to have been personality cults based on the charisma and patronage of prominent leaders (who may or may not have had differences of emphasis in theology and spirituality). Paul's description of them as σχίσματα (along with his further depiction of them in vv. 11–12) has affinities with the language traditionally used to depict strife between members of rival Greco-Roman political factions, and conflicts such as these would probably have been among the most likely associations evoked by Paul's language in the minds of his readers.[25]

1:11. In verse 11 we learn that the appeal in verse 10 is a response to an account of rivalries among the Corinthians that has been reported to Paul by "members of Chloe's people." "Chloe's people" were probably not members of her family, since, as Gerd Theissen points out, the members of a family would normally be identified by the name of the father, even

---

[23] Cf. the more detailed discussion of these verses in David I. Starling, *UnCorinthian Leadership: Thematic Reflections on 1 Corinthians* (Eugene: Cascade, 2014), 45–47, and Starling, "In the Same Mind." Also worth noting are the explicitly egalitarian implications of the similar expression, τὸ αὐτὸ ... φρονοῦντες, in Rom 12:16.

[24] Cf. F. C. Baur, *Paul the Apostle of Jesus Christ*, 2 vols. (London: Williams & Norgate, 1873–1876), 1:268–320.

[25] Cf. L. L. Welborn, *Politics and Rhetoric in the Corinthian Epistles* (Macon: Mercer University Press, 1997), 2–11.

after his death.[26] The most probably scenario is that Chloe was a wealthy Ephesian businesswoman, with business interests in Corinth, and that her "people" were slaves, agents, or associates of hers who had visited Corinth and brought back a report to Paul.[27]

The word "rivalry" (ἔριδες) that Paul uses to refer to the quarrels that Chloe's people have informed him about is a term that occurs frequently in the vice-lists that he warns believers against (Rom 1:29; 13:13; 2 Cor 12:20; Gal 5:20; 1 Tim 6:4; Titus 3:9) and was clearly a problem that he viewed with great seriousness. Its use by writers of the period to describe the rivalries between competing orators (and between their students and admirers) suggests that this too, along with the dynamics of factional politics, may well have been the kind of phenomenon that Paul viewed as being replicated among the Corinthian believers.[28]

1:12. Paul goes on in verse 12 to unpack the nature of the quarrels in Corinth, linking them with the attitudes that members of the Corinthian church took toward the various leaders that they associated themselves with. Paul may be quoting actual slogans used by the Corinthians, as he does elsewhere in the letter, or perhaps caricaturing or impersonating their attitudes by putting them into words.[29] There is no evidence that the leaders themselves had any role at all in encouraging this factionalism—Paul, for his part, immediately turns to the members of his own faction in verses 13–17 to undercut their position, not to encourage it, and he is at pains to present Apollos and himself as partners, not rivals, in chapters 3–4 (cf. 16:12).

---

[26] Gerd Theissen, *The Social Setting of Pauline Christianity: Essays on Corinth* (Philadelphia: Fortress, 1982), 57.

[27] Cf. Fee, *First Epistle to the Corinthians*, 55. The facts that Chloe is not mentioned in the greetings of Romans 16 and that Paul accepts and quotes the report from Chloe's people as objective and reliable are reasons for hypothesizing that Chloe is an Ephesian, not a Corinthian.

[28] See especially the discussion in Bruce W. Winter, *Philo and Paul among the Sophists*, 2nd ed. (Grand Rapids: Eerdmans, 2002), 175–76; Winter, *After Paul Left Corinth*, 31–43, and Dio Chrysostom's mocking description (ostensibly of Corinth in the time of Diogenes but almost certainly colored by his own experiences there) of "crowds of wretched sophists around Poseidon's temple shouting and reviling one another, and their disciples, as they were called, fighting with one another" (*Or.* 8.9). Also relevant in this connection is the reference Paul makes in 2 Cor 10–11 to the adverse comparisons that some in Corinth were drawing between Paul's lack of prowess as an orator and the superior skills of others.

[29] Cf. Raymond F. Collins, *First Corinthians*, Sacra Pagina (Collegeville: Liturgical Press, 1999), 73.

Much energy has been expended on trying to identify the membership and theological tendencies of the four groups Paul refers to. The Paul group has been painted by some (e.g., F. C. Baur) as a group that championed radical emancipation from the Mosaic law, in opposition to the "Judaizing" tendency of the Cephas group,[30] while others (e.g., Wilhelm Lütgert) viewed the defining attribute of the Paul group as its anti-gnostic or anti-elitist stance. The Apollos group has frequently been linked with those in Corinth who placed a high value on rhetorical skill and Hellenistic-Jewish wisdom (cf. Acts 18:24). The Christ group has variously been identified as referring to a "Judaizing" faction who held that the only genuine apostles were those who had a first-hand acquaintance with Jesus (Baur) or a group of "ultra-spiritual pneumatics" claiming their own unmediated connection with Christ, independent of the apostles (Lütgert, Hans Conzelmann); others have interpreted the slogan, "I belong to Christ," as a piece of ironic Pauline rhetoric, reducing to absurdity the notion that Paul, Apollos, or Cephas could become the exclusive property of one faction by applying a similar slogan to Christ (Wolfgang Schrage).[31]

While there may have been some doctrinal content to the factionalism in Corinth, Paul does not spring to the defense of the Paul group or critique the theological distinctives of the others; his response is profoundly and pervasively theological, but he applies the same theological critique to all four factions at once, suggesting (as argued above) that the core problem was not theological deviation from the correctness of the "Paul" group or the "Christ" group, but an ungodly factionalism and personality-politics that he perceived as being common to all four groups.[32]

1:13. The string of rhetorical questions that follows in verse 13 (the first in the letter, but by no means the last) is one of the devices Paul turns to when he is at his most forceful. Here, the questions expose the absurdity of factions in the church of Christ. The first question (worded in Greek to imply the answer "yes")[33] expresses Paul's shock that Christ's own body (the church) has been torn apart. The following questions,

---

[30] Cephas is the Aramaic name for Peter.

[31] Cf. the discussion and evaluation of these various proposals in Thiselton, *First Corinthians*, 123–33.

[32] Cf. Clarke, *Secular and Christian Leadership*, 89–105.

[33] Cf. Lightfoot, *Notes*, 154; Ciampa and Rosner, *The First Letter to the Corinthians*, 72; Gardner, *1 Corinthians*, 82; contra Brookins and Longenecker, *1 Corinthians 1–9*, 18.

however, are worded to imply the answer "no"[34] and to express the blasphemous absurdity of putting Paul (or, by implication, Apollos or Cephas or anyone else) in the place of Christ as the one who was crucified for the Corinthians and into whose name they were baptized.

1:14–16. The absurd idea of the Corinthians having been "baptized in Paul's name" (as the behavior of some of them implies) is the trigger for a brief reflection on Paul's original ministry in Corinth and how few of the Corinthians he had in fact personally baptized. Perhaps in view of the Greco-Roman religious context, in which initiates into a mystery cult owed a continuing devotion to the "mystagogue" who inducted them (e.g., Apuleius, *Metam.* 11), Paul is thankful for this, because it reinforces his desire that he be seen as a coworker with others (cf. 3:6) and a preacher of Christ (1:17), rather than as a traveling sophist or mystagogue recruiting disciples and initiates of his own.

Crispus was probably the "leader of the synagogue" referred to in Acts 18:8, and Gaius the same Gaius mentioned in Romans 16:23 as "host to me and the whole church." The "household of Stephanas" (v. 16) is also mentioned in 16:15–18, where Paul describes its members as "the first-fruits of [the gospel in] Asia" and recalls the way in which they "devoted themselves to serving the saints."[35] The aside in verse 16 is revealingly (and deliberately?) offhand; by forgetting (or rhetorically "forgetting"?)[36] such a prominent group within the congregation, Paul makes it clear that he does not consider it particularly important who baptized whom, and he does not view the people he baptized as his own personal protégés. "No one," he insists (presumably including even the anomalous few whom he happened to baptize), can say that they were baptized in his name (v. 15).

---

[34] As signaled by the particle μή that introduces the second rhetorical question in the sequence and the "or" (ἤ) that links the second and third questions together.

[35] Paul's reference to the fact that he baptized the "household" of Stephanas has been used by some (e.g., Jeremias, *Infant Baptism*, 19–24, 40–41) as evidence for the argument that the early church baptized infants, but there is no direct evidence here or in the other "household baptism" texts that the households baptized included infants or that the infants were included among those who were baptized. Certainly, in the most detailed household-baptism narratives such as Acts 10:34–11:18 and Acts 16:25–34, it is "all" the members of the household who are baptized, but it is also "all" the members of the household who are said to have heard the message, rejoiced (16:34), and received the Spirit, speaking in tongues! (10:46–47). Cf. G. R. Beasley-Murray, *Baptism in the New Testament* (London: Macmillan, 1962), 314–15.

[36] Cf. Richard B. Hays, *First Corinthians*, Interpretation (Louisville: Westminster John Knox, 1997), 23.

1:17. Verse 17 is not a denigration of baptism (see §8.1), but it does reveal the priority Paul gives to the gospel as the power of God for salvation (cf. Rom 1:16) and the centrality of gospel proclamation within his commission as an apostle (cf. Rom 1:1; Gal 1:16). Important to Paul's argument is not only that he was sent as a preacher, not a baptizer, but also the content and manner of his preaching—that he proclaimed the gospel "not with eloquent wisdom" (literally "not with wisdom of word"; οὐκ ἐν σοφίᾳ λόγου).[37] The implication is that Paul's aim in preaching was not to win admirers of his own cleverness and rhetorical skill, but to convey the content of the message about the cross. This important addition provides a transition from the issue of factions to the underlying issue of the contrast between human wisdom and the message about the cross, which will be the focus of the paragraphs that follow in 1:18–2:16. In Paul's mind, the Corinthians' factionalism is an expression of the fact that they are viewing their various leaders as wisdom-merchants, competing in the market-place for admirers and adherents. To preach the gospel in this manner would be, in Paul's view, a fundamental denial of the message that is being preached, with the inevitable consequence that "the cross of Christ" would be "emptied of its effect."

Bridge

Although the reports that Paul has received (vv. 11–12) and the events that he recalls in response to them (vv. 14–16) are both pointedly specific in their application to the Corinthian church, the problems of factionalism and the competitive adulation of speakers and leaders are hardly uniquely Corinthian phenomena, and the basic convictions that inform Paul's response to them are of relevance far beyond the immediate context

---

[37] Timothy Brookins is probably correct (as discussed below) in highlighting the points at which Paul's critique of the "wisdom" (σοφία) that the Corinthians adulated embraces matters of philosophical content as well as matters of rhetorical form; cf. Brookins, "Rhetoric and Philosophy," 233–52; Timothy A. Brookins, *Reading 1 Corinthians: A Literary and Theological Commentary*, RNT (Macon: Smyth & Helwys, 2020), 21. Nevertheless, the form of words Paul uses in describing it here, along with the even more pointed descriptions of it in 2:1–5 as "brilliance of speech" (ὑπεροχὴ λόγου) and "persuasive words of wisdom" (πειθοί σοφίας [λόγοί]), suggests that matters of rhetorical form are uppermost in his mind at this point in the discussion. Cf. the discussions in Will N. Timmins, "The Centrality of the Cross in Proclamation," in *Theology Is for Preaching: Biblical Foundations, Method, and Practice*, ed. Paul Grimmond and Chase Kuhn (Bellingham: Lexham, 2021), 142–54; Adam G. White, *Where Is the Wise Man? Graeco-Roman Education as a Background to the Divisions in 1 Corinthians 1-4*, LNTS (London: T&T Clark, 2015), 83–106.

he is addressing in this letter. The primary allegiance of all Christians is to the one name of the Lord Jesus. That overarching commitment does not rule out the possibility of a multitude of subsidiary connections of affection and debts of gratitude that we may (and should) feel in relation to those who have served us and served alongside us in his name (cf. 4:14–17; 16:16–18; Gal 4:14–15; 6:6). None of these loyalties, however, should be allowed to compromise or compete with the fundamental loyalty that believers have to Christ. When we elevate and adulate gifts of charisma, popularity, and intelligence, and when we divide Christians into competing factions based on their differing assessments of those who possess them, we behave in a manner that is dangerously similar to the Corinthians and merit a response of the same kind as Paul's outraged reaction to the factionalism that had arisen among them.

B. Reframing Wisdom in Light of the Cross (1:18–2:16)

> [18] For the word of the cross is foolishness to those who are perishing,
> but it is the power of God to us who are being saved. [19] For it is written,
>
> > **I will destroy the wisdom of the wise,**
> > **and I will set aside the intelligence of the intelligent.**
>
> [20] Where is the one who is wise? Where is the teacher of the law? Where
> is the debater of this age? Hasn't God made the world's wisdom foolish?
> [21] For since, in God's wisdom, the world did not know God through wis-
> dom, God was pleased to save those who believe through the foolishness
> of what is preached. [22] For the Jews ask for signs and the Greeks seek
> wisdom, [23] but we preach Christ crucified, a stumbling block to the Jews
> and foolishness to the Gentiles. [24] Yet to those who are called, both Jews
> and Greeks, Christ is the power of God and the wisdom of God, [25] because
> God's foolishness is wiser than human wisdom, and God's weakness is
> stronger than human strength.
>
> [26] Brothers and sisters, consider your calling: Not many were wise from
> a human perspective, not many powerful, not many of noble birth.
> [27] Instead, God has chosen what is foolish in the world to shame the
> wise, and God has chosen what is weak in the world to shame the strong.
> [28] God has chosen what is insignificant and despised in the world—what
> is viewed as nothing—to bring to nothing what is viewed as something,
> [29] so that no one may boast in his presence. [30] It is from him that you are
> in Christ Jesus, who became wisdom from God for us—our righteousness,
> sanctification, and redemption [31] —in order that, as it is written: **Let
> the one who boasts, boast in the Lord.**

2:1 When I came to you, brothers and sisters, announcing the mystery
of God to you, I did not come with brilliance of speech or wisdom. 2 I
decided to know nothing among you except Jesus Christ and him crucified. 3 I came to you in weakness, in fear, and in much trembling. 4 My
speech and my preaching were not with persuasive words of wisdom
but with a demonstration of the Spirit's power, 5 so that your faith might
not be based on human wisdom but on God's power.

6 We do, however, speak a wisdom among the mature, but not a wisdom
of this age, or of the rulers of this age, who are coming to nothing. 7 On
the contrary, we speak God's hidden wisdom in a mystery, a wisdom
God predestined before the ages for our glory. 8 None of the rulers of
this age knew this wisdom, because if they had known it, they would
not have crucified the Lord of glory. 9 But as it is written,

> **What no eye has seen, no ear has heard,**
> **and no human heart has conceived—**
> **God has prepared these things for those who love him.**

10 Now God has revealed these things to us by the Spirit, since the Spirit
searches everything, even the depths of God. 11 For who knows a person's thoughts except his spirit within him? In the same way, no one
knows the thoughts of God except the Spirit of God. 12 Now we have
not received the spirit of the world, but the Spirit who comes from
God, so that we may understand what has been freely given to us by
God. 13 We also speak these things, not in words taught by human wisdom, but in those taught by the Spirit, explaining spiritual things to
spiritual people. 14 But the person without the Spirit does not receive
what comes from God's Spirit, because it is foolishness to him; he is not
able to understand it since it is evaluated spiritually. 15 The spiritual
person, however, can evaluate everything, and yet he himself cannot
be evaluated by anyone. 16 For

> **who has known the Lord's mind,**
> **that he may instruct him?**

But we have the mind of Christ.

Context/Structure/Form

Within a larger section (1:10–4:21) in which Paul responds to the reports he has received of factionalism within the Corinthian church, 1:18 introduces an extended discussion of the cross and human wisdom that seems at first to be a digression from the issue at hand (see §§2, 4). However, when Paul does return to speaking explicitly about "envy and strife" in chapter 3, it is clear that for Paul the two issues are inextricably linked and the core problems underlying the Corinthians' factionalism are their devotion to the wisdom of this world and their consequent tendency to "boast in human leaders" (3:21).

Some commentators suggest that Paul is employing a rhetorical *schēma* in this section, "lull[ing] them into enjoying the derision of Jewish and Greek wisdom before unveiling in 3:18–19 that they are being denounced as well."[38] This is possible, but it is more likely, given the Corinthians' reverence for "wisdom" and aspirations to social status and power, that Paul would have expected them to find the paradoxes of 1:18–25 confronting from the start, a reaction that would have been intensified by the blunt reminders of 1:26–28.

Thiselton helpfully summarizes the rhetorical structure of 1:18–2:5 like this: "How can the gospel of Christ be a form of σοφία when (a) *the message* concerns a *crucified* Christ (1:18–25); (b) its *recipients* at Corinth are *far from 'wise' or influential* in the sense understood by the world at large (1:26–31); and (c) Paul's own *preaching* when he came to Corinth was not characterized by *the kind of cleverness designed to impress an audience* (2:1–5)?"[39]

Having made those three points, Paul goes on in 2:6–16 to make it clear that he is not rejecting wisdom per se. The real conflict is not between the gospel and wisdom but between the "wisdom of this age" (2:6) and "God's hidden wisdom" (2:7), which has now been revealed by the Spirit in the message of the gospel. Those to whom this wisdom of God is revealed are described as "the mature" (2:6) and "spiritual people" (2:13)—categories on which Paul will elaborate in the immediately following paragraph.

Comments

1:18. The "for" (γάρ) that links verse 18 with the sentence that precedes it suggests that the function of this verse (and indeed the entire paragraph) is to provide support for Paul's words in verse 17 about the pursuit of "eloquent wisdom" and its tendency to empty the cross of Christ of its power. The reason that is the case, Paul explains, is the fundamental inconsistency between the message of the cross and the wisdom of the world; if a preacher can succeed in making the gospel of Christ sound wise to unbelieving ears, it can only be by avoiding or downplaying the gospel's core content, which is the "foolish" message of the cross (see §2).

---

[38] David E. Garland, *1 Corinthians*, BECNT (Grand Rapids: Baker, 2003), 59–61.

[39] Thiselton, *First Corinthians*, 148, emphasis original.

Paul's contrasting depictions of the gospel's two audiences—"to those who are perishing" (τοῖς ... ἀπολλυμένοις) and "to us who are being saved" (τοῖς ... σῳζομένοις ἡμῖν)—both make use of present participles, picturing the present condition of the two groups as a work in progress, en route to salvation or destruction. The contrast between their two divergent assessments of the message is not (as we might expect) between foolishness and "wisdom" (σοφία) but rather between foolishness and "power" (δύναμις). The close association throughout this paragraph between "wisdom" and "power" is probably, in part, a reflection of the way in which the two ideas are interrelated in the cultural context Paul is addressing (and most other cultural contexts too). At a more basic level, however, it also reflects Paul's underlying soteriological concern: The "wisdom" he is most interested in here is not speculative philosophical wisdom or the superficial eloquence of sophistry but the saving and transformative knowledge of God (cf. 1:30; 4:20; 1 Thess 1:5–10).

1:19. Verse 19 is Paul's first explicit Scripture quotation in 1 Corinthians and comes from Isaiah 29:14.[40] Isaiah is Paul's most frequently quoted Old Testament book within 1 Corinthians,[41] partly because Isaiah's polemic against human arrogance and "wisdom" (especially in chs. 28–33) coheres so closely with Paul's purposes in 1 Corinthians. The words of Isaiah 29:14 in their original context are directed against Hezekiah's political advisors and the self-congratulatory cleverness that lies beneath the superficial veneer of their professed piety. God fulfils his promise to "destroy" their wisdom by allowing Jerusalem to be besieged and all but crushed when their alliance with Egypt backfires and precipitates an Assyrian invasion, before bringing about salvation in a manner that was unmistakably his work and not in any way attributable to their political cunning. It may well be that Paul has not merely the words of the verse but this wider

[40] The wording of Paul's quotation corresponds verbatim to the LXX, except for the final word, ἀθετήσω ("I will set aside"), which takes the place occupied by κρύψω ("I will hide") in almost all surviving manuscripts of the LXX. The difference in wording could be either because Paul is following another textual tradition or because he is paraphrasing the original, perhaps under the influence of Ps 33:10 (LXX Ps 34:10). Cf. the brief discussions in Garland, *1 Corinthians*, 64; Thiselton, *First Corinthians*, 160–61; Florian Wilk, "Isaiah in 1 and 2 Corinthians," in *Isaiah in the New Testament*, ed. Steve Moyise and Maarten J. J. Menken (London: T&T Clark, 2005), 136.

[41] Isaiah is the source of six of the seventeen direct quotations that the UBS[5] editors list within this letter.

context in mind when he draws out the parallel between the words of the prophet and the way in which God acts through the message of the cross.[42]

1:20. Paul hammers home the point of the Scripture quotation with a series of rhetorical questions, echoing the cadences of similar questions elsewhere in Isaiah (e.g., Isa 19:12; 33:18). "The one who is wise" (σοφός) may intend a particular reference to the Sophists or the philosophers of the Greek tradition[43] or perhaps a broader, all-encompassing reference to all of the various perceived experts in human wisdom.[44] The "teacher of the law" (γραμματεύς) probably refers specifically to Jewish Torah scholars,[45] though some take it has referring to the Greco-Roman γραμματεύς, who was not a scholar or theologian but an administrator.[46] The "debater" (συζητητής) may refer to an expert in rhetoric,[47] a philosopher engaged in the quest for truth through debate and discussion,[48] or a category broad enough to embrace both of the previous terms.[49]

Depending on how the three words are understood, the "wise" ones Paul is focusing on may be a consistently Greco-Roman list,[50] a consistently Jewish list,[51] or a deliberate mixture of both Greco-Roman and Jewish types (the most likely option, given the generality of "the world" in v. 20b and the balanced Jews/Greeks structure of v. 22).[52] Whatever is decided about whether the "wise ones" are Greco-Roman, Jewish, or both, the more important issue is that their wisdom is the wisdom "of this age." Grammatically, the phrase is connected only to the third term ("the debater of this age"), but most commentators plausibly suggest that it is intended by Paul to reflect on all three.[53] "This age" is apocalyptic language for the present world order and its rulers, contrasted with the

---

[42] Cf. Hays, *First Corinthians*, 29.

[43] Cf. Winter, *Philo and Paul*, 187–94 (Sophists); Brookins, *Reading 1 Corinthians*, 22–23 (philosophers).

[44] E.g., Gardner, *1 Corinthians*, 97.

[45] Fee, *First Epistle to the Corinthians*, 74.

[46] Thiselton, *First Corinthians*, 163–64.

[47] E. A. Judge, "The Reaction Against Classical Education in the New Testament," *Journal of Christian Education* 77 (1983): 11; White, *Where Is the Wise Man?*, 72.

[48] Garland, *1 Corinthians*, 65.

[49] Fee, *First Epistle to the Corinthians*, 74.

[50] E.g., Thiselton, *First Corinthians*, 163–64, who points out that it is Greeks in v. 22 who "seek wisdom."

[51] Martin Hengel and Roland Deines, *The Pre-Christian Paul* (London: SCM, 1991), 42.

[52] E.g., Fee, *First Epistle to the Corinthians*, 74; White, *Where Is the Wise Man?*, 72.

[53] E.g., Garland, *1 Corinthians*, 65; Fee, *First Epistle to the Corinthians*, 74–75.

coming kingdom of God. A similar sense is carried by "the world," whose wisdom (according to the final sentence in this verse) God has made foolish through the actions Paul goes on to describe in the remaining verses of the paragraph.

1:21. The "for" (γάρ) that links this verse to the sentence that precedes it suggests that its function is to provide us with an explanation of how God has "made the world's wisdom foolish" (v. 20). The explanation Paul offers contains a number of important propositions, bound together in a tight logical relationship:

(1) the world's wisdom did not lead it to know God ("the world did not know God through wisdom");
(2) this was something that God himself wisely foresaw and intended to be the case ("in God's wisdom");
(3) because of this, God decided to save not the cleverest or the most highly esteemed of humanity, but simply those who believe ("since ... the world did not know God through wisdom, God was pleased to save those who believe");
(4) and to do this through the apparently foolish message of the gospel ("through the foolishness of what is preached").

"In God's wisdom" has been variously understood;[54] the most likely interpretation is that it is roughly equivalent in meaning to "God was pleased" in the second half of the verse and is a reference to the sovereign wisdom of God, working out his plans and purposes in human history (cf. Rom 11:33–34; Eph 1:8–11).[55] In Paul's view, it is not a failure on God's part that he has not been found by human philosophy or science or religion; rather, it is exactly what God intended as a judgment on the arrogance of human pretensions to autonomous and all-knowing wisdom.

"The world did not know God through wisdom" is probably not intended by Paul as a denial that human wisdom can uncover any correct theoretical knowledge about God at all; rather, it is a denial that human wisdom (or, more precisely, the wisdom of "the world," i.e., what is counted as wisdom by the intellectual/political/religious gatekeepers who exercise hegemony over the present world order) has ever been

[54] Cf. the survey of scholarly views in Thiselton, *First Corinthians*, 168–69.

[55] Fee, *First Epistle to the Corinthians*, 76.

successful in leading to a genuine, saving knowledge of the true God. (Note the salvation language in the second half of the verse, the salvific content of "wisdom" in v. 21, and the parallel discussion of wisdom, foolishness, and the knowledge of God in Rom 1:19–23.)

"The foolishness of what is preached" is contrasted with "the world's wisdom" (v. 20) and—given the way in which the phrase is unpacked in the following verses—is almost certainly a reference to the *content* of what was preached by the apostles (with a particular focus on its claims about Jesus as a crucified Messiah) rather than to the *method* of "preaching" (as distinct from conversation, argument, writing, etc.). The "foolishness" of the message's content does, however, have implications for the form in which it is communicated and for the way in which those who communicate it ought to be regarded and assessed (cf. 1:17; 2:1–5; 4:1–5).

1:22. The sweeping generalizations of verse 22 unpack the mindset of "the world" of Paul's day. While it is likely that Paul does have in mind the particular achievements and pretensions of "the Greeks" (whom he distinguishes elsewhere not only from Jews but also from "barbarians" and "Scythians"; cf. Rom 1:14; Col 3:11), there is almost certainly also a broader sense in which he is using "Jews" plus "Greeks" as a summary of all humanity, with "Greeks" serving as a synonym for "Gentiles" (cf. v. 23).

"The Jews ask for signs" is probably a reference to the triumphalist messianism of Paul's day and may reflect Paul's awareness of the stories recounted in the Gospels about the Pharisees and others demanding miraculous signs from Jesus. The language of "signs" (σημεῖα) echoes the "signs and wonders" (σημεῖα καὶ ... τέρατα) of the Exodus story (e.g., Exod 7:3; 11:9–10; cf. Josephus, *J.W.* 6.5.2; *Ant.* 10.8.6) and refers to powerful and miraculous acts of judgment and salvation performed by God. "The Greeks seek wisdom" expresses not only Paul's perception of the Greek culture but its own self-perception. Herodotus, for example, recounts an anecdote about the Scythian philosopher Anacharsis reporting to the king of Scythia that "all Greeks" (except for the Spartans!) "were zealous for every kind of learning" (*Hist.* 4.77). Within that broader tradition, Paul may be focusing his description more particularly on the shallow, exhibitionist "wisdom" of the Sophists as he had encountered it in first-century Corinth.

1:23–25. In deliberate contrast ("but," not "so") to the demands Paul has described in the previous verse, Paul now sets forth the content of the apostles' proclamation, with a particular accent on the fact that it is

"Christ *crucified*" that they proclaim. "We preach" is the first instance of a first person plural verb in the letter, marking a subtle shift from Paul's words in v. 17 about his own particular calling and commissioning to an account of the gospel that he shares with all the apostles (cf. 1 Cor 15:10–11).

"Christ crucified" (as a figure whose victory is announced in a "gospel" as the source of salvation for others) would have fallen on Jewish and Greco-Roman ears alike as an absurd and offensive contradiction—"Christ" implying chosenness and victory and "crucified" implying curse (cf. Deut 21:23) and defeat.[56] "A stumbling block" (σκάνδαλον) is the same word used by Paul when he paraphrases Isaiah 8:14 in Rom 9:33 and Psalm 69:22 (LXX Ps 68:23) in Romans 11:9, where, in both cases, it carries a meaning that goes beyond merely an insult or offence to the sensibilities, implying something so provocative as to become the occasion of disastrous consequences.[57] The message of Christ crucified is equally "foolishness to Gentiles," given the shame of crucifixion, a penalty reserved for slaves and the worst of criminals,[58] and the fact that Greek philosophy was about the quest for "mastery" of life, bringing "success, honour and esteem."[59]

Although the cross is rejected as a "stumbling block" and "foolishness" by the world at large, it is embraced and experienced as "the power of God and the wisdom of God" by "those who are called" (v. 24). The latter expression is another way of describing "us who are being saved" (v. 18) and "those who believe" (v. 21), but with the accent on God's initiative in (effectually) "calling" them to salvation through the message of the gospel (cf. 1:9, 26, 30). "Christ the power of God and the wisdom of God" paradoxically locates true power and wisdom not in the "signs" and "wisdom" sought after by unbelieving Jews and Greeks, but in the apparent

---

[56] Cf. N. T. Wright, *The Climax of the Covenant: Christ and the Law in Pauline Theology* (Edinburgh: T&T Clark, 1991), 61. Matthew Novenson offers a number of helpful correctives and qualifications to the commonly made claim that the very idea of a crucified messiah was, in and of itself, a logical impossibility, but his arguments do not overturn the more specific claim that the proclamation, as a "gospel," of a [victorious, saving] "Christ crucified" would have fallen on Jewish and Greco-Roman ears as an irreducibly contradictory combination of ideas. Cf. Matthew V. Novenson, *Christ Among the Messiahs: Christ Language in Paul and Messiah Language in Ancient Judaism* (New York: Oxford University Press, 2012), 160–64.

[57] Ciampa and Rosner, *The First Letter to the Corinthians*, 100.

[58] Cf. the examples discussed in Martin Hengel, *Crucifixion in the Ancient World and the Folly of the Message of the Cross* (London: SCM, 1977).

[59] Thiselton, *First Corinthians*, 170.

foolishness of the cross. To say that the crucified Christ is "the power of God and the wisdom of God" is simultaneously to make a statement about the cross (not a failure but a victory), about true power and wisdom (not to be found in self-assertion but in self-sacrifice), and about God (not a God whose power and wisdom are a magnification of human power and wisdom, but a God whose power and wisdom are a contradiction of power and wisdom as they are understood and exercised by the world).

Verse 25 draws together the paradoxes of the paragraph, forcing home its main point by claiming not simply that God's wisdom is wiser than human wisdom or that God's strength is stronger than human strength but that God's "foolishness" and "weakness" are wiser than human wisdom and stronger than human strength. This, Paul asserts, is the reason why—despite the demands of the world for "signs" and "wisdom"—he and his fellow apostles persist with proclaiming the seemingly weak and foolish message of "Christ crucified" (v. 23).[60]

1:26. Verse 26 introduces a new paragraph in which Paul continues the contrast between the message about the cross and human wisdom that he commenced in 1:18. Having focused in 1:18–25 on the *content* of the message, he now goes on to talk about its *recipients*—still with the aim of showing that the message of the gospel is not a form of human wisdom (like all the other philosophies competing for adherents in first-century Corinth) but a contradiction of human wisdom.[61]

Having begun on the broadest canvas in 1:18–25, speaking about the quest of Jews and Greeks for signs and wisdom, Paul now speaks more

---

[60] Cf. Ciampa and Rosner, *The First Letter to the Corinthians*, 101. The logical function of the οτι ("because") linking v. 25 to the preceding sentence is obscured somewhat by the decision of the CSB to place a full stop at the end of v. 23 and treat v. 24 as a separate, freestanding sentence. A translation of vv. 22–24 that more closely reflected the syntax of the original would be something like this: "For the Jews ask for signs and the Greeks seek wisdom, 23 but we preach Christ crucified, a stumbling block to the Jews and foolishness to the Gentiles, 24 but to those who are called, both Jews and Greeks, Christ, the power of God and the wisdom of God. 25 For God's foolishness is wiser than human wisdom, and God's weakness is stronger than human strength."

[61] More precisely, given the untranslated "for" (γάρ) that links v. 26 with the preceding paragraph, Paul is not merely offering a second, parallel reason in vv. 26–31 to sit alongside vv. 18–25; rather, he is illustrating and confirming in vv. 26–31 what he has said in vv. 18–25. The fact that the gospel preached in Corinth attracted (for the most part) not the high-status but the low-status people of the city gives an example of how God has acted through the proclamation of the gospel in a manner that has "made the world's wisdom foolish" (v. 20) and has itself been rejected as foolishness by the world.

directly to the Corinthians about their own conversion and their pre-conversion social position—not only to further his argument about the "foolishness" of the cross but also to prick the bubble of their pretensions in so doing. Here, for the first time, Paul introduces the language of "boasting" (vv. 29, 31), which he will later use to describe the Corinthians' way of speaking about their leaders (3:21; 4:7).

The invitation to the Corinthians to "consider" the events that Paul goes on to remind them of is a metaphorical use of βλέπω ("look at"). "Consider your calling" is an invitation to the Corinthians to recall the story and circumstances of their conversion (cf. vv. 2, 9, 24 for "calling" [κλῆσις] as Pauline language for conversion, with the accent on God's initiative in the process). The trio of terms that Paul uses to describe what most of the Corinthians were not ("wise ... powerful ... of noble birth") starts with two adjectives derived from the "wisdom" and "power" that were the key words of the previous paragraph.[62] To these two, Paul adds a third word, "of noble birth" (εὐγενής), perhaps chosen because of the high premium placed on ancestry in determining a person's social status, especially in a city like Corinth where wealth was common but aristocratic ancestry was rare.[63] Fee suggests that this may be the reason Paul chooses "of noble birth" rather than "rich" (πλούσιος), which is the word that completes a similar trio of terms in Jeremiah 9:23 [LXX Jer 9:22], the verse that immediately precedes the one Paul quotes in v. 31.[64]

Paul's reminder that "not many" of the Corinthians were wise, powerful, or of noble birth is not quite the same as an assertion that "not any" of them possessed this kind of status. There were some notable exceptions in the Corinthian church, including Crispus, Erastus, Gaius, and Stephanas, all of whom seem to have possessed significant wealth and influence. Nevertheless, it would seem that the majority of the congregation (including, perhaps, a number who had pretensions or aspirations to a similar standing for themselves) were from lower social and

---

[62] The phrase, "from a human perspective" (κατὰ σάρκα), while attached grammatically to "wise," probably covers all three terms in a similar way to the phrase "of this age" in v. 20. Nevertheless, it may still have a special relevance in Paul's mind to the word "wise," anticipating the distinctions he will go on to draw in 2:8 and 3:18 between the wisdom of this age and the true, hidden wisdom of God, and the related distinction in 2:13–15 and 3:1–4 between "spiritual people" and "people of the flesh."

[63] Cf. Thiselton, *First Corinthians*, 12–13.

[64] Fee, *First Epistle to the Corinthians*, 84. The second of the three terms in Jeremiah's trio is translated in the LXX as ἰσχυρός, which is a near-synonym of Paul's δυνατός.

economic strata than these, and the social solidarity that Paul goes on to insist on in later chapters of the letter (e.g., 6:4; 8:7–13; 10:17; 11:2–34; 12:12–26) would have required the wealthy and wellborn members of the congregation to behave in a manner that unavoidably connected them with the lower social status of their brothers and sisters.

1:27–29. "God has chosen" (repeated three times) emphasizes that this state of affairs was no accident but the plan of God (cf. "in God's wisdom ... God was pleased" in v. 21). Intriguingly (for both Calvinists and Arminians!), Paul seems here to describe God choosing people for salvation not randomly but with a rationale and purpose in mind—though not one that leaves any room at all for human merit or boasting or implies a strong metaphysical assertion about the libertarian freedom of the human will (see §6).

The people whom God chose are described by Paul as "what is foolish in the world ... what is weak in the world ... what is insignificant and despised in the world—what is viewed as nothing"—a deliberate reversal of the "wise ... powerful ... of noble birth" in verse 26, but with a rhetorical heightening and generalization of the third term.[65] God's purpose in doing this, Paul asserts, was "to shame the wise ... to shame the strong ... to bring to nothing what is viewed as something." Once again, the third term in the sequence is heightened and generalized (not "those of noble birth" but "what is viewed as something" in contrast with "what is viewed as nothing"); this rhetorical heightening is reinforced by the shift from "to shame" (ἵνα καταισχύνῃ) to "to bring to nothing" (ἵνα ... καταργήσῃ).

The language of "shame" is important throughout the letter; Paul does not repudiate the "honor/shame" structure of the Corinthian culture but exposes the radical inconsistencies between what is honored (and despised) among humans and what is honored (and despised) in God's eyes. Behind this purpose of "shaming" and "bring[ing] to nothing" the

---

[65] "In the world" (τοῦ κόσμου), repeated three times in vv. 27–28, is probably used with the sense of "in the world's estimation" rather than as a straightforward partitive genitive, implying that there is an objective standard of what is "foolish," "insignificant," "weak," and "despised" that served as the common criterion for divine and human assessments; cf. Garland, *1 Corinthians*, 76, citing C. K. Barrett, *A Commentary on the First Epistle to the Corinthians*, 2nd ed., BNTC (London: A&C Black, 1971), 58, and the similarly functioning phrase, "from a human perspective" (κατὰ σάρκα), in v. 26. It would be a mistake, however, to read into Paul's words an entirely subjective or socially constructed set of distinctions; the differences implied by his categories probably included elements of both objective economic/physiological reality and subjective sociocultural status.

wise and strong and the things that are "viewed as something," God's ultimate purpose (v. 29) is "so that no one [literally "no flesh"] may boast in his presence." This is a crucially important issue for Paul, informing both his critique of the circumcision party in Galatians, Romans, and Philippians (cf. Rom 2:17, 23; 3:27; 4:2; Gal 6:13–14; Phil 3:3) and his response to the encroachment of Greco-Roman cultural values in 1–2 Corinthians (cf. 2 Cor 10:17; 11:12, 16, 18, 30; 12:9) and functioning as a kind of axiom in his theological reasoning (e.g., Rom 4:2).

1:30–31. Paul's repeated assertions that the starkly different human responses to the gospel described in the preceding paragraphs are the outworking of "God's wisdom" (v. 21) and what God was "pleased" (v. 21) and "has chosen" (vv. 27 –28) to do stand behind his reminder to the Corinthians in verse 30 that "it is from him that you are in Christ Jesus."[66] His depiction of believers as "in Christ" is one of his favorite ways of describing Christian existence, implying a relationship of belonging and corporate solidarity like the relationship of a limb to a body.

The relationship between "wisdom" and "righteousness, sanctification, and redemption" is probably not that they are simply four items side by side in a list; rather, as the syntax of the Greek implies (and as the CSB correctly reflects), the last three items are probably an unpacking of the first.[67] The "wisdom" that the Corinthians need is the saving knowledge of God. "Righteousness" (δικαιοσύνη), as it is used here, is probably to be understood as a forensic term, referring to a status that results from a positive verdict pronounced by God;[68] "sanctification" (ἁγιασμός) here refers not to progressive sanctification but positional sanctification, i.e., being set apart by God as belonging to him (cf. 1:2); "redemption" (ἀπολύτρωσις) has an exodus background and describes salvation in terms of liberation from slavery. The order in which the three terms are placed alongside one another here suggests that they are not intended by Paul to be understood as sequential steps in the process of salvation

---

[66] Cf. the arguments in Thiselton, *First Corinthians*, 188–89, for a causal interpretation of Paul's brief and elliptic expression, ἐξ αὐτοῦ δὲ ὑμεῖς ἐστε ἐν Χριστῷ Ἰησοῦ (literally: "but from him you are in Christ Jesus").

[67] Cf. Fee, *First Epistle to the Corinthians*, 89–90; Archibald Robertson and Alfred Plummer, *A Critical and Exegetical Commentary on the First Epistle of St. Paul to the Corinthians*, ICC (New York: Scribner, 1911), 27.

[68] Cf. Thiselton, *First Corinthians*, 193.

but as complementary metaphors expressing the various dimensions and entailments of the same event.[69]

Verse 31 concludes the paragraph with a quotation from Jeremiah 9:24, a verse that has already been alluded to in the "wise ... powerful ... of noble birth" triad in verse 26. Paul makes a number of alterations to the wording of the verse, the most significant of which is to replace the final phrase of the original ("boast in this: that he understands and knows me") with the shorter and simpler "boast in the Lord"—perhaps in order to eliminate the risk that the Corinthians might take from the verse an endorsement of their own illegitimate boasting in what they "understand" and "know" (cf. 1 Cor 8:1–3).

2:1. This verse introduces the last of three paragraphs that together compose a section extending from 1:18 to 2:5, in which Paul contrasts the message of the gospel ("the word of the cross"; 1:18) with the wisdom of the world. In this section Paul distinguishes the gospel he preached in Corinth from the "wisdom" of the Sophists (and from all other worldly wisdom) in terms of its *content* (the "foolishness" of the cross) (1:18–25), its *recipients* (not the wise and powerful and wellborn but—for the most part—the people who are "viewed as nothing") (1:26–31), and now, third, in terms of the *manner* in which Paul proclaimed it—a manner that, in its power-in-weakness, corresponded with the content of Paul's cross-centered message. Thus, the generalities about the message in 1:18–25 are illustrated and explained in terms of the specific story of the beginnings of the Christian community in Corinth—first in terms of the Corinthians and their "calling" (1:26–31) and then in terms of Paul and his preaching (2:1–5).

Having told the story of the Corinthians' "calling" in terms of their experience in the second person plural (1:26–31), Paul now turns to the first person to narrate the beginnings of the Corinthian community from the perspective of his own experience as the one who brought them the gospel.[70] This return to the first person singular (last used in 1:17), together with the echoes throughout this paragraph of the language and ideas of 1:17, signals that this paragraph completes Paul's unpacking of the pregnant statement in that earlier verse ("For Christ did not send me

---

[69] Cf. Fee, *First Epistle to the Corinthians*, 90.

[70] This turn to the first person singular is even more marked in the Greek (Κἀγὼ ἐλθὼν πρὸς ὑμᾶς, ἀδελφοί) than it is in the English. A more literal translation of the verse's first few words would read something like: "And I, when I came to you, brothers and sisters ... ."

to baptize, but to preach the gospel—not with eloquent wisdom, so that the cross of Christ will not be emptied of its effect.")

Paul describes the gospel that he came to Corinth to proclaim as "the mystery of God,"[71] drawing on the use of μυστήριον in OT apocalyptic contexts (e.g., Dan 2:28, 30, 47) to describe something inaccessible to human reason and investigation but revealed by God as he chooses (frequently involving content regarding the future plans and purposes of God).[72] By making use of this language in writing to the church in Corinth, Paul is probably also intending an implied contrast between the "mystery of God" contained in the message of the cross and the arcane and elitist mystery cults of pagan Corinth. Paul's proclamation of that mystery, he reminds the Corinthians, was "not ... with brilliance of speech or wisdom" (οὐ καθ' ὑπεροχὴν λόγου ἢ σοφίας; literally, "not ... in superiority of word or wisdom")—language that "refers not only to elaborate rhetoric ... but also to speech that pretends to some superior social status."[73]

2:2. The simplicity and unpretentiousness of Paul's presentation was no accident, as he goes on to emphasize in verse 2, but the result of a deliberate decision, based on the content of the message: "Jesus Christ and him crucified." It is unlikely that this decision was a reaction to his relatively unsuccessful experience of evangelism in Athens; the description he gives here of the content and manner of his evangelism is very similar to the descriptions he gives in letters that predate the Athens experience (e.g., 1 Thess 2:1–10; Gal 3:1), and the report of Paul's visit to Athens in Acts 17:16–34 makes it clear that Luke, for his part, did not regard the visit as a failure.[74]

The syntax of the Greek suggests that a more literal translation would not be "I decided to know nothing ... except Jesus Christ," but rather, "I

[71] The evidence of the early manuscripts is divided between those that read "the mystery [μυστήριον] of God" (cf. CSB; NRSV) and those that read "the testimony [μαρτύριον] of God" (cf. NIV). Arguments in favor of μυστήριον include that this appears to be the reading in the earliest surviving manuscript (𝔓[46]), the further development of the "mystery" concept in 2:6–16, and the possibility that a later copyist could have corrected the potentially ambiguous μυστήριον (occurring here for the first time in the letter) to μαρτύριον to harmonize with the language previously used in 1:6. Cf. Benjamin L. Gladd, *Revealing the Mysterion: The Use of Mystery in Daniel and Second Temple Judaism with Its Bearing on First Corinthians*, BZNW (Berlin: De Gruyter, 2009), 123–26.

[72] Cf. Collins, *First Corinthians*, 115–16; Gladd, *Revealing the Mysterion*, 17–50.

[73] Garland, *1 Corinthians*, 82.

[74] Cf. Fee, *First Epistle to the Corinthians*, 97.

did not decide to know anything ... except Jesus Christ." Thus, as Thiselton points out, Paul is not saying that he deliberately expelled all other knowledge from his mind and his preaching; rather, he is simply saying that the one thing he was determined to focus on was the crucified Jesus, and that this focus was inconsistent with the kind of grandiloquence that a visiting orator would normally have been expected to display.[75]

2:3–5. Paul's account of the manner and purpose of his preaching during his original visit to Corinth is further developed in verses 3–5. The "weakness," "fear," and "much trembling" in which Paul came to Corinth contrasts sharply with the conventions that surrounded the initial visit to a city by an orator wanting to establish a reputation and a following.[76]

Paul's "fear ... and much trembling" are understood by most commentators as referring—at least partly—to the anxieties and inadequacies that Paul felt in the face of his audience and his opposition (cf. Acts 18:9–11).[77] Alternatively, given the more common use of "fear and trembling" language in the LXX and the New Testament, Timothy Savage suggests that Paul's accent may be more on his fear of God and its implications for the humility and transparency with which he carried himself as a preacher (cf. 2 Cor 4:2; 5:11).[78] Either way, the addition of the first term, "weakness," suggests that at least part of what Paul is describing was his human vulnerability and inadequacy, which he made no attempt to hide from the Corinthians.

"My speech and my preaching" (ὁ λόγος μου καὶ τὸ κήρυγμά μου) are probably not describing two different things (e.g., conversation and public preaching, or content and presentation); more likely, Paul is simply treating the two words as roughly synonymous, in a kind of repetition for emphasis.[79] "Not with persuasive words of wisdom" (or, as in 𝔓[46] and some other early MSS, "not in the persuasiveness of wisdom")[80] expresses

---

[75] Thiselton, *First Corinthians*, 211–12.

[76] cf. Dio Chrysostom, *Or.* 47, and the discussion in Winter, *Philo and Paul*, 143–71.

[77] E.g., Fee, *First Epistle to the Corinthians*, 98–99; Witherington, *Conflict and Community*, 123.

[78] Timothy B. Savage, *Power Through Weakness: Paul's Understanding of the Christian Ministry in 2 Corinthians* (New York: Cambridge University Press, 1996), 73; Ciampa and Rosner, *The First Letter to the Corinthians*, 115–16.

[79] Thiselton, *First Corinthians*, 217–18.

[80] i.e., πειθοῖς σοφίας with πειθοῖς read not as an adjective ("persuasive") but as a misspelled dative singular form of the noun πειθώ ("persuasiveness"), the final sigma having been added in error by a copyist doubling the initial sigma of σοφίας. Cf. Fee, *First Epistle to the Corinthians*, 92–93.

something similar to what Paul said in verse 1 ("not ... with brilliance of speech or wisdom"), but with a more particular focus on what provided the persuasiveness of Paul's message—not specious human wisdom but the Spirit's power.

Paul's description of that supernaturally enabled dynamic makes up the remainder of verse 4: "but with a demonstration of the Spirit's power." Despite the fact that Paul's evangelism in Corinth was accompanied by "signs and wonders and miracles" (2 Cor 12:12), most commentators suggest that Paul is not talking here in verse 4 about miracles accompanying the message but about the power of the Spirit at work in the message itself.[81] Paul is not contrasting the power of miracles with the power of wisdom, but the power of God's Spirit (at work in the message of the cross) with the power of rhetoric and human cleverness.[82] This leads very naturally to the concluding verse, expressing Paul's (and/or God's) purpose: "so that your faith might not be based on human wisdom but on God's power."

2:6. Having completed the argument of 1:18–2:5 (an explanation and elaboration on 1:17, in which he emphatically distinguishes between the message of the cross and the wisdom of the world), Paul now goes on in 2:6–16 to make it clear that he is not rejecting wisdom itself (see §4).[83] The real conflict, as Paul sees it, is not between the gospel and wisdom but between the "wisdom of this age" (v. 6) and "God's ... wisdom" (v. 7), revealed by the Spirit in the message of the gospel. Those to whom this wisdom of God is revealed are described as "the mature" (v. 6) and as "spiritual people" (v. 13), referring not to a privileged subset of the Christian community, but to everyone who has received the Spirit of God (v. 12).

---

[81] E.g., Garland, *1 Corinthians*, 87; Fee, *First Epistle to the Corinthians*, 100; Thiselton, *First Corinthians*, 221–22.

[82] "Demonstration" (ἀποδείξις) is a semitechnical term from the realm of rhetorical theory, the normal meaning of which is not "manifestation" but "convincingness" or "proof." "The Spirit's power" (CSB) is probably a correct translation of the intended sense of the original (more literally, "the Spirit and power"), interpreting it as a hendiadys (a single concept conveyed through two words). The genitive construction ("the demonstration of the Spirit's power") is probably not an objective genitive (the Spirit was demonstrated—i.e., manifested—by Paul) but a subjective genitive (the Spirit did the demonstrating—i.e., convincing—in the Corinthians' hearts).

[83] The CSB's "however" correctly captures the adversative sense that is carried by the Greek conjunction δέ as it is used in this context and the close link that it suggests between this paragraph and the preceding ones.

Paul's description of the people among whom he and his fellow teachers (or perhaps more broadly, his fellow Christians?)[84] speak their message as "the mature" (οἱ τέλειοι) is possibly borrowed from the language of the elitists within the Corinthian congregation, who used the word to mark out their superiority to the rest of the congregation (in social status, knowledge, and/or spiritual gifts).[85] If that is the case, Paul takes the word back and redefines it (along with the "wisdom" that went with it) in terms of the message of the cross.

The wisdom that they speak is "not a wisdom of this age, or of the rulers of this age, who are coming to nothing" (v. 6b). "This age," as in 1:20, is apocalyptic language, contrasting the power structures and belief systems of the present world with those that are established and informed by the coming kingdom of God. Paul's further characterization of the wisdom that he disavows as "a wisdom ... of the rulers of this age" reflects the particular role of the powerful in shaping the "wisdom of this age." While some read this as a reference to demonic or angelic powers,[86] it is more likely that Paul is referring, as he does in Romans 13:3, to earthly rulers and power brokers (cf. Pss 2:2; 33:10 [LXX Ps 32:10]), epitomized (v. 8) by the earthly rulers who were involved in the crucifixion. Given the context here in 1 Corinthians, Paul probably also includes within the scope of the term a broader reference to the cultural, economic, and political elites that the Corinthians admired and emulated. All these powers are depicted by Paul as "coming to nothing" (καταργουμένων)—a present participle, picturing them as already under the shadow of their eschatological condemnation (cf. his use of the same verb in 1:28).

2:7. The true wisdom that Paul and his fellow teachers make known is described in verse 7 as "God's hidden wisdom in a mystery" (cf. 2:1) and as the unveiling of a plan that "God predestined before the ages"—language that echoes the emphasis of 1:21 on the "wisdom" and "pleas[ure]" of God and locates that decision "before the ages." His further description of that plan as being purposed "for our glory" expresses the fact that Paul's eschatological vision included not only the manifestation of the

[84] If the "we" in vv. 12–13 is referring to the same group as the "we" in v. 6 (i.e., if the scope of the "we" who communicate the message is the same as the scope of the "we" who receive and understand it), then the implication of those verses is that Paul's words apply to all who have received the Spirit, not just to his fellow apostles or fellow teachers.

[85] Cf. Brookins, *Reading 1 Corinthians*, 28–29; Fee, *First Epistle to the Corinthians*, 109–10.

[86] E.g., Barrett, *First Corinthians*, 70; Collins, *First Corinthians*, 129.

glory of God but also the glorification of his people (cf. Rom 8:30; 2 Cor 3:18; 2 Thess 1:12).

2:8. Verse 8 makes it clear that the cross is still at the heart of Paul's thinking when he speaks in this paragraph about "God's wisdom" (cf. 1:18–25). The failure of the rulers of this age to understand God's wisdom is partly to be understood in terms of God's sovereignty—they do not understand, because he has "hidden" it from them (v. 7); but it is also to be understood as an outworking of their own evil and arrogance—they do not understand because their high position is achieved and maintained through a "wisdom" that is precisely the opposite of the humble, sacrificial servant wisdom of the cross (cf. Isa 52:13, where it is the "wisdom" of the servant that is praised in the opening line of the song). That this is the case is confirmed in the second half of the verse: "because if they had known it, they would not have crucified the Lord of glory."

2:9–11. The "but" (ἀλλά) at the start of verse 9 contrasts the rulers of this age, who did not understand God's wisdom, with "us" (v. 10), to whom he has revealed it. The Scripture quotation is a composite one, drawn mainly from Isaiah 64:4 (LXX Isa 64:3), the words of which are combined with traces of other similar verses, chiefly from Isaiah (e.g., Isa 48:6; 52:15; 65:17 [LXX 65:16]; Jer 3:16).[87] Paul's extended version makes the thing that no human has seen or heard or conceived not God himself (as in Isa 64:4) but God's saving work in Christ (as it is in Isa. 52:15) "prepared ... for those who love him."

Paul goes on in verse 10 to identify the recipients of God's revelation as "us," and then concentrates in verses 10–13 on the means by which this revelation takes place, through the work of the Spirit (see §3). Because the revealing Spirit is God's own Spirit, who "searches everything, even the depths of God" (v. 10), he is able to fully comprehend (and therefore reveal) "the thoughts of God" (v. 11b). Verse 11a illustrates this by means of an analogy with human beings, and the unique access to a human person's inner thoughts that his or her own spirit possesses. In the context of Paul's argument, the primary content of "the thoughts of God" is the divine wisdom expressed in the eschatological plans and purposes that

[87] Cf. Garland, *1 Corinthians*, 103; Roy E. Ciampa, "Composite Citations in 1–2 Corinthians and Galatians," in *New Testament Uses*, vol. 2 of *Composite Citations in Antiquity*, ed. Sean A. Adams and Seth M. Ehorn (London: T&T Clark, 2018), 186–87.

have found their (stunningly unforeseen) fulfillment through the events of the crucifixion and resurrection of Christ.

2:12–13. The contrast in verse 12 between "the spirit of the world" and "the Spirit who comes from God" echoes the contrast in verses 6–7 between the "wisdom of this age" and "God's ... wisdom." "The spirit of the world" could possibly refer to a disposition or mindset or perhaps to the personal spirit of this world's ruler (cf. Eph. 2:2),[88] but Paul's language does not necessarily imply an assertion that there exists a "spirit of the world" that is comparable and opposed to the Spirit of God; his point is simply that the Spirit believers have in fact received is "not ... of the world ... but ... from God" (cf. the similar contrastive construction in Rom 8:15).[89]

The purpose for which we have been granted the Spirit, according to verse 12b, is "so that we may understand what has been freely given to us by God." The expression Paul uses here probably includes within its scope the "spiritual gifts" Paul has already referred to in 1:4–7 (though the word used here—χαρισθέντα—is not quite the same as the word χάρισμα that Paul uses in that passage and in ch. 12). If it does, then (as is the case in 1:4–7) Paul seems to include the "gifts" within the larger framework of everything we have received through the grace of God in Christ. Here, the purpose of the Spirit's bestowment is not so that we might manifest the gifts but so that we might understand them with the mind of Christ—an understanding that the Corinthians had not yet arrived at. Even the words we use to speak of these things (as Paul goes on to say in v. 13) are not the "words taught by human wisdom" (presumably a reference to the pretentious, superior rhetoric described in 2:1) but "[words] ... taught by the Spirit"—i.e., in humble reliance on what God has revealed in the message of "Jesus Christ and him crucified" (2:2).

Those who understand and expound the gifts of God in accordance with his wisdom are described by Paul in verse 13b as "explaining spiritual things to spiritual people" (πνευματικοῖς πνευματικὰ συγκρίνοντες). A difficult translation decision needs to be made here between two possible meanings of συγκρίνειν, which can mean either "interpret" (in the LXX, usually referring to the God-enabled interpretation of dreams) or "combine" (a common meaning of συγκρίνειν in classical Greek). Furthermore, πνευματικοῖς, the first word of the phrase in the Greek original, could be

[88] Cf. Ciampa and Rosner, *The First Letter to the Corinthians*, 131–32.

[89] Cf. Fee, *First Epistle to the Corinthians*, 120–21.

referring either to "spiritual things" (neuter plural) or "spiritual people" (masculine plural)—hence the difference between the CSB ("explaining spiritual things to spiritual people") and the NIV ("explaining spiritual realities with Spirit-taught words"). The CSB translation is probably the more likely one, given the references in 2:6, 2:15, and 3:1 to "mature" (τέλειοι) and "spiritual" (πνευματικοί) people and the closeness of the LXX συγκρίνειν passages to the ideas of this passage (Gen 40:8; Dan 5:7).

Paul's description of those who receive the wisdom of God as "spiritual" people is probably, like the earlier description of them in v. 6 as "mature," a deliberate (re)appropriation of language that a subset of the Corinthian church used to distinguish themselves from other, less spiritual, Christians (cf. 14:37). The source of this elitist self-description may have been a misappropriation of Paul's own language (cf. Gal 6:1) or an adoption of categories used in the Greco-Roman context to describe the enlightened adherents of a favored philosophical school,[90] reinforced under either scenario by the superior social status that they possessed relative to some other believers and their exercise of gifts that they considered to be commensurate with that status.

2:14–15. The things that "the person without the Spirit" (ψυχικὸς ... ἄνθρωπος; more literally "the natural person") does not receive "what comes from God's Spirit." Instead, such a person considers them to be "foolishness"—language that echoes 1:23 and reminds us once again that the heart of what Paul has in mind by "what comes from God's Spirit" is the message of Christ crucified (along with all of its various entailments). In rooting this rejection in the inability of the natural person to understand the things of the Spirit ("[and] he is not able to understand it since it is evaluated spiritually"), Paul echoes the point of 1:21 that the underlying dynamic at work is not one of sovereign human reason rejecting the claims of the gospel, but one of a sovereign God rejecting the foolishness of human reason.

The "spiritual person" (ὁ ... πνευματικός), to whom Paul goes on to refer in verse 15, is not a member of a privileged subset within the Christian community but (at least potentially; cf. 3:1–5) anyone who has the Spirit (cf. v. 12); because of the revealing work of the Spirit, they are able to "evaluate everything"—i.e., not just the things of human experience and awareness but even the very "depths of God" (v. 10) that have

---

[90] Cf. Brookins, *Reading 1 Corinthians*, 29–30.

been communicated to believers by the Spirit through the message of the cross. Paul's further claim in verse 15b that such a person "cannot be evaluated by anyone" is probably a reference to the invalidity of the world's assessment of Christ's people (a lesson that some at least among the Corinthians have been slow to learn; cf. 4:1–5; 6:1–11; 2 Cor 10:12–18).

2:16. Verse 16 begins with another quotation from Isaiah (a slightly abbreviated version of the LXX of Isaiah 40:13—a verse that perfectly fits Paul's point, with its sharp critique of human arrogance in the form of a sarcastic, rhetorical question.) The final sentence of the paragraph—"but we have the mind of Christ"—contrasts the true wisdom of Christ's people with the foolish arrogance of the world. What we do not have is the sort of knowledge that would be required for us to become the judges and teachers of God; what we do have is "the mind of Christ," which we receive by humble dependence on the revealing work of God's Spirit (cf. vv. 10–13). By "the mind of Christ" Paul probably has in mind the "mind-set" of Christ, centered on the cross and its entailments for the shape of Christian existence (cf. Phil 2:5–11).[91]

Bridge

Paul's reframing of what counts as wisdom in 1:18–2:16 is directed at a particular set of problematic attitudes and behaviors within the Corinthian church, but its implications reach far beyond the original context into which it was originally written. What God has done in Christ and caused to be proclaimed in the message of the gospel not only undercuts the elitism of a handful of first-century Corinthian Christians; it comprehensively overturns all human hierarchies of status and worth and calls into question every kind of human wisdom that claims to offer a comprehensive explanation of reality or a path of access to the divine through human knowledge, virtue, or spiritual experience. Equally, as Paul stresses in 2:1–5, it excludes as illegitimate all attempts to package and promote the Christian faith in a form that is calculated to appeal in the marketplace of competing spiritualities by diminishing or decentering the scandal of the cross. Christians in all times and places, including our own, need to give careful heed to the reminders that Paul gives to the Corinthians within these paragraphs of the letter, so that we might be warned against the danger of adopting or perpetuating a version of

---

[91] Cf. Thiselton, *First Corinthians*, 275.

Christianity that is inconsistent in form and content with the gospel that has been entrusted to us.[92]

Without weakening or diminishing the force of those warnings, however, Christians in our time should also take on board the clarifying comments that Paul goes on to give in 2:6–16 about the positive role that wisdom still plays within the life and ministry of those who have understood and embraced the word of the cross. Paul's critique of arrogant and overblown human wisdom should not be taken as a warrant for embracing irrationality or exalting unaccountable religious experience over careful reasoning and communal judgment.[93] John Webster's comments are apt and worth quoting at length:

> Reason is "a grace, and gift of love," and continues to be such despite our descent into depravity, because God has contradicted reason's contradiction of itself and God. The rehabilitation of reason is among the benefits that accrue to creatures from the Word's redeeming work which the Spirit is now realizing in the creaturely realm. By this unified saving action and presence of Word and Spirit, reason's vocation is retrieved from the ruins: its sterile attempt at self-direction is set aside; its dynamism is annexed to God's self-manifesting presence; it regains its function in the ordered friendship between God and creatures. ... The sanctifying Spirit must reorient reason to the divine Word, and only after that reorientation is reason authorized and empowered to judge and direct. Yet, as it is reoriented, reason really is authorized and empowered. And Christian theology is an instance of this redeemed intellectual judgement.[94]

C. Reframing Leadership in Light of God's Judgment (3:1–4:5)

> [3:1] For my part, brothers and sisters, I was not able to speak to you as spiritual people but as people of the flesh, as babies in Christ. [2] I gave you milk to drink, not solid food, since you were not yet ready for it. In fact, you are still not ready, [3] because you are still worldly. For since

---

[92] Cf. the warnings and encouragements in Timmins, "Centrality of the Cross," 152–54.

[93] I have argued for this claim at greater length in Starling, "As to Sensible People," 113–26. Also relevant and insightful is the extended discussion of 1 Cor 2:6–16 in Scott, *Paul's Way of Knowing*, 34–48.

[94] John Webster, *The Domain of the Word: Scripture and Theological Reason* (London: T&T Clark, 2012), 122–23.

there is envy and strife among you, are you not worldly and behaving
like mere humans? [4] For whenever someone says, "I belong to Paul," and
another, "I belong to Apollos," are you not acting like mere humans?

[5] What then is Apollos? What is Paul? They are servants through whom
you believed, and each has the role the Lord has given. [6] I planted, Apollos watered, but God gave the growth. [7] So, then, neither the one who
plants nor the one who waters is anything, but only God who gives the
growth. [8] Now he who plants and he who waters are one, and each will
receive his own reward according to his own labor. [9] For we are God's
coworkers. You are God's field, God's building.

[10] According to God's grace that was given to me, I have laid a foundation
as a skilled master builder, and another builds on it. But each one is
to be careful how he builds on it. [11] For no one can lay any foundation
other than what has been laid down. That foundation is Jesus Christ. [12] If
anyone builds on the foundation with gold, silver, costly stones, wood,
hay, or straw, [13] each one's work will become obvious. For the day will
disclose it, because it will be revealed by fire; the fire will test the quality
of each one's work. [14] If anyone's work that he has built survives, he will
receive a reward. [15] If anyone's work is burned up, he will experience
loss, but he himself will be saved—but only as through fire.

[16] Don't you yourselves know that you are God's temple and that the
Spirit of God lives in you? [17] If anyone destroys God's temple, God will
destroy him; for God's temple is holy, and that is what you are.

[18] Let no one deceive himself. If anyone among you thinks he is wise in
this age, let him become a fool so that he can become wise. [19] For the
wisdom of this world is foolishness with God, since it is written, **He
catches the wise in their craftiness**; [20] and again, **The Lord knows
that the reasonings of the wise are futile**. [21] So let no one boast in
human leaders, for everything is yours— [22] whether Paul or Apollos
or Cephas or the world or life or death or things present or things
to come—everything is yours, [23] and you belong to Christ, and Christ
belongs to God.

[4:1] A person should think of us in this way: as servants of Christ and
managers of the mysteries of God. [2] In this regard, it is required that
managers be found faithful. [3] It is of little importance to me that I should
be judged by you or by any human court. In fact, I don't even judge
myself. [4] For I am not conscious of anything against myself, but I am not
justified by this. It is the Lord who judges me. [5] So don't judge anything
prematurely, before the Lord comes, who will both bring to light what
is hidden in darkness and reveal the intentions of the hearts. And then
praise will come to each one from God.

Context/Structure/Form

In chapter 3, the explicit focus of the letter returns to the "envy and strife" (3:3) that is the overall theme of this whole section (1:10–4:21). Having set up the distinction in 2:12–16 between the "spiritual" people and the "natural" people of the world, Paul now applies it to the situation in Corinth in a surprising way: For all their pretentions to superior wisdom and spirituality, the "mature" and "spiritual" members of the Corinthian church are—in the very elitism that underlies their quarreling and jealousy—behaving precisely like people of the flesh. Recalling the factional slogans quoted in 1:12 and focusing now more particularly on two of them (v. 4: "I belong to Paul ... I belong to Apollos"), Paul sets out to reframe the Corinthians' understanding of the status and role of leaders in the church of God through a series of analogies that he develops in 3:6–17 (the church as God's field, God's building, God's temple), the implications of which are summed up and applied to the Corinthians in 3:18–4:5.

Comments

3:1. The CSB's "for my part," introducing verse 1, correctly conveys the effect of the emphatic "and I" (κἀγώ) that begins the sentence in Greek (cf. 2:1), marking the transition from the general truths of 2:6–16 to their specific application in Paul's dealings with the Corinthians. In contrast to the application that the Corinthians may have wanted or expected ("And so, brothers and sisters, I addressed you as spiritual people ..."), Paul applies the spiritual/fleshly contrast in exactly the opposite direction: "[Yet] for my part, brothers and sisters, I was *not* able to speak to you as spiritual people but as people of the flesh, as babies in Christ" (emphasis added).

In saying that the Corinthians needed to be addressed "as people of the flesh" (ὡς σαρκίνοις)—indeed, in verse 3, saying that they not only need to be *addressed* as fleshly but that they *are* fleshly (σαρκικοί)—Paul is not backing away from his earlier assumption (cf. 2:12–16) that everyone who has received the Spirit of God is in fact, as a matter of their status before God and the resources that he has made available to them, a spiritual person. He does, however, want to expose the Corinthians as being profoundly fleshly in their behavior (cf. v. 3), in a way that is radically inconsistent with their true identity in Christ.

Paul's claim that he was "not able to speak to" the Corinthians as spiritual people is a reference not to this present letter but to earlier communications—presumably his teaching during the time when he was in Corinth, establishing the community (though in vv. 2–3 Paul goes on to say that the situation still applies). The modifying phrase, "as babies in Christ," that Paul adds at the end of the verse does two things. On the one hand, it pointedly undercuts the Corinthians' elitist self-description as "the mature" (οἱ τέλειοι), just as his description of them as "people of the flesh" (σάρκινοι) undercuts their self-description as "spiritual" (πνευματικοί); on the other hand, it softens the spiritual/fleshly contrast by making it clear that the Corinthians are in fact "in Christ" and that their fleshliness is not a permanent condition but something he expects (and urges) them to grow out of.

3:2–4. Verse 2a elaborates on the remarks in the previous verse about the way in which Paul approached his communication to the Corinthians during his initial time of residency among them. "I gave you milk to drink" is Paul's way of describing the teaching that he conveyed during the establishment phase of the Corinthian church (simple, in the Corinthians' minds, because of its lack of oratorical flourish—cf. 2:1–5; simple, in Paul's mind, because it was focused on the earliest things that the new converts in Corinth needed to be established in). The Corinthians, it seems, having since progressed (in their own self-estimation) to a more mature faith, look back on the message Paul preached and deride it as mere milk for spiritual infants. Paul counters that the reason his message to them focused on no more than the most basic entailments of the gospel was not because the gospel lacks profound implications; rather, it was because they were "not yet ready for [solid food]," needing first to learn to digest the very simplest applications of the gospel to their community life.

This state of affairs, as Paul goes on to lament in verses 2a–4, is still the case: "In fact, you are still not ready, because you are still worldly. For since there is envy and strife among you, are you not worldly and behaving like mere humans? For whenever someone says, 'I belong to Paul,' and another, 'I belong to Apollos,' are you not acting like mere humans?" The particular focus of Paul's critique and the sign, in his mind, that the Corinthians are still "worldly" (σαρκικοί) and "like mere humans" (κατὰ ἄνθρωπον) in their attitudes and conduct is the "envy and strife" (ζῆλος καὶ ἔρις) that is present among them, manifested in the boasts that they make about their leaders ("I belong to Paul" and "I belong to Apollos"; cf. 1:12).

3:5. Having returned in verse 4 to the slogans that epitomize the Corinthians' factionalism and personality-focused politics, Paul now commences a lengthy section (3:5–4:5) in which he seeks to reframe the Corinthians' understanding of his ministry and Apollos's, and indeed their way of viewing all human ministries within God's church (see §9). Verse 5 introduces this discussion, establishing the basic point Paul plans to develop: that leaders are to be viewed as "servants" to whom the Lord has assigned their various tasks. The two questions by means of which Paul approaches that point both commence with the interrogative "What ... ?" (τί) rather than "Who ... ?" (τίς), shifting the focus from personality to function.[95] Paul's answer—"servants" (διάκονοι)—is a deliberately status-lowering term;[96] at the same time, it makes it clear that their ultimate accountability is not to any human master but to the Lord ("and each has the role the Lord has given"), a point Paul will develop in 4:1–5. The fact that "each" has been assigned his own distinctive role prepares the way for the agricultural analogy in verses 6–9, with its focus on the different but complementary roles of God's various servants. "Through whom" (δι' ὧν) frames the leaders' roles as channels or means of God's work, not as its ultimate source or end.

3:6–8. Having spoken in general terms of himself and Apollos as "servants ... each [of whom] has the role the Lord has given" (v. 5), Paul develops that idea in verses 6–9 through the more particular analogy of agricultural laborers at work on a farm. The image of agricultural laborers sharpens and increases the low-status connotations of the more general term "servants."

As Garland points out, the three statements in verses 6–8 have a parallel structure, speaking of the planting and watering work of Paul and Apollos in the first half of the verse and the undergirding, enabling, and rewarding work of God in the second half.[97] The aorist tenses of "planted" (ἐφύτευσα) and "watered" (ἐπότισεν) in verse 6, in contrast with the imperfect tense of "God gave the growth" (ὁ θεὸς ηὔξανεν), encourages a perspective that views the contributions of the various human ministers as sequential events in a narrative, but God's involvement as the ongoing constant at work through them all.[98]

---

95 Clarke, *Secular and Christian Leadership*, 119.

96 Cf. Garland, *1 Corinthians*, 111; Clarke, *Secular and Christian Leadership*, 119–20.

97 Garland, *1 Corinthians*, 111.

98 Cf. Thiselton, *First Corinthians*, 302.

While the analogy makes it clear that the two roles (planting and watering) are complementary and interdependent and (emphatically) that only God is the one who gives the growth to the point that "neither the one who plants nor the one who waters is anything" (v. 7), it also leaves room for human responsibility and (eschatological) reward: "Each will receive his own reward according to his own labor" (v. 8). "Labor" (κόπος) is a favorite Pauline word for the effort and toil involved in ministry (cf. 15:10, 58; 16:16), and it is this (not skill or privilege or good fortune) that God will reward in the age to come.

3:9. Verse 9 functions as a seam, reiterating the basic point from verse 5 ("for we are God's coworkers"), concluding the agricultural analogy of verses 6–8 ("you are God's field") and introducing the building analogy that will be developed in verses 10–15 ("God's building"). "God's coworkers" translates the Greek phrase θεοῦ ... συνεργοί, which could mean either "fellow workers [with God]" or "fellow laborers [with each other] who belong to God," as implied by the translations of the verse in the NRSV ("God's servants, working together") and NIV ("co-workers in God's service"). While the former has the parallel with 2 Cor 6:1 on its side, the latter is probably to be preferred, as it preserves the parallelism between the three instances of θεοῦ in the verse, understanding them all as possessive genitives (i.e., "belonging to God") and giving equal weight and equivalent effect to the emphasis implied, in each case, by the placement of θεοῦ as the first word of the phrase to which it belongs.

The word συνεργοί ("coworkers") is a favorite Pauline term for the men and women with whom he partners in ministry (cf. Rom 16:3, 9, 21; 2 Cor 8:23; Phil 2:25; 4:3; Col 4:11; 1 Thess 3:2; Phlm 1, 24) and is one of a number of different συν- compounds that he adopts or (possibly, in some cases) coins as part of his ministry vocabulary. "You are God's field" reflects a common Old Testament use of field or vineyard imagery to refer to the nation of Israel (e.g., Exod 15:17; Num 24:5–6; Isa 5:1–2; Jer 2:21; Amos 9:15). "God's building" adds a parallel metaphor, anticipating its further development in verses 10–15. The kind of building Paul has in view is not yet specified, though the possible (but unlikely) allusion in verse 12 to the building materials of Solomon's temple is taken by some as offering a hint that Paul already has a building of that sort in mind before he makes that further specification of the metaphor explicit in verses 16–17.

3:10. As foreshadowed in the final phrase of verse 9, Paul now moves on from the agricultural analogy in verses 6–8 to develop two more analogies—an extended analogy of the Corinthians as "God's building" (vv. 10–15) and a briefer, related analogy (or elaboration of the building analogy) in verses 16–17, where Paul pictures the Corinthians as "God's temple." The basic point underlying all three analogies has already been stated at the start of the section in verse 5: Paul and Apollos (and all who serve as leaders in God's church) are to be viewed as servants, who work together in complementary, interdependent roles and who are accountable to God for their work. The building analogy, like the agricultural analogy before it, develops both aspects of the metaphor (interdependence and accountability), though with the emphasis this time much more on the second aspect; the final, briefest analogy in verses 16–17 grows out of the second one and focuses only on the accountability/judgment aspect, which it heightens and intensifies.

For Paul's original readers in first-century Corinth, the language and imagery of a building project would have been very familiar, along with the politics of the various roles played by the patrons, beneficiaries, architects, and assessors of the buildings that were constructed.[99] In the century or so since Corinth had been refounded under Julius Caesar, the city had seen a vigorous and impressive series of such projects, and the boom had by no means come to an end in the time when Paul wrote his letter to the Corinthians; if anything, the surviving evidence suggests that building activity peaked during the time between Augustus and Nero.[100]

Paul's role within the metaphorical building project is that of a "skilled master builder" (σοφὸς ἀρχιτέκτων). The choice of the word "skilled" (σοφός) may hark back to the wisdom language of chapters 1–2 and

[99] Cf. Bradley J. Bitner, *Paul's Political Strategy in 1 Corinthians 1–4: Constitution and Covenant*, SNTSMS (New York: Cambridge University Press, 2015), 197–301. The metaphor of a community as a building would also have been familiar to Paul's readers through its frequent use in the language of ancient Greek politics (cf. Mitchell, *Paul and the Rhetoric of Reconciliation*, 99–111). Paul's use of the metaphor here has some similarities to the standard political commonplaces but is focused more on the status, agency, and accountability of the builders than it is on the harmonious interrelationship of the various parts of the building with one another. While the disunity of the Corinthian church is certainly in view within this chapter (cf. 3:4), Paul's more immediate focus is on the worldly arrogance and adulation of human leaders that underlie the Corinthian factionalism.

[100] Cf. John Harvey Kent, *Corinth: The Inscriptions, 1926–1950* (Princeton: American School of Classical Studies at Athens, 1966), 23–26; Savage, *Power Through Weakness*, 35–36.

provide Paul with an opportunity to remind them of the true nature of "wisdom" in ministry—not oratorical flourish but hard, careful, costly work, resting on the foundation of Christ. Paul has this role "according to God's grace that was given to me"—language that echoes the idea of verse 5 ("each has the role the Lord has given") and reflects Paul's understanding of all opportunities to serve as gifts of God's grace (cf. 1:4–7; 12:4–11; 15:9–10; 2 Cor 4:1) (see §§5, 9).

The second half of the verse goes on to refer to the work of those (including Apollos) who came after Paul, all of whom are described as "build[ing] on" the foundation Paul laid. While Paul elsewhere expresses his reluctance to build on foundations laid by others (e.g., Rom 15:20; cf. 2 Cor 10:15–16), the point in those passages seems to be related to his own particular calling as a pioneer and church planter (Rom 15:20) and to the inappropriateness of capitalizing on someone else's work and then boasting as if it were one's own (2 Cor 10:15–16). Here there is no hint at all that he resents or disapproves of the fact that others are building on the foundation he laid. He does, however, stress that "each one is to be careful how he builds on it"—a sober warning that is expanded on in the verses that follow.

3:11–13. The first way in which Paul develops the idea of the care with which after-comers must build is by stressing how important it is that they stick to the one true foundation, Jesus Christ (v. 11). Other foundations, according to Paul, are not merely inferior but impossible. A church built on any foundation other than Christ is not the church of God.

The second way in which builders need to take care is with regard to the quality of the materials with which they build. While the list of materials is arranged in a downward sequence from the most expensive (gold) to the least (straw), the more important feature of its arrangement is the two groups into which it is divided: three incombustible materials (gold, silver, costly stones) followed by three combustible (wood, hay, straw). Certainly, that distinction is what is revealed by the "fire" of the judgment day (v. 13).

While the majority of English versions have traditionally translated λίθους τιμίους as "precious stones," conjuring up images of diamonds, rubies, and other such gems, the more likely reference is (as the CSB and NIV translations put it) to "costly stones" like marble. The suggestion of some commentators that Paul intends an echo of the materials used in Solomon's temple (e.g., 1 Chr 29:2) is possible but unlikely, given that Paul includes some materials that are not in that list (hay, straw) and omits others (bronze, iron, onyx, antimony).[101]

Verse 13 makes it clear that the judgment spoken of here is a judgment of the "work" of each builder. Here, as elsewhere in his writings, Paul speaks of judgment as an event of revelation that discloses the true reality of things (e.g., Rom 2:15–16; 1 Cor 4:5) and "test[s] the quality of each one's work." Paul does not tell us here what constitutes the difference between work that stands the test of eschatological judgment and work that will be destroyed; the main points he wants to make here are simply that there will be a judgment and that the judgment that counts is not the present judgment of humans but the future judgment of God. The implication, in the context of the wider discussion of 1:10–4:21, is that much that is impressive to human eyes (e.g., ministries that are built on the charisma and rhetorical impressiveness of Christian leaders; cf. 2:1–5) is worthless in the sight of God and will not stand on the judgment day.

3:14–15. Verses 14–15 elaborate on the two contrasting outcomes of the judgment referred to in verse 13, for those whose work survives (v. 14) and for those whose work does not (v. 15). While it is possible to read verse 14 as speaking of some additional reward paid to those whose work survives the test of the judgment, it is more likely that what Paul has in mind is the survival of their work into eternity. This, along with the "praise ... from God" that will accompany it (4:5), is in itself the reward (cf. 1 Thess 2:19–20; Phil 2:19; 4:1; 1 Cor 15:58).

Verse 15, in contrast, speaks of the builder whose work is burned up. That person suffers real "loss" (presumably the lack of the reward experienced by the other)[102] but is still saved, though only as through fire. In context, the image of salvation "as through fire" is most unlikely to refer to purgatorial fires of suffering;[103] rather, it is the fire spoken of in verse 13, which destroys the ministry that was the person's life's work.

---

[101] Commentators who favor an allusion to Solomon's temple include Fee, *First Epistle to the Corinthians*, 151–52; Ciampa and Rosner, *The First Letter to the Corinthians*, 151. Commentators who reject such an allusion as unlikely include Thiselton, *First Corinthians*, 311; Garland, *1 Corinthians*, 117; Schnabel, *Erster Korintherbrief*, 207.

[102] On the word ζημιωθήσεται ("will experience loss") and its use in the penalty clauses of contemporary building contracts, see Bitner, *Paul's Political Strategy*, 218–21; Jay Shanor, "Paul as Master Builder: Construction Terms in First Corinthians," *NTS* 34 (1988): 461–71.

[103] Cf. Witherington, *Conflict and Community*, 134.

3:16–17. The final analogy of this section heightens the seriousness of the judgment warning in two ways: first, it pictures the church as not just any building but "God's temple," the dwelling place of his Spirit (cf. 2 Cor 6:16; Eph 2:22); and second, it speaks of the possibility of a person not merely building poorly and being saved "as through fire" but (far worse) acting in such a way as to destroy God's church and, in consequence, being "destroy[ed]" by God.

The rhetorical question, "Don't you ... know?" (οὐκ οἴδατε) with which Paul introduces the warning in verse 16, is the first of ten similarly worded questions in this letter (cf. 5:6; 6:2, 3, 9, 15, 16, 19; 9:13, 24). It is used by Paul, here and elsewhere in the letter, to express shock and to shame the readers by reminding them of something so fundamental that they have no excuse for failing to act on the basis of it.[104]

3:18–20. The two paragraphs that compose 1 Corinthians 3:18–4:5 conclude the section in 3:5–4:5 in which Paul reframes the Corinthians' view of himself and Apollos and their ministries (and Christian ministry and leadership more broadly). Having begun in 3:5 with the general point (Paul and Apollos, and all who serve as leaders in God's church, are to be viewed as servants of God, working together in complementary, interdependent roles and accountable to God for their work) and having illustrated it in 3:6–17 by means of three analogies (God's field, God's building, God's temple), Paul now hammers home its relevance to the Corinthians with two warnings: a warning against boasting (3:18–23) and a warning against premature judgment (4:1–5). Together, these two paragraphs play an important structural role within this section of the letter, linking the themes of wisdom/folly (3:18–23; cf. 1:18–2:16) and eschatological judgment (4:1–5; cf. 3:5–17) and making explicit their connection with the Corinthians' factionalism, the issue that is being dealt with in the larger section (1:10–4:21) to which this passage belongs.

The opening words of the first paragraph, "Let no one deceive himself" (Μηδεὶς ἑαυτὸν ἐξαπατάτω), are a variation on a common Pauline admonition, "Do not be deceived" (μὴ πλανᾶσθε), which introduces some of

---

[104] The question does not, in all instances, imply that the Corinthians *do* in fact know the thing that Paul is alerting them to or reminding them of, but it does suggest the implication that they *should* (especially since they boast so confidently in their knowledge; cf. 8:1). For a discussion of the range of ways in which Paul deploys this question within 1 Corinthians and the rhetorical effect of the expression, see Benjamin A. Edsall, "Paul's Rhetoric of Knowledge: The ΟΥΚ ΟΙΔΑΤΕ Questions in 1 Corinthians," *NovT* 55 (2013): 252–71.

his sternest warnings (e.g., 1 Cor 6:9; 15:33; Gal 6:7; cf. Eph 5:6). Like this initial admonition, the third person imperative that follows ("If anyone among you thinks he is wise in this age, let him become a fool so that he can become wise") is framed grammatically in a form that addresses it not merely to the whole community but to each individual within it. The paradoxical language harks back to the ideas of 1:18–25, which also form the basis for Paul's statement in verse 19 that "the wisdom of this world is foolishness with God." The admonition is directed not so much at teachers who have an inflated sense of their own wisdom as at those within the congregation who pride themselves on the cleverness that they display in evaluating and comparing their various teachers. Here, as in 1:20 and 2:6, the false wisdom in view is characterized eschatologically as belonging to those who think they are wise "in this age" (v. 18).

The admonition in verse 19a is supported by a pair of scriptural quotations in verses 19b–20: "since it is written, 'He catches the wise in their craftiness'; and again, 'The Lord knows that the reasonings of the wise are futile.'" The first, taken from Job 5:13, pictures the wise of the world being captured in the trap that their own craftiness has created.[105] (It is difficult to say whether Paul intends an added irony in that the speaker in this verse, in its original context, is Job's friend Eliphaz, who ends up living out the truth of his own words; cf. Job 12:2; 13:5; 42:7).[106] The second, from Psalm 94:11 (paraphrased by Paul to replace "of mankind" with "of the wise"),[107] emphasizes the futility of worldly wisdom. The

105 Paul's version of the verse differs slightly from the wording in surviving manuscripts of the LXX, with δρασσόμενος ("catches") taking the place of its near-synonym καταλαμβάνων and the more unambiguously negative πανουργία ("craftiness") taking the place of φρονήσις ("prudence"), in line with the negatively colored Hebrew original (חָכָם).

106 Hays thinks not, noting that "there is no evidence that Paul is paying any attention to the larger literary structure of Job, in which Eliphaz's words are discounted as facile counsel; instead, Paul cites them here as an authoritative disclosure of the truth about God's debunking of human wisdom." Hays, *First Corinthians*, 59. In either case the words are, as Fee points out, "the common assumption of all the 'players' in the book of Job, which is what makes the dialogue possible." Fee, *First Epistle to the Corinthians*, 165.

107 Paul's paraphrase is in keeping with the meaning of the psalm, which describes the schemers in view as "fools" (v. 8) who "pour out arrogant words" (v. 4), and urges them instead to "be wise" (v. 8; cf. 1 Cor 3:18). Cf. Ciampa and Rosner, *The First Letter to the Corinthians*, 164–65.

word διαλογισμοί ("reasonings") is used here in a sense that includes schemes and machinations[108] rather than merely thoughts and opinions.[109]

3:21–23. Verse 21a is the central injunction of the paragraph as the syntax would suggest ("so" [ὥστε] introducing v. 21a as the implication of vv. 18–20; "for" [γάρ] introducing vv. 21b–23 as further grounds for v. 21a). "Human leaders" (cf. NIV, NRSV) draws out the specific reference to human *leaders* that is implied but not stated in the original (ἐν ἀνθρώποις; "in humans"). Verse 22 makes it clear that the "humans" in whom the Corinthians are boasting are Paul, Apollos, and Cephas, maintaining the connection between the general application of the warning and its specific relevance to the problem Paul is addressing in Corinth. Paul has already condemned illegitimate boasting in 1:29–31; now, he makes it explicit that the particular kind of boasting he has in view here is the boasting in human leaders that is at the heart of the Corinthians' factionalism.

"Everything is yours" (v. 21b) introduces a new and surprising argument against boasting in human leaders. In their boastful slogans ("I belong to Paul/Apollos/Cephas") the Corinthians are turning their relationship with the three leaders upside down. By signing up to a faction identified with one of them, the Corinthians are missing the point that, in fact, the teachers (all three) belong to all of them.

Paul's point is bigger than this, however. In a rhetorical flourish (and a theological crescendo), he expands the list beyond Christian leaders to "the world or life or death or things present or things to come," and then adds, "everything is yours, and you belong to Christ, and Christ belongs to God" (vv. 22–23). Because they belong to Christ, and because Christ in turn belongs to God, "all things" (πάντα) belong to them (even the cosmic powers of life and death that tyrannize human existence; cf. Rom 8:28, 32, 38–39). Thiselton sums up: "The Christian shares in the Lordship of Christ, whereby creation and the church are restored into cooperative agencies for the well-being of humankind and for the glory of God-in-Christ, set within the providential dimension of the new order in Christ."[110]

It is difficult to escape the implication of verse 23b ("and Christ belongs to God") that Paul's Christology includes an element of "functional" (Fee),

---

[108] As implied by the verdict on them as "futile" (μάταιοι).

[109] Cf. Fee, *First Epistle to the Corinthians*, 165.

[110] Thiselton, *First Corinthians*, 327.

or even "ontological" (Thiselton), order, which applies not only to the temporary self-humbling of the incarnation but also to the eschatological (and eternal) shape of the relationship between Christ and God (cf. 1 Cor 8:6, 11:3, 15:28).[111] This christological crescendo is no mere rhetorical decoration or theological digression; it sets the privileged status of verse 22 within a pattern of ordered relationships and humble service, modeled on the relationship between Christ and God (see §2).

4:1–2. The warning against boasting in 3:18–23 is followed by a warning against premature judgment in 4:1–5. The opening statement ("A person should think of us in this way: as servants of Christ and managers of the mysteries of God," v. 1) reiterates the general principle that was stated at the start of this section of the letter in 3:5 ("What then is Apollos? What is Paul? They are servants through whom you believed"), which has been illustrated and applied throughout 3:5–23. The two terms Paul uses each have particular nuances: "servants" (ὑπηρέται) means "subordinates," emphasizing their position under Christ's authority, receiving instruction from him; the second term, "managers" (οἰκονόμοι), evokes the image of the steward of a household, with authority that is delegated and accountable. In referring to himself and Apollos as stewards of "the mysteries of God," Paul is using the plural form of the word he used in 2:7 to describe the message of the gospel, which reveals the hidden wisdom of God now made plain in the cross. In Paul's mind, the heart of his commission as a leader and teacher among God's people is to keep expounding and applying the message of the gospel.

The issue of accountability is the one that Paul goes on to emphasize in verse 2: "In this regard, it is required that managers be found faithful." "It is required" (literally: "it is sought") uses the passive form of the verb to

---

[111] Cf. Fee, *First Epistle to the Corinthians*, 168; Thiselton, *First Corinthians*, 329. Complicating the picture is the fact that Paul switches in 15:23–28 between "Christ" (vv. 23, 28a) and "the Son" (v. 28b), and between "God the Father" (v. 24) and "God" (vv. 27–28), with the possible implication (depending on how each of those titles is interpreted) that there is a correspondence, or a partial correspondence, between the Christ/God relationship of salvation history and the Son/Father relationship within the eternal being of God. Ciampa and Rosner sum up: "Like the Corinthian leaders and the Corinthians themselves, even Christ is an agent or instrument of God. The Son, though no less than the Father in being, serves the Father in obedience. His death, resurrection, and reign are all dedicated to destroying all of God's enemies and establishing a world in which all things, including Christ himself, are in perfect subjection to God (1 Cor. 15:21–28)." Ciampa and Rosner, *The First Letter to the Corinthians*, 168.

express a general (proverbial?) principle, applied here to what God looks for in the stewards of his gospel. "That [they] be found" (ἵνα ... τις εὑρεθῇ) is probably a reference to the final judgment, viewed here as involving a kind of audit of the stewardship of Christian leaders (cf. 3:8, 10–15). The key requirement of stewards is that they be "faithful" (πιστός); given that the stewards in view here are "managers of the mysteries of God," the main aspect of trustworthiness that is in view here is the faithful handing on of the message of the gospel rather than impressive flights of rhetoric and invention aimed at pleasing a human audience (cf. 2:1–5; 2 Cor 4:1–6; 5:9–12).

4:3–4. Verse 3a ("It is of little importance to me that I should be judged by you or by any human court") does not necessarily indicate that the whole Corinthian church has passed a negative judgment on Paul and rejected or called into question his apostolic authority (the inference that Fee draws from it).[112] The point here is rather that by dividing into factions based on their allegiance to Paul, Apollos, and Cephas, the Corinthians are setting themselves up like a kind of adjudication panel. This applies as much to those who admire Paul as it does to those whose attitude to him is less positive. "By any human court" (ὑπὸ ἀνθρωπίνης ἡμέρας) is, translated more literally, "by any human day," in implied contrast with "the Day" of 3:13.

"I am not conscious of anything against myself" (οὐδὲν ... ἐμαυτῷ σύνοιδα, v. 4) reflects Paul's characteristic understanding of the idea of conscience (συνείδησις) as a form of self-awareness, particularly the painful awareness of having done wrong. Paul's words here make it clear that he is not being cavalier in verse 3 when he says that he is not judged by the Corinthians, by any human court, or even by himself. Of course, he does expect the Corinthians to make assessments of him and other leaders, and he cares about what conclusions they come to (hence the lengthy self-defense in letters like 2 Corinthians and Galatians); he also quite frequently makes reference to the self-assessment of his own conscience (v. 4; cf. 2 Cor 1:12; 1 Thess 2:1–12). But these judgments, whether made by him or by others, are all merely human judgments, which are provisional and interim compared with the one judgment that really matters, which is God's. "I am not justified by this" (οὐκ ἐν τούτῳ δεδικαίωμαι) is not talking about a comprehensive and salvific verdict of justification

---

112 Fee, *First Epistle to the Corinthians*, 175.

in the sense that the word carries in texts such as Galatians 2:16 and Romans 3:24 but about the particular verdict of God on the rightness or wrongness of his conduct in specific instances of life and ministry. (In both instances of course, the same point still stands: The verdict that counts is God's verdict, not the verdict of Paul's own self-assessment or the views and opinions of others.)

4:5. Verse 5 sums up 4:1–5 and calls on the Corinthians to refrain from premature judgments about him and other leaders. The point is not that they are to stop making all assessments of the theology, ministry, and lifestyle of others; later in the letter he very explicitly requires them to make such judgments (e.g., 5:12; 6:5; 14:29) and sometimes to take painful and decisive action on the basis of them. Rather, he is warning them against the kind of worldly assessments they have been making of him and other leaders, which use the wrong criteria in judging, because they are more interested in the present judgments of pagan onlookers and the power brokers of the present age than they are in the eschatological judgment of God. (Of course, even when our human judgments are a genuine attempt to apply the criteria of God's eschatological judgment, as is the self-assessment of Paul's conscience in v. 4, they need to be made with fear and trembling and a humble recognition of the fallibility and interim status of such human assessments.)

One major reason why human judgments are at worst superficial and presumptuous and at best provisional is that God alone sees beneath the surface of things to "what is hidden in darkness" and "the intentions of the hearts"—realities that are certainly hidden to others and even, to a degree, hidden from ourselves. A day is coming, however, when these hidden realities will be brought to light at the coming of the Lord. On that day, Paul goes on to say in verse 5b, "praise will come to each one from God"—a reminder that echoes the ideas of 3:10–15 and suggests that the "reward" spoken of in that passage includes not only the survival of a person's ministry into eternity but also the "praise" (ἔπαινος) of God for that work.[113]

[113] Bitner sees in this verse a further extension of the building metaphor in the previous chapter and an allusion to the *adprobatio operis,* pronounced at the completion of the project by the magistrate-patron who originally commissioned the building. Bitner, *Paul's Political Strategy*, 257–58.

Bridge

The question of how we are to understand and exercise leadership within the community of God's people continues to fascinate and concern Christians in our own time, across a wide variety of denominational traditions and cultural contexts.[114] The Corinthians, it seems, were by no means the last Christians to succumb to the temptation of uncritically absorbing the leadership-related values and practices of the surrounding culture and perpetuating them within the church. Paul's reframing of leadership in 1 Corinthians 3:5–4:5 is an immensely helpful resource for contexts in which this is the case (and can serve as a prophylactic in any rare instances where it is not!).

The value of this subsection of the letter, for the Corinthians and for us, is enhanced by several factors: (1) It is not the kind of bitter and destructive critique that is voiced by an alienated outsider but a word of warning spoken against the worldly adulation of leaders by an insider, who has skin in the game and has himself been the recipient of such adulation from some, at least, within the Corinthian church; (2) it is not only a critique of the factors that have distorted the Corinthians' perspective on their leaders but also a positive statement of how their leaders, Paul included, should in fact be regarded; (3) it addresses the specifics of the Corinthian situation in an unmistakably concrete, practical, and personal manner, but its critique and countervision are at the same time deeply grounded in an explicitly theological and eschatological perspective that is relevant far beyond the particularities of first-century Corinth.

Those of us who exercise roles of leadership among God's people and those of us who have influence in some way over the processes by which leaders are formed, recognized, and evaluated should therefore make a habit of reading and rereading these paragraphs in 1 Corinthians, absorbing Paul's reminders, imprinting his analogies on our imagination, and taking heed to his warnings. To the extent that we participate in and perpetuate a leadership culture that fosters the kind of poor-quality building work that Paul warns against in these verses or—still worse—enables and rewards practices that damage and destroy the church, these paragraphs in Paul's letter call us to urgent self-examination and repentance and a serious, collective commitment to pursue a better and more biblical way.

---

[114] I have discussed these issues in greater detail in Starling, *UnCorinthian Leadership*, 1–28, 72–86.

D. A Climactic Challenge to the Corinthians' Boasting (4:6–21)

> [6] Now, brothers and sisters, I have applied these things to myself and Apollos for your benefit, so that you may learn from us the meaning of the saying: "Nothing beyond what is written." The purpose is that none of you will be arrogant, favoring one person over another. [7] For who makes you so superior? What do you have that you didn't receive? If, in fact, you did receive it, why do you boast as if you hadn't received it? [8] You are already full! You are already rich! You have begun to reign as kings without us—and I wish you did reign, so that we could also reign with you! [9] For I think God has displayed us, the apostles, in last place, like men condemned to die: We have become a spectacle to the world, both to angels and to people. [10] We are fools for Christ, but you are wise in Christ! We are weak, but you are strong! You are distinguished, but we are dishonored! [11] Up to the present hour we are both hungry and thirsty; we are poorly clothed, roughly treated, homeless; [12] we labor, working with our own hands. When we are reviled, we bless; when we are persecuted, we endure it; [13] when we are slandered, we respond graciously. Even now, we are like the scum of the earth, like everyone's garbage.
>
> [14] I'm not writing this to shame you, but to warn you as my dear children. [15] For you may have countless instructors in Christ, but you don't have many fathers. For I became your father in Christ Jesus through the gospel. [16] Therefore I urge you to imitate me. [17] This is why I have sent Timothy to you. He is my dearly loved and faithful child in the Lord. He will remind you about my ways in Christ Jesus, just as I teach everywhere in every church.
>
> [18] Now some are arrogant, as though I were not coming to you. [19] But I will come to you soon, if the Lord wills, and I will find out not the talk, but the power of those who are arrogant. [20] For the kingdom of God is not a matter of talk but of power. [21] What do you want? Should I come to you with a rod, or in love and a spirit of gentleness?

Context/Structure/Form

The final paragraphs of chapter 4 provide a forceful rhetorical climax to the whole section of the letter in 1:10–4:21, in which Paul responds to the reports of leadership-focused divisions within the Corinthian church. Having discussed in 3:5–4:5 how the Corinthians should view himself and Apollos (and all teachers and leaders within God's church), Paul now underlines that his primary concern in all this is not the narrow issue of the Corinthians' view of himself and Apollos but the underlying issue of their own arrogance and boasting and its outworking in the way they lionize and belittle their various teachers.

The rhetoric of this section is among the most forceful to be found in the whole letter, with the string of rhetorical questions in verse 7 followed by the sharp sarcasm of verses 8–13, the warm pathos of verses 14–17, and the blunt ultimatum with which the passage concludes in verses 18–21. According to these verses, the key problems with the Corinthians' arrogance are (1) its failure to acknowledge the Corinthians' complete dependence on God's grace (v. 7); (2) its assumption that the Corinthians are entitled in the present to the comfort and glory that belong, in reality, to the eschatological future (vv. 8–13); (3) its departure from the pattern of life "in Christ Jesus" that Paul sought to teach and model in Corinth and in all the churches (vv. 14–17); and (4) its superficial and vacuous focus on matters of mere talk, in contrast with the integrity and power of the true message and ministry of the kingdom of God (vv. 18–21).

Comments

4:6. Verse 6 signals a point of transition, referring back to the things Paul has written within the preceding paragraphs about himself and Apollos ("these things") and indicating that Paul will now shed further light on their significance for the Corinthians and his intentions in writing them. The scope of what Paul has in mind by "these things" is probably the immediately preceding section of the letter (3:5–4:5), though some (e.g., Thiselton) read it as referring more broadly to everything about Paul and Apollos in 1:10–4:5.[115]

Paul's explanation that he has "applied these things to [himself] and Apollos for [the Corinthians'] benefit" suggests that the previous section is not only about the Corinthians' attitude to Paul and Apollos but also (and perhaps even primarily?) relates to a broader or an underlying issue. Some commentators read this statement as an indication that the whole discussion about Paul and Apollos was a covert device for making a point about the real problem, which is the Corinthians' attitude to other teachers and leaders presently in Corinth.[116] This interpretation relies on an overly narrow interpretation of the verb translated here

[115] Thiselton, *First Corinthians*, 348.

[116] Cf. David R. Hall, "A Disguise for the Wise: Μετασχηματισμός in 1 Corinthians 4.6," *NTS* 40 (1994): 144; David R. Hall, *The Unity of the Corinthian Correspondence*, JSNTSup (London: T&T Clark, 2003), 4–8; Collins, *First Corinthians*, 175–76.

as "I have applied" (μετεσχημάτισα); it also neglects the fact that Paul seems to regard the Corinthians' judgments about him as a real, not just a hypothetical issue (4:1–5; cf. 9:3) and seems to be quoting real Corinthian slogans (or, at least, slogans that impersonate real Corinthian attitudes) in 1:12. More likely, Paul is saying here that alongside the issue of the Corinthians' attitude to Paul and Apollos is the broader issue of their attitude to all teachers and leaders, and underneath it is the deeper issue of their arrogant forgetfulness of grace and eschatology.

It is difficult to be certain of the origin or the meaning of the saying whose meaning Paul wants the Corinthians to learn ("Nothing beyond what is written"). The likeliest explanation of its origin is that it was a kind of slogan current within the circles in which Paul and the Corinthians moved.[117] Its meaning was most probably (1) a call to humble dependence on the Old Testament Scriptures as the boundary marker of true wisdom;[118] (2) a more particular appeal to the specific verses from Isaiah, Jeremiah, Job, and Psalms that Paul has already cited in chapters 1–3 in his polemic against fleshly wisdom and illegitimate boasting;[119] or (3) a combination of both these senses.[120] Regardless of which of these options is to be preferred, Paul clearly expects humility before God to translate to humility before his words in Scripture; this attitude of humble submission to God and his word is modeled by the "servant" categories that Paul uses in 3:5–4:5 to frame his and Apollos's leadership. The concluding clause—"that none of you will be arrogant, favoring one person over another"—fits well with any of the three interpretations suggested above and echoes the sentiments of 3:21. The word translated as "be arrogant" (φυσιοῦσθε; more literally, "become puffed up") is used only by Paul in the New Testament; six of the seven instances are in 1 Corinthians, suggesting that Paul considered the word particularly apt as a description of the Corinthians.

4:7. The string of rhetorical questions in verse 7 continues Paul's assault on the Corinthians' arrogance. The first, "For who makes you so superior?" (τίς γάρ σε διακρίνει; more literally, "For who makes you different?"), may be a general attack on the Corinthians' sense of superiority

---

117 As signaled by the article τό (CSB: "the saying"); cf. Thiselton, *First Corinthians*, 354–55.

118 E.g., Barrett, *First Corinthians*, 106.

119 E.g., Hays, *First Corinthians*, 69; Ciampa and Rosner, *The First Letter to the Corinthians*, 176.

120 E.g., Thiselton, *First Corinthians*, 355; Schnabel, *Erster Korintherbrief*, 243; Inkelaar, *Conflict over Wisdom*, 62–63; Starling, "Nothing Beyond What Is Written?," 54–55.

or more likely—given what Paul goes on to say in verses 8–13 and the close connection with verse 6 implied by the conjunction γάρ ("for")—a more specific question about what makes the Corinthians different from himself and Apollos.[121] If humility is appropriate for Paul and Apollos, it is certainly appropriate for the Corinthians. The second and third questions focus particularly on the issue of grace; like Paul and Apollos, and like all human beings, the Corinthians have nothing at all that they did not receive as a gift from God, a sobering fact that is intended to point out the folly of boasting in gifts as if they were achievements (see §5).

4:8. Not only does the Corinthians' attitude reveal their forgetfulness of their dependence on grace; it also shows how comfortable they are in the present age and how far removed they are from the apocalyptic categories that shape Paul's lifestyle. Interpreters of 1 Corinthians debate over whether the Corinthians have consciously subscribed to an overrealized eschatology that originated as a variant version of Christian teaching[122] or whether the problem is simply that they lack an eschatological perspective on the present age.[123] In favor of the latter view is that Paul seems to focus in verses 8–13 on issues of material comfort and social position rather than the details of eschatological teaching, reminding them of the eschatological perspective that they have forgotten rather than correcting an explicit eschatological error that they have consciously subscribed to (see §7).

"Already" flags the eschatological focus of Paul's corrective in these verses. The Corinthians, it seems, are expecting comforts and privileges in the present that Paul still waits for as part of the promised eschatological future. "You are already full" translates an expression (κεκορεσμένοι ἐστέ) with ugly connotations, describing someone who is bloated and overfed. "Without us" (χωρὶς ἡμῶν) probably does not mean "without our help"[124] but rather (given what Paul goes on to say) "without us sharing

[121] The switch from second-person plural to second-person singular pronouns in v. 7 makes the language more vivid and the rhetorical questions even more sharply pointed and may possibly imply that Paul has a particular member of the Corinthian elite in mind as he speaks. Cf. Welborn, *An End to Enmity*, 419.

[122] E.g., Fee, *First Epistle to the Corinthians*, 187–88; Thiselton, *First Corinthians*, 357–58; Thiselton, "Realised Eschatology at Corinth,"510–26.

[123] E.g., Garland, *1 Corinthians*, 138–39; Ciampa and Rosner, *The First Letter to the Corinthians*, 179–80.

[124] Contra Barrett, *First Corinthians*, 108.

in the same experience."[125] The description of the Corinthians as having "begun to reign as kings" (ἐβασιλεύσατε), with its eschatological overtones, is another clue that, although there is probably no dispute about the details of eschatological teaching, Paul still interprets and responds to their arrogance in eschatological categories.

4:9. The "us" of verse 8 is further specified and expanded in verse 9 as "us, the apostles," presenting the experience of Paul and Apollos in solidarity with that of the other apostles.[126] The description of the apostles in this verse as "displayed … in last place, like men condemned to die … a spectacle to the world, both to angels and to people," evokes an image of the Roman theater, in which condemned criminals were executed in ghastly spectacles and gladiators fought to the death as an entertainment for the crowds.[127] The apostles are displayed "in last place" (ἐσχάτους); this may be either a reference to the customary scheduling of the gladiatorial combats as the grand finale of the day's program in the theater or to the scheduling of the most gruesome and shameful executions as the final items of the midday spectacle, which was devoted entirely to

---

[125] Garland, *1 Corinthians*, 138–39.

[126] The group of "apostles" that Paul has in mind here probably includes Apollos (on the assumption that the "us" in v. 9 is a specification and expansion of the "us" in v. 8 and that the "us" in v. 8 refers, like the "us" in v. 6, to Paul and Apollos). Paul likely uses the term to refer to a category of itinerant missionaries that includes but is not limited to the narrower circles of the Twelve (cf. 15:5) and any additional witnesses to the resurrection whose apostleship had its origins in their face-to-face commissioning by the risen Jesus (cf. 9:1; 15:7).

[127] Ciampa and Rosner, *The First Letter to the Corinthians*, 181–82; Thiselton, *First Corinthians*, 359–60; V. Henry T. Nguyen, "The Identification of Paul's Spectacle of Death Metaphor in 1 Corinthians 4.9," *NTS* 53 (2007); Harrison, *Paul and the Ancient Celebrity Circuit*, 213; cf. K. M. Coleman, "Fatal Charades: Roman Executions Staged as Mythological Enactments," *JRS* 80 (1990); Donald G. Kyle, *Spectacles of Death in Ancient Rome* (London: Routledge, 1998); Courtney J. P. Friesen, "Paulus Tragicus: Staging Apostolic Adversity in First Corinthians," *JBL* 134 (2015). Some other commentators read Paul's language here as evoking the same image as the one in 2 Cor 2:14, where the apostles are pictured as prisoners of war paraded through the streets in a triumphal procession en route to their execution, or propose that Paul is drawing eclectically on both these scenarios as sources for his language and imagery here. Cf. Fee, *First Epistle to the Corinthians*, 190–91; Garland, *1 Corinthians*, 140. Somewhat less likely (given the prominence Paul gives to the statement that the apostles are exhibited "like men condemned to die") is Welborn's proposal that the primary figure evoked in v. 9 is the fool of the theatrical mime shows. The language of the following verses, however, may well suggest this as an additional cultural reference that Paul intended to evoke. Cf. Welborn, *Paul, the Fool of Christ*, 246–47.

the execution of criminals.[128] The focus of the image is not merely on the sufferings and eventual death of the apostles but on the way in which they are "displayed" (ἀπέδειξεν) as a "spectacle" (θέατρον), with all of the associated connotations of public visibility and disgrace.

4:10–13. While the catalog of afflictions that follows in verses 10–13 has some similarities with similar lists of sufferings in Greek descriptions of Cynic and Stoic sages, the trajectory toward a shameful death that is set up in verse 9 is a reminder that (in keeping with the theology of the cross in chs. 1–2) Paul's emphasis here is quite different from the emphasis of the lists of sufferings in the Greek literature. As Schrage correctly emphasizes, the theme here in 1 Corinthians 4 is not "heroic autonomy" but "the reflection of the cross."[129] It is no accident that the sufferings Paul lists echo at a number of points the sufferings of Christ as described in the Gospel tradition.

Paul's description of himself and his fellow apostles as "fools for Christ" (v. 10) recalls the earlier references to fools and folly in 1:25 and 3:18;[130] here, as there, the heart of the "folly" in the world's eyes is the message of the cross and its embodiment in the lives of those who follow and imitate Christ. By contrast, the Corinthians are "wise in Christ," the contrast with the apostles and the sharp sarcasm of the context suggesting that the "wisdom" of the Corinthians is in fact the world's wisdom, not Christ's. Two more contrasts follow in the remainder of verse 10: "We are weak, but you are strong! You are distinguished, but we are dishonored!" The first of these recalls the earlier contrast between "weakness" and "strength" in 1:25 and 2:3–5. The second concludes the sequence of contrasts and makes more explicit the focus on social position and reputation that was already implied by the "fools/wise" contrast at the start of the sequence.

The remaining list of the apostles' hardships and responses to abuse, cataloged in verses 11–13, are framed at the beginning and end by time references ("Up to the present hour ... Even now") that maintain the eschatological orientation implied by the "already ... already" of verse

[128] The NIV's translation of this word as "at the end of the procession" implies the alternative scenario, under which the apostles are viewed as prisoners of war led captive in a Roman triumph.

[129] Wolfgang Schrage, *Der erste Brief an die Korinther*, 4 vols., EKK (Zürich: Benziger, 1991–2001), 1:342, as cited and translated in Thiselton, *First Corinthians*, 368.

[130] Cf. the discussion of the theatrical background to the figure of the fool in Welborn, *Paul, the Fool of Christ*, 25–48.

8.[131] "We are both hungry and thirsty" contrasts starkly with the bloated comfort of the Corinthians (v. 8). "We are poorly clothed" (γυμνιτεύομεν; literally, "we are naked") describes by way of hyperbole the material inadequacy of the apostles' dress and the low social status implied by it (cf. Rom 8:35; 2 Cor 11:27). "We are ... roughly treated" (κολαφιζόμεθα) may refer specifically to the instances in which Paul and the other apostles were the victims of physical violence or more broadly to all the ways in which they were the victims of aggression and mistreatment. "We are ... homeless" (ἀστατοῦμεν) brings to mind the words of Jesus about his own homelessness (cf. Matt 8:20) as the background to the apostles' itinerant missionary work. "We labor, working with our own hands" draws attention to Paul's manual labor (cf. 9:15–18; 2 Cor 11:7, 27; 12:14; 1 Thess 2:9; 2 Thess 3:8–9; Acts 18:3; 20:34), which was generally regarded by members of the Greco-Roman elite as an occupation that was inferior to the purely intellectual pursuits that could be followed by those with leisure to do so.[132]

Three parallel descriptions of the apostles' response to opposition and hostility follow in verses 12b–13a: "When we are reviled, we bless; when we are persecuted, we endure it; when we are slandered, we respond graciously." Here, Paul recalls an important theme of the teaching of Jesus, of which he was almost certainly aware (cf. Rom 12:14), along with the example left for his followers by his conduct on the way to the cross.

The summary phrases in verse 13b ("Even now, we are like the scum of the earth, like everyone's garbage") vividly epitomize the apostles' low status in the hierarchies of the present age. "The scum of the earth" (περικαθάρματα τοῦ κόσμου) refers to the filthy residue that is removed by scraping around a utensil. Similarly, "everyone's garbage" (πάντων περίψημα) describes the offscourings that are scraped off something. Because these words can sometimes be used in the Greek literature to describe victims of human sacrifice (usually condemned criminals, chosen as worthless people who can be sacrificed to ward off evil for the good of the city), some commentators suggest that there is an overtone of

---

[131] In the word order of the Greek original, the two phrases (ἄχρι τῆς ἄρτι ὥρας and ἕως ἄρτι) are positioned at the start of v. 11 and the end of v. 13.

[132] E.g., Plutarch, *Per.* 2.1; Cicero, *Off.* 1.42, and the discussions in Steve Walton, "Paul, Patronage and Pay: What Do We Know About the Apostle's Financial Support?," in *Paul as Missionary*, ed. Trevor J. Burke and Brian S. Rosner, LNTS (London: T&T Clark, 2011), 221–23, and Garland, *1 Corinthians*, 417–19.

expiatory suffering in this verse.[133] If that is the case, then the context here would suggest that it is an additional connotation of the verse, not its primary meaning.

4:14–16. The paragraph that commences in verse 14 concludes the first major section of the letter (1:10–4:21), in which Paul responds to the reports of divisions within the Corinthian church. While the presenting issue of the Corinthians' factionalism is at no point forgotten throughout this section, Paul addresses most of his response toward what he considers to be the underlying issues: the worldly "wisdom" that has shaped the Corinthians' thinking in place of the true wisdom of the cross, the false estimation that they have of the role and status of leaders, the lack of eschatological perspective in their thinking, and the boastful arrogance with which "some" at least in the church have become puffed up. Here in the final paragraph of the section, it is these last two issues that dominate. Having drawn a sharp, sarcastic contrast in 4:8–13 between the prosperity and comfort of the Corinthians and the cruciform lifestyle of the apostles, Paul now admonishes the Corinthians, in a fatherly tone, to imitate him and his "ways in Christ Jesus" (which he has described in the previous paragraph and of which they will also be reminded by Timothy when he visits them); he then warns them that if they do not respond to this admonishment, he will be forced to act in stern confrontation when he visits, as he plans to soon.

The clarification with which Paul begins this paragraph ("I'm not writing this to shame you") should probably not be read as an attempt to deny that there is something shame inducing about the previous paragraph. Rather, as Paul explains, his purpose is not (merely) to shame them but to "warn" them as his "dear children." Paul's desire in giving the Corinthians the confronting reminder of the apostles' lifestyle, as he has described it in verses 8–13, is not merely that they will absorb the shame of being associated with the apostles or admire their heroism from a distance; his intention is that his readers will become imitators of the apostles (v. 16). The "spectacle" of apostolic suffering to which Paul refers in verse 9 may be intended by the synagogue rulers and Roman magistrates as a ritual of shame and humiliation, but Paul insists that it is not they who are ultimately responsible for staging the show. It is (ultimately) God who has put the apostles on display, and he has done so, in part at least, in order

---

[133] E.g., Barrett, *First Corinthians*, 112–13.

that they might serve as an example to be imitated by others, including the Corinthians, to whom Paul became a "father" through the gospel.[134]

The "father/children" language that Paul employs here, along with the accompanying call for the Corinthians to imitate him, has been criticized by some interpreters as manipulative, authoritarian, and paternalistic.[135] Certainly, it implies a relationship of authority (as vv. 18–21 make even more explicit); but, as Paul points out in verse 15, there is a real and legitimate foundation for the fatherly authority that he claims in the history of his dealings with the Corinthian church. Both the warmth of affection and the right to exercise authority are real, not something Paul is pretending to; in addition, the way in which he exercises his authority in relation to the Corinthians is deliberately frank and transparent, is directed toward their good rather than toward the promotion of his own comfort or status, and is expounded in terms of a cruciform pattern of practice that sharply subverts the "great man" paradigm of the Greco-Roman cultural context.[136]

4:17. Paul's decision to send Timothy (the aorist tense of ἔπεμψα, "I have sent," probably suggests that Paul has already sent Timothy, perhaps on a roundabout route that will take longer than the letter to reach Corinth; cf. 16:10) is for the reason that he has stated in verse 16, i.e., to facilitate their imitation of Paul. In keeping with the "father/children" language of verses 14–16, Timothy is described as "my dearly loved and faithful child in the Lord." Like the Corinthians, he is "dearly loved" (ἀγαπητόν) and a "child" (τέκνον) of Paul (cf. the description of the Corinthians in v. 14 as "my dear children"; τέκνα μου ἀγαπητά). Unlike the Corinthians, he is described as a "faithful" (πιστόν) child—probably indicating that he is a believer in Jesus but also, in this context, that he is a faithful imitator of Paul's pattern of life.

Because this is the case, when Timothy visits Corinth he can "remind" the Corinthians (not only by his words but also—primarily?—by his life)

---

134 The contrast between the Corinthians' many "instructors" (παιδαγωγόι) and their few "fathers" (just one, in fact) implies a distinction between the host of teachers and leaders who have exercised influence in the church since Paul's departure and the founding role that Paul played as apostle and church planter ("For I became your father in Christ Jesus through the gospel").

135 See especially Elizabeth A. Castelli, *Imitating Paul: A Discourse of Power* (Louisville: Westminster John Knox, 1991), 89–118.

136 Cf. Harrison, *Paul and the Ancient Celebrity Circuit*, 250–55.

of "my ways in Christ Jesus, just as I teach everywhere in every church." "My ways in Christ Jesus" describes the pattern of Paul's lifestyle insofar as it is shaped by his participation in Christ and in the community of Christ's people; these are the things in which he is to be imitated by the Corinthians, as he is by Timothy. The concluding phrase ("just as I teach everywhere in every church") expresses an emphasis that recurs repeatedly in this letter, reminding the Corinthians that they are called to live out the same pattern that all the churches are called to (cf. 1:2; 7:17; 11:16; 14:33, 36). It is also an important indication that Paul consciously and deliberately taught lifestyle as well as doctrine to the congregations that he established and that he taught by example as well as by word and expected his coworkers and emissaries to do the same.

4:18–21. Verses 18–21 present the hearers of the letter (or, more precisely, the "arrogant" members of the congregation) with a blunt ultimatum: continue as they are and experience Paul's imminent visit as a painful confrontation or take to heart his warnings and allow Paul to visit "in love and a spirit of gentleness."

"Arrogant," in verses 18–19, like "arrogant" in verse 6, translates a word that suggests an image of the Corinthians as having become metaphorically "puffed up" (ἐφυσιώθησαν/πεφυσιωμένων) with self-importance. The focus of Paul's language on "some" (τινες) and "those who are arrogant" (τῶν πεφυσιωμένων) suggests that his critique (throughout this whole section from 1:10–4:21?), while addressed to the whole congregation, is particularly intended for the ears of an elite within the church (cf. chs. 8–10, addressed to the whole congregation but particularly intended for the "strong"; likewise 11:17–34, which is correcting a practice of the wealthier members of the congregation, and chs. 12–14, which express a particular concern for the way in which the "weaker" and "less honorable" parts of the body are treated).

Paul's statement that he will come "if the Lord wills" (v. 19) is in line with his typical, explicit submission of his plans to the outworking of God's sovereign purposes (cf. 1 Cor 16:7; Rom 1:10; 15:32; 1 Thess 3:11; Phlm 22). While the threats of forceful confrontation in verse 21 are not to be minimized, they should not be read as implying that the "power" spoken of in verses 19–20 is a reference to the sort of self-serving bullying that epitomizes the way power is used by "the rulers of this age" (2:8). Rather, as Thiselton suggests, the meaning of "power" in verses 19–20 is best understood in terms of the contrast with mere "talk" (λόγος).[137] The implication of verses 19–20 is that the talk of the "arrogant" (literally, "puffed up") members of the Corinthian church is empty, lacking the accompanying power in the lives of speaker and hearers that comes from the work of the Spirit (cf. 1 Cor 2:1–5; 1 Thess 1:5–6).

"The kingdom of God" (v. 20) is an expression Paul can use to refer to the both the future reality (e.g., 6:9–10; 15:24, 50) and the present effect (e.g., Rom 14:17) of the reign of God established in Christ. Paul's use of "kingdom" language here may be prompted by the earlier description of the Corinthians as having "begun to reign as kings" in verse 8: Paul is contrasting the solid, powerful reality of God's kingdom work in Christ with the empty boasts and rhetoric of the Corinthian elite.

The "rod" that Paul threatens in verse 21 is obviously metaphorical, not literal, and is probably a continuation of the "father" metaphor from earlier in the paragraph. Clearly Paul's preference is not for painful confrontation, but he is prepared to exercise (moral and psychological) force if he has to in calling the Corinthians to repentance.

Bridge

These final, climactic paragraphs of the first section of 1 Corinthians are among the most intensely personal and rhetorically heightened moments within the letter. Paul is speaking to the Corinthians as a "father" to his "dear children," responding to reports he has received about the arrogant and entitled mindset that some among them have fallen into, foreshadowing an imminent visit to Corinth that he plans to make, and describing his hopes for the role that Timothy, his emissary, will play among them in the meantime. It is impossible to read these paragraphs without an awareness that this is a piece of personal correspondence, written within a preexisting relationship between Paul and the Corinthians and addressing a particular set of circumstances in Corinth.

But an awareness of these relational and rhetorical dynamics should not insulate us as twenty-first century readers from feeling the force of Paul's reminders and warnings or their relevance to our own situation. The pattern of life that Paul describes in verses 8–13 is, after all, one he shares with all the other apostles, in keeping with their participation "in Christ," and makes a practice of teaching and modeling "everywhere

---

137 Thiselton, *First Corinthians*, 376–77.

in every church" (v. 17). We, like the Corinthians, are called to become imitators of that pattern, translating the specifics of how it plays out in the mission of a first-century, itinerant, church-planting missionary into the various different situations in which we have been called to follow Christ. And to the extent that we, like some among the Corinthians, have succumbed to a mindset that presumes upon an entitlement to comfort, ease, and respectability in the present age, Paul's invitation to imitate him comes to us with the same edge of urgency and rebuke as it was intended by Paul to carry for the arrogant, puffed-up members of the Corinthian congregation.

III. Response to Reports of Immorality and Predatory Lawsuits (5:1–6:20)

Having responded in 1:10–4:21 to reports of division within the Corinthian church, Paul now deals in chapters 5–6 with reports about sexual immorality and predatory lawsuits. While the transition from the previous section to this one seems quite abrupt, there are a number of connections between them (beyond the obvious fact that they are both responses to what has been reported to Paul):

(1) the importance in both sections of Paul's authority, which is asserted implicitly throughout the previous section and explicitly in the concluding verses (4:14–21) and is now put to the test in particular situations addressed within chapters 5–6 (cf. especially 5:3–5);
(2) the challenge in both sections to the "arrogance" that underlies the Corinthian behavior (5:2, 6; cf. 4:6, 18–19).
(3) the contrast between the lack of "power" in the empty words of the arrogant in 4:19–20 and the "power of our Lord Jesus" in 5:4.[138]

Mitchell's suggestion that the main connection is the threat that the man's immorality poses to the unity of the church is unconvincing and is driven by her attempt to read the whole letter within an overarching framework of "the rhetoric of reconciliation."[139] Important as that theme

---

[138] All three connections are pointed out in Fee, *First Epistle to the Corinthians*, 212.
[139] Cf. Mitchell, *Paul and the Rhetoric of Reconciliation*, 112.

is (especially within chapters 1–4) the primary focus here in chapters 5–6 is not on the church's unity but on its holiness.

A. Egregious Immorality (5:1–13)

> [1] It is actually reported that there is sexual immorality among you, and the kind of sexual immorality that is not even tolerated among the Gentiles—a man is sleeping with his father's wife. [2] And you are arrogant! Shouldn't you be filled with grief and remove from your congregation the one who did this? [3] Even though I am absent in the body, I am present in spirit. As one who is present with you in this way, I have already pronounced judgment on the one who has been doing such a thing. [4] When you are assembled in the name of our Lord Jesus, and I am with you in spirit, with the power of our Lord Jesus, [5] hand that one over to Satan for the destruction of the flesh, so that his spirit may be saved in the day of the Lord.
>
> [6] Your boasting is not good. Don't you know that a little leaven leavens the whole batch of dough? [7] Clean out the old leaven so that you may be a new unleavened batch, as indeed you are. For Christ our Passover lamb has been sacrificed. [8] Therefore, let us observe the feast, not with old leaven or with the leaven of malice and evil, but with the unleavened bread of sincerity and truth.
>
> [9] I wrote to you in a letter not to associate with sexually immoral people. [10] I did not mean the immoral people of this world or the greedy and swindlers or idolaters; otherwise you would have to leave the world. [11] But actually, I wrote you not to associate with anyone who claims to be a brother or sister and is sexually immoral or greedy, an idolater or verbally abusive, a drunkard or a swindler. Do not even eat with such a person. [12] For what business is it of mine to judge outsiders? Don't you judge those who are inside? [13] God judges outsiders. **Remove the evil person from among you.**

Context/Structure/Form

The first issue Paul responds to in this section of the letter is the way in which the Corinthians have responded (or failed to respond) to a particular case of sexual immorality in which a man has been involved in a sexual relationship with his father's wife. Within chapter 5, the progression of thought moves from a statement of the problem (vv. 1–2) to a prescription for how it is to be dealt with (vv. 3–5), followed by a theologically grounded rebuke to the Corinthians' underlying arrogance and complacency (vv. 6–8) and a more general word (clarifying an instruction in a previous letter) about judging insiders, not outsiders (vv. 9–13).

Comments

5:1–2. The opening words of verse 1, "It is actually reported" (Ὅλως ἀκούεται), signal the beginning of a new section in the letter, once more responding to reports that have come to Paul (cf. 1:11). "Actually" translates the Greek word ὅλως, which usually means "wholly" or "altogether" but can also function idiomatically in later Greek to mean "really" or "actually" (cf. 6:7; 15:29);[140] here it expresses Paul's shock at the extremity of the immorality that is tolerated within the Corinthian church.

The word πορνεία (CSB: "sexual immorality") was generally used by speakers and writers outside of Jewish and early Christian circles to refer narrowly and specifically to the practice of selling one's body as a prostitute.[141] In Hellenistic-Jewish usage the range of meanings that it can carry widens significantly, so that it becomes an umbrella term for all sexual activity that is outside of marriage or in some other way improper.[142] Paul's use of the word has a similar breadth of meaning and is informed by a similar understanding of marriage as the sole context for legitimate sexual activity (cf. 6:16; 7:1–2).

The CSB translation of the following phrase, "and the kind of sexual immorality that is not even tolerated among the Gentiles," supplies the word "tolerated" on the basis that incestuous liaisons like the one in Corinth were certainly found in Greco-Roman culture but were not generally approved of.[143] An interpretive addition of this sort is probably not required, however: while it is unlikely that Paul is claiming that this sort of incest *never* occurs among the pagans, it is reasonable to allow him a little hyperbole in pointing out to the Corinthians that sexual immorality of this nature is not even part of the (normal, customary) way of life of the pagans.

The situation Paul is referring to is one in which "a man is sleeping with his father's wife" (more literally, "a certain one has his father's wife"). The language Paul uses to describe the situation almost certainly

---

[140] Cf. BDAG s.v. "ὅλως," 2.

[141] E.g., Demosthenes, *Fals. leg.* 200.7; Dionysius of Halicarnassus, *Ant. rom.* 4.24.4; cf. Kyle Harper, "*Porneia*: The Making of a Christian Sexual Norm," *JBL* 131 (2011): 366–69. Hippocrates, *Epid.* 7.122, which appears, on one possible reading, to use the word to refer to the visiting of prostitutes, is of uncertain date and may be influenced by later Jewish and Christian usage.

[142] E.g., T. Reu. 1.6; 6.1–2; T. Jos. 3.8; T. Benj. 9.1; T. Iss. 7.1–2; cf. T. Reu. 4.1.

[143] Thiselton, *First Corinthians*, 385; Garland, *1 Corinthians*, 157, and the similar translation in the 2011 NIV.

refers to an ongoing sexual relationship, given the present infinitive form of ἔχειν ("has") and the use of πορνεία in the previous clause. "His father's wife" (γυναῖκα ... τοῦ πατρός) echoes the language of Leviticus 18:8 ("You are not to have sex with your father's wife"; LXX: ἀσχημοσύνην γυναικὸς πατρός σου οὐκ ἀποκαλύψεις) and does not necessarily imply that the man's father is still alive. The focus on the man's actions and how he is to be disciplined by the church probably implies that the man and not the woman is part of the church.

Paul's outrage is generated not only by the egregiousness of the situation but also by the way in which the Corinthian church has responded to it: "And you are arrogant!" he declares with astonishment in verse 2, using the same word (literally "puffed up") that he has already used several times, in various forms, in the previous chapter (cf. 4:6, 18, 19). Although some commentators suggest that the Corinthians' arrogance is *because of* the man's sin (i.e., that they are indulging in a theologically motivated boast about the way in which his sin demonstrates his liberation from the old moral constraints of life in the flesh),[144] this reading is unlikely, given Paul's response in the following verses. Paul seems to presuppose that he and the Corinthians are in basic theological agreement and calls on them simply to act on the basis of what they know to be true. A simpler reading would be to understand Paul as saying that the Corinthians' arrogance is *despite* (rather than *because of*) the scandal in their midst.[145]

In place of the arrogant complacency that the Corinthians have shown, Paul suggests that the correct response should have been one of communal mourning: "Shouldn't you be filled with grief and remove from your congregation the one who did this?" Rosner interprets Paul's statement that the Corinthians should have been "filled with grief" (ἐπενθήσατε) against the background of the LXX, in which the word Paul uses frequently describes the contrite mourning in which the community confesses the sin of one of its members as if it was the sin of all.[146] Against this background, it is possible (as Thiselton points out) that the "grief" Paul speaks of might involve not only inward sorrow but also outward expressions of contrition—a public, visible act of mourning that "would

---

[144] E.g., Barrett, *First Corinthians*, 122; Thiselton, *First Corinthians*, 388–89; Fee, *First Epistle to the Corinthians*, 221–22.

[145] Cf. Clarke, *Secular and Christian Leadership*, 77; Garland, *1 Corinthians*, 160–61.

[146] Rosner, *Paul, Scripture and Ethics*, 72–73.

thereby make it intolerable for the offender to remain."[147] This kind of scenario may be behind the concluding clause, "and remove from your congregation the one who did this" (ἵνα ἀρθῇ ἐκ μέσου ὑμῶν ὁ τὸ ἔργον τοῦτο πράξας; more literally, "so that he who has done this would have been removed from among you"), which is worded by Paul in a way that appears to express the (intended) consequence of the community's mourning.

5:3–5. Having commenced by stating his assessment of the problem that has been reported to him (vv. 1–2), Paul now gives the Corinthians his instructions for how it is to be dealt with (vv. 3–5). He begins by reminding the Corinthians that despite his physical absence, which some might take as a reason for disregarding his instructions or delaying their response to them (cf. 4:18–19), he is even now "present in spirit" (παρὼν ... τῷ πνεύματι) with the Corinthians. The meaning of this phrase seems to include both the general sense in which Paul is always present "in spirit" with the Corinthians, because they are in his thoughts and prayers (cf. Col 2:5), and a more particular sense in which his presence will be manifested among the Corinthians as his letter is read in the congregation. Fee may be correct in suggesting that there is an additional reference intended to the Spirit of God as the one by whom Paul's presence is effected (though note the reference to "my spirit" in v. 4 (author translation), suggesting that Paul cannot only be referring to the Spirit of God in v. 3).[148]

The syntactical relationship between the various remaining parts of the sentence that follow in verses 3b–4 is a matter of some debate. The main question at issue is the function of the phrase "in the name of our Lord Jesus" (v. 4a), and the debate boils down to a choice between three main options:

(1) linking the phrase to the participle κατεργασάμενον ("has been doing") that immediately precedes it and interpreting it as an expression of the outrage Paul feels at the fact that "the one who has been doing such a thing" has been doing so "in the name of

[147] Thiselton, *First Corinthians*, 388.

[148] Fee, *First Epistle to the Corinthians*, 224–25, pointing out the similar interplay between "the Spirit" and "my spirit" in 14:14–16.

our Lord Jesus," claiming or tacitly assuming that his Christian freedom gives him the right to act in this way with impunity;[149]

(2) linking the phrase to the verb κέκρικα ("I have pronounced judgment"), which occurs slightly earlier in verse 3, and interpreting it as an assertion that the judgment Paul has already pronounced has been delivered "in the name of our Lord Jesus";[150]

(3) linking the phrase to the participle συναχθέντων ("assembled") in the genitive absolute construction that follows it and interpreting it as a depiction of the Corinthian assembly gathering "in the name of our Lord Jesus."[151]

Option (1) is the most natural way of taking the word order but sits less well with the primary themes and emphases of the sentence, which focuses more on the disciplinary action that the community needs to take than on the justifications that the man has given for his actions. Option (3) is consistent with this focus and with the scenario Paul appears to have in mind but has the effect of overloading συναχθέντων with multiple qualifying phrases that precede and follow it. Option (2) has against it the distance between κέκρικα and ἐν τῷ ὀνόματι τοῦ κυρίου [ἡμῶν] Ἰησοῦ but is probably to be preferred, given Paul's tendency to use the phrase "in the name of our Lord Jesus" or its close equivalents to modify a verb that precedes it rather than one that follows it (cf. 6:11; 2 Thess 3:6; Col 3:17).[152] This reading also has the advantage of preserving the parallelism in verses 3–4 between Paul's judgment "in the name of our Lord Jesus" (v. 4a) and the corresponding action he asks the Corinthians to take in the presence of "the power of our Lord Jesus" (v. 4b). While Paul has already "pronouced judgment," he is keen that the action be taken by the assembled congregation, in harmony with his judgment.[153]

---

[149] Cf. Hays, *First Corinthians*, 84; J. Murphy-O'Connor, *Keys to First Corinthians: Revisiting the Major Issues* (Oxford: Oxford University Press, 2009), 11–19.

[150] NIV, NRSV; cf. Ciampa and Rosner, *The First Letter to the Corinthians*, 206; Fee, *First Epistle to the Corinthians*, 228.

[151] CSB; cf. Barrett, *First Corinthians*, 124.

[152] Cf. Ciampa and Rosner, *The First Letter to the Corinthians*, 206. Garland also points out that the other three genitive absolute constructions in 1 Cor that are accompanied by a prepositional phrase all precede, rather than follow, that phrase (cf. 4:18; 11:18, 20). Garland, *1 Corinthians*, 165.

[153] The infinitive παραδοῦναι ("hand ... over") at the start of v. 5 is best understood as indirect discourse governed by the verb κέκρικα ("I have ... pronounced judgment"), with

The action Paul has called for the Corinthian assembly to take ("hand that one over to Satan") implies some sort of exclusion from the community of God's people (cf. v. 13: "Remove the evil person from among you"), leaving him exposed, unprotected to the Satanic forces of evil within the world (cf. 2 Cor 4:4; Gal 1:4; Col 1:13), whose activities God permits as an outworking of his judgment on human sin and for the testing, chastening, and strengthening of his own people (cf. 1 Tim 1:20; 2 Cor 12:7; Job 2:6). This action, Paul tells the Corinthians, is to be taken "for the destruction of the flesh, so that his spirit may be saved in the day of the Lord." The first of these two closely connected phrases ("for the destruction of the flesh") is probably not, as some commentators have argued, a description of a curse that Paul intends to lead to the man's physical death (i.e., "the destruction of [his] flesh").[154] More likely, it states Paul's intention in disciplining the man: to destroy the stranglehold that the flesh (i.e., the mindset of the world in its opposition to God) has gained over his life (cf. Gal 5:24; Rom 8:12–13), and so, Paul hopes, to lead to his eventual salvation.[155]

5:6. As he did in the previous section of the letter (1:10–4:21), Paul now digs beneath the presenting issue on the surface to the "boasting" that he regards as the real, underlying problem of the Corinthian church. "Don't you know ... ?" (οὐκ οἴδατε) is a question that occurs ten times in this letter (cf. 3:16; 6:2, 3, 9, 15, 16, 19; 9:13, 24), each time reminding the Corinthians of things they ought to know (especially since they claim, in 8:1, that they "all have knowledge") and that ought to shape their behavior.

The truth of which Paul reminds them on this occasion is that "a little leaven leavens the whole batch of dough"—a maxim or proverb (cf. Gal 5:9), similar to a number of sayings of Jesus about the influence (for good and for bad) of a little leaven over the whole lump (cf. Matt 13:33; 16:6–12).

"you" as the implied subject of the infinitive. The relevant parts of the sentence thus read: "I have ... pronounced judgment on the one who has been doing such a thing ... that you are to hand that one over to Satan ...". Cf. Fee, *First Epistle to the Corinthians*, 225.

154 E.g., Robertson and Plummer, *First Corinthians*, 99–100; Barrett, *First Corinthians*, 126.

155 Garland, *1 Corinthians*, 175–76; Fee, *First Epistle to the Corinthians*, 233. While Paul clearly has the purity of the whole community in view (cf. vv. 6–8), it is forcing the meaning of the word "saved" (σωθῇ) well beyond the range it normally covers in Paul's letters to read this second phrase, as some commentators do, as describing Paul's desire that the discipline taken by the congregation will lead to the Spirit's presence being "preserved" among them. Cf. the arguments against this view in Garland, *1 Corinthians*, 174.

Here, Paul uses it to refer to the pervasive, disastrous influence on the community of unrepentant sin that is condoned in one of its members. While Paul is concerned (v. 5) for the salvation of the individual sinner, he is also concerned for the corporate holiness of the community as he now goes on to spell out in verses 6–8.

5:7–8. The "leaven" metaphor that Paul introduces via the saying that he quotes in verse 6 is further developed in verses 7–8, with an evocation of the image of the unleavened bread that was eaten in conjunction with the Passover festival. The way in which Paul develops the metaphor suggests that the precise image he has in mind is communicated better by the word "leaven" (CSB, ESV) than by the commonly used alternative of "yeast" (NIV, NRSV); an integral component of the metaphor is the process by which leaven (unlike yeast) was made, which involved keeping back a portion of the previous batch of dough and promoting its fermentation.[156] In verses 7–8 Paul makes explicit this added dimension of the analogy, drawing a contrast between the "old" leaven of the Corinthians' former life in paganism and the "new" (unleavened) batch, which represents the redeemed and transformed life that they have now been called to in Christ. While the precise metaphor shifts a little from verse 7 to verse 8 (in v. 7a the Corinthians are the "new unleavened batch"; in vv. 7b–8 they are the Israelites who eat the unleavened bread as they celebrate the festival), the main point (the new life of the people saved in Christ and the implications for their lifestyle) is clear.

Verse 7 is characteristic of Paul's ethics, with its explicit grounding of the imperative of ethics ("Clean out the old leaven so that you may be a new unleavened batch") in the indicatives of salvation and ecclesiology ("as indeed you are. For Christ our Passover lamb has been sacrificed").[157] In speaking of Christ as "our Passover lamb," Paul is evoking an exodus typology that speaks of the salvation accomplished in Christ as a new exodus event and the people of Christ as a new Israel, who "observe the feast." While it is quite possible that it is Passover time in Ephesus as Paul writes (cf. 16:8 "I will stay in Ephesus until Pentecost," and 4:19, "I will come to you soon"), it is unlikely that Paul is referring here to a ritual celebration of the Passover as an annual festival or (narrowly) to

---

[156] Cf. Garland, *1 Corinthians*, 178–79, citing Plutarch, *Quaest. rom.* 289F; Pliny the Elder, *Nat.* 18.26.

[157] Cf. Barrett, *First Corinthians*, 128; Hays, "Ecclesiology and Ethics," 38–39, 41.

the Lord's Supper as a Christian Passover; more likely, given the context here in chapter 5, he is describing the whole common life of the Christian community as a kind of Passover celebration.[158] It is possible, of course, given the seriousness with which Paul regarded the symbolism of table fellowship (cf. 10:14–22), that he sees this reality as being symbolized in the shared meal of the Lord's Supper; certainly, there is a reference to some sort of table fellowship in verse 11, in connection with the expulsion of a person from the community.[159]

That Paul describes the old leaven as characterized by "malice" (κακία) and "evil" (πονηρία) suggests that he is laying down a general principle in these verses, not restricted to the particular instance of this man and his sexual immorality. The narrower focus in verse 8b on "sincerity" (εἰλικρίνεια) and "truth" (ἀλήθεια) as the essence of what is represented by the "unleavened bread" in his Passover metaphor may be intended as a contrast to the deception and pretense involved in treating a person living in unrepentant sin (of any kind) as if the sin were of no consequence.

5:9–10. Having called on the Corinthians to take action in response to the unrepentant sexual misconduct of a man within the congregation (vv. 1–5), and having grounded the instruction theologically in the corporate holiness of the saved people of God as a "new unleavened batch" of bread (vv. 6–8), Paul clarifies the principle at stake, making reference to an instruction in a previous letter in which he had urged the Corinthians not to associate with sexually immoral persons. Lest they (willfully?) misunderstood his earlier instruction to be about disassociation from the immoral of this world, he now makes it clear that he was speaking only about the situation of a person who "claims to be a brother or sister" yet lives a life inconsistent with that claim.

That Paul has already written to the Corinthians about this issue (the general principle, if not the specific instance) makes the Corinthians' complacency even more inexcusable. (The letter from the Corinthians to Paul that he refers to in 7:1 was probably a response to this earlier letter, which helps to explain the focus on issues to do with sexual relationships in both chs. 5–6 and ch. 7). Given the other indications in this letter of the Corinthians' attitude toward Paul and their approach to relationships

---

[158] Cf. Fee, *First Epistle to the Corinthians*, 239–40; Ciampa and Rosner, *The First Letter to the Corinthians*, 215.

[159] Cf. Fee, *First Epistle to the Corinthians*, 239–40.

with the surrounding pagan society, it is unlikely that they were seriously attempting to cut off all relationship with "the immoral people of this world," in obedience to what they thought Paul to be saying; more likely, as Thiselton suggests, "some may have maliciously applied a *reductio ad absurdum* of which Paul now shows himself fully aware."[160]

"Sexually immoral people" (v. 9) and "immoral people" (v. 10) both translate the Greek word πόρνοι (from the same root as πορνεία, the word used in 5:1 to describe the man's incestuous relationship with his stepmother),[161] suggesting a close connection between this clarification and Paul's rebuke in verses 1–8. Paul's instruction to the Corinthians not to "associate with" (συναναμίγνυσθαι) such people is expressed by means of a compound verb derived from μίγνυμι ("mix"/"mingle"), with the addition of two intensifying prefixes (συν- and ἀνα-). Thiselton suggests that what Paul is prohibiting is not all "association" altogether (what should a slave do, for example, if his master fell into this category?) but rather the kind of conduct that implies that a person is included indiscriminately within the community of the church.[162]

Paul's clarification of the earlier instruction also includes a generalization of the principle: the kind of disassociation he has in mind applies not only to the sexually immoral but also to "the greedy and swindlers or idolaters" (v. 10). As Rosner points out, the examples chosen may reflect the influence of the passages in Deuteronomy about sins that led to a person being cut off from the community of Israel (Deut 22:21–22; 24:7; 17:2–7).[163] It probably also reflects Paul's analysis of the sins that were particularly endemic in the culture of Corinth. "Swindlers" (ἅρπαγες) is commonly used to mean people who rob by fraud or take advantage of others financially (as distinct from λῃσταί, who rob by violence); the

---

[160] Thiselton, *First Corinthians*, 409.

[161] On the meaning of the word πορνεία in Jewish and early Christian usage, see the comments on 5:1. A similar difference between normal Greco-Roman usage and usage of the word by Jews and early Christians applies in the case of πόρνος, which in standard usage was the word for a male prostitute but in Jewish and early Christian usage had a much wider semantic range, including any (male) person who practiced πορνεία (as Jews and Christians understood that word). Cf. Sir 23:17, and the discussion in Harper, "*Porneia*," 377–79.

[162] Thiselton, *First Corinthians*, 409, citing (among other examples) the use of the cognate adjective to refer to the inclusion of a tract of land as an unbounded portion of a larger landholding, in P. Oxy. 4.718.16, in J. H. Moulton and G. Milligan, *The Vocabulary of the Greek New Testament* (repr., Peabody: Hendrickson, 1997), 602.

[163] Rosner, *Paul, Scripture and Ethics*, 69–70.

word refers (as Thiselton suggests) to "precisely the kind of 'stealing' which genuinely tempted early Christians in business or property" (cf. 6:1–11).[164] The close syntactical connection between "greedy" and "swindlers" (joined by "and," not "or") suggests that Paul is linking both words together to describe the same people.[165] "Idolaters" (εἰδωλολάτραι) also refers to a sin that would have been a real temptation for Corinthian Christians (cf. chs. 8–10). Verse 10b ("otherwise you would have to leave the world") expresses the impossibility that would confront anyone who attempted to avoid interacting with all such people, irrespective of whether they made any profession of Christian faith—an absurdity that some of the Corinthians may already have pointed out in a bid to dismiss Paul's earlier instruction.

5:11. If verses 9–10 clarify what Paul is *not* saying in his earlier letter, verse 11 makes it clear what he *is* saying. To the list in verse 10, Paul now adds "anyone ... who is ... verbally abusive" (λοίδορος; i.e., a person whose habitual mode of speech is to insult and revile others) and "a drunkard" (μέθυσος, probably intended to conjure up an image of the extravagant social drinking common in Greco-Roman culture and frequently associated with idol worship and sexual immorality; cf. 1 Cor 10:8). "Do not even eat with such a person," read within the context previously established by the instruction not to "associate [indiscriminately]" (συναναμίγνυσθαι), is probably best taken as prescribing exclusion from the hospitality of the shared table of the gathered congregation (and possibly also the household table, where such hospitality would be construed as a sign of fellowship in the community of God's people).[166] If that is the outer limit of the discipline imposed, then it makes sense to assume that there was still room for the normal social interactions that would occur if the person were not a believer.

5:12–13. In disavowing any responsibility or right to judge unbelievers (v. 12a), Paul is not only keeping the door open for missional friendship (cf. 10:27–11:1) but also backhandedly reinforcing the tightness of the community boundaries—the reason he has no business to judge them is precisely because they are "outsiders."[167] This does not mean renounc-

---

[164] Thiselton, *First Corinthians*, 411–12.

[165] Ciampa and Rosner, *The First Letter to the Corinthians*, 217.

[166] Thiselton, *First Corinthians*, 415; Ciampa and Rosner, *The First Letter to the Corinthians*, 218.

[167] See especially Paul R. Trebilco, *Outsider Designations and Boundary Construction in the New Testament: Early Christian Communities and the Formation of Group Identity* (New York:

ing all responsibility for making moral assessments and prophetic criticisms of the secular society; it simply means that formal decisions about exclusion and disfellowshipping would be inappropriate and meaningless for those who are already outside. Outsiders are not left without moral accountability, of course—they have God as their judge (v. 13)—and one important dimension of the church's prophetic critique of society is to bear witness to that coming judgment and urge others (including rulers and authorities) to act in the light of it.[168] On the other hand, "those who are inside" must definitely be judged (v. 12b). The "you" in the second question reinforces the implication of verses 3–5 that the whole community of believers is to be involved, in some measure at least, in sharing the responsibility of such decisions.

The Old Testament quotation supporting the exhortation to judge insiders comes from Deuteronomy 17:7, helping to confirm Rosner's thesis about the Deuteronomic background of this chapter.[169] The words from Deuteronomy are appropriated by Paul in a manner that addresses them directly to his readers in Corinth, prompting the following comment from Hays:

> [For Paul] there always has been and will be only one Israel. Into that Israel Gentile Christians such as the Corinthians have been absorbed. For that reason Paul can deploy the words of Deut 17:7 (LXX) as a direct word of exhortation to the Corinthians to guard the purity of their community … . No introductory formula intrudes between Moses and the Corinthians, no conjunction weakens the command to a simile. Paul could have written, "Just as Moses commanded Israel to drive out the wicked person, so you too … ." But … the scriptural command is treated as a valid word addressed immediately to these Gentiles.[170]

Hays's observations regarding the function of Scripture as a living word that continues to address Christian believers (in this instance, without

---

Cambridge University Press, 2017), 216–17

[168] The UBS[5] editors accentuate the verb κριvεῖ in a manner that suggests a future tense ("will judge") rather than the present tense form (κρίνει) implied by the CSB's "judges." Given the recurring references across the letter to the coming judgment on the day of the Lord, the future tense is probably to be preferred.

[169] Cf. Rosner, *Paul, Scripture and Ethics*, 69–70, and the comments on v. 10, above.

[170] Hays, *Echoes of Scripture*, 97.

the intrusion of any kind of introductory formula or analogical distance) are acute. There is, however, room for debate about his claim that "[for Paul] there always has been and will be only one Israel,"[171] and the dynamics observable in this instance of Scripture's function need to be placed alongside the wide variety of other, less immediate ways in which it functions elsewhere in Paul's letters before any more general conclusions can be drawn.[172]

Bridge

The situation to which Paul is responding in this passage is, as he points out to the Corinthians in the opening verse, an extreme and unusual one, and this is reflected in the forcefulness of his rhetoric and the urgency of the actions that he calls on the Corinthians to take. But the grounds on which he bases his response, as they are expressed in the Passover typology of verses 6–8, and the explicit generality of the clarifying comments that he makes in the final paragraph (vv. 9–13) make it clear that Paul's instructions to the Corinthian church in this chapter of the letter have a broad and continuing relevance, extending far beyond the unique circumstances of first-century Corinth and applying to a wide range of sinful behaviors, where they are persisted in unrepentantly by a professing Christian.

The precise way in which we respond to the instructions and reminders Paul gives in this chapter will need to take into account the relevant differences that exist between our own circumstances and those of the Corinthians. Unlike Paul's readers, for example, many twenty-first century Christians live in contexts where there are numerous churches, belonging to a multiplicity of denominational traditions, in which membership of a local church is (in some instances) given formal, institutionalized expression in a variety of different ways. These realities need to be taken into account in the practices of church discipline we follow

[171] Cf. Rom 9:6–7; 1 Cor 10:18; Gal 4:21–31.

[172] See, for example, the complex interplay between elements of continuity and discontinuity in salvation history that is stated or implied in passages within 1 Corinthians such as 10:1–22 and 15:44–45. For a discussion of the implications for how we are to understand the functions of Scripture in Paul's letters, see Starling, "Nothing Beyond What Is Written?," 55–62; David I. Starling, *Not My People: Gentiles as Exiles in Pauline Hermeneutics*, BZNW (Berlin: de Gruyter, 2011), 209–13.

and in the way we explain them to one another and to those who are affected by them.

But our acknowledgment of those differences between the Corinthians' context and our own does not do away with the basic reality that the visible, local church, then and now, is called to be a holy community, with communal boundaries, inscribed as a circumference around the center of the saving, ruling presence of Christ, that give visible, social expression to that reality.[173] Such boundaries, if they are to be consistent with Paul's instructions and reminders here and elsewhere in 1 Corinthians, should accurately represent the distinctions and disciplines of confession and conduct that mark out those who follow Jesus from those who do not know him, make explicit the covenantal commitment of a community of believers to live under those disciplines together, and allow for the missional involvement of God's people in the world and the hospitable welcome within the church of those who are in the process of learning about Christ but have not yet made a public profession of faith in him and become members of the covenant community.[174]

B. Predatory Lawsuits (6:1–11)

> 1 If any of you has a dispute against another, how dare you take it to
> court before the unrighteous, and not before the saints? 2 Or don't you
> know that the saints will judge the world? And if the world is judged by
> you, are you unworthy to judge the trivial cases? 3 Don't you know that
> we will judge angels—how much more matters of this life? 4 So if you
> have such matters, do you appoint as your judges those who have no
> standing in the church? 5 I say this to your shame! Can it be that there
> is not one wise person among you who is able to arbitrate between
> fellow believers? 6 Instead, brother goes to court against brother, and
> that before unbelievers!
>
> 7 As it is, to have legal disputes against one another is already a defeat
> for you. Why not rather be wronged? Why not rather be cheated? 8 In-
> stead, you yourselves do wrong and cheat—and you do this to brothers
> and sisters! 9 Don't you know that the unrighteous will not inherit God's
> kingdom? Do not be deceived: No sexually immoral people, idolaters,
> adulterers, or males who have sex with males, 10 no thieves, greedy
> people, drunkards, verbally abusive people, or swindlers will inherit
> God's kingdom. 11 And some of you used to be like this. But you were

[173] Cf. Gardner, *1 Corinthians*, 242–43.

[174] Cf. the discussion of these issues in Starling, "Good Fences, Good Neighbours?," 19–26.

> washed, you were sanctified, you were justified in the name of the Lord Jesus Christ and by the Spirit of our God.

Context/Structure/Form

The transition from chapter 5 to chapter 6 is somewhat abrupt and the connection not immediately obvious. Presumably Paul is aware of the litigation through reports that has heard, though there is no "report" language here (as there is in 1:11 and 5:1) to suggest that he is simply moving on from one problem reported to him to the next. It is possible but highly speculative to propose that the man spoken of in 5:1–2 is the same person taking other members of the congregation before the secular courts. More likely connections that have been suggested include

(1) that this case, like the previous one, is another example of the shameful realities within the Corinthian church (note the "shame" language in 6:5) that ought to have deflated their arrogant complacency;
(2) that this case, like the previous one, is an instance of the dysfunctional relationship between the Corinthian church and the surrounding society;
(3) that this case is an example of the greed and swindling that Paul has just spoken about as having no place within the community of God's people (5:10–11; cf. 6:8); and
(4) that the failure of the community to provide its own internal mechanisms for judging this kind of greed and extortion parallels the failure of the community to act in judging the immorality of one of its members (5:12).[175]

The language throughout this paragraph is forceful; most of the paragraph is made up of a string of rhetorical questions including three of the letter's ten "Don't you know ... ?" questions.

Comments

6:1. While verse 1 is expressed in quite general terms ("If any of you has a dispute against another"), it is clear from verses 5–6 that there is at least one specific instance that has already occurred, to which Paul is

---

[175] Cf. the discussion in Garland, *1 Corinthians*, 150–52; Fee, *First Epistle to the Corinthians*, 212–13; Ciampa and Rosner, *The First Letter to the Corinthians*, 226.

responding (and probably more if, as argued below, the "you yourselves" in v. 8 is directed at the initiators of litigation in cases such as this). "How dare you ... ?" (Τολμᾷ) is the first word in the Greek, expressing Paul's sense of outrage at this situation even more emphatically than the English. "Take it to court" is more literally "get [it] judged" (κρίνεσθαι), a form of the same verb κρίνω that Paul used in 5:12–13, supporting the theory that community matters is one of the main connecting themes between chapter 5 and chapter 6.

In describing the pagan magistrates as "the unrighteous" (οἱ ἀδίκοι), Paul chooses a word that not only distinguishes them as pagans from the people of God, but also implies that they are an unlikely source of justice (given the semantic overlap between "justice" and "righteousness"). As Winter has highlighted, the local civil magistrates' courts of the Roman empire had a well-attested reputation for being manipulated by the patronage networks of the wealthy, supporting the impression that many of the plaintiffs who took cases before these courts were not looking for justice but rather were seeking to make use of the courts to perpetrate injustice (cf. Jas 2:6).[176]

6:2–3. As he does throughout this letter, Paul addresses issues of conduct and relationships in the present in the light of the eschatological future. Here, he points out the inappropriateness of God's people going to the secular courts to seek justice against each other in the light of the fact that one day "the saints will judge the world."

The expectation that the saints will judge the world goes back to Daniel 7:22 and would have been reinforced in early Christian circles by the saying of Jesus recorded in Matthew 19:28.[177] It is difficult to be certain of the precise meaning and background to Paul's additional assertion in the following verse that the saints will judge not only the world but also "angels" (v. 3). Commentators variously suggest that Paul has followed a similar line of thought to the argument in Hebrews 2:5–9, based on Psalm 8, that the "angels" here are the patron angels of the nations or that the angels are fallen angels, subject to God's condemnation (cf. 1 En. 10:12–14; 19:1; 21:1–10; 2 En. 7; 18).[178] Whatever is the case, the rhetorical function of verse 3a is to up the ante on what Paul has said in verse 2a (cf. "human

[176] Winter, *After Paul Left Corinth*, 58–75.

[177] Cf. Trebilco, *Self-Designations*, 131–32.

[178] Cf. the discussion and evaluation of these options in Garland, *1 Corinthians*, 202–3.

or angelic tongues" in 13:1, or "even ... an angel from heaven" in Gal 1:8), making it even more outrageous that Christian would regard their brothers and sisters, who will one day judge even angels, as unworthy to sit in judgment on their disputes with a fellow believer.

Paul's understanding of the solidarity of believers as a single body in Christ (and possibly also the Dan 7 background, depending on how one interprets the relationship between the Son of Man and "the holy ones of the Most High") would suggest that he is not asserting that the saints will judge the world (and angels) as independent individuals but as participants in the rule and judgment of the risen Christ (cf. 1 Cor 15:20–28; Eph 1:20–23). Nevertheless, the eschatological vision painted here still has implications in the present for the appropriateness of God's people, rather than the power brokers of the world, as a source of just judgments. "If the world is judged by you," he asks the Corinthians in an incredulous rhetorical question, "are you unworthy to judge the trivial cases?"[179] In describing cases such as the one that has been taken before the secular courts as "trivial" (ἐλάχιστος), Paul is describing all such earthly disputes ("matters of this life" [vv. 3, 4])[180] as trivial compared to the great issues that will be at stake in the eschatological judgment; in doing so, as Garland suggests, he implicitly "berates the eager plaintiff who has so maltreated a brother Christian and exposed the community to shame over what amounts to nothing."[181]

6:4. Verse 4 could be translated either as a question, expressing outrage at the Corinthians' conduct (CSB: "So if you have such matters, do you appoint as your judges those who have no standing in the church?"), as a statement or exclamation expressing similar outrage (NJB: "But when you have matters of this life to be judged, you bring them before those

---

[179] The CSB's "unworthy," reflecting the issues of status and honor that are at stake, is to be preferred over the NIV and NRSV's "incompetent" as a translation for the Greek word ἀνάξιος. The present tense verb form κρίνεται ("is judged") that Paul uses in v. 2b is best taken as functioning in a gnomic sense, taking a reality that has just been spoken of as a future event in v. 2a and holding it in view before the hearers to provide the premise for an omnitemporal logical inference that Paul is now drawing. Cf. David Mathewson and Elodie Ballantine Emig, *Intermediate Greek Grammar: Syntax for Students of the New Testament* (Grand Rapids: Baker, 2016), 128; Andreas J. Köstenberger, Benjamin L. Merkle, and Robert L. Plummer, *Going Deeper with New Testament Greek: An Intermediate Study of the Grammar and Syntax of the New Testament* (Nashville: B&H Academic, 2016), 258–59.

[180] βιωτικά, referring in vv. 3, 4a to the issues and logistics of everyday life.

[181] Garland, *1 Corinthians*, 204.

who are of no account in the Church!"), or as an imperative (NIV 1984: "Therefore, if you have disputes about such matters, appoint as judges even men of little account in the church!").

While the first two alternatives have some strong arguments in their favor (e.g., the argument that translating v. 4b as a question coheres neatly with the barrage of outraged rhetorical questions in vv. 1–6),[182] the version that translates it as an imperative also has some strong support (most of the patristic commentators, including Chrysostom and Theodoret)[183] and a number of good arguments in its favor:

(1) Paul nowhere uses the verb ἐξουθενέω ("despise"; here, in its passive participle form, translated by the CSB as "have no standing") to describe how Christians are to view outsiders, but rather to describe how Christians are viewed by the world and sometimes—scandalously—by their fellow believers (cf. 1 Cor 1:28; 16:11; Rom 14:3, 10);
(2) it makes better sense of the way in which the phrase μὲν οὖν (the normal meaning of which is something more like "rather" or "instead") connects the verse to its immediately preceding context; and
(3) Paul would be unlikely to refer to the Corinthians "appoint[ing]" the magistrates of the secular courts as judges.[184]

If the imperative reading is the best way to translate verse 4, the instruction seems to be a rebuke to the elite and aspiring members of the congregation who think that their more lowly fellow believers are "unworthy" (v. 2) to adjudicate their disputes.[185] In Paul's mind, the lowliest believer would be a better source of justice than the corrupt and ungodly city magistrates.

---

[182] Cf. Fee, *First Epistle to the Corinthians*, 259.

[183] Cf. Chrysostom, *Hom. 1 Cor.* 16:6, Theodoret, *Interp. Ep. 1 ad Cor.*, 195A, cited in Thiselton, *First Corinthians*, 433.

[184] Cf. Brent Kinman, "'Appoint the Despised as Judges!' (1 Corinthians 6:4)," *TynBul* 48 (1997): 345–54; Garland, *1 Corinthians*, 205; Brookins and Longenecker, *1 Corinthians 1–9*, 135–36.

[185] Paul may have in mind people such as Fortunatus and Achaicus, members of Stephanas's household whose names suggest their status as slaves or freedmen—a circumstance that may have contributed to the need Paul felt to give such a strong endorsement to their leadership role within the church in 16:15–18.

6:5–6. Paul's exclamation at the start of verse 5, "I say this to your shame!" could refer backward to verse 4 (especially if verse 4 is read as a statement or rhetorical question) or, more likely, could refer forward to what Paul goes on to say in verses 5b–6. The extent of Paul's outrage is such that he is quite content simply to say that he is writing to "shame" the Corinthians (in contrast with the more nuanced statement in 4:14). What follows in verse 5b is another biting, rhetorical question ("Can it be that there is not one wise person among you who is able to arbitrate between fellow believers?"), worded in a manner that implies a sarcastic challenge to the Corinthians' confidence in their own wisdom. "Believers" is literally "brothers" (cf. the repeated use of the same word in v. 6) carrying connotations of fictive kinship that further heighten the inappropriateness of the Corinthians' actions.[186] "And that before unbelievers" (v. 6b) may refer not only to the unbelieving magistrates before whose tribunal the cases are taken for judgment, but also, more broadly, to the watching pagan society before whose eyes the Christians are treating each other like this, to the shame of the church.

6:7. Having argued that the church ought to take responsibility for resolving disputes among its members, Paul now goes a step farther, suggesting that the very existence of such quarrels is already a "defeat," demonstrating a shameful unwillingness to renounce personal rights and possessions for the good of the other.

The ethic of nonretaliation and nonresistance implied by Paul's rhetorical questions ("Why not rather be wronged? Why not rather be cheated?"; cf. 4:12–13; Rom 12:17–21; 1 Thess 5:15) does not negate the responsibility of the congregation to provide justice for its members, which has been presupposed and strongly reinforced by Paul's first response to the situation in verses 1–6. It would be a grave mistake to read verse 7 as warrant for the rest of the church to impose pressure on a victim of abuse or exploitation at the hands of a fellow Christian to simply absorb the loss and allow the misconduct to continue. Such a reading would ignore the fact that Paul's forceful rhetoric is spoken into a context in which the plaintiff is in all probability the more powerful one, using the pagan courts as a vehicle to inflict injustice rather than a

[186] Cf. Kar Yong Lim, *Metaphors and Social Identity Formation in Paul's Letters to the Corinthians* (Eugene: Pickwick, 2017), 81–85; Trebilco, *Self-Designations*, 34–35; David G. Horrell, "From ἀδελφοί to οἶκος θεοῦ: Social Transformation in Pauline Christianity," *JBL* 120 (2001): 299–300.

powerless victim looking to the courts for redress of a real wrong; more importantly, it wrongly assumes that the willingness of an individual to forgo rights is morally the same as the apathy of a community, willing to stand by and allow that person to be deprived of justice.

6:8. In stark contrast to the posture of nonretaliation and nonresistance implied by Paul's questions in verse 7, he goes on in verse 8 to accuse the congregation members in question of actively "do[ing] wrong and cheat[ing]" (ἀλλ' ὑμεῖς ἀδικεῖτε καὶ ἀποστερεῖτε), and of doing so to their own brothers and sisters. It is grammatically possible that Paul is referring here to the actions of the defendants who have been dragged before the courts.[187] This is unlikely, however, given the strong adversative ἀλλά ("Instead") and emphatic ὑμεῖς ("you yourselves") that contrast verse 8 with the preceding verse and the heavy weight of condemnation that has fallen on the plaintiffs in verses 1–7; it would seem strange, after all that, for the climactic conclusion of the paragraph to suddenly be directed at the defendants. The far more likely reading of these verses is that Paul is still speaking in verse 8 of the conduct of the plaintiffs, who are using the court system to "do wrong and cheat."[188] Paul's additional outrage at the fact that this is being done "to brothers and sisters" is an example of the ethical distinction that he draws between the general responsibility to treat all people rightly and the even greater responsibility of believers toward fellow members of the household of faith (cf. Gal 6:10).

6:9–10. While 6:9–11 anticipates some of the issues and ideas of 6:12–20, its closer connection is with 6:1–8, reinforcing the distinction Paul has drawn between "the unrighteous" and "the saints" (vv. 9–10; cf. v. 1) and grounding it in the gracious work of God in Christ, by the Spirit (v. 11). There appear to have been at least two key influences on Paul's selection of the vices that he includes in the list in verses 9–10: (1) the commands and warnings in Exodus, Leviticus, and Deuteronomy about ethical and religious practices that are incompatible with the holiness of God's people and (2) the behaviors that were practiced by some, at least, within the Corinthian church.

"Don't you know ... ?" (v. 9), like the other five such questions in this chapter, functions to remind the Corinthians of something they ought to

[187] As is assumed, for example, by Fee, *First Epistle to the Corinthians*, 263–64.

[188] Cf. Garland, *1 Corinthians*, 210; Thiselton, *First Corinthians*, 437–38.

know and to rebuke them for not living out the implications of it. In this case, the immediate issue that provokes this reminder is the way in which believers have been suing fellow believers before the pagan magistrates.[189]

The word translated as "the unrighteous" (ἄδικοι) is the same word Paul has already used in verse 1 and is from the same root as the verb translated as "wronged" and "wrong" in verses 7–8. While some commentators (e.g., Garland) highlight the connection with verse 1 and imply that the main function of verses 9–11 is to remind the Corinthians that the pagan magistrates to whom they are taking their cases will have no part in God's kingdom,[190] the stronger and more immediate connection is with verses 7–8: Paul is reminding the Corinthians that those who persist in a lifestyle of "wronging" others (e.g., by using their economic and social power to take advantage of them in the court system) show by their conduct that they have no place in the kingdom of God. The twofold warning that such people "will not inherit God's kingdom" (vv. 9–10) echoes the language of Jesus's teaching (e.g., Matt 25:34), using the phrase here to refer to the future consummation of God's rule (cf. the "kingdom" language of Dan 7, to which Paul has already alluded in v. 2).[191] In speaking of believers as a people who "will … inherit" (κληρονομήσουσιν) the kingdom (cf. 15:50; Gal 5:21), Paul (like Jesus) is drawing on the Deuteronomic picture of the land of Israel as the "inheritance" of God's people, fulfilled eschatologically in the eternal kingdom that will be received and possessed by the saints (cf. Dan 7:18, 22, 27). The admonition, "Do not be deceived" (v. 9; cf. 15:33, Gal 6:7; also the similar phrase in Eph 5:6) that precedes the first of these two warnings is a characteristically Pauline phrase that typically introduces a solemn warning about the consequences of sinful behavior and reflects Paul's assumption that temptation to sin is frequently accompanied by the deceptive message that it is possible to sin without consequences (cf. Gen 3:4).

The vice catalog that follows in verses 9b–10, listing categories of people whose unrepentant conduct will exclude them from inheriting the kingdom, includes the six kinds of people already spoken of in 5:10–11 ("sexually immoral people" [πόρνοι], "idolaters" [εἰδωλολάτραι], "greedy

---

[189] The NIV correctly includes the "or" (ἤ) at the start of v. 9, which suggests a slightly stronger connection between vv. 9–11 and vv. 1–8 than the CSB translation implies.

[190] Cf. Garland, *1 Corinthians*, 196.

[191] Cf. Brian S. Rosner, "The Origin and Meaning of 1 Cor 6:9–11 in Context," BibZeit 40 (1996): 252.

people" [πλεονέκται], "drunkards" [μέθυσοι] "verbally abusive people" [λοίδοροι], and "swindlers" [ἅρπαγες]) and inserts four more into the middle of the list: "adulterers" (μοιχοί), "males who have sex with males" (μαλακοί and ἀρσενοκοῖται), and "thieves" (κλέπται).

"Adulterers" (μοιχοί) is a narrower term than "sexually immoral people" (πόρνοι) and refers specifically to married people who engage in sexual activity outside of marriage. "Thieves" (κλέπται) is the general word for people who commit theft, without the more particular connotations of theft by deception carried by ἅρπαγες ("swindlers"). The two remaining words, μαλακοί and ἀρσενοκοῖται ("males who have sex with males") have been the subject of much discussion in recent decades, in the context of the larger controversy about the Bible's teaching on homosexuality and its implications for Christians today. Proponents of alternative theories about the meaning of these words have included John Boswell, who suggests that μαλακός is a derogatory epithet for moral weakness (with no necessary connection to male homosexuality) and ἀρσενοκοῖται refers to (heterosexual) male prostitutes;[192] Robin Scroggs, who suggests that the combination of terms refers narrowly to young male prostitutes (μαλακοί) and the men who use them (ἀρσενοκοῖται);[193] and Dale Martin, who suggests that the meaning of ἀρσενοκοῖται is irretrievable and that μαλακοί is an ambiguous insult-word, meaning something like "effeminate," and that the two terms, taken together, are irredeemably useless as a foundation for Christian ethical arguments.[194]

All three arguments have met with convincing refutation in the scholarly literature. A careful examination of the available evidence suggests the following conclusions:

(1) μαλακοί (which, when not used in contexts relating to matters of sex or gender, usually means "soft") is used in the Greek literature to refer pejoratively to young men who adopt effeminate

---

[192] Cf. John Boswell, *Christianity, Social Tolerance, and Homosexuality: Gay People in Western Europe from the Beginning of the Christian Era to the Fourteenth Century*, 2nd ed. (Chicago: University of Chicago Press, 2015), 341–44.

[193] Robin Scroggs, *The New Testament and Homosexuality: Contextual Background for Contemporary Debate* (Philadelphia: Fortress, 1983), 106–9. An interpretation of this sort is followed by a number of others, including James V. Brownson, *Bible, Gender, Sexuality: Reframing the Church's Debate on Same-Sex Relationships* (Grand Rapids: Eerdmans, 2013), 274.

[194] Dale B. Martin, *Sex and the Single Savior: Gender and Sexuality in Biblical Interpretation* (Louisville: Westminster John Knox, 2006), 37–50.

styles and mannerisms; in many (though not all) cases, μαλακοί acted as the passive partners in homosexual activity, and the use of the word by Paul in combination with ἀρσενοκοῖται (see below) strongly suggests that it has that meaning here.[195]

(2) ἀρσενοκοῖται is not found in the surviving literature earlier than 1 Corinthians and appears to be a word coined within Hellenistic Judaism (possibly by Paul himself) as a compound term formed from ἄρσενος ("with a man") and κοίτην ("sleeps" [in a sexual sense]) as they occur in Leviticus 18:22 ("You are not to sleep with a man as with a woman") and Leviticus 20:13 ("If a man sleeps with a man as with a woman …").

(3) While much Greco-Roman male homosexuality was between an older active partner and a younger passive partner, and this sort of relationship may well have been in the forefront of Paul's thinking here in 1 Corinthians 5, the LXX background of Paul's terminology and the parallel with mutual adult lesbianism in Romans 1:26–27 make it very unlikely that his condemnation is limited to pederasty or prostitution.[196]

Bruce Winter plausibly suggests that the reason Paul here describes men who engage in homosexual activity by means of not one general term but two terms, referring to the passive and the active partner respectively, is that Roman society drew a distinction between the passive partner (who was despised) and the active partner (whose activity was considered entirely unproblematic, provided the passive partner was a slave or a noncitizen). This distinction, which was of fundamental significance for Greco-Roman attitudes toward male homosexuality, appears to have been of no ethical consequence in Paul's mind, and his choice of words here may well have been made in order to emphasize that fact.[197]

---

[195] Cf. William R. G. Loader, *Sexuality in the New Testament: Understanding the Key Texts* (Louisville: Westminster John Knox, 2010), 31.

[196] Similar conclusions are argued for, on similar grounds, in Robert A. J. Gagnon, *The Bible and Homosexual Practice: Texts and Hermeneutics* (Nashville: Abingdon, 2001), chs. 5–6; Thiselton, *First Corinthians*, 440–53; Gardner, *1 Corinthians*, 264–69.

[197] Winter, *After Paul Left Corinth*, 110–20. Kyle Harper comments, somewhat similarly: "Early Christian literature—with one exception—offers none of the vicious attacks on sexual passivity that can be found in Lucian or Achilles Tatius, because the precise synthesis of machismo and sexual moralism was wholly absent from Christian discourse. Yet none of this means that the Christian posture towards same-sex love was uncertain. From Paul onward,

6:11. After the stark picture Paul has painted in verses 9–10, verse 11 goes on to remind the Corinthians that these behaviors were once the lifestyle of some of them, but that their identity and situation have since been radically changed by the gracious work of God in Christ, through the Spirit. The reminder is simultaneously a rebuke to any self-righteous amnesia and an urgent encouragement to all the Corinthians to live up to their new identity. "But" (ἀλλά) is repeated three times in the Greek ("But you were washed, [but] you were sanctified, [but] you were justified") adding emphasis to the once/now contrast that verse 11 establishes between the Corinthians' preconversion existence and their life in Christ. "Washed" (ἀπελούσασθε), "sanctified" (ἡγιάσθητε), "justified" (ἐδικαιώθητε) are three terms (all aorist tense verb forms) used by Paul to describe the various aspects of the Corinthians' conversion: they were forgiven and made new ("washed"),[198] set apart as God's holy people ("sanctified"), and declared to be in right standing with God ("justified"). The concluding phrases describe these three dimensions of the Corinthians' conversion as an expression of the sovereign authority of Christ ("in the name of the Lord Jesus Christ") brought about by the activity of the powerful Spirit of God ("and by the Spirit of our God").

Bridge

Paul's fierce response to the predatory and litigious conduct of the Corinthians should serve as a warning against any teaching (or unspoken assumption) that restricts the gospel's implications to the private and domestic sphere and leaves matters of business and finance to be conducted according to the logic of the marketplace, restricted only by the limits of what the legal system will permit. Christians are, of course, to uphold and abide by the law, except in circumstances where doing so

---

Christian sexual ideology collapsed all forms of same-sex contact, whether pederastic or companionate, into one category." Harper, *From Shame to Sin*, 99. The "one exception" to which Harper is referring is Clement of Alexandria (cf. Harper, *From Shame to Sin*, 114–15).

198 Thiselton correctly emphasizes that the forgiveness Paul has in mind here is not just the forgiveness for which the believer asks day by day but "*a wiping clean of the slate once-for-all*" (emphasis original) as symbolized by the ritual of Christian baptism; Thiselton, *First Corinthians*, 454. Paul uses similar imagery in Eph 5:25b–27 to describe a work of Christ that includes not only the remission of past sins but also an initiation of a process of renewal by the word, aimed at a present and enduring transformation of conduct; it is likely that the image carries a similar sense here. Cf. David I. Starling, *Reading Ephesians and Colossians: A Literary and Theological Commentary*, RNT (Macon: Smyth & Helwys, 2020), 144–45.

would be unjust or otherwise disobedient to God; Paul's words here do not take away from the legitimate and necessary role that the state has been charged by God to perform, protecting the vulnerable by deterring and punishing wrongdoing (cf. Rom 13:1–7). But the responsibilities of Christians do not stop at the bare minimum requirement that they comply with the letter of the law, nor does the existence of legal machinery that can be exploited by those with the economic and social power to do so justify its use by Christians to advance their own interests at the expense of others. In such matters, as in all things, Christians are to be driven by the priorities of the kingdom of God, pursuing the welfare of others (and especially of the vulnerable and powerless), willing to set aside their rights and forgo retaliation, and committed to exercising their collective responsibility to behave as a just and peaceable community (cf. Rom 12:9–21; 13:8–14).

C. Permissiveness and Prostitution (6:12–20)

> [12] "Everything is permissible for me," but not everything is beneficial.
> "Everything is permissible for me," but I will not be mastered by any-
> thing. [13] "Food is for the stomach and the stomach for food," and God
> will do away with both of them. However, the body is not for sexual
> immorality but for the Lord, and the Lord for the body. [14] God raised
> up the Lord and will also raise us up by his power. [15] Don't you know
> that your bodies are a part of Christ's body? So should I take a part of
> Christ's body and make it part of a prostitute? Absolutely not! [16] Don't
> you know that anyone joined to a prostitute is one body with her? For
> Scripture says, **The two will become one flesh.** [17] But anyone joined
> to the Lord is one spirit with him.
>
> [18] Flee sexual immorality! Every other sin a person commits is outside
> the body, but the person who is sexually immoral sins against his own
> body. [19] Don't you know that your body is a temple of the Holy Spirit
> who is in you, whom you have from God? You are not your own, [20] for
> you were bought at a price. So glorify God with your body.

Context/Structure/Form

Chapter 6 verses 12–20 serves as a conclusion to the section in chapters 5–6, in which Paul responds to reports of sexual immorality and litigation. In this paragraph, rather than beginning with the behavior of the Corinthians that has been reported to him, he begins at the level of attitudes and assumptions, makes brief mention of πορνεία ("sexual immorality") in verse 13, and only in verses 15–17 introduces the more specific issue of sex with a "prostitute" (πόρνη), before returning in verse 18 to the language of πορνεία and, in verses 19–20, to theological general principles.

Because πορνεία and πόρνη are such closely related words, it could be the case that within this paragraph Paul is using πορνεία to refer narrowly to sex with prostitutes. It is more likely, however, that he is still using it with the broad, general sense that it has carried throughout the rest of chapters 5–6. If that is the case, then reports about sex with prostitutes may not be the starting point of this paragraph at all; rather, sex with prostitutes (vv. 15–17) may simply be a particular example of a more general point about sexual immorality (vv. 13–18), which is in turn an example of the general principles that Paul reminds the Corinthians of in verses 12–20, in response to the permissiveness of the slogan that he quotes in the opening verse of the paragraph. Still, the force and immediacy of Paul's language ("Flee sexual immorality!"; v. 18) suggests that the example is not merely a theoretical one but one Paul knows or suspects to be a real problem among the Corinthian Christians.

Comments

6:12. Paul commences this paragraph with a twice-stated declaration—"Everything is permissible for me"—which most commentators (and most English versions, including the CSB) plausibly interpret as a Corinthian slogan that Paul quotes and then responds to.[199] Various suggestions have been made as to the source of the slogan:

(1) Many suggest that the slogan was originally Paul's own, referring to the freedom of Christians from the ritual purity laws of the Mosaic covenant, and that the Corinthians have generalized its application far beyond Paul's intention, making use of it to justify behaviors such as eating idol meat (cf. 10:23) and engaging in sexual immorality.[200]

(2) Some suggest that it was based on gnostic ideas, relying on the unlikely hypothesis of a pre-Christian gnostic movement that was already influential in first-century Corinth.[201]

---

[199] For an argument against this view, see Garland, *1 Corinthians*, 226–28.

[200] E.g., Fee, *First Epistle to the Corinthians*, 278; Robertson and Plummer, *First Corinthians*, 121–22.

[201] E.g., Barrett, *First Corinthians*, 144–45; Rudolf Bultmann, *Theology of the New Testament*, 2 vols. (New York: Scribner, 1951–1955), 1:341.

(3) A number of commentators offer the more likely suggestion that it was based on Greek philosophical ideas (e.g., a simplified and misappropriated version of the Stoic doctrine of the wise man's freedom, combined with an exaggerated version of anthropological dualism in which bodily functions were regarded as morally irrelevant).[202]

(4) Bruce Winter has argued plausibly that it would have been understood by Paul and the Corinthians as an expression of the cultural values and assumptions of the Greco-Roman elite—in particular, the attitude of the freeborn male who had reached adulthood and had put on the toga virilis, which gave him the right to eat and drink at banquets and sleep with the prostitutes (variously referred to as πόρναι and ἑταῖραι) who were routinely present at such occasions.[203]

Whatever the source of the slogan, Paul counters it with two responses: "but not everything is beneficial ... but I will not be mastered by anything." The first replaces a self-centered focus on what is "lawful for me" with a concern for what is beneficial for others (cf. 10:23, 33, where it is clear that Paul's concept of what is "beneficial" includes the good of others, not merely one's own personal advantage);[204] the second is a reminder that "freedom" used to indulge selfish desires becomes a new and worse enslavement to the thing that one craves.[205] Both replies make use of language and ideas that have affinities with the Stoic traditions that seem to have influenced the Corinthians with whom Paul is taking issue; Paul, it seems, is "selecting his words with special awareness of his audience's

---

[202] E.g., Albert V. Garcilazo, *The Corinthian Dissenters and the Stoics*, SBL (New York: Peter Lang, 2007), 50–62; Brookins, *Reading 1 Corinthians*, 55–56; Brookins, "The Wise Corinthians," 64–70; Hans Conzelmann, *1 Corinthians: A Commentary on the First Epistle to the Corinthians*, Hermeneia (Philadelphia: Fortress, 1975), 108–9.

[203] Winter, *After Paul Left Corinth*, 76–109. On the blurry line between πόρναι and ἑταῖραι in the Roman period, see McClure, *Courtesans at Table*, 9–17; Harper, *From Shame to Sin*, 47–50; Montserrat, *Sex and Society*, 107–8.

[204] On the traditional use of in συμφέρειν in ancient political discourse as an appeal to the common advantage of the community, see Mitchell, *Paul and the Rhetoric of Reconciliation*, 29–31.

[205] On self-mastery as a theme in Stoic philosophy (and the Greco-Roman philosophical tradition more broadly), see Stanley K. Stowers, "Paul and Self-Mastery," in *Paul in the Greco-Roman World: A Handbook*, vol. 2, ed. J. Paul Sampley (London: T&T Clark, 2016), 270–300; C. Kavin Rowe, *One True Life: The Stoics and Early Christians as Rival Traditions* (New Haven: Yale University Press, 2016), 30–36.

proclivities," alerting them that even the pagan philosophies they have been influenced by do not provide clear and unequivocal support for their conduct.[206]

6:13–14. Once again, most commentators and English versions read verse 13 as a Corinthian slogan. Thiselton plausibly suggests that the quotation should continue right to the end of the sentence (as it does in the NIV), expressing the Corinthians' superficially Christianized version of the traditional Greek contempt for the material, physical, and mortal.[207] Based on this reading, he paraphrases the Corinthian attitude to mean: "all this is transitory and without permanent significance for people of the Spirit such as us."[208]

If this is the case, then the slogan about food and the body is really being used by the Corinthians to make two interrelated points about sex: (1) the body exists merely as a vehicle for physical functions and appetites like food and sex ("food is for the stomach and the stomach for food"), and (2) these physical appetites and activities are of no enduring significance, because God is interested in only the eternal, spiritual dimension of a person ("and God will do away with both of them"). In response to these two subpoints of the Corinthian slogan, Paul responds that (1) the body does not exist merely for its appetites (and certainly not for the illicit satisfaction of those appetites) but for the Lord Jesus, and he values and cares about it ("the body is not for sexual immorality but for the Lord, and the Lord for the body" [v. 13b]); and (2) the body is indeed mortal, but the God who raised Jesus bodily will also raise us bodily with him ("God raised up the Lord and will also raise us up by his power" [v. 14]).[209]

6:15–17. The close relationship between the believer's body and the Lord expressed in verses 13–14 is developed further in verses 15–17. The bodies of Christians, Paul tells his readers, are "a part of Christ's body" (μέλη Χριστοῦ). When he goes on in verse 15b to speak of "tak[ing]" the members of Christ, he uses a verb (αἴρω) that typically means "remove"

---

[206] Brookins, *Reading 1 Corinthians*, 57; Brookins, *Corinthian Wisdom*, 176, 200.

[207] Similarly, Ciampa and Rosner, *The First Letter to the Corinthians*, 254; Brookins, *Reading 1 Corinthians*, 57.

[208] Thiselton, *First Corinthians*, 462.

[209] Cf. Brookins, *Reading 1 Corinthians*, 57. An alternative (or additional) suggestion as to why Paul associates food and sex so closely in these verses is that Paul has in view the context of a Greco-Roman convivium, in which the host provided his guests with food and alcohol in excess and prostitutes for them to have sex with as part of the after-dinner entertainment. Winter, *After Paul Left Corinth*, 86–93.

or "take away"; the image is of wrenching or tearing a limb from Christ's body to unite it instead with the body of a prostitute.

The force of the metaphor in verse 15b relies on two assumptions, which are made explicit in verses 16–17: (1) sex, even casual sex, is a unitive act that makes two people (at least temporarily) "one body" (ἓν σῶμα) (v. 16); and (2) a believer is "joined to the Lord"(κολλώμενος τῷ κυρίῳ) and consequently "one spirit with him" (ἓν πνεῦμα) (v. 17). In speaking of a man being "joined to" (κολλώμενος) a prostitute, the verb Paul uses (κολλάω) normally refers to the literal joining or gluing together of two objects and can be used metaphorically to express joining in relationship, including sexual relationships (e.g., Matt 19:5) and economic ones (e.g., Luke 15:15).

To support his claim that "anyone joined to a prostitute is one body with her," Paul quotes from LXX Genesis 2:24: "For Scripture says, 'The two will become one flesh.'" While Paul clearly does not draw the conclusion that every casual sexual encounter creates a marriage, with all the corresponding ethical entailments, he is saying that sex, even casual sex, creates a bodily unity between two people that was originally created by God to be an expression of the permanent unity of marriage.

A Christian who uses his body to have sex with a prostitute forgets or ignores the fact that he is not an independent, autonomous person. He already belongs to Christ—"joined to the Lord ... one spirit with him" (v. 17). In speaking of the Christian as "one spirit" with Christ, Paul is not saying that it is only the "spirit" of a person that is affected by union with Christ. Rather, while distinguishing the sexual, bodily union that a person has with a prostitute from the union with Christ that is effected by the Spirit,[210] Paul goes on in the immediately following verses (as he has already foreshadowed in v. 13) to stress the implications that this spiritual union with Christ has for the whole embodied person.

6:18. The explanations, argumentation, and rhetorical questions of verses 12–17 are followed in verse 18a by an imperative—"Flee sexual immorality!" (φεύγετε τὴν πορνείαν)—that is forceful, succinct, and urgent. The verb Paul uses, along with the metaphor that it implies, suggests a possible allusion to the story of Joseph (literally) fleeing from

---

[210] Cf. Fee, *First Epistle to the Corinthians*, 287.

the advances of Potiphar's wife and contributes to the vividness of the warning.[211]

The statement that follows—"Every other sin a person commits is outside the body"—could possibly be another Corinthian slogan, expressing the idea that physical acts are ultimately inconsequential because they are about the external interactions of the body rather than the internal life of the soul.[212] On this reading, the Corinthian slogan expresses an idea that Paul rejects outright, citing sexual immorality as one case at least where the Corinthian slogan breaks down. More likely, however, the whole sentence is Paul's own statement, setting up a contrast between sexual sins (which are "against [one's] own body") and other sins (which are "outside the body"). The contrast is not so much a quantitative difference as a qualitative one.[213] While numerous other sins (e.g., drunkenness and gluttony) may have negative bodily consequences, there is still something uniquely damaging about sexual immorality, because there is something uniquely self-exposing and self-committing about sex.[214]

6:19–20. Verse 19a builds on the statement in verse 17 that "anyone joined to the Lord is one spirit with him," making explicit its implications for the bodily existence and activities of believers by reminding the readers (via another "Don't you know?" rhetorical question) that the body of each of them is "a temple of the Holy Spirit."[215] While the similar image in 3:16 is a corporate one, in which "God's temple" is the whole Christian

---

[211] Cf. the use of the same verb, φεύγω, in LXX Gen 39:12 and the identically worded command in T. Reub. 5, both of which are discussed in Roy E. Ciampa and Brian S. Rosner, "1 Corinthians," in *Commentary on the New Testament Use of the Old Testament*, ed. G. K. Beale and D. A. Carson (Grand Rapids: Baker, 2007), 714.

[212] Cf. Collins, *First Corinthians*, 248; Hays, *First Corinthians*, 105.

[213] Cf. Garland, *1 Corinthians*, 237, citing Ernst Käsemann, *Essays on New Testament Themes* (London: SCM, 1964), 133; Brendan Byrne, "Sinning Against One's Own Body: Paul's Understanding of the Sexual Relationship in 1 Corinthians 6:18," *CBQ* 45 (1983): 613.

[214] Cf. Brian Brock and Bernd Wannenwetsch, *The Malady of the Christian Body*, vol. 1 of *A Theological Exposition of Paul's First Letter to the Corinthians* (Eugene: Cascade, 2016), 129 (emphasis original): "To sin against the body is to turn the body into a liar by overriding its own communicative action by means of a supervening edict ('This has no strings attached/ it is off the books'). To sin against the body lies in this perversion of its communicative meaning in the interest of sustaining illicit *social* bonds."

[215] Here and in v. 20b, "body" (σῶμα) is singular and "your" (ὑμῶν) is plural, in what is almost certainly, in both cases, to be understood in a distributive sense as "the body of each of you." Cf. Fee, *First Epistle to the Corinthians*, 291, citing Rom 8:23 as a parallel example. Brookins and Longenecker, *1 Corinthians 1-9*, 148–49, read the first instance distributively and the second as a reference to the corporate body of the church.

community, its application here is to the individual Christian. Against the idea that spiritual people have risen to a plane in which their bodily existence is now unimportant, Paul argues that the indwelling of the Spirit has exactly the opposite effect, making their bodies a sacred place in which God dwells and is worshiped. The further elaboration on the Holy Spirit as the one "who is in you, whom you have from God" emphasizes in passing that the Christian's experience of the Spirit is not a matter of human accomplishment or technique but a gift of God's grace (cf. 1:4–9; 2:12; 4:7) and a reminder of the authority that God has over believers as the source of their life and holiness (cf. 1 Thess 4:8).

The temple metaphor of verse 19a is followed by a slave metaphor in verses 19b–20a: "You are not your own, for you were bought at a price." The picture is drawn from the slave market and describes conversion as a kind of purchase, in which a slave is transferred by sale from one owner to another. Paul does not expand on the image to tell us what the price was or to whom it was paid—presumably the previous owner was sin (cf. Rom 6:12) and the price paid was the blood of Jesus (cf. Eph 1:7)—but the point here in 1 Corinthians 6 is simply that a transfer of ownership has taken place and that the believer in Jesus is now the possession of Christ.

The imperative with which Paul concludes the chapter—"So glorify God with your body"—continues the emphasis implied in verse 13b and verse 19a on the positive significance of the body as a place of God's presence, belonging to him, and speaks of the bodily existence of the believer as a sphere in which to "glorify" God by actions in the world that express praise toward God and contribute to the public honor of his name.

Bridge

For those of us who live in the post-Christendom West, Paul's teaching on sexual ethics, here and elsewhere in 1 Corinthians, has a striking and powerful resonance. In the not too distant past, when Christianity was still (in theory) the dominant religious and ethical tradition of our culture, it made sense, at least at a superficial level, to preach as if the content of Christian morality could safely be assumed as self-evident and the gospel was simply a remedy for our failure to live up to it.

But the gradual unravelling of Christendom and the emergence of the new cultural/political order that is replacing it have exposed the fact that something more is needed (and always was). The gospel was never meant to be merely a remedy for when we fail to live up to a moral code that we are all instinctively aware of. The gospel is the center of our whole moral vision as Christians, the touchstone against which we measure all the various fragments of moral intuition that we were shaped by, and the criterion by which we reform them into something true and coherent and beautiful. A consistently evangelical ministry is informed by the gospel from start to finish, and a consistently evangelical account of sexual ethics will be pervasively shaped by the grand narrative of Scripture and its climax in the message of the gospel.[216]

That this is the case is evident at multiple points within 1 Corinthians 5–7 and especially in the challenge that Paul issues to the Corinthians' self-serving permissiveness in 6:12–20. Sex means what it means because, Scripture informs us, the Creator's purpose in the beginning was that "the two will become one flesh" (v. 16). What we do with our bodies matters, because "the body is ... for the Lord, and the Lord for the body" (v. 13). We know this because "God raised up the Lord and will also raise us up by his power" (v. 14). The gospel not only gives us a motivation for obeying a moral code we already know and forgiveness for when we fail to do so; it also reframes our whole understanding of morality and teaches us a new vision for how to live in the world.

A key part of that vision is what the gospel teaches us about belonging. The good news includes the news that we have been set apart as the special possession of God, sanctified "in the name of the Lord Jesus Christ" (v. 11). The body is "for the Lord" (v. 13), and the body of each one of us is "part of Christ's body" (v. 15). "You are not your own," Paul reminds the Corinthians. "You were bought at a price" (vv. 19–20). And this is good news. Within a culture like our own, in which the forces of both economics and ideology conspire to tear us apart and isolate us from one another, the gospel gives us roots and a home and a family and a name. Becoming a Christian means being called to be Christ's and being given the gift of belonging. For us, as for the Corinthians, this is a precious and fundamentally important reality, with the power to transform our perspective not only on our sexuality but on the whole of our lives.

---

[216] See especially O'Donovan, *Resurrection and Moral Order*, and the application of O'Donovan's paradigm for evangelical ethics to matters of marriage and sexuality in Christopher Ash, *Marriage: Sex in the Service of God* (Leicester: Inter-Varsity Press, 2003), and Glynn Harrison, *A Better Story: God, Sex And Human Flourishing* (Downers Grove: InterVarsity Press, 2017).

IV. Responses Regarding Marriage and Virgins (7:1–40)

In chapter 7 Paul (finally) turns to the matters raised in the letter that the Corinthians wrote to him. By dealing with the reports of divisions, immorality, and predatory litigation first, he has implicitly asserted his pastoral authority over the Corinthians and reminded them that the theories and opinions of the group that wrote the letter are not necessarily the most important or urgent issues that need to be addressed. There is an elephant in the room (several elephants, actually!) that cannot just be politely ignored.

Fee is probably correct to argue, based on the tone and content of Paul's responses, that the Corinthian letter was not simply a respectful request for spiritual advice but a combative response to his previous letter (cf. 5:9): "In light of their own theology of 'S/spirit,' with heavy emphasis on 'wisdom' and 'knowledge,' they apparently have answered Paul with a kind of 'Why can't we?' attitude, in which they are looking for his response."[217]

Paul addresses the matters raised in the letter one by one. Note the plural "matters" that is implied by the Greek grammar in verse 1[218] and the περὶ δέ formula that is repeatedly used throughout the remaining chapters (7:1, 25; 8:1, [4]; 12:1; 16:1, 12), which most commentators take as a reference to items raised by the Corinthians.[219] The sequence in which Paul deals with the issues has a certain logic to it in relation to the rest of the letter, suggesting that Paul may not be simply working his way through the issues in the same order that they were raised in the Corinthians' letter.

The first two matters Paul addresses (in 7:1–24 and 7:25–40) both relate to questions of marriage, sex, and celibacy. Paul deals with these issues first, perhaps because they relate closely to the reports of sexual immorality to which he has been responding in chapters 5–6. Although he addresses a wide range of marriage-related questions within the chapter, he is not presenting a systematic Christian theology of marriage; rather, he is responding to a specific set of questions, ideas, and practices that appear to have been prevalent within the Corinthian church.

---

[217] Fee, *First Epistle to the Corinthians*, 295.

[218] Specifically, the plural relative pronoun, ὧν.

[219] For an example of the περὶ δέ formula performing a similar function in a surviving papyrus letter from the late first century BC, see *BGU* 4 1141, lines 31, 40.

Among the philosophers of the Greco-Roman world there had been a long-running, vigorously argued discussion about marriage, which educated and semieducated people in first-century Corinth could hardly have been unaware of. The debate, as it had played across the two or three preceding centuries and continued to play out in Paul's day, was in essence an argument between two competing philosophies—the philosophy of the Cynics and that of the Stoics. The Stoic position, in its classical form, was to praise marriage as one of the fundamental duties that the wise man should perform. Because humans are by nature political beings, because the wise man lives in accordance with nature, and because the household was the basic unit of society, a wise and morally upright young man should consider marrying and establishing a household to be "among the primary and most necessary actions."[220] The Cynics, on the other hand, placed the highest value on the freedom of the individual and pictured the wise man not as a citizen of the city but of the world. In keeping with that perspective, the philosophers of the Cynic tradition were famously opposed to marriage and deeply skeptical about the value of sex. According to Diogenes, the most famous of the Cynics, married love was "the business of the idle," and the wise would be better occupied with other pursuits.[221] Epicurus, who was influenced by the Cynic view on this issue, counseled the wise man not to marry, because marrying and caring for a family would distract him from the life of a philosopher.[222] Christians living in Corinth—or at least the more educated and aspirational ones among them—would have been exposed to both of these views and would have felt the pressure to declare themselves in favor of one view or the other.

The slogan Paul quotes in verse 1b is probably indicative of a perspective that had gained some adherents among the Corinthian elite to which he is responding. Some, it seems (influenced perhaps by Cynic philosophical opinion, reinforced by their self-perception as "spiritual"), are advocating a policy of celibacy for the sake of spirituality, even for the married, questioning the sanctity of marriages to nonbelievers and placing pressure on widows, widowers, and virgins to stay single and

---

220 Antipater of Tarsus, *On Marriage* (*Stoicorum Vetica Fragmenta* 3.254–57).

221 Diogenes Laertius, *Lives* 6.51; cf. 6.54.

222 Diogenes Laertius, *Lives*, 10.119; cf. the comments on the Cynic view of marriage in Epictetus, *Diatr.* 3.22.70.

celibate.[223] It is this philosophy that appears to have been advocated within the portion of the Corinthian letter that dealt with matters of marriage, sex, and celibacy, and it is in response to a viewpoint of this sort that Paul frames his own words of command, concession, and advice giving within this chapter.

The chapter falls into three main sections:

(1) a series of words of command and concession, addressed primarily to the married members of the congregation, together with a brief aside in verses 8–9 to the unmarried and widows (vv. 1–16);
(2) a statement and explanation of the general principles that inform Paul's commands and advice giving (vv. 17–24); and
(3) a series of words of advice relating primarily to the situation of virgins (betrothed and unbetrothed), stressing the advantages of remaining single in view of the "present distress" and the "limited" time that remains in the last days (vv. 25–40).

A. Commands and Concessions, Primarily Addressed to the Married (7:1–16)

> 1 Now in response to the matters you wrote about: "It is good for a man not to have sexual relations with a woman." 2 But because sexual immorality is so common, each man should have sexual relations with his own wife, and each woman should have sexual relations with her own husband. 3 A husband should fulfill his marital duty to his wife, and likewise a wife to her husband. 4 A wife does not have the right over her own body, but her husband does. In the same way, a husband does not have the right over his own body, but his wife does. 5 Do not deprive one another—except when you agree for a time, to devote yourselves to prayer. Then come together again; otherwise, Satan may tempt you because of your lack of self-control. 6 I say this as a concession, not as a command. 7 I wish that all people were as I am. But each has his own gift from God, one person has this gift, another has that.

[223] On the possibility that the Corinthians' attitudes to marriage and celibacy were influenced by Cynic philosophical ideas, see especially Will Deming, *Paul on Marriage and Celibacy: The Hellenistic Background of 1 Corinthians 7*, 2nd ed. (Grand Rapids: Eerdmans, 2004), 107–12. On the influence of the self-perception of the elite members of the Corinthian church as "spiritual," see especially Judith M. Gundry Volf, "Controlling the Bodies: A Theological Profile of the Corinthian Sexual Ascetics (1 Cor 7)," in Bieringer, *The Corinthian Correspondence*, 519–41.

> 8 I say to the unmarried and to widows: It is good for them if they remain as I am. 9 But if they do not have self-control, they should marry, since it is better to marry than to burn with desire.
>
> 10 To the married I give this command—not I, but the Lord—a wife is not to leave her husband. 11 But if she does leave, she must remain unmarried or be reconciled to her husband—and a husband is not to divorce his wife. 12 But I (not the Lord) say to the rest: If any brother has an unbelieving wife and she is willing to live with him, he must not divorce her. 13 Also, if any woman has an unbelieving husband and he is willing to live with her, she must not divorce her husband. 14 For the unbelieving husband is made holy by the wife, and the unbelieving wife is made holy by the husband. Otherwise your children would be unclean, but as it is they are holy. 15 But if the unbeliever leaves, let him leave. A brother or a sister is not bound in such cases. God has called you to live in peace. 16 Wife, for all you know, you might save your husband. Husband, for all you know, you might save your wife.

Context/Structure/Form

Paul's words in the first section of the chapter are addressed primarily to the married members of the congregation (with the exception of a brief aside to the unmarried and widows in vv. 8–9). After quoting what appears to have been a Corinthian slogan in verse 1a, Paul responds with a series of commands and concessions, punctuated by the occasional word of explanation (e.g., vv. 4, 7, 14b, 15b–16) and advice (e.g., v. 8).

The commands and concessions in verses 1b–7 are addressed (by implication, given their content) to married people and focus on sexual relations within marriage. Verses 8–9 are addressed to the unmarried and widows, offering them a word of advice about the benefits of singleness and a command that those who are not exercising self-control should marry. Verses 10–16 return the focus to the situation of the married, addressing them directly with a series of commands and concessions (with brief supporting explanations) regarding the permanence of marriage.

Comments

7:1. The opening sentence of verse 1 ("Now in response to the matters you wrote about") introduces a new section of the letter, in which Paul addresses the issues raised by the Corinthians' letter. The περὶ δέ ("Now in response to ...") formula recurs on multiple occasions in the remaining chapters of the letter (7:25; 8:1, [4]; 12:1; 16:1, 12), on each occasion signaling a new topic that Paul will address.

Verse 1b ("It is good for a man not to have sexual relations with a woman") is placed in quotation marks in most English versions, including the CSB, reflecting the view of most recent commentators that it is a Corinthian slogan to which Paul responds in the following verses (cf. the similar pattern in 6:12–13; 8:1–4; 10:23).[224] Judging from the advice and instructions Paul gives in the following verses (and the remainder of the chapter), Paul is happy to affirm that a decision for celibate singleness is advisable for some but resists the idea that it is the best course for all and strongly rejects the notion that it is an option available to those who are already married.

7:2. Paul begins his response to the Corinthians' slogan by reminding them that "sexual immorality is so common" (i.e., not only in the surrounding culture of the city but within the community of believers as well, as has been painfully evident in the reports to which Paul is responding in chs. 5–6; cf. 2 Cor 12:21).[225] Their lofty-sounding theories about spiritual celibacy clash embarrassingly with the shameful realities of their own sexual immorality and express a naïve underestimate of the power of sexual desire (or, alternatively, a hypocritical double standard that practices celibacy within marriage and promiscuity outside it).[226]

---

[224] E.g., Fee, *First Epistle to the Corinthians*, 307; Thiselton, *First Corinthians*, 498–99; Garland, *1 Corinthians*, 247–51. For an interpretation that presupposes the contrary position, reading v. 1b as an expression of Paul's own view, see Conzelmann, *1 Corinthians*, 114–15.

[225] The CSB's translation ("because sexual immorality is so common") accurately expresses the likely sense of the plural noun πορνείας in the original (διὰ … τὰς πορνείας). The addition of the article (τάς) may be intended to function as a reference back to the particular instances of πορνεία that have been discussed in the immediately preceding chapters of the letter. Cf. Brookins and Longenecker, *1 Corinthians 1–9*, 151.

[226] The difficulty of explaining a scenario in which the asceticism implied by the slogan in 7:1b coexists with the promiscuity to which Paul is responding in 6:12–20 prompts Dale Martin to propose that the asceticism advocated by the elite members of the Corinthian church is a path that they believe only they, as the "strong," are capable of following; on this reading, the earlier slogans quoted by Paul in 6:12–13 are used by them to justify not their own sexual license but their indifference to the promiscuity of their weaker brothers and sisters. Cf. Dale B. Martin, *The Corinthian Body* (New Haven: Yale University Press, 1995), 207–8. This interpretation is possible but unlikely, given the lack of any distinction in Paul's rhetoric between the two different subaudiences that he would need to be addressing in his response to the slogans of 6:12–13 and his warnings against sexual immorality in 6:14–20. The simpler and more likely explanation is that the proponents of the philosophy

In contrast with the approach advocated in the slogan Paul quotes in verse 1b, his own instruction (expressed in the form of a third person imperative) is that "each man should have sexual relations with his own wife, and each woman should have sexual relations with her own husband" (more literally, "let each man have his own woman, and let each woman have her own man").[227]

7:3–6. The general rule Paul lays down in verse 2 is unpacked and explained in verses 3–4, then qualified with a carefully worded concession in verse 5. In speaking of sexual intercourse as a "marital duty" (ὀφειλή) that husbands owe to wives (and wives to husbands), Paul is consistent with rabbinic interpretation of the reference to the "marital rights" (LXX: ὁμιλία) that are said to be owed by a husband to a wife in Exodus 21:10.[228] Paul's assumption that marriage creates a sexual "duty" owed by husbands to wives and wives to husbands is articulated and applied in verses 3–4 in carefully mutual language and in terms of the responsibility of each to give, not the right of either to demand or take. The stress that he places on this point suggests that some of the married members of the Corinthian church were making the (unilateral?) decision to embrace a celibate lifestyle as an outworking of their view that "it is good for a man not to have sexual relations with a woman."[229]

The strong insistence of verses 3–4 on the intrinsically sexual nature of marriage is further reinforced by a prohibition in verse 5a on "depriv[ing] one another," which is qualified in verse 5b by a carefully defined exception that Paul goes on in verse 6 to describe as "a concession, not a command."[230] The scope of the exception that Paul is prepared to concede

---

expressed in the slogan of 7:1b are (in some cases, at least) inconsistent in their adherence to it, abiding by it within their marriages but disregarding it in their liaisons with prostitutes.

[227] In light of the direction that Paul's instructions go on to take in vv. 3–7 and parallels including Deut 28:30 and 1 Cor 5:1, the CSB plausibly reads "have" not as a reference to marriage but a euphemism for sexual intercourse. On this reading, the principal conclusion drawn from the sexual immorality within and surrounding the Corinthian church is not that this is a reason (or the only reason) for single people to get married, but that this is a reason for married people to enjoy sexual relations within (and only within) marriage.

[228] Cf. m. Ketub. 5:8–9; t. Qidd. 3:7; Mek. Rab Ishmael, tractate Nezikin 3 on Exod 21:10; Tg. Onq. on Exod 21:11, cited in Garland, *1 Corinthians*, 258.

[229] Cf. John C. Poirier and Joseph Frankovic, "Celibacy and Charism in 1 Cor. 7:5–7," *HTR* 89 (1996): 2, cited with agreement in Garland, *1 Corinthians*, 257.

[230] The "concession" Paul is referring to in v. 6 is read by most commentators as a reference to something Paul has just said in the preceding verses (most plausibly, to the exception he has granted in v. 5b to the prohibition in v. 5a). Cf. Fee, *First Epistle to the*

to the ascetics is tightly limited: "except when you agree for a time, to devote yourselves to prayer. Then come together again; otherwise, Satan may tempt you because of your lack of self-control." A unilateral decision for celibacy would entail "depriv[ing]" one's spouse (v. 5a),[231] and even if the decision for abstinence is mutual, it is only to be "for a time" and "to devote yourselves to prayer"; to embark on a joint decision for long-term or permanent abstinence would be (as Paul goes on to warn the readers in v. 5b) to underestimate the strength of sexual desire, unnecessarily exposing oneself and one's spouse to temptation.

7:7. Paul concludes the paragraph with a brief statement of his own perspective on the issue as an explanation for the room that he leaves for individual difference in the advice and instructions of the chapter: "I wish that all people were as I am. But each has his own gift from God, one person has this gift, another has that." His point regarding the differing "gift[s]" that he speaks of in verse 7b could either be:

(1) that singleness and marriage (in and of themselves, considered objectively as life situations) are both gifts from God;
(2) that God gives some people (but not others) "that singular gift of freedom from the desire or need of sexual fulfillment that made it possible for him to live without need for marriage at all";[232] or
(3) that God gives some people what they need to serve him joyfully and contentedly in singleness and he gives other people what they need to serve him joyfully and contentedly in marriage.[233]

The symmetrical structure of verse 7b ("one person has this gift, another has that") suggests that either the first or the third of these three options

---

Corinthians, 314–15; Thiselton, *First Corinthians*, 511. Garland reads it as referring forward to the wish that Paul goes on to express in v. 7a, where he grants that there is something advantageous in being "as I am" (i.e., single and celibate), for those who have the gift; cf. Garland, *1 Corinthians*, 268–70. This reading of the verse is syntactically unlikely, however (cf. Brookins and Longenecker, *1 Corinthians 1-9*, 155), and is further undermined by the fact that what Paul goes on to say in v. 7a is not expressed in a form that would be easily mistaken for a "command" (ἐπιταγή).

[231] The verb ἀποστερέω that Paul uses here is a strong one, that can also be translated as "defraud" or "rob", cf. its earlier use in 6:7–8 and the comments in Fee, *First Epistle to the Corinthians*, 312; Garland, *1 Corinthians*, 260.

[232] Fee, *First Epistle to the Corinthians*, 316.

[233] Thiselton, *First Corinthians*, 513; Ciampa and Rosner, *The First Letter to the Corinthians*, 286.

is closest to Paul's intended meaning, i.e., that the two different scenarios he has in mind are not the presence of the gift of (unfrustrated) singleness and the absence of that gift, but the gift of (joyful and contented) singleness and the gift of (joyful and contented) marriage. The fact that Paul tends (usually, though perhaps not always) to use the language of χαρίσματα ("gifts") to refer not to life situations ordained by God in his providence but to the new-creation enablings given by God to his people, together with the fact that there seems to be a distinction in Paul's mind between those for whom the circumstance of singleness is likely to be experienced as a "gift from God" and those for whom it is likely to be experienced mainly as a frustration and a grief (cf. v. 9), would suggest that option (3) is to be preferred over option (1). As Thiselton puts it, "the parallel is not celibacy versus marriage, but the gift of a positive attitude which makes the most of the freedoms of celibacy without frustration, and the positive attitude which caringly provides the responsibilities, love, and 'dues' of marriage while equally living out the gospel."[234]

7:8–9. In verses 8–9 Paul turns briefly to the unmarried and the widows, taking what he has said in verse 7 to the married and applying it to their different situation.

The "unmarried" (ἄγαμοι) has traditionally been understood as an umbrella category for all who are not currently married. Some recent interpreters argue that it should be taken more narrowly as referring to widowers.[235] (In the New Testament period, the word ἄγαμος could be used in some contexts to fill the gap left by the classical Greek word χήρος, "widower," which had fallen out of usage.) Within the rest of the chapter, however—in line with typical Koine Greek usage—Paul appears to use the word quite flexibly (in v. 11, to refer to the no longer married condition of a wife separated from her husband; in v. 32 to refer generally to "unmarried" men, in contrast to married men; and in v. 34, to refer specifically to no longer married women, as distinct from not yet married "virgins"), so it probably makes best sense to assume that a broad reference is intended here. If that is the case, then the singling out of "widows" (who have already been included within the larger category of the "unmarried") may be, as Garland suggests, because of the special

[234] Thiselton, *First Corinthians*, 513.

[235] E.g., Fee, *First Epistle to the Corinthians*, 318–19; Deming, *Paul on Marriage and Celibacy*, 128; Collins, *First Corinthians*, 268.

place that widows had within the welfare structures and ministry roles of the church (cf. Acts 6:1; 1 Tim 5:3–16).[236]

Given that Paul has already told the married that he wishes "that all people were as I am," it comes as no surprise when he tells the unmarried that "is good for them if they remain as I am" (v. 8.) This much he is happy to concede to the Corinthian advocates of celibacy. But he goes on immediately to insist that "if they do not have self-control, they should marry," offering the reason that "it is better to marry than to burn with desire" (v. 9). The proviso, "if they do not have self-control" (εἰ δὲ οὐκ ἐγκρατεύονται; more literally, "if they are not controlling themselves"), may refer narrowly to those who are already engaged in actual πορνεία (cf. v. 2), perhaps as the extreme instance of those for whom marriage is self-evidently better than their current situation. Alternatively, it may refer more broadly to those who struggle to bring their passions under control, whether or not they are currently sexually active.[237] Writers in Paul's time could certainly use the language of "burn[ing]" as a metaphor for sexual or romantic desire (e.g. the description of the agonies suffered by the lovesick Habrocomes and Anthia in Xenophon of Ephesus's Ephesiaca).[238] Nevertheless, given the wide range of contexts in which the same language could be used by Paul (e.g., 2 Cor 11:29) and other Hellenistic Jewish writers (e.g., 2 Macc 4:38; 10:35; 3 Macc 4:2) as a metaphor for intense emotion, it would seem likely that Paul is intending not a narrow and exclusive reference to the "burning" of an uncontrollable libido but a broader reference to frustrated desire that may also include the related longings for intimate companionship and childbearing.

7:10–11. Paul now turns his attention back to the married, addressing first those who are married to fellow believers (vv. 10–11),[239] then "the

---

[236] Garland, *1 Corinthians*, 272.

[237] If Paul's assessment of the Corinthians' situation is the same as his assessment of the situation of the young widows in Ephesus, the advice that he gives in 1 Tim 5:11–15 may suggest a fairly broad reading of the category that he has in mind in v. 9; given the workings of our reproductive biology and the way in which most human societies are organized, the ability to live joyfully and contentedly in singleness would seem to be a rarer gift than the ability to live joyfully and contentedly in marriage.

[238] Xenophon of Ephesus, *Eph.* 1.5.8.

[239] The fact that Paul is not yet addressing those readers who are in mixed marriages is not made explicit within vv. 10–11 but is made clear in retrospect by the contrast in v. 12 between the group addressed in vv. 10–11 and "the rest" (i.e., those who are married to unbelievers and are addressed in vv. 12–16).

rest," i.e., those who are married to unbelievers (vv. 12–16). His command to the first group (which he presents as actually a command from the Lord) is briefly worded, emphasizing the permanence of marriage and prohibiting divorce and separation, except for the temporary separation that is aimed at reconciliation.

The language of "command" (παραγγέλλω) that Paul uses in verse 10 is unmistakably strong and is further reinforced by his claim that the true speaker of the command is "not I, but the Lord"—most likely a reference to the teaching of Jesus (e.g., the sayings regarding marriage and divorce that later came to be preserved in Mark 10:2–12).[240] Given the content of the surrounding paragraphs, it seems likely that the problem in Corinth that he is responding to in these verses is another application of the attitudes expressed in the slogan quoted in verse 1b; not only were some married people practicing celibacy within marriage but others were separating (or contemplating separation) from their spouses altogether.[241] The focus on "a wife" that is maintained for most of verses 10–11 (apart from the brief parallel word about "a husband" at the end of v. 11) probably implies that the instance(s) in Corinth that Paul is responding to involved a wife separating from her husband, not vice versa.

The proviso in verse 11 implicitly grants that there may be circumstances in which separation is required but rules out separation/divorce for the sake of remarriage. The distinction of language between "leave" (χωρισθῆναι) and "divorce" (ἀφιέναι) should not be read as implying a sharp, clear, legal distinction,[242] but the terms in which Paul frames the proviso ("But if she does leave, she must remain unmarried or be reconciled to her husband") suggest something that would have worked out in practice more like what we would call a separation than what we would call a divorce.

7:12–13. Paul's word to the second group is elaborated at somewhat greater length, with the general principle stated symmetrically: first to

[240] Cf. Fee, *First Epistle to the Corinthians*, 519–27; Craig Blomberg, "Quotations, Allusions, and Echoes of Jesus in Paul," in *Studies in the Pauline Epistles: Essays in Honor of Douglas J. Moo*, ed. Matthew S. Harmon and Jay E. Smith (Grand Rapids: Zondervan, 2014), 136–37.

[241] Ciampa and Rosner propose an alternative theory, which views v. 10 as a response to instances of Christians separating from spouses who had been sexually promiscuous before marriage, perhaps because of a misunderstanding of the earlier letter referred to in 5:9. Ciampa and Rosner, *The First Letter to the Corinthians*, 290.

[242] Cf. the examples of χωρίζω used in Hellenistic legal texts to mean "divorce," cited in Garland, *1 Corinthians*, 281.

husbands, then to wives in verses 12–13, followed by a justification of the principle in verse 14, an exception in verse 15a, then two further justifications of the general principle in verses 15b–16.

"The rest" (v. 12), in view of the explicit references to mixed marriages in every verse of the paragraph, almost certainly refers to those who are married to unbelievers. What Paul goes on to say to them, speaking this time as "I (not the Lord)," is not a direct word from Jesus but an (authoritative, apostolic) interpretation of the implications of the command from Jesus for those who have nonbelieving spouses. Here, Paul returns to the same balanced, roughly symmetrical form ("If any brother ... Also, if any woman ...") that he used in verses 3–4. The rationale he goes on to offer in verses 14–16 suggests that the impetus to separate from unbelieving spouses came, at least in part, from the notion that there was something unclean about marriage and sexual contact with them.[243] Against such thinking, Paul insists that a mixed marriage between a believer and an unbeliever, no less than a marriage between two believers, should be regarded as a permanent and binding commitment. The provisos with which Paul qualifies the two parallel commands that articulate this principle in verses 12–13 ("and she is willing to live with him ... and he is willing to live with her") anticipate the concession that Paul makes explicit in verse 15.

7:14–16. Verse 14 offers the first reason for the general principle that has been expressed in the commands of verses 12–13: Marriage to an unbeliever does not make a believer unholy; rather, marriage to a believer makes an unbeliever holy. The point Paul is making is not that the unbelieving spouse who has been "made holy" in this manner is automatically saved through marriage to a believer—that notion is expressly ruled out by the uncertainty of the premise that underlies Paul's rhetorical questions in verse 16. Rather, the point is that the unbelieving spouse is someone with whom the believing husband or wife can live, eat, and sleep without fear of being rendered impure. The reference to children of the marriage in verse 14b functions within Paul's explanation as a reductio ad absurdum, highlighting the absurdity of the notion that living in a familial relationship with someone who is not yet a believer renders a person unclean; if that were the case, as Paul points out, the people contemplating divorce from unbelieving partners should also be

---

[243] A similar attitude appears to be implied in Jos. Asen. 8:5–7.

contemplating the expulsion of their not yet believing children, which would be a patently wrongheaded idea.

Verse 15 expresses an exception to the general rule: "But if the unbeliever leaves, let him leave." The meaning of the following sentence ("A brother or a sister is not bound in such cases") is debated,[244] but the similar (though not identical) language in 7:39 and Romans 7:1–4 supports the idea that "not bound" (οὐ δεδούλωται) implies the option of remarriage.[245] "God has called you to live in peace" is taken by some to be a rationale for the permission to "let him leave" if the unbeliever makes a decision to abandon the marriage.[246] The normal meaning of the language of "peace" (εἰρήνη) in Jewish and early Christian usage, however, includes not just inner tranquility and the absence of strife but the maintenance or restoration of harmonious relationships; if (as is most likely) that is the sense in which Paul is using the word here, verse 15c should probably be read as a reminder that even if the unbeliever may choose divorce, that is never the preferred or ideal option for a Christian; where possible, the Christian instinct should always be for reconciliation (cf. Rom 12:18).[247]

The questions that follow, in verse 16, are linked by the conjunction γάρ (left untranslated in the CSB and most other English versions) with the preceding statement in verse 15b, suggesting that they function as

---

244 Fee, for example, insists strongly that Paul could not possibly have thought of marriage as a condition in which a person is "bound" (δεδούλωται) in a kind of slavery; on his reading of this phrase, Paul is not granting an exception to his general prohibition on remarriage after divorce but simply stating that a believer is not "under bondage" to the impossible task of trying to maintain a marriage to a spouse who has departed. Fee, *First Epistle to the Corinthians*, 334–35.

245 Cf. the arguments for this reading of v. 15 in Garland, *1 Corinthians*, 296–97; David Instone-Brewer, "1 Corinthians 7 in the Light of the Jewish Greek and Aramaic Marriage and Divorce Papyri " *TynBul* 52 (2001): 225–43. The verb used in 1 Cor 7:39 and Rom 7:1–4 is δέδεται not δεδούλωται, but in both cases it is serving as an antonym to ἐλευθέρα, suggesting a meaning that is functionally equivalent, in context, to δεδούλωται. (The same verb, δέω, is also used in v. 27, where it is contrasted with the noun that corresponds to its more literal antonym, λύω.)

246 On this reading, the "peace" in which believers are called to live is the inner tranquility that comes from letting go of the futile effort to resist an unbelieving spouse's decision to leave.

247 Cf. Fee, *First Epistle to the Corinthians*, 335–36; Garland, *1 Corinthians*, 291–93. On this reading, the δέ linking v. 15b to the preceding sentence should be taken as mildly adversative in force, and the statement in v. 15b understood as anticipating the encouragement of verse 16 to remain, if possible, in the marriage (i.e., "But God has called you to live in peace. Wife, for all you know, you might save your husband. Husband, for all you know, you might save your wife").

support for the point Paul is making in that statement. If (as some interpret it) the statement in verse 15b is an encouragement to believers who have been abandoned by an unbelieving spouse to let them go without offering any resistance, the questions in verse 16 are presumably to be understood in a pessimistic sense (e.g., NIV: "How do you know, wife, whether you will save your husband? Or, how do you know, husband, whether you will save your wife?"). If, on the other hand (as argued above), the statement in verse 15b is an encouragement to believers in mixed marriages to pursue the "peace" of a harmonious, continuing marriage relationship, the questions in verse 16 require a more optimistic slant, or at least an openness to the genuine possibility of a spouse's salvation (cf. the statements with which the CSB and NRSV paraphrase Paul's questions: "Wife, for all you know, you might save your husband. Husband, for all you know, you might save your wife"). Nothing in the grammar of verse 16 requires an interpretation that is unambiguously optimistic or pessimistic in its slant—on either reading, the uncertainty of the outcome is integral to the point Paul is making—but supporters of the more optimistic reading can point to a number of examples in the LXX and other ancient sources in which the question τί οἶδας ("How do you know?") is asked with an emphasis on the positive possibility, not the negative.[248] In light of these examples of the idiom's normal function and the context in which Paul uses it here (i.e., the encouragement in verse 15b to "live in peace" and the fact that the paragraph's primary emphasis is on reasons for staying in a marriage, not reasons for leaving), it makes the best sense to read the questions of verse 16 as genuinely open, but with an emphasis on the possibility of a positive outcome. The main function they serve, on this reading, is as an encouragement to the readers to keep their minds open to the possibility of a spouse's salvation and stay in the marriage with that hope in mind rather than abandoning the marriage on the assumption that their spouse's situation is irreversible.[249]

Bridge

Twenty-first century readers seeking to discern the relevance of Paul's words in this portion of 1 Corinthians for the marriage-related issues that

---

[248] E.g., LXX 2 Sam 12:22; Esth 4:14; Joel 2:4; Jonah 3:9; Jos. Asen. 11; LAB 9.6; Epictetus, *Diatr.* 2.20.30.

[249] Cf. Fee, *First Epistle to the Corinthians*, 337–38; Garland, *1 Corinthians*, 294; Ciampa and Rosner, *The First Letter to the Corinthians*, 305.

we grapple with in our own context need to take into account both the occasional nature of the words that Paul addresses to married believers in Corinth (as a response to a specific set of questions, ideas, and practices arising within a particular cultural and legal context) and the deeply theological premises that inform his response (as a series of commands and concessions, shaped by the teachings of Scripture and the words of Jesus, and given by Paul in his authoritative role as an apostle).

Paul is not setting out in this chapter to write a treatise on marriage or a body of canon law that covers every possible contingency and addresses every possible question that may arise. The commands and prohibitions that he gives in verses 10–11, for example, while explicitly based on the words of Jesus, do not go out of their way to mention the exception that Jesus makes reference to in Matthew 19:9 (relevant in Jesus's context because of the focus of rabbinic discussion on the interpretation of Deut 24:1, but not a matter of controversy among believers in Corinth); Paul does, however, go beyond the words of Jesus to address the scenario of abandonment by a nonbelieving spouse (relevant for the Corinthians but of less immediate relevance for Jesus's audience in Matt 19). It would be a mistake to read either Paul's words or Jesus's as if the single exception referred to in each case were the only possible scenario under which divorce (and remarriage after divorce) could be contemplated as a possibility by a believer.

The main points Paul wishes to make are clear, however, and are grounded in the words of Jesus and the teachings of the Genesis creation narratives that inform both Jesus's understanding and Paul's. Believers are called to be enduringly faithful to the marriage vows that they have made and to the mutual responsibilities that those vows give rise to. Integral to marriage is the committed and exclusive sexual relationship Paul speaks of in verses 2–5, in language that makes it clear he has in mind a dynamic of free and mutual giving, not unilateral imposition or coercion. Marriage (and sex within marriage) should not be viewed as a pollution from which believers should seek to be purified but as a context within which obedience to Christ is to be worked out in faithfulness and love. All of these points are of enduring relevance and fundamental importance for twenty-first century believers as we seek to live out a coherently and authentically Christian understanding of marriage.

B. The General Principle: Remain with God Where You Were Called (7:17–24)

> [17] Let each one live his life in the situation the Lord assigned when God called him. This is what I command in all the churches. [18] Was anyone already circumcised when he was called? He should not undo his circumcision. Was anyone called while uncircumcised? He should not get circumcised. [19] Circumcision does not matter and uncircumcision does not matter. Keeping God's commands is what matters. [20] Let each of you remain in the situation in which he was called. [21] Were you called while a slave? Don't let it concern you. But if you can become free, by all means take the opportunity. [22] For he who is called by the Lord as a slave is the Lord's freedman. Likewise he who is called as a free man is Christ's slave. [23] You were bought at a price; do not become slaves of people. [24] Brothers and sisters, each person is to remain with God in the situation in which he was called.

Context/Structure/Form

At first glance, this paragraph sits rather oddly within the chapter, given that it says nothing explicitly about celibacy, marriage, or divorce, talking instead about circumcision and slavery. The generality of Paul's language in verse 17, however, suggests that these verses should be taken not as a digression from the main theme of the chapter but as the centerpiece of the chapter's argument, stating and illustrating a general principle ("what I command in all the churches") in favor of remaining contentedly and faithfully within the situation in which one was called by God. The general rule is stated in verse 17; two illustrations follow in verses 18–19 (circumcision) and 21–23 (slavery), sandwiched by restatements of the general principle in verses 20, 24.

Comments

7:17. Verse 17 states the broad and generally applicable principle ("what I command in all the churches"—cf. 1:2; 4:17; 11:16; 14:33) that informs all of Paul's commands, concessions, and advice giving in the remainder of this chapter: "Let each one live his life in the situation the Lord assigned when God called him."[250] The way in which Paul applies and qualifies this "command" within the remainder of this paragraph (e.g., v. 21b) and in

---

[250] The verse begins with an expression (Εἰ μή) that is left untranslated in the CSB but probably means something roughly equivalent to the NRSV's "However that may be." Its function here appears to be to acknowledge the uncertain answer to the questions in v. 16 and signal a transition to a general statement that can be made regardless of the outcome

the rest of the chapter suggests that it is not an unbendable absolute but a strong default assumption: in the absence of strong reasons to the contrary, it is best for believers to assume that they can, and should, continue to serve God within the circumstances in which he originally called them.

When Paul speaks of God having "called" believers, his language usually refers not to an event in which believers were inwardly and specifically "called" to become circumcised, married, enslaved, and so forth but to the event in which they heard the gospel and were called to belong to Christ (cf. 1:26; 7:18–24). This is almost certainly the primary sense here, though the fact that this calling to become a believer took place within a situation that was (providentially) "assigned" (ἐμέρισεν) by God creates a secondary implication that the believer's calling included a divine intention that they be a follower of Christ within that situation (cf. the discussion of v. 20, below).

7:18–20. The general principle stated in verse 17 is now illustrated by means of two specific example, the first of which (circumcision, discussed in vv. 18–20) would probably have been relatively uncontroversial and obvious to the Corinthians and therefore useful to Paul in his argument. The call to Jews to follow Christ does not entail a call to abandon their Jewishness, nor does the call to gentiles to follow Christ entail a call to abandon their uncircumcision.[251] For Paul, what counts is not circumcision or uncircumcision but "keeping God's commands," whether as a circumcised Jew or as an uncircumcised gentile (cf. Gal 5:6; 6:15).[252]

---

of that particular issue. Cf. Brookins and Longenecker, *1 Corinthians 1–9*, 167; Thiselton, *First Corinthians*, 548.

251 The notion of a circumcised Jew "undo[ing] his circumcision" is not a ludicrous or impossible one; there was a surgical procedure, called epispasm, that upwardly mobile, Hellenized Jews could—and sometimes did—undergo to have their circumcision reversed; cf. 1 Macc 1:15; Josephus, *Ant.* 12.241; and the discussion in Bruce W. Winter, *Seek the Welfare of the City: Christians as Benefactors and Citizens* (Grand Rapids: Eerdmans, 1994), 147–52.

252 The parallel sayings in Gal 5:6 and Gal 6:15 offer a clue as to why Paul did not think that "keeping God's commands" required gentiles to submit to the commandment of circumcision. "Faith working through love" was, in Paul's view, the fulfillment of the law and the summing up of the commandments (Rom 8:4; 13:8–10). The "new creation" inaugurated in Christ does away with the covenantal distinction between Jew and gentile that circumcision signified. Believers, who participate in that new creation by virtue of their incorporation into Christ, keep God's commands by submitting to "the law of Christ" (Gal 6:2; cf. 1 Cor 9:21), informed by the commands of the Torah but not directly under their covenantal authority. Cf. the discussions in Rosner, *Paul and the Law*, ch. 1; Schreiner, *1 Corinthians*, 147–48.

Verse 20 ("Let each of you remain in the situation in which he was called") reinforces Paul's main point by reiterating the principle originally stated in verse 17. The word translated as "situation" in the CSB is actually the same word κλῆσις that Paul used in 1:26 (translated there as "calling") to refer to the event of the readers' conversion and is cognate with the verb καλέω ("call") that is used repeatedly throughout verses 17–24. Here, it is unlikely to carry the sense of a station in life or professional vocation to which believers have been specifically and directly "called" by God, through a divine communication distinct and separate from the gospel. The more likely sense that the word carries here is in line with its earlier use in 1:26 and the "calling" language throughout the rest of this paragraph: Paul is reminding the readers of their original call to follow Christ, which came to each one of them within a particular set of circumstances and (initially, at least) implied a summons to follow Christ within that situation.[253] Focusing on that call (i.e., the call to follow Christ) relativizes all other questions and concerns, creating a context in which the readers can contentedly "remain" within the circumstances in which they were originally converted, freed from the anxiety that might otherwise compel them to focus on changing their situation.[254]

7:21–23. The second illustration, in verses 21–23, deals with slavery and freedom. Within the context of the socially stratified Corinthian congregation (cf. 11:17–22), in which a "strong," "spiritual," privileged elite seem to have looked down on their poorer brothers and sisters as spiritually inferior (cf. 6:4; 12:21–26), Paul's words here would have functioned in part to reassure slaves within the Corinthian church that they were the spiritual equals of their freed and freeborn brothers and sisters: "He who is called by the Lord as a slave is the Lord's freedman. Likewise he who is called as a free man is Christ's slave" (v. 22). The menial work that most slaves would have been occupied with day by day did not make their lives less spiritual than the lives of their more leisured brothers and sisters, who had the luxury of time for lengthy prayers, spiritual exercises, and theological conversations. Believers who were slaves when they were called to follow Christ are urged by Paul in verse 21a not to let this "concern" them (i.e., not to let themselves be consumed by anxieties

---

[253] Cf. Garland, *1 Corinthians*, 303.

[254] Cf. the parallel between μενέτω ("let [him] remain"; v. 20) and μή σοι μελέτω ("Don't let it concern you"; v. 21) and the comments in Brookins and Longenecker, *1 Corinthians 1–9*, 171.

about their social position and any spiritual inferiority that this is thought to entail in the eyes of their fellow believers).

The proviso in verse 21b is somewhat obscure in the wording of the original (more literally: "but if you are able to become free, rather [or perhaps, 'all the more...'] make use"). Some English versions read verse 21b not as a proviso but as a reinforcement of the general principle (e.g., NRSV: "Even if you can gain your freedom, make use of your present condition now more than ever").[255] While there are some good arguments for this translation, the "but" (ἀλλά) that introduces verse 21b is probably a signal that the CSB translation ("But if you can become free, by all means take the opportunity") is to be preferred, with the words εἰ καί understood as "if indeed" (cf. 4:7; 7:11) rather than the NRSV's "even if."[256]

7:24. Verse 24 closes the paragraph with a further restatement of the general principle, this time with the addition of the phrases, "brothers and sisters" (perhaps as an implicit reminder of the equal status of believers with one another, whether slave or free) and "with God" (παρὰ θεῷ). The latter phrase pushes back against the notion that a person's life situation (e.g., slavery) can make them alienated from God and render their daily labor inconsequential and unspiritual.

Bridge

The rule Paul lays down within this paragraph (and that, he tells the Corinthians, he teaches "in all the churches") is as relevant to twenty-first century Western Christians as it was to the original recipients of the letter. Like the Corinthians we exist within a cultural context that is pervaded by hierarchies of status and all of the attendant ambitions and anxieties that they generate.[257] And like the Corinthians we are all too easily influenced by attitudes that denigrate mundane, earthly, and ordinary pursuits and spiritualities that privilege the pursuits and possibilities of the wealthy and well educated. We, like they, need to hear Paul's reminder that the call to belong to Christ is not a call to leave the ordinariness of everyday life and ascend into a more exalted, more spiritual situation; it is (for

255 Cf. the arguments in support of this interpretation in Thiselton, *First Corinthians*, 555–57.

256 Cf. Ciampa and Rosner, *The First Letter to the Corinthians*, 322; Brookins and Longenecker, *1 Corinthians 1-9*, 172–73.

257 Cf. the discussions in Alain De Botton, *Status Anxiety* (London: Hamish Hamilton, 2004); Thiselton, *First Corinthians*, 12–17; Wayne A. Meeks, *The First Urban Christians: The Social World of the Apostle Paul* (New Haven: Yale University Press, 1983), 51–73

most of us at least) a call to remain in the context God has placed us in, sanctifying the ordinary by the presence of his Holy Spirit.

C. Advice Relating Primarily to the Situation of Virgins (7:25–40)

> [25] Now about virgins: I have no command from the Lord, but I do give an opinion as one who by the Lord's mercy is faithful. [26] Because of the present distress, I think that it is good for a man to remain as he is. [27] Are you bound to a wife? Do not seek to be released. Are you released from a wife? Do not seek a wife. [28] However, if you do get married, you have not sinned, and if a virgin marries, she has not sinned. But such people will have trouble in this life, and I am trying to spare you.
>
> [29] This is what I mean, brothers and sisters: The time is limited, so from now on those who have wives should be as though they had none, [30] those who weep as though they did not weep, those who rejoice as though they did not rejoice, those who buy as though they didn't own anything, [31] and those who use the world as though they did not make full use of it. For this world in its current form is passing away.
>
> [32] I want you to be without concerns. The unmarried man is concerned about the things of the Lord—how he may please the Lord. [33] But the married man is concerned about the things of the world—how he may please his wife— [34] and his interests are divided. The unmarried woman or virgin is concerned about the things of the Lord, so that she may be holy both in body and in spirit. But the married woman is concerned about the things of the world—how she may please her husband. [35] I am saying this for your own benefit, not to put a restraint on you, but to promote what is proper and so that you may be devoted to the Lord without distraction.
>
> [36] If any man thinks he is acting improperly toward the virgin he is engaged to, if she is getting beyond the usual age for marriage, and he feels he should marry—he can do what he wants. He is not sinning; they can get married. [37] But he who stands firm in his heart (who is under no compulsion, but has control over his own will) and has decided in his heart to keep her as his fiancée, will do well. [38] So, then, he who marries his fiancée does well, but he who does not marry will do better.
>
> [39] A wife is bound as long as her husband is living. But if her husband dies, she is free to be married to anyone she wants—only in the Lord. [40] But she is happier if she remains as she is, in my opinion. And I think that I also have the Spirit of God.

Context/Structure/Form

Paul's focus now turns, in the final part of the chapter, to "virgins" (i.e., adults who have not yet been married, though some may have been pledged in betrothal). His advice regarding their situation takes the general principle from verses 17–24 (cf. v. 26: "it is good for a man to remain as he is") and applies it in the form of an argument for the advantages of remaining single. Three (interrelated and overlapping) reasons are given for this advice: "the present distress" and the additional "trouble" to which married people are exposed in a context such as this (vv. 26–28); the "limited" duration of the present time (vv. 29–31); and the "divided" interests of married believers (vv. 32–35). Along the way, Paul offers several qualifications to the advice that he gives as a general principle (vv. 28a, 36, 38), reassuring those who choose to marry that they are not sinning and making it clear that under some circumstances marriage is not only a permissible option (v. 36b: "he is not sinning") but the right option (v. 36c: "they should get married"; CSB: "they can get married").

Finally, in verses 39–40, Paul returns briefly to the subject of married women and widows, reminding them that a wife is "bound" to her husband as long as he lives but "free" to remarry after he dies and advising them that "she is happier if she remains as she is, in my opinion."

Comments

7:25. The περὶ δέ formula at the start of verse 25 signals a change of topic from the predominantly marriage-focused discussion in verses 1–16 and the generalities of verses 17–24 to the issues "about virgins" (τῶν παρθένων) that were raised by the questions asked (or views expressed) in the Corinthians' letter. There is debate about the scope of the term "virgins" (only women, or men too? Only the betrothed, or also the unbetrothed?),[258] but the range of scenarios Paul seems to address in verses 25–38 supports Thiselton's fairly broad interpretation: "those not yet married, especially unmarried women."[259]

As was the case in verse 12, Paul acknowledges that he has no direct command (ἐπιταγή) from the Lord; what he offers, instead, is his own "opinion" (γνώμη) as a piece of advice from "one who by the Lord's mercy is faithful." The remainder of the chapter includes a series of indications

---

[258] Cf. the survey of views in Fee, *First Epistle to the Corinthians*, 360–62.

[259] Thiselton, *First Corinthians*, 568.

that its content (or at least the majority of its content) is intended by Paul to be received in that spirit, as opinion and advice aimed at promoting the well-being of the readers and sparing them unnecessary trouble and distraction (cf. especially vv. 28, 32, 35, 40).

7:26. Verse 26b ("I think that it is good for a man to remain as he is") is a restatement of the general principle that was articulated in vv. 17–24. Verse 26a is a much-debated expression, offered by Paul as an additional rationale of some sort for the benefits of applying this mode of thinking to the question of whether it is better for virgins to enter into a marriage or remain single.

"The present distress" (ἡ ἐνεστῶσα ἀνάγκη) could mean either (1) a particular crisis of which Paul and the Corinthians are aware (e.g., the social instability caused by recent and continuing grain shortages)[260] or (2) the troubles and turmoils that Paul considered to be a perennial feature of life in the last days or an imminent prospect to be anticipated as part of the eschatological buildup to the parousia.[261] As a number of commentators point out, the two options need not be regarded as altogether mutually exclusive (especially if ἐνεστώς is understood as "present" rather than as "imminent"). Garland, for example, suggest that "it is most likely that [Paul] has in view a present crisis (perhaps the famine) interpreted as an end-time event."[262] On this reading, the "present distress" faced by the believers in Corinth should not be viewed as a unique, anomalous event—it is exactly the kind of thing that Christians ought to anticipate as a recurring feature of the last days before Christ's return—but neither should it be regarded as the permanent, standard set of circumstances within which all Christians everywhere will need to make their decisions about marriage and singleness.[263]

---

[260] Tacitus describes AD 51 as an "ominous" year, featuring a shortage of corn due to bad harvests in Egypt and, as a consequence, famine (*Ann.* 12.43; cf. Suetonius, *Claud.* 18). All this, Tacitus writes, was taken by the general population as a "supernatural warning." The famines appear to have continued intermittently across the next couple of years, recurring in AD 53 and 54; cf. Winter, *After Paul Left Corinth*, 216–25.

[261] Cf. Conzelmann, *1 Corinthians*, 132, interpreting ἐνεστώς as "imminent" rather than as "present" (which is the sense it most commonly carries in Paul's letters; e.g., Rom 8:38; 1 Cor 3:22; Gal 1:4).

[262] Garland, *1 Corinthians*, 324; cf. Ciampa and Rosner, *The First Letter to the Corinthians*, 337–38; Fee, *First Epistle to the Corinthians*, 364.

[263] Cf. Ciampa and Rosner's comment: "Paul's negative stance on getting married here and throughout the chapter is to some extent a 'refraction' of his ethics ... assum[ing] 'the character of a necessary emergency measure' rather than being his sober direction for

7:27–28. Within these circumstances, Paul advises, betrothal pledges are to be honored (v. 27a: "Are you bound to a wife? Do not seek to be released"), but those who are not bound by such commitments are best off if they remain single and do not go looking for a wife (v. 27b: "Are you released from a wife? Do not seek a wife").[264] This advice is immediately followed in verse 28 by an assurance that those who do choose to marry do not sin; the purpose of the advice is not to bind the Corinthians to an unwanted, frustrating predicament of singleness but to spare them from "trouble."

Paul's reference in verse 28 to "trouble" (θλίψις—a strong word, often translated as "tribulation" or "distress" in contexts of persecution or other extreme sufferings) faced by those who are married should not be taken simply as a jaundiced reflection, along the lines of Proverbs 21:9, 19, on the inconveniences and intrusions that are imposed by a spouse. In context (i.e., in light of the "present distress"), the "trouble" Paul has in mind is more likely to be the additional complications and heartaches that a person is exposed to in times of turmoil and persecution if they are responsible not only for themselves but also for a spouse and possibly children (cf. Luke 21:23; 23:27–29).

7:29–31. Verses 29–31 are interpreted by many commentators not as a new, additional reason for the preferability of singleness but as an elaboration or explanation of what Paul has in mind by his advice on how to take into account the "present distress" and the "trouble" referred to in verses 26–28.[265] This interpretation is also implied by the majority of English versions, which translate the opening words of verse 29 (τοῦτο δέ φημι) with an expression such as "This is what I mean ..." (CSB). But the particle δέ which Paul employs to link verses 29–31 with the preceding paragraph suggests a new, additional point rather than an explanation or clarification of what Paul has already said, and the timeframe, "from now on" (ὁ καιρὸς ... τὸ λοιπόν), is distinguished by Paul from the immediately prevailing circumstances suggested by the

all the churches." Ciampa and Rosner, *The First Letter to the Corinthians*, 338, quoting from Helmut Thielicke, *Theological Ethics* (Philadelphia: Fortress, 1966), 380.

[264] For arguments in favor of reading v. 27 as advice to betrothed and unbetrothed (male) virgins rather than as a reiteration of the commands to married and unmarried men and women that Paul has already given in vv. 8–16, see Fee, *First Epistle to the Corinthians*, 366–67; Ciampa and Rosner, *The First Letter to the Corinthians*, 338–40.

[265] E.g., Garland, *1 Corinthians*, 317; Fee, *First Epistle to the Corinthians*, 370.

"present distress," to which he has referred in verse 26.[266] The specific counsel Paul gives in verses 26–28 to betrothed and unbetrothed virgins may be conditioned by the particular circumstances of "present distress" that they are faced by, but even after the immediate crisis has passed, the mentality that Paul urges in verses 29–31 will still apply. The time is still "limited" (συνεσταλμένος), i.e., heading toward the abrupt end that it will be brought to at Christ's return (cf. Rom 13:11–12; 1 Thess 5:2–3). The current world order is not the permanent and enduring reality that some, at least among the Corinthians, appear to have taken it to be. As Paul goes on to remind them in verse 31: "This world in its current form is passing away" (παράγει ... τὸ σχῆμα τοῦ κόσμου τούτου).

The eschatological mindset that Paul encourages within these verses clashes strongly with the comfortable, worldly assumptions of the Corinthian elite (cf. 4:8–13) and applies far more broadly than merely to questions of marriage and singleness (see §7). Life in the urgent, tumultuous conditions of the last days places pressures on those who live faithfully to Christ's call, in ways that impact marriage, bereavement, possessions, business interests, and every part of life. Paul offers a list of examples in verses 29b–31a: "From now on those who have wives should be as though they had none, those who weep as though they did not weep, those who rejoice as though they did not rejoice, those who buy as though they didn't own anything, and those who use the world as though they did not make full use of it." The list touches on both emotional responses ("those who weep"; "those who rejoice") and economic behaviors ("those who buy"; "those who use") and suggests a complex and paradoxical stance that applies in both arenas. Believers are not to "disinvest" altogether from the involvements and commitments of the present age,[267] but they are to participate in a manner that takes account

---

[266] Cf. Robertson and Plummer, *First Corinthians*, 154; Ciampa and Rosner, *The First Letter to the Corinthians*, 342–43.

[267] John Barclay uses the language of material and emotional "disinvestment" to describe the stance that Paul is urging believers to take in these verses but applies it selectively: In the emotional sphere, for example, believers are to free themselves from "emotional reactions to events or conditions of this currently configured world," saving their emotional energy instead for "things that matter for Christ or for the church." John M. G. Barclay, "Apocalyptic Allegiance and Disinvestment in the World: A Reading of 1 Corinthians 7:25–35," in *Paul and the Apocalyptic Imagination*, ed. Ben C. Blackwell, John K. Goodrich, and Jason Maston (Minneapolis: Fortress, 2016), 269. The kind of "selective investment" he argues for is, perhaps, part of what Paul has in mind, but the picture Paul paints may not

of the impermanence of the present order and the promise of the age to come (cf. 2 Cor 6:8–10; 1 Thess 4:13; 1 Tim 6:17–19) and does not look to marriage (or any other this-worldly relationship or possession) as the guarantee of the permanence and security that are in reality given only in Christ.[268]

7:32–34. Having spoken in general terms about the shortening of the times, Paul now focuses once again on the specific question of marriage and singleness. His desire, he assures the Corinthians, is for their good: "I want you to be without concerns" (v. 32; θέλω δὲ ὑμᾶς ἀμερίμνους εἶναι). The "concern" Paul wishes the Corinthians to be free from is not in itself an ungodly state of mind; Paul is deeply appreciative, for example, of the fact that Timothy "will genuinely care" (μεριμνήσει) for the Philippians' welfare (Phil 2:20), and Paul himself suffers the daily pressure of his "concern" (μέριμνα) for all the churches (2 Cor 11:28). But it is not a pleasant or easy burden to carry, and wise people will not needlessly expose themselves or others to it.

Within the eschatological context that Paul has established in verses 29–31, concern for "the things of the Lord" is probably focused principally on the priorities of mission within the "limited" time of the last days. His intention is probably not to imply that the household duties of a married person are of no interest to God. In other contexts (e.g., Eph 6:5–8; Col 3:20; 22–25), he can state emphatically that the mundane duties of the household are precisely a way of "pleas[ing] the Lord" (cf. Eph 5:10). Rather, his point appears to be that there will inevitably be points at which the particular, urgent, last-days task of proclaiming of the gospel among the nations and building up the church will pull against the responsibilities of home and family. In such circumstances, a married

---

be quite as neat as Barclay would like it to be. The line between "events or conditions of this currently configured world" and "things that matter for Christ or for the church" is not always sharply and clearly drawn, and Paul's picture is not of believers as people who "weep (and rejoice) at some things but not at others"; the picture, rather, is of believers as people whose emotional responses (and practical/material involvements in the world) are shot through with paradox: "weep[ing] as though they did not weep, ... rejoic[ing] as though they did not rejoice, ... buy[ing] as though they didn't own anything, ... us[ing] the world as though they did not make full use of it."

[268] Cf. Sarah K. Whittle, "'Let Even Those Who Have Wives Be as Though They Had None' (1 Cor. 7:29)," in *Marriage, Family and Relationships: Biblical, Doctrinal and Contemporary Perspectives*, ed. Thomas A. Noble, Sarah K. Whittle, and Philip S. Johnston (London: InterVarsity Press, 2017), 93–97; Garland, *1 Corinthians*, 329–31.

person (who—rightly—wants to "please his wife" or "please her husband") who is also devoted to the Lord Jesus (and therefore longs to see the gospel proclaimed in new territory and the church built up) will inevitably feel painfully "divided" (μεμέρισται).

7:35. In verse 35 Paul reiterates the point that his desire is for the Corinthians' good (cf. vv. 28, 32). The expression that he uses in verse 35a (πρὸς τὸ ὑμῶν αὐτῶν σύμφορον; CSB: "for your own benefit") implies not so much what is morally good and right but what is advantageous and profitable: Paul has the Corinthians' own best interests at heart. Nevertheless, in the second half of the verse he makes it clear that what is advantageous for the Corinthians themselves is to be understood in the light of what is "proper" (εὔσχημον) as part of a life of consistent devotion to the Lord that is lived out "without distraction" (ἀπερισπάστως).

7:36–38. It is not easy to be certain about the precise nature of the scenario Paul addresses in these verses. Several questions arise:

(1) What is the nature of the relationship that Paul envisages between the person he has in mind and τὴν παρθένον αὐτοῦ (literally: "his virgin")? The CSB and NIV both translate the expression as "the virgin he is engaged to" (cf. NRSV "his fiancée"),[269] but it could also possibly be "his virgin daughter" (e.g., NASB).[270]

(2) What kind of behavior might constitute "acting improperly" (ἀσχημονεῖν).[271] An unjust delay in honoring a promise of marriage to a fiancée?[272] A failure to maintain sexual purity?[273]

---

[269] Most recent commentators, e.g., Thiselton, *First Corinthians*, 597–98; Garland, *1 Corinthians*, 337–38.

[270] Cf. the arguments for this reading in Robertson and Plummer, *First Corinthians*, 158–60, including that in v. 38 Paul uses the verb γαμίζω, which is used elsewhere in the New Testament to mean "give in marriage" rather than "marry" (e.g., Matt 22:30; 24:38). Proponents of the majority view point out that the sharp distinction between γαμέω and γαμίζω had broken down by the first century (cf. BDAG, s.v. "γαμίζω," 2) and argue that the reason for the switch from γαμέω in v. 36 to γαμίζω in v. 38 is that the verb is used with a direct object in v. 36, whereas it is used intransitively in v. 36 and elsewhere in the chapter. Cf. Garland, *1 Corinthians*, 339.

[271] The word ἀσχημονεῖν is the antonym of the verb that corresponds to the word εὔσχημον ("what is proper"), which Paul uses in the immediately preceding verse. It can refer to behavior that is immoral or contrary to social expectation and obligations.

[272] E.g., Ciampa and Rosner, *The First Letter to the Corinthians*, 358.

[273] E.g., Garland, *1 Corinthians*, 341.

(3) How should we translate ἐὰν ᾖ ὑπέρακμος, and should we take it as referring to the man in the scenario or to "his virgin"? The CSB opts for "if she is getting beyond the usual age for marriage,"[274] but other possible alternatives include the NIV's "if his passions are too strong" (cf. NRSV).[275]

On balance, the arguments in favor of the way the verse is rendered in the CSB are stronger than the arguments for the alternative translations of the verse, given the lack of clear examples in which ὑπέρακμος is used to refer to men (or women) whose sexual passions are excessively strong and the connotations of social obligation implied by the phrase, "and he feels he should" (καὶ οὕτως ὀφείλει γίνεσθαι).[276]

The complicated set of "ifs" that Paul envisages in the clauses that he strings together in verse 36a make it clear that he is aware of the nuances of circumstances and personalities that can create exceptions—even in the midst of "the present distress" (cf. v. 26)—in which it is better to marry than to remain single. Similarly, the long series of qualifications that precedes Paul's statement in verse 37b leaves the readers in no doubt that Paul is not wishing to place any pressure on those who are already betrothed to cancel or defer their marriage plans against their will. Nevertheless, in situations where personality, circumstance, and social responsibility do not tip the scales in favor of marriage and where the decision is made in genuine freedom, without coercion or compulsion, there are good reasons to stay single. In fact, in the absence of good reasons to marry, remaining single is, in Paul's view, the better option (v. 38).

7:39–40. Paul has already addressed the situation of widows in verses 8–9, but he returns to that topic again here, combining the advice that he gave to them in verses 8–9 (permission to marry if they wish or need to, but a preference for staying single if they can) with a reminder of the binding nature of marriage while the husband is still alive (cf. vv. 10–16) and a proviso that remarriage ought only to be "in the Lord" (i.e., to a fellow believer).[277] Verse 40 offers another statement of advice in favor of singleness, before closing with a reminder to the readers that "I think

[274] E.g., Ciampa and Rosner, *The First Letter to the Corinthians*, 358–59.

[275] E.g., Garland, *1 Corinthians*, 341.

[276] Cf. Ciampa and Rosner, *The First Letter to the Corinthians*, 358–59.

[277] Fee characterizes this proviso as "good sense" rather than as a command or rule (Fee, *First Epistle to the Corinthians*, 392), but that Paul embeds the proviso in a sentence that

that I also have the Spirit of God"—presumably a rhetorical understatement, directed primarily at those within the Corinthian congregation who were more conscious of their own status as "spiritual" people than they are of Paul's authority as an apostle (cf. the more strongly worded rebuff to this group in 14:37–38).[278]

Bridge

The eschatological perspective Paul commends to the Corinthians is as foreign to our cultural context as it was to the Corinthians', and we ourselves as twenty-first century Christians are (in many cases, at least) as deeply shaped by our cultural context as the Corinthians were by theirs. Like the Corinthians, too, we live in a context in which attitudes toward marriage and singleness are a contested topic, especially among the educated elite.

In a context of cultural and philosophical controversy regarding matters of sex and marriage, Paul endorses neither the Stoic perspective nor the Cynic perspective in its entirety, refusing to be constrained by the dichotomy that the debate created or controlled in his thinking by the shared assumptions that generated it. If the Stoics and the Cynics shared the assumption that this world is a self-contained, undisturbed cosmos and that the scrutiny of the philosopher is sufficient to discover the freedoms and the duties of the wise man, and if they end up in dichotomous positions on the value of sex and marriage based on whether the defining identity of the wise man is as a citizen of the city or a citizen of the world, then Paul's response is to resist both the dichotomy that they construct and the assumption that makes it fundamental. Borrowing a term from the Christian philosopher Christopher Watkin, we may say that Paul "diagonalizes" the dichotomy,[279] refusing to let himself be coopted into either the ethic of the Stoics or the opposing view of the Cynics and arguing instead for a view that cuts diagonally across both of their positions. So he insists that marriage has a good purpose, that wives and husbands belong to one another, that they should honor the promises they have made and the debts that they owe to each other. But he also

---

is about circumstances in which a person is "bound" or "free" suggests that something stronger than mere advice is being offered here.

278 Garland, *1 Corinthians*, 344–45.

279 Cf. Christopher Watkin, *Thinking Through Creation: Genesis 1 and 2 as Tools of Cultural Critique* (Phillipsburg: P&R, 2017), 149.

insists, equally, that there are reasons why a wise person, depending on their circumstances, would choose singleness over marriage. And he emphasizes to everyone, slave or free, married or single, that they are to live in this world and make use of the things of this world as people who know that the world in its present form is passing away.

In our own time, under the pressure of an enormous cultural shift and a continuing set of debates about marriage and sexuality, we can learn something important from the way that Paul navigates a similar set of issues in 1 Corinthians 5–7. On particular matters of law and public policy we will, of course, need to pick a side. But on the larger question of the constellation of values and assumptions that drive and define the culture war within our society, we need to be wary of letting ourselves be drafted into either party, squeezed into the mold of either the "family values" of suburbia or the new moral code emerging out of the sexual revolution of the last half century. We believe that families matter and marriage should be honored by all. We care about the circumstances in which children grow up, and we take seriously the connections between sex and marriage and child-rearing. But we also believe in the church—in a family that is bigger than the nuclear family—and we believe in the resurrection and the life to come, and we embrace a way of life that involves tensions and risks and vulnerabilities that are unknown to those for whom everything orbits around the center of a safe and happy home.

Those of us who are preachers have the task of articulating that kind of diagonal, countercultural vision—exposing the ways in which the vision of the coming kingdom of God cuts across all the varieties of worldliness, critiquing their shared assumptions and refusing their artificial dichotomies. Our task, in imitation of Paul, is to take up the particulars of everyday life—what the church should do about a man who is in a sexual relationship with his stepmother, believers who are visiting prostitutes, married people who are splitting up or electing for a kind of celibate marriage—and frame them, as Paul does in 1 Corinthians 5–7, within the larger picture of what we believe about life and the world, the present age and the age to come, and the identity that we have as people called by Jesus.

V. Response Regarding Food Sacrificed to Idols (8:1–11:1)

Having dealt in chapter 7 with the first cluster of issues raised by the Corinthians' letter, Paul now turns to a new set of issues that he responds to in 8:1–11:1. The umbrella category under which the issues are grouped by Paul (and were probably also grouped in the Corinthians' letter) is "food sacrificed to idols" (τὰ εἰδωλόθυτα, 8:1; cf. 8:4, 7, 10; 10:19). The "knowledge[able]" members of the Corinthian church, to whom these chapters are primarily addressed,[280] appear to have justified their freedom to eat such food in any and every context, by appealing to theological slogans such as the ones Paul quotes in 8:1, 4, and 10:23.

In his response, however, Paul rejects the sweeping, careless, and self-serving logic with which they have used these slogans to assert their freedom, working his way through the nuances of a range of different scenarios that could arise for believers living in a first-century Greco-Roman city, including meals eaten in an idol's temple (8:10; 10:14–22), food purchased at the meat market (10:25–26), and meals eaten in the home of an unbeliever (10:27–30), before concluding with his own statement of the overarching goals that direct his own conduct and a call to the Corinthians to imitate him in living by them (10:31–11:1).

Here, as elsewhere in the letter, the content and emphases of Paul's response make it clear that he is interested not only in the ideas that the Corinthians espouse but also in the attitudes that motivate them and the allegiances that are communicated by their behavior. In keeping with that interest, Paul chooses first, in chapter 8, to address the attitudinal issues of the Corinthians' arrogance and lack of love, assuming for the sake of the argument that the "knowledge" they are boasting in gives them the freedom that they think they have to participate in temple meals. Only subsequently, when he returns to the issue in 10:14–22, does he make it clear that in his view their theological understanding is naïve and inadequate and that eating at the table of a pagan god is out of the question

---

[280] Unlike Rom 14–15, where parallel sets of exhortations are addressed to "the strong" and "the weak," the only use of "strong"/"weak" language in 1 Cor 8–10 is the references to the "weak conscience" (8:7, 12) of "the weak ... brother or sister" (8:9, 10, 11; cf. 9:22) against whom the readers addressed in this section of the letter are warned not to sin. The implied scenario is not one in which a vocal minority of "weak" believers are judging and condemning the behavior of a self-confident majority who see themselves as "strong" and are, in turn, despising the weak. It is, rather, a situation in which a self-assured elite who pride themselves on their knowledge and freedom are acting without regard for the vulnerabilities of the weak (who are defined, in this case, not by their adherence to rules derived from the Old Testament and Jewish tradition but by the vulnerabilities that derive from their preconversion experience of pagan religious practice). See especially the discussion in Fee, *First Epistle to the Corinthians*, 394–401, and Garland, *1 Corinthians*, 350–62.

for believers in Jesus, quite apart from its potential to cause a "weaker" brother or sister to stumble.[281]

At the center of his response, inserted between the paragraphs in which he responds to the Corinthian slogans and teases out the issues involved in these various scenarios, is an extended discussion of his own example in chapter 9, focusing on the freedoms that he forgoes and the self-discipline that he exercises for the sake of the gospel (and, in the case of the disciplines to which he refers in 9:24–27, for his own salvation's sake). This is followed in 10:1–13 by a second example, derived from the history of Israel in the wilderness, to which Paul appeals in support of his warning to the Corinthians that what is at stake is not only the cause of the gospel and the conscience of their brothers and sisters but (potentially at least) their own salvation too.

A. Food, Idols, and the Loving Use of Knowledge (8:1–13)

> [1] Now about food sacrificed to idols: We know that "we all have knowledge." Knowledge puffs up, but love builds up. [2] If anyone thinks he knows anything, he does not yet know it as he ought to know it. [3] But if anyone loves God, he is known by him.
>
> [4] About eating food sacrificed to idols, then, we know that "an idol is nothing in the world," and that "there is no God but one." [5] For even if there are so-called gods, whether in heaven or on earth—as there are many "gods" and many "lords"—[6] yet for us there is one God, the Father. All things are from him, and we exist for him. And there is one Lord, Jesus Christ. All things are through him, and we exist through him.
>
> [7] However, not everyone has this knowledge. Some have been so used to idolatry up until now that when they eat food sacrificed to an idol, their conscience, being weak, is defiled. [8] Food will not bring us close to God. We are not worse off if we don't eat, and we are not better if we do eat. [9] But be careful that this right of yours in no way becomes a stumbling block to the weak. [10] For if someone sees you, the one who has knowledge, dining in an idol's temple, won't his weak conscience be encouraged to eat food offered to idols? [11] So the weak person, the brother or sister for whom Christ died, is ruined by your knowledge. [12] Now when you sin like this against brothers and sisters and wound their weak conscience, you are sinning against Christ. [13] Therefore, if

[281] In opting for this reading of Paul's rhetorical and pastoral strategy, I am following the argument of Gordon Fee (among others) that the scenario envisaged in 8:10–12 falls within the category that Paul goes on in 10:14–22 to describe as "shar[ing] in ... the table of demons." Cf. Fee, *First Epistle to the Corinthians*, 394–401, and the further comments on v. 10, below.

food causes my brother or sister to fall, I will never again eat meat, so that I won't cause my brother or sister to fall.

Context/Structure/Form

Paul begins this new section of the letter with a third instance of the περὶ δέ formula first introduced in 7:1, signaling that he is now turning to the topic of "food sacrificed to idols" (τὰ εἰδωλόθυτα). Judging from the tone and content of Paul's response, it appears that the treatment of this issue in the Corinthians' letter was not a request for him to adjudicate between groups who held differing views but an emphatic assertion of the letter writers' own view (expressed as either a statement or a pointed question), insisting on their right to eat such food whenever and wherever they chose and basing their claim on slogans such as the ones Paul quotes in 8:1, 4, and 10:23.

Paul begins with the Corinthians' slogans, partially affirming their content but taking issue with the inadequate understanding they imply of the way in which such knowledge should be used by Christians (see §4). The primary focus of his criticism at this point is the failure of those who use the slogans in this manner to take into consideration the effect on others (and in particular the "weak" brothers and sisters who are still vulnerable to pressures and temptations to revert to the pagan practices of their preconversion lives). This criticism is foreshadowed in verses 1–3, with their contrast between knowledge, which "puffs up," and love, which "builds up," then further developed in verses 7–13 via the case study of the "weak" brother or sister that Paul asks his readers to consider. In between, in verses 4–6, Paul affirms the fundamental theological principle that is at the heart of true Christian knowledge and serves as the basis for both the freedom that Christians possess from the enchantments and enslavements of idolatry (cf. vv. 5, 8) and the obligation that Christians are under to give uncompromised allegiance to the one Lord Jesus (cf. 10:14–22).

Comments

8:1. Having introduced the issue to which he is now turning his attention ("Now about food sacrificed to idols ..."), Paul proceeds to quote the first of the slogans on which the writers of the Corinthian letter based their assertion of the freedom that they claimed: "We know that 'we all have knowledge.' "[282]

Given the way in which Paul goes on to speak about "knowledge" in the following verses (esp. v. 7), the content of the knowledge that the Corinthian slogan is almost certainly referring to—at least primarily—is the theological understanding that is summed up in the additional slogans Paul quotes in verse 4b. It is possible, as some commentators note, that the introductory οἴδαμεν ὅτι ("We know that ...") in 8:1, 4 could have been part of the Corinthian slogan or a quotation from their letter, rather than a Pauline introductory formula,[283] but whichever way the precise boundaries of the quotation are delimited, the structure of Paul's argumentation across the paragraph as a whole suggests that the meaning is much the same: Paul's quarrel, in the case of each of the slogans that he quotes in 8:1, 4 is not with the content of the Corinthian slogan but with the inferences (both theological and practical) that they draw from it and the uses to which they put it.

Paul's critique of the way in which the Corinthian elite are regarding and using the knowledge they claim to have is signaled immediately by his response to their slogan in verse 1b: "Knowledge puffs up, but love builds up." The attitude expressed in the slogan of the Corinthian letter writers is, in Paul's view, a further instance of their inflated, puffed-up arrogance (cf. 4:6, 18, 19; 5:2; 13:4). The arrogance Paul sees in the attitude of the Corinthians is a combination of several overlapping and interrelated problems: their brash overestimation of the extent of their understanding (cf. v. 2), their casual disregard for the conscience and salvation of their fellow believers (cf. vv. 7–13), their complacency regarding their own spiritual standing and security (cf. 10:12), and the inflated sense of self-importance and social aspiration that fuels their desire for unrestricted participation in occasions at which they can eat and drink with their pagan peers and superiors (cf. 4:8–13; 15:33–34). In contrast to this arrogant and entitled approach to the possession and use of knowledge,

---

[282] The CSB, like the majority of English versions, encloses the words at the end of v. 1a in quotation marks, representing them as a Corinthian slogan or a quotation from their letter; the same approach is generally taken to the brief maxims in v. 4 ("an idol is nothing in the world," and "there is no God but one"). For arguments in support of this approach, see the comments in Ciampa and Rosner, *The First Letter to the Corinthians*, 373–80; Fee, *First Epistle to the Corinthians*, 403–10; Schnabel, *Erster Korintherbrief*, 439–45; Schrage, *1 Korintherbrief*, 2:221.

[283] Cf. the discussion in Ciampa and Rosner, *The First Letter to the Corinthians*, 374.

Paul urges an attitude of love, which "builds up" (οἰκοδομεῖ) the other and the community (8:10 [ironically]; 10:23; 14:4, 17; cf. 14:3, 5, 12, 26), rather than puffing up the self.

8:2–3. The implication of verse 1b that the Corinthian letter writers know less than they think they do is reinforced in verse 2, where Paul asserts that the person who "thinks he knows" something "does not yet know it as he ought to know it" (cf. 3:18; 10:12; 14:37). Those who are most fulsome in their claims to knowledge ironically reveal the shallowness of their understanding; those, by contrast, who have begun to grasp something more than a few glib slogans realize that their knowledge is earthbound and limited, awaiting its completion in the age to come (cf. 13:12). In contrast to the person whose boasts of knowledge are depicted in verse 2 as spurious and delusionary, the person who loves God is, as Paul goes on to assert in verse 3, "known by" God—a far more important (and far more secure) reality.

Paul's reminder that the person who "loves God" is "known by him" serves partly as a reassurance for the whole congregation (including those who lack the theological sophistication of those who boast in their knowledge) that the relationship with God that that they enjoy in Christ is real and not illusory, based on God's sovereign and electing knowledge of them (cf. 13:12; Gal 4:9) rather than on the rickety foundation of their knowledge about God. At the same time, by implication, it functions as a humbling rebuke to those whose boast is encapsulated in the slogan of verse 1a, reminding them that "what counts is not so much our knowledge of God as God's knowledge of us."[284] More than that: by reminding the readers of the covenantal commitment ("lov[ing] God" and being "known by him") that is at the heart of true relationship with God, it anticipates the allusion to the Shema in the following verse (cf. Deut 6:4–5: "Listen, Israel: The Lord our God, the Lord is one. Love the Lord your God with all your heart, with all your soul, and with all your strength") and prepares the way for the call to loyal and exclusive allegiance that Paul goes on to amplify and develop in 10:1–22.[285]

8:4. Having voiced this initial rebuke to the underlying attitude that is expressed by the slogan quoted in verse 1, Paul now returns to the

---

[284] Hays, *First Corinthians*, 138; cf. Brian S. Rosner, "'Known by God': The Meaning and Value of a Neglected Biblical Concept," *TynBul* 59 (2008): 221–23.

[285] Cf. Ciampa and Rosner, *The First Letter to the Corinthians*, 378.

particular topic under discussion ("About eating food sacrificed to idols, then ..."), before quoting what appear to have been two more Corinthian slogans: "We know that 'an idol is nothing in the world,' and that 'there is no God but one.'" Here, as in verse 1, the opening words, οἴδαμεν ὅτι ("We know that"), are probably a Pauline introductory formula rather than part of the Corinthian slogan[286] and indicate once again that Paul is in basic agreement with the content of the slogans. Paul's agreement with the second slogan is immediately reinforced in verses 5–6, and his agreement with the first is confirmed when he returns to the subject in 10:19–20a (though in the latter instance his agreement with the claim that "an idol is nothing" is qualified by a reminder of the complicating reality that "what [worshipers of idols] sacrifice, they sacrifice to demons and not to God").

8:5–6. Paul's agreement with the second of the two slogans that he has quoted in verse 4 is reinforced in verses 5–6 by a carefully constructed statement (possibly an expanded version of a preexisting hymn or baptismal creed) summing up his understanding of the oneness of God and the sole lordship of Christ: "For even if there are so-called gods, whether in heaven or on earth—as there are many 'gods' and many 'lords'—yet for us there is one God, the Father. All things are from him, and we exist for him. And there is one Lord, Jesus Christ. All things are through him, and we exist through him."

Paul is happy to agree that the basic theological content of the slogans in verse 4 can still (and must still) be wholeheartedly affirmed by those who have come to confess Jesus as Lord. The meaning of the claim that "there is one God, ... all things are from him, and we exist for him" (with its unmistakable echoes of the Shema and its possible additional allusions to the language of Hellenistic Judaism and Stoic natural theology)[287] must now be freshly understood in a way that includes the distinctively Christian confession that "there is one Lord, Jesus Christ. All things are through him, and we exist through him."[288] Nevertheless, the function

[286] The repetition of the word ὅτι as an introduction to the second slogan in v. 4b further increases the likelihood that this is the case.

[287] E.g., Philo, *Cherubim* 125–126; *Spec. Laws* 1.208; Marcus Aurelius, *Med.* 4.23; Pseudo-Aristotle, *De Mundo* 6; Seneca, *Ep.* 65.

[288] See especially Bauckham, *God Crucified*, 36–40; Wright, *Paul and the Faithfulness of God*, 661–70.

of the confession as (among other things) a repudiation of the pagans' allegiance to "many 'gods' and many 'lords'" is unaltered (see §§1, 2).[289]

Although the gods of the pagan pantheon were only, as Paul is happy to grant, "so-called" (λεγόμενοι) gods (cf. Gal 4:8), the presence of their physical images was a pervasive and dominating feature of the urban landscape that the Corinthians inhabited and their influence was powerful and far-reaching.[290] The gods were as omnipresent in the social and cultural life of the city as their images and shrines were in its physical landscape, and the stance taken by Jews and Christians who insisted that "for us there is one God" placed them sharply at odds with the traditions and expectations of the culture that surrounded them, risking ostracism, social shame, and economic disadvantage.[291]

8:7. Having confirmed in verses 5–6 his basic agreement with the content of the slogans quoted in verse 4, Paul now goes on to criticize the inferences that the authors of the Corinthian letter appear to have drawn from them and the uses to which they have put the knowledge that they claim. His particular focus in verses 7–13 is on the thoughtlessness of those who have come to the conclusion that they have an unrestricted right to eat food that has been sacrificed to an idol, in any situation they wish, without taking into account the effect of their actions on those who

---

[289] Given the context, with its focus on questions of food and temple worship, the "lords" in view here are almost certainly, like the "gods," to be understood as deities to whom cultic worship was offered and not the living, human political authorities who could also be addressed as "lords" (κύριοι). The line between political allegiance and religious veneration was a blurry one, however, given the increasing tendency of Roman emperors in this period to associate themselves in various ways with the worship of the traditional gods and receive divine honors themselves. On the relationship between the veneration of the traditional Greek and Roman gods and the more recently introduced rites of the Roman imperial cult, see Bookidis, "Religion in Corinth," 156–57; Mary E. Hoskins Walbank, "Evidence for the Imperial Cult in Julio-Claudian Corinth," in *Subject and Ruler: The Cult of the Ruling Power in Classical Antiquity*, ed. Alistair Small, JRASup (Ann Arbor: Journal of Roman Archaeology, 1996), 201–14; Winter, *Divine Honours*, 1–123.

[290] Cf. the list of shrines in Pausanias, *Descr.* 2.1–5, and the discussion of the surviving archaeological evidence from Roman era Corinth in Bookidis, "The Sanctuaries of Corinth," 256–58, and Bookidis, "Religion in Corinth," 151–64.

[291] Even those among the educated elite who embraced some version of monotheism or panentheism as a matter of philosophical opinion rarely dissented or abstained from the traditional practices of cultic veneration; cf. the famous discussion of the tensions between Roman natural theology, civil theology, and mythical theology, in Augustine, *Civ.* 6.5–10, including quotations from a no longer extant treatise, *De Superstitione*, that he attributes to Seneca.

do not have the same knowledge that they have. Accordingly, he begins in verse 7 by reminding the Corinthian elite of the vulnerable situation that such people are placed in: "However, not everyone has this knowledge. Some have been so used to idolatry up until now that when they eat food sacrificed to an idol, their conscience, being weak, is defiled."

This is the first mention in chapter 8 of the category of a person with a "weak conscience" (cf. v. 12, and the references to "the weak ... brother or sister" in 8:9, 10, 11).[292] Here (in contrast to the description in Rom 14 of the person who is "weak in faith," observing sacred days and abstaining from certain foods in deference to rules that appear to have been based on Old Testament laws and Jewish interpretive tradition), the nature of the vulnerability that Paul has in mind is based on such persons' previous, and in some cases very recent,[293] experience of participation in the rituals of pagan religious practice. The enduring formative effects of this experience, combined with a lack of the kind of knowledge that might enable them to retrain their instincts and affections, create a situation in which such people are exposed to significant risk of acting in such a way that their conscience is "defiled" (μολύνεται) by continuing or returning to practices that (in their own minds, at least) signify a compromise of allegiances.[294]

---

[292] "Conscience" (συνείδησις) in Paul's letters typically refers to an individual's faculty of moral self-consciousness, which pronounces an internal, subjective verdict on the rightness or wrongness of his or her past actions (cf. Paul's use of the cognate verb, σύνοιδα, in 4:4) and can, via reflection or habituation, contribute to the processes of moral deliberation and character formation that inform future moral action. Cf. Fee, *First Epistle to the Corinthians*, 419–20.

[293] Note the phrase "uptil now" (ἕως ἄρτι).

[294] The CSB translation of v. 7b syntactically subordinates the first clause ("when they eat food sacrificed to an idol") to the second ("their conscience, being weak, is defiled"), translating ὡς as "when" and leaving the conjunction καὶ untranslated. A more natural reading of the syntax would be to take the two clauses as being in coordinate relationship with one other, in keeping with the LEB's more literal translation: "But some, being accustomed until now to the idol, eat this food as food sacrificed to idols, and their conscience, because it is weak, is defiled." On this reading, the word ὡς functions to communicate the idea that such people eat the food in question not merely as ordinary food, devoid of religious significance, but "*as* food sacrificed to idols" (i.e., as food whose consumption implies an act of participation in the cult of the god). Cf. Brookins and Longenecker, *1 Corinthians 1–9*, 199, and the more expansive paraphrase in the NIV: "Some people are still so accustomed to idols that when they eat sacrificial food they think of it as having been sacrificed to a god, and since their conscience is weak, it is defiled."

Paul's description of such people and their consciences as "weak" (ἀσθενής) would probably have carried resonances for the Corinthians of the way in which such terminology was used in popularized versions of Greco-Roman moral philosophy to refer to the defective faculties of judgment possessed by people who lack serious philosophical training (e.g., Epictetus's description of a "sickly soul" [ἀσθενὴς ψυχή] in *Diatr.* 2.15.20). Within the immediate literary context of the letter, however, his language is also colored by his use of the language of "weak" and "strong" to refer to the differing socioeconomic circumstances that distinguished some believers from others (e.g., 1:25, 27; 4:10; 9:22; 12:22), allowing some the leisure to cultivate a sophisticated theological understanding and denying that opportunity to others.

8:8–9. Verses 8–9 begin the process of unpacking the logical and practical entailments of verses 4–7. Verse 8 draws out the implications of the core theological convictions articulated in verses 4–6 for the particular matter of eating and drinking, and verse 9 draws out the practical implications of the description in verse 7 of the brother or sister with a weak conscience for the question of how the knowledgeable should regulate their own conduct.

The two short sentences in verse 8 express a viewpoint on which Paul and the Corinthian letter writers can presumably agree: given the foundational theological understandings summed up in verses 4–6, matters of food and drink can safely be regarded as indifferent, in and of themselves. If the idols worshiped in the pagan temples are "nothing" (v. 4), then they have no power to imbue food that has been consecrated to them with any intrinsic spiritual qualities, either positive or negative. And if Jesus Christ is the one Lord of all, Jew and gentile alike (v. 6), then the purity boundaries that once separated Israel from the nations are of no further consequence for determining what can be eaten and drunk by believers: "Food will not bring us close to God. We are not worse off if we don't eat, and we are not better if we do eat."

But Paul is not content to leave the matter there, at the level of sweeping, in-principle generalizations and the broad rights and freedoms that they have been taken by the Corinthian letter writers as implying. Just as he has earlier done in verses 1b–3 and verse 7, Paul follows a Corinthian slogan or a statement of theological common ground on which he and the letter writers can agree with a caveat or qualification.

Here, the qualification Paul gives to the sweeping generalizations of verse 8 takes the form of a warning: "But be careful that this right of yours in no way becomes a stumbling block to the weak." The language of Paul's warning assumes for the sake of the argument that the knowledge the letter writers possess grants them the "right" (ἐξουσία) that they lay claim to. This assumption is a broadly reasonable one to make, given the statements of the previous verse, though (as Paul will make clear when he revisits the issue in 10:14–22) the ἐξουσία of the Corinthians in matters of eating and drinking may not be as far-reaching as they think it is. At this point in the argument, however, the limits Paul will go on to set in chapter 10 are not yet directly in view: his immediate concern is with the way in which the letter writers use their freedom and the account that they need to take of others as they do so.

The danger he has in mind here is not the danger that another believer with excessively censorious opinions will "take offence"; it is that the conduct and example of a believer will become a "stumbling block" (πρόσκομμα) for a weaker brother or sister, placing their very salvation at risk (cf. Rom 9:32, 34; 14:13, 20). A risk this serious is not something Paul is prepared to countenance: the warning he gives requires active vigilance and concern (βλέπετε, "Be careful") and a willingness to err on the safe side in anticipating and avoiding such possibilities (μή πως, "in no way"; more literally, "lest in some way").

8:10–12. Verses 10–12 elaborate on the warning in verse 9 by asking the readers to imagine a particular hypothetical scenario that might arise under the policy that the letter writers are advocating. Here, for the first time in the discussion, Paul places the eating of food that has been sacrificed to idols within a particular social location: "dining in an idol's temple" (ἐν εἰδωλείῳ κατακείμενον, v. 10).

Paul gives no explicit indication at this point in the argument as to whether the activity he is describing would be off-limits for believers even in the absence of a weaker brother or sister. In view of that, some commentators draw the conclusion that Paul must be talking here about a mode of "dining in an idol's temple" that is fundamentally different from the kind of scenario described in 10:14–22, where the temple meal Paul has in mind clearly functioned as a form of ritual participation in the cult of the god such that those involved were unambiguously practicing "idolatry" (εἰδωλολάτρια, v. 14) and, like the worshipers in Israel's temple, "eat[ing] the sacrifices" (ἐσθίοντες τὰς θυσίας) as "particip[ants] in the altar" (κοινωνοὶ τοῦ θυσιαστηρίου, v. 18).[295]

In support of this claim, proponents point to examples of surviving papyrus letters in which the recipients are invited to meals at the temple that appear to have been of a primarily social rather than cultic nature. One such letter, for example, reads: "Apollonius requests you to dine at the table of the lord Sarapis on the occasion of the coming of age of his brothers in the temple of Thoeris."[296] Nevertheless, the fact that the invitation quoted above still describes the occasion as a meal "at the table of the lord Sarapis" (εἰς κλείνην τοῦ κυρίου Σαράπιδος)—possibly implying the inclusion of a ceremony in which the god was invoked or a sacrifice offered—supports the conclusion that Paul would have viewed participation in an occasion such as this as an activity involving a form of ritual communion with the god that was intrinsically incompatible with a Christian's exclusive allegiance to Christ (cf. 10:21).[297]

The simplest way to interpret the shape of Paul's argument, relating it to what we can reconstruct as the likely cultural context, is probably to assume that the kind of occasion he is referring to in 8:10 falls within the scope of the same category that he has in view in 10:14–22. There, he makes it clear that all such occasions are inadmissible for Christians, but

---

[295] Cf. Wendell Willis, *Idol Meat in Corinth: The Pauline Argument in 1 Corinthians 8 and 10* (Chico: Scholars Press, 1985); Wendell Willis, "1 Corinthians 8–10: A Retrospective After Twenty-Five Years," *ResQ* 49 (2007): 103–12; David G. Horrell, "Theological Principle or Christological Practice? Pauline Ethics in 1 Corinthians 8.1–11.1," *JSNT* 67 (1997): 99; Brookins, *Reading 1 Corinthians*, 99–101; Oropeza, *1 Corinthians*, 133; Andrew David Naselli, "Was It Always Idolatrous for Corinthian Christians to Eat εἰδωλόθυτα in an Idol's Temple? (1 Cor 8–10)," *STR* 9 (2018): 29–43. I followed this interpretation of v. 10 in an earlier publication (Starling, "As to Sensible People," 120–21) but have since become less convinced of the likelihood of the scenario that it presupposes.

[296] P. Oxy. 1484, quoted in Willis, *Idol Meat in Corinth*, 41. For other examples, including invitations to a birthday celebration in a Sarapeum (P. Oxy. 2791) and a marriage feast in a temple of Sabazius (P. Oxy. 2678), see Chan-Hie Kim, "The Papyrus Invitation," *JBL* 94 (1975): 391–402.

[297] Further complicating the picture is the fact that the occasion to which the guests are invited in P. Oxy. 1484 is located not at the temple of Sarapis but at the temple of Thoeris (i.e., the Egyptian goddess Taweret); other surviving papyri invite guests to "the table of the lord Sarapis" (e.g., P. Oslo. 157) and "the consecrated meal (ἱέρωμα) of the lady Isis" (e.g., P. Fouad 76) but specify that the occasions are held in private homes. These examples suggest the likelihood that the formula "the table/consecrated meal of the lord/lady X" was a way of referring to the god who would be ceremonially honored as part of the occasion, not (directly or necessarily) to the location in which the meal would be eaten.

at this point in the argument he is still focusing on the effect that such an activity would have on the weak conscience of a fellow believer, not on the question of whether this particular mode of eating food previously sacrificed to idols is permissible in and of itself.[298]

In the hypothetical scenario Paul is exploring, the effect on the weaker brother or sister of observing their more knowledgeable fellow believer dining in an idol's temple is dangerously emboldening: "won't his weak conscience be encouraged to eat food offered to idols?" (v. 10b).[299] The word Paul uses to speak of the weak believer being "encouraged" (οἰκοδομηθήσεται; more literally, "built up" or "edified") is a favorite Pauline word, which he uses elsewhere in an exclusively positive sense (e.g., in this letter, 8:1; 10:23; 14:4, 17; cf. 14:3, 5, 12, 26). Here, given the close proximity to its use in an unambiguously positive sense in 8:1, its use is probably deliberate and ironic (i.e., the weaker believer's conscience is being "built up" toward his or her ruin [cf. v. 11]).[300]

8:11–13. Verses 11–13 elaborate on the scenario that Paul has asked the readers to imagine in verse 10, highlighting its gravity in several interrelated ways. The real effect of the action by which the weaker believer's conscience was "encouraged" (v. 10) was not to strengthen or educate the conscience but to "wound" (τύπτοντες, v. 12) it. The consequence (assuming the weaker believer acts on the example given and continues to walk down that path) is that the person is "ruined" (ἀπόλλυται, v. 11)—language Paul uses elsewhere to speak of death under God's judgment and/or the loss of eternal salvation (e.g., Rom 2:12; 14:15; 1 Cor 1:18; 10:9–10; 15:18; 2 Cor 2:15; 4:3; 2 Thess 2:10).[301] The person who has suffered this fate is no stranger but a "brother or sister" (vv. 11, 12; cf. v. 13); a person "for whom

---

[298] Cf. Fee, *First Epistle to the Corinthians*, 394–401; Garland, *1 Corinthians*, 388–89; Schnabel, *Erster Korintherbrief*, 426–33.

[299] More literally: "Will not his conscience, him being weak, be built up to eat food offered to idols?"

[300] Paul's use of the term here in v. 10 is unlikely to be an appropriation of language that the Corinthian letter writers used in a positive sense to refer to their own project of educating the consciences of their weaker brothers and sisters. The rhetorical question that he poses in v. 10 seems to be framed on the basis of an assumption that the letter writers were not giving any thought at all to their weaker brothers and sisters, not that they were engaged in an intentional campaign aimed at educating and enlightening them. Cf. Garland, *1 Corinthians*, 389; contra Fee, *First Epistle to the Corinthians*, 426–27.

[301] The situation Paul appears to have in mind is one in which the weaker brother or sister, emboldened by the example of a fellow believer whom they have seen participating in a meal of some sort at an idol's temple, draws the conclusion that they can return without

Christ died" (v. 11). To sin in this manner against such a person is, given the solidarity between Christ and his people, to sin against Christ (v. 12).

If this is what is at stake then Paul draws the inescapable practical conclusion: "Therefore, if food causes my brother or sister to fall, I will never again eat meat, so that I won't cause my brother or sister to fall." The verb σκανδαλίζω ("cause ... to fall"), which Paul uses twice in this verse, can sometimes be used with the relatively weak sense of "shock" or "give offence to" (e.g., Matt 15:12; 17:27; John 6:61), but its use here to refer to an action by which a brother or sister is "ruined" (v. 11) suggests a significantly stronger meaning, in line with the use of the cognate noun σκάνδαλον in the LXX to refer to the deadly risk that the people of Israel would be led astray into the worship of idols (e.g., Judg 2:3; Josh 23:13; Ps 105:36; Deut 7:16).[302]

The policy of total abstention from meat that Paul envisages as a course he would be willing to adopt almost certainly goes farther than is likely to be required and is, in that sense, hyperbolic;[303] it is entirely plausible to assume that there will still be plenty of occasions that Paul is able to put into practice the advice that he goes on to give in 10:25–27 and continue with the adaptability of practice that he describes in 9:19–23.[304] But if circumstances were such that he could not eat meat of any kind without creating a serious risk of leading fellow believers into sin and imperiling their salvation, then the decision to abstain altogether from meat would be, in his view, the obvious and necessary course to take. Compared with that possibility, the more modest sacrifice that he is in fact asking the Corinthian letter writers to make—abstaining from food that has been sacrificed to idols when it is eaten in a context (e.g., in a meal at an idol's temple) that would lead other believers into sin and potential apostasy—seems far from extreme or onerous.

---

harm to the cultic practices in which they participated before their conversion, sliding back across the line into the ranks of "those who are perishing" (1 Cor 1:18).

302 Cf. Garland, *1 Corinthians*, 390, citing Willis, *Idol Meat in Corinth*, 108–9.

303 Cf. Garland, *1 Corinthians*, 390.

304 As Fee points out, the shift in v. 13 from "food" (βρῶμα) to "meat" (κρέα) reflects the fact that he is reflecting with real seriousness on the decisions he himself makes to limit the exercise of freedoms that he does in fact possess (cf. 9:19–23): "He has been dealing right along with a form of 'eating'; but since he generalizes in the first person singular (i.e., with reference to his own conduct) and since he would never have participated in the cultic meals as such, he must broaden the principle to refer to scruples about food in general, and animal flesh in particular." Fee, *First Epistle to the Corinthians*, 430.

Bridge

For some twenty-first century readers of 1 Corinthians (particularly those whose primary cultural context is a non-Western one), the issues Paul is addressing in chapters 8–10 will bring to mind immediate and obvious points of potential applicability, evoking thoughts of closely comparable situations that involve the overlap between social interaction, familial obligation, and traditional religious practices. For other readers (including many of those who live in contexts that have been shaped primarily by Western cultural traditions), the issues addressed in these chapters will appear, at least at first glance, to lack any directly comparable equivalent in our own situation.

In both cases the assumption of total equivalence or total nonequivalence is worth examining. Not all expressions of ritualized respect are necessarily the kind of veneration that belongs exclusively to God, nor are the cherished traditions of some Western cultural contexts beyond scrutiny as to whether they are compatible with faithful allegiance to Christ. But even when due allowance has been made for both of these considerations, it remains the case that most Christians living in non-Western cultural contexts will find it easier to identify scenarios that are closely comparable with the scenarios Paul addresses in these chapters than will most Christians in Western contexts.

For all readers, however, the basic stance that Paul is urging the Corinthians to adopt is of the utmost relevance and importance. The knowledge that we are given in the gospel (along with all the knowledge that we derive from the various sources of information and understanding that are available to us) is not to be received as a possession that we exploit for our own personal advantage. It is, rather, to be used in love and with a consciousness of the particular responsibility that we owe to our brothers and sisters. Paul is not an enemy of knowledge or of rational reflection and deliberation; it is, after all, in this same letter that he repeatedly asks his readers, "Do you not know ... ?", reminding them of essential points of memory and understanding that ought to shape their conduct in the world, and goes out of his way to say that he is addressing his arguments to them "as to sensible people" (ὡς φρονίμοις, 10:15).[305] He is, however, a sharp critic of the elitist and irresponsible approach to

[305] Cf. the discussion of this aspect of the letter in Starling, "As to Sensible People," 113–26.

knowledge that appears to have been adopted or assumed by the writers of the Corinthian letter.

Those of us who are the least (or least obviously) confronted with questions such as those concerning food offered to idols may well be, in many cases, the most deeply formed by cultural assumptions regarding the rights and freedoms of the autonomous individual and, in consequence, the most commonly prone to the kind of attitudes that Paul is warning against in this chapter. A passage that seems, at first glance, to be remote from our situation and the issues that we face may turn out to be one of the portions of the letter that engages most searchingly and unsettlingly with values and behaviors that are second nature to us. For all of us, whatever our situation, the challenges and reminders Paul gives to the Corinthians in this chapter of the letter touch on matters that are of fundamental importance for the way in which we interpret the world we live in, the way in which we regard the knowledge that we possess (or claim that we possess), and the way in which we make use of the power and the freedoms that our knowledge grants to us.

B. Paul's Example: Freedom, Rights, and Self-Discipline (9:1–27)

> 1 Am I not free? Am I not an apostle? Have I not seen Jesus our Lord?
> Are you not my work in the Lord? 2 If I am not an apostle to others, at
> least I am to you, because you are the seal of my apostleship in the Lord.
>
> 3 My defense to those who examine me is this: 4 Don't we have the right
> to eat and drink? 5 Don't we have the right to be accompanied by a
> believing wife like the other apostles, the Lord's brothers, and Cephas?
> 6 Or do only Barnabas and I have no right to refrain from working?
> 7 Who serves as a soldier at his own expense? Who plants a vineyard
> and does not eat its fruit? Or who shepherds a flock and does not drink
> the milk from the flock?
>
> 8 Am I saying this from a human perspective? Doesn't the law also say
> the same thing? 9 For it is written in the law of Moses, **Do not muzzle
> an ox while it treads out grain.** Is God really concerned about oxen?
> 10 Isn't he really saying it for our sake? Yes, this is written for our sake,
> because he who plows ought to plow in hope, and he who threshes
> should thresh in hope of sharing the crop. 11 If we have sown spiritual
> things for you, is it too much if we reap material benefits from you? 12 If
> others have this right to receive benefits from you, don't we even more?
> Nevertheless, we have not made use of this right; instead, we endure
> everything so that we will not hinder the gospel of Christ.

13 Don't you know that those who perform the temple services eat the
food from the temple, and those who serve at the altar share in the
offerings of the altar? 14 In the same way, the Lord has commanded
that those who preach the gospel should earn their living by the gospel.

15 For my part I have used none of these rights, nor have I written these
things that they may be applied in my case. For it would be better for
me to die than for anyone to deprive me of my boast! 16 For if I preach
the gospel, I have no reason to boast, because I am compelled to preach—
and woe to me if I do not preach the gospel! 17 For if I do this willingly,
I have a reward, but if unwillingly, I am entrusted with a commission.
18 What then is my reward? To preach the gospel and offer it free of
charge and not make full use of my rights in the gospel.

19 Although I am free from all and not anyone's slave, I have made myself a slave to everyone, in order to win more people. 20 To the Jews I
became like a Jew, to win Jews; to those under the law, like one under
the law—though I myself am not under the law—to win those under
the law. 21 To those who are without the law, like one without the law—
though I am not without God's law but under the law of Christ—to win
those without the law. 22 To the weak I became weak, in order to win
the weak. I have become all things to all people, so that I may by every
possible means save some. 23 Now I do all this because of the gospel, so
that I may share in the blessings.

24 Don't you know that the runners in a stadium all race, but only one
receives the prize? Run in such a way to win the prize. 25 Now everyone
who competes exercises self-control in everything. They do it to receive
a perishable crown, but we an imperishable crown. 26 So I do not run
like one who runs aimlessly or box like one beating the air. 27 Instead,
I discipline my body and bring it under strict control, so that after
preaching to others, I myself will not be disqualified.

Context/Structure/Form

As is frequently the case in Paul's letters, the final verse of one section becomes a kind of springboard from which he launches into the next. Here, the shift Paul makes in 8:13 to the first person singular in his assertion of willingness to give up meat altogether, if required, prompts an extended discussion in chapter 9 of Paul's stance with regard to his freedom and rights (9:1–23) and the self-discipline that he exercises over the appetites and practices of his body (9:24–27).[306] Nowhere in this chapter

[306] Cf. David G. Horrell, *The Social Ethos of the Corinthian Correspondence: Interests and Ideology from 1 Corinthians to 1 Clement* (Edinburgh: T&T Clark, 1996), 205; Hall, *Unity*, 179; Joel White, "Meals in Pagan Temples and Apostolic Finances: How Effective Is Paul's Argument in 1 Corinthians 9:1–23 in the Context of 1 Corinthians 8–10?," *BBR* 23 (2018): 540.

does he state or imply that he sometimes eats in idol temples and sometimes does not.[307] Instead, he focuses on the particular entitlements that he possesses by virtue of his work as an apostle (vv. 1–18) and the freedom from Torah-based rules that he shares with all believers (vv. 19–23).

The discussion commences on an apologetic note, with Paul seeking first to assert his freedom as a Christian and to defend and confirm the rights that he possesses as an apostle (vv. 1–14), before going on to highlight and justify the ways in which he has chosen not to fully exercise those rights (vv. 15–18) and the freedom that he possesses as one "not under law" (vv. 19–23). Finally, in verses 24–27, Paul shifts the focus from the decisions he makes to forgo his rights for the sake of others to the athlete-like disciplines that he practices for the sake of his own perseverance in faith, "so that after preaching to others, I myself will not be disqualified" (v. 27).

Comments

9:1–2. Having introduced the subject of his own practice in 8:13, Paul now feels the need to expand on that topic at some length partly (and necessarily) as a defense against the criticisms that appeared to have been leveled at him by the people he refers to in verse 3 and partly as an example for the Corinthians to imitate. The defense that he offers is hardly routine or perfunctory: as Fee points out, the tone is urgent, earnest, and combative, suggesting that he is responding to real, not merely hypothetical, questions and criticisms.[308]

Paul's defense commences in verses 1–2 with a barrage of rhetorical questions (four in these verses, which are followed by eight more in vv. 4–8 and another four in vv. 9b–12). The first ("Am I not free?") relates directly to the scenario he has already referred to in 8:13 and implies an assertion that he will return to and build on in verses 19–23. In addition to this freedom, however (which he shares with the Corinthians and with all believers, Jew and gentile alike), Paul goes on to assert an additional set of rights that he possesses by virtue of his calling as an apostle—a calling that appears to have been questioned by some in Corinth, apparently on

[307] That he does not say this offers further support for the view (argued for below) that eating in idol temples is not, in Paul's opinion, a matter of indifference in which enlightened believers can participate with impunity, provided there are no weaker brothers or sisters present.

[308] Fee, *First Epistle to the Corinthians*, 433–35.

the basis of his failure to exercise the full range of his apostolic prerogatives (cf. 2 Cor 11:7–11; 12:13).

Before he turns in verses 3–18 to the explicit subject of those rights, however, he begins in verses 1–2 by shoring up the basic premise of his apostleship, first asserting it in the form of a rhetorical question ("Am I not an apostle?") and then offering support for that assertion via two more rhetorical questions ("Have I not seen Jesus our Lord? Are you not my work in the Lord?"). The first of these reminds the readers of the event that was the occasion of his apostolic commissioning and the primary basis for his authority as an apostle (cf. 15:5–11).[309] The second question adds an additional reason why the Corinthians, of all people, should acknowledge him as such, given that their existence as a church is the result of work that he did in fulfillment of his apostolic commissioning. This inference, already implied in the rhetorical question of verse 1b, is drawn out explicitly in verse 2: "If I am not an apostle to others, at least I am to you, because you are the seal of my apostleship in the Lord."[310]

9:3–7. Having reasserted his apostleship and the reasons the Corinthians should acknowledge it (vv. 1–2), Paul now commences the "defense" (ἀπολογία) to the criticisms and questions of those who have taken it upon themselves to "examine" (ἀνακρίνουσιν) him.[311] Both terms have courtroom connotations, the former being used for the speech that an accused person or their legal representative made in defense against

---

309 Not all who saw the risen Jesus were commissioned as apostles (cf. 15:6), and not all those who were called "apostles" in the early church were witnesses of the risen Jesus; in some cases, the term appears to have been used for men and women who were commissioned and sent out by churches as church-planting missionaries or special envoys of various sorts (cf. Phil 2:25; 2 Cor 8:23; 1 Cor 9:6; Acts 14:14; cf. Acts 13:2–3). Paul's own apostleship was located within the intersection of those two categories, as a witness, representative, and emissary of the Lord Jesus who had been personally commissioned in the context of a face-to-face encounter with the risen Christ. Cf. Gal 1:15–17.

310 It is difficult to say whether the "others" referred to here are critics of Paul who have come from outside the Corinthian church but have begun to gain influence among them (Fee, *First Epistle to the Corinthians*, 437–38; Hall, *Unity*, 13; cf. v. 3; 2 Cor 10–12) or simply the members of other churches that Paul did not establish (Garland, *1 Corinthians*, 405). Either way, Paul's emphasis in v. 2 is not the concessive clause that begins the sentence ("If I am not an apostle to others ...") but on the assertions that conclude it ("at least I am to you, because you are the seal of my apostleship in the Lord").

311 The present participle construction that Paul uses to refer to "those who examine" (τοῖς ... ἀνακρίνουσιν) him suggests strongly that the group to whom he is referring is an actual and not a merely hypothetical or fictive group; cf. Hall, *Unity*, contra Mitchell, *Paul and the Rhetoric of Reconciliation*, 246.

an allegation (e.g., Acts 22:1; cf. Paul's use of the cognate verb in 2 Cor 12:19), the latter being used for the questions and deliberations of an investigative or judicial authority (e.g., Acts 12:19; 28:18; cf. 1 Cor 4:3–5). The combination of the two terms here suggests a suspicious, inquisitorial, or accusing stance that some have taken toward Paul, requiring him to respond in his own defense.

The primary focus of the questioning directed at Paul by these people appears to have related to the material support that an apostle was entitled to receive. The core accusation, it seems, was not that Paul was demanding support that he was not entitled to but that his failure to demand such support (or to accept it if offered)[312] was evidence that he was not an authentic apostle—and, consequently, that the rights he was refraining from exercising did not belong to him anyway.[313]

Paul therefore begins his defense by seeking to confirm the existence of the rights that he has chosen not to exercise, launching into a second string of rhetorical questions that commences in verse 4 and extends through to the end of verse 8. The first question, in verse 4, implies an assertion that Paul takes as self-evidently true: "Don't we have the right to eat and drink?"[314] The μὴ οὐκ construction with which Paul introduces the question gives it a heavy rhetorical slant ("Surely you're not saying that we *don't* have a right to food and drink?"), consistent with the self-evident character of the proposition that it is asserting.[315] The word ἐξουσία that he uses here to refer to the "right" to food and drink that he possesses is the same word he used in 8:9 to refer to the "right" that members of the Corinthian church are asserting to eat food that has been

---

312 As Ryan Schellenberg correctly points out, we do not have enough evidence to say with certainty whether Paul was offered support and refused it or simply refrained from requesting that the Corinthians provide it. Ryan S. Schellenberg, "Did Paul Refuse an Offer of Support from the Corinthians?," *JSNT* 40 (2018): 312–36.

313 Cf. 2 Cor 11:7–11; 12:13, and the discussions in Hall, *Unity*, 174–98; Fee, *First Epistle to the Corinthians*, 440–43.

314 Paul's shift from the first person singular ("I") in vv. 1–3 to the first person plural ("we") in vv. 4–12 probably reflects the fact that—at some points at least in the discussion—he has Barnabas in mind as well as himself (cf. v. 6) and may also at other points (e.g., vv. 11–12) have in mind traveling companions such as Silas and Timothy who shared with him in the initial planting of the Corinthian church.

315 Cf. Brookins and Longenecker, *1 Corinthians 1–9*, 207; Thiselton, *First Corinthians*, 678–79, who translates the question, "Surely it cannot be that we have no 'right' to eat or drink?" (Thiselton, *First Corinthians*, 676). The same construction introduces the question in verse 5, implying a similar sense of incredulity on Paul's part.

offered to idols—a correspondence that prepares the way for Paul to use his own example of not fully exercising rights as an encouragement to the Corinthians to do the same (9:15–18).[316]

The second question, in verse 5, continues the focus on matters of material support for apostles who serve as traveling missionaries, asking this time: "Don't we have the right to be accompanied by a believing wife like the other apostles, the Lord's brothers, and Cephas?" Given the close proximity of chapters 8–9 to the immediately preceding discussion of marriage and singleness (in which Paul repeatedly makes reference to his own unmarried situation), some commentators have suggested that Paul may here be responding to criticisms based on his failure to (re)marry, raised as an additional objection to his legitimacy as an apostle.[317] This is unlikely to be his meaning, however, or the criticism that he is responding to: the verb περιάγειν that he uses reads far more naturally as "be accompanied by" than as "marry," and the close syntactical connection between the question in verse 5 and the immediately following question in verse 6, signaled by the "or" (ἤ) that introduces the latter, suggests that the focus in both questions is on matters of financial support, not marital status.[318] The function of the question is not to respond to a criticism of Paul's singleness but simply to make the point that, if Paul has the same rights as the other apostles to material support, then (like the other apostles, who travel with their wives) he would be entitled to support not only for himself but also for a wife, if he chose to marry one; if that is the case, then how much more obviously is he entitled to the smaller amount of support that would be required for him as a single person!

The third question of the sequence, in verse 6, presses home the point Paul has been making in the previous question by highlighting the inconsistency that would be created if the right asserted by the question in verse 5 were denied: "Or do only Barnabas and I have no right to refrain from working?" Given what Paul goes on to say about the way in which he has refrained from exercising this right and intends to continue doing so (vv. 12b, 15–18), his point here is not to defend himself against criticisms

---

316 Given the close connection between the three questions in 9:4–6, it makes best sense to read "the right to eat and drink" in v. 4 as referring to the right Paul has to the support required for basic sustenance, not to the freedom that he has from Old Testament food laws or superstitions regarding food that has been offered to idols.

317 Cf. the brief comments in Fee, *First Epistle to the Corinthians*, 445.

318 Cf. Brookins and Longenecker, *1 Corinthians 1–9*, 208.

that he illegitimately accepted support in the past or to request that the Corinthians now begin giving him the support that he has previously been denied. Paul's aim, rather, is to confirm that his practice of not receiving material support from the Corinthians (choosing rather to labor at a trade with his own hands, demeaning both himself and his potential patrons by so doing) has been a matter of free and deliberate choice on his part and not a sign that he lacked the right to ask for such support.

The right to material support that Paul has asserted as self-evident in verse 4 and defended in verses 5–6 on the basis of consistency with the treatment of other apostles is now given further support by an analogy that he draws in verse 7 between the support received by apostles and the reward that is owed to other workers in a variety of secular occupations: "Who serves as a soldier at his own expense? Who plants a vineyard and does not eat its fruit? Or who shepherds a flock and does not drink the milk from the flock?" The questions are obviously rhetorical in nature, implying the answer "no one" in each case.[319] A soldier is provided with the rations that he consumes day by day;[320] agricultural laborers and shepherds derive their living from the work that they do, including the sustenance that they (legitimately) take directly from the produce of the vines or the milk of the flock. In the same way, by implication, Paul as an apostle "should expect to be sustained by his 'produce' or 'flock'—the church that owes its existence to him."[321]

9:8–10. Having supported his point in verse 7 with illustrations drawn from everyday life, Paul now turns to the first of two appeals that he makes to the testimony of Scripture (vv. 9, 13), offering divine endorsement for what might otherwise be dismissed as arguments that he is making merely "from a human perspective" (κατὰ ἄνθρωπον, v. 8a). The source of the first piece of scriptural testimony is identified by Paul as "the law" (v. 8b) and further specified in the following verse as "the law of Moses" (v. 9a)—language that reflects the fact that Paul still views the

[319] The force of the first question is strengthened in the Greek by the addition of the indefinite adverb ποτέ ("Who [*ever*] serves as a soldier at his own expense?").

[320] The word ὀψώνια could be used in the sense of both "wages" and "provisions," but it is the latter sense that corresponds most closely to the grapes and milk Paul goes on to refer to in the questions that follow and best conveys the sense of what Paul has in mind regarding the kind of support that he viewed apostles as being entitled to. Cf. C. C. Caragounis, "ὀψώνιον: A Reconsideration of Its Meaning," *NovT* 16 (1974): 47–49, 51–52.

[321] Fee, *First Epistle to the Corinthians*, 447.

Old Testament law (including the law codes of the Sinai covenant, the larger Pentateuchal narrative in which they are embedded, and the Old Testament Scriptures as a whole) as divine testimony (cf. 14:21, 34), even if believers are no longer "under the law" as a covenantal authority (v. 20; cf. Gal 3:24–25; 5:18; Rom 6:14; 7:1–6).[322]

The text Paul goes on to quote is from Deuteronomy 25:4 and corresponds closely to the wording of that verse in surviving manuscripts of the LXX, with the only difference being that the word κημώσεις stands in place of its synonym φιμώσεις for "muzzle."[323] His use of that verse to support the point he is making about the right of apostles to receive material support from churches raises obvious questions about his approach to the interpretation and use of the Old Testament, particularly given the questions in verses 9b–10a with which he seeks to bridge the hermeneutical gap between oxen and apostles ("Is God really concerned about oxen? Isn't he really saying it for our sake?"). While some interpreters point to this verse as an example of Paul playing fast and loose with his Old Testament quotations,[324] Hays correctly notes that the original surrounding context of the verse in Deuteronomy 24–25 is full of provisions aimed at securing just and compassionate treatment of men and women (e.g., Deut 24:6–7, 10–22; 25:1–3), arguing that "it is not surprising that Paul would have read this verse also as suggesting something about justice in human economic affairs."[325]

Fee builds on this observation, pointing out that the law codes of the Old Testament (like most ancient legal codes) frequently function in a paradigmatic manner, with a concrete and particular legal enactment (in this instance, about oxen threshing) expected to provide a basis for extrapolation by judges and other interpreters (e.g., to animals other than oxen and activities other than threshing).[326] Arguing in a similar vein,

---

[322] Cf. Ciampa and Rosner, *The First Letter to the Corinthians*, 403–4; Christopher D. Stanley, *Arguing with Scripture: The Rhetoric of Quotations in the Letters of Paul* (New York: T&T Clark, 2004), 181.

[323] There is strong manuscript support for φιμώσεις in 1 Cor 9:9 (e.g., 𝔓[46], א, A), but that is easily explained as a scribal assimilation to the wording of the LXX. The different verb used by Paul may be a sign that he was quoting from memory, either imperfectly recalling the Greek or recalling the Hebrew text and translating it himself. Cf. Ciampa and Rosner, "1 Corinthians," 720.

[324] Cf. Collins, *First Corinthians*, 339; Stanley, *Arguing with Scripture*, 183.

[325] Hays, *First Corinthians*, 151.

[326] Fee, *First Epistle to the Corinthians*, 244.

David Instone-Brewer has highlighted the way in which later talmudic interpreters appealed to Deuteronomy 25:4 as one of the twin pillars on which they based their defense of the mishnaic rule (m. B. Meṣ. 7.2) that "these may eat [of the crop in which they labour] by virtue of what is enjoined in the Law: he who labours on what is still growing after the work is finished [i.e., from ploughing to reaping], and he who labours on what is already gathered before the work is finished [i.e., threshing]." The ruling in the Mishnah, the talmudic interpreters argued, was based on the logic that "if an ox, which does not eat of what is attached, may nevertheless eat of what is detached, then a man, who may eat of what is attached, may surely eat of what is detached!"[327]

Paul's application of Deuteronomy 25:4 to his own situation as a laboring apostle is probably best explained by an extrapolating logic of that sort, arguing from the lesser to the greater (*qal wachomer*). If that is the case, then his question in verse 9b ("Is God really concerned about oxen?") is to be understood as asking, in effect, "Is God really concerned *only* about oxen?" and the answer in verse 10a ("Isn't he really saying it for our sake?") as drawing out the extended application of the verse, based on the far greater concern that God has for humans,[328] including Paul and his fellow apostles.[329]

Verse 10b offers the answer to the question in verse 10a: "Yes, this is written for our sake, because he who plows ought to plow in hope, and he who threshes should thresh in hope of sharing the crop." Paul's twice-repeated statement that the scriptural text under discussion was written "for our sake" (δι' ἡμᾶς) anticipates the similar assertions in the following chapter that the stories of Scripture were written down "for our instruction" (πρὸς νουθεσίαν ἡμῶν, 10:11), and the events that they narrate took place as "examples for us" (τύποι ἡμῶν, 10:6). The logic of

---

[327] b. B. Meṣi'a 87a–91b (the talmudic interpretation of m. B. Meṣi'a 7.2) as translated with explanatory interpolations in David Instone-Brewer, "1 Corinthians 9.9–11: A Literal Interpretation of 'Do Not Muzzle the Ox,'" *NTS* 38 (1992): 559.

[328] Cf. Matt 10:29–31; Philo, *Virtues*, 160. This reading of v. 10a relies on the assumption that Paul is using the word πάντως to mean something like "really" or "surely" (cf. Luke 4:23; Acts 28:4) rather than "exclusively." Cf. BDAG, s.v. "πάντως," 1.

[329] Paul's δι' ἡμᾶς ("for our sake") is probably best taken as referring primarily to himself and his fellow apostles (cf. Hays, *Echoes of Scripture*, 165–68), but with that group understood as a subset of "us, on whom the ends of the ages have come" (10:11), and that group, in turn, as a subset of the humans with whom the oxen of v. 9 are being contrasted. Cf. Ciampa and Rosner, *The First Letter to the Corinthians*, 406.

qal wachomer extrapolation from a biblical commandment is, of course, different from the logic of typological correspondences drawn from a biblical narrative, but in both cases Paul is working from the same basic conviction: Scripture was written not only for its original readers but also "for our sake," with a continuing authority and applicability that extends beyond the immediate circumstances of its original addressees and culminates in the situation of New Testament believers, "on whom the ends of the ages have come" (10:11).[330]

The clauses that conclude the verse ("because he who plows ought to plow in hope, and he who threshes should thresh in hope of sharing the crop") could be taken in one of two ways, depending on how the conjunction ὅτι, which introduces them, is understood. If (in line with the CSB and most English versions) the ὅτι is understood as meaning "because" or "for," then the clauses are to be taken as statements of basic principles, distilled from Scripture (or from universal and self-evident moral intuitions) and offered as support for Paul's interpretive decision to apply Deuteronomy 25:4 to humans such as himself.[331] On balance, this is the more likely interpretation. Alternatively, if the ὅτι is translated as "because" (in line with the KJV and the punctation of the verse in the NA[28] edition of the Greek New Testament), then the clauses provide the content of what Paul says is "written for our sake"—either Paul's very loose paraphrase of the gist of Deuteronomy 25:4, a quotation from a text that is no longer extant, or (less likely) a quotation from the oral traditions of the rabbis.[332]

9:11–12. In verse 11, Paul expands on the agricultural metaphor underlying his application of the principle in verse 10b to his own ministry activity as an apostle: "If we have sown spiritual things for you, is it too much if we reap material benefits from you?" In keeping with

---

[330] Cf. Paul R. House, "To Them, for Us: The Bible's Continuing Relevance," in Kuhn and Grimmond, *Theology Is for Preaching*, 98–110; Hays, "Conversion of the Imagination," 391–412; Brian S. Rosner, "'Written for Us': Paul's View of Scripture," in *A Pathway into the Holy Scripture*, ed. Philip E. Satterthwaite and David F. Wright (Grand Rapids: Eerdmans, 1994), 81–106.

[331] Cf. Garland, *1 Corinthians*, 411; Gardner, *1 Corinthians*, 395–96.

[332] Instone-Brewer suggests that Paul may be quoting in v. 10b from the original rabbinic tradition that was later recorded in m. B. Meṣi'a 7.2. The suggestion is intriguing and the conceptual similarity between 1 Cor 9:10b and m. B. Meṣi'a 7.2 is close, but his proposal relies on the unlikely hypothesis that Paul is using the phrase ἐγράφη ὅτι ("it is written that") to refer to an oral tradition.

the metaphor Paul has already utilized in 3:5–8, he pictures his work among the Corinthians as a kind of metaphorical "sowing."[333] The logic underlying Paul's rhetorical question in verse 11 is, once again, a kind of *qal wachomer* extrapolation: If those who sow material seed have a right to share in the material harvest, how much more should those who sow the (far more precious) spiritual seed of the gospel?[334] The disproportion between the value of the spiritual seed Paul and his traveling companions have sown and the material support they are entitled to is highlighted by the interrogative phrase μέγα εἰ ("is it too much if ... ?") that introduces the question in the second half of the verse. The implied answer to the question is clearly: Of course not![335] A further rhetorical question follows in verse 12a ("If others have this right to receive benefits from you, don't we even more?"), revisiting the argument from consistency that Paul has already made in verses 5–6 but applying it this time to unnamed "others" who have received from the Corinthians the support they are entitled to[336]

---

[333] Although, grammatically speaking, the CSB's "for you" is the most obvious possibility for the dative pronoun ὑμῖν, it sits awkwardly with the earlier metaphor (explicit in 3:8 and implied in 9:7) in which the Corinthians were the field in which Paul sowed the gospel, not the landowners for whom Paul labored in sowing the crop. Rigorous consistency in the use of metaphors is not always a hallmark of Paul's writing, but in this instance the implied metaphor of the Corinthians as the field in which Paul sowed is established so explicitly in chapter 3 and the alternative metaphor of the Corinthians as the landowners in whose field Paul labored sits so uncomfortably with the way in which he has framed his ministry throughout the letter that it is probably best to read ὑμῖν as a dative of location, broadly equivalent to ἐν ὑμῖν , and translate the phrase as "among you" (cf. NIV, NRSV). This is how the phrase is taken in Ciampa and Rosner, *The First Letter to the Corinthians*, 408, Gardner, *1 Corinthians*, 396, and Garland, *1 Corinthians*, 402. Brookins and Longenecker, *1 Corinthians 1–9*, 212, interpret the phrase as a dative of advantage, in line with its translation in the CSB, as do Schnabel, *Erster Korintherbrief*, 489, and Thiselton, *First Corinthians*, 676.

[334] Cf. Garland, *1 Corinthians*, 412. The distinction that Paul draws here between "spiritual" (πνευματικά) and "material" (σαρκικά) things does not imply the sort of conflict between spirit and flesh that it does in some other places in Paul's letters (e.g., Gal 5:16–26). Here, it serves merely to highlight the contrast between the Spirit-empowered, life-creating ministry of gospel preaching (cf. 2:6–16) and the earthly, material benefits that Paul is entitled to as a servant of the gospel. Cf. the closely similar contrast in Rom 15:27 between the "spiritual blessings" (πνευματικά) that gentiles have received from the Jews and the "material things" (σαρκικά) in which they ought to be of service to them in return.

[335] Cf. the similarly constructed question (though without the additional force of the μέγα εἰ idiom) in 6:2.

[336] The way in which Paul frames the conditional clause in 9:12a and places the question of v. 12a in parallel with the question in v. 11 suggests that the "others" in view are a real and not merely hypothetical group, probably including Apollos and the unnamed "instructors" of 4:15 and possibly also including Cephas (cf. 1:12; 9:5). The verb μετέχουσιν that

and pressing the even greater claim (μᾶλλον, "even more") that Paul and his traveling companions have to the same kind of support.[337]

Nevertheless, as Paul goes on to say in verse 12b, he and his companions have not made use of this right that they possess; instead, "we endure everything so that we will not hinder the gospel of Christ." The language he uses to speak of his willingness to "endure everything" (πάντα στέγομεν) anticipates his later use of the same phrase in 13:7 and implies a choice made in love to suffer hardship and deprivation for the sake of others. In this instance, the hardship that Paul and his companions endured included both the material deprivation that resulted from their decision not to receive material support from the Corinthians and the hard work that this policy required of them (cf. 4:11–12). The motive for this decision was their desire to ensure that their actions did not create a hindrance (ἐγκοπή) to the gospel. The precise nature of the hindrance Paul was keen to avoid is not spelled out in detail here. In his letters to the Thessalonians he describes the similar practice that he followed in Thessalonica as having been motivated by his desire to avoid being a "burden" (βάρος) to the believers there (1 Thess 2:7–9; cf. 2 Thess 3:8), but the sarcasm with which he uses the same language in 2 Corinthians 12:13 suggests that the reasons motivating his decision in Corinth (where there was no shortage of resources that he could have called on if he chose to) were not the same as the reasons that motivated his decision in Thessalonica.[338] The explanation that lies closer to hand is Paul's statement in verse 18 that he desired to communicate the gospel in a manner that made it clear that it was offered "free of charge," without any constraints based on the social standing of those to whom it could be preached and free of the kind of strings that could potentially be attached to the patronage that was given by wealthy and influential Corinthians to others who "market[ed] the word of God for profit" (2 Cor 2:17).[339]

Paul uses to say that they "have" this right probably implies more than just a theoretical right that they possess but an actual provision that they have partaken of (cf. the use of the same verb in 9:10; 10:17, 21, 30) and, given the present tense form of the verb, continue in at least some cases to partake of.

[337] The basis for Paul's "even more" is presumably the quantity and kind of labor that were involved in his work as the one who originally "planted/sowed" the crop (cf. 3:6, 8).

[338] Cf. Fee, *First Epistle to the Corinthians*, 454.

[339] Cf. Ciampa and Rosner, *The First Letter to the Corinthians*, 410–11; Peter Marshall, *Enmity in Corinth: Social Conventions in Paul's Relations with the Corinthians*, WUNT (Tübingen: Mohr-Siebeck, 1987), 232–43.

9:13–14. Having already moved on in verse 12b from the first part of his argument (establishing his right to material support from the Corinthians) to the second (explaining his decision not to exercise it), Paul returns in verses 13–14 to the topic that was the focus of verses 4–12a, offering one more additional argument in support of the right that he claims but has not exercised.

The first premise of the argument, in verse 13, is framed as a rhetorical question—the seventeenth and last in the first half of the chapter, and the ninth of the ten οὐκ οἴδατε ("Do you not know ... ?") questions that Paul asks the Corinthians within the letter (cf. 3:16; 5:6; 6:2, 3, 9, 15, 16, 19; 9:24). In this instance, the knowledge Paul thinks the Corinthians ought to have possessed is knowledge that was available to them from several sources, including the stipulations in the law of Moses regarding the rights of priests and Levites (e.g., Num 18:8–32; Deut 18:1–8) and the common knowledge that most first-century people would have had regarding the standard practice in both the Jerusalem temple and the shrines of the Greco-Roman deities.

The conclusion of the argument is stated in verse 14 ("In the same way, the Lord has commanded that those who preach the gospel should earn their living by the gospel") and is based in part on the implied premise that the work of gospel preaching is a kind of priestly service (cf. Rom 15:16) or sufficiently analogous to it for the practice described in verse 13 to be applicable "in the same way" (οὕτως) to the work of those who preach the gospel. But the force of verse 14 derives not only from its function as a conclusion drawn from valid premises; it is also, as Paul reminds the Corinthians, a practice that "the Lord has commanded" (ὁ κύριος διέταξεν). The language Paul uses here is similar to the expressions he has already used in 7:10 (employing a different verb) and 7:25 (using the cognate noun, ἐπιταγή); here, as is the case in 7:10, the source of the command appears to have been a saying handed down from Jesus and—presumably, based on the way in which Paul can refer to it without elaboration or explanation—already familiar to the Corinthians (cf. Luke 10:7; 1 Tim 5:18).[340]

9:15–18. In verse 15 Paul finally reaches the turning point toward which the argument of the chapter has been heading, reiterating and strengthening the point that he began to make in verse 12b, when he

[340] Fee, *First Epistle to the Corinthians*, 455–56.

signaled an intention to move in that direction. The statement that he now makes builds on the earlier statement in several ways. First, and most obviously, it begins with an emphatic first person singular pronoun, ἐγώ ("For my part"), resuming the narrower focus of verses 1–3 on Paul's own personal conduct as both a matter to be defended and (now) an example for the Corinthians to imitate (cf. 8:13). Second, it replaces the aorist tense verb of verse 12 (οὐκ ἐχρησάμεθα; more literally, "we did not use") with the perfect tense verb, οὐ κέχρημαι ("I have [not] used"), bringing into closer focus the present settled stance that continues to be his policy.[341] Third, it replaces verse 12b's reference to "this right" (τῇ ἐξουσίᾳ ταύτῃ) with the more emphatic and generalized claim that "I have used none of these rights" (οὐ κέχρημαι οὐδενὶ τούτων). Fourth, and finally, it adds the further statement, "nor have I written these things that they may be applied in my case," emphasizing that Paul's purpose in defending the existence of his rights is not to begin exercising them but to explain his reasons for not exercising them.

The verse concludes with an intensely worded explanatory statement through which he begins the process of unfolding his reasons for persisting with this policy: "For it would be better for me to die than for anyone to deprive me of my boast!"[342] The content of his boast is not yet spelled out, but the context, read against the backdrop of Paul's earlier statements about the illegitimacy of those who boast in human power and eloquence (cf. 1:17–2:5; 3:21), suggests that his word choice is tinged with a deliberate irony and hints at an implied critique of those who base their claim to legitimacy as apostles partly on the extravagance of the patronage they receive (cf. 2 Cor 1:12–14; 5:12; 10:12–12:8).

The content of Paul's "boast" is spelled out a little more in verses 16–18: "For if I preach the gospel, I have no reason to boast, because I am compelled to preach—and woe to me if I do not preach the gospel! For if I do this willingly, I have a reward, but if unwillingly, I am entrusted with a commission. What then is my reward? To preach the gospel and offer it free of charge and not make full use of my rights in the gospel."

---

[341] Cf. Garland, *1 Corinthians*, 422; Brookins and Longenecker, *1 Corinthians 1–9*, 215.

[342] The awkwardness of Paul's grammar (more literally: "For it would be better for me rather to die than—no one will make my boast empty!") is probably the reason for the variant readings in F, G (τίς κενώσει, "For it would be better for me rather to die than anyone will make my boast empty!") and א[2], C, D[2] (ἵνα τις κενώσῃ, "For it would be better for me rather to die than that anyone should make my boast empty!").

Gospel preaching, in and of itself, is merely the discharge of Paul's duty and the fulfillment of the bare minimum of his commission (vv. 16–17). In this sense, it is something he does as one who is "compelled" (ἀνάγκη γάρ μοι ἐπίκειται; more literally, "for necessity is laid upon me") and not as one who acts as a volunteer, of his own initiative.[343] To do any less would be to rebel against the inescapable compulsion that is laid upon him by the command of Christ (cf. Jer 20:9; Amos 3:8), rendering him liable to divine condemnation (hence Paul's "and woe to me if I do not preach the gospel!" v. 16b).

What Paul can do voluntarily is "preach the gospel and offer it free of charge and not make full use of my rights in the gospel" (v. 18).[344] Paul's willingness to forgo the support that he is entitled to as a preacher of the gospel is an act of love for others and devotion to the cause of Christ that he can perform of his own initiative, not as one commanded to do so by Christ. By adopting and persevering with this policy he gains a paradoxical "reward" (μισθός): his payment is the delight that he can take (now and on the last day) in not receiving payment and in the ability that he gains to preach the gospel "free of charge" (ἀδάπανον) to anyone who will hear it.[345]

The implications of Paul's sense that accepting patronage (or some other form of remuneration from his hearers) would "hinder the gospel" (v. 12) and diminish his ability to proclaim it "free of charge" (v. 18) clearly go beyond merely the avoidance of scenarios in which unbelievers are

---

[343] The CSB's use of "willingly" and "unwillingly" to translate Paul's ἑκών and ἄκων implies the unfortunate connotation that if Paul were to accept financial support his evangelism would be undertaken begrudgingly or against his will.

[344] The CSB is probably correct to translate the verb καταχρήσασθαι as "make full use of" rather than (as some propose) the more negatively slanted "misuse" (cf. TNIV; Fee, *First Epistle to the Corinthians*, 465). Paul's use of the same verb elsewhere (e.g., in 7:31) suggests that the κατα- prefix carries an intensifying meaning (i.e., "make *full* use of") rather than an intrinsically pejorative sense (i.e., "*mis*use"), and there is nothing in the immediate context to suggest that Paul views those who accept the support that the Lord Jesus said they should be given are acting corruptly or exploitatively. Cf. Ciampa and Rosner, *The First Letter to the Corinthians*, 420.

[345] Gardner is probably correct to say that the primary timeframe in which Paul envisages himself as receiving this reward is eschatological (cf. 3:8, 14, and the eschatological context implied by Paul's "woe" in 9:16b), but that there is an anticipatory experience of that reward in the present age, in the pleasure that Paul can take here and now in his ability to preach the gospel free of charge. Cf. Gardner, *1 Corinthians*, 402; Scott J. Hafemann, *Suffering and Ministry in the Spirit: Paul's Defense of his Ministry in II Corinthians 2:14–3:3* (Grand Rapids: Eerdmans, 1990), 142–43.

charged for admission to hear the gospel preached. The primary and most controversial form of support he refrained from requesting or accepting when he was first among the Corinthians (and which he continues not to accept or request) appears to have been not a speaker's fee charged to unbelievers but the patronage that could have been provided by wealthy converts. Support of this kind detracted from the freedom of the gospel in at least three ways: first, it risked conveying the sense that Paul's ministry was to be understood like that of the Sophists, competing in the marketplace for patronage and popularity; second, it risked placing him under obligation to wealthy and influential supporters, diminishing the freedom with which he could communicate the gospel's demands to them; and third, it risked confining his mission activities within a kind of gilded cage, created by his patronage arrangements, requiring him to focus his activities on the peers and dependents of his patrons and reducing his capacity to make the gospel known to those whose circumstances were poorer or more precarious.[346]

9:19–23. Having spoken in verses 15–18 of the way in which he has chosen to forgo the exercise of the "right" (ἐξουσία) to material support that he had as an apostle (and the various associated rights that went with it), Paul now turns in verses 19–23 to the closely related topic of his status as a "free" (ἐλεύθερος) person and his paradoxical willingness to use it by enslaving himself to others for the sake of the gospel. Unlike his rights as an apostle, which Paul needed to defend and confirm at some length in vv. 4–14, Paul's freedom, which he shares with the Corinthians and with all believers,[347] is a status that he can confidently presuppose here, as in 9:1a, without fear of contradiction.

Although the theme of Paul's freedom harks back most obviously to the earlier reference to it in verse 1, the conjunction γάρ ("for," untranslated in the CSB) that links verse 19 with the previous verses suggests a close connection between the ideas of this paragraph and those of the preceding one and raises the possibility that Paul's status as "free from all and not anyone's slave" is also connected, in his mind, with the freedom from reciprocal obligations that he is able to secure by refusing

[346] Cf. Thiselton, *First Corinthians*, 697; White, "Meals in Pagan Temples," 541–45; Horrell, *Social Ethos*, 215–16, citing Lucian, *Merc. cond.* 1–4.

[347] Even those whose earthly status is that of an enslaved person have the status of ἀπελεύθερος κυρίου ("the Lord's freedman," 7:22) in Christ.

the patronage of those in Corinth who might otherwise have made him their dependent.[348]

The reason Paul gives to explain his willingness to voluntarily make himself "a slave to everyone" (v. 19) is his desire to "win" (κερδήσω) more people—language that he goes on to use repeatedly throughout verses 19b–22a before substituting the verb σώσω ("save") in verse 22b, making it clear (if the context did not make it clear enough already) that his goal is not to gain admirers or clients but to gain men and women as believing and obedient followers of Christ (cf. 10:33; Rom 1:5; 15:18; 16:26). The examples Paul offers in verses 20–22 make it clear that the freedom he has in mind derives from and relates closely to the freedom that he has in Christ from the restrictions and demands of the law of Moses (cf. Gal 3:19–5:15; Rom 7:1–6), but his language in introducing the theme ("free from all and not anyone's slave ... made myself a slave to everyone") suggests that his primary interest is in the social entailments of that freedom and of the ways in which he chooses to limit his exercise of it.

The concrete social practices involved in "ma[king] [him]self a slave" are described by Paul in terms of a series of actions in which he "became like" (ἐγενόμην ... ὡς, vv. 20–21) or "became" (ἐγενόμην, v. 22) a member of four different categories of people: "the Jews" (v. 20), "those under the law" (v. 20), "those without the law" (v. 21), and "the weak" (v. 22).

The language Paul uses to identify the first two of these categories suggests meanings that are closely similar, with the former expression, "the Jews" (οἱ Ἰουδαίοι), perhaps referring in this context to those whose Jewish identity derived from their birth and the latter, "those under the law" (οἱ ὑπὸ νόμον), stretching a little wider to include those who had chosen to take on the yoke of the law as proselytes.[349] The fact that Paul can speak of himself needing in some situations to "be[come] like" a Jew indicates the extent to which his allegiance to Christ has relativized all other markers of identity for him (cf. Gal 3:28; Col 3:11; Phil 3:4–8). Paul's ethnic identity as an Israelite (his preferred ethnic self-identifier in Rom 9:3–4; 11:1; 2 Cor 11:22) is not obliterated by the gospel, but he does distinguish between his present identity in Christ and his previous way of life "in Judaism" (ἐν τῷ Ἰουδαϊσμῷ, Gal 1:13), i.e., as a person committed to a theopolitical vision centered on loyalty to a community defined by torah

[348] Cf. Fee, *First Epistle to the Corinthians*, 468; contra Garland, *1 Corinthians*, 428.

[349] Cf. Ciampa and Rosner, *The First Letter to the Corinthians*, 426.

and ancestral tradition.[350] While he is fierce in opposing the activities of those for whom Jewish identity requires the exclusion of uncircumcised gentiles from the church or the denial of table fellowship between believers, he is happy to honor the consciences of fellow believers who continue to observe traditions such as the Mosaic Sabbath and food laws in their own conduct (cf. Rom 14) and to abide by restrictions such as these when necessary if it enables him to gain a hearing from Jews who have not yet become believers in Jesus. Verse 20b reiterates the point, affirming that he observes the same flexibility in his dealings with those who belong in the slightly wider, proselyte-inclusive category of "those under the law" and adding the parenthetical clarifying statement, "though I myself am not under the law" (cf. Gal 3:24–25; 5:18; Rom 6:14; 7:1–6).

In verse 21 Paul turns to "those who are without the law" (οἱ ἄνομοι), affirming that he observes a similar freedom in his dealings with them, while adding another clarifying parenthesis ("though I am not without God's law but under the law of Christ") aimed at averting any misunderstanding that his freedom from the law of Moses makes him exempt from the obligation to live in obedience to God. For Paul, obedience to "the law of Christ" does not require the promulgation of a new torah; it is, rather, a matter of walking in love, informed by Scripture and by the commands and example of Christ and his apostles, interpreted and applied with the wisdom given by the Spirit. Those who live in this manner fulfill the core requirement that was at the heart of the Mosaic law, under the new and different circumstances of the new covenant community (cf. Rom 8:1–17; 13:8–14; Gal 5:1–6:10; Col 1:9–10).

A fourth category, "the weak" (οἱ ἀσθενεῖς), is added in verse 22. Given the earlier pattern of the word's usage in 1 Corinthians, it is unlikely to be functioning here as a third way of referring to those who live according to a rule of conduct governed by rules derived from Old Testament law and Jewish tradition (as it appears to function in Rom 14). The most recent use of the language of "weakness" in 1 Corinthians was in the previous chapter, where "the weak" were those whose recent preconversion experience made them especially vulnerable to the temptation of returning to their past associations with idolatry. As discussed in the comments on that

---

350 See especially the discussion of the key terminological issues in Lionel J. Windsor, *Paul and the Vocation of Israel: How Paul's Jewish Identity Informs His Apostolic Ministry, with Special Reference to Romans*, BZNW (Berlin: De Gruyter, 2014), 44–95.

chapter above, it is also likely that Paul's description of them as "weak" is informed by their socioeconomic circumstances, which denied them the leisure that would have been required for them to develop the kind of sophisticated theological understanding that would permit a nuanced evaluation of the various shades of gray associated with the issue of food sacrificed to idols. Paul's adaptability in mission in his dealings with this group is expressed in stronger terms than those he used in relation to the previous three groups: he did not merely become "like the weak"; he "became weak"—language that probably includes a reference not only to his willingness to curtail dietary freedoms where necessary but also to his far more wide-reaching embrace of a lifestyle of struggle, manual labor, and deprivation, in solidarity with their experience (cf. 2:1–5; 4:9–13; 2 Cor 4:7–18; 11:16–12:10).[351]

Finally, in verse 22b, Paul offers one last generalizing statement, "I have become all things to all people, so that I may by every possible means save some," once more (as he did in v. 15) shifting from the aorist tense (ἐγενόμην, "I became"; vv. 20–22a) to the perfect tense (γέγονα, "I have become"; v. 22b) to highlight his present and continuing adherence to this practice. The contrast between the threefold "all" ("all things [πάντα] to all people [πᾶσιν], so that I may by every possible means [πάντως] …") and the "some" (τινάς), whom he strives by every possible effort to save, reflects the fact that Paul's flexibility in mission is not, in his view, a strategy that one can master to generate assured results. It is, rather, an expression of loving, cruciform willingness to sacrifice personal preferences and comfort in order to remove every possible obstacle from the gospel's path (cf. v. 12b).

Verse 23 completes the paragraph by stating Paul's motive for this flexible, self-sacrificial conduct: "Now I do all this because of the gospel, so that I may share in the blessings." Strictly speaking, the word "blessings" does not occur in the Greek, and it is possible to translate the verse without making use of it at all, so that Paul is understood as saying something more like: "I do it all for the sake of the gospel, so that I may participate [fully] in its proclamation."[352] But even if that more strictly literal translation is adopted, it still carries the implication that, as a συγκοινωνός—a full participant, or shareholder—in the enterprise of the

---

[351] Cf. Horrell, *Social Ethos*, 215–16.

[352] Cf. the argument for this reading in Thiselton, *First Corinthians*, 707.

gospel, Paul would have looked forward to the prospect of sharing in its profits.[353] The references in the following verses to the "prize" (v. 24) and "crown" (v. 25) of the athlete and Paul's desire not to be "disqualified" (v. 27) confirm, in a parallel pattern of imagery, the likelihood that verse 23 would have carried this implication. Paul's allegiance to the cause of the gospel is loyal but not disinterested: he serves Christ not only because it is a good and virtuous thing to do but also because he is eager to enjoy the blessings in which he will one day share as a participant in the gospel enterprise, who can take eternal delight in the harvest that it has yielded (cf. 3:8; 15:58).

9:24–27. The final paragraph of the chapter picks up the thread of eschatological expectation from verse 23b ("so that I may share in the blessings"), developing and expanding on the thought by introducing a pair of new and interrelated metaphors (that of a runner and a boxer, and the disciplines that they exercise) and a new danger to be averted (that Paul, after preaching to others, might find himself "disqualified" at the end of the race). The imagery Paul uses would have been familiar to the Corinthians, not only through the opportunities they had to witness the athletic contests of the biennial Isthmian games firsthand but also through the frequent use of athletic imagery as a metaphor or example in popular philosophical discourse and its widespread representation in a variety of visual media.[354]

The aspects of the athletic contest Paul emphasizes (and that were also highlighted in various ways within the popular philosophical literature and the surviving visual representations of athletes) are the disciplines exercised by the athlete, who "exercises self-control in everything" (πάντα ἐγκρατεύεται), and the "prize" (βραβεῖον) or "crown" (στέφανος) for which the athletes compete. In the stadium,[355] Paul reminds the read-

[353] Cf. the discussion of the social and legal expectations regarding partnerships in Julien M. Ogereau, *Paul's Koinonia with the Philippians: A Socio-Historical Investigation of a Pauline Economic Partnership*, WUNT (Tübingen: Mohr Siebeck, 2014), 332–38.

[354] For examples of the former, see Epictetus, *Diatr.* 1.24.1–2; 3.15.2–4; Seneca, *Ep.* 78.16; Dio Chrysostom, *Or.* 8.9–12. On the latter see especially Philip Francis Esler, "Paul and the Agon: Understanding a Pauline Motif in Its Cultural and Visual Context," in *Picturing the New Testament: Studies in Ancient Visual Images*, ed. Annette Weissenrieder, Friederike Wendt, and Petra von Gemünde (Tübingen: Mohr Siebeck, 2005), 356–84; Harrison, *Paul and the Ancient Celebrity Circuit*, 109–34.

[355] Or perhaps in the 200m sprint (στάδιον), from which the arena in which the contests were held took their name; cf. Esler, "Paul and the Agon," 376; Harrison, *Paul and the Ancient*

ers, "all race, but only one receives the prize" (v. 24). The point of this reminder is not to endorse the agonistic ethos of competitive quest for honors that was celebrated at the games and encourage believers to imitate it within the church;[356] nor is he going out of his way to "democratize" the idea of victory by making this a point of explicit contrast between the games and the race that is run by believers.[357] His point (anticipating the similar statements in 9:27 and 10:1–5) is simply that "entering a race and running does not automatically qualify one as a winner. ... Christians must not only joint the race, but also must put forth every effort to finish it well, because the laurels only go to the victor, in this case a multitude of victors."[358] With regard to the "crown" that is awarded to the victors, Paul does draw a contrast between the perishability of the crown awarded to the athletes at the games and the "imperishable crown" to which believers look forward, highlighting the latter as a reason for even greater sacrifice and self-discipline than that displayed by the athletes.[359]

In verse 26b the focus of Paul's imagery shifts from the runners to the boxers, whom he evokes as a comparison in his insistence that he does not "box like one beating the air." This comparison is further developed in verse 27a: "Instead, I discipline my body and bring it under strict control." The terms Paul uses are violent and forceful in their connotations: ὑπωπιάζω, translated as "discipline" in the CSB, can frequently be used to refer to the bruising blows that could be endured in a physical combat, and δουλαγωγῶ ("bring ... under strict control") carries connotations of enslavement and subjugation. The language is, of course, metaphorical, but the fact that the object of Paul's metaphorical beatings and subjugation is his own body suggests that physical bruises and batterings are not far from his mind—not as acts of self-punishment but as the bodily manifestations of the life of discipline, risk-taking, and self-deprivation

Celebrity Circuit, 121.

356 Contra Esler, "Paul and the Agon," 377.

357 Contra Harrison, *Paul and the Ancient Celebrity Circuit*, 124.

358 Garland, *1 Corinthians*, 440.

359 The wreaths awarded to victors at the Isthmian games were, in Paul's day, made of pine and had in earlier times been made of (even more obviously "perishable") wild celery; cf. Plutarch, *Mor.* 675D–677B; *Tim.* 26.1–5. Despite the perishability of the wreath with which he was crowned (and the short memories of the adoring public), a victor in the games could still boast of the "immortal crowns" (στέμμασιν ἀθανάτοις) with which he honored his father and his fatherland: L. Moretti, *Inscrizioni agonistiche greche* (Rome: Signorelli, 1953), §64, cited in Harrison, *Paul and the Ancient Celebrity Circuit*, 132.

to which Paul commits himself for the sake of the gospel (cf. 4:11–12; 15:30–32; 2 Cor 4:7–11; 6:4–10; 11:24–29).[360]

The purpose of these disciplines and self-deprivations is spelled out in verse 27b: "so that after preaching to others, I myself will not be disqualified." The worst-case scenario that he envisages here is not merely one in which he completes the race but others do not, depriving him of the fulness of the reward to which he had looked forward (though this is clearly a scenario he is eager to avoid);[361] the even darker possibility is that he himself might end up "disqualified" (ἀδόκιμος), judged unworthy of the very prize for which he urges the Corinthians themselves to strive. The fact that he can elsewhere speak with great confidence about the assured hope that he has, both for himself and for his readers (e.g., Phil 1:6, 19–20; 1 Cor 10:13; Rom 8:28–39), should not detract from the seriousness of his warnings regarding the risk of apostasy—which are themselves one of the means through which God secures the perseverance of his people.[362]

Bridge

For those of us among his twenty-first century readers who have been formed by cultural contexts that privilege the rights and freedoms of the individual and economic systems that revolve around the demand of the consumer for choice, convenience, and instant gratification, Paul's example, as he describes it in this chapter, is both essential and unsettling reading. Paul is not averse to the idea of rights and entitlements and goes out of his way within this chapter to defend the basic principle that "those who preach the gospel should earn their living by the gospel" (v. 14). Nor is he an enemy of the idea of freedom; on the contrary, he begins the chapter with an assertion of his own freedom (which he shares with all believers) and returns to that theme in verse 19. But he insists in the strongest possible terms that the mere fact that one possesses

---

360 Cf. Garland, *1 Corinthians*, 442–43; David I. Starling, "'The Weapons of Righteousness': Righteousness and Suffering in 2 Corinthians," in *Suffering in Paul*, ed. Siu Fung Wu (Eugene: Wipf & Stock, 2019), 51–63.

361 Nor, given the close proximity to his references to the "prize" and "imperishable crown" in vv. 24–25, is he simply referring to the possibility that he might be judged unworthy of his office as an apostle; contra Judith M. Gundry Volf, *Paul and Perseverance: Staying In and Falling Away*, WUNT (Tübingen: Mohr Siebeck, 1990), 237.

362 Cf. Ciampa and Rosner, *The First Letter to the Corinthians*, 442; Schreiner, *1 Corinthians*, 196–97.

rights and freedoms does not in itself answer the question of how they should be used.

In his own case, Paul tells his readers, he has made a deliberate decision not to use his right to material support as an apostle, motivated by his desire to make the gospel "free of charge" in the mode by which he proclaims it (vv. 15–18); he has made use of his freedom as one "not under the law" by voluntarily enslaving himself to others in costly and self-sacrificial practices of flexibility and solidarity for the sake of mission (vv. 19–23); and he has committed himself to a larger set of disciplines and practices that involve risk, pain, and self-deprivation, imitating the athletes and boxers at the games in his determination to complete the race that has been laid out for him to run (vv. 24–27).

His motive in so doing is not a kind of Kantian disinterestedness in the idea of obtaining any benefit or reward for himself. He is frank and explicit about the rewards toward which he looks forward and upon which he draws as motivations for a life of discipline and self-sacrifice: the "boast" that he is determined not to be deprived of (v. 15); the (paradoxical) "reward" that consists in and derives from his practice of offering the gospel free of charge (v. 18); the blessings that he hopes to "share in" as a full participant in the enterprise of the gospel (v. 23); and the "prize" and "crown" that he is eager to obtain and not to be disqualified from gaining (vv. 24–27). His deep, loyal allegiance to the cause of the gospel and his thirsty, passionate desire to share in its blessings are not competing drives but harmonious aspects of the one quest. He knows that it is gain, not loss, to serve the cause of Christ; hence, the sacrifices he describes can be made willingly and gladly, without any sense of self-pitying virtuousness.[363]

Those of us who, like the Corinthians, need to be persuaded (or repersuaded) to commit to a lifestyle such as the one Paul describes in this chapter can find within this chapter both a powerful example and a compelling set of motives for adopting it. Its stark contrast to the values and practices of late modern consumer capitalism underlines both the extent of the challenge we face in adopting it and the brightness with which a Christian community that lives by this pattern will shine against the backdrop of its environment.

---

[363] Cf. Starling, *UnCorinthian Leadership*, 34–36; John Piper, *Desiring God: Meditations of a Christian Hedonist*, 4th ed. (Colorado Springs: Multnomah, 2011), 239–52.

C. Israel's Example: Idolatry, Immorality, and Apostasy in the Wilderness (10:1–13)

> [1] Now I do not want you to be unaware, brothers and sisters, that our ancestors were all under the cloud, all passed through the sea, [2] and all were baptized into Moses in the cloud and in the sea. [3] They all ate the same spiritual food, [4] and all drank the same spiritual drink. For they drank from the spiritual rock that followed them, and that rock was Christ. [5] Nevertheless God was not pleased with most of them, since they were struck down in the wilderness.
>
> [6] Now these things took place as examples for us, so that we will not desire evil things as they did. [7] Don't become idolaters as some of them were; as it is written, **The people sat down to eat and drink, and got up to party.** [8] Let us not commit sexual immorality as some of them did, and in a single day twenty-three thousand people died. [9] Let us not test Christ as some of them did and were destroyed by snakes. [10] And don't grumble as some of them did, and were killed by the destroyer. [11] These things happened to them as examples, and they were written for our instruction, on whom the ends of the ages have come. [12] So, whoever thinks he stands must be careful not to fall. [13] No temptation has come upon you except what is common to humanity. But God is faithful; he will not allow you to be tempted beyond what you are able, but with the temptation he will also provide the way out so that you may be able to bear it.

Context/Structure/Form

In the final paragraph of chapter 9, Paul concluded the section in which he offered himself as an example to the Corinthians by speaking of the disciplines he subjected himself to, "so that after preaching to others, I myself will not be disqualified" (9:27).[364] What follows in 10:1–13 now builds on that paragraph and its concluding verse. Just as 8:13 had earlier provided a springboard from which Paul launched into the discussion of his own practice and example in chapter 9, his mention in 9:27 of the apostasy that he is determined to avoid now becomes, in turn, a springboard for a reminder of the story of the Israelites' apostasy in the wilderness, which he offers in 10:1–13 as a second (and, this time, negative) example for the Corinthians to learn from.

---

[364] The close connection between 9:24–27 and 10:1–13 is signaled by the conjunction γάρ ("for," untranslated in the CSB) that links the sentence in 10:1–2 to its immediately preceding context as an illustration offering explanation and support for what Paul has said about the danger of apostasy in 9:24–27. Cf. Gardner, *1 Corinthians*, 425; Fee, *First Epistle to the Corinthians*, 489.

The passage comprises two paragraphs. The first, in verses 1–4, offers a brief synopsis of the story of the Israelites' apostasy, highlighting that "all" (πάντες, five times repeated) of the Israelites were "baptized into Moses," ate the same "spiritual food," and drank the same "spiritual drink," and yet most of them were struck down in the wilderness under divine judgment. The second, in verses 6–13, draws out the significance of the story for the Corinthians, encouraging them to view the Israelites and the events in their story as "examples" (τύποι, vv. 6, 11) to be avoided, with a particular focus on the sins of idolatry (v. 7), immorality (v. 8), "test[ing] Christ" (v. 9), and grumbling (v. 10), before summing up in verses 12–13 with a word of warning and reassurance.

Comments

10:1–4. Paul follows the discussion of his own example in 9:1–27 with a second example, that of the wilderness generation of the Israelites (10:1–13), which—unlike his own example—he holds out to the readers in Corinth for their avoidance rather than their imitation. The reminder of that story that he offers in a compressed, synopsis form in verses 1–4 commences with a double negative construction, Οὐ θέλω γὰρ ὑμᾶς ἀγνοεῖν, ἀδελφοί ("Now I do not want you to be unaware, brothers and sisters"), that probably carries an edge of irony, given the self-perception of the Corinthian letter writers as the "knowledgeable" members of the congregation (cf. 8:1).[365]

The story of which Paul reminds his readers is framed as a story about "our ancestors" (οἱ πατέρες ἡμῶν, literally, "our fathers"), a description that relies upon the assumption that the gentile believers whom Paul is addressing have been grafted by faith into the people of God and have, consequently, become the spiritual descendants of the Old Testament Israelites.[366] They share in this identity with Paul, as spiritual (and in his case physical) descendants of the same "fathers"—a fact that he reinforces by addressing them as "brothers and sisters."[367]

---

[365] On the rhetorical function of Paul's Οὐ θέλω ... ὑμᾶς ἀγνοεῖν construction, here and elsewhere in his letters (esp. Rom 1:13; 11:25; 1 Cor 12:1; 2 Cor 1:8), see David I. Starling, "'We Do Not Want You To Be Unaware ... ': Disclosure, Concealment and Suffering in 2 Cor 1–7," *NTS* 60 (2014): 9–11.

[366] Cf. especially Hays, "Conversion of the Imagination," 398–400.

[367] Ciampa and Rosner, *The First Letter to the Corinthians*, 445–46; cf. Hays, *First Corinthians*, 160.

The primary source of the story that Paul asks the Corinthians to remember is the Old Testament Scriptures, and its particular focus is on the events narrated in the book of Exodus. Paul alludes to those events in the same sequence as they occur in the unfolding narrative of that book (and with an allusion in verse 4 to the rock that "followed" them on their journey that suggests an awareness on his part of the way the story was interpreted and recounted in Jewish tradition).[368] The compressed and allusive form in which Paul reminds them of the events in the Exodus story suggests the likelihood that the story was already familiar to the Corinthians, allowing him to toss out a string of allusions without needing to recount the whole narrative.[369]

Paul wants the Corinthians to reflect on the fact that "all" of the Israelites participated in the salvific events in which they were (figuratively) "baptized into Moses" as they traveled "under the cloud" (v. 1; cf. Exod 13:21; Ps 105:39) and passed "through the sea" (v. 1; cf. Exod 14:29), "all" of the Israelites ate the "spiritual food" of the manna provided for them from heaven (v. 3; cf. Exod 16:4, 31; Ps 105:40), and "all" of the Israelites drank the "spiritual drink" of the water from the rock (v. 4; Exod 17:6; Num 20:7–13; Ps 105:41). The correspondences between the Israelites' experiences and the Corinthians' are highlighted by Paul's description of the journey under the cloud and through the sea as events in which they were "baptized" into Moses (v. 2) and his identification of the rock from which the Israelites drank (both at Rephidim and at Kadesh) as "Christ" (v. 4). Given Paul's threefold use of the word "spiritual" to describe the food, the water, and the rock in Israel's story and the focus of the paragraph on laying groundwork for his use of the Israelites and the events in their story as "examples" (τύποι) for the Corinthians, it would be a mistake to read his claim that "that rock was Christ" in an overly literal manner. His point is not that Christ was, in a material or literal

[368] The interpretive tradition of the "following rock" derived from the fact that at two different points in the biblical narrative (Exod 17 and Num 20), referring to events that occurred in two different locations, mention is made of a rock from which water was provided for the Israelites. Cf. Peter E. Enns, "The 'Moveable Well' in 1 Corinthians 10:4: An Extra-Biblical Tradition in an Apostolic Text," *BBR* (1996): 23–38, and the discussion in Ciampa and Rosner, *The First Letter to the Corinthians*, 450–51, citing examples of later texts including LAB 10:7; 11:15; t. Sukkah 3.11, b. Šabb. 35a; b. Pesaḥ. 54a; Gen. Rab. 62:4; Num. Rab. 1:2; 9:14; 19:25–26 in which the rabbinic interpretive tradition of the "following" rock is received and passed on.

[369] Cf. Hays, *Echoes of Scripture*, 92.

sense, accompanying the Israelites in the form of a physical rock but that he was spiritually present with them as the "rock" of divine faithfulness and provision by whom they were preserved through their wilderness wanderings (cf. Deut 32:4, 15, 18, 30–31, 37).[370]

Given those multiple correspondences between the Israelites' experiences and the Corinthians' and the strong sense of continuity and solidarity implied by speaking of the Israelites as "our ancestors," there is an unmistakable note of warning sounded by what Paul goes on to say in verse 5: "Nevertheless God was not pleased with most of them, since they were struck down in the wilderness." The language Paul uses to speak of the Israelites being "struck down in the wilderness" (κατεστρώθησαν … ἐν τῇ ἐρήμῳ) is closely similar to the language with which the LXX translates Moses' description in Numbers 14:16 of what the nations would say (κατέστρωσεν αὐτοὺς ἐν τῇ ἐρήμῳ) if the plague announced in Numbers 14:12 were to eventuate. On that occasion Moses's intercession was successful and the judgment was averted; the exodus project was not defeated by Israel's grumbling and threats of mutiny, and the nation was not destroyed "with a single blow" (Num 14:15). Nevertheless, for the vast majority of the adult individuals within the nation (all but Caleb and Joshua!), the combined effect of forty years' wilderness wandering and the various events to which Paul alludes in verses 7–10 was equivalent to what would have been the fate of the nation as a whole if Moses's intercession had not been heeded.

10:6–11. Verses 6–11 spell out explicitly what is already implicit in the summary Paul has given in verses 1–5 of the story of the Israelites who died in the wilderness. Verses 6 and 11 bracket the paragraph with generalizing statements about the function of the various events in the story of the Israelites as "examples" (τύποι, v. 6; τυπικῶς, v. 11) for Paul and the Corinthians. The focus of Paul's attention within the intervening verses is on the various actions of the Israelites that incurred the judgment of God and their function as warnings to Paul and the Corinthians, "so that we will not desire evil things as they did" (10:6b). This would suggest that he is using the word τύποι not in the more technical hermeneutical sense of "symbolic foreshadowings" (e.g., Rom 5:14) or "allegorical symbols" (e.g., Philo, *Creation* 157) that the word can sometimes carry but in the more widely attested sense of "examples," which it most commonly has within

[370] Cf. Garland, *1 Corinthians*, 456–57.

his letters (e.g., Phil 3:17; 1 Thess 1:7; 2 Thess 3:9; 1 Tim 4:12; Titus 2:7). If that is the case, then "these things" (ταῦτα, v. 6; cf. v. 11) probably refers not so much to the objects Paul has mentioned or alluded to in verses 1–4 (the cloud, the sea, the manna, the rock) but to the events of divine judgment that came upon the Israelites and (by implication) the precipitating actions of the Israelites with which God was displeased (v. 5).[371]

In verses 7–10 Paul zeroes in on four examples of events in which the Israelites "desire[d] evil things" (v. 6) and came under the fatal judgment of God. The first example, in verse 7, is the making of the golden calf, in which Paul says the Israelites became "idolaters" (εἰδωλολάτραι). The particular verse of the exodus narrative that he chooses to quote in verse 7b ("The people sat down to eat and drink, and got up to party") focuses not on the demand that the Israelites bring to Aaron (Exod 34:1), the request and donation of their gold earrings (Exod 34:2), or the fashioning of the calf (Exod 34:4), but on the feasting and celebration in which the people participated after the burnt offerings and fellowship offerings had been presented on the altar of the idol—suggesting an obvious point of connection with the meals at the pagan temples in which the Corinthians were asserting their right to participate.

The second example, in verse 8, is the event at Shittim, narrated in Numbers 25 and recalled in Psalm 106, in which the Israelite men "began to indulge in sexual immorality with Moabite women, who invited them to the sacrifices to their gods" (Num 25:1–2, NIV). Although the events at Shittim involved a direct and immediate connection to the worship of the gods of the Moabites, Paul is content to leave that in the background as an additional resonance that his allusion carries for those who know the story, focusing his warning in this verse on the immorality that the Israelites indulged in (μηδὲ πορνεύωμεν, καθώς τινες αὐτῶν ἐπόρνευσαν; more literally, "let us not commit sexual immorality, as some of them committed sexual immorality"), not on the idolatry that accompanied it. The consequence for the Israelites, as Paul reminds his readers in verse

---

[371] Cf. Gardner, *1 Corinthians*, 433; Collins, *First Corinthians*, 369–70; contra Leonhard Goppelt, *Typos: The Typological Interpretation of the Old Testament in the New*, trans. Donald H. Madvig (Grand Rapids: Eerdmans, 1982), 17–20. There is, of course, a "typological" dimension to Paul's reading of the Old Testament narrative, here and elsewhere, but his use of the words τύποι (v. 6) and τυπικῶς (v. 11) here in this paragraph is probably not referring directly to that aspect of his hermeneutic.

8b, was that "in a single day twenty-three thousand people died" (cf. Num 25:9; Ps 106:29).[372]

The third example, in verse 9, is the event narrated in Numbers 21:4–9, in which the Israelites spoke against God and Moses, and venomous snakes came among them as a judgment. Paul appeals to that event as a warning not to "test Christ," drawing on the language with which the grumbling and impatience of the Israelites is described elsewhere (e.g., Exod 17:2–3, 7; Pss 78:18; 106:14). The language with which Paul connects his warning to the Corinthians with the allusion to the story in Numbers 21 (μηδὲ ἐκπειράζωμεν τὸν Χριστόν, καθώς τινες αὐτῶν ἐπείρασαν; literally, "And let us not test Christ, as some tested") leaves the object of the verb ἐπείρασαν unstated. Although the easiest and most obvious way for hearers to fill the ellipsis is by supplying "Christ," Hays is probably justified in suggesting that Paul would have expected his hearers to supply "God."[373]

The fourth and final example, in verse 10, recalls the various similar events in which the Israelites "grumble[d]" against God and Moses (cf. Num 11:33–34; 14:1–2, 27–38; 16:41–50; LXX Ps 105:25 [MT PS 106:25]) and "were killed by the destroyer" (language that recalls Exod 12:23 and presumably reflects the traditional assumption that all acts of divine judgment are carried out by a destroying angel; cf. 2 Sam 24:16; 1 Chr 21:15; Ps 78:49). The double reminder in verses 9–10 of the judgment of God on the actions in which the Israelites "test[ed]" God and "grumbled" against God and Moses may be intended to function as a warning against any further escalation of the tone of entitlement and insubordination already present in the letter that the Corinthians have sent to Paul.[374]

In verse 11 Paul returns to the point that he made in verse 6 ("These things happened to them as examples"), going on to elaborate that "they were written for our instruction, on whom the ends of the ages have come." The claim Paul is making need not be read as an assertion that Scripture was written exclusively for the sake of the last days community. To assert that would be to fly in the face of the numerous indications within the Old Testament Scriptures that they were written, in the first

---

[372] There is no obvious explanation for why Paul describes the number who fell under God's judgment as 23,000 when the number is given in Num 25:9 as 24,000, but the precise number who fell is, of course, immaterial to the point he is making.

[373] Cf. Hays, *First Corinthians*, 165.

[374] Cf. Ciampa and Rosner, *The First Letter to the Corinthians*, 464; Fee, *First Epistle to the Corinthians*, 505–6.

instance at least, for the people of Israel (e.g., Pss 78:1–8; 103:7; 147:19–20)—a claim with which Paul happily concurs elsewhere (cf. Rom 3:2, 19; 9:4). But it does make explicit the claim, already implied by his description of the Israelites in verse 1 as "our ancestors," that the gentile-inclusive community of believers in Christ has become the inheritor of Israel's Scriptures—and therefore of the reminders and warnings that accompany Scripture's prophecies and promises. More than that: by describing the community of believers as those "on whom the ends of the ages have come," Paul implies that the church not only receives Israel's Scriptures but participates in their (inaugurated) fulfillment, understanding them in light of "the revelation of the mystery kept silent for long ages but now revealed and made known" (Rom 16:25–26; cf. Eph 3:3–7).

Hays helpfully sums up the "bifocal" nature of the awareness Paul seeks to inculcate in his readers:

> [Paul] calls his converts to understand that they live at the turning point of the ages, so that all the scriptural narratives and promises must be understood to point forward to the crucial eschatological moment in which he and his churches now find themselves. His eschatological reasoning calls upon the Corinthians to perform a complex imaginative act: on the one hand, they are to see in their own experience the typological fulfilment of the biblical narrative. ...
>
> But this is only the first half of the complex imaginative act to which Paul summons his readers. The Corinthians are not only to see how Scripture points to its fulfilment in their own community but also to see that God's final judgment stands over their present experience. The prospect of future apocalyptic judgment, symbolized by the destruction that came upon the idolatrous Israelites in the wilderness, hovers over the entire passage. ... Because Paul and his readers stand at the turn of the ages, they must envision their present experience both as the fulfilment of the scriptural figures and, at the same time, as a hint of the eschatological consummation that is still to come. Thus, Paul's reading of Scripture is "bifocal," corresponding to the dialectical ("already/ not yet") character of his eschatology.[375]

[375] Hays, "Conversion of the Imagination," 400–401. As argued above, I do not think that Paul's statements in vv. 6, 11 are (in and of themselves) a direct assertion of typological

10:12–13. In verses 12–13 Paul concludes the paragraph with a word of warning (v. 12) and reassurance (v. 13). The warning follows as an inference (ὥστε, "So then") from the narrative Paul has summarized in vv. 1–5 and from which he has drawn out a series of examples in vv. 6–11 for the Corinthians to avoid. The wording of the warning is broad and generalized, distilling the essential point of the four more specific warnings in verses 7–10 against idolatry, immorality, testing Christ, and grumbling and stating it as a third person imperative addressed to anyone who "thinks he stands." The focus of the warning on the dangers of complacency is presumably informed by Paul's sense that the Corinthian letter writers are "puff[ed] up" (8:1) by the knowledge they think they have.[376]

The warning of verse 12 is followed by a reassurance in verse 13, acknowledging the reality of the temptation that the Corinthians are subject to but assuring them that there is no need for them to be overwhelmed or defeated by it. Paul may intend the language of "temptation" (πειρασμός), used in close proximity to the extended discussion of the wilderness experience of the Israelites, to allude to the words of Moses in Deuteronomy 8, where he tells the Israelites that YHWH led them on their wilderness wanderings "so that he might humble you and test (ἐκπειράσῃ) you" (Deut 8:2, 16; cf. Exod 15:25)—a statement that is accompanied by a reminder of the numerous ways in which YHWH was at work during the journey to support, strengthen, and provide for them (Deut 8:3–4) and a warning against the fresh temptations that are still ahead of them (Deut 8:7–20). Within the Corinthians' context, the particular temptation they are most obviously subject to in relation to the sins against which Paul has warned in verses 7–10 is the social pressure to conform to the

---

correspondence between the Corinthians and the "scriptural figures" that they fulfill but the typologically framed summation of the story of the wilderness generation in vv. 1–4 implies much the same point.

[376] Some commentators (e.g., Barrett, *First Corinthians*, 228; Conzelmann, *1 Corinthians*, 168) also suggest that the Corinthians' overdeveloped sense of security may have been reinforced by the notion that their participation in the rituals of baptism and the Lord's Supper immunized them against the risk of spiritual harm. This may well have been the case, and a mirror reading of vv. 1–4 would suggest it as one possible explanation for Paul's description of the Israelites as having been "baptized" into Moses and provided with "spiritual food" and "spiritual drink," but it is not a diagnosis that Paul himself explicitly states, and when he returns to the theme of the Lord's Supper in vv. 16–21, the tendency of his rhetoric is, if anything, to strengthen rather than to weaken the Corinthians' sense of the ritual's participatory significance.

practices of their pagan neighbors. Paul assures them that they are not alone in this predicament—the temptations they experience are "common to humanity" (ἀνθρώπινος)—and God, who is "faithful" (cf. Deut 7:9), can be counted on to honor his commitments to them, limiting the temptations they experience so that they are not beyond their capacity to endure and providing a "way out" (ἔκβασις) that will enable them to persevere to the end (cf. 1:8–9).

Bridge

The hermeneutical bridge Paul builds between the story of the Israelite wilderness generation and the situation of the Corinthian believers extends across the divide of centuries and cultures to us, as well. Like the Corinthians, we are to regard the Israelites not as strangers but as "our ancestors" (v. 1). Like the Corinthians, too, we are among those "on whom the ends of the ages have come" (v. 11). And like the Corinthians we may therefore receive the Scriptures of the Old Testament as having been written down "for our instruction" (v. 11).

The particular lesson Paul draws from the story of the wilderness generation is as relevant to us as it was to the believers in Corinth. For those of us who live within the context of the post-Christendom West, the Corinthians' situation presents a particularly illuminating pre-Christendom analog to our own "awkwardly intermediate stage of having once been culturally established but not yet clearly disestablished."[377] Like us, and to a greater extent than many of the early Christians addressed within the New Testament,[378] the Corinthians have something to cling onto, a place within the city (or, for some, a pretension or an aspiration to a place) that they are anxious to avoid losing. In striking and significant ways, the Corinthians are our contemporaries, subject to strong social pressures to conform to the idolatry and immorality of their surrounding social context and yet liable to a dangerous overconfidence about the strength

[377] George A. Lindbeck, *The Nature of Doctrine: Religion and Theology in a Postliberal Age* (Philadelphia: Westminster, 1984), 134, quoted in Stanley Hauerwas, *After Christendom? How the Church Is To Behave If Freedom, Justice, and a Christian Nation are Bad Ideas* (Nashville: Abingdon, 1991), 23.

[378] Cf. especially Barclay, "Thessalonica and Corinth," 49–74; Winter, "Gallio's Ruling," 213–24.

of the position in which they stand.[379] The warnings and encouragements of verses 6–13 were written for them but apply with no less force to us.

D. Eating and Abstaining in Various Scenarios (10:14–11:1)

> 14 So then, my dear friends, flee from idolatry. 15 I am speaking as to sensible people. Judge for yourselves what I am saying. 16 The cup of blessing that we bless, is it not a sharing in the blood of Christ? The bread that we break, is it not a sharing in the body of Christ? 17 Because there is one bread, we who are many are one body, since all of us share the one bread. 18 Consider the people of Israel. Do not those who eat the sacrifices participate in the altar? 19 What am I saying then? That food sacrificed to idols is anything, or that an idol is anything? 20 No, but I do say that what they sacrifice, they sacrifice to demons and not to God. I do not want you to be participants with demons! 21 You cannot drink the cup of the Lord and the cup of demons. You cannot share in the Lord's table and the table of demons. 22 Or are we provoking the Lord to jealousy? Are we stronger than he?
>
> 23 "Everything is permissible," but not everything is beneficial. "Everything is permissible," but not everything builds up. 24 No one is to seek his own good, but the good of the other person.
>
> 25 Eat everything that is sold in the meat market, without raising questions for the sake of conscience, 26 since **the earth is the Lord's, and all that is in it.** 27 If any of the unbelievers invites you over and you want to go, eat everything that is set before you, without raising questions for the sake of conscience. 28 But if someone says to you, "This is food from a sacrifice," do not eat it, out of consideration for the one who told you, and for the sake of conscience. 29 I do not mean your own conscience, but the other person's. For why is my freedom judged by another person's conscience? 30 If I partake with thanksgiving, why am I criticized because of something for which I give thanks?
>
> 31 So, whether you eat or drink, or whatever you do, do everything for the glory of God. 32 Give no offense to Jews or Greeks or the church of God, 33 just as I also try to please everyone in everything, not seeking my own benefit, but the benefit of many, so that they may be saved. 11 Imitate me, as I also imitate Christ.

[379] I have argued for this claim at greater length in Starling, "Not a Wisdom of This Age," 81–98, esp. 84–88.

Context/Structure/Form

In verses 14–22 Paul returns explicitly to the particular issue of meals eaten at the table of a pagan god (v. 21; cf. 8:10) and to the implications of the knowledge that believers have about the ontological status of idols and the food that has been offered to them (v. 19; cf. 8:4–6). Paul's initial treatment of the issue in 8:7–13 was informed primarily by his opening words about the loving use of knowledge (8:1–3) and supported by the discussion in 9:1–23 of his willingness to curtail the exercise of his rights and freedoms for the sake of others. The warning that he gives in 10:14–22 has a different focus, shaped by the subsequent discussions in 9:24–27 and 10:1–13 regarding the discipline Paul exercises in order not to be "disqualified" at the end of the race and the judgments that fell upon the wilderness generation of the Israelites.

The final paragraphs of the chapter, in 10:23–11:1, shift the focus away from the topic of meals at the table of an idol to a brief selection of other scenarios in which the possibility of eating food that had been sacrificed to idols might arise (vv. 25–30). Paul precedes his advice on these matters by giving his response to the slogan that encapsulates the approach that the Corinthian letter writers have taken to them (vv. 23–24) and follows it with a summation of his own approach to this and all such matters (10:31–11:1).

Comments

10:14. Paul begins the paragraph with the inferential conjunction Διόπερ ("Therefore"), signaling that he is drawing out the implications of the illustrations and warnings in verses 1–13, and a summarizing exhortation to the readers as his "dear friends" (ἀγαπητοί), urging them to "flee from idolatry." (Cf. the similarly worded exhortation to "flee sexual immorality" that Paul gives to his readers in 6:18 as he draws together the threads of his discussion regarding that topic.)

This exhortation sets the tone for the rest of the paragraph; building on what he has said about his own example in 9:24–27 and the story of Israel in 10:1–13, Paul now goes significantly farther than he had earlier gone in his initial, brief treatment of the topic in 8:7–13. In that earlier discussion, Paul's focus was on the loving use of knowledge and the need to take account of the situation of a weaker brother or sister; the inferences that the Corinthians have drawn from the theological principles Paul affirms in 8:4–6 regarding the freedom they have to participate in a meal at an idol temple are, at that stage of the discussion, still assumed for the sake of the argument. Now, however, Paul exposes the inadequacy of the Corinthians' understanding of what is taking place in such a situation and the perils that eating at an idol's table involves, not only for the weaker brother or sister but for the person participating.

10:15. Despite the preparatory groundwork that he has already laid in 9:24–27 and 10:1–13, Paul still frames the point that he is making within this paragraph not as a bare word of exhortation but as an argument presented to the Corinthians for their assessment: "I am speaking as to sensible people [ὡς φρονίμοις λέγω]. Judge for yourselves what I am saying." There is no need to assume that Paul expects the Corinthians to have forgotten the sharp edge of sarcasm with which the same word φρόνιμος ("sensible"/"wise") was used earlier in the letter, in 4:10 ("We are fools for Christ, but you are wise [φρόνιμοι] in Christ!"); Paul's aim is not to bolster the Corinthians' delusional assurance of their own wisdom. But the function of his comment is not merely to deflate their pretensions; in choosing to frame his appeal "*as* to sensible people," Paul is simultaneously summoning them to think with the true wisdom and clear-sighted reasoning that they have hitherto failed to exercise.[380] The goal he hopes that his letter will accomplish is not only the conversion of their imaginations but also the renewal of their reasoning and the reauthorization of their judgment.[381]

10:16–17. The argument Paul presents for the Corinthians' consideration in this paragraph begins with a reflection on the significance of their participation in the common meal of the Lord's Supper: "The cup of blessing that we bless, is it not a sharing in the blood of Christ? The bread that we break, is it not a sharing in the body of Christ? Because there is one bread, we who are many are one body, since all of us share the one bread." The rhetorical questions of verse 16 are both framed as questions anticipating a positive answer—a slant that is signaled in Greek by the repeated οὐχί ... οὐχί ("is it not ... ? is it not ... ?"). Together they function to assert a single proposition: that participation in the "cup of

---

[380] There is no need to discount the likelihood that there is a sarcastic or critical edge to Paul's language here, but the context makes it clear that his intent is not *merely* sarcastic: cf. Schnabel, *Erster Korintherbrief*, 548; Ciampa and Rosner, *The First Letter to the Corinthians*, 471.

[381] Cf. Starling, "As to Sensible People," 119–23.

blessing" and the broken bread implies κοινωνία ("sharing") in the blood and body of Christ.[382]

As Fee correctly highlights, the double symbolism of the meal suggests a double κοινωνία—the cup focusing primarily on the "vertical" communion established through the atoning death of Jesus (cf. 11:25) and the bread focusing not only on that but also on the "horizontal" communion that believers share with one another as fellow members of Christ's body (cf. v. 17).[383] The assertion implied by Paul's questions is not one that he appears to have considered particularly controversial, requiring a lengthy argument to justify it: he supports it simply with a brief statement in verse 17 of the symbolism of the "one bread" in which participants in the Lord's Supper share to signify that they are "one body" in Christ (see §8.2).

10:18. Paul adds to his case in verse 18 by reminding the Corinthians of a second instance of communal eating that functions as a symbol of participation: "Consider the people of Israel. Do not those who eat the sacrifices participate in the altar?" In this instance, the meal Paul wishes his readers to consider is the meal that the people of Israel (Ἰσραὴλ κατὰ σάρκα; literally, "Israel according to the flesh")[384] shared in when they ate the food that had previously been offered in sacrifice on the altar (e.g., Lev 7:15; Deut 12:26–28; 1 Sam 1:4).[385] To "participate in the altar" is, by implication, to share in the worship that was offered up through the sacrifice that was made on it.[386]

---

382 Paul's description of the cup as "the cup of blessing that we bless" probably reflects a custom of recalling the traditional Jewish blessing pronounced by Jesus over the cup he shared with the disciples at the Passover meal that they celebrated on the eve of his crucifixion (cf. Mark 14:23).

383 Fee, *First Epistle to the Corinthians*, 516.

384 Paul's description of them as "Israel according to the flesh" is probably intended to communicate that he has in mind the visible solidarity of national Israel as a community defined by common ancestry and participation in a shared set of ritual practices including circumcision and the sacrificial system associated with the Jerusalem temple (cf. Rom 1:3; 2:28; 4:1; 9:3, 5, 8; Gal 4:23, 29).

385 Some commentators (e.g., Gardner, *1 Corinthians*, 452; Garland, *1 Corinthians*, 478–79) argue that Paul is returning to the incident that he recalled earlier in the chapter, when the Israelites "sat down to eat and drink" after the sacrifices had been offered to the golden calf (10:7; cf. Exod 32:6). This reading sits uncomfortably with the present tense forms of ἐσθίοντες ("eat") and κοινωνοὶ … εἰσίν ("participate"), which are most naturally read in a gnomic sense, making statements of a permanent or timeless nature rather than as recounting an incident in a narrative. Cf. Ciampa and Rosner, *The First Letter to the Corinthians*, 477; Schreiner, *1 Corinthians*, 211.

386 Ciampa and Rosner, *The First Letter to the Corinthians*, 477.

10:19–20. Paul's statements about the participatory symbolism of the Lord's Supper and the meals in which the people of Israel consumed sacrifices previously offered on the altar carry an obvious and intended implication regarding the similar significance attached to the act of eating a meal at the table of a pagan god. But before Paul spells that implication out, he anticipates a question that it would inevitably have raised for the Corinthian letter writers: How does the analogy that he is implying sit with the earlier statements that he made in chapter 8, where he was happy to agree with the Corinthians that "an idol is nothing in the world" and "there is no God but one" (8:4)? If a parallel can be drawn between the participation that is symbolized by a meal at the table of an idol and the participation with the (risen and real) Jesus that is symbolized by the Lord's Supper, or the participation with the (true and living) God of Israel that is symbolized by the eating of the sacrifices that have been offered to him, is Paul then implying that an idol is something after all or that the ritual of sacrificing food to an idol has the power to transform it into something other than ordinary food (v. 19)?

Paul's answer to that question in verse 20 is an (unstated) "No!"—implied by the "but" (ἀλλά) with which the verse commences and correctly inserted by the translators of most English versions (including the CSB). But there is more to be said than that: "But I do say that what they sacrifice, they sacrifice to demons and not to God. I do not want you to be participants with demons!" (v. 20). The idols themselves are a deception, not a substantial and authentic reality, but they are a deception that has been propagated and believed under the influence of demons. The worship offered to them is, therefore, worship that can be described as being offered "to demons and not to God" (δαιμονίοις καὶ οὐ θεῷ), and those who participate in that worship by sharing in a meal at the idol's table are "participants with demons" (κοινωνοὺς τῶν δαιμονίων).

The words Paul uses to describe the worship of the pagan cults as offered "to demons and not to God" correspond verbatim to the words used in LXX Deuteronomy 32:17 (cf. Bar 4:7) to describe the unfaithfulness of the people of Israel (an event that Moses describes in the previous verse as one in which they "provoked [the Lord's] jealousy with different gods"; Deut 32:16). The "demons" Paul has in mind as the instigators and recipients of idolatrous worship are probably to be understood, in line with second temple Jewish interpretation of Deuteronomy 32:17 (e.g., Bar

4:7; 1 En. 19:1; T. Sol. 5:5), as personal and malevolent beings, supernatural but not transcendently divine in their nature.[387]

10:21. Given that this is, in Paul's mind, the significance of eating a meal at the table of a pagan god, it is no surprise that he goes on to say in verse 21 that participation in a meal of this kind is incompatible with the allegiance that is communicated through participation in the meal eaten by believers at the Lord's table: "You cannot drink the cup of the Lord and the cup of demons. You cannot share in the Lord's table and the table of demons." The Lord's Supper is, in Paul's view, to be understood as an expression of belonging and allegiance that is functionally equivalent to the meals in which the people of Israel participated in the sacrifices that had been offered at "the Lord's table" (τράπεζα κυρίου; cf. the use of the same expression to refer to the temple of YHWH in LXX Mal 1:7, 12, and the similar language in Ezek 41:22; 44:16; T. Jud. 21:5; T. Levi 8:16).[388] His description of the meals connected with the veneration of pagan gods as meals eaten at "the table of demons" reflects the language that was used in the surviving papyri to invite guests to a variety of different kinds of celebration, some of which took place in the temple of the god at whose "table" the meal was eaten and others of which took place in a private home or (in one instance) at the temple of another god.[389]

10:22. Verse 22 concludes the paragraph with a pair of rhetorical questions ("Or are we provoking the Lord to jealousy [παραζηλοῦμεν τὸν κύριον]? Are we stronger than he?"). The first of the two questions echoes the description in LXX Deuteronomy 32:16, 21 of Israel as having "provoked the jealousy" (παρώξυνάν) of the Lord, denying him the exclusive allegiance that they owed under the covenant he had made with them; the second returns the focus to the arrogant overconfidence of the Corinthian letter writers' self-estimation (cf. v. 12), which Paul clearly views as dangerously delusional. Together, they warn the Corinthians in the strongest possible terms against the view that the "knowledge" they possess entitles them to eat with impunity at the table of a pagan god.

---

387 Cf. BDAG, s.v. "δαιμόνιον," 2; Garland, *1 Corinthians*, 480; Ciampa and Rosner, *The First Letter to the Corinthians*, 481.

388 Cf. Gardner, *1 Corinthians*, 455.

389 Cf. P. Oxy. 2592, P. Oxy. 110 (meals "at the table of the lord Sarapis," celebrated in the Sarapeum); P. Oxy. 1484 (a coming of age party "at the table of the lord Sarapis," celebrated in the temple of Thoeris); P. Oslo. 157 (a meal "at the table of the lord Sarapis," celebrated in a private home), and the discussion in Kim, "The Papyrus Invitation," 391–402.

10:23–24. Having brought to a conclusion his warning against participating in meals "at the table of" the pagan gods (the issue that appears to have been the point of sharpest controversy between Paul and the Corinthian letter writers), Paul now turns in the final verses of the chapter to consider two other scenarios in which believers might encounter the possibility of eating food previously offered in sacrifice to idols (vv. 25–30). Before turning to those matters, however, he offers his response to the slogan that epitomizes the approach that the letter writers appear to have taken to them (vv. 23–24).

The slogan Paul (twice) quotes and (twice) responds to in verse 23 (Πάντα ἔξεστιν, "Everything is permissible") is closely similar to the slogan he has already twice quoted and twice responded to in 6:12 (Πάντα μοι ἔξεστιν, "Everything is permissible for me"). In both cases, the first response that he gives to the slogan is the same: "but not everything is beneficial" (ἀλλ' οὐ πάντα συμφέρει)—language that implies a concern not only for what is beneficial to the individual but also for what is beneficial to the community.[390] This focus on the benefit of the community is further reinforced by Paul's second response to the slogan, which replaces the response that he gives in 6:12b ("but I will not be mastered by anything") with a reminder that "not everything builds up" (οὐ πάντα οἰκοδομεῖ; cf. Paul's use of the same verb in 8:1; 14:4, 17, and the cognate noun in 14:3, 5, 12, 26). The same emphasis continues in verse 24: "No one is to seek his own good, but the good of the other person" (more literally, "Let no one seek his own, but that of the other"). In Romans 15:1–3 Paul directs a closely similar exhortation to the "strong" members of the churches in Rome, grounding it explicitly in the example of Christ, who "did not please himself" but submitted instead to "the insults of those who insult you" (Rom 15:3, quoting Ps 69:9). A similar exhortation can also be found in Philippians 2:4, where, once again, it is framed as a call to imitate the example of Christ (cf. Phil 2:5–9). Here, the scope of "the other" is not limited to fellow believers but explicitly includes the unbelieving neighbor who might invite a believer to dinner (10:27) and the "Jews" and "Greeks" whose salvation the readers are to seek (10:32),

---

[390] Cf. the comments on 6:12, above, regarding the likely source of the slogan and the thinking that it expresses. For a discussion of the traditional use of συμφέρειν in political discourse focused on the common advantage of the community, see Mitchell, *Paul and the Rhetoric of Reconciliation*, 29–31.

and the explicit reference to Christ's example comes at the end of the paragraph, in 11:1.

10:25–26. The first scenario Paul goes on to discuss, in verses 25–26, is straightforward. Meat that has been purchased in the meat market can be eaten without the need to raise any questions of conscience (v. 25), since "the earth is the Lord's, and all that is in it" (v. 26, quoting from Ps 24:1). Paul's advice here presupposes that a good deal of what was sold at the meat market had previously been offered to an idol but would not have been visibly identifiable as such.[391]

His advice against "raising questions for the sake of conscience" is probably (given the way in which Paul connects it with the statement in the following verse that "the earth is the Lord's, and all that is in it") intended primarily as an affirmation of the freedom that believers genuinely do have.[392] The discussion that follows in verses 27–30, however, suggests that it may also have a secondary function as a way of helping believers to avoid scenarios in which asking the question and having it answered in the affirmative could frame their purchase of the meat, in the eyes of others, as an indication that they are happy to participate indirectly in the worship of the idol.[393] In a scenario such as this, as in the case that Paul envisages in verse 29, the "conscience" Paul has in mind is probably not the conscience of the purchaser but the conscience of an observer who may misconstrue the purchaser's intention.

10:27–30. Verses 27–30 explore a slightly different scenario, in which the meal is eaten in the private home of an unbeliever (presumably not as a cultic occasion along the lines of the celebration to which guests are invited in P. Oslo. 157). Here, as in the meat market, Paul's advice to the readers is that they should feel free to eat whatever is set before them, "without raising questions for the sake of conscience" (v. 27). Paul's encouragement to the readers to accept such invitations (if they wish to) is in line with his earlier clarification statement in 5:9–13 that they should not set themselves up to "judge outsiders" (5:12) or attempt to withdraw from social interactions with "the immoral people of this world or the greedy and swindlers or idolaters" (5:10); it coheres, too, with his

[391] Cf. Murphy-O'Connor, *St. Paul's Corinth*, 30.

[392] Cf. Fee, *First Epistle to the Corinthians*, 531.

[393] Cf. Ciampa and Rosner, *The First Letter to the Corinthians*, 487–88.

own example of becoming "like one without the law" to those who are themselves "without the law" (9:21).

But this scenario, unlike the transaction Paul asks the readers to imagine in the meat market, is potentially complicated by the presence of fellow diners, the questions they may ask and the responses they may receive, and the various possible interpretations that they may place on the religious significance of the food eaten as part of the meal. Paul goes on to explore one such possible complication in the case study of verses 28–30, which is generated by a gratuitous piece of information that someone offers to the guests,[394] informing them that a particular item of food is ἱερόθυτον ("food from a sacrifice"). The most likely identity of the informant Paul envisages is the host, since they would have been in the best position to know the source of the various dishes being served at the table, but the indefiniteness of Paul's "someone" (τις) leaves other possibilities open. The fact that the word used to describe the food is ἱερόθυτον ("food from a sacrifice") rather than εἰδωλόθυτος ("food that has been sacrificed to an idol") suggests that Paul is picturing a pagan rather than a Jewish or Christian person as the speaker.

In a scenario such as this, Paul tells the Corinthians they should refrain from eating that item "out of consideration for the one who told you, and for the sake of conscience. I do not mean your own conscience, but the other person's" (vv. 28–29a). It is certainly grammatically possible that (as most commentators assume) the "other person" in verse 29a is referring to the same person as "the one who told you" in verse 28b and that the two phrases in verse 28b ("out of consideration for the one who told you, and for the sake of conscience") are intended to express a single idea (i.e., "out of consideration for the conscience of the informant").[395] This is a somewhat forced reading of the grammar of verse 28b, however, and it is difficult (though not impossible) to reconstruct a plausible scenario under which Paul envisaged the conscience of the unbelieving informant

---

[394] The pronoun second person pronouns throughout vv. 25–28 are all plural. It is difficult to say with certainty whether this is because Paul is envisaging scenarios in which his readers are consuming food (at home and in the homes of others) in groups and not as isolated individuals, or simply because he is addressing the advice to the whole gathered congregation as they hear the letter read. In either case, the social context of the meal appears to be one in which both the group dynamics of the communicative context and the responsibilities of the individual believer toward "the other person" (v. 29) are in play.

[395] E.g., Fee, *First Epistle to the Corinthians*, 534–35; Ciampa and Rosner, *The First Letter to the Corinthians*, 493; Garland, *1 Corinthians*, 496.

being vulnerable in a manner even broadly comparable in nature and seriousness to the kind of vulnerability of conscience that Paul discusses earlier in 8:7–13.

The more natural reading of verse 28b is to take it as offering two distinct reasons for refraining from the food that has been identified as deriving from a sacrifice: first, out of consideration for the informant, who has (presumably) made an attempt to show a courteous concern for the scruples of a Christian guest, and second, "for the sake of conscience." Paul immediately goes on to add in verse 29a that the particular conscience he has in mind is not "your own conscience, but the other person's." Given the earlier discussion of conscience as a motivating concern in 8:7–13, it is probably best to take the "other person" of verse 29a as referring back to the generic "other person" of verse 24,[396] rather than to "the one who told you" in verse 28b, and to interpret Paul's concern here as a desire to protect the vulnerable conscience of a fellow believer who might otherwise be emboldened in a manner similar to the emboldening Paul envisaged as a dangerous possibility in 8:7–13.

Having reintroduced the issue of conscience as a reason for abstaining, Paul hastens to add the clarifying explanation in verses 29b–30 that his intention is not to burden the conscience of believers themselves but to encourage them to be concerned for the consciences of others: "For why is my freedom judged by another person's conscience? If I partake with thanksgiving, why am I criticized because of something for which I give thanks?" The "I" of verses 29b–30 is probably the generic "I," through which Paul imagines himself participating in the scenario he has been describing in verses 27–29a,[397] rather than a directly self-referring "I" functioning in the same way as the "I" of 9:1–3 and resuming the defense Paul commenced in those verses.[398] The focus of the rhetorical question in verse 30 on "thanksgiving" (χάρις) probably reflects traditional Jewish

---

[396] Cf. Brookins and Longenecker, *1 Corinthians 10-16: A Handbook on the Greek Text*, BHGNT (Waco: Baylor University Press, 2016), 24.

[397] Cf. Ciampa and Rosner, *The First Letter to the Corinthians*, 493–94, who point out the close link that the conjunction "for" (γάρ) signals between v. 29b and v. 29a.

[398] See Fee, *First Epistle to the Corinthians*, 535–37, for an argument in favor of taking vv. 29b–30 as a reference to actual and current controversies to which Paul is responding in an abrupt return to the "defense" he mounted in the opening paragraphs of ch. 9.

interpretation of Psalm 24:1 (quoted by Paul in v. 26) as a reason for blessing God before the consumption of every meal.[399]

10:31–11:1. Paul concludes this section of the letter with a statement of the overarching goals and principles that are to shape believers' conduct in all such matters, including both the relatively straightforward situations such as those discussed in 10:14–22, where a line can (and must) be drawn in black and white, and the more complicated situations such as those discussed in 10:23–30. The bottom line of his counsel to the Corinthians is expressed in the three imperatives contained within these verses: "do everything for the glory of God" (v. 31); "give no offense to Jews or Greeks or the church of God" (v. 32); and "imitate me, as I also imitate Christ" (11:1).

While the first imperative is introduced with an inferential conjunction οὖν ("So"), suggesting that it should be taken as a conclusion drawn from the argument and explanation that precedes it in chapters 8–10, it is framed in the broadest possible terms ("whether you eat or drink, or whatever you do, do everything ..."), signaling an applicability that extends well beyond the bounds of that particular discussion (see §1).

The second imperative, in verse 32, spells out one particular entailment of the first, as it applies to situations such as the ones discussed in the preceding paragraphs. The admonition to "give no offence" (ἀπρόσκοποι ... γίνεσθε) harks back to the earlier warning against allowing one's own freedom to become a "stumbling block [πρόσκομμα] to the weak" (8:9); here, however, the scope of the concern is broadened beyond the situation of the weaker brother or sister to include the stumbling blocks that might be placed in the way of (unconverted) "Jews" and "Greeks" as well as "the church of God" (i.e., all believers, including weak and strong, Jew and gentile, and every other possible subcategory). Given that the "stumbling block" of 8:9 was no mere annoyance but a circumstance that endangered a fellow believer's salvation, a similar level of seriousness should probably be attached to the cognate verb here, and a similar focus on matters of salvation: the Corinthians are to take care not to act in a manner that endangers the salvation of their fellow believers or places a barrier in the path of unbelievers hearing the gospel and coming to salvation.

---

[399] Ciampa and Rosner, *The First Letter to the Corinthians*, 494; Fee, *First Epistle to the Corinthians*, 531–32, 37, citing *b. Ber.* 35a; *t. Ber.* 4.1.

Verse 33 expands on the imperative in verse 32, offering Paul's own conduct (which he has already described in 9:19–23) as a lived example of what he has in mind. Paul's description of his own example confirms the focus on salvation as the primary "benefit" (σύμφορον) that he wishes to secure for others and prioritizes over the more immediate and mundane benefits he might otherwise have sought for himself. Paul's conduct as he describes it in this verse also illustrates the general principle that he has earlier laid down in verse 24 ("No one is to seek his own good, but the good of the other person") and, like that verse, resembles the similar language used by Paul in Romans 15:1–3 and Philippians 2:4.

The paragraph (and the entire discussion in chs. 8–10) is brought to a conclusion in 11:1 with Paul's third imperative: "Imitate me, as I also imitate Christ." The appeal to Paul's example echoes a similar, earlier appeal in 4:16 but is, in this instance, expanded by an explicit reference to the fact that Paul's example, in turn, is modeled on that of Christ.[400] Based on the parallel appeals in Romans 15:3–4 and Philippians 2:5–11, the impulse at the core of what is to be imitated is the willingness of Christ to seek the good (and, supremely, the salvation) of others ahead of his own immediate and personal advantage, sacrificing material wealth and advantage, social esteem, and ultimately life itself in order that others might be saved.

Bridge

Paul's instructions and advice to the Corinthians within these final paragraphs of chapter 10 is, on the one hand, tightly focused on the kind of situations that might arise within the specific cultural and religious context that they inhabited. It presupposes a particular set of connections between the slaughter of animals, the sacrificial rituals of the city's temples, the operations of the meat market, and the conventions of the dining room. Here, as elsewhere in the letter, Paul's primary interest is not in writing pure theoretical theology but in offering direction for the faithful performance of the readers' roles as believers in Jesus within the particular social context they inhabit.

[400] Something similar is probably implied by the reference in 4:17 to "my ways in Christ Jesus" (though that phrase is probably referring primarily to the way in which Paul's conduct is shaped by his participation in Christ and in the community of Christ's people rather than directly to the idea of imitating Christ).

Nevertheless, the advice that he gives, here as elsewhere in the letter, is thought through from first theological principles (in this case, the creational monotheism of Ps 24:1, the salvation-historical continuity between Israel and the church, the jealous commitment of God to the covenant that he has with his people, the relationship of solidarity and exclusive allegiance that is represented by participation in the Lord's Supper, and the example of Christ as the pattern of sacrificial love to be imitated by believers) that are embedded within these paragraphs as the basis of Paul's counsel. We too will encounter scenarios (different from those faced by the Corinthians) in which we will need to draw sharp, clear lines such as Paul calls the Corinthians to draw in verses 14–22, exercise the freedom Paul encourages in verses 25–27, and practice the care and caution that Paul advises in verses 28–30.

The detail of the scenarios will differ, but the convictions and commitments that ought to inform our practice should be the same; like the Corinthians, in imitation of Paul and of Christ, we are to seek the glory of God above all things and act in accordance with that quest for God's glory within all our social relationships, demonstrating within our own context a missionary engagement with our neighbors (including a holistic concern for their good and a particular desire for their salvation), a loving solidarity with our fellow believers, and a loyal allegiance to Christ.

VI. Instructions on Issues Relating to the Gathering (11:2–34)

In chapter 11 Paul addresses two issues that both relate to the way in which believers honor one another (and therefore honor God) in the regular gatherings of the church. The two issues appear to have been connected in Paul's mind by the fact that they both arise when the Corinthians "come together" (vv. 17, 18, 20, 33, 34) and to aspects of their interaction that he can "praise" (v. 2, albeit with significant qualifications and corrections!) or "not ... praise" (v. 17). Further connections between verses 2–16 and verses 17–34 are suggested by the fact that in both halves of the chapter Paul is addressing issues relating to behaviors that involve the honoring or dishonoring of others (cf. vv. 4–7, 13–15, 22, 29, 33) and (as will be argued below in relation to vv. 2–16 as well as vv. 17–34) the equal honor that is owed to all believers, regardless of wealth or social status.

It is difficult to be certain as to whether the issues addressed in this chapter were raised in the Corinthians' letter (cf. 7:1) or brought to

Paul's attention in oral reports that he received, like the matters that he addresses in 1:10–4:21 and 5:1–6:20. The commendation in verse 2 for the fact that "you remember me in everything and hold fast to the traditions just as I delivered them to you" reads a little more easily as a reference to a claim they have made in their letter, and the qualifications and corrections that follow ("But I want you to know that ...") resemble the way in which Paul responds to what appear to have been Corinthian slogans and/or quotations from their letter in earlier chapters (cf. 6:12–13; 7:2; 8:1b–3, 7; 10:23). The statement in verse 18, "I hear that when you come together as a church there are divisions among you," however, is almost certainly a reference to an oral report Paul has received. The entire chapter appears to hang together in Paul's mind as a set of "instruction[s]" (vv. 17, 34) that he is giving to the Corinthians, and the final verse makes reference to "the other matters" (Τὰ ... λοιπά), on which he will give further instructions in person when he is able to visit—language that suggests a shared awareness of other outstanding (but presumably less urgent) matters that may have been addressed in the Corinthian letter and raises the possibility that the Lord's Supper may have been raised as an issue in the letter as well as in the oral reports Paul has received.[401]

A. Men, Women, and Head Coverings in Prayer and Prophecy (11:2–16)

> [2] Now I praise you because you remember me in everything and hold fast to the traditions just as I delivered them to you. [3] But I want you to know that Christ is the head of every man, and the man is the head of the woman, and God is the head of Christ. [4] Every man who prays or prophesies with something on his head dishonors his head. [5] Every woman who prays or prophesies with her head uncovered dishonors her head, since that is one and the same as having her head shaved. [6] For if a woman doesn't cover her head, she should have her hair cut off. But if it is disgraceful for a woman to have her hair cut off or her head shaved, let her head be covered.
>
> [7] A man should not cover his head, because he is the image and glory of God. So too, woman is the glory of man. [8] For man did not come from woman, but woman came from man. [9] Neither was man created for the

[401] The matters to which he is referring here could perhaps involve further details regarding the conduct of the Lord's Supper; alternatively, Paul may have in mind other traditions that the Corinthians have been keeping, but on which they require further instruction. Cf. Fee, *First Epistle to the Corinthians*, 629.

> sake of woman, but woman for the sake of man. [10] This is why a woman should have a symbol of authority on her head, because of the angels. [11] In the Lord, however, woman is not independent of man, and man is not independent of woman. [12] For just as woman came from man, so man comes through woman, and all things come from God.
>
> [13] Judge for yourselves: Is it proper for a woman to pray to God with her head uncovered? [14] Does not even nature itself teach you that if a man has long hair it is a disgrace to him, [15] but that if a woman has long hair, it is her glory? For her hair is given to her as a covering. [16] If anyone wants to argue about this, we have no other custom, nor do the churches of God.

Context/Structure/Form

Paul's treatment of the first issue he deals with in this chapter commences with a broadly framed word of praise for the way in which the Corinthians have remembered him "in everything" and held fast to the traditions he delivered to them. He goes on immediately, however, to raise a matter on which he considers the Corinthians to require further instruction and correction. The difficulty we face as twenty-first century readers in interpreting the instructions Paul gives lies partly in the cultural distance between us and the Corinthians and partly in the fact that Paul's instructions are part of an ongoing conversation that he is engaged in with his readers, not all of which we are privy to.

Most commentators (whatever their ideological stance in relation to the gender issues raised by Paul's instructions) read 11:2–16 on the assumption that Paul is responding to a scenario in which a group of high-status Corinthian women are objecting to the custom of wearing a head covering when they pray and prophesy in the Corinthian gathering. One major difficulty with this reconstruction, however, is that the conclusion toward which Paul is arguing in verses 3–10 is stated not as a *repudiation* of the authority that a woman has over her own head but as an *affirmation* of that authority.[402] An additional difficulty lies in the fact that the hypothetical objector to whom Paul addresses his rebuke in verse 16 is described with a grammatically masculine adjective φιλόνεικος ("contentious"; CSB: "wants to argue"), a choice that need not be taken as

---

[402] The translation of the relevant phrase in the CSB (and the NIV 1984) as "a symbol of authority on her head" is unlikely; see the comments on v. 10, below.

implying an exclusively male source of opposition envisaged by Paul[403] but is difficult to square with the hypothesis of an exclusively female resistance to the custom of the head covering. An alternative reconstruction that fits more neatly with the direction of Paul's argument is that the position of the elite congregation members to whom he is responding is not a *rejection* of the head covering but a *restriction* of the right to wear it, limiting the privilege of wearing the head covering to those women whose social status permitted it.[404]

If that alternative reconstruction is accepted, it helps to explain not only the way in which Paul frames the conclusion for which he is arguing as a defense of the "authority" (ἐξουσία) that a woman possesses over her head (v. 10) but also the prominence of the word "every" (παντός/πᾶς/πᾶσα) within the sentences in which Paul frames the premises from which he is arguing (vv. 3, 4, 5). Within a context in which head coverings functioned as a symbol of both gender differentiation and class distinction, signifying and safeguarding the honor of a respectable, freeborn woman (and, by extension, the honor of her husband or father),[405] Paul insists on the right of *every* woman in the congregation to cover her head in that manner, without distinction between freeborn women and those who are freedwomen or slaves.

In support of that assertion, Paul marshals arguments from a variety of sources, including the creation narratives to which he alludes in verses 7–12, the observations regarding custom and nature in verses 5–6 and 13–15, and the nested sequence of relationships to which he refers in

---

403 The grammatical gender of the adjective is probably a generic masculine, which would be compatible with the possibility of objectors who were either male or female.

404 For arguments in favor of this alternative reconstruction, see Cynthia Long Westfall, *Paul and Gender: Reclaiming the Apostle's Vision for Men and Women in Christ* (Grand Rapids: Baker Academic, 2016), 24–43; Janelle Peters, "Veiling in Corinth: A Surprising Sign of Equality," in *The Biblical World of Gender: The Daily Lives of Ancient Women and Men*, ed. Celina Durgin and Dru Johnson (Eugene: Cascade, 2022), 112–15; Janelle Peters, "Slavery and the Gendered Construction of Worship Veils in 1 Corinthians," *Biblica* 101 (2020): 431–43. For a critical assessment of the historical reconstruction that Westfall proposes (pointing out, for example, the scarcity of evidence for Westfall's claim that the distinction of social status signified by head coverings was universally observed and legally enforced), see Rodney Kilgore and Josiah D. Hall, "Veiling Within the Corinthian Context: An Examination of Cynthia Long Westfall's Reading of 1 Corinthians 11:2–16," *BBR* 33 (2023): 162–85.

405 Cf. Judith Lynn Sebasta, "Symbolism in the Costume of the Roman Woman," in *The World of Roman Costume*, ed. Judith Lynn Sebasta and Larissa Bonfante (Madison: University of Wisconsin Press, 2001), 46–53; K. Olson, *Dress and the Roman Woman: Self-Presentation and Society* (New York: Routledge, 2008), 33–36; Harper, *From Shame to Sin*, 38–45.

verses 3–5, in each of which the conduct and treatment of one person reflects—either positively or adversely—on the honor of the person who is their "head" (κεφαλή). The passage concludes with a firmly worded preemptive response to anyone who might wish to argue against the position Paul is advocating, informing (or reminding?) them that "we have no other custom, nor do the churches of God" (v. 16).

Comments

11:2. Paul begins this section of the letter with a warm statement of commendation, praising the Corinthians for the fact that "you remember me in everything and hold fast to the traditions just as I delivered them to you." The breadth of this statement, its position at the start of a new section of the letter, and the lack of obvious commendation in the following verses suggest that the "traditions" Paul speaks of here need not be taken as a specific reference to traditions regarding head coverings, gender relationships, or prayer and prophecy.[406] The way in which Paul responds, by giving a general affirmation followed by a qualification or correction (cf. 6:12–13; 7:2; 8:1b–3, 7; 10:23), suggests the likelihood that the sweeping claim to which Paul is responding was part of the Corinthians' letter.[407] While this verse is the only place within 1 Corinthians in which the noun "traditions" (παραδόσεις) occurs,[408] he uses the cognate verb παραδίδωμι in 11:23 and 15:3 to refer to teachings and verbal formulations that he received and passed on to the Corinthian believers. By praising the Corinthians for holding fast to the traditions, Paul both reinforces the importance of doing so and secures a measure of good will in preparation for its expenditure in the coming verses, where he will call them to task for the instances in which they have not adhered to the traditions as faithfully as they claim.[409]

11:3–6. Having praised the Corinthians for their (professed?) adherence to the traditions he passed on to them, Paul now turns to an issue

[406] Cf. Garland, *1 Corinthians*, 512; Fee, *First Epistle to the Corinthians*, 552; Gardner, *1 Corinthians*, 478.

[407] Cf. Fee, *First Epistle to the Corinthians*, 552; Ciampa and Rosner, *The First Letter to the Corinthians*, 505.

[408] Cf. its use in 2 Thess 2:15; 3:6 to refer to Christian traditions passed on by Paul, in Gal 1:14 to refer to Jewish ancestral traditions, and in Col 2:8 to refer to the "human tradition" on which the philosophy against which Paul is warning was based.

[409] Cf. Mitchell, *Paul and the Rhetoric of Reconciliation*, 260; Garland, *1 Corinthians*, 513, citing Plutarch, *Mor.* 73C–74E.

on which some correction or further instruction is required ("But I want you to know that …"). The starting point that he chooses for the corrective that he offers to their understanding and practice is a carefully constructed statement in which he juxtaposes three sets of relationships, in each of which one party is said to be the "head" of the other: "But I want you to know that Christ is the head of every man, and the man is the head of the woman, and God is the head of Christ."

The precise meaning Paul has in mind by speaking of Christ as the "head" (κεφαλή) of the man (and the man of the woman, and God of Christ) has been a matter of much scholarly conversation and debate with a variety of options proposed as alternatives to the traditional assumption that "head" in this context means "ruler" or "authority."

The claim made by a line of late twentieth-century interpreters that the word κεφαλή is functioning here as a metaphor meaning "source" (without any sense of authority, prominence, or representation) is not well supported by the evidence that is typically cited.[410] It is true, for example, that Herodotus can refer to "the headwaters of the river Tearus" (Τεάρου ποταμοῦ κεφαλαί) (Hist. 4.91.2), but the context of the metaphor in that instance is very different from those places where it is a person that is referred to as "head." Closer to the mark is the frequently quoted Orphic fragment in which Zeus is acclaimed as "head" (κεφαλή) and the one "from whom comes all that is" (δ' ἐκ πάντα τέτυκται) (e.g., Pseudo-Aristotle, De Mundo 401b). Even here, however, the relationship between Zeus and the cosmos that the hymn describes is one in which derivation (e.g., "root [ῥίζα] of the sea … root of the sun and the moon") and rule (e.g., "Zeus the king, ruler of all, ruling the thunder") are inextricably linked. In the LXX, although it is true that the Hebrew word ראשׁ, used in the sense of "ruler," is more frequently translated as ἄρχων, it is not difficult to find examples of places in which κεφαλή does carry that sense (e.g., LXX Judg 11:11; 2 Kgdms 22:44), and these would have contributed to the range of possibilities that Paul and his readers could draw upon for the metaphorical use of the word.

---

[410] For arguments in favor of that claim, see Catherine Clark Kroeger, "Head," in *Dictionary of Paul and His Letters*, ed. Gerald F. Hawthorne, Ralph P. Martin, and Daniel G. Reid (Downers Grove: IVP, 1993), 375–77; Alvera Mickelsen and Berkeley Mickelsen, "What Does *Kephalē* Mean in the New Testament?," in *Women, Authority, and the Bible*, ed. Alvera Mickelsen (Downers Grove: IVP, 1986), 108–10. For a discussion of the way in which Paul uses the metaphor in Ephesians and Colossians, see Starling, *Reading Ephesians and Colossians*, 141–42.

Here in 1 Corinthians 11, Paul does not go on to say anything directly about "authority" (except for the statement in v. 10 that a woman ought to have authority over her own head), and the context, unlike the household code of Ephesians 5:21–6:9, does not address the question of submission within relationships. Nor does the idea that one party is the "source" of the other appear to be the heart of what Paul has in mind at this point in the argument (though a notion along those lines is present in v. 8, complicated somewhat by the carefully balanced set of statements in v. 12). The primary sense of the metaphor as Paul uses it in verses 3–5 appears to be the notion of representation, and his main point is that, in a relationship between a person and the one who is their "head," the way in which the first party acts or is treated reflects—either positively or negatively—on the honor of the second.[411]

What is emphasized in the word order of the Greek but obscured in most English translations of verse 3 is the word "every" (παντός), which is brought forward to the front of its clause to highlight that Christ is the head of every man.[412] The point is reiterated in the following two sentences, in which Paul insists that "every man who prays or prophesies with something on his head dishonors his head" (v. 4), and "every woman who prays or prophesies with her head uncovered dishonors her head" (v. 5a).[413] Paul's point is not merely that a "man who prays or prophesies with something on his head dishonors his head" and a "woman who prays or prophesies with her head uncovered dishonors her head" but

---

[411] Cf. A. C. Perriman, "The Head of a Woman: The Meaning of Κεφαλή in 1 Cor. 11:3," *JTS* 45 (1994): 621; Garland, *1 Corinthians*, 516; Thiselton, *First Corinthians*, 816–18; Brian Brock and Bernd Wannenwetsch, *The Therapy of the Christian Body*, vol. 2 of *A Theological Exposition of Paul's First Letter to the Corinthians* (Eugene: Cascade, 2018), 40. This meaning is entirely compatible with uses of the metaphor to designate one party as an authority over or a source of life and benefit for the other (both of which are aspects of the metaphor's meaning as it is used in Ephesians and Colossians), but neither of these appears to be the core sense that the word denotes here.

[412] The fact that Paul commences with a statement about the relationship between "every man" and Christ, before he introduces the relationship between "the woman" and "the man" in v. 3b, supports the decision made by the translators of most English versions (including the CSB) to translate ἀνήρ as "man" rather than "husband" and γυνή as "woman" rather than "wife," even though the particular relationship in view in v. 3b is almost certainly the relationship between a wife and a husband (cf. Eph 5:22–33, where the clear and explicit focus is on the relationship between wives and their own "husbands" [τοῖς ἰδίοις ἀνδράσιν]).

[413] For a discussion of what Paul had in mind by the verb προφητεύω ("prophesy") and the noun προφητεία ("prophecy"), see the comments on 12:10, below.

that this is the case for every man and every woman, not merely the freeborn men and women whose honor was displayed and safeguarded by the traditional head covering.

It is difficult to know whether the scenario depicted in verse 4 (i.e., a man praying or prophesying "with something on his head")[414] is one that has been occurring within the Corinthian congregation or merely a hypothetical situation created by Paul to make a point. The latter is probably more likely, given the relative lack of elaboration on the importance of men praying and prophesying with uncovered heads in the verses that follow and the much clearer emphasis on the issue of women's head coverings as the point at issue (cf. vv. 6, 10, 13). Paul does not spell out what exactly it is about a man praying or prophesying with a covered head that dishonors Christ. One possibility suggested by some commentators is that a man covering his head in this context could be taken as an imitation of the practice of elite Roman males who covered their heads in the context of pagan worship, dishonoring Christ by importing pagan customs into the Christian gathering.[415] If that were the case, however (as Ciampa and Rosner point out), it would be difficult to see why the same problem was not created by women covering their heads, since women as well as men covered their heads within the context of Roman cultic rituals. An explanation lying closer to hand is suggested by verses 14–15, where the differing cultural evaluations placed on long and short hairstyles worn by men and women are appealed to as a sign and outworking of what "nature itself" teaches regarding the distinction between the sexes. If the customary head coverings worn by women are understood as in some way analogous to the natural head covering of long hair, then a man praying with his head covered might be understood to be obscuring or erasing

[414] Paul's wording here (κατὰ κεφαλῆς ἔχων; literally, "having [something] extending down from the head") has been variously interpreted. Some commentators (e.g., Murphy-O'Connor, *Keys to First Corinthians*, 142–47) argue that it refers simply to hair worn long, but are not able to cite any examples of an expression like this used to convey that meaning. The most closely similar expressions that can be found elsewhere in the extant literary sources (e.g., LXX Esth 6:12; Plutarch, *Mor.* 200F) refer to a garment used as a head covering, and this sense of the word is probably the most likely here. Cf. Fee, *First Epistle to the Corinthians*, 558–59; Benjamin A. Edsall, "Greco-Roman Costume and Paul's Fraught Argument in 1 Corinthians 11.2–16," *JGRChJ* 9 (2013): 133–38.

[415] Cf. Garland, *1 Corinthians*, 517.

a traditional sign of distinction between the genders, dishonoring the intentions of the creator (and thereby dishonoring Christ).[416]

The scenario Paul envisages in verse 4 is matched by a complementary scenario in verses 5–6: "Every woman who prays or prophesies with her head uncovered dishonors her head, since that is one and the same as having her head shaved. For if a woman doesn't cover her head, she should have her hair cut off. But if it is disgraceful for a woman to have her hair cut off or her head shaved, let her head be covered." Paul gives no indication that he is concerned about the idea of a women praying or prophesying within the gathered assembly of the church; his concern lies in the fact that in the scenario he envisages she is praying or prophesying "with her head uncovered."[417] Here, as in verse 4, the "head" that Paul depicts as being dishonored is not only the literal head of the woman but her metaphorical head (i.e., her husband), whose honor was either enhanced or diminished by the way in which his wife acted in public and was regarded by others. For a woman to perform a public role of this sort without the customary head covering would be to attract shame to herself and her husband, equivalent (in Paul's view) to the shame conveyed by cutting off a woman's hair or shaving her head.[418] This is the case, Paul insists, for "every woman," not merely for the freeborn, married women whose honor (and whose husbands' honor) was signified and protected by the traditional Roman dress codes. If men and women, slave and free alike, were to participate alongside one another by praying and prophesying in the gathered assembly of the church, then Paul is insistent that they be allowed to do so in a manner that does not expose them to shame by

---

[416] Ciampa and Rosner, *The First Letter to the Corinthians*, 514.

[417] Here too, as in v. 4, there is debate over the precise meaning of the expression Paul uses to describe the hairstyle or (lack of) head covering that he has in mind. In this instance, the expression Paul uses is ἀκατακαλύπτῳ τῇ κεφαλῇ (CSB: "with her head uncovered"). The adjective ἀκατακάλυπτος is used in LXX Lev 13:45 to refer to the uncovered or unbound hair of a person with a skin disease, and the cognate verb ἀποκαλύπτω is used in LXX Num 5:18 to refer to the loosed hair of a woman who has been accused of marital infidelity, leading some to argue that this is the meaning Paul has in mind here. This meaning is, however, difficult to square with the alternative Paul prescribes in v. 6b (κατακαλυπτέσθω, "let her head be covered"; cf. v. 7; LXX Gen 38:15; Sus 32 [Theodotion]), suggesting that the more likely meaning of the phrase in v. 5 is "with her head uncovered." Cf. Fee, *First Epistle to the Corinthians*, 562.

[418] Cf. Ciampa and Rosner, *The First Letter to the Corinthians*, 520–22, citing Aristophanes, *Thesm.* 838; T. Job 24:10; Sib. Or. 3:356–62.

excluding all but the freeborn from the customary signifiers of sexual modesty and social propriety.[419]

11:7–12. In verses 7–12 Paul turns to Scripture (and, in particular, the creation narratives of Gen 1–2) as a source of explanation and support for the assertions that he has made in the previous paragraph.[420] He begins by evoking Genesis 1:27 as support for his original assertion that "Christ is the head of every man" (v. 3a) and the entailment he deduces from it, that "every man who prays or prophesies with something on his head dishonors his head" (v. 4): "A man should not cover his head, because he is the image and glory of God" (v. 7a; cf. Gen 1:27). By adding the phrase "and glory" to the language that he borrows from Genesis 1:27, he highlights the link that he wishes his readers to see between the creation story and the issues of honor and dishonor that he has early communicated through the metaphor of headship. Humanity was created in the beginning to bear the image of God and so to reflect his honor and glory in the world (cf. Ps 8:1, 5). For a man to cover his head in a manner that obscures the created distinction between male and female is to dishonor the intention of the creator and thereby to dishonor his head, Christ (cf. 8:6).

Just as the man bears God's image and so brings him glory, so the woman brings glory to the man.[421] Paul's point is not to deny that the woman, like the man, is created in God's image (the clear and explicit teaching of Genesis 1:27, presupposed by Paul as applying to men and women alike in 15:49), but to draw a parallel between the glory that a man brings to his creator and the honor that a woman brings to her husband (cf. LXX Prov 11:16; 4 Ezra 4:17). This asymmetry in the role relationship (expressed in v. 3 by the image of the man as the "head" of the woman) is explained by Paul in verses 8–9 as an outworking of the order in which

---

[419] It is possible that the elite members who were denying women of enslaved or slave-born status the right to cover their heads were also tacitly assuming the ineligibility of such women to participate in the prayers and prophesying that took place within the gathering. If that was the case, then Paul's insistence on the right of all women to cover their heads within the gathering of the church may also have served the function of alerting them to a consequence they might not have considered as an implication of restricting the right to wear the head covering.

[420] A relationship of this sort between v. 7 and the preceding verses is implied by the conjunction γάρ ("For ..."), left untranslated in the CSB.

[421] The function of Paul's μὲν ... δέ construction is not merely to draw a contrast between the man's role as "the image and glory of God" and the woman's as "the glory of man" but (as the CSB seeks to highlight by translating δέ as "so too") to suggest an analogy between the "glory" that one party gives to the other in both relationships.

the man and the woman were created in the narrative of Genesis 2: "For man did not come from woman, but woman came from man. Neither was man created for the sake of woman, but woman for the sake of man" (vv. 8–9). As the one created first and originally addressed with the words of command and commissioning in Genesis 2:15–17, the man is framed within the narrative of Genesis 2–3 as carrying a kind of representative role,[422] and the woman who is taken from his side and brought to him by YHWH is given to him as a "helper" to rectify the deficiencies of his aloneness and enable the fulfillment of the task with which he had been charged (Gen 2:18). In this sense, therefore, Paul can speak of the woman as having been created "for the sake of man"—not as his personal chattel, but as a helper and companion given to him by God—and insist on the maintenance of customs that reflect that distinction and the role of a wife as the "glory" of her husband (v. 7).

In verse 10 Paul states the conclusion toward which he has been arguing: "This is why a woman should have [authority over] her head, because of the angels." The CSB translation (like the NIV 1984) renders Paul's ἐξουσίαν ἔχειν ἐπὶ τῆς κεφαλῆς as "have a symbol of authority on her head," but this is a most unlikely meaning for the expression to carry. In all the previous instances in the letter in which Paul has spoken of a person "hav[ing] authority" (7:37; 9:4, 5, 6; cf. Rom 9:21; 2 Thess 3:9), the expression clearly refers to a right or authority that the person possesses, not to a symbol of someone else's authority that is placed on them. The expression ἐξουσία ... ἐπί, throughout the New Testament, consistently carries the sense of "authority over" (Luke 9:1; Rev 2:26; 6:8; 11:6; 13:7; 14:18; 22:14) or, in several instances referring to the earth as the sphere in which authority is exercised, "authority on" (Matt 9:6 and parallels; 28:18).

The main difficulty with giving the expression its grammatically obvious meaning is that Paul frames his statement as a conclusion drawn from the preceding verses (διὰ τοῦτο, "For this reason"),[423] which do

[422] This role played by Adam within the narrative is also reflected also in the sequence of the cross-examinations in Gen 3:9–13 and the way in which the final, climactic word of judgment on all of humanity is spoken to Adam, rather than to Eve his wife, in Gen 3:19b. Cf. the discussion in Gordon J. Wenham, *Genesis 1–15*, WBC (Dallas: Word, 1987), 50–51.

[423] It is possible that τοῦτο ("this") could be pointing forward to διὰ τοὺς ἀγγέλους ("because of the angels") in v. 10b rather than backward to the preceding verses, but even on this reading a logical or rhetorical relationship of some sort between v. 9 and v. 10 would still need to be inferred.

not appear in any immediately obvious way to offer an argument for a woman's authority over her own head. But this difficulty is not fatal, and an equivalent difficulty needs to be overcome by those who read v. 10 as referring to "a symbol of [her husband's] authority" and struggle to explain why Paul needs to offer the immediate balancing statement in v. 11 that "in the Lord ... woman is not independent of man." If ἐξουσίαν ἔχειν ἐπὶ τῆς κεφαλῆς in verse 10 is to be understood as "have authority over her head," the best explanation of the διὰ τοῦτο that commences the verse is probably that verses 8–9 are an explanatory parenthesis that Paul offers in support of the assertion in verse 7b that "woman is the glory of man." Because that is the case (and because it is a truth that Paul derives from the Genesis narrative and applies, in consequence, to every marriage and not merely to those of the respectable, freeborn elite), Paul draws the conclusion that he states in verse 10 as the bottom line of the argument: a woman ought to have the right to cover her head so as not to bring dishonor to herself and her husband (and this right should not be restricted to the narrow circle of those who already possessed it as a matter of Roman custom).

The final phrase in verse 10, διὰ τοὺς ἀγγέλους ("because of the angels"), has also occasioned a good deal of scholarly discussion. The theory that this phrase is referring to the (human) "messengers" from other congregations or outside observers who might visit the Corinthian assembly from time to time is unlikely, especially given the absence of any indication as to whose "messengers" they are.[424] A more likely explanation is the role that angels played in Jewish tradition as guardians of the created order and as participants in and observers of the worship of God's people (e.g., 1 Enoch 99:1–3; 2 Enoch 19; 1QSa 2:8–9; 1QM 7:4–7).[425]

In verse 11 Paul offers a balancing statement (commencing in Greek with the word πλὴν; literally, "Nevertheless") that guards against the risk that readers might draw the false conclusion that the "authority" to which he has referred in the previous verse implies a kind of autonomous disconnection of the woman from the man (or, for that matter, of the man from the woman): "In the Lord, however, woman is not independent

[424] For arguments in favor of a reading along these lines, see J. Winandy, "Un curieux *casus pendens*: 1 Corinthiens 11.10 et son interpretation," *NTS* 38 (1992): 621–29; Winter, *After Paul Left Corinth*, 133–38.

[425] Cf. the discussions in Garland, *1 Corinthians*, 526–29; Ciampa and Rosner, *The First Letter to the Corinthians*, 530–31; Thiselton, *First Corinthians*, 839–41.

of man, and man is not independent of woman."[426] The word order of the CSB translation, which brings the phrase "in the Lord" forward to the beginning of the verse, conveys the impression that Paul is drawing a contrast between the order of creation (which he has invoked in vv. 8–9) and the interdependence of men and women "in the Lord" as a new creation order that replaces or coexists with the order of the original creation. This is an unlikely reading of the logic of the paragraph, however, as the phrase ἐν κυρίῳ ("in the Lord") is in fact positioned at the end of verse 11, not the beginning, and the supporting statement Paul goes on to give in verse 12 ("For just as woman came from man, so man comes through woman, and all things come from God") is still grounded in the order of creation, within which "woman came from man" (cf. Gen 2:21, 23), "man comes through woman" (cf. Gen 3:20), and "all things come from God" (cf. Gen 1:1). Given the role played by Christ in the creation of all things (1 Cor 8:6), relationships "in the Lord" are not an undoing of the order given in creation but a redemption of that order from the oppressive distortions introduced by the fall.[427]

11:13–16. If verse 10 is the conclusion toward which Paul has been arguing and verses 11–12 are a clarification guarding against a possible misunderstanding of that conclusion, verses 13–16 are a kind of coda in which Paul acknowledges the possibility that not all of his audience may yet have been convinced by what he has to say and urges them to consider two more closely interconnected reasons for adopting the viewpoint that he has been advocating.

The first, in verses 13–15, is an appeal for them to reflect on the impropriety that would be created by placing restrictions on the right of women to cover their heads, given the cultural conventions of shame

---

[426] Cf. Westfall, *Paul and Gender*, 41: "However, he is quick to say that his pronouncement does not mean he is declaring that woman is independent from man, or vice versa (11:11). This last statement may indicate Paul's awareness that his support for 'women's rights' to cover their heads may override the conventional authority of some of the Corinthian men over their wives, sisters, daughters, or slaves, and he is making it clear that he is not empowering women to operate independently without consideration of their family or masters."

[427] Cf. Michael Lakey, *Image and Glory: 1 Corinthians 11:2–16 as a Case Study in Bible, Gender and Hermeneutics*, LNTS (London: T&T Clark, 2010), 115–16, and the broader discussions in David I. Starling, "Restoring All That Was Broken: Gender, Gospel, and the New Creation," in *The Gender Conversation: Evangelical Perspectives on Gender, Scripture, and the Christian Life*, ed. David I. Starling and Edwina Murphy (Eugene: Wipf & Stock, 2016), 377–85; Wright, *Paul and the Faithfulness of God*, 475–94.

and glory that Paul encourages his readers to view as manifestations of what "nature itself" teaches. Paul introduces this first argument with an invitation for the readers to "judge for [them]selves" (cf. 10:15) and, in keeping with that invitation, frames the question in terms of categories that would have been familiar to the Stoic-influenced elite with whom he is in dialogue.[428] If "nature itself" (through the manifest distinctions between male and female that can be seen in human bodies and their refraction in human customs and cultural values) teaches that "if a man has long hair it is a disgrace to him, but that if a woman has long hair, it is her glory" (vv. 14 –15),[429] then the Corinthian elite should be able to judge for themselves what the answer should be to the rhetorical question of verse 13. The long hair that functions for women as a kind of "covering" (περιβόλαιον) given by nature provides a pointer in the direction of the seemliness of women wearing the head covering provided by cultural convention when they stand up in the assembly to pray (v. 15b).[430]

The second reason Paul offers, in verse 16, is closely connected to the first.[431] If some among the Corinthians remain unconvinced by Paul's appeal to nature (and to the cultural conventions from which Paul derives the form and detail of his conclusions in vv. 14–15 about what "nature itself teach[es]"), Paul points them in verse 16 to the consensus of the Christian community, as it can be seen in the conventions observed uniformly by the apostles (ἡμεῖς, "we")[432] and "the churches of God" (αἱ

[428] Cf. Timothy Brookins, "'Natural Hair': A 'New Rhetorical' Assessment of 1 Cor 11:14–15," in *Paul and the Greco-Roman Philosophical Tradition*, ed. Andrew W. Pitts and Joseph R. Dodson, LNTS (London: T&T Clark, 2017), 173–95, citing Epictetus, *Diatr*. 1.16.9–14 for an example of a Stoic argument from nature regarding the visible distinctions between male and female. Stoic-flavored terminology within vv. 13–16 includes the reference in v. 13 to what is "proper" (πρέπον), the question in v. 14 about what "nature itself teach[es]" (ἡ φύσις αὐτὴ διδάσκει), and the appeal in v. 16 to (apostolic and Christian) "custom" (συνήθεια).

[429] Cf. Lakey, *Image and Glory*, 120.

[430] Cf. Oropeza, *1 Corinthians*, 149; Lakey, *Image and Glory*, 121.

[431] Contra Brookins, "Natural Hair," 179, who reads v. 16 as "a separate argument, added independently of those with which Paul precedes [it]."

[432] Paul's ἡμεῖς ("we") could possibly refer more narrowly to his own circle or even just to himself and Barnabas (cf. 9:6), but the particular kind of argument he is making here, as an appeal to the consensus of a large group ("we have no other custom, nor do the churches of God"), suggests that he has all of the apostles in mind, in line with the similar appeals and reminders in 4:8–17 and 15:1–11.

ἐκκλησίαι τοῦ θεοῦ): "If anyone wants to argue about this, we have no other custom, nor do the churches of God."[433]

Bridge

The task of applying Paul's instructions regarding gender and head coverings in 1 Corinthians 11:2–16 within a twenty-first century context is a case study in the complexities of the role played by cultural context in interpreting and responding to Scripture. When speaking of the "cultural context" of a biblical text, it is worth pausing at the outset to recognize that the notion of "culture" is a synthetic concept that we use to speak of a number of distinct but related realities, including (1) the language- and symbol-systems with which the members of a particular community make and understand meaning; (2) the practices that are customary within that community; (3) the social structures within which relationships in that community are ordered and the way in which power is distributed within those social structures; and (4) the values and beliefs that prevail within that context.

The fact that a biblical text is expressed within the language- and symbol-systems of a particular culture, or that it presupposes the practices and social structures of its time, does not necessarily mean that the values and beliefs of the biblical writer are simply absorbed uncritically from those of the dominant culture. Reading a text in relation to its cultural context requires us to ask what perspective the writer invites us to take toward that context and to draw a distinction between those aspects of the text in which a particular set of social arrangements is simply being assumed (without a judgment being made for or against them) and those aspects of a text in which a set of values of a way of ordering relationships is being taught as an expression or outworking of the writer's basic theological convictions (either with or against the grain of the culture).

In the case of the instructions Paul gives to the Corinthians regarding gender and head coverings in the gathered assembly it is necessary, on the one hand, to take into account the symbol-systems and social conventions that were operative within the context in which he expects

[433] The redundant ἡμεῖς ("we"), added for emphasis and placed at the beginning of the clause, suggests that the movement from vv. 14–15 to v. 16 is not, in Paul's mind, a movement from φύσις ("nature") to συνήθεια ("custom") but a movement from an argument based on what "nature" teaches, interpreted through the lens provided by the συνήθειαι of the gentile nations, to an argument based on the συνήθεια of the Christian community.

the Corinthians to interpret and apply his instructions. To simply replicate the detail of the practices he prescribes regarding head coverings and hair lengths (to the extent that we can ascertain what they were) without reference to the meanings Paul intended them to communicate and the social functions he intended them to perform would be, in most twenty-first century contexts, to communicate a message widely at variance with the message Paul intended the Corinthian men and women to communicate.

Nor are we at liberty, on the other hand, to dismiss these verses altogether and treat them as if their significance were confined to the original context in which they were written. To do so would fly in the face of the repeated appeals Paul makes to universally relevant authorities and sources of meaning, including the creation narratives to which he alludes in verses 7–12, the message of what "nature teaches" regarding sexual differentiation (vv. 13–15), and the theologically grounded assertions about the relations and responsibilities of headship that he asserts in verse 3 as the foundational premise of the whole discussion.

For most of us, the cultural context we inhabit is one in which the meanings that are communicated by hair lengths and head coverings (and the associated cultural evaluations of honor and disgrace) differ widely from the meanings and values that were prevalent within the shared context inhabited by Paul and the Corinthians. Our task is not to replicate the symbolic behaviors that were required within the Corinthians' context to communicate the meanings that Paul wished them to communicate, irrespective of the different message they would communicate in our context. But we do have the task of translating those same meanings into the symbolic language of our own context (just as we are to translate the words of Paul's letter into our own vernacular), and of finding a way of communicating in our words, deeds, customs, and symbols the same complex and multilayered set of realities that Paul wished the Corinthians to communicate in theirs: that men and women are interdependent and equal members of the family of God's people, with the differences inscribed in their bodies to be received as a good gift of God, the Creator, and reflected in appropriate distinctions of custom and dress; that husbands carry a particular responsibility of headship within a marriage that is to be understood and practiced as analogous to the headship that Christ exercises in his relation to them;[434] and that all members of God's people, regardless of wealth or social rank, should be treated with equal honor, working together with a shared concern for the way in which the conduct of the church reflects on the honor of the name of Christ.

B. Status-Based Divisions at the Lord's Supper (11:17–34)

> [17] Now in giving this instruction I do not praise you, since you come together not for the better but for the worse. [18] For to begin with, I hear that when you come together as a church there are divisions among you, and in part I believe it. [19] Indeed, it is necessary that there be factions among you, so that those who are approved may be recognized among you. [20] When you come together, then, it is not to eat the Lord's Supper. [21] For at the meal, each one eats his own supper. So one person is hungry while another gets drunk! [22] Don't you have homes in which to eat and drink? Or do you despise the church of God and humiliate those who have nothing? What should I say to you? Should I praise you? I do not praise you in this matter!
>
> [23] For I received from the Lord what I also passed on to you: On the night when he was betrayed, the Lord Jesus took bread, [24] and when he had given thanks, broke it, and said, "This is my body, which is for you. Do this in remembrance of me."
>
> [25] In the same way also he took the cup, after supper, and said, "This cup is the new covenant in my blood. Do this, as often as you drink it, in remembrance of me." [26] For as often as you eat this bread and drink the cup, you proclaim the Lord's death until he comes.
>
> [27] So, then, whoever eats the bread or drinks the cup of the Lord in an unworthy manner will be guilty of sin against the body and blood of the Lord. [28] Let a person examine himself; in this way let him eat the bread and drink from the cup. [29] For whoever eats and drinks without recognizing the body, eats and drinks judgment on himself. [30] This is why many are sick and ill among you, and many have fallen asleep. [31] If we were properly judging ourselves, we would not be judged, [32] but when we are judged by the Lord, we are disciplined, so that we may not be condemned with the world.
>
> [33] Therefore, my brothers and sisters, when you come together to eat, welcome one another. [34] If anyone is hungry, he should eat at home, so that when you gather together you will not come under judgment. I will give instructions about the other matters whenever I come.

---

[434] For a discussion of Paul's instructions in Eph 5:21–32 regarding the significance of the metaphor within that relationship, see Starling, *Reading Ephesians and Colossians*, 134–49.

Context/Structure/Form

In verses 17–34 Paul turns to give instructions regarding a second matter, responding to reports that he has received of "divisions" (σχίσματα) within the congregation when they gather as a church to celebrate the Lord's Supper (v. 18). The statement with which Paul commences the discussion ("Now in giving this instruction I do not praise you"; cf. v. 22b) is a clear reference back to verse 2 ("Now I praise you because you remember me in everything and hold fast to the traditions just as I delivered them to you"). It would be a mistake to read this as a suggestion that verses 3–16 should somehow be interpreted as praise rather than as correction or censure, but it does imply a connection of some sort in Paul's mind between the two matters addressed in this chapter, perhaps because they were both addressed (among "other matters"; cf. v. 34) in a section of the Corinthians' letter that commenced with a broad claim about the way in which they "remember" Paul in everything and "hold fast to the traditions" as he delivered them (v. 2). Certainly, the second half of the chapter includes an explicit reference to one of the traditions Paul "received" (παρέλαβον) from the Lord and "passed on" (παρέδωκα) to the Corinthians (v. 23), the meaning of which Paul reminds them of and applies as a corrective to their conduct of the community meal.

Paul's treatment of this issue falls into three parts: (1) an initial response to the reports of division, including a sharp rebuke to those who "despise the church of God and humiliate those who have nothing" (vv. 17–22); (2) a reminder of the traditions regarding the Last Supper that Paul passed on to the Corinthians (vv. 23–26); and (3) instructions and warnings regarding the conduct of the Lord's Supper, highlighting its gravity and significance in light of the Last Supper traditions that Paul has made reference to in the preceding paragraph (vv. 27–34) (see §8.2).

Comments

11:17–19. Paul commences the second half of the chapter with a sharply worded statement that "in giving this instruction" (Τοῦτο ... παραγγέλλων) he does not have any praise for them.[435] The "instruction" Paul is referring to is not given until verses 27–34 (more specifically, vv.

[435] Barrett, *First Corinthians*, 260, reads τοῦτο as referring backward to the matter on which Paul has instructed the Corinthians in vv. 2–16 (in line with the usual function of τοῦτο, e.g., in 7:6). Here, however, the repetition of "this" (ἐν τούτῳ, "in this matter") in v. 22—by now referring unambiguously to the matter of the Corinthians' Lord's Supper

28, 33–34), because before he is in a position to give it Paul feels compelled to elaborate on his initial assertion that the instruction is given with censure rather than with praise.

The problem Paul is addressing is one that he views with great seriousness—so much so that, in his view, their gatherings are "not for the better but for the worse" (v. 17b). The occasions Paul is referring to are gatherings of the believers ἐν ἐκκλησίᾳ ("as a church," v. 18), ἐπὶ τὸ αὐτὸ ("in the same place," v. 20 [untranslated in the CSB])—language that suggests a meeting in which all of the believers in the city (who may well also have met on other occasions in smaller groups in houses, tenement buildings, or other meeting places) joined with one another to share the Lord's Supper.[436] Paul has received reports ("For to begin with, I hear ... " v. 18)[437] that when they gather for this purpose there are "divisions" (σχίσματα) among them—language that echoes the terminology used in 1:10 in the context of Paul's response to the report that "one of you says, 'I belong to Paul,' or 'I belong to Apollos,' or 'I belong to Cephas,' or 'I belong to Christ'" (1:12) but turns out in this instance to be referring to divisions based on socioeconomic status rather than on attachment to different leaders.[438]

Paul's response in verses 18b–19 is ambiguous in its tone and meaning. It is possible that his statement that "in part" he believes the reports is an expression of charitable or judicious caution[439] and that the verse that follows expresses his sincere desire that "those who are approved [by

---

celebrations—makes it clear that τοῦτο is in this instance referring forward, to the new issue that Paul is now turning to address.

[436] Cf. Rom 16:23, where Paul (writing from Corinth) refers to Gaius as "host to me and to the whole church," and the reference in 1 Cor 14:23 to occasions in which "the whole church assembles together." For a discussion of the variety of possible locations in which smaller or larger groups of Christians may have assembled, see Adams, *Earliest Christian Meeting Places*, 198–202; M. Bruce Button and Fika J. Van Rensburg, "The 'House Churches' in Corinth," *Neot* 37, no. 1 (2003): 1–29; Bradly S. Billings, "From House Church to Tenement Church: Domestic Space and the Development of Early Urban Christianity—The Example of Ephesus," *JTS* 62 (2011): 541–69.

[437] The expression "to begin with" (πρῶτον) possibly alludes to the existence of the same "other matters" that Paul goes on to refer to in v. 34.

[438] It is possible, of course, that the two kinds of "divisions" could have been interrelated, e.g., if the adherents of one or more of the leaders referred to in 1:12 prided themselves on the superior erudition and sophistication of that leader's teaching as a badge of their own social superiority.

[439] E.g., Robertson and Plummer, *First Corinthians*, 239; Simon Kistemaker, *1 Corinthians*, NTC (Grand Rapids: Baker, 1993), 387.

God] may be recognized among you."[440] The fierceness of the rhetoric in the surrounding context suggests a more sarcastic tone, however,[441] and Richard Horsley's suggested paraphrase fits convincingly within that context: "For of course there must be 'discrimination' among you so that it will become clear who among you are 'the distinguished ones.'"[442]

11:20–22. The details of the scenario that has been reported to Paul become clearer in verses 20–22. Here, for the first time, we learn that the divisions he is referring to relate to the way in which the community meal of the gathered church is being celebrated and that they have the effect of making the meal "not … the Lord's Supper" (v. 20) but rather an occasion in which "each one eats his own supper" (v. 21). Here, too, we learn that the divisions involve one person being left "hungry" while another "gets drunk" (v. 21) and that Paul's outrage is directed toward those who "have homes in which to eat and drink" and yet behave at the Lord's Supper in a manner that "despise[s] the church of God and humiliate[s] those who have nothing" (v. 22).

The verb Paul uses in the context of his description of the meal as an occasion in which "each one eats [προλαμβάνει] his own supper" is read by some commentators in connection with the instruction to "welcome one another" (ἐκδέχεσθε; literally, "wait for one another") and taken as implying a scenario in which the wealthier members of the congregation were able to arrive first and eat the best of the food.[443] There are no surviving examples, however, of the compound verb προλαμβάνει being used in a manner that suggests that the prefix προ- carried this sort of temporal force,[444] and the verb ἐκδέχομαι, when used in relation to meals and other social occasions, appears to have carried the meaning of "welcome" rather than "wait,"[445] so it is difficult to be certain as to whether or not the staggered arrival times hypothesized under this scenario were a factor that contributed to the problem Paul is responding to.[446] Other com-

---

440 Robertson and Plummer, *First Corinthians*, 240

441 Cf. Hays, *First Corinthians*, 195; Ciampa and Rosner, *The First Letter to the Corinthians*, 544.

442 Richard A. Horsley, *1 Corinthians* (Nashville: Abingdon, 1998), 159.

443 E.g., Murphy-O'Connor, *St. Paul's Corinth*, 185.

444 There are two instances in Athenaeus, *Deipn.* 2,445c; 3.84, in which the verb is used to speak of one item of food or drink being consumed before another, but there are no surviving examples of the verb being used to speak of one person taking food before another person does.

445 Cf. Winter, *After Paul Left Corinth*, 151–52, citing 3 Macc 5:26 and P. Tebt. 33 as examples.

446 Cf. the discussion in Fee, *First Epistle to the Corinthians*, 598–601.

mentators point (instead or in addition) to the spatial arrangements of a typical large Roman home, in which a small number of high-status guests could be accommodated in the triclinium and a much larger number of lower-status guests would be fed in the outdoor atrium.[447] Whatever the precise combination of temporal and spatial factors may have been, the outcome was that the meal was subject to "divisions" between the eaters that had the effect of making it an occasion in which it was no longer the Lord's Supper but "each one['s] ... own supper,"[448] with some going hungry and others taking the opportunity to eat and drink to excess.

The focal point of the disapproval Paul expresses is not the immoderation of those who ate and drank excessively (though that would no doubt have been a behavior that he frowned on) but the humiliating distinction that was made between the privileged and the poor—as he makes clear in the first two of the four rhetorical questions he strings together in verse 22: "Don't you have homes in which to eat and drink? Or do you despise the church of God and humiliate those who have nothing?" The contrast Paul had in mind may well have been those who had "homes" and those who had "nothing," with the latter word plausibly supplied by the translators of the English versions as the implied object of Paul's τοὺς μὴ ἔχοντας ("those who do not have"). Another possibility—still referring to broadly the same group—may be that the word "homes," which Paul has already supplied as the object of ἔχετε ("have") in the first half of the verse, is the implied object of the same verb in the verse's second half and that Paul is referring to members of the ἐκκλησία who were not the owners of homes or secure in the patronage of the homes they were attached to as slaves or clients.[449] In either case, the conduct of the meal is such that it "humiliate[s]" this group and, by so doing, shows that the privileged members of the group "despise the church of God" (v. 22a).

The paragraph concludes in verse 22b with two more rhetorical questions and a final indignant exclamation: "What shall I say to you? Shall

[447] E.g., Murphy-O'Connor, *St. Paul's Corinth*, 178–85; Ciampa and Rosner, *The First Letter to the Corinthians*, 545. Cf. the methodological cautions expressed in David G. Horrell, "Domestic Space and Christian Meetings at Corinth: Imagining New Contexts and the Buildings East of the Theatre," *NTS* 50 (2004)

[448] For a discussion of the kind of "private banquet" to which Paul may be alluding here, see Winter, *After Paul Left Corinth*, 154–58; Theissen, *Social Setting*, 147–50.

[449] Cf. Brookins and Longenecker, *1 Corinthians 10–16*, 50; Garland, *1 Corinthians*, 543; Bruce W. Winter, "The Lord's Supper at Corinth: An Alternative Reconstruction," *RTR* 37 (1978): 81.

I praise you? Certainly not in this matter!" (NIV). The implied tone of dumbfoundedness with which Paul returns (yet again!) to the idea of "praise" for the Corinthians (cf. vv. 2, 17) suggests the possibility that he has discerned a note of self-congratulation or an expectation of approval from him in their claim that they have remembered him and maintained the traditions he handed on to them. In this matter, at least, there is no cause for praise at all.

11:23–26. In verses 23–26 Paul turns to remind the Corinthians of the account of the Last Supper that he had "received" (παρέλαβον) and "passed on" (παρέδωκα) to them—presumably as one of the "traditions" to which he has referred in verse 2. The close connections between these verses and the paragraphs that precede and follow them are indicated by the conjunctions "For" (γάρ) in verse 23 and "So then" (Ὥστε) in verse 27. The Corinthians may well have maintained a tradition of remembering the Last Supper and (perhaps) reciting a form of words narrating the events of Jesus's last meal with his disciples in connection with their own community meal,[450] but the significance of the former meal and its implications for the latter seem to have escaped them.

Paul therefore reminds them of the tradition that he handed on to them, apparently as an institution narrative that he gave to them in order to explain the origins and establish the significance of the meal they ate when they gathered.[451] Paul's claim that he received the tradition "from the Lord" is unlikely to mean that the story was told directly to Paul by the Lord Jesus on the occasion of their encounter on the road to Damascus, but it does stress the role of Jesus himself as the originator of the tradition that was subsequently handed on to Paul.

The wording that follows is similar but not identical to the words that are used by the evangelists in their accounts of the Last Supper. Distinctive features of Paul's version include the succinct introductory

---

[450] We do not know for certain whether there was a distinction within the Corinthian gathering between a "sacramental meal" of bread and wine and a "common meal" comprising the various other dishes that may have been eaten or (if there was such a distinction) what the relationship was between the two within the order of proceedings. For a discussion of the various possibilities see Garland, *1 Corinthians*, 546.

[451] A connection of this sort between the narrative of the Last Supper and the ritual of the Lord's Supper appears to be implied by the references to "this bread" and "the cup" in v. 26 and the subsequent references in vv. 27–28 to "eat[ing] the bread" and "drink[ing] the cup."

phrase ("on the night when he was betrayed"),[452] establishing a narrative context that is already in place within the synoptic passion narratives, and the explanatory postscript in verse 26 that draws an explicit connection between the Last Supper and its reenactment in the Corinthians' community meal ("For as often as you eat this bread and drink the cup, you proclaim the Lord's death until he comes").[453] Other elements of the narrative recounted in the Synoptic Gospels (e.g., the references to Jesus giving the bread and wine to the disciples) are omitted by Paul, presumably to focus in more closely on the words of Jesus that he quotes in verses 24b and 25b ("This is my body, which is for you. Do this in remembrance of me. ... This cup is the new covenant in my blood. Do this, as often as you drink it, in remembrance of me"). Here too, the accent falls heavily on the significance of the Corinthian meal as a remembrance of Jesus, with words similar to those in Luke 22:19 but absent from the accounts in Matthew and Mark retained and repeated, with the additional phrase "as often as you drink it" (ὁσάκις ἐὰν πίνητε) included in verse 25b in anticipation of the similar phrase in verse 26.[454] The descriptions of the bread as "my body, which is for you (ὑπὲρ ὑμῶν)" and the cup as "the new covenant in my blood" resemble most closely the language of Luke's account ("my body, which is given for you [ὑπὲρ ὑμῶν διδόμενον]" ... "the

[452] The word παρεδίδετο ("betrayed") that Paul uses here is also used within the passion narratives of the Gospels to refer to the events in which Jesus was "handed over" by the chief priests to Pilate (Mark 15:1) and by Pilate to the soldiers (Mark 15:15), but its repeated use to refer to the actions of Judas in close proximity to the Passover meal (Mark 14:10, 42, 44) and the likelihood (given the significance of the passion narrative as a core tradition the within the early Christian community) that Paul and the Corinthians would have known the story of Judas's betrayal suggest that this is probably the primary reference intended here. For an argument against this reading and in favor of a wordplay on παρεδίδετο ("handed over") and παρέδωκα ("passed on"), see Hays, *First Corinthians*, 198.

[453] The command in Luke 22:19 to "do this in remembrance of me" (depending on how it is interpreted) probably also suggests a connection of this sort.

[454] In speaking of wordings "retained" by Paul, I am not, of course, suggesting that he is working from an original version that is identical to one of the surviving accounts in the Synoptic Gospels (which were, at any rate, written later than 1 Corinthians). The wording that we have here in 1 Cor 11 is as close as we can get, barring speculative reconstructions, to the version of the Last Supper narrative that was handed on to Paul and originally delivered to the Corinthians. For discussions of the relationship between the wording here in 1 Cor 11 and the wordings preserved in the Synoptic Gospels and attempts to reconstruct the original traditions behind them, see especially Joachim Jeremias, *The Eucharistic Words of Jesus* (London: SCM, 1990); I. Howard Marshall, *Last Supper and Lord's Supper* (Exeter: Paternoster, 1980).

new covenant in my blood, which is poured out for you"; Luke 22:19–20)—language that, in both cases, includes explicit reference to the benefactive and salvific nature of Jesus's death and the new covenant that was inaugurated through it.[455]

The explanatory sentence in verse 26 that concludes the paragraph draws out the key point Paul wishes to highlight in reminding the Corinthians of the Last Supper tradition that stands behind their community meal: "For as often as you eat this bread and drink the cup, you proclaim the Lord's death until he comes." Given the context of the statement, embedded as it is within Paul's critique of what is communicated by the actions of the Corinthians in their conduct of the meal, it is unlikely that his point here in verse 26 is merely that the eating and drinking of the Lord's Supper ought to be accompanied by a verbal proclamation of the message about Christ's death: his emphasis, rather, is on the crucicentric symbolism of the meal itself,[456] which is being scandalously obscured by the elitist and self-serving actions of the privileged members of the Corinthian church.[457] By saying that the meal retains this function "until he comes," Paul is probably not complicating the discussion by taking a passing shot at the Corinthians' "over-realized eschatology"[458] or "soften[ing] ... the harsh idea of proclaiming the Lord's death"[459] but simply highlighting the enduring significance of the meal as a perpetual ordinance of God's people (cf. Exod 12:14, 24) (see §8.2).

11:27–32. Having reminded the Corinthians of the tradition and its significance, Paul now spells out the implications for their community

---

455 Cf. Paul's descriptions elsewhere of Jesus's death as having taken place ὑπὲρ ἡμῶν ("for us"; Rom 5:8; 8:32; 2 Cor 5:21; Gal 3:13; Eph 5:2; Titus 2:14), ὑπὲρ πάντων ("for all"; 2 Cor 5:14–15; 1 Tim 2:6), or ὑπὲρ τῶν ἁμαρτιῶν ἡμῶν ("for our sins"; 1 Cor 15:3; Gal 1:4), and the discussions in Thiselton, *First Corinthians*, 877–78, and Michael J. Gorman, *The Death of the Messiah and the Birth of the New Covenant: A (Not So) New Model of the Atonement* (Eugene: Cascade, 2014), 53–56.

456 Note the way in which Paul brings forward the phrase τὸν θάνατον τοῦ κυρίου ("the Lord's death"), placing it ahead of the verb καταγγέλλετε ("you proclaim") to highlight its significance as "the emphatic focus of the clause" (Brookins and Longenecker, *1 Corinthians 10–16*, 55).

457 Cf. Garland, *1 Corinthians*, 548–49; Michael J. Gorman, *Apostle of the Crucified Lord: A Theological Introduction to Paul and His Letters*, 2nd ed. (Grand Rapids: Eerdmans, 2017), 321–22.

458 Contra Collins, *First Corinthians*, 434; Witherington, *Conflict and Community*, 251.

459 Contra Troels Engberg-Pedersen, "Proclaiming the Lord's Death: 1 Corinthians 11:17–34 and the Forms of Paul's Theological Argument," in *1 and 2 Corinthians*, ed. David M. Hay, vol. 2 of *Pauline Theology* (Minneapolis: Fortress, 1993), 116; Garland, *1 Corinthians*, 550.

meal, commencing in verses 27–31 with an urgent call for self-examination on the part of those who have been eating and drinking unworthily. The instructions Paul gives in this paragraph and the one that follows are clearly connected closely with the abuses that he has described in verses 17–22 and that he is seeking to correct. To eat the bread or drink the cup "in an unworthy manner" (ἀναξίως) is not to bring to the table unconfessed and unforgiven sins from the week preceding the meal (though Paul would, no doubt, have been in favor of periodic self-reflection and confession of sin) but to participate in the meal itself in a manner that is "unworthy" of its significance as a proclamation of Christ's death.[460] Those who do so, Paul tells the Corinthians, are "guilty of sin against the body and blood of the Lord"—an assertion that he makes based on the words of institution that he has highlighted in the previous paragraph and the symbolic significance of the meal as a proclamation of Jesus's death.[461] The charge is a weighty one: by behaving in a manner that suggests their allegiance is not with the people of the Lord Jesus but with "the rulers of this age" who crucified him (2:8), the Corinthian elite are placing themselves in solidarity with those who are "guilty" (ἔνοχος) of his body and blood and liable to God's judgment.[462]

The call for self-examination Paul issues in verse 28 is, therefore, an urgent one. The verb δοκιμαζέτω ("Let [a person] examine ...") that Paul uses here is cognate with the adjective δόκιμοι that he used in an ironic sense in verse 19 to refer to the members of the congregation who were recognized as being "approved" members of a more socially elevated subgroup. If the reuse of that word here in verse 28 is a deliberate echo of its earlier use, Paul's point may be that the members of the Corinthian elite should shift their focus away from examining others to determine if they are worthy to join them at the best table for the meal and redirect it instead toward examining themselves, to see if their approach to the meal is in keeping with the message of the crucified Jesus. Those who fail to do so risk eating and drinking "without recognizing the body" (μὴ διακρίνων τὸ σῶμα, v. 29a), a phrase that almost certainly refers not to an attitude

---

[460] Cf. Fee, *First Epistle to the Corinthians*, 619–20.

[461] This is what is implied by the inferential conjunction Ὥστε ("So then ...") that introduces v. 27.

[462] The words "sin against" are added by the CSB translators as an interpretive paraphrase; the phrase "guilty of his body and blood" probably implies the stronger meaning of "liable for his death"; cf. Cf. Garland, *1 Corinthians*, 550; Fee, *First Epistle to the Corinthians*, 621.

that fails to distinguish the sacramental bread from the ordinary food of a common meal but rather to an attitude and a manner of conducting the meal that fails to acknowledge the double significance of the bread they eat as a symbol of Christ's body given in death (cf. 11:24, 27) and the "one body" of his people to whom they belong (cf. 10:16–17; 12:12–27).[463] The one who eats and drinks in this manner "eats and drinks judgment on himself" (v. 29b; cf. v. 27).

Paul's assertion in verse 29b is supported in verse 30 by his statement that "this is why many are sick and ill among you, and many have fallen asleep." It is difficult to say with certainty whether the sicknesses and deaths Paul is referring to are to be understood as judgments from God, possibly—though not necessarily—falling on those who have been guilty of the kind of conduct Paul describes in verses 17–22,[464] or natural consequences of the hunger and malnutrition experienced by the poorest members of the congregation due to the unwillingness of wealthier believers to share their resources with them (and/or the self-inflicted sickness suffered by the rich as a result of overconsumption).[465] The two alternatives are not necessarily mutually exclusive: in many cases, the narratives of divine judgment recorded in the Old Testament make reference to the natural causes through which they were occasioned, and the sufferings experienced by the community do not necessarily fall exclusively on the heads of those who committed the sins that are being punished. If a version of the second hypothesis is accepted and the sicknesses and deaths to which Paul is referring are taken as being in some way a natural consequence of the malnutrition of some and the overconsumption of others, the language of the surrounding verses (especially the reference in v. 32 to "when we are judged by the Lord"

---

463 Cf. Ciampa and Rosner, *The First Letter to the Corinthians*, 555–56; Fee, *First Epistle to the Corinthians*, 622–24. Evidence in the text that supports this understanding includes not only the description of the church in ch. 12 as the "body of Christ" (12:27), the connection in ch. 10 between that metaphor and the symbolic significance of the "one bread" (10:17), and Paul's censure in 11:22 of those who "despise the church of God and humiliate those who have nothing" but also the way in which Paul narrows his focus from "the bread and ... the cup" in vv. 27–28 and "the body and blood" in v. 27 to "the body" in v. 29.

464 Cf. Ciampa and Rosner, *The First Letter to the Corinthians*, 556; Gardner, *1 Corinthians*, 519–20.

465 Cf. Herm. Vis. 3.9.3–5a and the discussions in Garland, *1 Corinthians*, 553–54; Welborn, "Inequality in Roman Corinth," 66–67; David J. Downs, "Physical Weakness, Illness and Death in 1 Corinthians 11.30: Deprivation and Overconsumption in Pauline and Early Christianity," *NTS* 65 (2019): 572–88.

and "disciplined") suggests that Paul wants the Corinthians to understand these events not merely as evidences of the greedy behavior that merits God's judgment but as constituting in themselves the disciplinary judgments of God on the community.[466]

The concluding sentences of the paragraph, in verses 31–32, thus leave the Corinthians with three alternative scenarios: a best case scenario (only a hypothetical possibility at present, as signaled by the syntax of the second-class, counterfactual condition),[467] under which they would be "properly judging" themselves, as Paul has urged in verse 28, and would not need to come under God's judgment (v. 31); a second-best case scenario, under which they experience the present judgment of God as a merciful and corrective discipline on the community; and a worst case scenario (hopefully also one that turns out to be merely hypothetical),[468] under which they fail to respond to God's corrective discipline and end up "condemned with the world" (v. 32).

11:33–34. In the final two verses of the chapter Paul gives a second instruction regarding the way in which the Corinthians should approach the meal, once again framing it as an inferential conclusion from the preceding discussion.[469] When the Corinthians come together to eat they are to "welcome one another" (ἀλλήλους ἐκδέχεσθε). As discussed in the comments above on verse 21, there is insufficient evidence for us to draw a conclusion with any certainty about whether one of the exacerbating causes of the problem Paul is responding to was the ability of some congregation members to arrive at the meal before other, less wealthy

---

[466] In this respect, the function of Paul's appeal to the evidence of the sicknesses and deaths would differ from the function of the corresponding appeal in Herm. Vis. 3.9.3–5a, where the sicknesses and deaths are framed as evidences of sin that merits God's coming judgment, not as disciplinary judgments that God has permitted the church to experience in the present.

[467] Cf. Brookins and Longenecker, *1 Corinthians 10–16*, 58.

[468] The syntax of the ἵνα μή clause frames the event as the outcome that the disciplines visited upon the Corinthians are intended (by God) to avert.

[469] Fee reads the first Ὥστε ("So then ..."), in v. 27, as signaling a response in vv. 27–32 to the words of institution that Paul has reminded the Corinthians of in vv. 23–26 and the second, in v. 33, as signaling a response in vv. 33–34 to the abuse that he has described in vv. 17–22 (cf. Fee, *First Epistle to the Corinthians*, 588–89), but this distinction is a little too neat. The instruction in vv. 33–34 certainly recalls and reverses language Paul has used in the earlier description of the problem that he has given in vv. 17–22, but the purpose he states in v. 34 ("so that when you gather together you will not come under judgment") suggests that vv. 33–34 are also to be read as following inferentially from their immediately preceding context in vv. 27–32.

fellow believers. Furthermore, the verb ἐκδέχομαι, which Paul uses here, appears to have carried the meaning of "welcome" rather than "wait" when it was used in relation to meals and other social occasions.[470] If it was in fact the case that wealthier congregation members were arriving at the meal while others were still occupied with the labors of the day, then waiting for their brothers and sisters to arrive would almost certainly have been part of what was involved in welcoming them honorably, but it is unlikely to have been the entirety of what Paul had in mind. In addition to any waiting that may have been required, Paul's instructions would also have carried the sense that wealthier believers should welcome poorer and less well-connected brothers and sisters to the same table as the one at which they are eating and share with them the same food and drink as they are consuming. If they really are hungry, then they should eat at home rather than turning the Lord's Supper into an occasion for their own overconsumption (v. 34a).[471]

The chapter concludes in verse 34b with a brief, but opaque reference to a number of other unspecified issues on which he will "give instructions" (διατάξομαι) to the Corinthians when he comes and is able to speak with them face to face. He provides us with no details as to what these other issue were, but the definiteness with which he refers to them as "the other matters" (Τὰ ... λοιπά) suggests that he and the Corinthians shared a common awareness of a number of other outstanding matters (possibly though not necessarily relating to the community meal), perhaps because they had been addressed in the Corinthian letter.

Bridge

The primary application of Paul's instructions in these verses (and of the rebukes, warnings, and reminders that accompany them) is to the conduct of the regular gatherings of the local community of believers. Applied within that context, Paul's words to the Corinthians provide a perennial challenge to structures, traditions, and behaviors that create

---

470 Cf. Winter, *After Paul Left Corinth*, 151–52, citing 3 Macc 5:26 and P. Tebt. 33 as examples.

471 That Paul tells them they should avoid this problem, if necessary, by "eat[ing] at home" (ἐν οἴκῳ ἐσθιέτω) makes it clear, if there was any doubt, that he is speaking here to the privileged members of the congregation, not to the poorer members who may well have come to the meal in the grips of real hunger and would not have had the option of simply eating a meal at home before they came. Cf. Fee, *First Epistle to the Corinthians*, 629.

or perpetuate hierarchies of status within the congregation of believers, elevating some above others by formal or informal distinctions and segregations.

The passage also suggests additional lines of extended significance, based on the assumptions in which Paul grounds his response to the Corinthian situation or on extrapolations from what he says about the regular gathering of the local congregation to other spheres of application.

Remaining (in the first instance) within the context of the local church gathering, it is worth pondering whether the assumptions about the significance of the Lord's Supper on which Paul's instructions are based might raise questions about the conduct of that meal within many contemporary churches that are quite unrelated to the problematic issues in the Corinthian church that Paul was addressing in his letter to them. Paul's assumption, for example, that the community's ritual remembrance of the death of Jesus and his last meal with the disciples would take the form of (or be celebrated in conjunction with) a real, shared meal raises obvious questions about the thinly symbolic token meal that constitutes the Lord's Supper in most churches today. A meal of this sort may well function adequately as an occasion for reciting the words of institution and joining in thankful remembrance for the saving death of Christ, but it is difficult to avoid the conclusion that it lacks some of the additional layers of meaning that a genuine community meal can carry as "a foretaste of the future messianic banquet" and "a microcosm of the new-covenant life effected by cross."[472]

If we step beyond the regular gatherings of the local community of believers, it is possible to identify other points at which an extended application of what Paul writes within these verses can (and probably should) be made. Within the urban and suburban contexts in which many local congregations of believers gather in our own time, there is little evidence of the kind of socioeconomic diversity that appears to have been present in the Corinthian congregation; the social arrangements of late modernity have a tendency to segregate people into residential enclaves that are largely homogeneous in their makeup, and the churches that meet in those contexts typically reflect the homogeneity of their environment. In a context of this sort there is often little opportunity for the gathered community of believers to enact and demonstrate the kind

[472] Gorman, *Death of the Messiah*, 54.

of solidarity in diversity that Paul is calling on the Corinthians to display through their community meal. Reflection on that situation poses the question of whether more of us who possess the necessary social mobility (and do not have responsibilities that tether us tightly to the situation we are currently placed in) should consider relocating to a context in which resources are scarcer or believers less numerous, in order to further the work of the gospel and better demonstrate the dynamics of the coming kingdom of God. In addition, moving beyond the decisions of individuals to the structures and practices in which we engage collectively with one another, it poses the question of whether there might be other ways in which privileged communities of believers might be more generous in sharing their resources with other less privileged communities, so that there might be equal honor and equal provision not only within the congregation but between congregations and across the world.

VII. Response Regarding Matters of the Spirit (12:1–14:40)

In 12:1 Paul turns to a new topic (Περὶ δὲ τῶν πνευματικῶν, "Now concerning spiritual gifts ... ," or perhaps, as argued below, "Now concerning matters of the Spirit ...") that he deals with in chapters 12–14. The περὶ δέ formula (cf. 7:1, 25; 8:1, [4]; 16:1, 12) is probably an indication that Paul is responding to a question or assertion regarding the topic that was contained in the Corinthians' letter. While Paul commences the section in verse 1 by stating that "I do not want you to be unaware" (οὐ θέλω ὑμᾶς ἀγνοεῖν), it would be a mistake to read these chapters as if Paul were simply filling in the gaps in the Corinthians' knowledge in response to polite and respectful questions. Rather, as Fee correctly stresses, "Paul's answer is intended to be *corrective*, not instructional or informational. Thus, even if they presented themselves to Paul with a question (or questions), his response seems to take *exception* to their viewpoint, not simply to inform them in areas where they lack understanding."[473]

The polemical, corrective nature of chapters 12–14 becomes increasingly clear across the section and is most evident in chapter 14, where Paul turns to the specific issues in which he urges change in how the Corinthians behave when they gather. (Note especially the combative tone of Paul's conclusion in 14:36–40, but there are ample indications in

[473] Fee, *First Epistle to the Corinthians*, 632, emphasis original.

the rhetoric of the whole section that Paul's intention is more than just informative.)

Like a number of earlier sections of the letter,[474] chapters 12–14 are structured concentrically, with an initial (and primarily descriptive) response to the question about matters of the Spirit in chapter 12, a central section regarding the priority and indispensability of love in chapter 13, and a more explicitly corrective and instructive treatment of the practical and behavioral aspects of the topic in chapter 14 (with a particular focus on the gifts of tongues and prophecy).

A. The Spirit, the Gifts, and the Body of Christ (12:1–31)

[1] Now concerning spiritual gifts: brothers and sisters, I do not want you
to be unaware. [2] You know that when you were pagans, you used to be
enticed and led astray by mute idols. [3] Therefore I want you to know
that no one speaking by the Spirit of God says, "Jesus is cursed," and
no one can say, "Jesus is Lord," except by the Holy Spirit.

[4] Now there are different gifts, but the same Spirit. [5] There are different ministries, but the same Lord. [6] And there are different activities,
but the same God works all of them in each person. [7] A manifestation
of the Spirit is given to each person for the common good: [8] to one is
given a message of wisdom through the Spirit, to another, a message of
knowledge by the same Spirit, [9] to another, faith by the same Spirit, to
another, gifts of healing by the one Spirit, [10] to another, the performing
of miracles, to another, prophecy, to another, distinguishing between
spirits, to another, different kinds of tongues, to another, interpretation
of tongues. [11] One and the same Spirit is active in all these, distributing
to each person as he wills.

[12] For just as the body is one and has many parts, and all the parts of that
body, though many, are one body—so also is Christ. [13] For we were all
baptized by one Spirit into one body—whether Jews or Greeks, whether

---

[474] Fee (Fee, *First Epistle to the Corinthians*, 16) identifies the following three A/B/A structures in earlier chapters of the letter. Example 1: A. 1:10–2:5 / B. 2:6–16 / A. 3:1–23; Example 2: A. 7:25–28 / B. 7:29–35 / A. 7:36–40; Example 3: A. 8:1–13 / B. 9:1–27 / A. 10:1–22. In all three instances there is room for debate about the precise boundaries of the subsections in the A/B/A structure. In relation to example 1, Fee himself proposes a slightly different analysis later in the commentary (Fee, *First Epistle to the Corinthians*, 51), suggesting a break-up of A. 1:10–2:5 / B. 2:6–3:4 / A. 3:5–23, and in my own analysis, above, I have suggested yet another break-up of A. 1:10–17 / B. 1:18–2:16 / A. 3:1–4:21. In relation to example 2, I would suggest that the more obvious concentric structure discernible in ch. 7 is A. 7:1–16 / B. 7:17–24 / A. 7:25–40, and in relation to example 3, I would tentatively incline toward the slightly different break-up of A. 8:1–13 / B. 9:1–10:13 / A. 10:14–11:1.

slaves or free—and we were all given one Spirit to drink. [14] Indeed, the body is not one part but many. [15] If the foot should say, "Because I'm not a hand, I don't belong to the body," it is not for that reason any less a part of the body. [16] And if the ear should say, "Because I'm not an eye, I don't belong to the body," it is not for that reason any less a part of the body. [17] If the whole body were an eye, where would the hearing be? If the whole body were an ear, where would the sense of smell be? [18] But as it is, God has arranged each one of the parts in the body just as he wanted. [19] And if they were all the same part, where would the body be? [20] As it is, there are many parts, but one body. [21] The eye cannot say to the hand, "I don't need you!" Or again, the head can't say to the feet, "I don't need you!" [22] On the contrary, those parts of the body that are weaker are indispensable. [23] And those parts of the body that we consider less honorable, we clothe these with greater honor, and our unrespectable parts are treated with greater respect, [24] which our respectable parts do not need.

Instead, God has put the body together, giving greater honor to the less honorable, [25] so that there would be no division in the body, but that the members would have the same concern for each other. [26] So if one member suffers, all the members suffer with it; if one member is honored, all the members rejoice with it.

[27] Now you are the body of Christ, and individual members of it. [28] And God has appointed these in the church: first apostles, second prophets, third teachers, next miracles, then gifts of healing, helping, leading, various kinds of tongues. [29] Are all apostles? Are all prophets? Are all teachers? Do all do miracles? [30] Do all have gifts of healing? Do all speak in tongues? Do all interpret? [31] But desire the greater gifts. And I will show you an even better way.

Context/Structure/Form

The opening paragraphs of chapter 12 point us to the central theme of chapters 12–14: the correct view of "matters of the Spirit" (including both spiritual gifts and spiritual people) (see §3). The tendency of some in Corinth seems to have been to view the possession of spectacular miraculous gifts (particularly tongues) as the essence of spirituality and to speak of the elite who possessed them as the πνευματικοί ("spiritual people"). In response, Paul emphasizes that the criterion that marks the presence of the Spirit is not miraculous phenomena or inspired speech but confession of Jesus as Lord (12:1–3), and that behind all the different ministries within the body of Christ is the work of the one Spirit (12:4–11).

In verse 12 Paul introduces the metaphor of the body of Christ (cf. its earlier use in 5:15 [implied]; 10:16–17; 11:29 [probably]), into which believers have been baptized by the Spirit—a metaphor that remains in explicit focus for the remainder of the chapter as the primary frame for the discussion of the issues of diversity, unity, solidarity, and honor that Paul discusses. In doing so, he borrows an image that was a standard feature of Greco-Roman political discourse, but the way in which he develops the metaphor across the remaining paragraphs of chapter 12 includes elements that are sharply at variance with the value connotations that it usually carried when used in Greco-Roman political contexts.

The chapter concludes with another list of the multiple and richly varied gifts with which God has blessed the church, an encouragement to the readers to desire the "greater" gifts, and an announcement that Paul will show the Corinthians (in the immediately following chapter) "an even better way."

Comments

12:1–3. The περὶ δέ formula with which verse 1 commences introduces a new topic and probably signals that Paul is taking up a matter that was raised in the Corinthians' letter (cf. 7:1, 25; 8:1, [4]; 16:1, 12), though on this occasion (unlike 7:1 and 8:1) he does not appear to include a Corinthian slogan or a quotation from the letter at the start of his response. Paul addresses his response to the Corinthians as ἀδελφοί ("brothers and sisters"), which is his preferred term of address within this letter (cf. 1:10, 11, 26; 2:1; 3:1; 4:6; 7:29; 10:1), implying his solidarity with and affection for them as children of the same Father.

The phrase τῶν πνευματικῶν could be referring either to "spiritual people" (if the genitive plural is read as a generic masculine; cf. 2:13, 15; 3:1; 14:37) or to "spiritual things/gifts" (if it is read as neuter; cf. 2:13; 9:11; 10:3–4; 14:1). It is difficult to decide between the two options. Given the close connection that seems to have existed in the Corinthians' thinking between "spiritual gifts" and "spiritual people," it is probably reasonable to treat the gender of the word as neuter and translate it as "spiritual things" but to take it as functioning not in a narrow or technical sense to refer exclusively to "spiritual gifts" but as embracing within its meaning both "spiritual gifts/manifestations" and "spiritual people."[475] This interpretation of the phrase fits well with the way Paul commences his

[475] Cf. Thiselton, *First Corinthians*, 910–11; Fee, *First Epistle to the Corinthians*, 638; Barrett, *First Corinthians*, 278.

discussion of the topic in the remainder of verses 1–3, where the next two references to the Spirit (both in v. 3) are expressed in terms of people who claim to be "speaking by the Spirit of God" (ἐν πνεύματι θεοῦ λαλῶν) or "[speaking] by the Holy Spirit" ([εἰπεῖν] ... ἐν πνεύματι ἁγίῳ)—language that implies the ideas of both (putatively) "spiritual people" and the exercise of (what is asserted by the speaker to be) a "spiritual gift."

As argued above, Paul's statement in verse 1 that he "do[es] not want [the Corinthians] to be unaware" (οὐ θέλω ὑμᾶς ἀγνοεῖν) should not be read as implying that Paul is merely filling in gaps in the Corinthians' knowledge. Given the pride taken by the Corinthian elite in their "knowledge" (cf. 8:1) and their claim to be "spiritual people" (3:1; 14:37), it is likely that there is a note of deliberate irony in Paul's choice of words: Witherington goes as far as to suggest that it would have functioned "like a slap in the face" for these members of Paul's audience.[476]

In verse 2 Paul commences the task of remedying the deficiencies that he sees in the Corinthians' understanding of the issue, reminding them of experiences they had before their conversion as participants in pagan religious practices (using the word ἔθνη to refer not to their gentile ethnic identity but to their past, pagan existence).[477]

The syntax of the last half of the verse (πρὸς τὰ εἴδωλα τὰ ἄφωνα ὡς ἂν ἤγεσθε ἀπαγόμενοι) is difficult to unravel, given the absence of a finite verb in the principal clause. The simplest and most likely solution, given the frequency with which copulative verbs such as εἰμί were elided in Ancient Greek, is for the reader to supply the ellipsis by assuming an additional ἦτε between ἤγεσθε and ἀπαγόμενοι. On this reading, ὡς ἂν ἤγεσθε can be understood as a subordinate clause ("when you were being led"), and [ἦτε] ἀπαγόμενοι as a periphrastic imperfect ("you were being led astray"). Thus, the sentence would read: "You know that when you were pagans, when you were being led, you were being led astray to dumb idols."[478]

---

476 Witherington, *Conflict and Community*, 256. On the rhetorical function of Paul's Οὐ θέλω ὑμᾶς ἀγνοεῖν construction, here and elsewhere in his letters (esp. Rom 1:13; 11:25; 1 Cor 10:1; 2 Cor 1:8), see Starling, "We Do Not Want You To Be Unaware," 9–11.

477 Cf. the earlier reference in 10:32 to "Jews," "Greeks," and "the church of God."

478 An alternative option, originally suggested by Westcott and Hort, is to assume that ὅτε ("when") was originally πότε ("once"), so that the sentence would read: "You know that at one time you were pagans, being led astray to dumb idols, when you were being led." This alternative is less likely because (1) it involves a conjectural emendation of the text rather than simply requiring the reader to supply the verb ἦτε to fill the ellipsis, and

Some commentators suggest that the experience of being "led astray by mute idols" refers to the Corinthians' previous experiences of participation in pagan cultic processions (in which they were literally "led ... to" idols), viewed in retrospect as a kind of enslavement.[479] More likely, and more obviously relevant to Paul's argument, is the traditional interpretation, in which Paul is reminding the Corinthians that the experience of being (metaphorically) "led" and acted on by spiritual powers is not a uniquely Christian one; it was something they experienced before their conversion, under the influence of mute idols.[480] Forbes's cautions about the use of evidence from Greco-Roman sources culturally remote from first-century Corinth need to be taken seriously,[481] and there is room for argument about whether or not the speech Paul is referring to was "ecstatic"—in chapter 14 Paul certainly views Christian prophecy as an experience in which prophets were capable of exercising control over their speech—but it still seems to make the best sense of Paul's argument to understand him as referring to some sort of inspired speech (note the irony implied in "dumb idols" and the focus on the content of spoken words in v. 3).

Verse 3 draws out the implications of what Paul has said in the previous verse for how the Corinthians should regard and evaluate claims about inspired speech within their own community.[482] Because of the fact (as Paul has reminded the Corinthians in v. 2) that spiritual phenomena and inspired speech can be just as much a phenomenon of paganism as an experience of the Spirit of Christ, a test of allegiance and content must be applied as the basic criterion for evaluating such claims: "Therefore I want you to know that no one speaking by the Spirit of God says, 'Jesus is cursed,' and no one can say, 'Jesus is Lord,' except by the Holy Spirit." While some commentators have tried to construct scenarios under

---

(2) Paul's main purpose in v. 2 appears to have been not merely to remind the Corinthians of the *fact* that they used to be pagans but to draw their attention to the *nature and significance* of the spiritual experiences they used to have when they were. For discussion and evaluation of the various options, see Brookins and Longenecker, *1 Corinthians 10–16*, 63; Fee, *First Epistle to the Corinthians*, 639.

[479] E.g., Garland, *1 Corinthians*, 565–67, citing Terence Paige, "1 Corinthians 2:2: A Pagan *Pompē*?," *JSNT* 44 (1991): 57–65, and Wayne A. Grudem, *The Gift of Prophecy in 1 Corinthians* (Washington: University Press of America, 1982), 162–63.

[480] Cf. Fee, *First Epistle to the Corinthians*, 640.

[481] See especially Christopher Forbes, *Prophecy and Inspired Speech in Early Christianity and Its Hellenistic Environment* (Peabody: Hendrickson, 1997), 20–43, 44–74, 103–81.

[482] A logical relationship of this sort between v. 2 and v. 3 is signaled by the inferential conjunction Διό ("Therefore ...").

which a person within the Corinthian congregation may have actually said "Jesus be cursed" (e.g., in ecstatic speech or under the influence of a gnostic teaching that worshiped the exalted, heavenly Christ but repudiated the physical, human Jesus),[483] the scenarios suggested are far from convincing. Nor is it necessary to suggest that the language of Ἀνάθεμα Ἰησοῦς is drawn from the synagogue or from Paul's pre-Christian past. The simplest explanation is that it is a hypothetical literary device constructed by Paul as a contrast to the Christian confession, Κύριος Ἰησοῦς.[484] Paul's point can hardly be to give the Corinthians a fail-safe technique to use in judging prophecies. Rather, he is making the much more general point that supernatural phenomena and inspired speech in themselves are not the criterion of the work of the Spirit; instead, the work of the Spirit is seen where Jesus is exalted as Lord (and this is the case in the life of every Christian, not only those who have the more spectacular gifts).[485]

12:4–6. In verses 4–11 Paul turns explicitly to the subject of gifts given by the Spirit. The paragraph is structured concentrically, with the list of gifts in verses 8–10 preceded by the general principles of verses 4–7, which are repeated in summary form in verse 11.

The most obvious structural feature of verses 4–6 is the threefold contrast between "different" (διαιρέσεις; more literally, "different apportionments [of] ...") gifts/ministries/activities and "the same" (τὸ ... αὐτό / ὁ αὐτός) Spirit/Lord/God, emphatically making the point that within the church all the different kinds of ministry (not just the few that the Corinthian elite have focused on) are the work of the one God. Garland's attempt to read the three terms for gifts (χαρίσματα, διακονίαι, and ἐνεργήματα) as referring to three different "categories" of gifts is unconvincing;[486] in the absence of any obvious criteria for assigning the various gifts Paul goes on to list into one or other of these categories (or any reason why Paul would have chosen to do so), the more likely way of reading these verses is to understand the three terms as different ways of describing the same gifts. The variation is not merely stylistic, however. In starting with χαρίσματα, Paul may well be deliberately substituting his

[483] E.g., Barrett, *First Corinthians*, 279–80; James D. G. Dunn, *Jesus and the Spirit: A Study of the Religious and Charismatic Experience of Jesus and the First Christians as Reflected in the New Testament* (London: SCM, 1975), 234–35.

[484] Cf. Thiselton, *First Corinthians*, 920–21; Hays, *First Corinthians*, 209.

[485] Cf. Gardner, *1 Corinthians*, 529–31.

[486] Cf. Garland, *1 Corinthians*, 576.

own preferred word (which implies a focus on the origin of the gifts in the grace of God; cf. 1:4–7) for the Corinthians' preferred word πνευματικά (which implies a focus on the presence and power of the Spirit in those who possess them). The remaining two words have the effect of broadening the scope of what counts as "spiritual gifts" (διακονία, for example, is broad enough to include contributing financially to the needs of fellow believers; cf. 2 Cor 8:4; 9:1, 12, 13) and complementing the emphasis on the gifts that a person possesses with an emphasis on the service/activity that a person performs (though of course, as Paul goes on to emphasize, it is ultimately God who works "all of them in each person").

The Spirit/Lord/God variation is strikingly proto-Trinitarian (without making any explicit claim about the ontological unity of the three persons). The variation has the effect here of reminding the Corinthians that the activities they are accustomed to viewing as manifestations of the Spirit need also to be understood as ways of serving the Lord Jesus (and serving others in his name) and as work that participates in and is empowered by the work of God.

12:7. Verse 7 completes the initial statement of overarching general principles that precedes the list of gifts Paul goes on to give in verses 8–10. Despite Fee's arguments to the contrary, the most natural way of reading ἑκάστῳ is to infer that "every last person" within the community is in view. Against the elitism of the self-styled "spiritual" members of the Corinthian church (cf. 14:37) and reinforcing the implications of the ἐν πᾶσιν ("in each person") in the previous verse, Paul emphasizes that *all* the members of Christ's body are people through whom and in whom the Spirit's presence is manifested. Nevertheless (in broad agreement with the gist of Fee's point), it is important to note the articular form of Paul's expression, ἡ φανέρωσις, which probably counts against the idea that Paul thinks each person necessarily possesses "a" manifestation of the Spirit (i.e., a specific, singular, and clearly identifiable gift that can be listed in a catalog and identified through a survey). The final phrase of the verse, πρὸς τὸ συμφέρον ("for the common good"), continues Paul's project of reframing the Corinthians' view of gifts by reminding them that the manifestation of the Spirit given to each individual is not for elevating one above another but for the good of all, anticipating the emphasis on love and edification in chapters 13–14.

12:8–10. Having established in verses 4–7 the general principles that function as the frame through which Paul wishes the Corinthians to view the gifts of the Spirit, Paul goes on in verses 8–10 to provide a list of examples. The main function of the list is to illustrate the point made in verses 4–7 about the diverse manifestations of the Spirit given to the members of the community. When this list of gifts is compared with other gift-lists, later in this chapter and elsewhere in Paul's letters (cf. vv. 28, 29–30; Rom 12:4–8; Eph 4:11), it becomes evident that this is hardly intended to be an exhaustive catalog of spiritual gifts; rather, as Fee stresses, it is an ad hoc list of examples, reflecting the Corinthian situation and the particular gifts that would have been familiar to Paul's readers in Corinth.[487]

The stylistic variation between ἄλλῳ and ἑτέρῳ may also serve to structure the list by breaking it into three groups: Group A, a pair of word gifts imparting wisdom and knowledge; Group B, a diverse collection of assorted gifts; and Group C, a pair of gifts related to speaking in tongues.[488]

> A: ᾧ μὲν γὰρ διὰ τοῦ πνεύματος δίδοται λόγος σοφίας, **ἄλλῳ** δὲ λόγος γνώσεως κατὰ τὸ αὐτὸ πνεῦμα, ["to one is given a message of wisdom through the Spirit, to another, a message of knowledge by the same Spirit"].

> B: **ἑτέρῳ** πίστις ἐν τῷ αὐτῷ πνεύματι, **ἄλλῳ** δὲ χαρίσματα ἰαμάτων ἐν τῷ ἑνὶ πνεύματι, ἄλλῳ δὲ ἐνεργήματα δυνάμεων, **ἄλλῳ** [δὲ] προφητεία, **ἄλλῳ** [δὲ] διακρίσεις πνευμάτων, ["to another, faith by the same Spirit, to another, gifts of healing by the one Spirit, to another, the performing of miracles, to another, prophecy, to another, distinguishing between spirits"].

> C: **ἑτέρῳ** γένη γλωσσῶν, ἄλλῳ δὲ ἑρμηνεία γλωσσῶν· ["to another, different kinds of tongues, to another, interpretation of tongues"].

The order in which the three groups are arranged is probably deliberate: in the first place, anticipating Paul's emphasis in chapter 14 on gifts that edify others by imparting intelligible wisdom and knowledge, are "a message of wisdom" and "a message of knowledge"; in the last place (as is the case in all three lists of gifts within this chapter) are the tongues-related gifts that the Corinthians seem to have been particularly fixated on; and in the middle is the largest and most diverse group, reinforcing Paul's

[487] Cf. Fee, *First Epistle to the Corinthians*, 649.

[488] Cf. Robertson and Plummer, *First Corinthians*, 265.

point about the great variety of ways in which the Spirit's presence is manifested in his people.

The gifts Paul describes as "a message of wisdom" (λόγος σοφίας, v. 8a) and "a message of knowledge" (λόγος γνώσεως, v. 8b) are probably best understood in the light of what Paul says about σοφία and γνῶσις elsewhere in this letter: λόγος σοφίας is the ability to speak to others in a way that imparts the true wisdom of the mind of Christ, which is made known by the Spirit and centered on the message of the cross (cf. 2:6–16), and λόγος γνώσεως is the ability to convey to others the knowledge of the truth (e.g., 1 Cor 8:4, the truth about idols and the oneness of God) in a manner that informs and is informed by love and functions to shape Christian character and conduct.[489]

"Faith" (πίστις, v. 9a) cannot here refer to saving faith, since it is described here as being given to some and not others. Presumably what Paul has in mind here (and also in 13:2) is "not the saving faith which is basic to all Christian life, but a special endowment of faith for a special service."[490] "Gifts of healing" (χαρίσματα ἰαμάτων, v. 9b; more literally, "gifts of healings") is expressed in the plural, perhaps suggesting "not a permanent 'gift,' as it were, but that each occurrence is a gift in its own right."[491] "The performing of miracles" (ἐνεργήματα δυνάμεων, v. 10a), similarly plural, probably includes all sorts of miracles (a broader category than "healings").

"Prophecy" (προφητεία, v. 10b and throughout chs. 12–14) is a much-disputed term. There is general agreement among the majority of interpreters on a number of points, including (1) its intelligible verbal content (cf. 14:2–3); (2) its origin in the work of the Spirit (cf. 12:11); (3) its fundamentally different character from the uncontrollable,

---

[489] Cf. the interpretation of this gift argued for by Robert Banks, who proposes that λόγος γνώσεως refers to the gift of "understanding and exposition of the OT and Christian traditions." Banks, *Paul's Idea of Community*, 80.

[490] F. F. Bruce, *1 and 2 Corinthians*, NCBC (London: Oliphants, 1971), 119.

[491] Fee, *First Epistle to the Corinthians*, 659. Similarly Garland, *1 Corinthians*, 582, who lists examples of occasions in which Paul is involved in a wide variety of ways in the miraculous healing of others and other occasions (e.g., Phil 2:27; 2 Tim 4:20) in which there is no suggestion of any healing sought or effected and quotes a warning from Don Carson against the institutionalizing of the gift: "If a Christian has been granted the χάρισμα (*charisma*) to heal one particular individual of one particular disease at one particular time, that Christian should not presume to think that *the* gift of healing has been bestowed on him or her, prompting the founding of 'a healing ministry.'" D. A. Carson, *Showing the Spirit: A Theological Exposition of 1 Corinthians 12–14* (Carlisle: Paternoster, 1995), 39.

ecstatic speech that characterized some (though by no means all) pagan προφητεία (cf. 14:31–33); (4) its function in edifying and encouraging God's people (14:3); its distinction from the gift of teaching, but with sufficient overlap that those who prophesy can be said to "teach" (κατηχέω, 14:19) others and those who receive the prophecies of others can be said to "learn" (μανθάνω, 14:31) from them.

Within that broad consensus, commentators vary in some important matters of detail and emphasis. David Hill (among others) emphasizes the elements of "admonition and comfort" involved in prophecy and speaks of New Testament prophecy as "pastoral preaching."[492] Dunn and Fee emphasize spontaneity as an essential dimension of New Testament prophecy, both emphatically asserting (in identical words) that it is "*not* the delivery of a previously prepared sermon."[493] Grudem emphasizes the requirement in 1 Corinthians 14:29 and 1 Thessalonians 5:21–22 that believers "evaluate" (διακρίνω) or "test" (δοκιμάζω) prophecies and the implication that they are therefore to be regarded as fallible and of lesser authority than the canonical Scriptures.[494]

One reason for the variety of interpretations may be the tendency of modern readers to read their own various practices back into the text; another is the way in which Paul appears to have used the word προφητεία as an umbrella term for a variety of different Spirit-inspired word ministries.[495] Within the wide variety of intelligible word ministries Paul includes within the scope of the term, some appear to have been more spontaneous in nature (e.g., 14:30) and others less so (e.g., 14:26); some, too, appear to have been primarily revelatory in their content, conveying new and divinely disclosed information about the present or the future (e.g., 14:25, 30), while others appear to have been primarily or exclusively hortatory or didactic (e.g., 14:19, 31). Thiselton, accordingly, opts for a broad definition:

> **Prophecy**, as a gift of the Holy Spirit, combines pastoral insight into the needs of persons, communities and situations with the

---

[492] David Hill, *New Testament Prophecy* (London: Marshall, Morgan & Scott, 1979), 131. Cf. Thomas W. Gillespie, *The First Theologians: A Study in Early Christian Prophecy* (Grand Rapids: Eerdmans, 1994), 141.

[493] Dunn, *Jesus and the Spirit*, 228; Fee, *First Epistle to the Corinthians*, 660 (emphasis Fee's).

[494] Grudem, *The Gift of Prophecy in 1 Corinthians*, 110–11.

[495] Cf. Hays, *First Corinthians*, 237; similarly Ciampa and Rosner, *The First Letter to the Corinthians*, 515, 679.

> ability to address these with a God-given utterance or longer discourse (whether unprompted or prepared with judgement, decision, and rational reflection) leading to challenge or comfort, judgment or consolation, but ultimately building up the addressees.[496]

The gift of "distinguishing between spirits" (διακρίσεις πνευμάτων, v. 10c) is probably referring to the gift that assists the community with the responsibility to "evaluate" (διακρίνειν) prophecies that Paul speaks of in 14:29. Its close connection with προφητεία ("prophecy") in this list parallels the close connection between γένη γλωσσῶν ("different kinds of tongues") and ἑρμηνεία γλωσσῶν ("interpretation of tongues") in the following line. In describing the weighing of prophecies as a matter of "distinguishing between spirits," Paul is probably referring to the task of determining whether a prophecy is an expression of the cross-centered wisdom of the Spirit of Christ (cf. 12:2–3; 2:6–16) or of some other spirit (whether human or demonic). One example of such a discernment may be the judgment Paul makes in 2 Corinthians 11:4 that the message conveyed by the words and actions of the "super-apostles" amounts to "another Jesus ... a different Spirit ... a different gospel."

"Different kinds of tongues" (γένη γλωσσῶν, v. 10d) and "interpretation of tongues" (ἑρμηνεία γλωσσῶν, v. 10e) are placed last in the list, perhaps in a deliberate contrast to the prominence they seem to have been given by the Corinthians. As with prophecy, there is much debate over the nature of tongues. While some commentators insist that the tongues in 1 Corinthians 12–14 are real foreign human languages,[497] this argument runs into a number of problems: (1) Here in 1 Corinthians 12–14, tongues are spoken of as being addressed to God, not humans (e.g., 14:2, 14, 28); (2) outside the unusual, multilingual evangelistic context of Acts 2, it would be difficult to see the necessity or purpose for the tongues to be real human languages; and (3) the reference to foreign human languages in 14:10–11 is explained in verse 12 as an *analogy* with the Corinthian situation, not a literal description of what is taking place.[498]

---

[496] Thiselton, *First Corinthians*, 964 (emphasis original).

[497] E.g., Forbes, *Prophecy and Inspired Speech*, 53–74; Robert H. Gundry, "'Ecstatic Utterance' (NEB)?," *JTS* 17 (1966): 299–307.

[498] Forbes is correct, however, when he points out that the instructions in 14:28–29 presuppose that tongue speakers, while not able to understand what they were saying, were still able to control their speech and were not in a state of frenzied ecstasy. Forbes, *Prophecy*

The more likely interpretation, therefore, is that the "tongues" Paul is speaking of here should be understood as a language of prayer, unintelligible to human hearers (and, according to 14:14, to the speaker) unless "interpreted" in the form of articulate speech by a person with the gift of interpretation. If that is the case, then the gift of "interpretation of tongues" (ἑρμηνεία γλωσσῶν, v. 10e; cf. Paul's use of the cognate verb, διερμηνεύω ["interpret"], in 14:5, 13, 27, and the noun διερμηνευτής in 14:28) probably refers not to a miraculous ability to translate one language into another but rather to the capacity to "put into words" the burden of lament or praise that has been poured out in nonverbal form through the utterance of the tongue speaker.[499]

Verse 11 echoes the language and ideas of verses 4–7 (ἐνεργεῖ, "is active," cf. v. 6; διαιροῦν, "distributing," cf. διαιρέσεις, "different apportionments" in vv. 4, 5, 6; ἑκάστῳ, "to each person," cf. 7; τὸ αὐτὸ πνεῦμα, "the same Spirit," cf. v. 4), tying verses 4–11 together as a coherent and unified paragraph. Here, the main idea of verses 4–7 (that all the gifts are the work of the one Spirit) is reinforced, with additional emphasis on the sovereignty of the Spirit in distributing them (καθὼς βούλεται, "as he wills").[500]

12:12. In verse 12 Paul reintroduces a metaphor that he has already more fleetingly employed in 10:17 and that will frame the discussion for the remainder of the chapter, likening the members of the church in Corinth to the parts of a body (see §8). Greco-Roman readers would have been familiar with the image as a standard theme of political discourse, going back to Plato. Martin emphasizes the hierarchical and conservative connotations of the image as it was used in Greco-Roman political discourse,[501] and Thiselton and Witherington follow him in pointing out

---

and Inspired Speech, 103–81. For a discussion of the theory that tongues were understood by the Corinthians and/or Paul as a form of angelic speech, see the comments on 13:1, below.

[499] See especially the argument for this view in Thiselton, *First Corinthians*, 1098–100, citing examples including Josephus's description of the wonders of Herod's palace as "baffling all description" (παντός λόγου κρείσσων) and his subsequent claim that "it is impossible adequately to delineate [i.e., to put into words] the palace" (οὔθ' ἑρμηνεῦσαι δυνατὸν ἀξίως τὰ βασίλεια) (*J.W.* 5.176, 182), and the similar uses of ἑρμηνεύω in Philo, *Alleg. Interp.* 1.10; *Worse* 15, 39; *Migration* 21, 35.

[500] Cf. the brief comments on the implications of verses in 1 Corinthians such as this (and 2:10–13; 3:16; 6:11), in which Paul attributes "personal traits" to the Spirit, for our understanding of Pauline pneumatology, in Rabens, "Development of Pauline Pneumatology," 177.

[501] Martin, *The Corinthian Body*, 92–94

the way Paul's use of the image (e.g., in vv. 21–26) overturns these traditional connotations.[502]

While most commentators, drawing on the function of the image as it is used in the Greco-Roman political literature,[503] see Paul's emphasis falling on the unity of the body, Fee argues that Paul's main point here is not the unity ("despite the fact that you are diverse, it is important that you are united") but the diversity ("despite the fact that you are one, it is important that you welcome the diversity of how God has gifted you"). There is truth in both perspectives, but Fee's reading of the chapter makes better sense of the movement of ideas, which heads toward the string of rhetorical questions about diversity in verses 29–30. The point Paul makes is not merely about diversity but about diversity overlaid with hierarchies of status. The main target of his corrective in these verses is the way in which the Corinthians are competing with one another for status within the community, with an excessive focus on a small number of high-status gifts, and are thereby forfeiting the much richer diversity of gifts with which God has blessed them.[504]

Paul reintroduces the metaphor in language that frames it as a comparison or analogy (καθάπερ, "just as"), but the conclusion of the sentence raises the possibility of something stronger than that by drawing the comparison not with "the church" but with "Christ" (οὕτως καὶ ὁ Χριστός, "so also is Christ"). A number of influential twentieth-century commentators pointed to this as evidence of a "mystical" relationship between believers and Christ that was at the heart of Paul's ecclesiology,[505]

---

[502] Thiselton, *First Corinthians*, 993; Witherington, *Conflict and Community*, 259; Martin, *The Corinthian Body*, 94–96.

[503] E.g., Mitchell, *Paul and the Rhetoric of Reconciliation*, 267–70; Martin, *The Corinthian Body*, 92–94. Thiselton, *First Corinthians*, 996. Thiselton also points out the syntactical priority of ἕν ἐστιν σῶμα ("are one body") over the concessive participial phrase, πολλὰ ὄντα ("though many") in v. 12b, but this argument is undermined somewhat by the fact that v. 12b is preceded by the statement in v. 12a that "the body is one and has many parts"—a wording that suggests at least an equal emphasis on diversity and is compatible with Fee's claim that the primary emphasis of the passage as a whole is on diversity within unity rather than on unity despite diversity.

[504] Paul's corrective on this score is thus quite closely similar to the corrective he gives in 3:21–23 to the Corinthian tendency to boast competitively in individual human leaders rather than receiving them all as God's gifts to the whole church.

[505] E.g., Albert Schweitzer, *The Mysticism of Paul the Apostle*, trans. W. Montgomery (New York: Holt, 1931) and Hans Lietzmann and Werner Georg Kümmel, *An die Korinther I-II*, 4th ed., HNT (Tübingen: Mohr Siebeck, 1949), claiming v. 13 as evidence for "the factuality of the mystic idea" (cited and translated in Conzelmann, *1 Corinthians*, 211).

but the adjective does little to clarify exactly what meaning he (or they) intended. A simpler and more solidly grounded approach is to allow Paul's own development and application of the metaphor, here and elsewhere (e.g., 10:17 and, by implication, 6:15–17), to determine the nature and extent of the identification he has in mind.[506]

12:13–14. The origin of this unity is traced back by Paul to the event(s) in which the Corinthians "were all baptized by one Spirit into one body" and "were all given one Spirit to drink." There is considerable debate among commentators about what event or events Paul is referring to. Evaluation of the various possibilities needs to take into account both that the verb βαπτίζω was already in common use among first-century Greek speakers to convey the sense of "dip" or "immerse"[507] and, on the other hand, that no Christian was likely to understand the word, when used in a context relating to Christian initiation, without the ritual of water baptism being evoked in some way (either as a metaphor for initial experience of the Spirit or as an outward and visible event that accompanies or signifies it). Both of these meanings are likely to be present here: the primary reference of the phrase is probably to the experience in which believers, at the point of their conversion, were (metaphorically) "washed" by/in the Spirit (cf. 6:11),[508] but Paul's choice to describe that event using the word "baptized" encourages his hearers to recall the

[506] Also relevant are those places (e.g., 8:12) where the idea of identification or solidarity is present without the body metaphor being used or implied at all, and the various phrases such as "in Christ," "into Christ," "with Christ," and "Christ in me" that imply (sometimes, though not always) the possibility of some sort of participationist meaning. Cf. the discussions in James D. G. Dunn, *The Theology of Paul the Apostle* (Grand Rapids: Eerdmans, 1998), 390–412; Campbell, *Paul and Union with Christ*; and Michael J. Thate, Kevin J. Vanhoozer, and Constantine R. Campbell, eds., *"In Christ" in Paul: Explorations in Paul's Theology of Union and Participation*, WUNT (Tübingen: Mohr Siebeck, 2014).

[507] Cf. LSJ, s.v. "βαπτίζω," 1, 2.

[508] In both 6:11 (ἐν τῷ πνεύματι) and 12:13 (ἐν ἑνὶ πνεύματι), the preposition ἐν is probably best understood as meaning "by" rather than "in." In the case of its use in 6:11, that the phrase qualifies not just the verb, "washed," but also the two parallel verbs, "sanctified" and "justified," counts strongly against understanding ἐν in a locative sense as "in." In the case of its use in 12:13, the decision is a little harder to make with certainty, but the juxtaposition of the two prepositional phrases, ἐν ἑνὶ πνεύματι and εἰς ἓν σῶμα, tips the scales in favor of taking the first in an instrumental sense ("by one Spirit") and the second in a (metaphorically) locative sense ("into one body").

event of their baptism in water as having accompanied or symbolized it (see §8.1).[509]

The description in verse 13b of the Corinthians as having been "given one Spirit to drink" is unlikely (given the lack of any other New Testament instances, within or beyond Paul's letters, in which being "given the Spirit to drink" carries this meaning)[510] to be referring to a separate and subsequent event. The more likely interpretation of this clause is to take it as supplying a second, parallel metaphor for the same event of Christian initiation (and as reinforcement for the view that the "bapti[sm]" referred to in v. 13a was—at least in the primary sense of the word—similarly metaphorical in nature).[511]

Whatever conclusion is drawn about the precise event or events Paul is referring to when he says that the Corinthians were "baptized by one Spirit into one body" and "given one Spirit to drink," the basic point is still the same: *all* believers in Christ, without distinction, have experienced the event(s) he is referring to (cf. Gal 3:27–28). The repetition of ἕν ("one") and πάντες ("all") and the explicit inclusions εἴτε Ἰουδαῖοι εἴτε Ἕλληνες, εἴτε δοῦλοι εἴτε ἐλεύθεροι ("whether Jews or Greeks, whether slaves or free"), reinforce the point that within this community there is no room for divisions of loyalty or hierarchies of status. It is therefore unlikely in the extreme that the baptism in/by the Spirit spoken of here is meant by Paul to refer to a postconversion "second blessing" experience. Thiselton comments: "Any theology that might imply that this one baptism in 13a in which believers were baptised by [or in] one Spirit might mark off some postconversion experience or status enjoyed only by some Christians attacks and undermines Paul's entire argument and emphasis."[512]

Verse 14 ("Indeed, the body is not one part but many") moves us back to the initial analogy and introduces an elaboration of the metaphor, with

[509] This association is strengthened, as Collins points out, by Paul's use of the same formula ("whether Jews or Greeks, whether slaves or free") that he uses in Gal 3:27–28 in connection with the ritual of Christian baptism. Collins, *First Corinthians*, 462–63.

[510] Carson points to LXX Isa 29:10 (πεπότικεν ὑμᾶς κύριος πνεύματι κατανύξεως; NETS: "the Lord has made you drink with a spirit of deep sleep") as a possible parallel, suggesting a metaphorical sense of "drenched" or "flooded" (Carson, *Showing the Spirit*, 46). A similar image is conveyed (using the verb πίνω, "drink") in John 7:37–39, where the experience of "drink[ing]" the Spirit is connected closely with "com[ing]" to Jesus and "believ[ing]" in him.

[511] Cf. Fee, *First Epistle to the Corinthians*, 670–71.

[512] Thiselton, *First Corinthians*, 997–98.

emphasis unambiguously placed on the plurality (and, by implication, the diversity) of the members.

12:15–20. In verses 15–16 Paul further develops the metaphor, personifying the parts of the body and constructing a dialogue between them in order to convey how ridiculous it is to envy the gifts and ministries of others, as if only those with the highest-status gifts truly belong.[513] The positive point that the dialogue is intended to support is clear (i.e., all are needed, and their diversity is essential to the well-being of the body), but the particular attitude being satirized in verses 15–16 as the opposite of it is less clear. Garland is probably correct to suggest that the point of view expressed by the foot and the ear is that of the (supposedly) inferior, or the view that the superior members of the body impose on them.[514] With the vast majority of English versions (and against the punctuation of the UBS[5] edition of the Greek text) it makes more sense to read verses 15–16 as negative statements ("If the foot/ear should say ... it is not for that reason any less a part of the body") rather than as rhetorical questions ("If the foot/ear should say ... would it not for that reason cease to belong to the body?").

Verse 17 continues the assault against the envying of gifts (and the boastfulness that encourages it) by pointing out the absurdity—indeed the monstrosity!—of a body that was all eye or all ear. If everyone in the Corinthian community envied the gifts of those who performed the highest-status ministries and if all who thus envied were given what they wished for (or if the assumptions of those who boasted in their own high-status gifts were extended to their logical conclusion), the result would be absurd and dysfunctional.

Verse 18 takes the argument a step farther by asserting that the diversity of gifts within the body is by God's deliberate design—a reminder of Paul's earlier point in verse 11 about God's sovereign distribution of gifts. The connective phrase νυνὶ δέ (literally, "But now") that commences the verse suggests a relationship with the preceding verse that is logical, not chronological, in nature: "But as it is ..." (i.e., in contrast with the absurd hypotheticals of the previous verses). Paul's stress on the fact that this applies to every single member of the community of believers is conveyed

[513] In doing so he echoes (and may be consciously alluding to) a popular fable, also appropriated by Livy (*Ab urbe cond.* 2.32) though with a very different political purpose.

[514] Garland, *1 Corinthians*, 594; contra Fee, *First Epistle to the Corinthians*, 676, who sees no element of inferiority or superiority in the distinctions between hand and foot, eye and ear.

by the way in which he words the phrase ἓν ἕκαστον αὐτῶν ("each one [of them]"), with the redundant ἕν ("one") included for emphasis. (An English equivalent would be "every single one" or "each and every one.")

Verses 19–20 conclude the first half of the paragraph by reiterating two points that Paul has already made earlier in the discussion: "And if they were all the same part, where would the body be?" (v. 19, which is a reiteration in generalized terms of the point made in v. 17); and "As it is, there are many parts, but one body" (v. 20, which is a reiteration of points already made, in closely similar language, in vv. 12, 14). Read in light of the points Paul has made in the intervening discussion in verses 16–18, the statement in verse 19 should now probably be taken as implying a slightly stronger claim than it carried in verses 12 and 14: that is that the unity of the body does not exist *in spite of* its diversity but *in reliance on* it.

12:21–24a. The distinctions of status implied in verses 15–17 here become explicit, with the words of the "eye" and the "head" representing the attitude of those in Corinth who are convinced of the superior status of their gifts relative to the gifts of others. Paul sharply rejects such a view, asserting in verse 22 the indispensability of the "weaker" parts of the body to its life and health. Martin reads these verses on the assumption that Paul's reference here to the body's "weaker" parts implies not only a perceived inferiority of gifting but also a lower social status, arguing plausibly that the two kinds of status hierarchy may well have overlapped within the value system of the Corinthian elite.[515]

In verses 23–24a Paul raises the stakes in his use of the body metaphor by shifting attention from the "weaker" parts of the body to those that are considered "less honorable" (ἀτιμότερα) and "unrespectable" (ἀσχήμονα). The parts he has in mind here are almost certainly the body's sexual organs, and the care we take to cover them is highlighted as a way in which we show them "greater honor" (τιμὴν περισσοτέραν) and "greater respect" (εὐσχημοσύνην περισσοτέραν).[516] Translated from the realm of the metaphor to its application in the life of the church, Paul's point here echoes his claim made earlier in the letter that "God has chosen what is foolish in the world to shame the wise, and God has chosen what is weak in the world to shame the strong" (1:27): the beauty of

[515] Martin, *The Corinthian Body*, 87–92; Dale B. Martin, "Tongues of Angels and Other Status Indicators," *JAAR* 59 (1991): 547–90.

[516] Cf. Garland, *1 Corinthians*, 596–97.

Christ is displayed within the church most clearly by the way in which it welcomes, honors, and receives the ministry of those whom the world considers ugly and unpresentable, and the wisdom of God is displayed in the way that the church embraces, esteems, and gives heed to those whom the world dismisses as weak and foolish.[517]

12:24b–26. The implication in verses 22–24a that the arrangement Paul describes is by divine intention and design is made explicit in verse 24b: "Instead, God has put the body together, giving greater honor to the less honorable." Here again (as earlier in vv. 11, 18) Paul stresses the sovereignty and purpose of God as an outworking of the paradoxical wisdom that he has expounded in 1:18–31 as a basic entailment of "the word of the cross" that he has been given to proclaim.

The purpose of this divine design, according to verse 25, is "so that there would be no division in the body, but that the members would have the same concern for each other." The reference here to "division" (σχίσμα) echoes the earlier references in 1:10 and 11:18 to σχίσματα within the church, further reinforcing the likelihood that the hierarchies of status erected by those with the more esoteric and exalted gifts corresponded to or are overlapped with the socioeconomic divisions Paul describes and denounces in 11:17–34. Here, as in 11:17–34, Paul pictures the unity of the body as being expressed in practices of solidarity and mutual care, extending without distinction to all members of the body, with a particular concern for those who are less impressively gifted and/or of lower social status. Verse 26 unpacks this "concern for each other" in terms of the empathetic identification that believers are to practice with those among them who are suffering and the shared honor that the whole body receives when one of its parts is honored (cf. Rom 12:15–16). Given the reinterpretation of honor Paul has argued for in the immediately preceding paragraph (cf. vv. 22–24), the picture in verse 26b ("if one member is honored, all the members rejoice with it") should probably be taken not as a reference to the collective dignity bestowed on the church by occasions when its high-status members are the recipients of civic honors in the wider society but as an assertion of the paradoxical honor that the church accrues when it relates to its weakest and least presentable members in the manner that it should.[518]

---

[517] Cf. Thiselton, *First Corinthians*, 1009; Brock and Wannenwetsch, *Therapy*, 115–18.

[518] Cf. Hays, *First Corinthians*, 216.

12:27–31. In the final verses of the chapter, Paul returns explicitly to the theme of the various gifts given by the Spirit and the different ways in which believers are appointed by God to serve one another within the community of faith (cf. vv. 4–11), with verse 27 linking this paragraph backward to the metaphor that framed the preceding discussion in verses 12–26 and verse 31b looking forward to what follows in chapter 13.

Verse 27 commences the paragraph with an emphatic assertion of the applicability of the previous metaphorically framed discussion to the Corinthians: community and the body of Christ are explicitly and emphatically asserted: "Now *you* [with the redundant pronoun Ὑμεῖς included for emphasis and placed first in the clause] are the body of Christ and individual members of it." The phrase ἐκ μέρους ("individually") reflects the fact that Paul is talking not merely about how to view the community as a whole (as he is, for example, in ch. 3) but about how to view the place of each member within it and the interrelationships between them.

In verse 28 Paul provides a second list of the gifts God has given to the church and the people whom he has appointed to serve within it. The list is noticeably different from the earlier list in verses 8–10, both in the examples it includes and in the way in which it is organized. The opening words ("And God has appointed these in the church …") reiterate the emphasis of earlier verses on God's sovereign role in distributing the gifts and appointing people to serve (cf. vv. 11, 18, 24) and make explicit the communal context in which they belong and are to be exercised (ἐν τῇ ἐκκλησίᾳ). The latter phrase probably refers to the community rather than more narrowly to the event of the gathering (as it does in 14:19). Given the previous verse ("Now you are the body of Christ …"), it probably makes more sense to read ἐκκλησία as referring primarily to the local church in Corinth rather than to the universal church.

The list begins with three numbered items referring to persons or offices ("first apostles, second prophets, third teachers"), reflecting Paul's emphasis on the indispensability of the gifts that build up the church by ministering the message of the gospel to it. As Fee points out, the plural "apostles" is probably a reminder that the local community is part of a larger work of God and is still, in a sense, the beneficiary of the collective testimony of all the apostles, not just Paul;[519] alternatively, Paul may be using the term to refer to himself and Barnabas as church-planting

[519] Fee, *First Epistle to the Corinthians*, 687.

missionaries, sent out by the church in Antioch. The "prophets" Paul is speaking of are almost certainly the prophets who are present and active within the Corinthian congregation (cf. 14:29, 32, 37). The "teachers" probably identifies a group that corresponds at least broadly to the "instructors" (παιδαγωγοί) of 4:15 and has a significant overlap with those within the congregation whose frequent or particular contribution is to minister the "message of wisdom" and "message of knowledge" Paul has spoken of in 12:8.

These three numbered person-gifts are followed in verse 28b by an unnumbered list of capacity-gifts, which juxtaposes overtly "spiritual" or supernatural gifts such as "miracles" (δυνάμεις), "gifts of healing" (χαρίσματα ἰαμάτων), and "various kinds of tongues" (γένη γλωσσῶν) with more mundane and ordinary gifts such as "[forms of] helping" (ἀντιλήμψεις) and "[forms of] leading" (κυβερνήσεις). The word ἀντιλήμψεις is quite general in its scope, perhaps with a particular accent on ministries that assist the weak and vulnerable (cf. the use of the cognate verb ἀντιλαμβάνεσθαι in Acts 20:35). κυβερνήσεις is a metaphor for leadership derived from the steering of a ship (e.g., Acts 27:11) and was used in the political discourse of ancient Greece as a stock image for a person whose task it is to steer the affairs of a city or a kingdom.[520] The plural form in which Paul uses the noun here suggests that he has in mind a variety of forms that this gift may take and a plurality of persons who may exercise it within the community of God's people.

The list in verse 28 is followed by a string of rhetorical questions in verses 29–30, which zero in on the first three persons/offices in the list from verse 27a and the more overtly spiritual or supernatural items from the remainder of the list in verse 27b (with interpretation of tongues added in connection with tongues at the end of the list): "Are all apostles? Are all prophets? Are all teachers? Do all do miracles? Do all have gifts of healing? Do all speak in tongues? Do all interpret?" All the questions are introduced by the interrogative particle μή, making it clear that a negative answer is expected to each of them.

Verse 31a is grammatically ambiguous, with some arguing in favor of reading ζηλοῦτε in the indicative mood and others in favor of reading

---

[520] E.g., Plato, *Resp.* 488a; Dio Chrysostom, *Or.* 48.14; Polybius, *Hist.* 6.4.2. In the LXX (e.g., Prov 11:14; 24:6) the word was used with a similar metaphorical sense to refer to the "guidance" provided to a nation or army by wise counselors. Cf. Starling, *UnCorinthian Leadership*, 6–7, 73.

it as an imperative. If the first option is taken, then the statement being made is almost certainly a critical one: "Yet you are desiring [what you think of as] the 'greater' gifts. But I will show you an even better way." If the second option is taken then the sentence reads as a positive command in favor of desiring the gifts: "But [despite what I have said about the diversity of gifts and the sovereignty of God in distributing them, you should nonetheless continue to] desire the [genuinely] greater gifts. And I will show you an even better way." Given the close similarity of verse 31a to what Paul goes on to say in 14:1 and 14:39 (both of which are clearly commands), the latter is probably the more likely option, with Paul's sharp words against status envy, competitiveness, and arrogance in 12:14–26 (and implicitly in vv. 29–30) making it clear that he wishes the Corinthians to understand μείζονα ("greater") in terms of usefulness, not status. Finally, in verse 31b, Paul concludes the chapter with a brief statement that acts as a bridge between the encouragement of verse 31a to pursue the greater gifts and the "even better way" (καθ' ὑπερβολὴν ὁδόν) that he will go on to show them in the following chapter.

Bridge

Paul's words in this chapter regarding the christological criterion by which true spirituality is to be recognized, the diversity of gifts with which the one Spirit has blessed the church, the equal concern that all members ought to have for one another, and the particular honor that should be shown to the body's weakest and least esteemed members have an obvious and enduring applicability, challenging both our individual habits and attitudes and the structural and cultural aspects of our communal life. In some contexts the primary corrective to be taken from this chapter will be to hierarchies of gifts that overvalue the spectacular, the spontaneous, and the supernatural; in other contexts the primary corrective will be to hierarchies that overvalue the cerebral, the formally educated, and the officially credentialed; and in other contexts still the primary corrective will be to distinctions of status that are based not on gifts and abilities but on wealth, lineage, or social connections.

In all cases, the foundational principle underlying contemporary application is the same: the first and most basic criterion for discerning the presence and work of the Spirit is authentic confession of Jesus as Lord (cf. vv. 1–3). It is that confession of Jesus's lordship over the church that fosters both a grateful openness to the diversity of gifts with which he blesses the church through the work of his Spirit and a jealous concern for the purity and authenticity of the ministry that is undertaken in his name. And it is the same confession of Jesus's lordship that overthrows all hierarchies of privilege and status that stand in contradiction to it and demands that special honor be given to the body's weakest and least presentable members, in keeping with the crucicentric wisdom by which Christ rules and orders his church.

B. An Encomium to Love (13:1–13)

> 1 If I speak human or angelic tongues but do not have love, I am a noisy
> gong or a clanging cymbal. 2 If I have the gift of prophecy and under-
> stand all mysteries and all knowledge, and if I have all faith so that I
> can move mountains but do not have love, I am nothing. 3 And if I give
> away all my possessions, and if I give over my body in order to boast
> but do not have love, I gain nothing.
>
> 4 Love is patient, love is kind. Love does not envy, is not boastful, is not
> arrogant, 5 is not rude, is not self-seeking, is not irritable, and does not
> keep a record of wrongs. 6 Love finds no joy in unrighteousness but
> rejoices in the truth. 7 It bears all things, believes all things, hopes all
> things, endures all things.
>
> 8 Love never ends. But as for prophecies, they will come to an end; as
> for tongues, they will cease; as for knowledge, it will come to an end.
> 9 For we know in part, and we prophesy in part, 10 but when the perfect
> comes, the partial will come to an end. 11 When I was a child, I spoke like
> a child, I thought like a child, I reasoned like a child. When I became a
> man, I put aside childish things. 12 For now we see only a reflection as
> in a mirror, but then face to face. Now I know in part, but then I will
> know fully, as I am fully known. 13 Now these three remain: faith, hope,
> and love—but the greatest of these is love.

Context/Structure/Form

First Corinthians 13 is a well-known and widely loved chapter, which takes the form of an encomium (i.e., a speech in praise of someone or something) that celebrates the excellences of love.[521] It is carefully

---

[521] Cf. James G. Sigountos, "The Genre of 1 Corinthians 13," *NTS* 40 (1994): 246–60; Brookins, *Reading 1 Corinthians*, 122–23; Ciampa and Rosner, *The First Letter to the Corinthians*, 621–23. For a textbook example from the fourth century AD, see the encomium to wisdom in Aphthonius, *Prog.* 8. Fee (quoting Ceslas Spicq) characterizes it as a "paraenetic exhortation" (Fee, *First Epistle to the Corinthians*, 693), and he is certainly correct that it serves a serious, paraenetic purpose and prepares the way for the exhortations and instructions of ch. 14,

constructed, internally coherent, and neatly bounded[522] but still shows multiple signs of being tightly and deliberately integrated into its context within the letter. The first and third paragraphs contain obvious connections to the topics discussed in the preceding and following chapters, contrasting love with tongues, prophecy, and faith, and preparing the way for the command in 14:1 to "pursue love and desire spiritual gifts" and the emphasis in chapter 14 on behavior that "builds up" the body.[523] Even the middle paragraph (vv. 4–7), which makes no explicit reference to the gifts and manifestations of the Spirit, has points of connection to the situation in Corinth via the contrasts that it draws between love and several of the behaviors and dispositions for which Paul rebukes the Corinthians elsewhere in the letter.

The chapter falls neatly into three paragraphs. The first functions as a kind of prologue and focuses on the indispensability of love (vv. 1–3); the second gives a description of the character of love as manifested in its acts and its abstentions (vv. 4–7); the third asserts the permanence of love, drawing comparisons on this score between the eternal significance of love and the ephemerality of gifts such as prophecy, tongues, and knowledge (vv. 8–13).[524]

Comments

13:1 2. The first paragraph acts as a kind of prologue to the encomium, introducing its theme (love) and highlighting its indispensability. It does so through a series of hyperbolically stated scenarios in which spiritual gifts or religiously motivated behaviors of various kinds are imagined, even in impossibly extreme forms, but asserted to be useless in the absence of love.

The first of these three scenarios focuses on the gift of tongues, reflecting (and critiquing) the inordinately high value placed on that gift by the Corinthians. The distinction between "human" and "angelic" tongues

but it does so by means of epideictic rhetoric in praise of the disposition and associated behaviors that Paul wishes to commend to the Corinthians, without (yet) directly exhorting or commanding the readers.

522 Note the use of asyndeton in 13:1 and 14:1 to create syntactical seams, the use of the two closely similar commands in 12:31a and 14:1 as an inclusio around ch. 13, and the foreshadowing in 12:31b of the new topic that is about to be introduced.

523 Cf. the connection between love and upbuilding in 8:1.

524 Cf. the form-based analysis in Sigountos, "The Genre of 1 Corinthians 13," 246–60 and the content-based analysis in Fee, *First Epistle to the Corinthians*, 692–96.

could be (1) a distinction between two different kinds of glossolalia, both of which were practiced by the Corinthians; (2) a distinction between ordinary human eloquence and glossolalia (on the assumption that Paul and/or the Corinthians understand glossolalia to be the language of angels);[525] or (3) a reference to glossolalia ("human ... tongues"), with the reference to "angelic tongues" to be understood as an impossible hypothetical, added for the sake of hyperbole.

The idea that some in Corinth may have viewed tongues as a form of angelic speech finds support in Testament of Job 48–50, where it is said of a daughter of Job that she spoke "ecstatically in the angelic dialect,"[526] but Paul's statement in verse 8 that tongues "will cease" suggests that, in his view at least, tongues were a phenomenon of this age, not the age to come (and probably, therefore, to be viewed as earthly rather than heavenly in nature).

Option (3) is the simplest explanation for Paul's introduction of the idea of angelic tongues at this point (and this point only) in the letter, though it need not be viewed as mutually incompatible with the possibility that some or all of the Corinthians themselves considered their tongues-speaking to be a manifestation of angelic speech. It is consistent with the syntax, in which καὶ τῶν ἀγγέλων is held back to the end of the clause for the sake of emphasis, and matches the pattern of hyperbolic escalation that Paul follows in constructing each of the scenarios of verses 1–3. It is also in line with other instances in his letters where Paul uses references to angels as a form of hyperbolic rhetorical heightening (1 Cor 4:9; 6:3; Gal 1:8).

The conclusion Paul draws is damning: tongues—even angelic tongues—without love are nothing more than "a noisy gong or a clanging cymbal." The first term, χαλκὸς ἠχῶν ("a noisy gong"; literally, "resounding brass"), suggests a loud but empty sound. The second, κύμβαλον ἀλαλάζον ("a clanging cymbal"), refers more specifically to an instrument that was regularly associated with the rites performed in pagan cults (especially that of Cybele, the mother goddess, whose rites involved extreme examples of ecstatic speech and behavior). If an allusion to those rites is intended here, then Paul is implying that tongues-speaking exercised without love is not only useless but potentially worse than useless, replicating within

---

[525] Cf. Martin, *The Corinthian Body*, 267

[526] Cf. the arguments in favor of this view in Fee, *First Epistle to the Corinthians*, 698–99.

the Christian assembly the kind of noise and chaos that was characteristic of pagan ritual.[527]

Verse 2 moves beyond the gift of tongues to consider two other gifts (prophecy and faith), both in scenarios in which they are possessed to a superlative degree but without love. "The gift of prophecy" is described with an accent on the insights that inform the prophetic utterance, which are here imagined in hyperbolic all-embracing terms ("and understand all mysteries and all knowledge"). "Faith" (presumably the same kind of special-purpose faith referred to earlier, in 12:9, as a gift of the Spirit) is described in similarly extreme terms as "all faith so that I can move mountains." In both cases, however, Paul's verdict is that, if he possesses these gifts in the absence of love, he is "nothing."

13:3. Verse 3 adds two more scenarios, both of which move beyond the exercise of spiritual gifts to the performance of extreme and extravagant acts of giving. The first ("And if I give away all my possessions ...") is relatively straightforward to interpret, with the verb ψωμίσω ("I give away") implying that the purpose for which Paul has given away his possessions (all of them) is to feed the hungry.[528] Interpretation of the second scenario is complicated by the fact that in some manuscripts (e.g., 𝔓[46], א, A, B) the principal verb is shown as καυχήσωμαι ("in order to boast") whereas in other manuscripts (e.g., C, D, F, G, Ψ) and in the writings of many of the church fathers it is shown as καυθήσομαι or καυθήσωμαι ("in order that I might be burned"). The former of these two options is almost certainly to be preferred, given the strength of its manuscript support and the fact that later copyists (reading the text at a time when burnings of Christian martyrs had become a widely recounted communal memory) would have been more likely to change "boast" to "burn" than vice versa.[529] The kind of scenario Paul has in mind, therefore, is probably not a martyrdom but an act of generosity even more extreme than the one he has imagined in the first part of the verse. Having pictured himself giving away all of his possessions, he now raises the stakes even further

---

[527] Cf. Barrett, *First Corinthians*, 300; Fee, *First Epistle to the Corinthians*, 700.

[528] Ψωμίσω is commonly used to refer to the kind of almsgiving that is aimed at supplying the needs of the hungry, or (even more directly) to refer to the physical act of feeding another person (e.g., Rom 12:20; LXX Num 11:4; T. Lev. 8:5). Cf. Ciampa and Rosner, *The First Letter to the Corinthians*, 634; Fee, *First Epistle to the Corinthians*, 702.

[529] Cf. the discussions of the text-critical issues in Thiselton, *First Corinthians*, 1042–44; Fee, *First Epistle to the Corinthians*, 702–3.

and imagines himself giving away even his own body, selling himself into slavery in order to ransom others or to benefit them in some other way.[530] He does this, under the imagined scenario, on the assumption that he is going above and beyond what anyone could reasonably consider to be his duty and, by so doing, giving himself legitimate grounds to "boast" (cf. 9:15–18). He does so, however, as one who "do[es] not have love," with a set of motives that do not include a genuine desire for the good of the people who are receiving the benefit of his actions.[531] Because of that, Paul concludes, "I gain nothing."

13:4–7. Having introduced his theme in verses 1–3, focusing on love's indispensability, Paul goes on in verses 4–7 to provide a sketch of the character of love, as demonstrated in the actions that it does and does not perform. In the Greek all fourteen of Paul's descriptions of love in verses 4–7 are expressed in the form of verbs ("Love endures patiently [μακροθυμεῖ]; love acts kindly [χρηστεύεται]; love does not envy [οὐ ζηλοῖ], does not boast [οὐ περπερεύεται], does not become puffed up [οὐ φυσιοῦται], etc.")—a fact that the majority of English versions obscure by translating most of the statements in verses 4–5 with adjectives ("patient"; "kind"; "not . . . boastful"; "not . . . jealous") supplied as the predicates of their respective clauses. The differences between these two ways of framing the assertions should not be overstated, however: many of the verbs in these verses are stative verbs that do not describe "actions" in the strict sense of that word; nor should we conclude that in describing love by the way it acts and refrains from acting, Paul is reducing love to mere outward actions, with no necessary involvement of the affections and no interest in questions of motive or purpose. (If that were the case,

---

[530] Clement of Rome, writing at the end of the first century, speaks of people he knew who had done exactly that, possibly under the influence of Paul's words in 1 Corinthians, to which he appears to be alluding (and interpreting as having this meaning): "We know that many among us have had themselves imprisoned (παραδεδωκότας ἑαυτοὺς εἰς δεσμά), so that they might ransom others, and with the price received for themselves have fed (ἐψώμισαν) others" (1 Clem. 55:2).

[531] The example of 9:15–18, discussed above, would suggest that in Paul's understanding, the fact that a person's actions are motivated in part by the desire that they might have a "boast" of some sort is not intrinsically incompatible with the possibility that they might also be motivated by a genuine love for others. But in the scenario he is imagining here in 13:3, love is not among the motives behind the action, despite the fact that its outcome confers benefit on others at the (material and personal) cost of the one who performs it.

then the scenarios Paul has just described in v. 3 would become almost impossible to interpret with any kind of convincing coherence.)

The first two verbs, in Fee's words, "represent respectively love's necessary passive and active responses toward others or difficulties in general."[532] The first, μακροθυμέω ("is patient"), along with its cognate noun μακροθυμία, is typically used by Paul to refer to the forbearance that is shown within social relationships (cf. 1 Thess 5:14; 2 Cor 6:6; Gal 5:22; 2 Tim 4:2; Col 1:11; 3:12) rather than to the patience that waits for the fulfillment of God's promises or the endurance that bears up under sufferings.[533] The second is χρηστεύομαι, which speaks of active goodness shown toward others, in acts of generous benefaction (cf. Luke 6:35) or in other forms of gentle and merciful conduct (cf. LXX Pss 85:5; 144:9). Paul uses both words in Romans 2:4, speaking of the kindness and patience of God.

The next seven statements, in verses 4b–5, all speak in negative terms about what love does not do: "Love does not envy, is not boastful, is not arrogant, is not rude, is not self-seeking, is not irritable, and does not keep a record of wrongs." The first verb, ζηλοῖ ("envy"), can sometimes be used in a positive sense to speak of the proper jealousy that is intrinsic to love (e.g., 2 Cor 11:2) and corresponds—albeit imperfectly—to the jealousy of God himself (e.g., LXX Zech 8:2). In other contexts, however, it carries a negative sense, referring (like its cognate adjective ζῆλος) to the kind of envious desire that gives rise to destructive rivalry and resentment (cf. 3:3; 2 Cor 12:20; Gal 5:20; Rom 13:13), and it is this sense that it carries here.

The second and third verbs of this sequence—περπερεύεται ("is ... boastful") and φυσιοῦται ("is ... arrogant")—describe similar behaviors. The verb περπερεύομαι is rarely attested within the surviving literature but is used by Marcus Aurelius to advise himself against "play[ing] ... the braggart,"[534] and Polybius uses the cognate noun πέρπερος in a similar sense, describing a person who is, in his view, "a chatterbox, a braggart, and a bore."[535] The third verb, φυσιοῦται, is all too familiar to readers of 1 Corinthians, due to its repeated use by Paul within this letter to speak

[532] Fee, *First Epistle to the Corinthians*, 705.

[533] The word Paul typically uses to speak of "patience" in that sense is ὑπομονή (or its cognate verb, ὑπομένω; cf. v. 7).

[534] Marcus Aurelius, *Med.* 5.5.4.

[535] Polybius, *Hist.* 32.2.5; cf. 39.1.2.

of the "puffed up" attitude taken by the Corinthian elite toward their own importance and abilities (cf. 4:6, 18–19; 5:2; 8:1).

The fourth verb, ἀσχημονεῖ ("is ... rude"), suggests treatment of others that lacks concern for their dignity and tramples on the kind of social customs that protect it,[536] and the verbal phrase that follows (ζητεῖ τὰ ἑαυτῆς, "is ... self-seeking") describes an attitude that is the opposite of the one Paul has commended in 10:24, 33.

Taken together, these first five items in the sequence of negative statements Paul strings together in verses 4b–5 are all uncomfortably reminiscent of the behaviors and attitudes for which Paul has reproved the Corinthians within the earlier chapters of the letter, suggesting the likelihood that even this portion of his description of love is composed with the Corinthian situation in mind.

The sixth and seventh items of the list (it "is not irritable, and does not keep a record of wrongs") are less obviously related to the problems Paul sees in the Corinthian church. Both of them recall the earlier, positive statement that love "is patient" (μακροθυμεῖ, v. 4) and speak of the way in which love responds to provocations that arise out of the actions of others. The statement that love "is not irritable" (οὐ παροξύνεται) focuses on the gentleness and self-control that love exercises in the moment of provocation, and the following statement, that love "does not keep a record of wrongs" (οὐ λογίζεται τὸ κακόν), focuses on the longer-term willingness of love to refrain from the kind of scorekeeping that records insults and injuries for the sake of future retribution.[537]

Verse 6 follows the seven negative statements of verses 4b–5 with a double-barreled statement that draws a contrast between what love does not do ("Love finds no joy in unrighteousness") and what love does do ("but rejoices in the truth"). Garland reads verse 6a as a reference to the attitude that takes pleasure in doing wrong to others so as to advantage oneself, recalling Paul's earlier rebuke to the congregation members who are initiating unjust lawsuits (6:8),[538] but this interpretation relies on a

---

[536] Cf. the cognate noun Paul has used in 12:24 to speak of God giving "greater honor" to the less honorable parts of the body, and his advice in 7:36 regarding situations in which a man "thinks he is acting improperly toward the virgin he is engaged to."

[537] Cf. Paul's statement in 2 Cor 5:19 that "in Christ, God was reconciling the world to himself, not counting their trespasses against them (μὴ λογιζόμενος αὐτοῖς τὰ παραπτώματα αὐτῶν)."

[538] Garland, *1 Corinthians*, 619.

slightly forced reading of the phrase ἐπὶ τῇ ἀδικίᾳ ("in unrighteousness"), which reads more naturally as a reference to someone else's wrongdoing as an external occasion for one's own rejoicing.[539] The most likely sense in which Paul is using the phrase is as a reference to pleasure taken in the exposure of the wrongdoings of others as an opportunity for one's own advancement and the other person's loss of status or reputation. Love, in contrast, is committed to the good of the other and "rejoices" (with them) "in the truth."[540] This last statement is a reminder that love, as Paul understands it, is not a balancing factor to be held in tension with a commitment to truth but is itself firmly wedded to the truth and eager to see justice and integrity upheld.

Verse 7 brings Paul's description of the character of love to a climax, with four parallel two-word statements: πάντα στέγει ("it bears all things"; cf. 9:12), πάντα πιστεύει ("believes all things"), πάντα ἐλπίζει ("hopes all things"), πάντα ὑπομένει ("endures all things"). The word πάντα is probably to be understood adverbially, with the sense of "always" or "in all circumstances,"[541] rather than as the object of each of the four verbs (which would make the second and third statements difficult to understand in any plausible and relevant way). As a number of commentators have proposed, the four statements appear to be arranged in a chiastic sequence, with the second and third verbs ("believes" and "hopes") speaking of the future-oriented faith and hope that motivate and enable the present perseverance and patience Paul speaks of in the first and fourth verbs ("bears" and "endures").[542]

13:8–13. The third paragraph of the encomium, in verses 8–13, praises the permanence of love, contrasting its enduring value and significance with the transitory function of gifts such as prophecy, tongues, and knowledge and illustrating that contrast with the examples in verses 11–12a. The opening statement in verse 8a that "Love never ends" (Ἡ ἀγάπη οὐδέποτε πίπτει; more literally, "love never falls" or "love never fails") builds on the

---

[539] Thiselton, *First Corinthians*, 1054.

[540] The compound verb συγχαίρει that Paul uses in v. 6b is unlikely to carry the sense of "rejoic[ing] with" the (personified) truth; the more likely meaning intended by Paul in this context is that love joins with others in rejoicing together in the truth (rather than turning against others to do them harm). Cf. Fee, *First Epistle to the Corinthians*, 708.

[541] Cf. BDAG, s.v. "πᾶς, πᾶσα, πᾶν," 1.d.β.

[542] Cf. Ciampa and Rosner, *The First Letter to the Corinthians*, 648; Fee, *First Epistle to the Corinthians*, 709.

statements in verse 7 about love's endurance through all the fluctuating circumstances of this age, making an assertion that turns out by the end of the chapter to embrace not only the present age but also the age to come. Verse 8b contrasts that assertion with three parallel statements about the impermanence of prophecies, tongues, and knowledge. Some interpreters have appealed to these statements as support for a claim that miraculous gifts ceased at the end of the apostolic era,[543] but the context (especially the image of seeing "face to face" in v. 12) makes it clear that what Paul has in mind as the time when prophecies, tongues, and (the gift of) knowledge will come to an end is not the close of the canon or the end of the apostolic era but the last day, when Christ returns. The stylistic variation between καταργηθήσονται/καταργηθήσεται ("will come to an end") and παύσονται ("will cease") should probably not be pressed for any distinction in meaning.[544]

The claims regarding knowledge and prophecy in verse 8 are supported in verses 9–10 by a distinction between our present experience of both, which is only "in part" (ἐκ μέρους), and the perfection that is to come, when everything "partial" (ἐκ μέρους) will be made redundant and come to an end. Here, as in 12:27, ἐκ μέρους (vv. 9, 10) means not merely "in part" (in a quantitative and static sense) but rather, "part by part," "piece by piece" (with additional qualitative and dynamic connotations). Luther's image of a *Stückwerk*—a patchwork, presumably still being put together—conveys the sense well.[545]

This statement, in turn, is supported by two illustrations in verses 11–12a: "When I was a child, I spoke like a child, I thought like a child, I reasoned like a child. When I became a man, I put aside childish things. For now we see only a reflection as in a mirror, but then face to face."[546] The first illustration affirms in a heavily qualified way the present legitimacy and validity of the gifts of prophecy and knowledge, with a focus on the activities of speech, thought, and reasoning in which the Corinthian elite

---

[543] E.g., Robert L. Thomas, "'Tongues ... Will Cease'," *JETS* 17 (1974): 81–89.

[544] Paul's statement here that "tongues ... will cease" helps to confirm the likelihood that, in his view at least, the tongues in which the Corinthians spoke were not literally "the language of angels" (cf. v. 1).

[545] Cited in Thiselton, *First Corinthians*, 1064; see also BDAG, s.v. "μέρος," 1.c.

[546] The "for" (γάρ) linking v. 12 to v. 11 suggests that, strictly speaking, v. 12 should be read not as a second and parallel illustration of the same idea as the one illustrated in v. 11 but as an explanation for why the statement Paul is asserting by means of the analogy in v. 11 is a valid one.

prided themselves. The concluding sentence of verse 11 ("When I became a man, I put aside childish things") is not a call for the Corinthians to "put aside" prophecy and knowledge. In terms of the metaphor, they (and Paul himself, as well) are still living under the "childish" conditions of the present age. But it does carry an implied rebuke to any arrogant overestimation they may have regarding the comprehensiveness and finality of their knowledge or the capacity of their reasoning powers to transcend the limits of their creaturely finitude.

The second illustration, in verse 12, likens the knowledge we have "now," in the present age, to the experience of seeing δι᾽ ἐσόπτρου ἐν αἰνίγματι ("only a reflection as in a mirror"), contrasting it with the knowledge we will have "then," in the age to come, when we will see πρόσωπον πρὸς πρόσωπον ("face to face"). Given that contrast between the indirectness and imperfection of our current knowledge and the perfect immediacy of the knowledge we will have in the age to come, it is entirely appropriate that the gifts we depend upon now will become redundant then. The contrast between seeing ἐν αἰνίγματι and seeing πρόσωπον πρὸς πρόσωπον, in the context of a discussion about the gift of prophecy, suggests an allusion to the words of God in LXX Numbers 12:6–8, where a contrast is drawn between the way in which God speaks to a prophet "in riddles" (δι᾽ αἰνιγμάτων) and the way in which he speaks with Moses "face to face" (στόμα κατὰ στόμα). Paul's use of the phrase πρόσωπον πρὸς πρόσωπον rather than στόμα κατὰ στόμα is consistent with the fact that his primary focus is on "seeing" rather than "speaking" and may also reflect the influence of the similar language used of Moses in Deuteronomy 34:10, where it is said of him that the Lord "knew [him] face to face" (πρόσωπον κατὰ πρόσωπον). The influence of Deuteronomy 34:10 may also be part of the reason for Paul's additional comment in verse 12b, "as I am fully known" (see also Num 12:6),[547] which underlines the relational focus of Paul's idea of knowledge, in line with his earlier statements in 1 Corinthians 8:2–3 regarding knowledge, love, and being known by God.

Verse 13 concludes the chapter with a climactic summary statement about the supreme excellence of love, first placing it alongside faith and hope in a triad that is a recurring feature of his letters (cf. Gal 5:5–6; Col 1:4–5; 1 Thess 1:3; 5:8), then singling it out for special mention as "the

[547] Cf. Ciampa and Rosner, "1 Corinthians," 739.

greatest of these." The opening phrase, νυνὶ δὲ μένει ("Now these three remain"), is probably logical and not temporal in its meaning,[548] picturing faith, hope, and love as remaining "on the table" in a logical or rhetorical sense.[549] It should not be read as making a statement about the eschatological permanence of faith and hope. If anything, the context probably implies the opposite, if "faith" and "hope" carry the same meaning here as they do in Romans 4:18–21; 8:24–25. Love, on the other hand, remains as an eternal bond between believers and God and between believers and one another, perfected rather than superseded in the age to come.

Bridge

Application of 1 Corinthians 13 needs to take into account both the features of this chapter that link it directly to its immediate context in the letter and the features that transcend or exceed the requirements of that context.

The description of love Paul gives within this chapter is, on the one hand, a pointed and powerful word against precisely the sorts of attitudes that the Corinthian elite were displaying in their misuse of the gifts that they prized and boasted in (and in the various other dysfunctions of the Corinthian community that Paul alludes to along the way). Most of us do not need to look far within our own contexts to see attitudes and practices that are closely similar (or legitimately analogous) to the Corinthian practices that Paul is implicitly rebuking within this chapter through the contrasting features that he highlights in his description of love. Nor is it difficult to identify habits and customs that have the effect (whether intentionally or unintentionally) of prioritizing charisma or ability over the kind of authentic love that Paul singles out in this chapter as the truly indispensable requirement for Christian life and ministry.

But 1 Corinthians 13 is not merely a word of rebuke or a narrowly targeted corrective to a particular set of dysfunctions in the Corinthians' understanding and practice of the things of the Spirit. Paul's decision to elaborate on the theme in the manner that he does within this chapter

[548] Cf. the logical rather than temporal sense in which the phrase νυνὶ δέ is used on the two other occasions in which it occurs in this epistle, in 1 Cor 12:18; 15:20. Also worth noting is Paul's choice to use νυνὶ δέ here rather than continue with the word ἄρτι ("now") that he has used on two occasions in an unambiguously temporal sense in the immediately preceding verse.

[549] Cf. Thiselton, *First Corinthians*, 1071–72.

and the encomium form that he chooses to adopt in so doing suggest the possibility of a wider form of application that includes, rather than displacing, the corrective use of the chapter as a remedy for Corinthian-style dysfunctions. Love, as Paul describes it in this chapter, is not merely a better approach to church and the gifts of the Spirit but an all-embracing "way" (cf. 12:31b) to be celebrated, delighted in, and "pursue[d]" (14:1) in all things, both in this age and in the age to come.[550] We are therefore entitled (and obliged) to apply this chapter broadly as well as narrowly, and in a celebratory as well as in a corrective fashion, tracing out examples from its limitless field of possible connections to the circumstances and scenarios of our world and training one another to view the whole of life through this lens.

C. Prophecy, Tongues, and Building Up the Body of Christ (14:1–40)

> Pursue love and desire spiritual gifts, and especially that you may
> prophesy. 2 For the person who speaks in a tongue is not speaking to
> people but to God, since no one understands him; he speaks mysteries
> in the Spirit. 3 On the other hand, the person who prophesies speaks
> to people for their strengthening, encouragement, and consolation.
> 4 The person who speaks in a tongue builds himself up, but the one who
> prophesies builds up the church. 5 I wish all of you spoke in tongues, but
> even more that you prophesied. The person who prophesies is greater
> than the person who speaks in tongues, unless he interprets so that
> the church may be built up.
>
> 6 So now, brothers and sisters, if I come to you speaking in tongues,
> how will I benefit you unless I speak to you with a revelation or knowl-
> edge or prophecy or teaching? 7 Even lifeless instruments that produce
> sounds—whether flute or harp—if they don't make a distinction in the
> notes, how will what is played on the flute or harp be recognized? 8 In
> fact, if the bugle makes an unclear sound, who will prepare for battle?
> 9 In the same way, unless you use your tongue for intelligible speech,
> how will what is spoken be known? For you will be speaking into the air.
> 10 There are doubtless many different kinds of languages in the world,
> none is without meaning. 11 Therefore, if I do not know the meaning of
> the language, I will be a foreigner to the speaker, and the speaker will
> be a foreigner to me. 12 So also you—since you are zealous for spiritual
> gifts, seek to excel in building up the church.

[550] Cf. Gardner, *1 Corinthians*, 583–84.

[13] Therefore the person who speaks in a tongue should pray that he
can interpret. [14] For if I pray in a tongue, my spirit prays, but my understanding is unfruitful. [15] What then? I will pray with the spirit, and
I will also pray with my understanding. I will sing praise with the spirit,
and I will also sing praise with my understanding. [16] Otherwise, if you
praise with the spirit, how will the outsider say "Amen" at your giving
of thanks, since he does not know what you are saying? [17] For you may
very well be giving thanks, but the other person is not being built up.
[18] I thank God that I speak in tongues more than all of you; [19] yet in the
church I would rather speak five words with my understanding, in order
to teach others also, than ten thousand words in a tongue.

[20] Brothers and sisters, don't be childish in your thinking, but be infants
in regard to evil and adult in your thinking. [21] It is written in the law,

> **I will speak to this people**
> **by people of other tongues**
> **and by the lips of foreigners,**
> **and even then, they will not listen to me,**

says the Lord. [22] Speaking in tongues, then, is intended as a sign, not for
believers but for unbelievers, while prophecy is not for unbelievers but
for believers. [23] If, therefore, the whole church assembles together and
all are speaking in tongues and people who are outsiders or unbelievers
come in, will they not say that you are out of your minds? [24] But if all
are prophesying and some unbeliever or outsider comes in, he is convicted by all and is called to account by all. [25] The secrets of his heart
will be revealed, and as a result he will fall facedown and worship God,
proclaiming, "God is really among you."

[26] What then, brothers and sisters? Whenever you come together, each
one has a hymn, a teaching, a revelation, a tongue, or an interpretation. Everything is to be done for building up. [27] If anyone speaks in
a tongue, there are to be only two, or at the most three, each in turn,
and let someone interpret. [28] But if there is no interpreter, that person
is to keep silent in the church and speak to himself and God. [29] Two or
three prophets should speak, and the others should evaluate. [30] But if
something has been revealed to another person sitting there, the first
prophet should be silent. [31] For you can all prophesy one by one, so
that everyone may learn and everyone may be encouraged. [32] And the
prophets' spirits are subject to the prophets, [33] since God is not a God
of disorder but of peace.

As in all the churches of the saints, [34] the women should be silent in
the churches, for they are not permitted to speak, but are to submit
themselves, as the law also says. [35] If they want to learn something,
let them ask their own husbands at home, since it is disgraceful for a

woman to speak in the church. [36] Or did the word of God originate from you, or did it come to you only?

[37] If anyone thinks he is a prophet or spiritual, he should recognize that what I write to you is the Lord's command. [38] If anyone ignores this, he will be ignored. [39] So then, my brothers and sisters, be eager to prophesy, and do not forbid speaking in tongues. [40] But everything is to be done decently and in order.

Context/Structure/Form

Paul has already introduced the topic of matters of the Spirit in chapter 12, emphasizing acknowledgment of Christ's lordship as the essential criterion of true spirituality, the diversity of gifts within the body as an indispensable gift from God, the solidarity and interdependence of all the body's members, and the special honor to be given to those who are weakest and least esteemed. The discussion of the topic in chapter 12 concludes with a command to the Corinthians to "desire the greater gifts" (12:31a) and a promise that Paul will show the Corinthians "an even better way" (12:31b).

Having delivered on the promise of 12:31b in the encomium to love that follows immediately in chapter 13, Paul now returns to the command of 12:31a, reiterating it in 14:1 in an expanded form that places it beneath an overarching exhortation to "pursue love" (14:1; cf. ch. 13) and begins the process of unpacking the reference in 12:31b to "the greater gifts," by adding the phrase, "and especially that you may prophesy."

What follows in the remainder of chapter 14 is focused largely on explaining, expanding on, and applying that command. The first half of the chapter, in verses 1–25, is composed chiefly of argument and explanation, giving reasons for the priority Paul places on the gift of prophecy, with a particular focus on its superiority over the gift of tongues for the purpose of "build[ing] up the church" (v. 4). After the epideictic interlude in chapter 13, the form of the argument in 14:1–25 is clearly deliberative, framed as an appeal to the collective advantage of the congregation.[551]

The second half of the chapter, in verses 26–40, gives a series of instructions that apply the general principle of verse 26 ("Everything is to be done for building up") to various aspects of the Corinthian gathering,

[551] Cf. Witherington, *Conflict and Community*, 274.

including the exercise of the gift of tongues (vv. 27–28) and the ordering and evaluation of prophecies (vv. 29–36). The latter section includes an excursus requiring women to maintain silence, asking questions of their husbands at home rather than speaking in the assembly (vv. 33b–36), which is probably focused specifically on the interrogative processes that the church followed as part of the evaluation of prophecies. It is followed by a brief word of warning addressed to members of the Corinthian church who consider themselves to be "prophets" or "spiritual" and may feel entitled to ignore or dissent from Paul's instructions (vv. 37–38) and a final summary word addressed to the whole congregation in verses 39–40, tying together the themes of the chapter.[552]

Comments

14:1. Paul begins chapter 14 by returning to the command that he gave at the end of chapter 12, where he encouraged the Corinthians to "desire the greater gifts" (ζηλοῦτε ... τὰ χαρίσματα τὰ μείζονα).[553] The original version of the command, in 12:31, was accompanied by a promise from Paul that he would show the Corinthians "an even better way" (which he immediately goes on to do in the encomium to love that follows in ch. 13). It also offers little detail on how the Corinthians are to determine which gifts count as the "greater gifts," though the preceding paragraphs (esp. 12:14–26) make it clear that what he does not have in mind is an endorsement of the status distinctions that have been the preoccupation of the Corinthian elite. Now, in the reiterated version of the command, Paul picks up both of these threads, preceding the command to "desire spiritual gifts" (ζηλοῦτε δὲ τὰ πνευματικά)[554] with an exhortation to "pursue love" (Διώκετε τὴν ἀγάπην) and commencing the process of explaining

---

[552] For a helpful and slightly more detailed analysis of the structure of vv. 26–40, see Garland, *1 Corinthians*, 655–56.

[553] See the discussion above in the comments on 12:31 for the arguments in favor of reading ζηλοῦτε as an imperative rather than an indicative and interpreting the sentence as a command rather than as a criticism.

[554] The shift of terminology from χαρίσματα in 12:31 (which is probably Paul's preferred term; see comments above on 12:4) to πνευματικά in 14:1 (which is probably the Corinthians' preferred term) probably reflects the fact that Paul is happy that he has now done enough work in chs. 12–13 to reframe the discussion and can return to the language that was used by the Corinthians in the relevant section of their letter (cf. 12:1).

what might be meant by "the greater gifts" by adding the phrase, "and especially that you may prophesy" (μᾶλλον δὲ ἵνα προφητεύητε).[555]

14:2–4. Verses 2–4 commence the argument Paul offers in verses 2–25 as support for the priority that he has placed on prophecy in the previous verse,[556] with a particular focus on the superior claims of prophecy over the tongues speaking that appears to have been so highly valued by those among the Corinthians who considered themselves to be "spiritual." He begins, therefore, with a description in verse 2 of the audience, content, and function of tongues speaking that he places in contrast with a parallel description in verse 3 of the audience and function of tongues speaking, before drawing a summary conclusion in verse 4 regarding the different contributions that both gifts make to the task of "building up" the people of God.

The description of tongues speaking in verse 2 is clearly positive in its tone and content, even as Paul lays the groundwork for the contrasts in verses 3–4 that will confirm the superior contribution that prophecy makes to the building up of the church: "The person who speaks in a tongue is not speaking to people but to God, since no one understands him; he speaks mysteries in the Spirit."[557] As Witherington correctly argues, Paul's description of the tongues speaker as "not speaking to people but to God," uttering "mysteries in the Spirit," suggests two likely inferences: (1) The "language" used is not an ordinary human language but a special mode of prayer; and (2) even after the utterance has been "interpreted" for the benefit of others, the end product is not equivalent to prophecy, since it is praise or lament poured out before God, not exhortation directed toward other people.[558]

---

[555] The context (particularly the heavy emphasis Paul has placed on the diversity of the gifts in ch. 12, the plural form of the "greater gifts" that Paul refers to in 12:31, and the closely similar—though not identical—use of the word in 14:5) supports the decision made by the translators of most English versions (including the CSB) to render μᾶλλον as "especially" (BDAG, s.v. "μᾶλλον," 2.b), not "rather" (BDAG, s.v. "μᾶλλον," 3.d). Cf. Brookins and Longenecker, *1 Corinthians 10–16*, 99. For a discussion of the meaning of "prophesy" and "prophecy" within chs. 12–14, see the comments above on 12:10.

[556] Hence the conjunction γάρ ("for") that connects v. 2 with the preceding sentence.

[557] The CSB's translation of πνεύματι as "in the Spirit" is probably the most likely sense in which Paul is using the word, given Paul's earlier reference in 12:3 to people "speaking by the Spirit of God" (ἐν πνεύματι θεοῦ λαλῶν), but given the way Paul goes on to use πνεῦμα in a similar context in 14:14–16, the NIV 1984 translation of the phrase ("with his spirit") is also a possibility.

[558] Witherington, *Conflict and Community*, 280–81.

The description of prophecy in verse 3 is the closest thing we have in 1 Corinthians to a functional definition of what Paul had in mind by the gift, but even here the detail Paul provides is scanty. This is presumably because Paul can work on the assumption that the Corinthians are already familiar with what prophecy is and he has no need to provide them with a full definition. His purpose is simply to highlight those features of the gift that are most salient to the point he is making in the contrast that he is drawing here between prophecy and tongues.[559]

Unlike tongues speaking, prophecy is directed "to people," and the content it conveys is not "mysteries" that "no one understands" (v. 2) but rather a message that is for the "strengthening, encouragement, and consolation" (οἰκοδομὴν καὶ παράκλησιν καὶ παραμυθίαν) of its human audience. These three terms should probably be understood as broadly synonymous in meaning and not as referring to three specific and distinct kinds of prophetic message. The first of the three (which is the cognate noun of the verb to "build up" that Paul uses repeatedly throughout this chapter) should certainly not be narrowly defined, since Paul goes on to say in verse 26 that "everything" is to be done "for building up" (πρὸς οἰκοδομήν).

Paul's introduction of the word οἰκοδομή ("strengthening," "building up") in verse 3 serves as a kind of bridge between his advocacy for prophecy in verses 2–25, his instructions regarding the orderly and edifying use of gifts in verses 26–40, and the command to "pursue love" with which the chapter commenced. As Paul has already said in 8:1, "love builds up" (ἡ ... ἀγάπη οἰκοδομεῖ); the building up of fellow believers through the prioritizing of prophecy and the orderly exercise of the gifts is the particular form that love takes when applied to the practice of "matters of the Spirit" within the assembly.

This focus on "building up" continues in verse 4, where Paul states the key point that he wishes to draw out from the comparison between tongues and prophecy that he has made in verses 2–3: "The person who speaks in a tongue builds himself up, but the one who prophesies builds up the church." Thiselton tentatively argues for the possibility that the

---

[559] A further reason for the vagueness of the description Paul gives may be that he is using the word as a kind of umbrella term for a variety of intelligible and edifying Spirit-enabled utterances (cf. Hays, *First Corinthians*, 237). See the comments above on 12:10 and the variety in form, content, and function that seems to be embraced by the reference to prophecy (and related terms) in the discussion here in ch. 14.

self-edification spoken of in verse 4a might be evaluated by Paul not as a positive phenomenon but as an altogether negative one—a matter of "building up" one's own ego and status within the community.[560] As Thiselton grants, however, this critique would apply only to untranslated tongues in the assembly, not to the use of tongues in private prayer,[561] and the other things said about tongues in the immediate context—e.g., the statement about his own use of tongues in verse 5a—would suggest that the latter is what Paul has in mind in verse 4a. It is probably best, therefore, to take 4a as attributing to tongues speaking (as a form of private prayer) a genuine, though limited, good that consists in the encouraging and consoling effect that it has for tongue speakers who have been able to pour out their hearts before God. This limited good is contrasted in verse 4b with the greater good accomplished through prophecy, which builds up not merely the speaker but the whole church.

14:5. Verse 5 draws out explicitly the implications of verse 4 for assessing the relative values of prophecy and tongues: "I wish all of you spoke in tongues, but even more that you prophesied. The person who prophesies is greater than the person who speaks in tongues, unless he interprets so that the church may be built up." The opening statement is both a warmly positive affirmation of the value of tongues speaking and a preparation for the much warmer affirmation of prophecy that follows immediately after it. Both statements (and especially the first) should be read against the background of the earlier discussion in chapter 12 regarding the essential diversity of gifts within the body and the sovereign freedom of the Spirit in distributing them: Paul's wish is sincere and is consistent with his own practice and the benefit that he derives from it (cf. vv. 4, 18), but he is aware that God does not bestow every gift on every member of the body.

The statement in verse 5b that the person who prophesies is "greater" (μείζων) than the one who speaks in tongues should likewise be read against the background of chapter 12, not as an attempt by Paul to replace one elitist status hierarchy with another but as a functional distinction based on the relative contributions made by the two gifts to the building up of God's people and a clarification of what he had in mind by his

[560] Cf. the negative use of the same verb οἰκοδομέω in 8:10 (though with a different kind of negativity in view in that instance) and the implied equation in 10:23–24 between "build[ing] up" and seeking the good of the other rather than one's own good.

[561] Thiselton, *First Corinthians*, 1094–95.

earlier encouragement to "desire the greater (μείζονα) gifts" (12:31). This assertion regarding the lesser benefit conveyed by the person who speaks in tongues is qualified by the proviso, "unless he interprets so that the church may be built up." The CSB's translation of the opening phrase of this proviso is a more obvious and natural way of reading the Greek than the NRSV's "unless someone translates," which imports into verse 5 the idea from verse 27 that the interpreter of an utterance spoken in a tongue might sometimes be a person other than the original tongue speaker.[562] The wording of verse 27 certainly allows for that possibility, but here, as in verse 13, Paul's assumption appears to be that under normal circumstances the most obvious candidate for the role of interpreter (i.e., for putting into words the motivating source of the praise or lament that was poured out inarticulately as an utterance in a tongue) is the person who has spoken the original utterance.[563]

14:6–12. In verses 6–12 Paul offers further support for his basic assertion regarding the superior benefit conferred to the community by prophecy rather than tongues. A hypothetical and rhetorical question regarding his own practice in verse 6 is followed by a pair of parallel illustrations in verses 7–8 (musical instruments used for entertainment or in military contexts) and verses 10–11 (meaningless sounds and foreign languages), each of which is applied directly to the Corinthians as either a rhetorical question and explanatory statement (v. 9) or as a command (v. 12). The central theme of the paragraph is intelligibility, which Paul stresses as an essential requirement for spoken communication that will build up the church.

The scenario Paul asks his readers to imagine in the rhetorical question of verse 6 is clearly a hypothetical one. Paul (as he goes on to make clear in v. 18) is an enthusiastic tongue speaker but, as the readers will no doubt be able to recall, his contributions to the gathered assembly of God's people are deliberately intelligible and focused on conferring benefit to his

---

[562] In the absence of an indication such as the indefinite article τις ("someone"), the NRSV's reading is an unlikely sense for Paul's language to be carrying. Cf. Brookins and Longenecker, *First Corinthians 10–16*, 103.

[563] As argued above in the comments on 12:10, Thiselton is convincing in his arguments for understanding διερμηνεύω ("interpret") as referring not to the "translating" of what was spoken by the tongue speaker into a message to the congregation but rather a "putting into words" of "the ground of prayer, praise, joy or longing" that was vocalized in the utterance originally spoken "in the Spirit" as a "mystery" addressed to God. Thiselton, *First Corinthians*, 1099.

hearers: "Now, brothers and sisters," he asks the Corinthians, "if I come to you speaking in tongues, how will I benefit you unless I speak to you with a revelation or knowledge or prophecy or teaching?" The focus of the question on how Paul's contribution "will ... benefit" (ὠφελήσω) the Corinthians is consistent with the deliberative tenor of Paul's rhetoric and the form of his argument as an appeal to advantage. Strictly speaking, the syntax of the question suggests the possibility of Paul coming to the Corinthians speaking in tongues and conferring a benefit on them by conveying "a revelation or knowledge or prophecy or teaching" in that form (presumably through an interpretation of the utterance), but to take his question that way would be to read Paul's ἐὰν μὴ ("unless") in an overly literalistic manner and ignore his statements elsewhere (e.g., vv. 3, 14–17) about the normal content and audience of an utterance spoken in a tongue. If Paul is to benefit the Corinthians, rather than a tongue he will bring them a message along the lines of the four words that he strings together in verse 6b ("a revelation or knowledge or prophecy or teaching").

Like the three words Paul links in verse 3 to speak about the beneficial effect of prophecy for its hearers, the four words Paul uses here to describe the kind of message that would confer such a benefit should probably not be teased out too precisely from each other as technical terms referring to different and neatly distinguishable activities. "Prophecy," in particular, appears to function throughout chapter 14 as an umbrella term for a variety of different intelligible and edifying word ministries, and Paul's use of the language of "revelation" (ἀποκάλυψις),[564] "knowledge" (γνῶσις),[565] and "teaching" (διδαχή)[566] and their cognates elsewhere in the letter suggests the likelihood of significant overlap between them.

Verses 7–8 reinforce the point by means of two illustrations relating to musical instruments ("lifeless instruments that produce sounds"). The first, in verse 7, asks the readers to imagine the sounds made by a flute or a harp, stressing the need for "distinction in the notes" (διαστολὴν τοῖς φθόγγοις) if the tune being played is to be "recognized" (γνωσθήσεται) by the hearers. The second, in verse 8, raises the stakes by changing the instrument from a flute or harp to a trumpet and shifting the scene to a

[564] Cf. 2:10; 14:26, 30.

[565] Cf. especially 1:5; 8:1, 7, 10, 11; 12:8; 13:2, 8.

[566] Cf. 14:26; 12:28–29.

battlefield: "In fact, if the bugle makes an unclear sound, who will prepare for battle?" This extension or adaptation of the metaphor reflects the urgency that Paul attaches to the task of edification; what is taking place in the gathering is not merely artistic expression or entertainment but encouragement for battle. Verse 9 makes the point of the analogy explicit, with an accent on the need for "intelligible speech" (εὔσημον λόγον) in order that the content of the message being spoken might be "known" (γνωσθήσεται) by the hearers. In the absence of that essential requirement (for example, in the case of untranslated tongues), the Corinthians will be merely "speaking into the air" (εἰς ἀέρα λαλοῦντες).

Verses 10–11 offer another illustration for the Corinthians to consider: "There are doubtless many different kinds of languages in the world, none is without meaning. Therefore, if I do not know the meaning of the language, I will be a foreigner to the speaker, and the speaker will be a foreigner to me." Here the comparison Paul draws is with speaking in an unknown language. (The fact Paul can use a foreign language as an *analogy* for tongues speaking further increases the likelihood that he understands the "tongues" given by the Spirit as something other than real human languages.) He begins by pointing out the vast diversity of languages spoken in the world,[567] all of which make a sound.[568] Verse 11 completes Paul's point: every language makes some kind of noise, but to those who do not understand it, it is meaningless babble.[569]

In verse 12 Paul draws the conclusion from the preceding illustrations, introducing his point with the same construction, οὕτως καὶ ὑμεῖς ("So also you"), he has previously used in verse 9 to draw out the point of his

---

[567] The expression εἰ τύχοι (CSB: "doubtless") that he uses to invite the Corinthians to contemplate their number is the aorist optative form of τυγχάνω (literally: "if it should so happen ..."). It functions idiomatically to convey the sense, "it may be that ..." or perhaps (as Conzelmann, Fee, and Garland suggest) "who knows how many, if one were to count them ..." Cf. Conzelmann, *1 Corinthians*, 232; Fee, *First Epistle to the Corinthians*, 736; Garland, *1 Corinthians*, 643.

[568] The phrase καὶ οὐδὲν ἄφωνον at the end of v. 10 is probably not (yet) making the claim that all of the languages have "meaning" (CSB); the more natural way of reading the expression is that Paul is continuing to play on the multiple senses of φωνή ("voice," "sound," "language") and using ἄφωνος here in its commonest sense of "mute" or "silent" to lay the groundwork for the simple point, made in the following verse, that mere sound, in and of itself, does not communicate meaning to the hearer. Cf. Conzelmann, *1 Corinthians*, 236.

[569] βάρβαρος ("foreigner") is a word that focuses on the *linguistic* foreignness of the other and is possibly onomatopoeic in origin, imitating the way in which foreign speech falls on the ear of the uncomprehending hearer like nonsense syllables. Cf. BDAG, s.v. "βάρβαρος."

earlier analogy. Here in verse 12, the conclusion Paul draws is explicitly practical and directed to the readers as an imperative: "Since you are zealous for spiritual gifts, seek to excel in building up the church." The wording Paul uses to frame the command is probably intended to imply a subtle critique of their current practice and attitude: unlike the earlier encouragements he has given to them to "desire ... the gifts" (ζηλοῦτε ... τὰ χαρίσματα) or "desire spiritual gifts" (ζηλοῦτε ... τὰ πνευματικά), Paul's description here pictures them as ζηλωταί ... πνευμάτων (literally, "desirous of spirits"). That expression carries uncomfortable connotations, suggesting the possibility that their competitive eagerness to excel one another and their eagerness for manifestations of spirituality are the outworkings of an impulse that is dangerously close to the ethos of pagan polytheism, replacing trust in the one, wise Spirit of God who sovereignly apportions the gifts with a mentality that chases after a multiplicity of "spirits" to be appropriated and tapped into by the worshipers.[570] In place of that competitive and divisive quest, Paul urges them (without abandoning their enthusiasm for things of the Spirit) to focus their energies on "seek[ing] to excel in building up the church."[571]

14:13–19. The broad and general exhortation of verse 12 is now given more focused and practical application to tongue speakers in verses 13–19. Once again (as earlier in v. 6) Paul appeals to his own example, but in this more developed discussion Paul's self-depiction as a tongue

---

[570] Cf. Richard Oster, *1 Corinthians* (Joplin: College Press, 1995), 320, and Lietzmann and Kümmel, *An die Korinther I-II*, quoted (without agreement) in Conzelmann, *1 Corinthians*, 237. Oster and Lietzmann both argue for a strong view of this interpretation, taking Paul's words as an indication that some of the Corinthians were in fact consciously holding to an "animistic" perspective, "as if it were each man's wish that a πνεῦμα [προφητικόν] would take up its abode in him" (Lietzmann, as translated in Conzelmann, *1 Corinthians*, 237). Ciampa and Rosner reject this interpretation, arguing that "if Paul had such a pagan perspective in mind, it hardly seems likely that he would have offered as mild a corrective as is found in the following clause." Ciampa and Rosner, *The First Letter to the Corinthians*, 685. Their point has some weight, and the argument probably holds good against strong versions of the interpretation such as Oster's and Lietzmann's. But a plausible case can still be made for Conzelmann's more modest claim that Paul's language here and there within chs. 12–14 is colored by connotations that suggest "a glimpse of an animistic background," and the idea that Paul might be hinting at paganizing tendencies in the Corinthians' attitude to spiritual phenomena is entirely consistent with his initial framing of the topic in 12:1–3.

[571] A similar rhetorical strategy, applied to a different (though not altogether dissimilar) problem, may be seen in Paul's paradoxical command in Rom 12:10 to "take the lead in honoring one another." Cf. Harrison, *Paul and the Ancient Celebrity Circuit*, 250.

speaker includes elements that are clearly more than hypothetical in nature.

He begins in verse 13 with an instruction for tongue speakers, drawn as an inference (διό, "therefore") from the argument of the previous paragraph: "Therefore the person who speaks in a tongue should pray that he can interpret." As was the case in his earlier reference in verse 5 to the "interpret[ing]" of an utterance spoken in a tongue, Paul's assumption here appears to be that the most natural candidate for the role of putting into words the underlying, precognitive ground of an utterance that has been spoken in a tongue is the original tongue speaker (if God grants that person the ability to do so).[572]

Verse 14 supplies a reason for that instruction: "For if I pray in a tongue, my spirit prays, but my understanding is unfruitful." Given that Paul goes on to claim that he speaks in tongues "more than all of you" (v. 18), this description in verse 14 should almost certainly be taken as a reflection on personal experience rather than as an a priori judgment or a hypothetical scenario. The description of tongues-speaking as an experience in which "my spirit prays" may be a reference to the deep, innermost workings of the subconscious mind (cf. 2:11), the breath that gives voice to those inward impulses (cf. Ps 150:6), or some combination of both of these. Although Paul's spirit is active when he prays in a tongue, his mind is "unfruitful" (ἄκαρπος): because he is pouring forth sound but his conscious mind is not at work to organize these outpourings into coherent thoughts and words, he is unable to give "fruit" (i.e., benefit) to others.

In verse 15 Paul draws the practical conclusion (τί οὖν ἐστιν; "What then?") from the reflection on his experience in the previous verse: "I will pray with the spirit, and I will also pray with my understanding. I will sing praise with the spirit, and I will also sing praise with my understanding."[573] The answer, as Paul sees it, is not to give up speaking in tongues but to complement the noncognitive outpourings of his tongues speaking with prayers and praises that can be brought before God with the conscious understanding of an active mind. The primary implied context in which

---

[572] Cf. Thiselton, *First Corinthians*, 1107–8.

[573] The references in vv. 15–16 to praying "with the spirit" are probably best understood as carrying the same meaning as the earlier reference in v. 14 to contexts in which "my spirit prays."

he will adopt this strategy (or at least the latter part of it) is the gathered assembly or other situations in which he is in the presence of others and wishes his prayers to be accessible to them (cf. vv. 16–17), though it may also be that he envisages a similar approach in his private prayers, so that he himself is able to experience the double benefit of an outpoured heart and a fruitful mind. It is not entirely clear, as Hays points out, whether the two forms of prayer Paul speaks of engaging in under this complementary approach are to be thought of as taking place simultaneously or sequentially, though the previous instruction in verse 13 would suggest that the latter is more likely if Paul's prayer "with the spirit" takes the form of praying in a tongue.[574] Alternatively, Paul may be speaking of an approach when he prays in the company of others of replacing the noncognitive outpourings of tongues-speaking with a mode of prayer and praise in which both his spirit (i.e., his innermost being and/or the breath that gives voice to his utterances) and his mind are simultaneously active—an approach that would appear to be consistent with the preference he goes on to state in verse 19.[575] Either way, whether the respective contributions of spirit and mind are simultaneous or sequential, the combined effect Paul seeks is one in which prayers and praises offered to God when Christians gather together involve both the heart (or as Paul puts it here, the spirit) and the mind, in harmony and interdependent cooperation: "If only the mind is active, everything remains at a theoretical level; if only the heart is active, the door lies open to self-deception and credulity. If both are open to the Holy Spirit, the result can build up the community and bear the fruit (v. 14a) of love for the other."[576]

Verses 16–17 underscore the importance of the advice in verses 13–15 by pointing out the adverse consequence where believers insist on bringing uninterpreted tongues into contexts of communal prayer and praise: "Otherwise, if you praise with the spirit, how will the outsider say 'Amen' at your giving of thanks, since he does not know what you are saying? For you may very well be giving thanks, but the other person is not being built up." The terms in which Paul describes that scenario are consistent with his earlier statement in verse 2 that tongues-speaking, as he

---

[574] Hays, *First Corinthians*, 237.

[575] This is the interpretation favored by Ciampa and Rosner, *The First Letter to the Corinthians*, 690.

[576] Thiselton, *First Corinthians*, 103.

envisages it, is a form of utterance (in this case, thanksgiving) that is directed primarily to God. The "outsider" (ὁ ἀναπληρῶν τὸν τόπον τοῦ ἰδιώτου; literally, "the one filling the place of the uninformed") is probably not to be pictured as one of the "unbelievers" (ἄπιστοι) to whom Paul later refers in conjunction with "outsiders" (ἰδιῶται) in verse 23. At this stage in the discussion the person Paul has in mind appears to be a fellow believer who would have wanted to join in saying "Amen" to the prayer of thanksgiving but has been left excluded from that by the fact that the utterance was spoken in a tongue and left uninterpreted. The effect of that was to put the hearer into "the place of the uninformed"—i.e., to push them (by the very act of praying in an uninterpreted tongue) into the situation of someone who is uninformed and excluded.[577] As a consequence, "you may very well be giving thanks, but the other person is not being built up"[578]—language that echoes the stress Paul has already placed on the importance of behavior that "builds up the other" and "builds up the church" (cf. 8:1; 10:23–24; 14:3–5) and makes it clear that in Paul's view the upbuilding function of the interactions within the gathering is fulfilled not only by the exercise of prophecy, narrowly defined, but by a variety of other activities (including, in this instance, the experience of joining together with fellow believers in a prayer of thanks to which all can say "Amen").

Verses 18–19 complete the paragraph, concluding the reflections offered by Paul on his own experience as an example to the Corinthians. They take the form of two complementary statements, both framed in hyperbolic terms, expressing Paul's respective evaluations of tongues (v. 18) and words spoken "with my understanding" (v. 19). The evaluation of tongues implied by verse 18 ("I thank God that I speak in tongues more than all of you") is enthusiastically positive and performs a rhetorical function similar to Paul's enthusiastic statements in chapter 7 regarding his own singleness (7:7–8), highlighting the common ground he shares with those whom he is about to correct and making it clear that his

---

[577] Cf. Ciampa and Rosner, *The First Letter to the Corinthians*, 692; Hays, *First Corinthians*, 237; Garland, *1 Corinthians*, 641.

[578] The first half of the statement ("you may very well be giving thanks") places the pronoun σύ "you" at the front of the clause for heavy emphasis and point/counterpoint contrast with "the other person" (ὁ ἕτερος) and inserts the adverb καλῶς ("very well") in a manner that suggests both a genuine concession and a note of mild sarcasm. Cf. Brookins and Longenecker, *1 Corinthians 10–16*, 113.

critique of the use of untranslated tongues in the gathering is not based on a dismissive attitude toward the practice, in and of itself.[579]

The positive evaluation of tongues that Paul implies by his statement in verse 18 is immediately placed in the shade, however, by the far more positive evaluation Paul gives of words that are spoken "with ... understanding" in verse 19: "yet in the church I would rather speak five words with my understanding, in order to teach others also, than ten thousand words in a tongue." The opening words, "yet in church" (ἀλλ' ἐν ἐκκλησίᾳ), make it clear that his assessment of the superior claims of intelligible communication is specific to that context and not an expression of a more global subordination of the "spirit" to the "mind." Although the immediately preceding context has been focused on speech acts of prayer (vv. 14–15a), praise (vv. 15b–16a), and thanksgiving (vv. 16b–17), the scope of verse 19 is wide and embraces a wide range of possible forms that could be taken by words spoken "with ... understanding." The effect of such words, according to Paul in this verse, is to "teach others also" (καὶ ἄλλους κατηχήσω), with the context implying a range of different ways in which believers might be said to "teach" one another that extends well beyond the boundaries of the specific gift and ministry of those who are "teachers" in the narrower sense of that word (cf. Col 3:16 [using the verbs διδάσκω and νουθετέω]; Rom 15:14 [using the verb νουθετέω]). The terms in which Paul frames the comparison do not rule out altogether the possibility of (interpreted) tongues within the gathering (cf. vv. 13, 27–28) but imply Paul's strong preference for other forms of utterance as more obviously and directly beneficial to others.[580]

14:20–25. Verses 20–25 begin with an initial exhortation to maturity, then direct the readers' attention toward a quotation from Isaiah 28:11–12, which Paul unpacks across the following verses, highlighting the alienating and unbelief-confirming effect of untranslated tongues and contrasting it with the convicting and potentially converting effect of prophecy.

The initial exhortation in verse 20 is framed in broad and general terms: "Brothers and sisters, don't be childish in your thinking, but be infants in regard to evil and adult in your thinking." The implication is that the Corinthians—or, more precisely, the elite within the congregation

---

[579] Cf. Garland, *1 Corinthians*, 642; Fee, *First Epistle to the Corinthians*, 748.

[580] Cf. Carson, *Showing the Spirit*, 105; Ciampa and Rosner, *The First Letter to the Corinthians*, 695.

who style themselves as "the mature" (cf. 2:6–3:4)—are altogether too "adult" in their tolerance of evil and "childish" in their grasp of the wisdom of the Spirit.[581] While this description could be applied to them in relation to a wide range of issues Paul touches on within the letter, its use in the present context is focused primarily on their attitude to the gift of tongues, which exhibits the egocentrism and thoughtlessness of little children rather than the mindset of adults whose roles require them to take responsibility for others and whose life experience and accumulated wisdom enable them to do so. The present tense prohibition (μὴ παιδία γίνεσθε) should probably be translated "stop being children" (with the implication that behaving childishly is exactly what the Corinthians are currently doing). [582]

Verse 21 is a quotation from Isaiah 28:11–12, introduced with the words "It is written in the law."[583] The wording of the quotation differs in several ways from extant versions of the LXX: (1) where the LXX reads διὰ φαυλισμὸν χειλέων διὰ γλώσσης ἑτέρας ("because of contempt from lips, through a different tongue"), Paul's quotation reads ἐν ἑτερογλώσσοις καὶ ἐν χείλεσιν ἑτέρων ("by people of other tongues and by the lips of foreigners"); (2) where the LXX reads ὅτι λαλήσουσιν ("because they will speak"), Paul's quotation reads λαλήσω ("I will speak"); (3) verse 12a in the LXX (λέγοντες αὐτῷ Τοῦτο τὸ ἀνάπαυμα τῷ πεινῶντι καὶ τοῦτο τὸ σύντριμμα, "saying to them, 'This is rest for the hungry, and this is the destruction'" NETS) is omitted altogether from Paul's quotation; and (4) verse 12b in the LXX (καὶ οὐκ ἠθέλησαν ἀκούειν, "yet they would not hear") is replaced in Paul's quotation by καὶ οὐδ' οὕτως εἰσακούσονταί μου, λέγει κύριος ("and even then, they will not listen to me, says the Lord").

The first of these differences may partly be due to the text type Paul is following or to his memory of (or access to) the Hebrew text, the meaning of which is closer to Paul's wording than that of the LXX,[584] but

---

[581] The word translated here as "adult" is the same word τέλειοι that was translated as "mature" in 2:6.

[582] Cf. Thiselton, *First Corinthians*, 1119.

[583] "The law" (ὁ νόμος) is used here to refer to the Scriptures in their entirety (cf. Rom 3:19) rather than more narrowly to the Pentateuch or the law codes contained within it.

[584] Cf. Wilk, "Isaiah in 1 and 2 Corinthians," 142; Ciampa and Rosner, "1 Corinthians," 741; Christopher D. Stanley, *Paul and the Language of Scripture: Citation Technique in the Pauline Epistles and Contemporary Literature*, SNTSMS (Cambridge: Cambridge University Press, 1992), 198; Fee, *First Epistle to the Corinthians*, 753, drawing attention to Origen's claim regarding the (later) translation by Aquila, which (according to Origen) shared with Paul's quotation

it is also worth noting that the different word order, which places ἐν ἑτερογλώσσοις at the start of the quotation, has the effect of highlighting the verbal connection it creates with the practice of tongues speaking. The omission of verse 12a is almost certainly Paul's doing and has the effect of focusing attention on the phenomenon of speech in "other tongues" and "by the lips of foreigners" and their effect on the hearers rather than on the content of the intelligible message previously spoken through the prophets. In Paul's version of the quotation, as in the Hebrew text, the speech in foreign tongues is represented as a form of communication from the Lord himself—a fact that Paul makes more vivid by the first person singular verb λαλήσω ("I will speak") and the added pronoun μου ("to me"). The final line of the quotation, too, appears to be a Pauline adaptation, transforming a report on the past failure of Israel to listen to the message YHWH has spoken to them into a prediction of their future failure to listen even to the new message, communicated through the lips of the "foreigners" who are the agents of his judgment (cf. the similar dark forecast in Isa 28:13).

Despite these multiple adaptations to the original wording (to the extent that we can reconstruct what it was), Paul's use of the quotation shows multiple, and probably deliberate, resonances with the context from which it was taken. In the original context, the sound of a foreign language (the foreign language of Assyrian invaders) is a work of God's judgment on an Israel that will not listen to the clear words of salvation that he has spoken to them through his prophets. Their failure to listen appears to have been the consequence of an overinflated estimation of their own wisdom and an arrogant dismissal of the prophets' message (cf. Isa 28:9–10)—an attitude distressingly similar to that of the Corinthians. Within that context, "the 'sign' of unintelligible speech is a prophetic sign of judgment,"[585] and (as Isaiah forecasts in Isa 28:13 and Paul anticipates in the reworked final line of the quotation in 1 Cor 14:21) its effect is merely to confirm the hearers in their unbelief.

It is that background that appears to be in view in the conclusion Paul draws in verse 22: "Speaking in tongues, then, is intended as a sign, not for believers but for unbelievers, while prophecy is not for unbelievers

---

the reversed order of the references to "tongues" and "lips" and the use of the compound noun ἑτερόγλωσσος.

[585] Hays, *First Corinthians*, 240.

but for believers." At first reading Paul's statement appears to be at odds with his earlier depictions of tongues as a form of speech employed, with self-edifying effect, by believers (vv. 2, 4a, 13–19) and the scenario he goes on to describe in verses 24–25, where prophecy is depicted as benefiting unbelievers, even leading to their conversion. The neatest way of resolving this apparent contradiction is to read Paul's point in verse 22 as focusing on the effect that (uninterpreted) tongues has on its hearers, placing them in the position of outsiders or unbelievers (and if they are already unbelievers, confirming them in that condition), whereas prophecy can have the effect of creating and sustaining faith (and is hence "for believers"). Hence the speech of the Corinthians in the assembly should not be speech that alienates and excludes the hearers but rather speech that fosters (and potentially creates) faith in those who listen.

Paul offers support for that implied conclusion in the two contrasting scenarios that he invites the readers to imagine in verses 23–25. In the first scenario, "the whole church assembles together and all are speaking in tongues and people who are outsiders or unbelievers come in."[586] Here, in contrast to the earlier scenario in verse 16, the ἰδιῶται appear to be genuine "outsiders," as yet uninitiated into an understanding of the Christian faith, rather than fellow believers who have been put into "the place of an outsider" by the exercise of uninterpreted tongues. A related and possibly overlapping category is the "unbelievers" (ἄπιστοι), who may or may not have an intellectual understanding of the content of the Christian faith but do not have a personal allegiance to Jesus.[587] In either case, the conclusion they draw from their encounter with the phenomenon of uninterpreted tongues speaking is that "you are out of your minds" (μαίνεσθε)—a term that can imply either madness (e.g., Acts 12:15;

---

[586] The reference to "all" speaking in tongues is probably not (contra Forbes, *Prophecy and Inspired Speech*, 180; Fee, *First Epistle to the Corinthians*, 758) intended to imply a cacophony of simultaneous tongues-speaking, given that the same language is used in the following verse to picture "all" prophesying, without any suggestion of chaos or confusion. Paul's point is simply that the entire focus of the gathering, in the scenario he is asking his readers to imagine, is on tongues-speaking (v. 23) or prophesying (vv. 24–25).

[587] The scenario is a hypothetical one and does not provide direct evidence that "outsiders" and "unbelievers" were commonly present within the gatherings of early Christians. Nevertheless, it is worth noting that Paul clearly regards their presence as a desirable thing and an opportunity for the kind of witness he goes on to envisage in vv. 24–25, and considers it important that the content of Christian gatherings be intelligible for this reason too, in addition to his desire that the gathering be an edifying experience for the believers who are present.

26:24–25) or a state of ecstasy, under which the speakers are "carried away by some external powerful force, as a devotee of Dionysus might be."[588]

The second scenario, which Paul depicts in verses 24–25, is constructed as a deliberate contrast to the scenario in verse 23. Once again, by implication, the whole church is gathered and an "outsider" or "unbeliever" is present, but in this scenario "all are prophesying" (presumably not simultaneously and not necessarily—given the likely numbers involved and the instructions Paul goes on to give in vv. 29–33—each and every member of the assembly).[589] The effect on the visitor is starkly different from the imagined effect of the encounter with uninterpreted tongues that Paul has described in the previous verse: "he is convicted by all and is called to account by all. The secrets of his heart will be revealed, and as a result he will fall facedown and worship God, proclaiming, 'God is really among you.'"

The description Paul gives in verses 24–25 of the message and its effect is probably not intended to imply that the content of the prophecies was directly targeted at the unbelieving visitor or (more broadly and generically) framed as an evangelistic message addressed to unbelievers. Rather, the visitor is depicted as having walked in on the ordinary content of a Christian gathering (as Paul wishes it to be conducted)—or, more precisely, a hypothetical version of the gathering that is given over entirely to the kind of prophesying activity that Paul wishes the Corinthians to prioritize in their meetings. The same message that communicates the gospel to its primarily intended audience of believers, with Spirit-given insight and applicability to "the secrets of the heart," has an equivalent effect on the visiting unbeliever, causing the visitor to "fall facedown and worship God, proclaiming, 'God is really among you.'" The words that Paul envisages the visitor responding with are an echo of language used in Isaiah 45:14 and Zechariah 8:23.[590] Both of these verses, in their

---

[588] Witherington, *Conflict and Community*, 284. Cf. Homer, *Iliad* 6.132; *Odyssey* 18.406; Achilles Tatius, *Leuc. Clit.* 2.3.

[589] Cf. Thiselton, *First Corinthians*, 1127.

[590] The word οντως ("surely"), added by Paul, implies the astonishment of the visitor at this unexpected encounter with the presence of God. Edwin Judge's comment is worth quoting at length: "[Paul's] only use of a technical term of worship [i.e., προσκυνέω] in connection with the church-meeting is to describe the reaction of the hypothetical unbeliever who is stunned to discover, contrary to what would have seemed obvious, that God was actually present there (1 Cor. 14:25). In that scene of lively social intercourse there was neither solitude nor mystery, no shrine, no statue, no cult, no ceremony, no offering

original contexts, place the words in the mouths of gentiles who wish to join themselves to a restored people of Israel—an aspect of the Old Testament's prophetic hope that Paul appears to have viewed as finding fulfillment in gentiles who become worshipers of Israel's God through their encounter with the people of Christ.[591]

14:26. Having mounted an argument in verses 1–25 in favor of the superiority of prophecy over tongues within the gathering and the indispensability of intelligible discourse that builds up the hearers, Paul now turns in verse 26–40 to draw out the practical implications of that argument. He lays these out in a series of instructions regarding various aspects of the Corinthian gathering, including the exercise of the gift of tongues (vv. 27–28) and the ordering and evaluation of prophecies (vv. 29–36).

The turn from argumentation and basic principles toward particular and practical implications is signaled at the start of verse 26 by the opening phrase, Τί οὖν ἐστιν, ἀδελφοί; ("What then, brothers and sisters?"; cf. v. 15). What comes next in verse 26 is a description of the various verbal contributions that different members of the congregation come to the gathering intending to contribute: "Whenever you come together, each one has a hymn, a teaching, a revelation, a tongue (γλῶσσα), or an interpretation (ἑρμηνεία)." The description should not be read over literally as implying that each and every member brought a contribution of some sort to every gathering of the church, nor should it be taken as a prescriptive list of the five essential components that must be present in every Christian gathering. It does, nevertheless, suggest a strikingly plurivocal and participatory form of meeting, and while the instructions that follow seek to impose a greater degree of order on the way in which the gathering was conducted, Paul's aim is clearly not to extinguish that dynamic (and the instructions in vv. 30–31 may well be intended to protect, rather than to diminish, the ability of multiple speakers to participate).

---

to ensure that all was well between gods and men. Instead there was talk and argument, disturbing questions about belief and behavior (two matters of little or no concern to religion in antiquity), conscious changes to accepted ways, and the expectation of a more drastic transformation soon to come. The purpose of classical religion was to secure what was already there against just such an upheaval." E. A. Judge, "Cultural Conformity and Innovation in Paul: Some Clues from Contemporary Documents," *TynBul* 35 (1984): 6.

[591] Cf. Hays, "Conversion of the Imagination," 391–93; Ciampa and Rosner, "1 Corinthians," 742–43.

The particular items in the list have all been previously mentioned or implied in earlier verses, with "hymn" (ψαλμός) implied by the cognate verb ψάλλω ("sing praise") in verse 15, "teaching" (διδαχή) and "revelation" (ἀποκάλυψις) both mentioned in verse 6, "tongue" (γλῶσσα) mentioned or implied on multiple occasions, and "interpretation" (ἑρμηνεία) implied by the cognate verb διερμηνεύω in verses 5 and 13. Paul's instructions do not give us enough information to say with certainty whether the term ψαλμός is used here to refer exclusively to the canonical hymns of the Psalter or to a wider category that also included other newly composed Christian hymns of praise, but the evidence of Colossians 3:16 would suggest that the songs sung within early Christian gatherings took a variety of forms. A "teaching" brought to the gathering was presumably a message that was composed through a process that involved prior study and reflection and involved the transmission and application of the core traditions of Scripture and the gospel (cf. Col 3:16; Titus 1:9). A "revelation," too, could in some instances be an insight given to the speaker prior to the gathering, though Paul also appears to go out of his way in verse 30 to leave room for the possibility that a revelation might be granted in the midst of the meeting. Paul's references elsewhere to the role played by the Spirit in granting revelation and understanding to believers suggest that the primary content of such revelations consisted in insights, either rational or intuitive in nature, into the entailments of the gospel message and its application to the circumstances of the congregation (cf. 1 Cor 2:10; 14:30; Eph 3:5; Phil 3:15), though texts such as Galatians 2:2 (cf. Acts 11:27–30) suggest the possibility that a "revelation" could also, on occasion, include the disclosure of specific and supernaturally revealed information.

Having listed a few examples of the kinds of contributions various congregation members would typically bring with them to the gathering, Paul lays down at the end of verse 26 the guiding principle that should govern the use of all of them: "Everything is to be done for building up [πρὸς οἰκοδομήν]." This principle is consistent with his earlier depiction of the church as a metaphorical building in the process of being constructed (3:9–17) and his repeated calls for the Corinthians to focus their behavior on what "builds up the other" and "builds up the church" (cf. 8:1; 10:23–24; 14:3–5, 12). Although Paul can on occasion use the language of "building up" to refer to the strengthening or formation of an individual (e.g., 10:23–24 and [ironically] 8:10), the implied context is always a communal one, and the ultimate object of edification is not just the individual but the church.[592]

14:27–28. Having laid down a general principle in verse 26, Paul proceeds to apply it in a series of specific instructions that he gives to the Corinthians in verses 27–36, dealing first with the gift of tongues (vv. 27–28). His instructions regarding tongues are framed in conditional terms ("If anyone speaks in a tongue …"), implying that in his view tongues speaking (with interpretation) is a legitimate but not essential element of the gathering.

If tongues speaking is to be included, Paul lays down three requirements: (1) the number of speakers should be limited to "two, or at the most three"; (2) those who speak in tongues should do so "each in turn" (ἀνὰ μέρος); and (3) there must be interpretation (i.e., the feelings or experiences that generated the impulse to give them expression in a tongue must be put into words so that the hearers can understand and join with the tongue speaker in saying "Amen" to the prayer).[593] The wording of this third requirement (καὶ εἷς διερμηνευέτω, "and let someone interpret" or, more literally, "and let one interpret") should not be taken as a requirement that one single person must be the interpreter of both or all of the utterances; it could, as Thiselton argues,[594] simply mean "someone" (in a sense roughly equivalent to that of the indefinite pronoun τις) and hence leave room for the possibility that the interpretations might be provided by the tongue speakers themselves—a scenario that Paul's earlier instructions seems to have presupposed as the typical or preferred option (vv. 5, 13). If no such interpretation is available (a fact that the tongue speaker is presumably required to be aware of before giving voice to the utterance), then "that person is to keep silent in the church and speak to himself and God." The most obvious meaning implied by this last instruction is that the utterance should be saved for a context of private prayer at home, though (less plausibly, given the communal context and Paul's implied desire for all of the gathered congregation to give their attention to each speaker, one at a time) it might still be

---

592 Cf. Paul S. Minear, *Images of the Church in the New Testament*, 2nd ed. (Louisville: Westminster, 2004), 164; Starling, *UnCorinthian Leadership*, 85–86.

593 Cf. the comments on 12:10, above, regarding the meaning of "interpretation of tongues," and the discussion in Thiselton, *First Corinthians*, 1098–100.

594 Cf. Thiselton, *First Corinthians*, 1137–39, citing BDF §129; cf. BDAG, s.v. "εἷς, μία, ἕν," 3a.

intended to leave room for tongues speaking that takes place silently or even (Witherington argues) "under one's breath" in the gathering.[595]

14:29–33a. In verses 29–36 Paul sets out a parallel and significantly more detailed set of instructions regarding prophecy and its evaluation. He begins in verse 29 with an initial instruction regarding the number of prophecies and the need for evaluation. Here, in contrast with the instructions on tongues speaking, there is no conditional construction of the kind found in verse 27 ("If anyone speaks in a tongue"); nor is the limit of "two or three" prophets qualified with the same "at most" (τὸ πλεῖστον) that Paul adds in that verse—features that combine to underline that Paul regards prophecy (unlike tongues) as an essential feature of the gathering.

Paul gives no instruction on the process or criteria by which to "evaluate" (διακρίνω) prophecies (cf. the range of different meanings that the verb can carry in 4:7; 6:5; 11:29, 31; 12:10 and Paul's use of the cognate verb κρίνω in 10:15 and 11:13 to invite the Corinthians to "judge" what he himself is saying to them in this letter), but the instruction certainly suggests that a word of prophecy was not to be accepted unconditionally.[596] The "others" (οἱ ἄλλοι) who are to evaluate the prophecy are presumably the whole congregation,[597] though Paul may well have assumed that the process through which all are assisted to weigh the prophecy would involve particular roles played by individuals within the congregation, including those who are gifted in "distinguishing between spirits" (διακρίσεις πνευμάτων, 12:10) and those who carry a responsibility of some sort for the pastoral oversight of the community (cf. 16:15–18).

---

[595] Witherington, *Conflict and Community*, 286.

[596] The fact that this evaluation can take place within the event of the gathering, immediately after the speaking of the prophecy, implies an assumption on Paul's part that the prophecies to be evaluated were typically (or at least primarily) exhortative rather than predictive in nature, since the evaluation of any predictive element in a prophecy would presumably need to wait until the fulfillment or non-fulfillment of the predicted events. A prophecy that involved the disclosure of some previously hidden fact could also, of course, be evaluated immediately under some circumstances, if the fact revealed were a matter capable of being verified in some way by the congregation members present within the gathering.

[597] Cf. Garland, *1 Corinthians*, 662–63; Barrett, *First Corinthians*, 328; Gardner, *1 Corinthians*, 627. Some (e.g., Horsley, *1 Corinthians*, 187; Gillespie, *The First Theologians*, 163) read οἱ ἄλλοι as "the other [prophets]," but this would seem inconsistent with the responsibility that Paul places on all to evaluate prophecy in 1 Thess 5:20–21, and the stress in 1 Cor 2:15 on the ability of all who have the Spirit to "evaluate everything."

Verses 30–31a add several more instructions regarding turn taking and orderliness, which is followed by a statement of their purpose in verse 31b and an elaboration on their rationale in verses 32–33a: "But if something has been revealed to another person sitting there, the first prophet should be silent. For you can all prophesy one by one, so that everyone may learn and everyone may be encouraged. And the prophets' spirits are subject to the prophets, since God is not a God of disorder but of peace." The instructions in verses 30–31 appear to be designed partly to preserve the possibility that God might grant insight instantaneously, within the gathering, to a member of the community and partly to avoid the occasion being dominated by a small number of self-important speakers.[598] Their purpose (or perhaps the purpose of the instruction in v. 31a, more specifically) is stated in verse 31b as being "so that everyone may learn and everyone may be encouraged"—with a clear emphasis on the benefit of the whole community. Paul's use of the two verbs μανθάνωσιν ("may learn") and παρακαλῶνται ("may be encouraged") here to describe the benefit that he wishes the community to receive from the prophecies suggests an assumption on his part that congregational prophecy typically included a combination of instructive and exhortative elements. Verses 32–33a conclude the paragraph by insisting that "the prophets' spirits are subject to the prophets" (probably a statement of the control that individual prophets have over their own spirits and, by implication, the ability they have to discipline themselves to speak or keep silence in accordance with the guidelines in the previous verses)[599] and supporting that claim with a reminder that "God is not a God of disorder but of peace" (in implied contrast with the pagan deities whose devotees—in some cultic contexts—spoke and acted in an uncontrollable ecstasy).

14:33b–36. In verses 33b–35 Paul continues the discussion commenced in 14:26 concerning the need for order within the conduct of gathering. Depending on how one understands the relationship between verses 29–33a and verses 33b–35 (or vv. 34–35 if v. 33b is read as belonging

---

[598] Cf. Forbes, *Prophecy and Inspired Speech*, 262.

[599] Garland, *1 Corinthians*, 661–62; Thiselton, *First Corinthians*, 1144–45; Fee, *First Epistle to the Corinthians*, 771. Horsley reads v. 32 as a statement about the need for those who prophesied to submit their prophecies to the evaluation of their fellow prophets, but this requires an unlikely meaning for οἱ ἄλλοι ("the others") in v. 29, as argued above, and fits less obviously with the more immediate context of the instructions regarding turn taking in vv. 30–31.

with the preceding paragraph), the instructions in verses 33b–35 (or vv. 34–35) are either a third, distinct subsection, concerning "the ordering of women," or (more likely) a continuation of the instructions regarding prophecy and the weighing of prophecy, addressing the role played by women/wives in that process.[600]

In a handful of Western manuscripts (D, F, and G, together with several Old Latin manuscripts and the commentary of Ambrosiaster), verses 34–35 are placed at the end of the chapter, after verse 40.[601] This phenomenon raises two important and interrelated questions: (1) whether these verses were part of the original letter at all or were a post-Pauline marginal gloss that was subsequently incorporated into the text but placed by copyists in two different locations and (2) whether verse 33b should be read as the beginning of the sentence in verse 34 or the conclusion to the clause commenced in verse 33a.

The first question, while originally raised by the existence of the alternative placement of these verses in D, F, and G is further complicated by the fact that the perspective taken in these verses appears, on the surface at least, inconsistent with the earlier instructions in 11:2–16, which presuppose that the participation of women, praying and prophesying (with heads covered), will be a standard and unproblematic feature of the gathering. While this apparent inconsistency on Paul's part is undoubtedly a difficult problem and must be grappled with in the exegesis of verses 34–35, it should not be allowed to outweigh the manuscript evidence, which is unanimous regarding the inclusion of these verses as part of the original text of the letter and differs only regarding their placement. Given the small number, relatively late date, and probable interdependence of the manuscripts that locate verses 34–35 at the end of the chapter, it seems unlikely that the variation in the placement of these verses is the result of a marginal comment being added into the text. For that to have been the case, the marginal comment would have

---

[600] Cf. the arguments in favor of this reading of the structure of vv. 26–40 in Garland, *1 Corinthians*, 655–56.

[601] Also relevant is the sixth-century Latin manuscript Codex Fuldensis, which includes vv. 34–35 in their traditional location but also adds a siglum after verse 33 directing readers to a note in the lower margin that reproduces vv. 36–40 (without vv. 34–35). Cf. Philip B. Payne, "Fuldensis, Sigla for Variants in Vaticanus, and 1 Cor 14.34–5," *NTS* 41 (1995): 240–62; Curt Niccum, "The Voice of the Manuscripts on the Silence of Women: The External Evidence for 1 Cor 14.34–5," *NTS* 43 (1997): 246–47.

had to be added extremely early in the text's transmission history, with no manuscripts surviving in which it was omitted altogether or retained as a comment in the margin. The more likely explanation of the surviving manuscript evidence is that the words of verses 34–35 were original, and the displacement in D, F, and G was the result of a copyist's uncertainty regarding the relationship of these verses to their immediate context.[602]

If verses 34–35 are a non-Pauline interpolation, then the answer to the second question must necessarily be that verse 33b should be read as the conclusion to the clause commenced in verse 33a (i.e., "since God is not a God of disorder but of peace, as in all the churches of the saints"). This would, however, be a rather odd way of stating things, as if Paul were contemplating (before ultimately rejecting) the notion that God might have different attributes in different congregations. If (as would seem more likely in light of the manuscript evidence) verses 34–35 are original, then both possible readings of the relationship between verse 33b to its context may be considered. On balance, the more likely reading is to take verse 33b as the commencement of the sentence that continues in verse 34 ("As in all the churches of the saints, the women should be silent in the churches"), since it prepares the way for verse 36 in a kind of inclusio around the instructions of verses 34–35 and the repetition of ἐν ... ταῖς ἐκκλησίαις ("in ... the churches") within verses 33b–34, though a little awkward, still makes more sense than the alternative.

Interpretation of verses 34–35 must be consistent with the earlier instructions in 11:2–16, where Paul appears untroubled by the idea of women praying and prophesying (providing the traditional head covering is worn and authority to wear it is granted to all the women of the congregation). One explanation that is sometimes put forward is that verses 34–35 are an extended quotation from the Corinthians' letter, which Paul

---

602 Bruce Manning Metzger, *A Textual Commentary on the Greek New Testament: A Companion Volume to the United Bible Societies' Greek New Testament (Fourth Revised Edition)*, 2nd ed. (Stuttgart: Deutsche Bibelgesellschaft, 1994), 499; Niccum, "Voice of the Manuscripts," 242–55; Antoinette Clark Wire, *The Corinthian Women Prophets: A Reconstruction Through Paul's Rhetoric* (Minneapolis: Fortress, 1990), 153–54; Garland, *1 Corinthians*, 675–77. For a contrary assessment, including an argument that the distigme markings in Codex Vaticanus represent indirect evidence for the existence of an earlier manuscript in which vv. 34–35 were omitted, see Philip B. Payne, "Vaticanus Distigme-Obelos Symbols Marking Added Text, Including 1 Corinthians 14.34–5," *NTS* 63 (2017): 604–25.

goes on to emphatically reject in verse 36,[603] but this relies on a very unlikely interpretation of the word "or" (ἤ) at the start of verse 36 and struggles to give a convincing explanation of the similarity of thought between verse 36 and verse 33b or the brevity of the response it sees Paul as giving to such a lengthy quotation from the Corinthian letter.[604]

If we assume that the words are Paul's and that the implied context of the praying and prophesying in 11:2–16 is within the assembly (which seems to be the most natural reading of those verses), then clearly the "silen[ce]" required of women in verse 34 cannot be absolute but must be (like the "silen[ce]" of vv. 28, 30) a decision to refrain from speaking in a particular situation within the gathering.

One explanation suggested by some commentators is that the kind of speaking Paul is asking the Corinthian women to refrain from was disruptive speaking (loud chatter or disruptive questioning, often on the assumption that the women were seated, synagogue-fashion, in a separate part of the room).[605] This theory has some contextual support in the concern expressed in verses 27 and 31 that tongue speakers and prophets speak one at a time and the general concern for decorum and order. However it has against it (1) the unlikeliness of the assumption that the seating and format of the Corinthian gathering were modeled on synagogue practice (and the fact that we know very little about the first-century synagogue at any rate); (2) the fact that Paul directs the instruction exclusively to women (when disruptive speaking by men would surely have been no less problematic); and (3) the elaboration Paul goes on to give in verse 34b ("but are to submit themselves, as the law also says"), which reads more naturally as something to do with gender roles and marriage (presumably an allusion to Gen 1–2, along the lines of the earlier allusion in 11:8–9) than as a reference to a word somewhere in the law of Moses forbidding disruptiveness and noisy chatter.

A more likely explanation (as a number of commentators argue, with varying details of interpretation, historical reconstruction, and hermeneutical approach) is that the point at which Paul requires the Corinthian women not to speak is when those who have brought a word of prophecy

---

[603] David W. Odell-Scott, "Let the Women Speak in Church: An Egalitarian Interpretation of 1 Cor 14:33b–36," *BTB* 13 (1983): 90–93; David W. Odell-Scott, "In Defense of An Egalitarian Interpretation of I Cor 14:34–36," *BTB* 17 (1987): 100-103.

[604] Cf. Gardner, *1 Corinthians*, 633–34.

[605] E.g., Bruce, *1 and 2 Corinthians*, 135.

are questioned as part of the process of evaluating the prophecy and that the reason behind the instruction has something to do with the submission of wives to husbands and the social shame that wives publicly interrogating their husbands' prophecies would have attracted in the first-century context.[606] (On this view, the questions Paul encourages wives to pursue at home are of a different nature from the public and inquisitorial questions asked in the course of the weighing of the prophecy.) Proponents of this view vary as to (1) whether γυναῖκες should be understood as "women" or more narrowly as "wives" (which is probably more likely, given the requirement that they "submit themselves" in v. 34b and the assumption in v. 35 that they have "their own husbands" at home); (2) whether the "submi[ssion]" Paul wishes to see upheld and expressed is to a broad principle of order that God has established or (probably more likely) the particular submission of a wife to her own husband. This explanation is not without its problems (e.g., that the evaluation of prophecies is mentioned only in v. 29 and that the wording of vv. 34–35, on the face of it, seems more general in application), but of the various theories on offer, it still seems to make best sense of the rationale Paul himself offers in verses 34–35 and the need to read Paul's words in a way that meshes with what he has already said in chapter 11.

Verse 36 concludes the paragraph with a sharply worded rhetorical question: "Or did the word of God originate from you, or did it come to you only?" The implied rebuke is presumably to the same sense of Corinthian specialness Paul has already challenged (explicitly or implicitly) on multiple occasions earlier in the letter (e.g., 1:2; 4:7, 17; 7:17; 11:16) and reinforces his earlier reminder that the instructions in verses 34–35 correspond with the customs that are observed "in all the churches of the saints" (v. 33b).

14:37–40. Verses 37–40 function as a kind of *peroratio* to chapters 12–14, concluding the discussion and urging the audience to make a favorable response. Paul begins in verses 37–38 with a word of warning that anticipates and gives a preemptive response to those within the congregation who consider themselves to be "prophet[s]" or "spiritual." If that is indeed true of them, Paul insists, then they will recognize that

[606] E.g., Garland, *1 Corinthians*, 666–73; Thiselton, *First Corinthians*, 1150–61; Gardner, *1 Corinthians*, 634–37;

what he has written in chapters 12–14 is "the Lord's command";[607] if they choose to ignore it, they themselves will be ignored (presumably by God himself, given the indicative rather than imperative form of the verb).[608]

The paragraph concludes in verses 39–40 with another restatement of the encouragement originally given in 12:31 (ζηλοῦτε δὲ τὰ χαρίσματα τὰ μείζονα, "But desire the greater gifts") and reformulated in 14:1 (Διώκετε τὴν ἀγάπην, ζηλοῦτε δὲ τὰ πνευματικά, μᾶλλον δὲ ἵνα προφητεύητε, "Pursue love and desire spiritual gifts, and especially that you may prophesy.") Now, in its third occurrence, the wording changes yet again and expands still further. In place of χαρίσματα ("gifts," 12:31) and πνευματικά, μᾶλλον δὲ ἵνα προφητεύητε ("spiritual gifts, and especially that you may prophesy," 14:1), Paul now focuses the encouragement exclusively on prophecy and tongues. The priority of the former is clearly signaled by the contrast between his encouragement to the readers to "be eager to prophesy" (ζηλοῦτε τὸ προφητεύειν) and the more muted word of permission that follows (καὶ τὸ λαλεῖν μὴ κωλύετε γλώσσαις, "and do not forbid speaking in tongues").

If the paired commands of verse 39 are, in essence, a summation of verses 1–25, the command in verse 40 is a summation of verses 26–36: "But everything is to be done decently and in order." The adverb εὐσχημόνως ("decently") echoes the concerns expressed earlier in the letter for the conventions of honor and propriety to be observed, with particular care being taken to preserve the dignity of those most vulnerable to shame and disrespect (cf. 7:35, 36; 12:23–24). Within verses 26–36 it probably

---

607 Although "the Lord's command" (κυρίου ... ἐντολή) is expressed in a grammatically singular form, the subject of the clause (ἃ γράφω ὑμῖν, "what I write to you") is grammatically plural and probably embraces all of the instructions regarding "spiritual matters" in chs. 12–14. Some (mostly Western) manuscripts and versions (e.g., D*, F, G; Ambrosiaster) omit ἐντολή and others make it plural (e.g., D[1], K), but the manuscript support for including it (e.g., 𝔓[46], ℵ[2], B) is stronger than for its omission, and its omission or conversion to a plural form can be explained as attempts by copyists to eliminate the tension between the verb's plural subject and singular complement. Cf. Fee, *First Epistle to the Corinthians*, 774.

608 Another text-critical issue arises in v. 38, with some manuscripts (e.g., ℵ[*], A[*vid], D[*]) reading ἀγνοεῖται ("he will be ignored") and others (e.g., 𝔓[46], ℵ[2], A[c], B) reading ἀγνοείτω ("let him ignore it"). The latter has strong manuscript support but support for the former is still fairly strong and quite diverse, and it is more plausible to imagine a copyist attempting to soften ἀγνοεῖται by amending it to ἀγνοείτω than to imagine the reverse occurring. Cf. Thiselton, *First Corinthians*, 1163. The verb form Paul uses (ἀγνοεῖται) is in the present tense, not the future tense, and probably refers gnomically to a stance taken by God, without distinction between its present and future manifestations.

reflects the concern behind verses 33b–35 for the avoidance of behaviors that are culturally shameful and may also recall the scenario Paul asked the readers to imagine earlier in the chapter, in verse 22. The phrase κατὰ τάξιν ("in order") captures the sense of the earlier words about turn taking and self-control, in keeping with the fact that "God is not a God of disorder [ἀκαταστασία] but of peace" (vv. 27–33a).

Bridge

The arguments and instructions of chapter 14 are not a step-by-step manual for the conduct of all Christian gatherings, in every time and every place; they are, rather, a response to a particular set of understandings and practices that were features of the Corinthians' gatherings and presuppose the dynamic of the context in which the Corinthians gathered. Nevertheless, here as elsewhere in the letter, the responses Paul gives to the particular and contingent circumstances of the Corinthian church are grounded in explicit and universally applicable theological convictions Paul makes explicit within the chapter.

The bedrock convictions that shape Paul's arguments and instructions in this chapter have to do with the nature of God (who is "not a God of disorder but of peace," v. 33a), the primary purpose of God for the gatherings of believers ("Everything is to be done for building up," v. 26), and the indispensable role in furthering those purposes that is played by intelligible words of prophecy that apply the truth of God to the circumstances of his people with Spirit-enabled wisdom and insight (vv. 2–25).

The particular instructions Paul gives to the Corinthians in verses 26–36 are an application of those basic convictions to the Corinthian context. The numbers of permitted words of prophecy and tongues, for example, are predicated on a particular, preexisting set of Corinthian practices, and the instructions in verses 33b–35, while grounded in what "the law ... says" and in keeping with first-century practice "in all the churches of the saints," are premised on cultural dynamics of honor and shame that differ widely from those that apply within most twenty-first century contexts. Nevertheless, even here, those of us whose church traditions are less participatory and plurivocal than the Corinthians' would be wise not to dismiss too quickly those aspects of the Corinthian gathering that Paul is aiming to regulate for the sake of edification, not to extinguish altogether. Similarly, those of us whose cultural context is shaped by gender norms and honor-shame dynamics that differ significantly from those of the first-century Greco-Roman world will still need to work out how, in our own context, we give expression to the distinct and complementary roles of husbands and wives that Paul (here and in chs. 7 and 11) derives from the Genesis creation narrative, interpreted in light of the gospel.

In all things, for us as for the Corinthians, the bottom line of application is that our gatherings should be in keeping with the character of the God whom we serve and be a vehicle for the saving and renewing work of his word. Where that is the case, we may legitimately hope (and should earnestly pray) that their effect will be to bring about the kind of scenario Paul describes in verses 24–25, drawing all who are present toward a transformative encounter with the true and living God, who is among us as we meet.

VIII. Response Regarding the Resurrection of the Dead (15:1–58)

In chapter 15 Paul turns to the subject of the resurrection of the dead. Unlike most of the issues that he addresses in chapters 7–14, this issue is not introduced by Paul with the same περὶ δέ formula that has previously functioned to introduce his responses to matters raised in the Corinthians' letter, and it is possible that he is responding here not to a viewpoint propounded in their letter but to an oral report that he has been given. Either way, Paul's decision to hold this issue back until almost the end of the letter has the effect of placing it in the climactic position of his argument. The majority of the letter body is thus framed by blocks of discourse about the cross (1:18–2:5) and the resurrection (ch. 15), with the former reflected in the cruciform pattern of life to which Paul calls his readers in the intervening chapters and the latter confirming the glorious final vindication of those who live by that pattern.[609]

The argument of the chapter begins in verses 1–11 with a reaffirmation of the shared convictions about Christ's death, burial, and resurrection to which Paul can appeal as common ground in the remainder of the chapter and a reminder of the basis on which those convictions are held. The central section of the chapter, in verses 12–34, responds to those who profess Christian faith but deny the future resurrection of believers, stressing the incompatibility of that position with the fundamentals of Christian faith and practice (vv. 12–19, 29–34) and tracing out the positive logic

[609] See especially Malcolm, *Paul and the Rhetoric of Reversal*, 231–66.

of correlation between Christ's resurrection and the resurrection of his people (vv. 20–28). The last part of the chapter, in verses 35–58, begins as a response to the skeptical question asked by those who dismiss the idea of future resurrection, because they consider its bodily nature irrational or unseemly. Paul's response to his imagined interlocutor begins in verses 35–49 as argument and explanation, then pivots in verses 50–58 toward a triumphant reproclamation of the divinely revealed "mystery" at the heart of the gospel and a final word of encouragement and application in verse 58.

A. The Gospel and the Resurrection of Christ (15:1–11)

> [1] Now I want to make clear for you, brothers and sisters, the gospel I
> preached to you, which you received, on which you have taken your
> stand [2] and by which you are being saved, if you hold to the message I
> preached to you—unless you believed in vain. [3] For I passed on to you
> as most important what I also received: that Christ died for our sins
> according to the Scriptures, [4] that he was buried, that he was raised
> on the third day according to the Scriptures, [5] and that he appeared to
> Cephas, then to the Twelve. [6] Then he appeared to over five hundred
> brothers and sisters at one time; most of them are still alive, but some
> have fallen asleep. [7] Then he appeared to James, then to all the apostles.
> [8] Last of all, as to one born at the wrong time, he also appeared to me.
>
> [9] For I am the least of the apostles, not worthy to be called an apostle,
> because I persecuted the church of God. [10] But by the grace of God I am
> what I am, and his grace toward me was not in vain. On the contrary,
> I worked harder than any of them, yet not I, but the grace of God that
> was with me. [11] Whether, then, it is I or they, so we proclaim and so
> you have believed.

Context/Structure/Form

In verses 1–11 Paul lays the groundwork for the response he will make in the remainder of the chapter to those among the Corinthians who say that "there is no resurrection of the dead" (v. 12). He does so by reminding the Corinthians of the core gospel traditions that he passed on to them and that they have believed (vv. 1–5) and of the witnesses (himself included) whose testimony to the postresurrection appearances of Christ is joined to the testimony of the Twelve as further support for the truth of those core traditions (vv. 6–11).

These reminders are not presented as arguments for a position that the Corinthians have rejected. They are, rather, a reassertion of fundamental convictions that the Corinthians have already committed themselves to (vv. 1–2, 11). Paul's primary reason for reasserting them here is to lay a platform on which he will build his response in the remainder of the chapter to those among the Corinthians who (presumably) continue to profess belief in the resurrection of Jesus but have rejected the notion of a future resurrection of believers. Nevertheless, that Paul spends more than half of this opening section of the chapter on listing the witnesses whose testimony supports these core convictions suggests that the anxiety he expresses in verse 2b ("unless you believed in vain") is real. Those who are professing faith in the resurrection of Jesus but rejecting a priori the possibility of a future resurrection of believers are (as Paul goes on to stress in vv. 12–19) attempting to hold together an unstable and internally incoherent set of beliefs. That instability will eventually resolve itself one way or another, and the extra care Paul takes in verses 6–11 to underscore the basis for continuing to hold to the core traditions regarding Christ's death, burial, and resurrection is insurance against the possibility that they might resolve the contradiction in favor of skepticism rather than faith.

Embedded within the list of witnesses to Christ's postresurrection appearances is a brief elaboration on Paul's own status as "one born at the wrong time" (vv. 8–10). The function of this digression almost certainly includes an apologetic dimension, responding to those in Corinth who are sitting in judgment on Paul's credentials as an apostle (cf. 9:1–3), but it also serves an exemplary purpose, illustrating the transformative power of the risen Christ through its effect in Paul's life and labors and introducing themes to which he will return in verses 30–32 and in the final exhortation of verse 58.[610]

Comments

15:1–2. The opening verses commence with a phrase (Γνωρίζω ... ὑμῖν, "I want to make clear for you"; more literally, "I make known to you") that typically precedes the announcement of a new piece of information.[611]

---

[610] Note especially the echo of v. 10's ἐκοπίασα ("worked") and οὐ κενή ("not in vain") in v. 58's κόπος ("labor") and οὐκ ἔστιν κενός ("is not in vain").

[611] Cf. BDAG, s.v. "γνωρίζω," 1; on the use of γνωρίζω in epistolary "disclosure formulae," see John L. White, "Introductory Formulae in the Body of the Pauline Letter," *JBL* 90 (1971): 94, and Stanley E. Porter and Andrew W. Pitts, "The Disclosure Formula in the Epistolary Papyri and in the New Testament: Development, Form, Function and Syntax,"

Here, however, Paul immediately makes it clear that the content of what he is "mak[ing] known" to the Corinthians is nothing new at all but the same message that he originally preached to them, which they received and on which they have taken their stand.

The language Paul uses in verses 1–2 to describe his original proclamation of the message is pervaded by recurring instances of εὐαγγέλιον and its cognates (τὸ εὐαγγέλιον ὃ εὐηγγελισάμην ὑμῖν, "the gospel I preached to you"; τίνι λόγῳ εὐηγγελισάμην ὑμῖν, "the message I preached to you"), in line with Paul's statement in the opening chapter of the letter that he was sent not to baptize but "to preach the gospel" (εὐαγγελίζεσθαι, 1:17). The Corinthians' reception of the message is described in verses 1–2a using a cluster of different verbs: they "received" (παρελάβετε) the gospel (a verb that anticipates the tradition-related language of verse 3); they "have taken [their] stand" (εστήκατε) on it (a perfect tense verb that highlights the present state that is a continuing consequence of their initial reception of the message); and they "are being saved" (σῴζεσθε) by it (a present tense verb that focuses attention on the gospel's ongoing effect among them, with a view toward their future and final destiny).

The orientation of this third verb toward the (eschatological) future is the springboard for two more verbs, placed by Paul in a pair of conditional clauses: "if you hold [κατέχετε] to the message I preached to you—unless you believed [ἐπιστεύσατε] in vain." The first of these echoes the language Paul has used earlier in the letter, probably referring on that occasion to a claim the Corinthians themselves had made about the fidelity and comprehensiveness with which they were "hold[ing] fast" to the traditions Paul had handed on to them. On that earlier occasion, Paul's response was to applaud the general sentiment that the claim expressed but to raise two significant instances of traditions that were not being fully and faithfully observed (11:2–16, 17–34). Here, in 15:2, Paul's focus is more narrowly concentrated on the core tradition of the gospel, the faithful preservation of which is essential to their final salvation (cf. the similar statement, expressed in different language, in Col 1:23). The alternative, if they do not continue to hold onto the message, is that they will turn out to have "believed in vain" (εἰκῇ ἐπιστεύσατε)—a phrase that suggests the dreadful possibility of a profession of faith in the message

in *The Language of the New Testament*, ed. Stanley E. Porter and Andrew W. Pitts (Leiden: Brill, 2013), 429–30.

and allegiance to Christ that turns out in the end to have been without effect (cf. Gal 3:4; 4:11),[612] either because it failed to endure or because it was spurious from the outset (or for both of these reasons in combination, with the latter becoming apparent only in retrospect).

15:3–5. In verses 3–5 Paul offers support or explanation for his statements in verses 1–2,[613] reminding the Corinthians that the message he preached to them was one that he passed on "as most important" (ἐν πρώτοις) and one that he himself had also received (by implication, from faithful and authoritative sources and as the core content of the faith). The expression ἐν πρώτοις could possibly carry a chronological sense (i.e., "from the very beginning"); but if that were Paul's intended meaning, the plural form of πρώτοις would have been a little unexpected, and a more obvious expression for him to choose would have been ἐν ἀρχῇ (cf. Phil 4:15). The context here is certainly consistent with a focus on the central importance of the tradition Paul goes on to recount.[614]

The tradition Paul goes on to recount probably extends from verse 3b to the end of verse 5, with a succession of assertions arranged in chronological sequence and introduced in each case by the conjunction ὅτι

---

[612] The adverb εἰκῇ can carry various meanings, including "without cause" (e.g., Col 2:18), "without result" (e.g., Gal 3:4; 4:11), "without purpose" (e.g., Rom 13:4), and "without due consideration" (e.g., 1 Clem. 40:2). Here, the prospect of eschatological judgment implied by σῴζεσθε suggests the likelihood that the second of these is in view, and Paul is picturing a scenario in which an initial profession of faith turned out to be without ultimate saving efficacy, either because it did not endure or because it was spurious from the outset. Thiselton argues for the fourth of these meanings ("such a superficial or *confused* appropriation of the gospel in which no **coherent** grasp of its logical or practical entailments for eschatology or for practical discipleship had been reached"; Thiselton, *First Corinthians*, 1186, emphasis original; cf. BDAG, s.v. "εἰκῇ," 4); but despite the careful argumentation Paul engages in across the following paragraphs, there is no suggestion within the chapter that he considers the main problem of the Corinthians to have been carelessness or confusion in their initial reception of the message. The simpler reading of Paul's language here is to assume that the adverb carries a meaning similar to the one that it has in Gal 3:4 and 4:11.

[613] The γάρ connecting v. 3 to its preceding context suggests that it offers some sort of explanation or support for what precedes. Precisely what it is explaining or supporting is open to various possible interpretations: v. 3 could be functioning epexegetically, to provide the content of the message Paul preached (Brookins and Longenecker, *1 Corinthians 10–16*, 137); alternatively, it could be offering an explanation for Paul's stated desire in v. 1 to remind the Corinthians of this core tradition or giving support for his assertions in v. 2 regarding the indispensability of faithful adherence to the message, grounded (in either case) in the fact that this particular tradition is "most important" and was passed on from faithful and authoritative sources.

[614] Cf. Fee, *First Epistle to the Corinthians*, 801–2; Thiselton, *First Corinthians*, 1186.

("that").[615] The subject of each clause is "Christ," a fact that is consistent with Paul's characterization of his message elsewhere as "the gospel of Christ" (Rom 15:19; 1 Cor 9:12; 2 Cor 2:12; 9:13; 10:14; Gal 1:7; Phil 1:27; 1 Thess 3:2). Paul's message is, at its heart, an announcement of the saving rule of Christ (which comes with an urgent call to respond with faith and repentance and an offer of salvation and the outpoured Spirit of God), rather than a formula for personal salvation (with Christ's death and resurrection included as the mechanism that makes that salvation possible).[616]

The first line of the gospel summary that Paul recounts is an assertion that "Christ died for our sins according to the Scriptures" (v. 3b). Included within it is the fact that Christ died, but the bulk of the content focuses not on the bare fact of his death but on its significance. As Paul has already acknowledged in the opening chapter of the letter, the death of Christ (and, even more, the shameful manner of his death as a victim of crucifixion) is an event that makes the Christian gospel "a stumbling block to the Jews and foolishness to the Gentiles" (1:23). In defiance of that verdict, however, the gospel summary Paul quotes here insists that Christ's death was not a humiliating defeat but an event of atoning significance, in faithful accordance with the message of the Old Testament Scriptures and not in contradiction to it. The description of Christ's death as having taken place "for our sins" (ὑπὲρ τῶν ἁμαρτιῶν ἡμῶν) suggests that the primary Old Testament text in view is the description of the sufferings, death, and vindication of the Servant in Isaiah 52:13–53:12, which speaks of him as the one who was crushed "because of our iniquities" (LXX: διὰ τὰς ἁμαρτίας ἡμῶν; 53:5), interpreting his death as a guilt offering (LXX: δῶτε περὶ ἁμαρτίας; 53:10), and depicting him as one who "bore the sin of many" (LXX: ἁμαρτίας πολλῶν ἀνήνεγκεν; 53:13).[617]

The statement in verse 3b about Christ's death is followed by three more, in verses 4–5, about his burial, his resurrection, and the witnesses of his postresurrection appearances. The statement in verse 4a regarding his

---

615 The adverb εἶτα ("then") in v. 5 may have been introduced by Paul as a replacement for a καί ("and") in the original formulation, in order to set up the εἶτα ... ἔπειτα ... ἔπειτα ... εἶτα ("then ... then ... then ... then") sequence that extends across vv. 5–7. Cf. Fee, *First Epistle to the Corinthians*, 803.

616 Cf. Ciampa and Rosner, *The First Letter to the Corinthians*, 745

617 The preposition ὑπέρ, when followed by the genitive case, usually carries the meaning of "for the sake of," or "for the benefit of." Its use in early Christian formulations such as "for sins" or "for our sins" probably involves a spillover of meaning from other traditional formulations such as "for us," "for many," or "for all."

burial is brief (just three words in Greek: καὶ ὅτι ἐτάφη, "[and] that he was buried"), lacking any explicit unfolding of the significance of that event or any statement that it was "according to the Scriptures." Although some commentators read verse 4a as relating primarily to the statement in verse 3b about Christ's death,[618] its brevity and lack of elaboration probably suggest that it is connected more closely to the statement in verse 4b about Christ's resurrection, in line with the close connection between the burial and resurrection narratives in the Gospels. This connection between burial and resurrection is also consistent with the emphasis later in the chapter on the fact that the kind of "resurrection" Paul has in view (in our case and, by implication, in Christ's) is one that implies an empty tomb and involves a transformation of the body that died and was buried (cf. especially vv. 36–37, 42–44).[619]

The statement in verse 4b about Christ's resurrection involves somewhat more elaboration, with the inclusion of the detail that it was "on the third day" and the assertion that it took place "according to the Scriptures." The verb used to narrate Christ's resurrection is in the perfect tense, implying the continuing, present significance of Christ's resurrection (though the mention of the fact that it took place "on the third day" makes it clear that the past, historical event is still in view).[620] The assertion that Christ's resurrection was "according to the Scriptures" probably alludes to a variety of texts in the psalms and the prophetic literature that speak of the victory and vindication of the righteous sufferer, the anointed king, or the Servant of YHWH (e.g., Pss 16:9–11; 110:1; 116:8; Isa 53:11–12).

It is possible, though unlikely, that Paul may also have in mind Old Testament texts that serve in some way as a prophecy or typological foreshadowing of the fact that Christ's resurrection took place "on the third day" (τῇ ἡμέρᾳ τῇ τρίτῃ). The two texts that are most frequently suggested as possible candidates are Hosea 6:2 ("He will revive us after two days, and on the third day he will raise us up [LXX: ἐν τῇ ἡμέρᾳ τῇ τρίτῃ ἀναστησόμεθα]") and Jonah 1:17 ("Jonah was in the belly of the fish three days and three nights"). The latter has in its favor that it is appealed to by Christ in Matthew 12:40 in connection with the prospect of

618 E.g., Conzelmann, *1 Corinthians*, 255; Garland, *1 Corinthians*, 686.

619 Cf. N. T. Wright, *The Resurrection of the Son of God*, COQG (London: SPCK, 2003), 321.

620 Cf. Ciampa and Rosner, *The First Letter to the Corinthians*, 748, citing Constantine R. Campbell, *Basics of Verbal Aspect in Biblical Greek* (Grand Rapids: Zondervan, 2009), 107–8.

his death and resurrection, but the verbal similarities with the language of 1 Corinthians 15:4 are very slim. The former is much closer to Paul's language but is never elsewhere connected with Christ's resurrection by Paul or any other New Testament writer, and the words of Israel quoted in that verse appear to be interpreted by YHWH in the lament that follows in Hosea 6:4–11 as a spurious and ephemeral expression of devotion rather than as a well-founded expectation of imminent deliverance. The simplest and most likely interpretation is probably to understand "according to the Scriptures" as modifying the verb "was raised" rather than the temporal phrase "on the third day."[621]

The final line of the gospel summary, in verse 5, asserts that "he appeared to Cephas, then to the Twelve." The inclusion of this line as part of the tradition that Paul says he received and passed on is suggested by the syntax of the verse, which introduces the statement with a fourth instance of the conjunction ὅτι ("that"), which is grammatically dependent, like its predecessors, on the verb παρέδωκα ("I passed on") in verse 3a. The syntax and content of the verse also suggest the likelihood that the traditional material extends to include the verse's second half ("then to the Twelve") rather than finishing with "to Cephas" and that the extended list of witnesses that follows in verses 6–8 is probably added by Paul.[622]

15:6–7. Verses 6–8 continue the list of witnesses to the postresurrection appearances of Christ, beginning in verse 6 with a reference to an appearance of Christ to "over five hundred brothers and sisters at one time." This event is nowhere else attested within the New Testament and Paul offers little detail concerning it here, except to say that of the "more than five hundred brothers and sisters" to whom Christ appeared on this occasion, "most of them are still alive, but some have fallen asleep."

---

621 Cf. Thiselton, *First Corinthians*, 1195–96; Hays, *First Corinthians*, 256.

622 It would seem unlikely that the traditional material made reference to Cephas as a witness to the resurrection but neglected to mention the other members of the Twelve (a collective term that occurs on numerous occasions within the Gospels but nowhere else in Paul's letters). That the one verb ὤφθη ("he appeared") governs both "to Cephas" and "to the Twelve" has the effect of binding both parts of v. 5 together as one clause, whereas the repetition of ὤφθη in v. 6 suggests the commencement of a new clause no longer governed by the ὅτι in v. 5. As mentioned above, however, it is possible that the adverb εἶτα ("then") in v. 5 has been introduced by Paul in place of a καί ("and") in the original formulation, in order to link the statement in v. 5 with the ἔπειτα ... ἔπειτα ... εἶτα ("then ... then ... then") sequence in vv. 6–7. Cf. Fee, *First Epistle to the Corinthians*, 803.

That Paul chooses to include this particular detail, in the absence of any others, probably reflects his interest in the function of those who are still alive as witnesses who can confirm the veracity of his claim regarding the event.

The following two appearances Paul goes on to recall in verse 7 are "to James" and, subsequently, "to all the apostles." The appearance to James is nowhere else attested but is consistent with his early emergence as a leader within the Jerusalem community of Christ followers, despite the fact that he was remembered as having been among those who had "not ... believed in" Christ during the time of his earthly ministry (cf. John 7:5). The group to which Paul is referring by the phrase "all the apostles" is presumably a larger one than "the Twelve," to which he has already referred in verse 5 (cf. the comments above on the meaning of "apostle" in 9:1), nor should it necessarily be taken as including all of the "more than five hundred brothers and sisters" referred to in verse 6, who witnessed an appearance of the risen Jesus but may not have been commissioned by him on that occasion as his messengers and representatives.[623] Fee's summation is probably about as much as we can say with confidence: "'The Twelve' were a definite group who had a special relationship to Jesus and in the early church probably served in some kind of authoritative capacity. But the 'apostles,' a term that included the Twelve, were a larger group who in Paul's understanding had seen the risen Lord and were commissioned by him to proclaim the gospel and found churches (cf. 9:1–2)."[624]

15:8–11. Finally, in verse 8, Paul adds his own name to the list of witnesses, describing himself as the one to whom Christ appeared "last of all, as to one born at the wrong time." The word ἔκτρωμα, which Paul uses here as a metaphor for the abnormality and untimeliness of his apostolic commissioning, normally refers to a baby cast out prematurely from the womb due to an abortion, a miscarriage, or a premature birth (e.g., LXX Num 12:12; Job 3:16; Eccl 6:3).[625] Given the negative associations that the word conveys, the self-deprecatory elaboration that follows in verse 9,

---

[623] Also excluded by implication from the scope of the term as used here are those such as Barnabas and Timothy who were subsequently sent out by churches in the name of Jesus and referred to as "apostles" but did not (as far as we know) meet with Jesus face to face after the resurrection and receive their commissioning first-hand from him.

[624] Fee, *First Epistle to the Corinthians*, 812.

[625] BDAG, s.v. "ἔκτρωμα."

and the defense Paul goes on to offer in verse 10, it seems likely (though not certain) that Paul is appropriating a term used of him by others in a pejorative sense, owning the judgment that it implies on his preconversion career and the abnormality of his apostolic commissioning but reframing those parts of his story within a larger narrative about the transforming grace of God (see §5).

The explanatory elaboration Paul offers in verse 9 on his abnormal status as a witness to the resurrection who was "born at the wrong time" (v. 8) focuses on the circumstances that gave rise to his belated encounter with Christ and the implications for his status as an apostle: "For I am the least of the apostles, not worthy to be called an apostle, because I persecuted the church of God." Paul is happy to concede that he is not only "least of the apostles" but also "not worthy to be called an apostle," grounding both of these judgments in the fact that before his encounter with the risen Christ he was a persecutor of the church. If, as seems likely, the labels of "least of all the apostles" and "not worthy to be called an apostle" were used or implied by the critics Paul has referred to earlier in the letter (cf. 9:3), the basis on which they cast those judgments may well have differed from the basis Paul states here. In choosing to focus attention on his preconversion activities as a persecutor, he may well be deliberately bypassing the other less valid reasons his critics may have put forward for their negative judgments, such as his unwillingness to request or accept financial support (cf. 9:3–18; 2 Cor 11:7–11; 12:13), his lack of stature or physical presence (cf. 2 Cor 10:10), or the weakness of his rhetorical powers (cf. 2 Cor 10:10; 11:6). In place of these invalid criteria of judgment, Paul zeroes in on something that is of far weightier significance in his evaluation but (unlike the other factors) has the nature of a sin that has been forgiven and a manifestation of character that has been redeemed by the work of God through the transformative call of Christ (cf. Gal 1:13–24; Phil 3:6; 1 Tim 1:12–16).

It is this transformation that Paul focuses on in verse 10: "But by the grace of God I am what I am, and his grace toward me was not in vain. On the contrary, I worked harder than any of them, yet not I, but the grace of God that was with me." The emphasis of the account falls on the "grace" of God as the agent of transformation, with the phrase χάριτι δὲ θεοῦ ("But by the grace of God") brought forward to the front of the sentence and the word χάρις ("grace") recurring twice in the following clauses. The reference in the previous verse to Paul's persecuting activities suggests that part of what Paul has in mind by "the grace of God" is the forgiveness he has received for these acts of violence and hostility (cf. 1 Tim 1:13, 16), but the account of the transforming and energizing work of God that Paul goes on to give in the remainder of the verse suggests that in his mind "the grace of God" was responsible for far more than the forgiveness of his sins: it was also, in his view, the creative force that commissioned and (re)made him (cf. Rom 1:5; 15:15; 2 Cor 5:17; Eph 2:10) and the energizing power that was present with him to enable his apostolic labors (cf. 2 Cor 12:9). This grace does not displace the need for his own labor but is at work within it: his labor is not merely a response of gratitude to God's gracious activity but a manifestation of it, both in the act of commissioning that entrusted him with his task and in the continuing divine presence that enables him to perform it.

Paul's statement that God's grace toward him was "not in vain" (οὐ κενή) and its supporting claim that he "worked harder than" (περισσότερον ... ἐκοπίασα) any of the other apostles combine to anticipate the exhortation at the end of the chapter in which he urges the readers to "be steadfast, immovable, always excelling in the Lord's work, because you know that your labor [ὁ κόπος ὑμῶν] in the Lord is not in vain [οὐκ ἔστιν κενός]" (v. 58). It also foreshadows his assertion in verse 14 that, if Christ has not been raised, "our proclamation is in vain, and so is your faith [κενὸν ... τὸ κήρυγμα ἡμῶν, κενὴ καὶ ἡ πίστις ὑμῶν]," and suggests a close connection in his mind between the actions that he attributes to the risen Christ and the actions that he attributes to the personified grace of God (cf. 2 Cor 12:9–10; Gal 2:20; Col 1:29).

Verse 11 concludes the paragraph by returning the focus from the unique aspects of Paul's commissioning and ministry to the common proclamation of all the apostles and the reception of that message by the Corinthians: "Whether, then, it is I or they, so we proclaim and so you have believed." Paul's primary emphasis, given the immediate context of the argument in chapter 15, is on the content of the message that he and the apostles preached and the Corinthians believed: "So [οὕτως] we proclaim and so [οὕτως] you have believed," with the twice-repeated οὕτως referring back in each case to the gospel summary Paul has recited in verses 3b–5. In addition to that, however, the stress that he places on his solidarity with the other apostles in preaching the one gospel also has the effect of reinforcing two other points that he has made earlier in the letter: first, the futility of dividing into factions based on competing loyalties to various different teachers and leaders (cf. 1:10–17; 3:1–23); and second, the foolishness of the Corinthian elite's desire to develop their own boutique version of the faith (cf. 1:2; 4:7, 17; 11:16; 14:33).

Bridge

Paul's reiteration of the core content of the gospel and his reminder of its indispensability are as essential for us as they were for the Corinthians. The language of traditioning in verses 1–3 implies that the same message Paul has received and passed on should be faithfully passed on, in turn, by the Corinthians, and that future generations, too, should faithfully receive, preserve, and hand on the same message. The reminder in the final verse of the united testimony of all the apostles gives further reinforcement to Paul's implied assertion that this a message for all churches in all times and all places, uniting all followers of Christ in a shared confession of the things that are of first importance.

The message Paul holds out to the Corinthians as the core of Christian faith includes more than merely an assertion of the bare historical facts of Jesus's death, burial, and resurrection. It also includes an affirmation of the messianic identity of Jesus as "Christ," an assertion of the meaning of his crucifixion as a death "for our sins," and a twice-repeated affirmation of the Old Testament Scriptures as the interpretive framework within which we are to understand the gospel events and as the arc of narrative, prophecy, and foreshadowing within which they belong as the culmination and fulfillment.

For us, as for the Corinthians, receiving this gospel involves more than merely giving mental assent to the truth of the propositions contained within it. To receive this gospel is (as Paul reminds his readers in these opening verses of ch. 15) to "take [one's] stand" upon it and (as he goes on to stress in the remainder of the chapter) to commit oneself to thinking through and living out all its various implications and entailments. In the twenty-first century, as in the first, that calls for a willingness to hold together the propositional and the personal, building on the foundation of the apostolic testimony not only valid arguments but also a lifestyle that is coherent with the truths we confess.[626]

---

[626] Cf. Kevin J. Vanhoozer, "The Trials of Truth: Mission, Martyrdom and the Epistemology of the Cross," in *To Stake a Claim: Mission and the Western Crisis of Knowledge*, ed. J. Andrew Kirk and Kevin J. Vanhoozer (Maryknoll: Orbis, 1999), 120–56.

B. Christ's Resurrection and the Resurrection of Believers (15:12–34)

[12] Now if Christ is proclaimed as raised from the dead, how can some of
you say, "There is no resurrection of the dead"? [13] If there is no resurrection of the dead, then not even Christ has been raised; [14] and if Christ has
not been raised, then our proclamation is in vain, and so is your faith.
[15] Moreover, we are found to be false witnesses about God, because we
have testified wrongly about God that he raised up Christ—whom he
did not raise up, if in fact the dead are not raised. [16] For if the dead are
not raised, not even Christ has been raised. [17] And if Christ has not been
raised, your faith is worthless; you are still in your sins. [18] Those, then,
who have fallen asleep in Christ have also perished. [19] If we have put our
hope in Christ for this life only, we should be pitied more than anyone.

[20] But as it is, Christ has been raised from the dead, the firstfruits of
those who have fallen asleep. [21] For since death came through a man,
the resurrection of the dead also comes through a man. [22] For just as
in Adam all die, so also in Christ all will be made alive.

[23] But each in his own order: Christ, the firstfruits; afterward, at his
coming, those who belong to Christ. [24] Then comes the end, when he
hands over the kingdom to God the Father, when he abolishes all rule
and all authority and power. [25] For he must reign until he puts all his
enemies under his feet. [26] The last enemy to be abolished is death. [27] For
God has put everything under his feet. Now when it says "everything"
is put under him, it is obvious that he who puts everything under him
is the exception. [28] When everything is subject to Christ, then the Son
himself will also be subject to the one who subjected everything to him,
so that God may be all in all.

[29] Otherwise what will they do who are being baptized for the dead? If
the dead are not raised at all, then why are people baptized for them?
[30] Why are we in danger every hour? [31] I face death every day, as surely
as I may boast about you, brothers and sisters, in Christ Jesus our Lord.
[32] If I fought wild beasts in Ephesus as a mere man, what good did that
do me? If the dead are not raised, **Let us eat and drink, for tomorrow
we die**. [33] Do not be deceived: "Bad company corrupts good morals."
[34] Come to your senses, and stop sinning; for some people are ignorant
about God. I say this to your shame.

Context/Structure/Form

Having commenced in verses 1–11 by reiterating and reinforcing the basic gospel convictions that he passed on to the Corinthians and the Corinthians received and have taken their stand on, Paul now begins building on that foundation, offering his response to the views of those among the Corinthians who profess faith in the resurrection of Christ but deny the future resurrection of believers. His stress within this section is on the incoherence and unsustainability of that combination of ideas—a point that he makes both negatively, by stressing the implications that follow if one accepts as a basic axiom that "the dead are not raised" (vv. 12–19, 29–34), and positively, by spelling out the narrative logic that connects Christ's resurrection with the future resurrection of his people (vv. 20–28) (see §7).

Comments

15:12–13. In verse 12 Paul makes explicit reference for the first time to the views of those among the Corinthians ("some of you") who say that "there is no resurrection of the dead" (ἀνάστασις νεκρῶν οὐκ ἔστιν). The absence of a περὶ δέ ("Now concerning ...") formula may be a clue that this viewpoint held by some of the Corinthians was not a theory espoused within their letter but a matter about which he has received an oral report (cf. 1:12; 5:1; 11:18), perhaps from Chloe's people or from Stephanas, Fortunatus, and Achaicus, but a reference to this topic within the letter cannot be ruled out with any certainty.

The implied logic of the rhetorical question in which Paul's allusion to this viewpoint is embedded makes it clear that what is being (consciously and explicitly) denied by those who hold to it is not the resurrection of Jesus but the future resurrection of believers: "Now if Christ is proclaimed as raised from the dead, how can some of you say, 'There is no resurrection of the dead'?" Some commentators take this verse (along with Paul's sarcastic depiction in 4:8 of the Corinthian elite as "already full ... already rich ... [already having] begun to reign as kings without us") as an indication that some of the Corinthians had become believers in an explicitly Christian heresy along the lines of the teaching attributed in 2 Timothy 2:17–18 to Hymenaeus and Philetus, whom Paul represents as having "departed from the truth, saying that the resurrection has already taken place."[627] Paul's argument across the remainder of the chapter, however (in keeping with his rebuke to the Corinthians in 4:8–13) suggests that the more likely source from which this sort of thinking made its way into the beliefs of the Corinthian Christians was the attitude of the educated and semi-educated elite among their pagan neighbors, the majority of

[627] Cf. Thiselton, "Realised Eschatology at Corinth," 510–26.

whom would have regarded ideas of embodied postmortem existence as distasteful, primitive, and irrational.[628]

Verse 13 spells out the logic underlying the assertion that is implied by the rhetorical question in verse 12: if it is accepted as a general principle that resurrection of dead bodies is an irrational, superstitious notion, then that basic axiom rules out not only the future resurrection of believers but also the resurrection within history of Jesus himself. Those who embrace that general principle while still professing Christian faith are sawing off the branch that they are sitting on.

15:14–19. Paul's unfolding of what is implied by a general denial of the resurrection of the dead continues in verses 14–19, beginning in with verse 14 with the preaching of the apostles and the faith of the Corinthians. If, as verse 13 has pointed out, a general denial of the resurrection of the dead implies a denial of Christ's resurrection, and if (as emphasized in vv. 1–11) the resurrection of the dead was at the heart of what was preached by the apostles and believed by the Corinthians, then "our proclamation is in vain, and so is your faith." The word κενός that Paul uses twice in this verse to describe the apostles' preaching and the Corinthians' faith as being "in vain" is the word he used in verse 10 to affirm that God's grace toward him was "not in vain" and will return to in verse 58 to affirm the same of the Corinthians' labor. Here, as in both of those places, its meaning includes an implication of uselessness or lack of (ultimate) effect similar to the meaning of the word εἰκῇ ("in vain") in verse 2. In addition, here in verse 14, it probably also carries a connotation of emptiness (i.e., lack of substantive truth-content), implied by the meaning that the adjective carries when it is used in its original, non-metaphorical sense (e.g., Mark 12:3; Luke 1:53).[629]

Verse 15 extends the series of implications one step farther: if the dead are not raised, and if (in keeping with that general principle) Christ has not been raised, then Paul and his fellow apostles are not only false witnesses about Christ but false witnesses about God, since the God whom they urged their hearers to place their trust in is the God who raised Jesus from the dead. If the resurrection did not take place, then a question mark hangs over the very identity and existence of the God whom Paul's gospel proclaimed. This statement offers an important insight into how Paul

[628] See especially Wright, *Resurrection*, chs. 2, 7.

[629] Cf. BDAG, s.v. "κενός," 1, 2.a.

understood the epistemic relationship between faith in the God of Israel and the testimony to the resurrection that was proclaimed in the gospel. While there is a sense in which convictions regarding the existence and identity of the one true God already, in Paul's view, had preexisting warrants in the evidence of the creation (cf. Rom 1:19–20) and the history of his dealings with Israel, the experience of life in a world oppressed by the powers of sin and death and the catastrophe of Israel's apostasy, exile, and enslavement to pagan empires raised fundamental questions about the presence and power of the God to whom they professed allegiance. In keeping with the message of Isaiah to the exiles of Israel (e.g., Isa 40:9; 52:7), Paul's gospel was not only an announcement about the vindication of Jesus (whom God had raised from the dead) but an announcement about the vindication of God himself against the accusation that he had forgotten his covenant and abandoned his people, that he had been overpowered by the gods of the nations, or that he was no true God at all.[630] But if Jesus has not in fact been raised, then those questions loom large and ugly once again, and the apostles are exposed as the proponents of a lying message offering false comfort to God's people.[631]

Verses 16–18 trace out another strand of the entailments of resurrection-denial, focusing this time on the implications that the idea poses for the faith of the Corinthians. The train of thought begins in verse 16 with a reiteration of the point Paul has made already in verse 13: "For if the dead are not raised, not even Christ has been raised." Verse 17 then restates the assertion of verse 14b ("and so is your faith" [i.e., in vain]), with the adjective κενός replaced here by its near-synonym μάταιος ("worthless"), unpacking that claim in verse 17b with the elaboration that "you are still in your sins." The predicament Paul pictures here probably embraces a combination of continuing liability to the penalty of unforgiven sin and continuing enslavement to its power—both of which Paul speaks of

---

630 Cf. the discussion of "eschatological monotheism" in Bauckham, *God Crucified*, 35, 48–49.

631 If the expression ἐμαρτυρήσαμεν κατὰ τοῦ θεοῦ is translated not as "we have testified wrongly about God" but, in line with the more typical sense that the word κατά carries in expressions such as this, "we have testified *against* God" (emphasis added), then the picture implied is not merely one in which false testimony has been offered in God's favor but one in which this false evidence has been offered *against* God in some sense. If that is Paul's meaning, then the sense he has in mind is probably that the claim of the apostles would have the effect, under this scenario, of tying the honor of God to the reputation of a false prophet (i.e., the unresurrected Jesus).

elsewhere as having been reversed for believers by the resurrection of Christ and their solidarity with him (cf. Rom 4:25; 6:5–14).[632]

Verse 18 traces out the logical thread still farther, focusing on the predicament of those who have "fallen asleep in Christ." If there is no resurrection and believers are still "in [their] sins,"[633] then they are not "asleep," awaiting resurrection and the fulness of life but have "perished" (along with all the rest of fallen humankind; cf. Paul's use of the same verb in 1:18).[634]

Verse 19 draws the paragraph to a close with a free-standing summary statement: "If we have put our hope in Christ for this life only, we should be pitied more than anyone." The CSB translation of this verse (along with most English versions) correctly renders the μόνον ("only") at the end of verse 19a as modifying ἐν τῇ ζωῇ ταύτῃ (i.e., "if we have put our hope in Christ *for this life* only"; emphasis added) rather than ἠλπικότες ἐσμέν (i.e., "if in this life we have only *hoped* in Christ"; emphasis added). The latter alternative (as Fee points out) relies on a meaning of "hoped" that is much weaker than Paul's usual use of ἐλπίζω.[635] Paul's statement here should not be taken as a denial of all the many joys and rewards that come with serving Christ within this lifetime, as foretastes and firstfruits of the age to come. It does, however, rely on the assumption that those who live by faith in the risen Jesus commit themselves to a way of life that involves daily sacrifices of comfort, status, and safety that make sense only if it is indeed true that God raises the dead (cf. vv. 30–32; 1 Cor 4:8–16; 2 Cor 4:1–18); if he does not, then by any outwardly visible measure they have thrown away their lives on the basis of a delusion and may be described (with an obvious element of hyperbole) as people who should be "pitied more than anyone."

15:20–22. In verse 20 Paul's argument turns a corner. Having focused in verses 12–19 on teasing out the various negative implications that follow if one embraces a general principle that "the dead are not raised,"

---

[632] A meaning of this sort is consistent with the multi-dimension picture of salvation implied in verses such as 1 Cor 1:30; 6:11.

[633] Note the inferential conjunction ἄρα, which presents v. 18 as a further logical implication of the conclusion reached in the previous verse.

[634] This picture of their fate, if there is no resurrection, is probably intended to stand in contrast to the expectation that the Corinthian resurrection-deniers would have shared with the majority of their pagan neighbors, who looked forward to some sort of disembodied postmortem existence.

[635] Fee, *First Epistle to the Corinthians*, 825.

highlighting the multiple ways in which a belief of this sort renders Christian faith incoherent and impossible, Paul now turns in verses 20–28 to a more positive line of argument, tracing the shape of the narrative arc implied by the story to which Christ's resurrection belongs and spelling out the reasons why that story requires not only Christ's resurrection but the resurrection of his people.

The phrase νυνὶ δέ (literally, "But now") with which verse 20 begins, is probably best understood here not as a chronological "now" but as marking a transition from the previous line of argument to a new one (cf. 12:18; 13:13): hence the CSB's translation, "But as it is … ." Paul begins by reasserting the fact of Christ's resurrection, which he has already affirmed in 15:1–11 as fundamental to the gospel, consistent with the testimony of the Old Testament Scriptures and supported by a long list of eyewitnesses. His focus now, however, is not simply on repeating that assertion but on tracing out the threads of connection between Christ's resurrection and the resurrection of believers. He begins here in verse 20 with the image of Christ's resurrection as "the firstfruits of those who have fallen asleep." The image of "firstfruits" (ἀπαρχή) is drawn from the world of agriculture and the law of Moses (e.g., Lev 23:10; Deut 18:4) and, as Paul uses it here and elsewhere in his letters, speaks of something that comes first in time, is representative in character, and carries the promise of more of the same kind that is still to come (cf. 16:15; Rom 8:23; 11:16; 16:5; 2 Thess 2:13).

Paul's explanation for why Christ's resurrection should be thought of in this way—as firstfruits of a larger harvest rather than merely as a unique and unrepeatable anomaly—begins in verses 21–22: "For since death came through a man, the resurrection of the dead also comes through a man. For just as in Adam all die, so also in Christ all will be made alive."[636] The γάρ ("for") that joins each of these two verses to its predecessor is explanatory in nature. Paul is not merely unpacking the content of verse 20 to make explicit the ideas that were already contained within that verse; he is also introducing new ideas that help to confirm the applicability of the "firstfruits" image and explain the logic

[636] The further elaborations that Paul offers across the following verses (and consistency with Paul's eschatological expectations as he unfolds them elsewhere) make it clear that his intent in v. 22 is not to assert that "all" (i.e., each and every human being) will be made alive in Christ, but that "all in Christ" (i.e., "[all] those who belong to Christ," v. 23) will be made alive with him.

that informs his use of it. The key idea here has to do with the solidarity of humankind as a family and the representative roles that Adam and Christ, respectively, play in relation to those members of the human family who are "in" each of them. Just as, in the beginning, "death came through a man" (cf. Gen 3:1–7; Rom 5:12–21) so now, through Christ, "the resurrection of the dead also comes through a man." The representative role played by Adam in relation to the family of his descendants is an obvious implication of the way in which the narrative of Genesis 1–3 depicts him as being commissioned (Gen 2:15) and judged (Gen 3:19) not merely in his own private capacity but as the bearer of his descendants' destiny. The representative role played by Christ is an outworking not only of his authentic and archetypal humanity (cf. v. 49) but also of his messianic office (cf. Rom 1:3–4) and his calling as the Servant of the Lord (cf. Rom 15:8–9; 1 Cor 15:3), by virtue of which he bears on his shoulders Israel's destiny and fulfills Israel's calling to bring God's blessing to the nations.[637]

15:23–28. Having sketched out the outlines of Christ's representative role in verses 20–22, Paul goes on in verses 23–28 to clarify the sequence of the events in which Christ fulfills it, first in his own person and then second, subsequently, for his people. The fact that he expresses his point here as a kind of qualification or clarification, using the mildly adversative particle δέ ("But") suggests that his intention in these verses is partly to rule out misunderstandings of the gospel that take Christ's vindication as a warrant for the idea that his followers are entitled to an expectation of honor and glory in the present age (cf. 4:8–13; Rom 8:17). The firstfruits metaphor from verse 20 thus reappears here in verse 23, serving now not only as an image for the connection between Christ and his people but also as reminder of the "order" (τάγμα) that is expressed in the distinction between Christ's resurrection, which has already taken place, and the resurrection of his people, which will occur "afterward, at his coming."

The word παρουσία, which Paul uses here and elsewhere to refer to the future "coming" of Christ (cf. 1 Thess 4:15; 5:23; 2 Thess 2:1, 8), can sometimes be used in cultic contexts to refer to the visible manifestation of a god[638] and sometimes in political contexts to refer to the visit of a king or emperor to a province.[639] Given the multiple references to "king-

---

637 Cf. Wright, *Resurrection*, 334–38.

638 E.g., Diodorus Siculus, *Bib. hist.* 3.65.1; 4.3.3; cf. BDAG, s.v. "παρουσία," 2.b.

639 E.g., Polybius, *Hist.* 18.48.4.

dom" (βασιλεία), "rule" (ἀρχή), "authority" (ἐξουσία), "power" (δύναμις), "reign[ing]" (βασιλεύειν), and "enemies" (ἐχθροί) in verses 24–26, it is almost certainly the political rather than the cultic use of the word that is closer to the front of Paul's mind here.[640] The culmination toward which Paul looks forward in verse 24 involves not merely the bodily resurrection of believers but the reordering of the entire universe, with "all rule and all authority and power" (i.e., all present, earthly rule, authority, and power) abolished when Christ "hands over the kingdom to God the Father." Chief among the various Old Testament texts that stand behind Paul's depiction of the abolition of all earthly kingdoms and their replacement by the coming kingdom of God is the vision in Daniel 2, the climax of which is an event in which "the God of the heavens will set up a kingdom that will never be destroyed," which "will crush all these kingdoms and bring them to an end, but will itself endure forever" (Dan 2:44).

The language of the following verse ("For he must reign until he puts all his enemies under his feet," v. 25) evokes echoes of both Psalm 110:1 ("Sit at my right hand until I make your enemies your footstool") and Psalm 8:6 ("you put everything under his feet"). Although it is the latter that Paul goes on to quote explicitly in verse 27, the references in verse 25 to "enemies" (ἐχθροί) and a reign that must continue "until" (ἄχρι οὗ) they have been subjugated and placed beneath Christ's feet make it clear that Psalm 110:1 is at least equally important in giving shape and content to the picture of the end that Paul is encouraging his readers to anticipate. The time of Christ's reign, between now and "the end," should not be thought of as a kind of empty interval between his first coming and his return. It is true that Paul encouraged his readers to view themselves as people who "wait" for the coming of Christ at the end of the age (cf. 1:7; 1 Thess 1:10), but this "wait[ing]" involves more than merely the passive endurance of hardships. Believers, according to Paul's gospel, are called by the gospel into an active allegiance in which they now "serve the living and true God" (1 Thess 1:9), "put on the armor of light" (Rom 13:12), and offer up to God their various powers and capacities as "weapons for righteousness" (Rom 6:13). Within that larger story Paul's own role as an "ambassador for Christ" involves him in an ongoing task of proclaiming

---

[640] Contra Fee, *First Epistle to the Corinthians*, 834. For a discussion of the relationship between these verses and the imperial eschatology of Rome (as illustrated, for example, in the Priene calendrical inscription), see Witherington, *Conflict and Community*, 295–98.

Christ's rule and participating in God's work of reconciling the world to himself (2 Cor 5:18–20).

It would be over-reading (and indeed misreading) Paul's language here to derive from it a story of smooth and inexorable progress in which the church steadily expands its territory, Christianizing the world in readiness for Christ's return; the picture of Paul and his fellow apostles in 4:8–13 hardly represents them as the generals of an army that marches from visible and manifest triumph to visible and manifest triumph, as measured by the criteria of the world. But it would be under-reading his language if we were to reduce it to nothing more than a story of grim endurance. The references in verses 25–27 to multiple "enemies" and a present reign of Christ that continues until all but the last have been placed beneath his feet suggests that in Paul's mind the story of the current age is one in which the reign of Christ within the world is progressively extended as the gospel is proclaimed and as believers devote their energies to promoting the cause of justice and righteousness, in anticipation of the final consummation in which even death itself, the last enemy, is defeated (see §7).

Verses 27–28 depict that final consummation in explicitly universal—and indeed cosmic—terms: "For God has put everything under his feet. Now when it says 'everything' is put under him, it is obvious that he who puts everything under him is the exception. When everything is subject to Christ, then the Son himself will also be subject to the one who subjected everything to him, so that God may be all in all." The story of messianic vindication and the triumph of Israel's God over the powers of oppressive empire evoked by the earlier echoes from Psalm 110 and Daniel 2 is expanded still further by a quotation in verse 27 from Psalm 8:6 (which has already been hinted at, in combination with Ps 110:1, in v. 25). The consummation Paul anticipates is not merely the vindication of Israel's messiah and the overthrow of Israel's enemies but the fulfillment and perfection of the original vocation of the whole human race, as it is depicted and celebrated in that psalm. "Everything" (i.e., the whole creation) is restored and placed under the feet of Christ, and Christ in turn subjects himself to the one who has placed all things under his feet, so that "God may be all in all."

Paul's choice of titles in verses 24–28 is intriguing. On the one hand, it is as "the Son" (ὁ υἱός)—not merely as "Jesus" or "the Christ"—that he is subject to the one who subjected all things to him (v. 28),[641] suggesting that something is being said not merely about the earthly, messianic vocation of Jesus but about the continuing loyal allegiance of the exalted Son to the Father.[642] On the other hand, the final consummation Paul depicts at the end of verse 28 is one in which it is not merely "the Father" but "God" (ὁ θεός) who is ultimately said to be "all in all" (v. 28): while the Son is subject to the Father, his rule over all things is not swallowed up or obliterated in the rule of the Father (as if his rule were somehow a rival or challenge to the Father's rule, which must be overcome by the superior force of the Father) but is perfected in the universal rule of (the Triune) God (see §§1, 2).[643]

15:29. In verses 29–34, having reached the eschatological climax of the grand narrative he sketches out in verses 20–28, Paul returns to a mode of argument similar to the one he pursued in verses 12–19. Once again, as in those earlier verses, his focus in this paragraph is on tracing out the logical consequences that follow "if the dead are not raised" (vv. 29–32) and exposing the contradictions that are generated with various elements of Christian faith and practice (with an accent, in this instance, on the latter). In particular, he directs the attention of the Corinthians toward two more practices that would be rendered absurd and pointless if the dead are not raised: first, the practice of those who are "baptized for the dead" (v. 29) and second, his own practices of suffering and self-endangerment for the sake of the gospel (vv. 30–32). Finally (vv. 33–34) he exhorts the Corinthians to "come to [their] senses" and "stop sinning."

The practice of baptism "for the dead" (ὑπὲρ τῶν νεκρῶν) to which Paul refers in verse 29 is otherwise unattested within the New Testament, leading to endless speculation on the part of interpreters. The idea of the argument and the language in which it is expressed may have been suggested to Paul by the account in 2 Maccabees 12 of an occasion when Judas Maccabeus found pagan religious artifacts hidden in the clothing of fallen soldiers whose bodies were being recovered from the battlefield. In response to the discovery, Judas offered prayers and sacrifices for the fallen soldiers. The narrator adds a comment that "in doing this he

[641] Cf. the reference in v. 24 to Christ handing over the kingdom "to God the Father" (τῷ θεῷ καὶ πατρί).

[642] As Garland observes, this is the one place in Paul's letters where ὁ υἱός ("the Son") is used absolutely in this way. Garland, *1 Corinthians*, 713.

[643] Cf. Thiselton, *First Corinthians*, 1137–38; Garland, *1 Corinthians*, 713–14.

acted very well and honorably, taking account of the resurrection (ὑπὲρ ἀναστάσεως διαλογιζόμενος)," and goes on to justify that comment by arguing that "if he were not expecting that those who had fallen would rise again, it would have been superfluous and foolish to pray for the dead (ὑπὲρ νεκρῶν)" (2 Macc 12:43–44, NRSV). While the basic idea of the argument that the writer of 2 Maccabees is making has obvious similarities with the point implied by Paul's rhetorical question (i.e., highlighting an action performed ὑπὲρ νεκρῶν ["for the dead"] that would make no sense if the person performing it did not believe in resurrection), the nature of the action depicted (i.e., the offering of prayers and atoning sacrifices in hope that the sins of the dead will be forgiven) is obviously different from the action that Paul is referring to here and the kind of benefit intended for the dead should not be assumed to be the same.

While some commentators argue that the practice Paul is alluding to here was probably some sort of vicarious baptism performed as a kind of prayer for the eternal salvation of loved ones who had died without professing Christ,[644] or had professed faith but had not been baptized,[645] there is no indication anywhere else in the New Testament to support the existence of a practice such as this, and it is hard to square with the meaning Paul attributes to Christian baptism elsewhere in his letters as a ritual of Christian initiation and an expression of personal allegiance. It is possible that Paul may be alluding to a practice of this sort, making use of it as part of an ad hominem argument without needing to either endorse or criticize it,[646] but the questions that would be raised by such a fleeting allusion to a practice of this sort would seem to outweigh its usefulness as support for the point Paul is making.[647] No proposal is without difficulty, but the simplest is probably the view advocated by Thiselton, who

---

[644] E.g., Conzelmann, *1 Corinthians*, 275.

[645] E.g., A. J. M. Wedderburn, *Baptism and Resurrection: Studies in Pauline Theology Against Its Graeco-Roman Background*, WUNT (Tübingen: Mohr Siebeck, 1987), 288–89.

[646] Cf. Conzelmann, *1 Corinthians*, 275.

[647] Also unlikely is the proposal advocated by Garland (following the majority of the Greek fathers), that the term "the dead" is being used metaphorically to refer to candidates for baptism as people who are "dead" in their sins. Cf. Garland, *1 Corinthians*, 717–18. On this view the phrase "the dead" would need to be interpreted in an entirely different sense here from the sense in which it is to be understood throughout the rest of the chapter, and the phrase ὑπὲρ τῶν νεκρῶν would be functioning (most unusually!) in a kind of reflexive manner to describe a baptism that the men and women being referred to were undertaking for their own sakes.

suggests that the people being referred to were not undergoing a kind of vicarious baptism intended to secure the salvation of the unbaptized or unbelieving dead but were seeking to benefit the (Christian) dead by turning to Christ and undergoing baptism as a belated answer to their prayers and pleadings, in the hope that they would be united with them at the resurrection.[648] A practice of this sort would have been entirely plausible in the context of a strongly communitarian culture and would have presumably been viewed by Paul as theologically unproblematic; it would also have made no sense if the dead are not, in fact, raised, and those being baptized with this expectation in mind would never live to see it fulfilled.

In verses 30–32 Paul turns to a second example of a practice that makes no sense if the dead are not raised: "Why are we in danger every hour? I face death every day, as surely as I may boast about you, brothers and sisters, in Christ Jesus our Lord. If I fought wild beasts in Ephesus as a mere man, what good did that do me? If the dead are not raised, Let us eat and drink, for tomorrow we die." Here, the basic sense of what he has in mind is easier to determine than in verse 29, even if the precise event to which he is alluding to in verse 32, when he "fought wild beasts in Ephesus," is unknown to us. The verb κινδυνεύω ("put oneself in danger") occurs only here in Paul's letters, though the cognate noun κίνδυνοι ("dangers") occurs eight times within the space of one verse in 2 Corinthians 11:26. On this occasion Paul does not list the dangers he has faced (apart from the reference in v. 32 to the "wild beasts" that he faced in Ephesus) but is content to speak in general terms, with the hyperbolic claim that he endangers himself "every hour" suggesting a pattern of life that is habitual and recurring, not one that is merely occasional and exception. A similar claim (expressed in similarly hyperbolic form) follows in verse 31, where Paul goes on to assert: "I face death every day" (καθ' ἡμέραν ἀποθνῄσκω; more literally, "I die every day")—language that implies not merely risk but suffering and affliction, and perhaps also the wearisome, enervating labors in which Paul poured out his life's energies in the service of Christ and his people (cf. 2 Cor 4:10–11, 16–17; 6:4–10; 13:15). Verse 31b underlines the earnestness with which Paul asserts this claim, while simultaneously reminding his readers in Corinth of the place they occupy in his affections and the "boast" he has

[648] Thiselton, *First Corinthians*, 1248–49.

in them as the one who brought the gospel to them and established them as a community of Christ's people.

The "wild beasts" to which Paul refers in verse 32a are presumably metaphorical (cf. Ps 22:12–13; Ignatius, *Rom.* 5:1), and although Paul does not give us enough information to confirm with any certainty the event to which he is referring, the riot reported in Acts 19 is a likely candidate (if that event has already occurred by the time Paul writes 1 Corinthians).[649] Verse 32b uses the words of Isaiah 22:13, suggesting a parallel between the hedonistic delusions of those who ignore the warning of judgment implicit in the resurrection and the Jerusalemites who ignore the warning of the coming Assyrian invasion, distracting themselves with self-indulgent luxuries.[650] A likely additional resonance of the saying for the Corinthians would have been an echo of the stereotypically Epicurean response to human mortality (as it was depicted in the caricatures of its critics).[651] Epicurus's attitude toward pleasure (which he viewed as the "first and kindred good" of humankind) was closely connected to his view on death; death, he insisted was not to be feared at all, since it was nothing but nonexistence and (consequently) the end of all pleasure and pain. The way to be happily mortal, according to Epicurus, was "not by adding to life an unlimited time, but by taking away the yearning after immortality."[652] Whether the popular opinion was fair to Epicurus's original vision or not,[653] most people in Paul's day would have viewed the philosophy of Epicureanism as amounting to something that closely resembled the attitude expressed in the saying Paul quotes from Isaiah.

---

[649] Barrett, *First Corinthians*, 366. The narrative in Acts 19 does not give us enough information to be certain about the precise chronological relationship we are intended to infer between the sending of Timothy and Erastus to Macedonia (Acts 19:22, possibly the same sending of Timothy to which Paul refers in 1 Cor 4:17; 16:10) and the riot narrated in Acts 19:23–41, which occurred "about that time" (κατὰ τὸν καιρὸν ἐκεῖνον). Both events appear to be represented by Luke as occurring toward the end of Paul's stay in Ephesus and both are connected in the narrative with statements about his decision to leave (cf. Acts 19:21; 20:1).

[650] Cf. Hays, *First Corinthians*, 268; Starling, *UnCorinthian Leadership*, 89–92.

[651] Plutarch, for example, disapprovingly quotes the Epicurean Metrodorus as asserting that the human calling is "not ... to save the nation or get crowned by it for wisdom [but merely] to eat and drink wine, gratifying the belly without harming it." *Mor.* 1098C; cf. 1100D, 1125D.

[652] Epicurus, *Letter to Menoeceus* 127.

[653] Note the protest that Epicurus registers against caricatures of his philosophy in *Letter to Menoeceus* 131–32.

The paragraph concludes in verses 33–34 with a stern word of rebuke, expressed in language and tone that resemble a father's rebuke to an undisciplined and wayward son. The content of the rebuke, including its focus on the "company" the Corinthians are keeping and the metaphor of drunken stupor implied by the call to the readers to "come to your senses" (ἐκνήψατε; literally, "sober up"), suggests that the kind of hedonistic escapism depicted by Paul in verse 32b is not merely a hypothetical possibility for the privileged subset of the church whom he is primarily addressing but an already-present tendency in their attitudes and behavior (cf. 4:8–13).

The terms in which Paul expresses his warning in verse 33 support the likelihood that the primary source of the attitude Paul is warning against is not an esoteric article of heretical Christian teaching but the influence of the ideas and lifestyle of the pagan neighbors whose approval the Corinthian believers wished to retain. The saying that he borrows as a vehicle for the warning is a Greco-Roman epigram that derived originally from the playwright Menander,[654] with the fitting (and possibly deliberate) consequence that the worldliness of the Corinthians' beliefs and lifestyle is condemned through the words of a pagan dramatist.[655]

The closing words of the paragraph, in verse 34, implicitly represent the attitude and lifestyle of the Corinthian believers who are saying by their words and their actions that "the dead are not raised" as a kind of metaphorical drunkenness from which they need to sober up, as a sinful pattern of speech and life from which they need urgently to turn aside, and as an evidence of a dangerous defection from true knowledge of God.[656] Accordingly, Paul does not shrink from rebuking them directly, in the

---

[654] Menander, *Thais*, frag. 187.

[655] For an argument in favor of the view that Paul is intending a deliberate allusion to the idioms and tropes of Menandrian comedy, see Michael Benjamin Cover, "The Divine Comedy at Corinth: Paul, Menander and the Rhetoric of Resurrection," *NTS* 64 (2018): 532–50.

[656] Paul's statement in v. 34 that "for some people are ignorant about God" (ἀγνωσίαν γὰρ θεοῦ τινες ἔχουσιν) is almost certainly, given its immediate context, referring to people within the Corinthian congregation—presumably the same people to whom he has already referred in v. 12 as "some of you" (ἐν ὑμῖν τινες). His depiction of them as "ignorant" (like his earlier statement in 12:1) is probably intended as a deliberate challenge to their self-estimation as the knowledgeable and spiritual members of the congregation (cf. 8:1; 14:37). Read against the backdrop of the warning in the immediately preceding verse, the depiction of them here as being ignorant "about God" implies not merely a lack of theological sophistication but a reversion to the mindset of the pagans, who do not know the true and living God. Cf. Fee, *First Epistle to the Corinthians*, 857.

context of a letter that is to be read before the whole congregation, with the deliberate and explicitly articulated intent of evoking their shame as a motive for urgent change in their thinking and their conduct (cf. 4:14; 6:5).

Bridge

Saying that "there is no resurrection of the dead" can occur within a wide variety of contexts, both ancient and modern, and can take a wide variety of forms. In some cases the belief expressed is a comprehensive denial of any kind of postmortem existence at all; in others it is a rejection of the idea of *resurrected* postmortem existence due to a philosophical or aesthetic prejudice against embodiment, or simply an unreflective acceptance of notions of the afterlife derived from folk religion and mythology; and in others still it is a denial that is expressed in actions more than in words and takes the form of a lifestyle that so starkly contradicts any verbal profession of resurrection belief as to reduce it to the level of empty lip-service.

Paul's arguments within this middle section of chapter 15 expose the inconsistency of all such forms of resurrection-denial with authentic Christian faith, as defined by the core traditions Paul has laid out in verses 1–11 as of first importance. Given the place that the gospel events occupy within the story that they belong to (as the pivotal moment in the fulfillment of God's purposes for Israel and humanity and the inauguration of his victory over the forces of sin and death) and the representative nature of Christ's role (as Israel's messiah, the Servant of the Lord, and the head of a renewed and redeemed humanity), belief in the resurrection of Christ is inextricably connected to belief in the promise of the future resurrection of his people.

Nor can that belief be reduced to a merely theoretical assent to an idea. The reminder Paul offers in verses 30–32 of his own lifestyle of suffering and self-endangerment for the sake of the gospel powerfully illustrates that faith in the resurrection manifests itself in a life that is shaped by the cross-centered story of the one whom God raised from the dead. The message of the resurrection that Paul affirms in chapter 15 as central to the Christian faith does not erase, dilute, or counterbalance the "word of the cross" that Paul described himself in chapter 1 as having been sent to preach. Rather, it underlines it and endorses it, affirming that those who pour out their lives in imitation of the Servant will not be put to shame but will be raised, vindicated, and glorified with him.

Paul's arguments, rebukes, and reminders in this middle section of the chapter are as relevant for us today as they were for their original readers in first-century Corinth. If we are to embrace the Christian gospel, we must embrace it with all its necessary entailments and practical implications. That means embracing a grand narrative that is full of hope, not only for ourselves but for all the world, and a way of life that stands out as a compelling contrast to the life of those who have nothing more to live by than "Let us eat and drink, for tomorrow we die."

C. Resurrection and the Transformation of Bodies (15:35–58)

> 35 But someone will ask, "How are the dead raised? What kind of body
> will they have when they come?" 36 You fool! What you sow does not
> come to life unless it dies. 37 And as for what you sow—you are not sow-
> ing the body that will be, but only a seed, perhaps of wheat or another
> grain. 38 But God gives it a body as he wants, and to each of the seeds its
> own body. 39 Not all flesh is the same flesh; there is one flesh for humans,
> another for animals, another for birds, and another for fish. 40 There are
> heavenly bodies and earthly bodies, but the splendor of the heavenly
> bodies is different from that of the earthly ones. 41 There is a splendor
> of the sun, another of the moon, and another of the stars; in fact, one
> star differs from another star in splendor. 42 So it is with the resurrec-
> tion of the dead: Sown in corruption, raised in incorruption; 43 sown in
> dishonor, raised in glory; sown in weakness, raised in power; 44 sown a
> natural body, raised a spiritual body. If there is a natural body, there is
> also a spiritual body. 45 So it is written, **The first man Adam became a
> living being**; the last Adam became a life-giving spirit. 46 However, the
> spiritual is not first, but the natural, then the spiritual.
>
> 47 The first man was from the earth, a man of dust; the second man is
> from heaven. 48 Like the man of dust, so are those who are of the dust;
> like the man of heaven, so are those who are of heaven. 49 And just as
> we have borne the image of the man of dust, we will also bear the image
> of the man of heaven.
>
> 50 What I am saying, brothers and sisters, is this: Flesh and blood cannot
> inherit the kingdom of God, nor can corruption inherit incorruption.
> 51 Listen, I am telling you a mystery: We will not all fall asleep, but we
> will all be changed, 52 in a moment, in the twinkling of an eye, at the
> last trumpet. For the trumpet will sound, and the dead will be raised
> incorruptible, and we will be changed. 53 For this corruptible body must
> be clothed with incorruptibility, and this mortal body must be clothed
> with immortality. 54 When this corruptible body is clothed with incor-

ruptibility, and this mortal body is clothed with immortality, then the saying that is written will take place:

> **Death has been swallowed up in victory.**
> [55] **Where, death, is your victory?**
> **Where, death, is your sting?**

[56] The sting of death is sin, and the power of sin is the law. [57] But thanks
be to God, who gives us the victory through our Lord Jesus Christ!

[58] Therefore, my dear brothers and sisters, be steadfast, immovable,
always excelling in the Lord's work, because you know that your labor
in the Lord is not in vain.

Context/Structure/Form

The final part of the chapter commences in verse 35 as a response to a question that Paul puts in the mouth of an imagined interlocutor, who asks: "How are the dead raised? What kind of body will they have when they come?" Paul's initial response to the question (after the scathing denunciation of v. 36a) takes the form of argument and explanation (vv. 36–49). He begins in verses 36–41 with a series of analogies, focusing on the varied forms that embodiment can take, the various kinds and degrees of glory that bodies can possess, and the transformations that can occur even within the present form of the world. In verses 42–49 he draws out the implications of those analogies for the claims that he is making about resurrection and embodiment, highlighting the transformations that resurrection involves and the contrast between bearing the image of Adam, "the man of dust," and bearing the image of Christ, "the man of heaven."

In verses 50–58 Paul pivots from argument and explanation toward a more triumphant and celebratory rhetoric that reproclaims the divinely revealed "mystery" at the heart of the gospel and applies it to the Corinthians with a final word of encouragement and application in verse 58.

Comments

15:35. The double-barreled question with which this last section of the chapter begins is placed in the mouth of an interlocutor whom Paul goes on in the following verse to describe as a "fool" (ἄφρων), with the clear implication that it should be taken not as a polite and sincere inquiry but as an expression of mocking incredulity. The second half of the question ("What kind of body will they have when they come?") explicates the intended meaning of the interrogative particle "How ... ?" (Πῶς) that introduces the first half of the question, implying that it has to do with *both* the possibility *and* the manner of the resurrection of the dead. The focus of the interlocutor's skepticism and disdain is clearly the idea of postmortem embodiment, and the implied assertion behind the question is that the notion of bodily resurrection is either absurd, distasteful, or (most likely, given the multi-dimensional response Paul offers in vv. 36–49) both of these.

15:36–38. Paul's initial response to the question is uncompromisingly negative, rebuking his interlocutor as a "fool" whose arrogance disguises a basic lack of understanding of God and of the world that God has made. (Cf. the use of the same word in texts such as LXX Pss 14:1; 93:8 to describe the stance of the practical atheist, who acts as if there is no God in heaven to see and judge human actions, and the rebukes that Jesus pronounces—or puts into the mouth of God—in Luke 11:40; 12:20. A similar sentiment is also expressed by Jesus in the answer that he gives to the Sadducees in Mark 12:24–27.)

The CSB's translation, "You fool!" implies a reading of the Greek that connects the pronoun σύ ("you") with the preceding word "fool" rather than with the phrase ὃ σπείρεις that follows (cf. the punctuation in the UBS5 and NA[28] texts).[657] Either reading is grammatically possible, but the latter is probably to be preferred, given that the pronoun σύ can be omitted as redundant in equally strong rebukes such as the one in Luke 12:20, whereas the inclusion of the pronoun as the explicit subject of the phrase that follows ("Fool! What you yourself sow does not come to life unless it dies ...") adds materially to the emphasis Paul is placing on the point that he is making. Fee's paraphrase helpfully brings out the force of the pronoun and its contribution to Paul's point: "Foolish man ... *You* hold the answer in your *own* hands. Simply look at the way God has arranged the natural order of plant life. In the everyday occurrence of the seed you have the evidence to answer your question."[658]

Verses 37–38 complete the point that was commenced in verse 36b: "And as for what you sow—you are not sowing the body that will be, but only a seed, perhaps of wheat or another grain. But God gives it a body as he wants, and to each of the seeds its own body."[659] The example of

---

[657] Cf. the argument for this reading in Thiselton, *First Corinthians*, 1263.

[658] Fee, *First Epistle to the Corinthians*, 863 (emphasis original).

[659] The phrase εἰ τύχοι (literally, "if it should so happen") in v. 37 makes use of the aorist optative form of τυγχάνω in an idiomatic fashion, with a meaning similar to the meaning

seeds and plants serves a double function within Paul's argument, as both a kind of metaphor for the idea of eschatological transformation and as an instance of the power of God that is able to effect a transformation of this sort, even within the natural order of the creation in its present form. Here, as elsewhere in his letters (e.g., 2 Cor 9:10), Paul depicts the regular processes of the natural order not as a closed and self-sufficient system but as a daily manifestation of the providential activity of God.[660] Essential to the point Paul is making is the idea of transformation: what is sown is not a miniature plant but a seed, and what emerges from the soil is not an enlarged replica of the seed but something remarkably and gloriously different.[661] Also important (and preparing the way for the point Paul goes on to make in vv. 39–41) is the reminder in verse 38 of the wide variety of "bodies" that can emerge from the seeds that are planted; the God who created and sustains these natural processes is not only the powerful source of the life-giving energy that they require but also the infinitely inventive author of all the rich diversity that his creation contains (cf. Gen 1:12).

15:39–41. Paul's point in verses 36–38 about transformation is followed in verses 39–41 by a second point about the variety of forms that embodiment can take and the differing kinds and degrees of glory that bodies can possess, both on the earth and in the heavens. He begins in verse 39 with a list of examples of the various different forms that "flesh" (σάρξ) can take, including the flesh of humans, animals, birds, and fish. His use of the word "flesh" in this context does not imply any of the negative moral connotations that it can carry elsewhere (Gal 5:17, 19) but may still hint at the conditions of mortality and vulnerability that are pervasive features of the bodies of earthly creatures in this age but will no longer be present in the age to come (cf. v. 50).

---

that it carries in 14:10; here, it means something like "perhaps" (CSB) or "for instance," introducing a list of examples that could have been made more complete or more precise if it had been more important.

[660] The variation in tenses between the present δίδωσιν ("God gives") and the aorist ἠθέλησεν (CSB "he wants"; more literally, "he willed") may suggest that the latter verb is referring to God's original design as creator and the former to his ongoing providential activity as the one who sustains and energizes his creation.

[661] Paul's description of the seed that is sown as "naked" (γυμνός, untranslated in the CSB) anticipates his later depiction of the resurrected body as being "clothed" (ἐνδύσηται) with incorruptibility and immortality.

Verses 40–41 build on this point and extend it: not only are there are various forms that even "flesh" can take, when comparing one earthly creature with another, but there is also the (far greater) difference that can be observed between "earthly bodies" (i.e., bodies of the sort referred to in v. 39) and "heavenly bodies" (probably, given the following verse, a reference to the sun, the moon, and the stars, not the bodies of angels). This difference is not only a difference of kind but a difference of "splendor" (δόξα), and even among the heavenly bodies the splendor of the sun differs in both kind and degree from the splendor of the moon and the stars, and star differs from star in splendor.[662] The accent in these verses on varieties and degrees of splendor is probably intended as a response to the aesthetic dimension of the thinking behind the question in verse 35: those who recoil from the idea of reanimated corpses as an intrinsically dishonorable notion have not reckoned on the glory that bodies can possess and the ability of God to redeem and recreate the earthly bodies of believers, clothing their present dishonor with a new and far greater glory than they currently possess.

15:42–44a. In verses 42–44 Paul draws out explicitly the implications of the analogies in the previous verses for the way in which he wishes the Corinthians to think about the resurrection of the dead. The fourfold repetition of "sown" (σπείρεται) and "raised" (ἐγείρεται) recalls the seed analogy of verses 36–38 and the contrasts between "corruption" (φθορά) and "incorruption" (ἀφθαρσία), "dishonor" (ἀτιμία) and "glory" (δόξα), "weakness" (ἀσθένεια) and "power" (δύναμις) recall the point made in verses 39–41 about different kinds of bodies and the differences in kind and degree of the glory that they possess.

The transformations Paul describes imply a material change from our present experience of embodiment in a world that is (as Paul puts it elsewhere) in "bondage to decay" (Rom 8:21), with a strong implication that those aspects of our present embodied experience that involve disability, degeneration, and disease will either no longer be present in the age to come or will no longer intersect with our social and material environment in a way that diminishes our ability to enjoy God and his creation. Our bodies will, indeed, be redeemed (cf. Rom 8:23). Nevertheless, in light of what Paul has already said in the previous chapters of this letter about

[662] The ideas and language of v. 41 probably reflect the influence of Sir 43:1–12. Cf. Thiselton, *First Corinthians*, 1268–69.

the divinely intended diversity within the body of Christ and the stark contrasts between God's estimation of weakness and strength, glory and honor, and the way in which these variables are measured by the world (1:18–31; 3:18–23; 12:21–26; cf. 2 Cor 12:7–10), it would be a mistake to conclude from these verses that the transformation Paul anticipates is simply the erasure of everything about our bodies that does not conform to what is conventionally regarded as strong, clever, beautiful, or honorable. Nor should we assume that the glorification of our bodies will involve the eradication of all those aspects of our character and identity that are the way they are because of our experiences of disability or disease in this age. The risen Christ whom the disciples meet in the resurrection narratives of John's Gospel still, after all, bears the scars of his crucifixion, and the one whom John sees on the throne in the visions he recounts in the book of Revelation is still recognizably and gloriously the one who was crucified.[663]

The transformations of verses 42–43 from "corruption" to "incorruption," "dishonor" to "glory," and "weakness" to "power," are followed in verse 44a by a fourth transformation, from "natural" (ψυχικός) to "spiritual" (πνευματικός). The first of these two words is difficult to translate. Given Paul's strong insistence in this section on the embodied nature of our experience in the age to come, the NRSV's choice of the word "physical" as a contrast to "spiritual" is unfortunate. "Natural" (e.g., CSB, NIV, ESV) is probably the best option available to us, though it should be remembered that the word it translates is derived not from φύσις ("nature") but from ψυχή ("person"/"soul"). The primary background against which Paul wishes the notion of a "natural" (ψυχικός) existence to be understood, as he makes clear in the following verse, is the creation narrative of Genesis. Read against that background, the contrast he has in mind appears to be between a form of embodied existence that is determined by the realities of the present creation (which we share with all living and breathing creatures) and a new form of embodied existence that is pervasively renewed by the presence of the Spirit. The contrast here in chapter 15 between a σῶμα ψυχικόν and a σῶμα πνευματικόν is therefore a consummation and perfection of what is already foreshadowed and anticipated by the contrast in 2:14–15 between the ψυχικὸς ... ἄνθρωπος ("the person without the Spirit") and the πνευματικὸς ...

[663] Cf. the discussion in Brock and Wannenwetsch, *Therapy*, 212–20.

ἄνθρωπος ("the spiritual person"), who has the firstfruits of the Spirit and is in the process of being inwardly (though not yet outwardly and bodily) transformed by the Spirit's presence.[664]

15:44b–49. The contrast in verse 44a between the "natural body" and the "spiritual body" is explained and elaborated on in verses 44b–49, with "the first man Adam" appealed to as a paradigm of the former and Christ, "the last Adam," appealed to as a paradigm of the latter. Paul begins in verse 44b with an assertion that is framed in the form of a first-class conditional sentence (i.e., a conditional sentence in which the truth of the protasis is assumed for the sake of the argument and a conclusion is drawn from it): "If there is a natural body, there is also a spiritual body."[665] The implied premise standing behind the sentence is not a general, a priori principle that everything natural has a spiritual counterpart. It is, rather, a truth that Christians have been made aware of a posteriori, through the gospel announcement of Christ's resurrection and the outpouring of the Spirit as a first instalment of God's work to renew the whole creation. Paul's claim is not that Adam's existence logically implies the necessity of Christ's, or of the new humanity who will be created in Christ's image. His claim is, rather, that the *embodied* nature of Adam's existence is a sign pointing forward to the *embodied* nature of human existence in the renewed, Spirit-transformed creation.

Verse 45 begins with a modified quotation from Genesis 2:7, offered partly as scriptural support for the reference in the previous verse to a σῶμα ψυχικόν ("spiritual body") and partly to set up a series of comparisons and contrasts between Adam and Christ (and between those who bear their respective images) that Paul unfolds across the following verses. The quotation from Genesis 2:7 is identified as such by the citation formula that introduces it ("So it is written"), but Paul alters it slightly by introducing the word "first" (πρῶτος) and identifying Adam by name, preparing the way for the corresponding statement about Christ in the second half of the verse. The key points Paul wishes to make from the quotation are signaled by the contrasts Paul draws between what is said of Adam in the first half of the verse and what is said of Christ in the second half. If Adam was the "the first man" (ὁ πρῶτος ἄνθρωπος), related to the

[664] Cf. the discussion in Wright, *Resurrection*, 348–54.

[665] Cf. Brookins and Longenecker, *1 Corinthians 10–16*, 175; Daniel B. Wallace, *Greek Grammar Beyond the Basics: An Exegetical Syntax of the New Testament* (Grand Rapids: Zondervan, 1996), 690, 711.

rest of humankind as their progenitor and the paradigm of their earthly existence, Christ is the "the last Adam" (ὁ ἔσχατος Ἀδάμ), who stands at the end of human history as its goal. If Adam became "a living being" (εἰς ψυχὴν ζῶσαν), sharing a "natural" (ψυχικός) existence with all the other living creatures made by God (cf. Gen 1:20, 21, 24, 30; 2:19), Christ, the last Adam, became "a lifegiving spirit" (εἰς πνεῦμα ζῳοποιοῦν)—a description that highlights his role as the giver of the Spirit and the source of resurrection life for his people.[666]

Verse 46 makes a point similar to the one Paul has already made in verse 23, insisting that "the spiritual is not first, but the natural, then the spiritual." The explicitly contrastive and corrective nature of the syntax of this verse suggests that Paul is not simply offering an uncontroversial and self-evident point about the shape of the grand narrative he is rehearsing for the Corinthians. Although, as argued above, the primary source for the thinking of those within the church who have rejected the idea of future bodily resurrection is probably the pagan thinking of their neighbors rather than an explicitly Christian heresy along the lines of the teaching referred to in 2 Timothy 2:18, it is still in keeping with Paul's statements elsewhere in the letter to those who considered themselves to be the "spiritual" members of the church that he would need to issue a warning of this sort, reminding them that the fulness of spiritual existence is reserved for the age to come. Wedderburn comments: "Taken in this way the verse becomes a polemic against an unrealistic spiritualizing of this present life, a blending of heaven and earth that does away with the earthiness of the latter; the Corinthians erred in holding to a one-stage soteriology, rather than in reversing the order of a two-stage one."[667]

Verses 47–49 further elaborate on the contrast between "the first man" (Adam) and "the second man" (Christ). The former, Paul says, was "from the earth, a man of dust" (with an obvious allusion to Gen 2:7). The latter, Paul goes on to say by way of contrast, is "from heaven" (ἐξ οὐρανοῦ). Paul's description of Christ as "from heaven" is probably not to be taken as referring primarily to his origin, as the one who came from heaven to

---

[666] It may also hint at his divine identity, echoing the description of the Lord God in Gen 2:7 as the one who "breathed the breath of life into [Adam's] nostrils." Cf. Wright, *Resurrection*, 354–55; Fee, *First Epistle to the Corinthians*, 873.

[667] A. J. M. Wedderburn, "Philo's 'Heavenly Man'," *NovT* 15 (1973): 302.

earth in the event of the incarnation;[668] if that were his intended meaning, it would be difficult to see how he could go on in the following verses to affirm the correspondence that he asserts between the "man of heaven" (ὁ ἐπουράνιος) and "those who are of heaven" (οἱ ἐπουράνιοι), who bear his image. The accent is, rather, on the heavenly nature of the body that he now has, which possesses an incorruptible and immortal glory that derive from the resurrecting work of God.[669]

What can be said of Adam and Christ can also be said, according to verses 48–49, of those who bear their image: "Like the man of dust, so are those who are of the dust; like the man of heaven, so are those who are of heaven. And just as we have borne the image of the man of dust, we will also bear the image of the man of heaven." The main interpretive difficulty associated with these verses lies in the final verb of verse 49. Here, the CSB translation (like the NIV and NRSV) is in keeping with the UBS5 text, which follows those manuscripts (e.g., B, I) in which the verb is shown as a future tense (φορέσομεν, "we will ... bear"), rather than an aorist subjunctive (φορέσωμεν, "let us ... bear"). The UBS committee's decision is based primarily on their interpretation of the immediate context, which is clearly didactic rather than hortatory in nature,[670] and despite the stronger manuscript support (e.g., 𝔓[46], א, A, C, D, F) for the aorist subjunctive form of the verb, the exegetical considerations they point to are probably a sufficient warrant for this decision.[671]

15:50–53. The opening words of verse 50 (Τοῦτο δέ φημι, "What I am saying ... is this"; more literally, "And this I say"), like the similar expression in 7:29, signal the transition to a new section in the flow of ideas rather than an explanatory conclusion to the previous paragraph.[672] Having

---

[668] Hence (correctly!) the decision of the CSB translators to supply "is" rather than "was" as the elided verb.

[669] Cf. Fee, *First Epistle to the Corinthians*, 877.

[670] Metzger, *Textual Commentary*, 502. Another relevant exegetical consideration is the insistence of Paul in v. 46 that "the spiritual is not first, but the natural, then the spiritual," which would seem to count against the idea that Paul views his readers as (already) no longer bearing the image of the man of dust.

[671] See Fee, *First Epistle to the Corinthians*, 879–80, for a contrary argument in favor of φορέσωμεν as original. The difference between the two readings should not be overstated; on either reading, the larger shape of Paul's argument across the chapter includes an exhortation to the Corinthians to allow their future bodily destiny to inform the shape of their present moral conduct.

[672] The latter understanding appears to have been held by the copyist whose alteration of δέ to γάρ is reflected in the reading of this verse shown in a number of Western manuscripts

focused in verses 44b–49 on the contrast between the "natural body" and the "spiritual body" and the typological relationship between Adam and Christ, Paul's focus now returns to the vulnerability of flesh and blood and its susceptibility to decay and corruption (cf. vv. 42–43)—attributes that he declares to be categorically incompatible with the incorruptible life of the coming kingdom of God. While the idea of transformation from "corruption" to "incorruption" was already present in verse 42, the new idea here is the *necessity* of this transformation. Flesh and blood "cannot" (οὐ δύναται) inherit the kingdom of God; the corruptible "must" (δεῖ) be clothed with incorruptibility and the mortal with immortality (v. 53).

The statement in verse 50 is followed in verses 51–52 by a bold declaration: "Listen, I am telling you a mystery: We will not all fall asleep, but we will all be changed, in a moment, in the twinkling of an eye, at the last trumpet. For the trumpet will sound, and the dead will be raised incorruptible, and we will be changed." Paul's description of this declaration as a "mystery" (μυστήριον) is in keeping with its use in the Old Testament and elsewhere in his letters to describe something that was once hidden but has now been made known by God (cf. the comments on 2:1, 7, above). Although it is possible that Paul is using that word here to refer to a particular and distinct word of prophetic revelation that the Spirit has made known to him (cf. 12:8; 13:2),[673] this is not a necessary implication of the way in which he phrases his claim. The simpler and more likely understanding of his meaning, in line with the way in which he has previously characterized the gospel itself as a μυστήριον that reveals the inbreaking of God's eschatological purposes in the resurrection of the crucified Jesus (cf. 2:1, 7–10), is that the "mystery" Paul is declaring here is an unfolding of what he understands to be a necessary entailment of that gospel, given the basic principle that he states in verse 50 and restates in verse 53. Given that mortal and corruptible flesh cannot pass unchanged into the incorruptible realm of the coming kingdom, we can *all* expect to undergo transformation, irrespective of whether we pass through death and resurrection or are simply "changed, in a moment, in the twinkling of an eye, at the last trumpet" (vv. 51–52). The "last trumpet" to which Paul refers in verse 52 is a reference to the trumpet blast that announces the arrival of the day of God's judgment in Old Testament and Second

---

including D, F, and G, and in Ambrosiaster's commentary on this verse.

[673] Cf. Fee, *First Epistle to the Corinthians*, 885.

Temple Jewish tradition (e.g., Joel 2:1; Zeph 1:16; Zech 9:14; 4 Ezra 6:23; Sib. Or. 4:173–175), and the fact that the transformation Paul envisages is described as taking place "in a moment, in the twinkling of an eye" (ἐν ἀτόμῳ, ἐν ῥιπῇ ὀφθαλμοῦ) emphasizes its nature as a miraculous work of God.

Verse 53 offers explanatory support for the statement in verses 51–52, reiterating the claim of verse 50 about the impossibility of corruptible flesh and blood passing unchanged into the coming kingdom but rephrasing it in positive terms: "For this corruptible body must be clothed with incorruptibility, and this mortal body must be clothed with immortality." Paul's picture of the body being "clothed" (ἐνδύσασθαι) with incorruptibility and immortality differs strikingly from the imagery used by writers such as Philo, who speak of the body being "stripped off" to enable the liberation of the immortal soul from its bodily imprisonment (e.g., *Alleg. Int.* 2.15.54–59; *Dreams* 1.8.43) and implies the redemption and glorification of the body rather than its being discarded and disposed of.[674]

15:54–57. This transformation is celebrated by Paul in verses 54–55 in words he borrows from Scripture in a composite quotation from Isaiah 25:8 and Hosea 13:14.[675] Paul's wording differs at several points from the wording of these verses in most surviving versions of the Hebrew and Greek textual traditions.[676] The two main changes he appears to have made (or derived from the textual tradition he is following) are (1) combining the LXX's language of "swallow[ing] up" (where it refers to the way in which death has "swallowed up" the nations) with the depiction in the Hebrew text of God as the one who has defeated death and (2) making double use of the word νῖκος ("victory"), which Paul, in common with Aquila and Theodotion, uses in place of ἰσχύσας ("having prevailed") in Isaiah 25:8 and substitutes in place of the LXX's "judgment" or "penalty"

---

[674] Cf. Garland, *1 Corinthians*, 744. Given the susceptibility of the earthly body to decay and destruction, the kind of continuity Paul has in mind is presumably a continuity of identity rather than a straightforwardly physical/material continuity of substance.

[675] Cf. especially Ciampa, "Composite Citations," 174–79.

[676] The variant readings of Isa 25:8 that are attested in the translations of Aquila, Symmachus, and Theodotion are significantly closer to Paul's rendition of the verse, suggesting the possibility that some of the differences between Paul's language and that of the LXX and MT may be due to the textual tradition he is following rather than a deliberate modification of the text on his part for rhetorical or interpretive purposes. Cf. Joseph Ziegler, ed., *Isaias*, vol. 14 of *Septuaginta: Vetus Testamentum Graecum* (Göttingen: Vandenhoeck & Ruprecht, 1967), 208.

(δίκη) in Hosea 13:14. The combined effect of both verses, in the version in which Paul quotes them, is unambiguously celebratory and triumphant: the readers are implicitly invited to join with Isaiah's song of victory over death, and the summoning of Death and Hades for judgment in Hosea 13:14 is transformed into a taunt over death, whose penal role has been made redundant by the work of Christ on behalf of those who are in him.[677]

Verses 56–57 explain and celebrate the way in which the work of Christ has brought about the transformation of believers' situation that Paul has already presupposed in his alteration of "penalty" (δίκη) to "victory" (νῖκος) in the quotation from Hosea. The "sting" of death (i.e., the circumstance that confers on it its venomous effect as a manifestation of the destructive judgment of God) is sin, and the "power" of sin (i.e., the framework within which it is authorized to carry out that condemning and alienating work) is the law.[678] But Christ (whose death has absorbed the condemnation of the law and whose resurrection has conquered the powers of sin and death) has overcome these powers once and for all (cf. Rom 5:21; 8:1–4, 31–39; Col 2:13–15), a triumph Paul celebrates in verse 57: "But thanks be to God, who gives us the victory through our Lord Jesus Christ!"

15:58. The chapter concludes in verse 58 with a word of exhortation Paul addresses to the whole community of believers in Corinth: "Therefore, my dear brothers and sisters, be steadfast, immovable, always excelling in the Lord's work, because you know that your labor in the Lord is not in vain." The activity Paul has in mind when he refers to "the work of the Lord" (τό ἔργον τοῦ κυρίου) is probably the shared task of building up of the people of God (cf. 3:10–15; 9:1; 16:10)—a task that (unlike the futile labors to build something eternal on any other foundation) withstands and overcomes all the predations of death and decay. It is possible that Paul is intending an even more specific reference to the work of gospel-proclamation (note the connection between "labor[ing]" and "preach[ing]" in 15:10–11)—a work that he has already declared to be "in vain" (κενός) if Christ has not been raised (v. 14). The former, slightly broader, interpretation is probably to be preferred, given Paul's earlier

[677] Cf. David I. Starling, *Hermeneutics as Apprenticeship: How the Bible Shapes Our Interpretive Habits and Practices* (Grand Rapids: Baker, 2016), 143–45.

[678] Cf. the similar statements regarding the interrelationship between sin, death, and the law in Rom 5:12–21.

statements in chapter 12 about the diversity of ways in which believers are gifted by God and contribute to the work of building up Christ's body.

This assurance clearly stands in obvious contrast to the situation of those who do not possess the hope of the resurrection (cf. the recurring use of ματαίος and κενός in vv. 10, 14, 17). While the exhortation of verse 58 is clearly directed to the whole community of believers, Paul has not forgotten the polemic against those who say that "there is no resurrection of the dead" (v. 12), which has made up the majority of the chapter. The exhortation with which the chapter concludes implicitly urges those who have subscribed to that idea to abandon it and return to the fulness of the hope entailed by the gospel and encourages the remainder of the audience to resist their influence, remaining "steadfast" (ἑδραῖοι) and "immovable" (ἀμετακίνητοι) in the gospel on which they have taken their stand (cf. vv. 1–2; Col 1:23).

Bridge

The story Paul retells and celebrates in verses 35–58 is the story of the whole human race, inasmuch as we are all among those who have "borne the image of the man of dust" (v. 49a), and the whole church, inasmuch as we will all one day "bear the image of the man of heaven" (v. 49b). It is therefore of the broadest possibility applicability, extending far beyond the particular set of ideas that were subscribed to by those in Corinth who recoiled from the idea of a future bodily resurrection.

The hope Paul contends for and celebrates within this chapter is an inseparable entailment of the gospel announcement of Christ's death, burial, and resurrection and is fundamental to the view of the world that Paul urges his readers to adopt and maintain. Oliver O'Donovan aptly summarizes the significance and scale of what is at stake:

> In proclaiming the resurrection of Christ, the apostles proclaimed also the resurrection of mankind in Christ; and in proclaiming the resurrection of mankind, they proclaimed the renewal of all creation with him. The resurrection of Christ in isolation from mankind would not be a gospel message. The resurrection of mankind apart from creation would be a gospel of a sort, but of a purely gnostic and world-denying sort which is far from the gospel that the apostles actually preached.[679]

[679] O'Donovan, *Resurrection and Moral Order*, 31.

Faithful Christian proclamation, and faithful Christian living, requires both a laser-like focus on the things that are of first importance, as Paul spells them out in the opening verses of the chapter, and a vast, expansive vision of the scope of the transforming and redeeming work that God has brought about in Christ and is in the process of bringing to its consummation.

Within that story, believers are both the joyful recipients of a salvation we could never have accomplished or merited on our own and the active participants in a work to which God calls us as his redeemed people. This climactic chapter of 1 Corinthians is both an affirmation of the grace that undergirds every part of our salvation and a summons to the labor that, because of that grace, is not in vain. It encourages and equips us to resist all the various forces, within and beyond the church, that tempt us to decenter or diminish the gospel that has been passed on to us or to grow weary in the work that it calls us to.

IX. Responses Regarding the Collection, Travel Plans, and Apollos (16:1–12)

The opening paragraphs of chapter 16 deal with two remaining issues that appear to have been raised in the Corinthians' letter: the collection Paul is organizing for the believers in Judea and the forthcoming visit of Apollos that the Corinthians—or, at least, some among them—have been eagerly anticipating.

After the grandeur and rhetorical power of the final paragraphs of chapter 15, the instructions and updates Paul gives in these opening paragraphs of chapter 16 are strikingly brief and matter-of-fact. The περὶ δέ formula that opens verse 1 is the fifth instance of the phrase within 1 Corinthians and, like the previous instances (7:1, 25; 8:1; 12:1), it appears to signal a response that Paul is making to a matter that was raised in the Corinthians' letter (cf. 7:1). A series of brief instructions regarding the way in which Paul wishes the Corinthians to participate (vv. 1–2) is followed in verses 3–4 by some information on Paul's plans to visit and convey the collection to Jerusalem. This update, in turn is followed in verses 5–11 by further detail and explanation regarding the timing and duration of Paul's visit and his hopes for the visit that he is intending for Timothy to make in the interim. Finally, in verse 12, Paul adds what appears to be another response to a matter raised in the Corinthians' letter, updating the readers on the circumstances behind the delay in a visit from Apollos that the Corinthians appear to have been expecting and assuring them that he will come when he is able.

A. The Collection and Paul's Travel Plans (16:1–11)

> [1] Now about the collection for the saints: Do the same as I instructed
> the Galatian churches. [2] On the first day of the week, each of you is to
> set something aside and save in keeping with how he is prospering, so
> that no collections will need to be made when I come. [3] When I arrive,
> I will send with letters those you recommend to carry your gift to Je-
> rusalem. [4] If it is suitable for me to go as well, they will travel with me.
>
> [5] I will come to you after I pass through Macedonia—for I will be trav-
> eling through Macedonia— [6] and perhaps I will remain with you or
> even spend the winter, so that you may send me on my way wherever
> I go. [7] I don't want to see you now just in passing, since I hope to spend
> some time with you, if the Lord allows. [8] But I will stay in Ephesus until
> Pentecost, [9] because a wide door for effective ministry has opened for
> me—yet many oppose me. [10] If Timothy comes, see that he has nothing
> to fear while with you, because he is doing the Lord's work, just as I
> am. [11] So let no one look down on him. Send him on his way in peace so
> that he can come to me, because I am expecting him with the brothers.

Comments

16:1–4. Paul begins the chapter with a formula (Περὶ δέ, "Now about …") that has become a familiar structural feature of the second half of the letter (cf. 7:1, 25; 8:1; 12:1; 16:12). The brevity and lack of detail in the reference that follows to "the collection for the saints"[680] supports the hypothesis that this is a response to a question that the Corinthians have asked within their letter and that Paul has already laid out the details of the collection and its rationale within an earlier communication. Paul's instructions here offer no explanation, for example, of who "the saints" are, and it is not until verse 3 that we are told that the collection will be taken to Jerusalem; nor does Paul provide the Corinthians with anything like the sort of summary of the collection's nature and rationale that he gives to his readers in Romans 15:25–27, on the assumption that some of

---

[680] The word λογεία ("collection") that Paul uses here is used in the papyri to refer to collections of money for a variety of different purposes, but most commonly for "religious collections for a god, a temple, etc." David J. Downs, *The Offering of the Gentiles: Paul's Collection for Jerusalem in Its Chronological, Cultural, and Cultic Contexts*, WUNT (Tübingen: Mohr Siebeck, 2008), 129. Cf. BDAG, s.v. "λογεία."

them will be hearing about the collection for the first time (even though, in their case, he is not asking for any contribution other than prayer for its acceptance).

The instruction in verse 1b to "do the same as I instructed the Galatian churches" is unlikely to have been intended as self-explanatory (unless the Corinthians were somehow aware of the instructions Paul had given to the Galatian churches). Rather, it points forward to the instructions that follow in the following verse and frames them with a subtle reminder that what Paul is asking of the Corinthians is consistent with what he asks of others (cf. 4:17; 7:17; 11:16; 14:33)—the Corinthians are not to think that they are somehow being singled out for a special burden or, for that matter, a special honor as distinguished benefactors.

The instructions that follow are simple and brief. All members of the church are encouraged to participate, offering contributions that are in proportion with their means ("each of you is to set something aside and save in keeping with how he is prospering"). They are to plan ahead, "so that no collections will need to be made when I come," setting aside an amount each week as they are able. This is to take place "on the first day of the week"—an instruction that, when read in conjunction with purpose clause that follows ("so that no collections will need to be made when I come") suggests that the process Paul had in mind in his instructions to "set ... aside" (τιθέτω) and "save" (θησαυρίζων) an amount each week probably involved bringing a sum of money to contribute to a common purse, rather than merely setting it aside at home;[681] it also offers a clue that the regular weekly gathering of the church took place not on the Jewish Sabbath but on the first day of the week (presumably in honor of Christ's resurrection).[682]

The reference in verse 2b to Paul's arrival is followed in verses 3–4 by a brief outline of Paul's plans for what will take place when he comes: "When I arrive, I will send with letters those you recommend to carry

---

[681] Cf. Ciampa and Rosner, *The First Letter to the Corinthians*, 843; Downs, *The Offering of the Gentiles*, 128–29; contra Fee, *First Epistle to the Corinthians*, 899. Fee points out that the phrase παρ' ἑαυτῷ can sometimes be used with the meaning "at home" (e.g., Xenophon, *Mem.* 3.13.3; Philo, *Cherubim* 48; *Embassy* 271), but when it is used, as here, in conjunction with the immediately preceding phrase, ἕκαστος ὑμῶν ("each of you"), the meaning conveyed by the phrase is not "at home" but "individually" (e.g., Aristotle, *Hist. an.* 511b; Herodian, *Hist.* 4.3.8; IG XI/4 1040, cited in Downs, *The Offering of the Gentiles*, 128).

[682] Cf. Acts 20:7; Rev 1:10, and the discussion in S. R. Llewelyn, "The Use of Sunday for Meetings of Believers in the New Testament," *NovT* 43 (2001): 205–23.

your gift to Jerusalem. If it is suitable for me to go as well, they will travel with me." The inclusion of Corinthian representatives in the party that conveys the gift to Jerusalem is presumably intended partly as a practical measure to assist with carrying the money and reducing the risk of theft, partly as way of safeguarding the transparency and integrity of the project (cf. 2 Cor 8:16–24; 12:14–18) and partly as a visible expression of the partnership (κοινωνία) between gentile and Jewish believers that Paul wished the collection to be a manifestation of (cf. 2 Cor 8:4; 9:13; Rom 15:26–27).

The uncertainty Paul expresses in verse 4 as to whether he himself will be accompanying the collection to Jerusalem is read by some as an indication that he will go only if the size of the collection is "worthy" (ἄξιος) of his presence.[683] As Fee argues, however, the syntax of the clause reads far more naturally as an impersonal construction ("if it is advisable"; cf. the CSB's "if it is suitable for me to go as well"), rather than with "your gift" (cf. v. 3) as the implied subject of the verb.[684] It would also seem oddly inconsistent with the resistance Paul offers elsewhere to the Corinthians' desire to be regarded as honored benefactors if he were to pander to that aspiration by making a promise of his personal participation in the delegation contingent on the size of their contribution.[685] The more likely scenario is that Paul is still weighing up the question of whether his presence in the delegation will help or hinder its chances of being positively received by the believers in Jerusalem and intends to make a final decision on that matter between the writing of the letter to the Corinthians and the departure of the delegation from Corinth (cf. Rom 15:30–31; Acts 21:20–30).

16:5–9. Having spoken in verses 2b–4 of his plan to visit the Corinthians (cf. 4:18–21; 11:34b), Paul goes on in verses 5–9 to offer some more detail on the timing of the visit and an explanation for the fact that it will not take place until some months' time. Paul's present location is in Ephesus,

---

[683] E.g., Robertson and Plummer, *First Corinthians*, 387; Schrage, *1. Korintherbrief*, 4:432.

[684] Fee, *First Epistle to the Corinthians*, 902. The neuter gender of ἄξιον fits much more naturally with an impersonal construction than with one in which the implied subject of the verb is the feminine noun χάρις in the preceding verse.

[685] This is not to say that Paul is entirely unconcerned about matters of honor and shame associated with the collection, but the expression that he gives in 2 Cor 9:1–4 to considerations such as this is framed as a desire to avoid the shame that would result from a failure of the Corinthians to contribute, rather than a promise of special honor as an incentive for a large contribution.

and he plans to remain there until the Feast of Pentecost, in late spring or early summer, because "a wide door for effective ministry has opened for me—yet many oppose me" (vv. 8–9). The "yet" with which the CSB translates Paul's καί assumes that the conjunction is being used here with an adversative meaning—i.e., that Paul is remaining in Ephesus *because of* the opportunities that are open to him, *despite* the opposition he is facing. This is a grammatically possible interpretation (the conjunction καί can sometimes be used in context where there is an obviously adversative relationship between the two elements of the sentence that are being connected), but the conjunction itself is certainly not "marked" as a way of signaling this sort of contrast and the context does not necessitate an adversative interpretation.[686] The opposition Paul makes mention of here (which would presumably have included the hostility alluded to by Paul in 1 Cor 15:32 and sort of resistance that led to the events described in Acts 19:21–41)[687] may well have factored in his thinking as an additional reason for remaining a little longer (in order to offer support and encouragement to the local believers) rather a counterbalancing consideration to be weighed against the opportunities he wished to exploit.[688]

After Paul's stay in Ephesus is completed, his plan is to travel through Macedonia, visiting the churches there (v. 5) before arriving in Corinth.[689] Under the timeline described in verses 5–7, this journey through Macedonia would take place prior to Paul's visit to Corinth, allowing him the possibility of an extended stay with the Corinthians (perhaps even

---

686 Cf. Brookins and Longenecker, *1 Corinthians 10–16*, 195; Steven E. Runge, *Discourse Grammar of the Greek New Testament: A Practical Introduction for Teaching and Exegesis* (Peabody: Hendrickson, 2010), 23–27.

687 The mysterious, allusive mention that Paul makes in 2 Cor 1:8–10 of "the affliction that took place in Asia" may be referring to a flare-up of this opposition, in keeping with the expectations Paul expresses here in 1 Cor 16. Cf. the discussion of that verse and its likely background in Starling, "We Do Not Want You To Be Unaware," 266–79.

688 Cf. Brock and Wannenwetsch, *Therapy*, 236–40.

689 It is possible, as David Gill has argued (based on Paul's claim in Rom 15:19 that he has "have fully proclaimed the gospel ... all the way around to Illyricum") that the travels Paul intended to make—and did in fact end up making—through Macedonia may have also included a missionary visit to the western parts of the province in order plant new churches there. Cf. David W. J. Gill, "Macedonia," in *The Book of Acts in Its Graeco-Roman Setting*, ed. David W. J. Gill and Conrad H. Gempf (Grand Rapids: Eerdmans, 1994), 398–99; Ciampa and Rosner, *The First Letter to the Corinthians*, 846. Under either scenario, the request of the Macedonian churches to contribute to the collection for Judea could have been either an additional reason for his visit to the province or (more likely, given the way in which Paul speaks about it in 2 Cor 8:1–5) a matter that they raised while Paul was visiting them as part of this trip.

spending the winter there)[690] before being sent on his way by them for the next stage of his journey.[691] In the event, Paul's plans did not work out as intended: he was compelled by a crisis in Corinth to make an emergency visit to the Corinthian church prior to his journey through Macedonia (cf. 2 Cor 2:1–4), and only subsequently (after that "painful visit," the delayed journey through Macedonia, and the writing of 2 Corinthians) to return with representatives of the Macedonian churches to spend a longer period of time with the Corinthians (cf. 2 Cor 9:4; 12:14; 13:1).

In the meantime, as Paul has already mentioned in 4:17, he has sent Timothy to the Corinthians (via Macedonia, if the sending of Timothy referred to here is the same event as the one recorded in Acts 19:22) and is anticipating that he will soon arrive there. In verses 10–11 he follows the update on his own travel plans with some instruction regarding Timothy's visit (presumably written on the assumption that the letter will likely arrive in Corinth before Timothy does). The first of these instructions urges the Corinthians to "see that [Timothy] has nothing to fear while with you" (v. 10) and is reinforced in the following verse by a command that no one should "look down on" Timothy. The inclusion of these two commands and the strength of the language they are couched in (particularly the second, which uses a verb Paul has previously employed on two occasions to describe the contemptuous attitude that the wealthy and privileged have toward their social inferiors) implies an apprehension on Paul's part that some of the more arrogant and overbearing members of the Corinthian church might be inclined to disregard or intimidate Timothy because of his youth and lack of personal authority.[692]

---

[690] Paul's reference in v. 6 to the possibility of "spend[ing] the winter" with the Corinthians reflects the fact that sea travel ceased almost completely across the winter months, until the arrival of the westerly winds in early February, when "spring open[ed] the sea to voyagers" (Pliny the Elder, *Nat.* 2.47).

[691] The verb προπέμπω, which Paul uses to express his hope that "that you may send me on my way" (ἵνα ὑμεῖς με προπέμψητε), is a semi-technical term that occurs in several places within his letters (Rom 15:24; 1 Cor 16:6, 11; 2 Cor 1:16; Titus 3:13) to describe the action of providing a traveler with assistance such as food, money, and (where needed) traveling companions or a means of transport. Cf. BDAG, s.v. "προπέμπω," 2.

[692] Cf. Paul's previous use of ἐξουθενέω ("look down on"; "despise") in 1:28; 6:4, and his later use of the same verb in 2 Cor 10:10 to describe the attitude that some of the Corinthians took toward Paul's own lack of rhetorical prowess. In Gal 4:14 Paul uses the same verb to express his gratitude for the fact that the Galatian believers did not "despise" him on the basis of his sickly physical condition.

In support of these two commands regarding the reception of Timothy, Paul reminds the Corinthians in verse 10b that "he is doing the Lord's work, just as I am"—language that echoes the way in which Paul has previously described the work that he and Apollos have performed among the Corinthians (cf. 3:13–15) and the work that he wishes the Corinthians themselves to persevere and abound in (15:58). In keeping with the correspondence Paul highlights between Timothy's work and his own, he concludes the paragraph of instructions regarding Timothy's visit by requesting that after Timothy's work among the Corinthians is complete they should "send him on his way in peace" (using the same verb Paul has previously used in v. 6 to request their assistance for himself) so that Timothy can return to Paul and rejoin him, "because I am expecting him with the brothers."[693]

B. Apollos's Forthcoming Visit (16:12)

> 12 Now about our brother Apollos: I strongly urged him to come to you with the brothers, but he was not at all willing to come now. However, he will come when he has an opportunity.

Comments

16:12. The περὶ δέ ("Now about …") that introduces the information in verse 12 about Apollos and his intended visit is the last occurrence of that formula within the letter and, in line with the pattern established by the previous instances of that phrase's use (7:1, 25; 8:1; 12:1; 16:1) is probably a reference to a matter that has been raised in the Corinthians' letter. The most likely scenario, in line with the earlier references to Apollos in chapters 1–4, is that the group behind the writing of the letter (who were presumably admirers of Apollos) had included within the letter a question about why a visit from Apollos that they had been hoping for

[693] We do not know who "the brothers" are that Paul is referring to here; most likely they include Erastus (cf. Acts 19:22) and one or more of the Ephesian believers that Paul has sent to Macedonia and Corinth with Timothy. Alternatively, they could be Ephesian believers or members of Paul's missionary team who are still with Paul and, like him, awaiting Timothy's return (if "with the brothers" is taken as qualifying "I am expecting" rather than as qualifying "him"). The former scenario rather than the latter is the simpler and more likely, and coheres with the mention of Erastus's departure from Ephesus with Timothy in Acts 19:22; cf. Brookins and Longenecker, *1 Corinthians 10–16*, 197–98.

had not yet eventuated (possibly with the insinuation that Paul had been discouraging or preventing him from coming).[694]

In reply, Paul informs the Corinthians that he had in fact "strongly urged" (πολλὰ παρεκάλεσα) Apollos to go to Corinth "with the brothers" (presumably Stephanas, Fortunatus, and Achaicus, who have visited Paul and are now returning to Corinth as the bearers of his letter).[695] It was, Paul insists, Apollos who resisted Paul's urgings, because "he was not at all willing to come now," but "he will come when he has an opportunity."

Bridge

The instructions and updates that compose the majority of the last chapter of 1 Corinthians are among the most obviously occasional elements of the letter, focused very specifically on events, places, and persons that are of little direct relevance to the lives of its twenty-first century readers.

Nevertheless, their combined effect is to offer a strong reminder and a rich set of examples of the kind of partnership that Paul viewed believers as having with him and with one another in the work of the gospel and in the labors of love and mutual care that the gospel produces as its fruit. The instructions regarding the collection do not tell us much about its rationale or aim (we can learn more of that elsewhere, in and 2 Cor 8–9 and Rom 15:25–27, 31) and would not be the first place to which we might turn for a theology of Christian giving, but they do go out of their way to stress the solidarity of the Corinthians with the other churches that are contributing to the collection (v. 1), the desire Paul has for all the members of the church to be participants, in proportion to their means (v. 2), and the arrangements Paul wishes to make to ensure that the bringing of the gift to Jerusalem will be authentically, visibly, and transparently an expression of partnership between the various churches that have been involved in it.

Similarly, the updates and instructions regarding the travel plans of Paul, Timothy, and Apollos illustrate and emphasize the multiple strands of relational partnership that were a pervasive feature of Paul's

---

694 Cf. the suggested reconstruction in Welborn, *An End to Enmity*, 411–12.

695 If, as I have argued in the introduction, the Corinthians' letter was brought to Paul by other members of the congregation and Stephanas, Fortunatus, and Achaicus had already been with him in Ephesus when it arrived, then "the brothers" sent back to Corinth with Paul's letter may have been a larger delegation that included both this trio and the people who had conveyed the Corinthians' letter to Paul.

missionary activity: his desire to revisit the churches of Macedonia and to spend time among the Corinthians—not just fleetingly, but for an extended stay—and his hope for their assistance in sending him on his way; his commitment to staying the course with the Ephesian believers, sharing with them in making the most of the opportunities God had opened up and standing firm in the face of opposition; his fatherly concern for Timothy and insistence that the Corinthians must receive him in the same way they would receive Paul; and his warm encouragement to Apollos and endorsement of the idea that Apollos should make a return visit to Corinth (as a coworker with Paul, and not a rival).

Those of us who live and minister within a context in which the values of the competitive marketplace are deeply ingrained in the ethos of our culture will find benefit in all of these lived examples of solidarity and partnership that we can glimpse through the window of these verses. Against the competitive and individualistic assumptions that will be second nature for many of us, Paul's instructions in these verses remind us that the work of the gospel is to be carried out in close and interdependent partnership and that it ties us to one another with strands of mutual connection and care that extend in multiple directions within, beyond, and between the congregations we are part of. Rightly receiving and responding to a letter such as 1 Corinthians includes our reflection on paragraphs such as these and the consequent actions that we take to create, restore, and maintain the networks of fellowship that unite us to other believers in the cause of the gospel and the community that the gospel creates.

X. Letter Closing (16:13–24)

The closing section of the letter comprises four paragraphs, each of which performs a distinctive task (or, in some cases, a cluster of interrelated tasks): (1) a brief set of five staccato exhortations that reinforce key themes and commands from earlier in the letter (vv. 13–14); (2) a commendation of the household of Stephanas (particularly Stephanas, Fortunatus and Achaicus, who have been with Paul in Ephesus) and their ministry among the Corinthians (vv. 15–18); (3) a cluster of greetings from the believers in Asia and Paul's coworkers, and an exhortation to the Corinthians to greet one another with a holy kiss (vv. 19–20); and (4) a final greeting Paul has written in his own hand, which includes a solemn anathema against the enemies of Christ, a prayer for Christ's return, a grace benediction, and an expression of Paul's love for the readers.

A. Exhortations and Commendations (16:13–18)

> [13] Be alert, stand firm in the faith, be courageous, be strong. [14] Do everything in love.
>
> [15] Brothers and sisters, you know the household of Stephanas: They are the firstfruits of Achaia and have devoted themselves to serving the saints. I urge you [16] also to submit to such people, and to everyone who works and labors with them. [17] I am delighted to have Stephanas, Fortunatus, and Achaicus present, because these men have made up for your absence. [18] For they have refreshed my spirit and yours. Therefore recognize such people.

Comments

16:13–14. The five succinctly stated commands in verses 13–14 occupy a similar place in the letter and perform a similar function to the five commands Paul strings together in 2 Corinthians 13:11 (cf. the similar fusillade of imperatives in 1 Thess 5:16–22). The commands need little elaboration, partly because they function (like the *peroratio* of a speech) to reiterate and reinforce what has already been said, rather than to introduce and explain new ideas.[696] The first four commands, in verse 13, focus mainly on reinforcing the reminders and imperatives of chapter 15: "Be alert" (Γρηγορεῖτε; cf. 15:33–34); "stand firm in the faith" (στήκετε ἐν τῇ πίστει; cf. 15:1, 58); "be courageous, be strong" (ἀνδρίζεσθε, κραταιοῦσθε; cf. 1 Cor 15:30–32, 58). The final command, in verse 14 ("Do everything in love"; πάντα ὑμῶν ἐν ἀγάπῃ γινέσθω), reiterates a series of earlier exhortations and reminders relating to that theme (e.g., 8:1–3; 10:33; 13:1–13; 14:1).

16:15–18. The commendation of Stephanas and his household is extended, emphatic, and specific, going well beyond the briefer and more generic remarks Paul makes on a similar theme in 1 Thessalonians 5:12–13a and Galatians 6:6. The extra elaboration and emphasis are probably an outworking of several interrelated factors, including the presence of Stephanas, Fortunatus, and Achaicus with Paul as he writes, their likely role in conveying this letter to Corinth and helping the church to understand and apply it, and the obvious confidence Paul has in their character and judgment. Paul goes out of his way to remind the church

[696] Cf. Witherington, *Conflict and Community*, 318.

of their history as "the firstfruits of Achaia" and their devotion to the service of God's people, despite the fact that (as he acknowledges) these things are already well known to his readers (v. 15).

The verses that follow also include further elements of repetition for emphasis: Paul urges the readers both to "submit to" (v. 16) and to "recognize" (v. 18) people such as Stephanas, Fortunatus, and Achaicus and informs them that he has been "delighted" to have these three members of Stephanas's household present with him, making up for the Corinthians' absence (v. 17) and that they have "refreshed my spirit and yours" (v. 18). Given the likelihood (based on their names) that Fortunatus and Achaicus were slaves or freedmen in Stephanas's household,[697] the elaborate and emphatic endorsement Paul gives to them and their ministry may also be an attempt to remedy the lack of respect that some of their social superiors within the Corinthian congregation were showing toward them (cf. 6:4; 11:17–34; 12:13). If that is the case, then the twice-repeated generalizing phrase, "[to] such people" (τοῖς τοιούτοις ... τοὺς τοιούτους), may be intended both as a reinforcement of the kind of criteria Paul wishes to see the Corinthians focusing on in identifying leaders to recognize and examples to imitate and as an implicit corrective to the specious criteria that (some of) the Corinthians have been fixated on instead.[698]

B. Final Greetings (16:19–24)

> [19] The churches of Asia send you greetings. Aquila and Priscilla send you greetings warmly in the Lord, along with the church that meets in their home. [20] All the brothers and sisters send you greetings. Greet one another with a holy kiss.
>
> [21] This greeting is in my own hand—Paul. [22] If anyone does not love the Lord, a curse be on him. Our Lord, come! [23] The grace of the Lord Jesus be with you. [24] My love be with all of you in Christ Jesus.

---

[697] On Fortunatus and Achaicus as names that were frequently given to slaves or taken by freedmen, see Fee, *First Epistle to the Corinthians*, 919; Meeks, *The First Urban Christians*, 56.

[698] For an extended discussion of these verses and their implications for understanding of Paul's view on local church leadership, see Allan Leslie Chapple, "Local Leadership in the Pauline Churches: Theological and Social Factors in Its Development: A Study Based on 1 Thessalonians, 1 Corinthians and Philippians" (PhD thesis, Durham, 1984), 393–445

Comments

16:19–20. The three greetings in verses 19–20a are all conveyed by Paul on behalf of other believers and congregations. The first, from "the churches of Asia," is the only instance in Paul's letters of a greeting from all of the churches in a province. Its presence here is probably a reflection of the role played by the city of Ephesus as the mother city of the province and the church(es) in Ephesus as the hub of a province-wide network of congregations (cf. Acts 19:10),[699] and may also be a further expression of Paul's desire to remind the Corinthians that they belong to a family of believers that extends far beyond their own small circle (cf. 1:2; 4:17; 11:16; 14:33).

The second greeting, in verse 19b, is from "Aquila and Priscilla ... along with the church that meets in their home." Paul's singling out of Aquila and Priscilla for special mention and the extra word πολλά ("warmly"), which he includes in the reference that he makes to their greeting, are probably both consequences of the fact that they were present in Corinth with Paul at the time of the Corinthian church's foundation (cf. Acts 18:1–3) and would have been personally known to many of the believers in Corinth.

The third greeting, in verse 20a, is from "all the brothers and sisters." Given that Paul has already conveyed the greetings of "the churches of Asia," the greeting here is probably not from the local Ephesian believers but from Paul's coworkers and traveling companions.[700] It is followed in verse 20b by an exhortation to the believers in Corinth to "greet one another with a holy kiss" (cf. 1 Thess 5:26; 2 Cor 13:12; Rom 16:16; 1 Pet 5:14)—a greeting that early Christianity took over from Old Testament tradition and Mediterranean culture more broadly and that was commonly used between family members (e.g., Gen 27:26–27; 29:13) and close friends (e.g., 1 Sam 20:41). The description of the kiss here (and in Paul's other references to it) as a "holy" kiss suggests that it signified more than just

---

[699] Other indications of the interconnectedness between the churches of Asia include the greeting in Rev 1:4 addressed to "the seven churches of Asia" and the seven letters in Rev 2–3, and the absence of the words "in Ephesus" from Eph 1:1 in the earliest manuscripts of the letter, suggesting the possibility that the letter functioned as a circular homily for all of the churches in the province (cf. Starling, *Reading Ephesians and Colossians*, 6–7). For a larger discussion of the role played by Ephesus in early Christianity, see Paul R. Trebilco, *The Early Christians in Ephesus from Paul to Ignatius*, WUNT (Tübingen: Mohr Siebeck, 2004).

[700] Cf. Fee, *First Epistle to the Corinthians*, 924.

an expression of standard social custom and was understood as a way of signifying the honor and welcome that believers extended to one another as fellow members of the community of God's holy people (cf. 1:2).[701]

16:21–24. The final paragraph of the letter contains a "greeting" (ἀσπασμός) that Paul has written in his own hand (cf. Gal 6:11; Col 4:18; 2 Thess 3:17)—a practice that Paul describes elsewhere as a sign of the letter's authenticity (2 Thess 3:17) and that probably also functioned as a way of expressing and intensifying the personal character of the letter's final words.

The first of these final remarks is a solemn curse Paul pronounces on "anyone [who] does not love the Lord" (v. 22a). Its function here at the conclusion of the letter is probably to underline the urgent and nonnegotiable nature of the commands and gospel reminders that the letter has conveyed and to call for the community to separate themselves from those who show by their departure from the gospel or their disregard of Paul's commands that they are not united in the bonds of allegiance to the Lord Jesus that connect believers with one another (cf. 14:37–38; Gal 1:8–9; 2 Thess 3:14–15).[702]

The anathema of verse 22a is followed in verse 22b by a traditional Aramaic prayer, Μαρανα θα ("Our Lord, come!"). The retention of the traditional Aramaic form of the prayer (carried across into Greek in a transliterated form) gives expression to the connectedness between the gentile churches planted by Paul and the Aramaic-speaking communities that had grown out of the original Jesus movement. Its content, as a prayer for Christ's return, is consistent with the central role that hope occupied within the response that the gospel called for from its hearers (cf. 1:7–8) (see §7).

This prayer is followed, in turn, by a benediction that takes the form of a prayer-wish that "the grace of the Lord Jesus" would be with the readers. This benediction, with occasional variations, is a characteristic element of Paul's letter closings (cf. Rom 16:20; 2 Cor 13:13; Gal 6:18; Eph 6:24; Phil 4:23; Col 4:18; 1 Thess 5:28; 2 Thess 3:18; 1 Tim 6:21; 2 Tim 4:22; Titus 3:15; Phlm 25)—just as a reference to the "grace and peace" of God the Father and the Lord Jesus is the standard greeting with which his

---

[701] Garland, *1 Corinthians*, 772–73.

[702] Cf. Fee, *First Epistle to the Corinthians*, 925–26. Garland also highlights the centrality of love for the Lord as the fundamental expression of covenant loyalty for the people of Israel (e.g., Deut 6:4–6). Garland, *1 Corinthians*, 774.

letters commence—and reflects the critical role played by the grace of God within Paul's gospel (see §5). Less standard is the expression of Paul's own love for the Corinthians that follows in verse 24 as the final word of the letter and is presumably added here by Paul as a reassurance that the strong rebukes and warnings the letter has contained are an expression of his love for them, not a sign of his alienation from them (cf. 4:14–15; 2 Cor 2:4; 13:10). This love Paul expresses for the Corinthians is a love that he has for them "in Christ Jesus." Like the grace benediction in the preceding verse, these final words of the letter recall the opening greetings with which it commences, reminding the readers of the bonds that connect them with Paul and with one another, and with all whose lives are lived "in Christ Jesus."[703]

Bridge

Like the updates and instructions that make up the first half of 1 Corinthians 16, the exhortations, commendations, and greetings of the chapter's second half are laced with names and details that are specifically related to the letter's original recipients and to the immediate circumstances of Paul as its sender. Nevertheless, these paragraphs too are not without significance for contemporary readers of the letter.

The most obviously and directly relevant portions of these final paragraphs for twenty-first century readers are the commands with which this closing section of the letter commences (vv. 13–14) and the words of warning and benediction with which it concludes (vv. 22–24). The former have the effect, for us as for the letter's original recipients, of reinforcing key reminders and exhortations from the letter body, underlining the gospel-shaped message of the letter as whole, which calls its readers to an energetic and courageous fidelity, in view of Christ's resurrection, and a life of love for others, in imitation of the cruciform pattern modeled for us in his death and resurrection. The latter, like the letter's opening words, remind us of the grace that initiates, enables, and completes the entirety of the Christian life, the hope of Christ's return that it looks forward to, and the loyal love for the Lord Jesus that is at its center.

Sandwiched between these more generically framed and universally applicable words of gospel-shaped exhortation and benediction are the more obviously particular and occasional contents of the

[703] Cf. Fee, *First Epistle to the Corinthians*, 928.

intervening paragraphs, containing Paul's commendation of the household of Stephanas (vv. 15–18) and his greetings from the believers who are with him in Asia (vv. 19–20). Even these, however, are framed by Paul in ways that hint at their continuing relevance for us. The commendation of Stephanas, Fortunatus, and Achaicus (along with the other members of their household) is not merely a character reference for a particular group of people but also a vehicle for a more broadly applicable reminder to recognize the leadership and honor the labors of others ("such people") who resemble them, and a reminder of the criteria on which this sort of recognition should be based (here, the longevity of their commitment to Christ, their willingness to "work" and "labor," and their devotion to the service of the saints).[704] For those of us who, like the Corinthians, inhabit a social context in which a very different set of criteria are often relied upon for the legitimation of leaders (not only in the surrounding secular culture but in the church, as well), the focus of Paul's commendation is a refreshing change and a spur for self-examination. The greetings of verses 19–20, too, merit reflection on our part, directing our thoughts once again (like the instructions and reminders of vv. 1–11) toward the relationships of gospel partnership in mutual love that connect us together as women and men, households, congregations, and mission teams, united in a common family of believers and involved together in a shared labor in the cause of Christ.

---

[704] Cf. Clarke, *Secular and Christian Leadership*, 126.

BIBLIOGRAPHY

Adams, Edward. *The Earliest Christian Meeting Places: Almost Exclusively Houses?* LNTS. London: T&T Clark, 2013.

Arzt-Grabner, Peter. *1. Korinther.* PKNT. Göttingen: Vandenhoeck & Ruprecht, 2006.

———. "Paul's Letter Thanksgiving." Pages 129–58 in *Paul and the Ancient Letter Form.* Edited by Stanley E. Porter and Sean A. Adams. Pauline Studies. Leiden: Brill, 2010.

Ash, Christopher. *Marriage: Sex in the Service of God.* Leicester: Inter-Varsity Press, 2003.

Banks, Robert J. *Paul's Idea of Community: Spirit and Culture in Early House Churches.* 3rd ed. Grand Rapids: Baker, 2020.

Barclay, John M. G. "Apocalyptic Allegiance and Disinvestment in the World: A Reading of 1 Corinthians 7:25–35." Pages 257–74 in *Paul and the Apocalyptic Imagination.* Edited by Ben C. Blackwell, John K. Goodrich and Jason Maston. Minneapolis: Fortress, 2016.

———. *Paul and the Power of Grace.* Grand Rapids: Eerdmans, 2020.

———. "Thessalonica and Corinth: Social Contrasts in Pauline Christianity." *JSNT* 47 (1992): 49–74.

Barrett, C. K. *A Commentary on the First Epistle to the Corinthians.* 2nd ed. BNTC. London: Black, 1971.

Barth, Karl. *The Resurrection of the Dead.* London: Hodder & Stoughton, 1933.

Bauckham, Richard. *God Crucified: Monotheism and Christology in the New Testament.* Grand Rapids: Eerdmans, 1999.

Baur, F. C. *Paul the Apostle of Jesus Christ.* 2 vols. London: Williams & Norgate, 1873–1876.

Beasley-Murray, G. R. *Baptism in the New Testament.* London: Macmillan, 1962.

Beker, J. Christiaan. "Recasting Pauline Theology: The Coherence-Contingency Scheme as Interpretive Model." Pages 15–24 in *Thessalonians, Philippians, Galatians, Philemon.* Edited by Jouette M. Bassler. Vol. 1 of *Pauline Theology.* Minneapolis: Fortress, 1991.

Billings, Bradly S. "From House Church to Tenement Church: Domestic Space and the Development of Early Urban Christianity—The Example of Ephesus." *JTS* 62 (2011): 541–69.

Bitner, Bradley J. *Paul's Political Strategy in 1 Corinthians 1-4: Constitution and Covenant.* SNTSMS. New York: Cambridge University Press, 2015.

Bjerkelund, C. J. *Parakalô: Form, Funktion und Sinn der Parakalô Sätze in den Paulinischen Briefen.* Oslo: Universitetsforlaget, 1967.

Blomberg, Craig. "Quotations, Allusions, and Echoes of Jesus in Paul." Pages 129–43 in *Studies in the Pauline Epistles: Essays in Honor of Douglas J. Moo.* Edited by Matthew S. Harmon and Jay E. Smith. Grand Rapids: Zondervan, 2014.

Bookidis, Nancy. "Religion in Corinth: 146 B.C.E. To 100 C.E." Pages 141–64 in *Urban Religion in Roman Corinth: Interdisciplinary Approaches.* Edited by Daniel N. Schowalter and Steven J. Friesen. Cambridge: Harvard University Press, 2005.

———. "The Sanctuaries of Corinth." *Corinth* 20 (2003): 247–59.

Boswell, John. *Christianity, Social Tolerance, and Homosexuality: Gay People in Western Europe from the Beginning of the Christian Era to the Fourteenth Century.* 2nd ed. Chicago: University of Chicago Press, 2015.

Brock, Brian, and Bernd Wannenwetsch. *The Malady of the Christian Body.* Vol. 1 of *A Theological Exposition of Paul's First Letter to the Corinthians.* Eugene: Cascade, 2016.

———. *The Therapy of the Christian Body.* Vol. 2 of *A Theological Exposition of Paul's First Letter to the Corinthians.* Eugene: Cascade, 2018.

Brookins, Timothy A. *Corinthian Wisdom, Stoic Philosophy, and the Ancient Economy.* SNTSMS. New York: Cambridge University Press, 2014.

———. "'Natural Hair': A 'New Rhetorical' Assessment of 1 Cor 11:14–15." Pages 173–95 in *Paul and the Greco-Roman Philosophical Tradition.* Edited by Andrew W. Pitts and Joseph R. Dodson. LNTS. London: T&T Clark, 2017.

———. *Reading 1 Corinthians: A Literary and Theological Commentary.* RNT. Macon: Smyth & Helwys, 2020.

———. "Rhetoric and Philosophy in the First Century: Their Relation with Respect to 1 Corinthians 1–4." *Neot* 44 (2010): 233–52.

———. "The Wise Corinthians: Their Stoic Education and Outlook." *JTS* 62 (2011): 51–76.

Brookins, Timothy A., and B. W. Longenecker. *First Corinthians 1-9: A Handbook on the Greek Text.* BHGNT. Waco: Baylor University Press, 2016.

———. *First Corinthians 10-16: A Handbook on the Greek Text.* BHGNT. Waco: Baylor University Press, 2016.

Brown, Alexandra R. *The Cross and Human Transformation: Paul's Apocalyptic Word in 1 Corinthians.* Minneapolis: Fortress, 1995.

Brownson, James V. *Bible, Gender, Sexuality: Reframing the Church's Debate on Same-Sex Relationships.* Grand Rapids: Eerdmans, 2013.

Bruce, F. F. *1 and 2 Corinthians.* NCBC. London: Oliphants, 1971.

Bultmann, Rudolf. *Theology of the New Testament.* 2 vols. New York: Scribner, 1951–1955.

Button, M. Bruce, and Fika J. Van Rensburg. "The 'House Churches' in Corinth." *Neot* 37 (2003): 1–28.

Byrne, Brendan. "Sinning against One's Own Body: Paul's Understanding of the Sexual Relationship in 1 Corinthians 6:18." *CBQ* 45 (1983): 608–16.

Campbell, Constantine R. *Basics of Verbal Aspect in Biblical Greek.* Grand Rapids: Zondervan, 2009.

———. *Paul and Union with Christ: An Exegetical and Theological Study.* Grand Rapids: Zondervan, 2012.

Caragounis, C. C. "A House Church in Corinth? An Inquiry into the Structure of Early Corinthian Christianity." Pages 365–418 in vol. 1 of *Saint Paul and Corinth: 1950 Years Since the Writing of the Epistles to the Corinthians.* Edited by C. J. Belezos. Athens: Psichogios, 2009.

———. "Ὀψώνιον: A Reconsideration of Its Meaning." *NovT* 16 (1974): 35–57.

Carson, D. A. *Showing the Spirit: A Theological Exposition of 1 Corinthians 12–14.* Carlisle: Paternoster, 1995.

Castelli, Elizabeth A. *Imitating Paul: A Discourse of Power.* Louisville: Westminster John Knox, 1991.

Chapple, Allan Leslie. "Local Leadership in the Pauline Churches: Theological and Social Factors in Its Development: A Study Based on 1 Thessalonians, 1 Corinthians and Philippians." PhD thesis, Durham, 1984.

Chester, Stephen J. *Conversion at Corinth: Perspectives on Conversion in Paul's Theology and the Corinthian Church.* London: T&T Clark, 2003.

Ciampa, Roy E. "Composite Citations in 1–2 Corinthians and Galatians." Pages 159–89 in *New Testament Uses.* Vol. 2 of *Composite Citations in Antiquity.* Edited by Sean A. Adams and Seth M. Ehorn. LNTS. London: T&T Clark, 2018.

Ciampa, Roy E., and Brian S. Rosner. "First Corinthians." Pages 695–752 in *Commentary on the New Testament Use of the Old Testament.* Edited by G. K. Beale and D. A. Carson. Grand Rapids: Baker, 2007.

———. *The First Letter to the Corinthians.* PNTC. Grand Rapids: Eerdmans, 2010.

Clarke, Andrew D. *Secular and Christian Leadership in Corinth: A Socio-Historical and Exegetical Study of 1 Corinthians 1–6.* Eugene: Wipf & Stock, 2006.

Coleman, K. M. "Fatal Charades: Roman Executions Staged as Mythological Enactments." *JRS* 80 (1990): 44–73.

Collins, Adela Yarbro. "Introduction: Early Christian Apocalypticism, Genre and Setting." *Semeia* 36 (1986): 1–11.

Collins, Raymond F. *First Corinthians.* Sacra Pagina. Collegeville: Liturgical, 1999.

———. "Reflections on 1 Corinthians as a Hellenistic Letter." Pages 39–61 in *The Corinthian Correspondence.* Edited by Reimund Bieringer. BETL. Leuven: Peeters, 1996.

Conzelmann, Hans. *First Corinthians: A Commentary on the First Epistle to the Corinthians.* Hermeneia. Philadelphia: Fortress, 1975.

Coutsoumpos, Panayotis. *Paul, Corinth, and the Roman Empire.* Eugene: Wipf & Stock, 2015.

Cover, Michael Benjamin. "The Divine Comedy at Corinth: Paul, Menander and the Rhetoric of Resurrection." NTS 64 (2018): 532–50.

De Botton, Alain. *Status Anxiety.* London: Hamish Hamilton, 2004.

De Vos, Craig Steven. *Church and Community Conflicts: The Relationships of the Thessalonian, Corinthian, and Philippian Churches with Their Wider Civic Communities.* SBLDS. Atlanta: Scholars Press, 1999.

Deming, Will. *Paul on Marriage and Celibacy: The Hellenistic Background of 1 Corinthians 7.* 2nd ed. Grand Rapids: Eerdmans, 2004.

Downs, David J. *The Offering of the Gentiles: Paul's Collection for Jerusalem in Its Chronological, Cultural, and Cultic Contexts.* WUNT. Tübingen: Mohr Siebeck, 2008.

———. "Physical Weakness, Illness and Death in 1 Corinthians 11.30: Deprivation and Overconsumption in Pauline and Early Christianity." NTS 65 (2019): 572–88.

Dunn, James D. G. *Jesus and the Spirit: A Study of the Religious and Charismatic Experience of Jesus and the First Christians as Reflected in the New Testament.* London: SCM, 1975.

———. *The Theology of Paul the Apostle.* Grand Rapids: Eerdmans, 1998.

Edsall, Benjamin A. "Greco-Roman Costume and Paul's Fraught Argument in 1 Corinthians 11.2–16." *JGRChJ* 9 (2013): 132–46.

———. "Paul's Rhetoric of Knowledge: The ΟΥΚ ΟΙΔΑΤΕ Questions in 1 Corinthians." *NovT* 55 (2013): 252–71.

Engberg-Pedersen, Troels. "Proclaiming the Lord's Death: 1 Corinthians 11:17–34 and the Forms of Paul's Theological Argument." Pages 103–82 in *1 and 2 Corinthians.* Edited by David M. Hay. Vol. 2 of *Pauline Theology.* Minneapolis: Fortress, 1993.

Enns, Peter E. "The 'Moveable Well' in 1 Corinthians 10:4: An Extra-Biblical Tradition in an Apostolic Text." BBR (1996): 23–38.

Esler, Philip Francis. "Paul and the Agon: Understanding a Pauline Motif in Its Cultural and Visual Context." Pages 356–84 in *Picturing the New Testament: Studies in Ancient Visual Images.* Edited by Annette Weissenrieder, Friederike Wendt, and Petra von Gemünde. Tübingen: Mohr Siebeck, 2005.

Fee, Gordon D. *The First Epistle to the Corinthians.* 2nd ed. NICNT. Grand Rapids: Eerdmans, 2014.

Forbes, Christopher. *Prophecy and Inspired Speech in Early Christianity and Its Hellenistic Environment.* Peabody: Hendrickson, 1997.

Friesen, Courtney J. P. "Paulus Tragicus: Staging Apostolic Adversity in First Corinthians." *JBL* 134 (2015): 813–32.

Friesen, Steven J. "The Wrong Erastus: Ideology, Archaeology, and Exegesis." Pages 231–56 in *Corinth in Context: Comparative Studies on Religion and*

Society. Edited by Steven J. Friesen, Daniel N. Schowalter, and James C. Walters. Leiden: Brill, 2010.

Gagnon, Robert A. J. *The Bible and Homosexual Practice: Texts and Hermeneutics.* Nashville: Abingdon, 2001.

Garcilazo, Albert V. *The Corinthian Dissenters and the Stoics.* SBL. New York: Lang, 2007.

Gardner, Paul. *First Corinthians.* ZECNT. Grand Rapids: Zondervan, 2018.

Garland, David E. "First Corinthians." Pages 97–107 in *Theological Interpretation of the New Testament: A Book-by-Book Survey.* Edited by Kevin J. Vanhoozer. Grand Rapids: Baker, 2008.

———. *First Corinthians.* BECNT. Grand Rapids: Baker, 2003.

Gill, David W. J. "Macedonia." Pages 397–417 in *The Book of Acts in Its Graeco-Roman Setting.* Edited by David W. J. Gill and Conrad H. Gempf. Grand Rapids: Eerdmans, 1994.

Gillespie, Thomas W. *The First Theologians: A Study in Early Christian Prophecy.* Grand Rapids: Eerdmans, 1994.

Gladd, Benjamin L. *Revealing the Mysterion: The Use of Mystery in Daniel and Second Temple Judaism with Its Bearing on First Corinthians.* BZNW. Berlin: De Gruyter, 2009.

Goodrich, John K. "Erastus of Corinth (Romans 16.23): Responding to Recent Proposals on His Rank, Status, and Faith." *NTS* 57 (2011): 583–93.

Goppelt, Leonhard. *Typos: The Typological Interpretation of the Old Testament in the New.* Translated by Donald H. Madvig. Grand Rapids: Eerdmans, 1982.

Gorman, Michael J. *Apostle of the Crucified Lord: A Theological Introduction to Paul and His Letters.* 2nd ed. Grand Rapids: Eerdmans, 2017.

———. *Cruciformity: Paul's Narrative Spirituality of the Cross.* 2nd ed. Grand Rapids: Eerdmans, 2021.

———. *The Death of the Messiah and the Birth of the New Covenant: A (Not So) New Model of the Atonement.* Eugene: Cascade, 2014.

Grudem, Wayne A. *The Gift of Prophecy in 1 Corinthians.* Washington: University Press of America, 1982.

Gundry, Robert H. "'Ecstatic Utterance' (NEB)?" *JTS* 17 (1966): 299–307.

Gundry Volf, Judith M. "Controlling the Bodies: A Theological Profile of the Corinthian Sexual Ascetics (1 Cor 7)." Pages 519–41 in *The Corinthian Correspondence.* Edited by Reimund Bieringer. Leuven: Peeters, 1996.

———. *Paul and Perseverance: Staying In and Falling Away.* WUNT. Tübingen: Mohr Siebeck, 1990.

Hafemann, Scott J. *Suffering and Ministry in the Spirit: Paul's Defense of His Ministry in II Corinthians 2:14–3:3.* Grand Rapids: Eerdmans, 1990.

Hall, David R. "A Disguise for the Wise: Μετασχηματισμός in 1 Corinthians 4.6." NTS 40 (1994): 143–49.

———. *The Unity of the Corinthian Correspondence.* JSNTSup. London: T&T Clark, 2003.

Harper, Kyle. *From Shame to Sin: The Christian Transformation of Sexual Morality in Late Antiquity.* Cambridge: Harvard University Press, 2013.

——. "Porneia: The Making of a Christian Sexual Norm." *JBL* 131 (2011): 363–83.

Harrison, Glynn. *A Better Story: God, Sex and Human Flourishing.* Downers Grove: InterVarsity Press, 2017.

Harrison, James R. *Paul and the Ancient Celebrity Circuit: The Cross and Moral Transformation.* WUNT. Tübingen: Mohr Siebeck, 2019.

Hauerwas, Stanley. *After Christendom? How the Church Is to Behave If Freedom, Justice, and a Christian Nation Are Bad Ideas.* Nashville: Abingdon, 1991.

Hays, Richard B. "The Conversion of the Imagination: Scripture and Eschatology in 1 Corinthians." NTS 45 (1999): 391–412.

——. "Ecclesiology and Ethics in 1 Corinthians." *ExAud* 10 (1994): 31–43.

——. *Echoes of Scripture in the Letters of Paul.* New Haven: Yale University Press, 1989.

——. *First Corinthians.* Interpretation. Louisville: Westminster John Knox, 1997.

Head, Peter M. "'Witnesses Between You and Us': The Role of the Letter-Carriers in 1 Clement." Pages 477–93 in *Studies on the Text of the New Testament and Early Christianity in Honor of Michael W. Holmes.* Edited by D. M. Gurtner, J. Hernández, and P. Foster. NTTSD. Leiden: Brill, 2015.

Hengel, Martin. *Crucifixion in the Ancient World and the Folly of the Message of the Cross.* London: SCM, 1977.

Hengel, Martin, and Roland Deines. *The Pre-Christian Paul.* London: SCM, 1991.

Hiigel, John L. *Leadership in 1 Corinthians: A Case Study in Paul's Ecclesiology*. SBEC. Lewiston: Mellen, 2003.

Hill, David. *New Testament Prophecy.* London: Marshall, Morgan & Scott, 1979.

Hill, Wesley. *Paul and the Trinity: Persons, Relations, and the Pauline Letters.* Grand Rapids: Eerdmans, 2015.

Hodge, Charles. *First Epistle to the Corinthians.* 5th ed. Edinburgh: Banner of Truth, 1958 [1858].

Horrell, David G. "Domestic Space and Christian Meetings at Corinth: Imagining New Contexts and the Buildings East of the Theatre." NTS 50 (2004): 349–69.

——. "From ἀδελφοί to οἶκος θεοῦ: Social Transformation in Pauline Christianity." *JBL* 120 (2001): 293–311.

——. *The Social Ethos of the Corinthian Correspondence: Interests and Ideology from 1 Corinthians to 1 Clement.* Edinburgh: T&T Clark, 1996.

——. "Theological Principle or Christological Practice? Pauline Ethics in 1 Corinthians 8.1–11.1." *JSNT* 67 (1997): 83–114.

Horsley, Richard A. *First Corinthians.* Nashville: Abingdon, 1998.

House, Paul R. "To Them, for Us: The Bible's Continuing Relevance." Pages 98–110 in *Theology Is for Preaching: Biblical Foundations, Method, and Practice.* Edited by Chase Kuhn and Paul Grimmond. Bellingham: Lexham, 2021.

Inkelaar, Harm-Jan. *Conflict over Wisdom: The Theme of 1 Corinthians 1–4 Rooted in Scripture.* CBET. Leuven: Peeters, 2011.

Instone-Brewer, David. "1 Corinthians 7 in the Light of the Jewish Greek and Aramaic Marriage and Divorce Papyri." *TynBul* 52 (2001): 225–43.

———. "First Corinthians 9.9–11: A Literal Interpretation of 'Do Not Muzzle the Ox.'" NTS 38 (1992): 554–65.

Jeremias, Joachim. *The Eucharistic Words of Jesus.* London: SCM, 1990.

———. *Infant Baptism in the First Four Centuries.* Philadelphia: Westminster, 1960.

Jewett, Robert. *Romans: A Commentary.* Hermeneia. Minneapolis: Fortress, 2007.

Jones, C. P. *The Roman World of Dio Chrysostom.* Cambridge: Harvard University Press, 1978.

Judge, E. A. "Cultural Conformity and Innovation in Paul: Some Clues from Contemporary Documents." *TynBul* 35 (1984): 5–23.

———. "The Reaction Against Classical Education in the New Testament." *Journal of Christian Education* 77 (1983): 7–14.

Käsemann, Ernst. *Essays on New Testament Themes.* London: SCM, 1964.

Keener, Craig S. *Acts: An Exegetical Commentary.* 4 vols. Grand Rapids: Baker, 2012–2015.

Kent, John Harvey. *Corinth: The Inscriptions, 1926–1950.* Princeton: American School of Classical Studies at Athens, 1966.

Kilgore, Rodney, and Josiah D. Hall. "Veiling Within the Corinthian Context: An Examination of Cynthia Long Westfall's Reading of 1 Corinthians 11:2–16." BBR 33 (2023): 162–85.

Kim, Chan-Hie. "The Papyrus Invitation." *JBL* 94 (1975): 391–402.

Kinman, Brent. "'Appoint the Despised as Judges!' (1 Corinthians 6:4)." *TynBul* 48 (1997): 345–54.

Kistemaker, Simon. *1 Corinthians.* NTC. Grand Rapids: Baker, 1993.

Kloppenborg, John S. *Christ's Associations: Connecting and Belonging in the Ancient City.* New Haven: Yale University Press, 2019.

Köstenberger, Andreas J., Benjamin L. Merkle, and Robert L. Plummer. *Going Deeper with New Testament Greek: An Intermediate Study of the Grammar and Syntax of the New Testament.* Nashville: B&H Academic, 2016.

Kroeger, Catherine Clark. "Head." Pages 375–77 in *Dictionary of Paul and His Letters.* Edited by Gerald F. Hawthorne, Ralph P. Martin, and Daniel G. Reid. Downers Grove: InterVarsity Press, 1993.

Kyle, Donald G. *Spectacles of Death in Ancient Rome.* London: Routledge, 1998.

Lakey, Michael. *Image and Glory: 1 Corinthians 11:2–16 as a Case Study in Bible, Gender and Hermeneutics.* LNTS. London: T&T Clark, 2010.

Lietzmann, Hans, and Werner Georg Kümmel. *An Die Korinther I–II.* 4th ed. HNT. Tübingen: Mohr Siebeck, 1949.

Lightfoot, J. B. *Notes on the Epistles of St. Paul.* 5th ed. London: Macmillan, 1895.

Lim, Kar Yong. *Metaphors and Social Identity Formation in Paul's Letters to the Corinthians.* Eugene: Pickwick, 2017.

Lindbeck, George A. *The Nature of Doctrine: Religion and Theology in a Postliberal Age.* Philadelphia: Westminster, 1984.

Llewelyn, S. R. "The Use of Sunday for Meetings of Believers in the New Testament." *NovT* 43 (2001): 205–23.

Loader, William R. G. *Sexuality in the New Testament: Understanding the Key Texts.* Louisville: Westminster John Knox, 2010.

Longenecker, Bruce W., ed. *Narrative Dynamics in Paul: A Critical Assessment.* Louisville: Westminster, 2002.

Malcolm, Matthew R. *Paul and the Rhetoric of Reversal in 1 Corinthians: The Impact of Paul's Gospel on His Macro-Rhetoric.* SNTSMS. Cambridge: Cambridge University Press, 2013.

Marshall, I. Howard. *Last Supper and Lord's Supper.* Exeter: Paternoster, 1980.

Marshall, Peter. *Enmity in Corinth: Social Conventions in Paul's Relations with the Corinthians.* WUNT. Tübingen: Mohr Siebeck, 1987.

Martin, Dale B. *The Corinthian Body.* New Haven: Yale University Press, 1995.

———. *Sex and the Single Savior: Gender and Sexuality in Biblical Interpretation.* Louisville: Westminster John Knox, 2006.

———. "Tongues of Angels and Other Status Indicators." *JAAR* 59 (1991): 547–90.

Mathewson, David, and Elodie Ballantine Emig. *Intermediate Greek Grammar: Syntax for Students of the New Testament.* Grand Rapids: Baker, 2016.

McClure, Laura. *Courtesans at Table: Gender and Greek Literary Culture in Athenaeus.* New York: Routledge, 2003.

Meeks, Wayne A. *The First Urban Christians: The Social World of the Apostle Paul.* New Haven: Yale University Press, 1983.

Metzger, Bruce Manning. *A Textual Commentary on the Greek New Testament: A Companion Volume to the United Bible Societies' Greek New Testament (Fourth Revised Edition).* 2nd ed. Stuttgart: Deutsche Bibelgesellschaft, 1994.

Mickelsen, Alvera, and Berkeley Mickelsen. "What Does Kephalē Mean in the New Testament?" Pages 97–110 in *Women, Authority, and the Bible.* Edited by Alvera Mickelsen. Downers Grove: InterVarsity Press, 1986.

Millis, Benjamin W. "The Local Magistrates and Elite of Roman Corinth." Pages 38–53 in *Corinth in Contrast: Studies in Inequality.* Edited by Steven J. Friesen, Sarah A. James, and Daniel N. Schowalter. NovTSup. Leiden: Brill, 2014.

Minear, Paul S. *Images of the Church in the New Testament.* 2nd ed. Louisville: Westminster, 2004.

Mitchell, Margaret Mary. *Paul and the Rhetoric of Reconciliation: An Exegetical Investigation of the Language and Composition of 1 Corinthians.* Louisville: Westminster John Knox, 1993.

Montserrat, Dominic. *Sex and Society in Græco-Roman Egypt.* London: Kegan Paul, 1996.

Moretti, L. *Inscrizioni Agonistiche Greche.* Rome: Signorelli, 1953.

Moulton, J. H., and G. Milligan. *The Vocabulary of the Greek New Testament.* Repr., Peabody: Hendrickson, 1997.

Murphy-O'Connor, J. *Keys to First Corinthians: Revisiting the Major Issues.* Oxford: Oxford University Press, 2009.

———. *Paul the Letter-Writer: His World, His Options, His Skills.* Collegeville: Liturgical, 1995.

———. *St. Paul's Corinth: Text and Archaeology.* 3rd ed. Collegeville: Liturgical, 2002.

Naselli, Andrew David. "Was It Always Idolatrous for Corinthian Christians to Eat Εἰδωλόθυτα in an Idol's Temple? (1 Cor 8–10)." STR 9 (2018): 23–45.

Nguyen, V. Henry T. "The Identification of Paul's Spectacle of Death Metaphor in 1 Corinthians 4.9." NTS 53 (2007): 489–501.

Niccum, Curt. "The Voice of the Manuscripts on the Silence of Women: The External Evidence for 1 Cor 14.34–5." NTS 43 (1997): 242–55.

Novenson, Matthew V. *Christ among the Messiahs: Christ Language in Paul and Messiah Language in Ancient Judaism.* New York: Oxford University Press, 2012.

O'Brien, Peter T. *Introductory Thanksgivings in the Letters of Paul.* Leiden: Brill, 1977.

Odell-Scott, David W. "In Defense of an Egalitarian Interpretation of I Cor 14:34–36." *BTB* 17 (1987): 100.

——. "Let the Women Speak in Church: An Egalitarian Interpretation of 1 Cor 14:33b–36." *BTB* 13 (1983): 90–93.

O'Donovan, Oliver. *Resurrection and Moral Order: An Outline for Evangelical Ethics.* 2nd ed. Leicester: Inter-Varsity Press, 1994.

Ogereau, Julien M. *Paul's Koinonia with the Philippians: A Socio-Historical Investigation of a Pauline Economic Partnership.* WUNT. Tübingen: Mohr Siebeck, 2014.

Olson, K. *Dress and the Roman Woman: Self-Presentation and Society.* New York: Routledge, 2008.

Oropeza, B. J. *First Corinthians.* NCCS. Eugene: Cascade, 2017.

Oster, Richard. *First Corinthians.* Joplin: College Press, 1995.

Paige, Terence. "First Corinthians 2:2: A Pagan Pompē?" *JSNT* 44 (1991): 57–65.

Pawlak, Marcin N. "Corinth After 44 BC: Ethnical and Cultural Changes." *Electrum* 20 (2013): 143–62.

Payne, Philip B. "Fuldensis, Sigla for Variants in Vaticanus, and 1 Cor 14.34–5." NTS 41 (1995): 240–62.

——. "Vaticanus Distigme-Obelos Symbols Marking Added Text, Including 1 Corinthians 14.34–5." NTS 63 (2017): 604–25.

Perriman, A. C. "The Head of a Woman: The Meaning of Κεφαλή in 1 Cor. 11:3." *JTS* 45 (1994): 602–22.

Peters, Janelle. "Slavery and the Gendered Construction of Worship Veils in 1 Corinthians." *Biblica* 101 (2020): 431–43.

——. "Veiling in Corinth: A Surprising Sign of Equality." Pages 112–15 in *The Biblical World of Gender: The Daily Lives of Ancient Women and Men.* Edited by Celina Durgin and Dru Johnson. Eugene: Cascade, 2022.

Pickett, Raymond. *The Cross in Corinth: The Social Significance of the Death of Jesus.* JSNTSup. Sheffield: Sheffield Academic, 1997.

Piper, John. *Desiring God: Meditations of a Christian Hedonist.* 4th ed. Colorado Springs: Multnomah, 2011.

Poirier, John C., and Joseph Frankovic. "Celibacy and Charism in 1 Cor. 7:5–7." *HTR* 89 (1996): 1–18.

Porter, Stanley E., and Andrew W. Pitts. "The Disclosure Formula in the Epistolary Papyri and in the New Testament: Development, Form,

Function and Syntax." Pages 421–38 in *The Language of the New Testament.* Edited by Stanley E. Porter and Andrew W. Pitts. Leiden: Brill, 2013.

Rabens, Volker. "The Development of Pauline Pneumatology: A Response to F. W. Horn." *BZ* 43 (1999): 161–79.

Rajak, Tessa, and David Noy. "Archisynagogoi: Office, Title and Social Status in the Greco-Jewish Synagogue." *JRS* 83 (1993): 75–93.

Richards, E. Randolph. *Paul and First-Century Letter Writing: Secretaries, Composition, and Collection.* Downers Grove: InterVarsity Press, 2004.

———. *The Secretary in the Letters of Paul.* WUNT. Tübingen: Mohr Siebeck, 1991.

Robertson, Archibald, and Alfred Plummer. *A Critical and Exegetical Commentary on the First Epistle of St. Paul to the Corinthians.* ICC. New York: Scribner, 1911.

Rosner, Brian S. "'Known by God': The Meaning and Value of a Neglected Biblical Concept." *TynBul* 59 (2008): 207–30.

———. "The Origin and Meaning of 1 Cor 6:9–11 in Context." BibZeit 40 (1996): 250–53.

———. *Paul and the Law: Keeping the Commandments of God.* NSBT. Downers Grove: InterVarsity Press, 2013.

———. *Paul, Scripture and Ethics: A Study of 1 Corinthians 5–7.* Leiden: Brill, 1994.

———. "'Written for Us': Paul's View of Scripture." Pages 81–106 in *A Pathway into the Holy Scripture.* Edited by Philip E. Satterthwaite and David F. Wright. Grand Rapids: Eerdmans, 1994.

Rowe, C. Kavin. *One True Life: The Stoics and Early Christians as Rival Traditions.* New Haven: Yale University Press, 2016.

Runge, Steven E. *Discourse Grammar of the Greek New Testament: A Practical Introduction for Teaching and Exegesis.* Peabody: Hendrickson, 2010.

Savage, Timothy B. *Power through Weakness: Paul's Understanding of the Christian Ministry in 2 Corinthians.* New York: Cambridge University Press, 1996.

Schellenberg, Ryan S. "Did Paul Refuse an Offer of Support from the Corinthians?" *JSNT* 40 (2018): 312–36.

Schnabel, Eckhard J. *Der erste Brief des Paulus an die Korinther.* HTA. Wuppertal: Brockhaus, 2006.

Schnackenburg, Rudolf. *Baptism in the Thought of St. Paul: A Study in Pauline Theology.* Translated by G. R. Beasley-Murray. New York: Herder & Herder, 1964.

Schrage, Wolfgang. *Der erste Brief an die Korinther.* EKK. 4 vols. Zürich: Benziger, 1991–2001.

Schreiner, Thomas R. *First Corinthians: An Introduction and Commentary.* TNTC. Downers Grove: InterVarsity Press, 2018.

Schweitzer, Albert. *The Mysticism of Paul the Apostle.* Translated by W. Montgomery. New York: Holt, 1931.

Scott, Ian W. *Implicit Epistemology in the Letters of Paul: Story, Experience and the Spirit.* WUNT. Tübingen: Mohr Siebeck, 2006.

———. *Paul's Way of Knowing: Story, Experience, and the Spirit.* Grand Rapids: Baker, 2009.

Scroggs, Robin. *The New Testament and Homosexuality: Contextual Background for Contemporary Debate.* Philadelphia: Fortress, 1983.

Sebasta, Judith Lynn. "Symbolism in the Costume of the Roman Woman." Pages 46–53 in *The World of Roman Costume*. Edited by Judith Lynn Sebasta and Larissa Bonfante. Madison: University of Wisconsin Press, 2001.

Shanor, Jay. "Paul as Master Builder: Construction Terms in First Corinthians." NTS 34 (1988): 461–71.

Sigountos, James G. "The Genre of 1 Corinthians 13." NTS 40 (1994): 246–60.

Spawforth, Antony. "The Achaean Federal Cult Part 1: Pseudo-Julian, Letters 198." *TynBul* 46 (1995): 151–68.

Stanley, Christopher D. *Arguing with Scripture: The Rhetoric of Quotations in the Letters of Paul*. New York: T&T Clark, 2004.

———. *Paul and the Language of Scripture: Citation Technique in the Pauline Epistles and Contemporary Literature*. SNTSMS. Cambridge: Cambridge University Press, 1992.

Starling, David I. " 'As to Sensible People': Human Reason and Divine Revelation in 1 Corinthians 8–10." Pages 113–26 in *Revelation and Reason in Christian Theology*. Edited by David I. Starling and Christopher C. Green. Bellingham: Lexham, 2018.

———. "'But We Have the Mind of Christ': 1 Corinthians, Wisdom, and the Interpretation of Israel's Scriptures." In *Paul in His Jewish and Graeco-Roman Contexts*. Edited by Constantine R. Campbell and James R. Harrison. Sydney: SCD Press, 2025.

———. "Good Fences, Good Neighbours? Holiness, Boundaries and Mission." *PJBR* 8 (2013): 19–26.

———. "'The Harvest of Your Righteousness': Scripture, Bread and Benefaction in 2 Corinthians 8–9." Pages 139–51 in *Scripture, Texts, and Tracings in 2 Corinthians and Philippians*. Edited by A. Andrew Das and B. J. Oropeza. Minneapolis: Fortress Academic, 2022.

———. *Hermeneutics as Apprenticeship: How the Bible Shapes Our Interpretive Habits and Practices*. Grand Rapids: Baker, 2016.

———. "'In the Same Mind and the Same Purpose': 1 Corinthians, Unity, and the Graeco-Roman Political Tradition." In *Paul in His Jewish and Graeco-Roman Contexts*. Edited by Constantine R. Campbell and James R. Harrison. Sydney: SCD Press, 2025.

———. "Meditations on a Slippery Citation: Paul's Use of Psalm 112:9 in 2 Corinthians 9:9." *JTI* 6 (2012): 241–55.

———. "Not a Wisdom of This Age: Theology and the Future of the Post-Christendom Church." Pages 81–98 in *Theology and the Future*. Edited by Trevor H. Cairney and David I. Starling. London: T&T Clark, 2014.

———. *Not My People: Gentiles as Exiles in Pauline Hermeneutics*. BZNW. Berlin: de Gruyter, 2011.

———. "'Nothing Beyond What Is Written'? First Corinthians and the Hermeneutics of Early Christian 'Theologia.'" *JTI* 8 (2014): 45–62.

———. *Reading Ephesians and Colossians: A Literary and Theological Commentary*. RNT. Macon: Smyth & Helwys, 2020.

———. "Restoring All That Was Broken: Gender, Gospel, and the New Creation." Pages 377–85 in *The Gender Conversation: Evangelical Perspectives on Gender,*

Scripture, and the Christian Life. Edited by David I. Starling and Edwina Murphy. Eugene: Wipf & Stock, 2016.
———. *UnCorinthian Leadership: Thematic Reflections on 1 Corinthians*. Eugene: Cascade, 2014.
———. "'We Do Not Want You to Be Unaware ...': Disclosure, Concealment and Suffering in 2 Cor 1–7." NTS 60 (2014): 266–79.
———. "'The Weapons of Righteousness': Righteousness and Suffering in 2 Corinthians." Pages 51–63 in *Suffering in Paul*. Edited by Siu Fung Wu. Eugene: Wipf & Stock, 2019.
Stowers, Stanley K. "Paul and Self-Mastery." Pages 270–300 in vol. 2 of *Paul in the Greco-Roman World: A Handbook*. Edited by J. Paul Sampley. London: T&T Clark, 2016.
Thate, Michael J., Kevin J. Vanhoozer, and Constantine R. Campbell, eds. *"In Christ" in Paul: Explorations in Paul's Theology of Union and Participation*. WUNT. Tübingen: Mohr Siebeck, 2014.
Theissen, Gerd. *The Social Setting of Pauline Christianity: Essays on Corinth*. Philadelphia: Fortress, 1982.
Thielicke, Helmut. *Theological Ethics*. Philadelphia: Fortress, 1966.
Thielman, Frank. *Theology of the New Testament: A Canonical and Synthetic Approach*. Grand Rapids: Zondervan, 2005.
Thiselton, Anthony C. *The First Epistle to the Corinthians: A Commentary on the Greek Text*. NIGTC. Grand Rapids: Eerdmans, 2000.
———. *The Hermeneutics of Doctrine*. Grand Rapids: Eerdmans, 2007.
———. "Realised Eschatology at Corinth." NTS 24 (1978): 510–26.
Thomas, Robert L. "'Tongues ... Will Cease.'" *JETS* 17 (1974): 81–89.
Thompson, James. *Pastoral Ministry According to Paul: A Biblical Vision*. Grand Rapids: Baker, 2006.
Timmins, Will N. "The Centrality of the Cross in Proclamation." Pages 142–54 in *Theology Is for Preaching: Biblical Foundations, Method, and Practice*. Edited by Paul Grimmond and Chase Kuhn. Bellingham: Lexham, 2021.
Treat, Jeremy R. *The Crucified King: Atonement and Kingdom in Biblical and Systematic Theology*. Grand Rapids: Zondervan, 2014.
Trebilco, Paul R. *The Early Christians in Ephesus from Paul to Ignatius*. WUNT. Tübingen: Mohr Siebeck, 2004.
———. *Outsider Designations and Boundary Construction in the New Testament: Early Christian Communities and the Formation of Group Identity*. New York: Cambridge University Press, 2017.
———. *Self-Designations and Group Identity in the New Testament*. Cambridge: Cambridge University Press, 2012.
Vanhoozer, Kevin J. "The Trials of Truth: Mission, Martyrdom and the Epistemology of the Cross." Pages 120–56 in *To Stake a Claim: Mission and the Western Crisis of Knowledge*. Edited by J. Andrew Kirk and Kevin J. Vanhoozer. Maryknoll: Orbis, 1999.
Wagner, J. Ross. *Heralds of the Good News: Isaiah and Paul "in Concert" in the Letter to the Romans*. NovTSup. Leiden: Brill, 2002.

Walbank, Mary E. Hoskins. "Evidence for the Imperial Cult in Julio-Claudian Corinth." Pages 201–14 in *Subject and Ruler: The Cult of the Ruling Power in Classical Antiquity*. Edited by Alistair Small. JRASup. Ann Arbor: Journal of Roman Archaeology, 1996.

Wallace, Daniel B. *Greek Grammar Beyond the Basics: An Exegetical Syntax of the New Testament*. Grand Rapids: Zondervan, 1996.

Walton, Steve. "Paul, Patronage and Pay: What Do We Know About the Apostle's Financial Support?" Pages 220–33 in *Paul as Missionary*. Edited by Trevor J. Burke and Brian S. Rosner. LNTS. London: T&T Clark, 2011.

Watkin, Christopher. *Thinking Through Creation: Genesis 1 and 2 as Tools of Cultural Critique*. Phillipsburg: P&R, 2017.

Watson, Francis. "Scripture in Pauline Theology: How Far Down Does It Go?" JTI 2 (2008): 181–92.

Webster, John. *The Domain of the Word: Scripture and Theological Reason*. London: T&T Clark, 2012.

Wedderburn, A. J. M. *Baptism and Resurrection: Studies in Pauline Theology Against Its Graeco-Roman Background*. WUNT. Tübingen: Mohr Siebeck, 1987.

———. "Philo's 'Heavenly Man.'" *NovT* 15 (1973): 301–26.

Welborn, L. L. *An End to Enmity: Paul and the "Wrongdoer" of Second Corinthians*. BZNW. Berlin: De Gruyter, 2011.

———. "Inequality in Roman Corinth: Evidence from Diverse Sources Evaluated According to a Neo-Ricardian Model." Pages 47–84 in *Roman Corinth*. Vol. 2 of *The First Urban Churches*. Edited by James R. Harrison and L. L. Welborn. Atlanta: Scholars Press, 2016.

———. *Paul, the Fool of Christ: A Study of 1 Corinthians 1–4 in the Comic-Philosophic Tradition*. JSNTSup. London: T&T Clark, 2005.

———. *Politics and Rhetoric in the Corinthian Epistles*. Macon: Mercer University Press, 1997.

Wenham, Gordon J. *Genesis 1–15*. WBC. Dallas: Word, 1987.

Westfall, Cynthia Long. *Paul and Gender: Reclaiming the Apostle's Vision for Men and Women in Christ*. Grand Rapids: Baker Academic, 2016.

White, Adam G. *Where Is the Wise Man? Graeco-Roman Education as a Background to the Divisions in 1 Corinthians 1–4*. LNTS. London: T&T Clark, 2015.

White, Joel. "Meals in Pagan Temples and Apostolic Finances. How Effective Is Paul's Argument in 1 Corinthians 9:1–23 in the Context of 1 Corinthians 8–10?" *BBR* 23 (2018): 531–46.

White, John L. "Introductory Formulae in the Body of the Pauline Letter." *JBL* 90 (1971): 91–97.

Whittle, Sarah K. "'Let Even Those Who Have Wives Be as Though They Had None' (1 Cor. 7:29)." Pages 86–100 in *Marriage, Family and Relationships: Biblical, Doctrinal and Contemporary Perspectives*. Edited by Thomas A. Noble, Sarah K. Whittle, and Philip S. Johnston. London: Inter-Varsity Press, 2017.

Wilk, Florian. "Isaiah in 1 and 2 Corinthians." Pages 133–58 in *Isaiah in the New Testament.* Edited by Steve Moyise and Maarten J. J. Menken. London: T&T Clark, 2005.

Williams, Charles K, II. "Corinth, 2011: Investigation of the West Hall of the Theater." Hesperia 82 (2013): 487–549.

———. "A Re-Evaluation of Temple E and the West End of the Forum of Corinth." Pages 156–62 in *The Greek Renaissance in the Roman Empire*. Edited by Susan Walker and Averil Cameron. London: University of London Press, 1989.

Willis, Wendell. "First Corinthians 8–10: A Retrospective after Twenty-Five Years." ResQ *49 (2007): 103–12.*

———. *Idol Meat in Corinth: The Pauline Argument in 1 Corinthians 8 and 10.* Chico: Scholars Press, 1985.

Wilson, Andrew. *The Warning-Assurance Relationship in 1 Corinthians.* WUNT. Tübingen: Mohr Siebeck, 2017.

Winandy, J. "Un curieux casus pendens: 1 Corinthiens 11.10 et son interpretation." NTS 38 (1992): 621–29.

Windsor, Lionel J. *Paul and the Vocation of Israel: How Paul's Jewish Identity Informs His Apostolic Ministry, with Special Reference to Romans.* BZNW. Berlin: De Gruyter, 2014.

Winter, Bruce W. *After Paul Left Corinth: The Influence of Secular Ethics and Social Change.* Grand Rapids: Eerdmans, 2001.

———. *Divine Honours for the Caesars: The First Christians' Responses.* Grand Rapids: Eerdmans, 2015.

———. "Gallio's Ruling on the Legal Status of Early Christianity." *TynBul* 50 (1999): 213–24.

———. "The Lord's Supper at Corinth: An Alternative Reconstruction." *RTR* 37 (1978): 73–82.

———. *Philo and Paul Among the Sophists.* 2nd ed. Grand Rapids: Eerdmans, 2002.

———. *Seek the Welfare of the City: Christians as Benefactors and Citizens.* Grand Rapids: Eerdmans, 1994.

Wire, Antoinette Clark. *The Corinthian Women Prophets: A Reconstruction Through Paul's Rhetoric.* Minneapolis: Fortress, 1990.

Witherington, Ben. *Conflict and Community in Corinth: A Socio-Rhetorical Commentary on 1 and 2 Corinthians.* Grand Rapids: Eerdmans, 1995.

———. *Paul's Narrative Thought-World: The Tapestry of Tragedy and Triumph.* Louisville: Westminster, 1994.

Wolter, Michael. *Paul: An Outline of His Theology.* Waco: Baylor University Press, 2015.

Wright, N. T. *The Climax of the Covenant: Christ and the Law in Pauline Theology.* Edinburgh: T&T Clark, 1991.

———. *Paul and the Faithfulness of God.* COQG. London: SPCK, 2013.

———. *Paul: A Biography.* San Francisco: HarperOne, 2018.

———. *The Resurrection of the Son of God.* COQG. London: SPCK, 2003.

Ziegler, Joseph, ed. *Isaias.* Vol. 14 of *Septuaginta: Vetus Testamentum Graecum.* Göttingen: Vandenhoeck & Ruprecht, 1967.

SCRIPTURE INDEX

OLD TESTAMENT

NEW TESTAMENT

1 Corinthians

2 Corinthians

Galatians

Ephesians

OTHER ANCIENT SOURCES INDEX

APOCRYPHA AND SEPTUAGINT

DEAD SEA SCROLLS AND RELATED TEXTS

OTHER SECOND TEMPLE JEWISH WRITINGS

TARGUMIC TEXTS

MISHNAH, TALMUD, AND OTHER RABBINIC WRITINGS

CLASSICAL AND ANCIENT CHRISTIAN WRITINGS

PAPYRI AND INSCRIPTIONS